CRIMINAL PROCESS

Part One—Investigation

THIRD EDITION

by

LLOYD L. WEINREB
Dane Professor of Law, Harvard University

Reprinted from Weinreb's Criminal Process (Seventh Edition)

FOUNDATION PRESS

NEW YORK, NEW YORK

2004

Reprinted from
Weinreb's Criminal Process
Cases, Comment, Questions
(Seventh Edition)
Pages 1–514

© 2004 By FOUNDATION PRESS
395 Hudson Street
New York, NY 10014
Phone Toll Free 1–877–888–1330
Fax (212) 367–6799
fdpress.com
Printed in the United States of America

ISBN 1–58778–802–0

 TEXT IS PRINTED ON 10% POST CONSUMER RECYCLED PAPER

PREFACE

This book is a complete, unchanged reprint of Part One of Weinreb, Criminal Process—Cases, Comment, Questions (seventh edition, 2004). It provides a close examination of the law of criminal investigation. Because so much of the law is federal, especially constitutional law, federal criminal investigation is used as the model.

All the important constitutional decisions are included. They are studied from the perspective of criminal investigation, however, and not, at least in the first instance, as matters of constitutional law. Accordingly, discussion in the opinions of issues like federalism, jurisdiction, and precedent, which do not have anything directly to do with criminal investigation, are usually omitted. The Federal Rules of Criminal Procedure, insofar as they affect criminal investigation, provide a model of such rules generally. State and local rules that affect criminal investigation rarely depart significantly from federal law. Some of the more significant departures are noted.

In order to bring rules and procedures down to earth, I have included descriptions of a large number of concrete factual situations, drawn from actual cases. Although citations to the cases are always given, students should not ordinarily need to refer to the opinions; it is the facts of the cases and how the rules and procedures in question ought to be applied in various contexts that are of principal concern, rather than the particular answer that the court gave. Forms used in connection with various aspects of criminal investigation are included in the appropriate place.

Notes are numbered consecutively through the book from 1 to 288. Footnotes are numbered consecutively in each chapter. I have generally omitted footnotes in reproduced materials. Those that appear are renumbered but are in the original materials unless the footnote number is enclosed in brackets. In Supreme Court cases, separate opinions of Justices that are not reproduced are indicated in a footnote at the end, along with the votes of Justices who did not join one of the reproduced opinions. I have corrected obvious typographical and similar errors and have made a few other small changes in reproduced materials not affecting their sense.

Cross-references to pages in Part Two of Criminal Process, which covers prosecution (including adjudication and post-adjudication proceedings) can generally be disregarded. If there is special reason to look up the reference in some instances, they can be found in that book or in a separate publication, Criminal Process—Prosecution, which is a companion volume to this one and contains only Part Two.

Police forms were provided by the Boston Police Department. Some of the police forms were prepared for the Boston Police Department by Comnetix Computer Systems, Inc. Robert Layfield, Director of Police Sales for Comnetix, kindly allowed me to use sample forms on which his name and picture appear for demonstration purposes. Forms used in the federal courts were provided by the Office of the Clerk of the United States District Court for the District of Massachusetts.

Lawrence Heftman, while a student at Harvard Law School, gave me substantial research and editorial assistance for this edition. Melinda Eakin was responsible for copy editing and for preparation of the manuscript in all its stages. Her assistance was invaluable. As in the past, I am grateful to Raymond S. Andrews ("Sherwood"), who did the illustrations.

LLOYD L. WEINREB

July 2004

SUMMARY OF CONTENTS

*

TABLE OF CONTENTS

TABLE OF CASES

Principal cases are in bold type. Non-principal cases are in roman type. References are to Pages.

*

CRIMINAL PROCESS

Part One—Investigation

*

PART ONE

INVESTIGATION

A crime is committed. How should the criminal process—official response to crime—begin? Consider the following cases:

(1) A policeman walking a beat at night stumbles across a man's body on the sidewalk. The man has been shot to death.

(2) A policeman walking a beat at night hears the burglar alarm of a jewelry store. When he arrives at the store no one is in sight. The store window is broken.

(3) A policeman walking a beat at night hears the burglar alarm of a jewelry store. As he arrives at the store, a woman rushes out the door.

(4) A policeman walking a beat at night hears a scream and the sound of a gun being fired. He goes to the place from which the sounds came and sees people rushing out of a house.

(5) An accountant reports to the president of a bank that there is a recurrent shortage in the daily cash receipts of one of the tellers.

(6) A tax examiner reports to her superior that a bank president has apparently understated his income on tax returns for the past three years.

(7) A bank president calls her husband on the telephone to report that their son has been kidnapped.

(8) The wife of a bank president tells him that for the past several weeks she has received anonymous threatening telephone calls.

(9) A woman reports to the police that her husband has beaten her up.

In each of the cases, a crime has apparently been committed. What should happen next? So far as the policemen know, the same crime has been committed in cases (2) and (3). Should the two policemen act alike? Why (not)? In cases (3), (5), (6), and (9) the identity of the apparent criminal is known. Should the official action taken in each case be the same? Why (not)?

What should be accomplished at the beginning of the criminal process? Who should be advised that the process has "begun"? Who should be asked to participate? Or required to participate? Why?

1

Contrast the cases above with some of the following situations:

(1) A mother finds her small son standing on a chair and, in violation of her strict rule, reaching into the cookie jar.

(2) A woman finds the housekeeper taking a nip from a bottle in the liquor cabinet.

(3) A student discovers her roommate in the act of stealing her class notes.

(4) A student discovers that his class notes are missing and suspects strongly that his roommate has taken them.

(5) A private on guard duty sees a prisoner climbing the camp fence.

(6) An army officer leading an attack on the enemy sees one of his men running away to the rear.

(7) A policeman sees a car parked in a "no parking" zone on a quiet Sunday when traffic is slight.

Is there any official function that *must* be performed before it can be said that criminal process has begun?

Boston Police
INCIDENT REPORT

HANDPRINT

ORIGINAL ☐   SUPPLEMENTARY ☐

01. KEY SITUATIONS ☐ DRUGS ☐ LICENSED PREMISES ☐ ELDERLY ☐ JUVENILE ☐ COMMUNITY DISORDERS ☐ DOMESTIC ☐ OTHER	02. COMPLAINT NO.	03. REPORT DIST.	CLEARANCE DIST	PAGE	OF

04. TYPE OF INCIDENT	05. CRIME CODE	06. STATUS ☐ INACTIVE ☐ UNFOUNDED ☐ ARREST ☐ UNDER 18 ☐ EXCEPT CL ☐ UNDER 18	07. DATE OF OCCUR. A. B.

08. LOCATION OF INCIDENT (NO STREET) (INTERSECTION-ALPHA ORDER)	APT	09. DISPATCH TIME ☐A ☐P	10. TIME OF OCCUR. A. ☐A ☐P B. ☐A ☐P

11. VICTIM-COMP. (LAST, FIRST, MI)	12. PHONE	13. SEX ☐M ☐F	14. RACE	15. MARITAL STATUS ☐ MARRIED ☐ UNMARRIED

16. ADDRESS (NO., STREET, CITY AND STATE IF OTHER THAN BOSTON OR MASS.)	APT.	OCCUPATION	17. AGE	18. D.O.B.

19. PERSON REPORTING (IF DIFFERENT THAN ABOVE)	20. ADDRESS	APT.	21. PHONE

PERSON INTERVIEWED	AGE	LOCATION OF INTERVIEW	APT. NO.	HOME ADDRESS	APT.	TEL	RES BUS
						TEL	RES BUS
						TEL	RES BUS

PERSONS

24. ☐ ARREST ☐ WARRANT ☐ MISSING ☐ SUMMONS ☐ SUSPECT	25. NAME (LAST, FIRST, MI)	26. S.B. NO.	27. BOOKING NO.	28. PHOTO NO.	29. ALIAS
30. WARRANT NO.	31. ADDRESS	32. SEX ☐M ☐F	33. RACE	34. AGE	35. HEIGHT	36. D.O.B.

37. SPECIAL CHARACTERISTICS (INCLUDING CLOTHING)	38. WEIGHT	39. BUILD	40. HAIR	41. EYES

VEHICLES

43. ☐ STOLEN ☐ RECOV. ☐ LV SCENE ☐ ABAND. ☐ IN CUST. ☐ TOWED ☐ USED IN CRIME ☐ OTHER	44. REG. STATE NO.	45. PLATE TYPE	YEAR (EXP.)	46. MODEL
47. VEHICLE MAKE-YEAR	48. VEHICLE NO.	49. STYLE	50. COLOR (TOP-BOTTOM)	
51. OPERATOR'S NAME	52. LICENSE NO.	53. OPERATOR'S ADDRESS		
54. OWNER'S NAME	55. OWNER'S ADDRESS			

PROPERTY

57. TYPE OF PROPERTY	58. SERIAL OR I-DENTI-GUARD NO.	59. BRAND NAME-DESCRIPTION	60. MODEL	61. VALUE	62. UCR	63. RECOV.

MO

65. TYPE OF WEAPON-TOOL	66. NEIGHBORHOOD	67. TYPE OF BUILDING	68. PLACE OF ENTRY
69. WEATHER	70. LIGHTING	71. TRANSPORTATION OF SUSPECT (CAR, FOOT, MBTA, ETC.)	72. VICTIM'S ACTIVITY
73. UNUSUAL ACTIONS AND STATEMENTS OF PERPETRATOR			RELATIONSHIP TO VICTIM

BLOCK NO.	76. NARRATIVE AND ADDITIONAL INFORMATION

77. UNIT ASSIGNED	78. TOUR OF DUTY	79. REPORTING OFFICER'S SIGNATURE	80. REPORTING OFFICER'S ID	81. PARTNER'S ID	F.I. ☐ YES ☐ NO
82. DATE OF REPORT	83. SPECIAL UNITS NOTIFIED (REPORTING)				TELETYPE NO.
84. TIME COMPLETED ☐A ☐P	85. SIGNATURE OF PATROL SUPERVISOR		86. PAT. SUP. ID	87. SIGNATURE DUTY SUPERVISOR	88. DUTY SUP. ID

BPD Form 1.1 Revised 86

HEADQUARTER'S COPY

CHAPTER 1

ARREST

Complaint

FEDERAL RULES OF CRIMINAL PROCEDURE

Rule 3

THE COMPLAINT

The complaint is a written statement of the essential facts constituting the offense charged. It must be made under oath before a magistrate judge or, if none is reasonably available, before a state or local judicial officer.

Rule 4

ARREST WARRANT OR SUMMONS ON A COMPLAINT

(a) Issuance. If the complaint or one or more affidavits filed with the complaint establish probable cause to believe that an offense has been committed and that the defendant committed it, the judge must issue an arrest warrant to an officer authorized to execute it. At the request of an attorney for the government, the judge must issue a summons, instead of a warrant, to a person authorized to serve it. A judge may issue more than one warrant or summons on the same complaint. If a defendant fails to appear in response to a summons, a judge may, and upon request of an attorney for the government must, issue a warrant.

(b) Form.

(1) *Warrant.* A warrant must:

(A) contain the defendant's name or, if it is unknown, a name or description by which the defendant can be identified with reasonable certainty;

(B) describe the offense charged in the complaint;

(C) command that the defendant be arrested and brought without unnecessary delay before a magistrate judge or, if none is reasonably available, before a state or local judicial officer; and

(D) be signed by a judge.

(2) *Summons.* A summons must be in the same form as a warrant except that it must require the defendant to appear before a magistrate judge at a stated time and place.

4

*A summons allows the person to appear. (used in white collar cases)

(c) Execution or Service, and Return.

(1) *By Whom.* Only a marshal or other authorized officer may execute a warrant. Any person authorized to serve a summons in a federal civil action may serve a summons.

(2) *Location.* A warrant may be executed, or a summons served, within the jurisdiction of the United States or anywhere else a federal statute authorizes an arrest.

(3) *Manner.*

(A) A warrant is executed by arresting the defendant. Upon arrest, an officer possessing the warrant must show it to the defendant. If the officer does not possess the warrant, the officer must inform the defendant of the warrant's existence and of the offense charged and, at the defendant's request, must show the warrant to the defendant as soon as possible.

(B) A summons is served on an individual defendant:

(i) by delivering a copy to the defendant personally; or

(ii) by leaving a copy at the defendant's residence or usual place of abode with a person of suitable age and discretion residing at that location and by mailing a copy to the defendant's last known address.

(C) A summons is served on an organization by delivering a copy to an officer, to a managing or general agent, or to another agent appointed or legally authorized to receive service of process. A copy must also be mailed to the organization's last known address within the district or to its principal place of business elsewhere in the United States.

(4) *Return.*

(A) After executing a warrant, the officer must return it to the judge before whom the defendant is brought in accordance with Rule 5. At the request of an attorney for the government, an unexecuted warrant must be brought back to and canceled by a magistrate judge or, if none is reasonably available, by a state or local judicial officer.

(B) The person to whom a summons was delivered for service must return it on or before the return day.

(C) At the request of an attorney for the government, a judge may deliver an unexecuted warrant, an unserved summons, or a copy of the warrant or summons to the marshal or other authorized person for execution or service.

———

If the complaint (and accompanying affidavits) must show probable cause "to believe that an offense has been committed and that the defendant committed it," it is apparent that the criminal process is well under way when the complaint is filed. The investigatory stage of the process, if not complete, has advanced to the point where officials have concluded that a crime has been committed, have identified a person who they are prepared to assert has probably committed it, and are able to show a basis for their assertion. The filing of a complaint that satisfies the requirements of Rule 4 may occur long after the commission of a crime, after police and prosecutorial officials have performed a variety of functions that may impose substantially on the person charged in the complaint or on others. Should officials who are investigating the commission of a crime but are not prepared to make a complaint showing probable cause be required to file an official statement that (they believe) a crime has occurred or that they are investigating the conduct of a specific person or persons in connection with the crime? Why (not)? If so, what form should "filing" take? With or without filing, should the officials be required to notify anyone that the investigation is taking place?

Giordenello v. United States

357 U.S. 480, 78 S.Ct. 1245, 2 L.Ed.2d 1503 (1958)

■ MR. JUSTICE HARLAN delivered the opinion of the Court.

Petitioner was convicted of the unlawful purchase of narcotics, see 26 U.S.C. (Supp. V) § 4704, after a trial without a jury before the Federal District Court for the Southern District of Texas. A divided Court of Appeals affirmed. . . . We granted certiorari to consider petitioner's challenge to the legality of his arrest and the admissibility in evidence of the narcotics seized from his person at the time of the arrest. . . .

Agent Finley of the Federal Bureau of Narcotics obtained a warrant for the arrest of petitioner from the United States Commissioner in Houston, Texas, on January 26, 1956. This warrant, issued under Rules 3 and 4 of the Federal Rules of Criminal Procedure . . . was based on a written complaint, sworn to by Finley, which read in part:

> The undersigned complainant [Finley] being duly sworn states: That on or about January 26, 1956, at Houston, Texas in the Southern District of Texas, Veto Giordenello did receive, conceal, etc., narcotic drugs, to-wit: heroin hydrochloride with knowledge of unlawful importation; in violation of Section 174, Title 21, United States Code.
>
> And the complainant further states that he believes that _____ _____ are material witnesses in relation to this charge.

About 6 o'clock in the afternoon of the following day, January 27, Finley saw petitioner drive up to his residence in a car and enter the house. He emerged shortly thereafter and drove away in the same car, closely followed in a second car by a person described by Finley as a "well-known police character." Finley pursued the cars until they stopped near another residence which was entered by petitioner. When petitioner left this residence, carrying a brown paper bag in his hand, and proceeded towards his car, Finley executed the arrest warrant and seized the bag, which proved to contain a mixture of heroin and other substances. Although warned of his privilege to remain silent, petitioner promptly admitted purchasing the heroin in Chicago and transporting it to Houston.

. . .

Petitioner challenges the sufficiency of the warrant on two grounds: (1) that the complaint on which the warrant was issued was inadequate because the complaining officer, Finley, relied exclusively upon hearsay information rather than personal knowledge in executing the complaint; and (2) that the complaint was in any event defective in that it in effect recited no more than the elements of the crime charged, namely the concealment of heroin with knowledge of its illegal importation in violation of 21 U.S.C. § 174.

It appears from Finley's testimony at the hearing on the suppression motion that until the warrant was issued on January 26 his suspicions of petitioner's guilt derived entirely from information given him by law enforcement officers and other persons in Houston, none of whom either appeared before the Commissioner or submitted affidavits. But we need not decide whether a warrant may be issued solely on hearsay information, for in any event we find this complaint defective in not providing a sufficient basis upon which a finding of probable cause could be made.

Criminal Rules 3 and 4 provide that an arrest warrant shall be issued only upon a written and sworn complaint (1) setting forth "the essential facts constituting the offense charged," and (2) showing "that there is probable cause to believe that [such] an offense has been committed and that the defendant has committed it. . . ." The provisions of these Rules must be read in light of the constitutional requirements they implement. The language of the Fourth Amendment, that ". . . no Warrants shall issue, but upon probable cause, supported by Oath or affirmation, and particularly describing . . . the persons or things to be seized," of course applies to arrest as well as search warrants. . . . The protection afforded by these Rules, when they are viewed against their constitutional background, is that the inferences from the facts which lead to the complaint "be drawn by a neutral and detached magistrate instead of being judged by the officer engaged in the often competitive enterprise of ferreting out crime." Johnson v. United States, 333 U.S. 10, 14. The purpose of the complaint, then, is to enable the appropriate magistrate, here a Commissioner, to determine whether the "probable cause" required to support a warrant exists. The Commissioner must judge for himself the persuasiveness of the facts relied on by a complaining officer to show probable cause. He should not accept without question the complainant's mere conclusion that the person whose arrest is sought has committed a crime.

When the complaint in this case is judged with these considerations in mind, it is clear that it does not pass muster because it does not provide any basis for the Commissioner's determination under Rule 4 that probable cause existed. The complaint contains no affirmative allegation that the affiant spoke with personal knowledge of the matters contained therein; it does not indicate any sources for the complainant's belief; and it does not set forth any other sufficient basis upon which a finding of probable cause could be made. We think these deficiencies could not be cured by the Commissioner's reliance upon a presumption that the complaint was made on the personal knowledge of the complaining officer. The insubstantiality of such an argument is illustrated by the facts of this very case, for Finley's testimony at the suppression hearing clearly showed that he had no personal knowledge of the matters on which his charge was based. In these circumstances, it is difficult to understand how the Commissioner could be expected to assess independently the probability that petitioner committed the crime charged. Indeed, if this complaint were upheld, the substantive requirements would be completely read out of Rule 4, and the complaint would be of only formal significance, entitled to perfunctory approval by the Commissioner. This would not comport with the protective purposes which a complaint is designed to achieve.

. . . [1]

———

Jaben v. United States

381 U.S. 214, 85 S.Ct. 1365, 14 L.Ed.2d 345 (1965)

[The petitioner Jaben was prosecuted for wilfully attempting to evade federal income taxes. The statute of limitations on that offense required that an indictment be obtained within six years after its commission, but provided that if a complaint were filed within that period the government should have an additional nine months after the complaint was filed within which to obtain an indictment. Internal Revenue Code of 1954, § 6531. On the day before the period expired, the government filed a complaint against Jaben:

The undersigned complainant, being duly sworn, states:

That he is a Special Agent of the Internal Revenue Service and, in the performance of the duties imposed on him by law, he has conducted an investigation of the Federal income tax liability of Max Jaben for the calendar year 1956, by examining the said taxpayer's tax return for the year 1956 and other years; by identifying and interviewing third parties with whom the said taxpayer did business; by consulting public and private records reflecting the said taxpayer's income; and by interviewing third persons having knowledge of the said taxpayer's financial condition.

[1] Justice Clark wrote a dissenting opinion, which Justice Burton and Justice Whittaker joined.

That based on the aforesaid investigation, the complainant has personal knowledge that on or about the 16th day of April, 1957, at Kansas City, Missouri, in the Western District of Missouri, Max Jaben did unlawfully and wilfully attempt to evade and defeat the income taxes due and owing by him to the United States of America for the calendar year 1956, by filing and causing to be filed with the District Director of Internal Revenue for the District of Kansas City, Missouri, at Kansas City, Missouri, a false and fraudulent income tax return, wherein he stated that his taxable income for the calendar year 1956 was $17,665.31, and that the amount of tax due and owing thereon was the sum of $6,017.32, when in fact his taxable income for the said calendar year was the sum of $40,001.76 upon which said taxable income he owed to the United States of America an income tax of $14,562.99.

[Signed] David A. Thompson

Special Agent

Internal Revenue Service
Kansas City, Missouri.

The commissioner before whom the complaint was filed determined that there was probable cause to believe that Jaben had committed the offense and issued a summons ordering Jaben to appear one month later for a preliminary examination on the complaint. Before the hearing was held, after the six-year period had expired but within the nine-month extension if it were applicable, the grand jury returned an indictment. Jaben moved to dismiss the indictment on the ground that, the complaint being invalid for failure to show probable cause, the indictment was untimely.]

■ MR. JUSTICE HARLAN delivered the opinion of the Court.

. . .

Under the Government's interpretation of § 6531, probable cause is not relevant to the complaint's ability to initiate the extension of the limitation period. Section 6531 provides that the nine-month extension is brought into play "[w]here a complaint is instituted before a commissioner of the United States" within the six-year period of limitations. . . . Rule 3 of the Federal Rules of Criminal Procedure defines a complaint as

. . . a written statement of the essential facts constituting the offense charged. It shall be made upon oath before a commissioner or other officer empowered to commit persons charged with offenses against the United States.

Since the Government's complaint stated the essential facts constituting the offense of attempted tax evasion and was made upon oath before a

Commissioner, the Government contends that regardless of the complaint's adequacy for any other purposes, it was valid for the purpose of triggering the nine-month extension of the limitation period whether or not it showed probable cause. The Government would, thus, totally ignore the further steps in the complaint procedure required by Rules 4 and 5. Indeed it follows from its position that once having filed a complaint, the Government need not further pursue the complaint procedure at all, and, in the event that the defendant pressed for a preliminary hearing and obtained a dismissal of the complaint, that the Government could nonetheless rely upon the complaint as having extended the limitation period.

We do not accept the Government's interpretation. Its effort to look solely to Rule 3 and ignore the requirements of the Rules that follow would deprive the institution of the complaint before the Commissioner of any independent meaning which might rationally have led Congress to fasten upon it as the method for initiating the nine-month extension. The Commissioner's function, on that view, would be merely to rubber-stamp the complaint. The Government seeks to give his role importance in its version of § 6531 by pointing out that he would administer the oath, receive the complaint, and make sure that it stated facts constituting the offense (a requirement which would be met by a charge in the words of the statute); but surely these matters are essentially formalities. The argument ignores the fact that the Commissioner's basic functions under the Rules are to make the judgment that probable cause exists and to warn defendants of their rights. Furthermore, if we do not look beyond Rule 3, there is no provision for notifying the defendant that he has been charged and the period of limitations extended. (Indeed, it is not until we reach Rule 4 that we find a requirement that the complaint must show who it was that committed the offense.) Notice to a criminal defendant is usually achieved by service upon him of the summons or arrest warrant provided for in Rule 4. Neither is appropriate absent a judgment by the Commissioner that the complaint shows probable cause, and no other form of notice is specified by the Rules.

More basically, the evident statutory purpose of the nine-month extension provision is to afford the Government an opportunity to indict criminal tax offenders in the event that a grand jury is not in session at the end of the normal limitation period. This is confirmed by the immediate precursor of the present section which provided for an extension "until the discharge of the grand jury at its next session within the district." I.R.C. 1939 § 3748(a). Clearly the statute was not meant to grant the Government greater time in which to make its case (a result which could have been accomplished simply by making the normal period of limitation six years and nine months), but rather was intended to deal with the situation in which the Government has its case made within the normal limitation period but cannot obtain an indictment because of the grand jury schedule. The Government's interpretation does not reflect this statutory intention, for it provides no safeguard whatever to prevent the Government from filing a complaint at a time when it does not have its case made, and then using the nine-month period to make it.

The better view of § 6531 is that the complaint, to initiate the time extension, must be adequate to begin effectively the criminal process prescribed by the Federal Criminal Rules. It must be sufficient to justify the next steps in the process—those of notifying the defendant and bringing him before the Commissioner for a preliminary hearing. To do so the complaint must satisfy the probable cause requirement of Rule 4. Furthermore, we think that the Government must proceed through the further steps of the complaint procedure by affording the defendant a preliminary hearing as required by Rule 5, unless before the preliminary hearing is held, the grand jury supersedes the complaint procedure by returning an indictment. This interpretation of the statute reflects its purpose by insuring that within a reasonable time following the filing of the complaint, either the Commissioner will decide whether there is sufficient cause to bind the defendant over for grand jury action, or the grand jury itself will have decided whether or not to indict. A dismissal of the complaint before the indictment is returned would vitiate the time extension.

In this case the Government obtained a superseding indictment before any preliminary hearing took place. Under the interpretation which we have adopted it follows that if the complaint satisfied the requirements of Rules 3 and 4, in particular the probable cause standard of Rule 4, then the nine-month extension had come into play and had not been cut off by any later dismissal of the complaint. We turn then to the question whether the complaint showed probable cause.

. . .

Petitioner argues that the complaint is basically indistinguishable from that which the Court found wanting in Giordenello v. United States, 357 U.S. 480. . . .

The complaints there and here are materially distinguishable. Information in a complaint alleging the commission of a crime falls into two categories: (1) that information which, if true, would directly indicate commission of the crime charged, and (2) that which relates to the source of the directly incriminating information. The *Giordenello* complaint gave no source information whatsoever. Its directly incriminating information consisted merely of an allegation in the words of the statute, and even then incomplete, supplemented by "on or about January 26, 1956, at Houston." If the *Jaben* complaint were as barren, it would have stated simply that "on or about April 16, 1957, at Kansas City, Missouri, Jaben willfully filed a false income tax return." In fact, it gave dollars-and-cents figures for the amounts which allegedly should have been returned and the amounts actually returned. As to sources, the affiant indicated that he, in his official capacity, had personally conducted an investigation in the course of which he had examined the taxpayer's returns for 1956 and other years, interviewed third persons with whom the taxpayer did business and others having knowledge of his financial condition, and consulted public and private records reflecting the taxpayer's income; and that the conclusion that Jaben had committed the offense was based upon this investigation.

Beyond the substance of the complaint there is a material distinction in the nature of the offense charged. Some offenses are subject to putative establishment by blunt and concise factual allegations, e.g., "*A* saw narcotics in *B*'s possession," whereas "*A* and *B* file a false tax return" does not mean very much in a tax evasion case. Establishment of grounds for belief that the offense of tax evasion has been committed often requires a reconstruction of the taxpayer's income from many individually unrevealing facts which are not susceptible of a concise statement in a complaint. Furthermore, unlike narcotics informants, for example, whose credibility may often be suspect, the sources in this tax evasion case are much less likely to produce false or untrustworthy information. Thus, whereas some supporting information concerning the credibility of informants in narcotics cases or other common garden varieties of crime may be required, such information is not so necessary in the context of the case before us.

Giordenello v. United States, supra, and Aguilar v. Texas, 378 U.S. 108, established that a magistrate is intended to make a neutral judgment that resort to further criminal process is justified. A complaint must provide a foundation for that judgment. It must provide the affiant's answer to the magistrate's hypothetical question, "What makes you think that the defendant committed the offense charged?" This does not reflect a requirement that the Commissioner ignore the credibility of the complaining witness. There is a difference between disbelieving the affiant and requiring him to indicate some basis for his allegations. Obviously any reliance upon factual allegations necessarily entails some degree of reliance upon the credibility of the source. . . . Nor does it indicate that each factual allegation which the affiant puts forth must be independently documented, or that each and every fact which contributed to his conclusions be spelled out in the complaint. . . . It simply requires that enough information be presented to the Commissioner to enable him to make the judgment that the charges are not capricious and are sufficiently supported to justify bringing into play the further steps of the criminal process.

In this instance the issue of probable cause comes down to the adequacy of the basis given for the allegation that petitioner's income was $40,001.76 instead of the $17,665.31 he had reported. This is not the type of fact that can be physically observed. The amount of petitioner's income could only be determined by examining records and interviewing third persons familiar with petitioner's financial condition. . . . Here the affiant, a Special Agent of the Internal Revenue Service, swore that he had conducted just such an investigation and thereafter swore that he had personal knowledge as to petitioner's actual income. In such circumstances, the magistrate would be justified in accepting the agent's judgment of what he "saw" without requiring him to bring the records and persons to court, to list and total the items of unreported income or to otherwise explain how petitioner's actual income was calculated.

We conclude that the challenged count of this indictment is not time-barred.

. . .[2]

———

Giordenello was prosecuted for the purchase of narcotics. Jaben was prosecuted for tax evasion. In *Jaben*, the Court says that "there is a material distinction in the nature of the offense charged" in the two cases, p. 12 above, which has a bearing on how the issue of probable cause is treated. Does the nature of the offenses also have a bearing on what official steps should be taken if there is probable cause to believe that the crime was committed? What official steps were taken in each case after the complaint was filed? Is the difference justified by the facts so far as they appear in the reports of the cases?

———

1.   Rule 4(a), p. 4 above, provides that probable cause may be established in "one or more affidavits filed with the complaint." When *Giordenello* and *Jaben* were decided, there was no reference in the rule to affidavits accompanying the complaint. If affidavits are used to show probable cause, does the complaint as such effectively begin the criminal process in any significant sense?

2.   Do the federal rules authorize the making of a complaint that does not itself or in accompanying affidavits show "probable cause to believe that an offense has been committed and that the defendant committed it"? Should a magistrate refuse to accept such a complaint for filing? If he accepts it, what should he do with it? Where and how should he "file" it? Is there any reason why anyone should want to file such a complaint?

3.   The Fourth Amendment requires that warrants be "supported by oath or affirmation." "The nearly unanimous view is that the Fourth Amendment requires that only information related to the magistrate on oath or affirmation is competent upon which to base a finding of probable cause; that unsworn oral statements may not form a basis for that decision." Frazier v. Roberts, 441 F.2d 1224, 1227 (8th Cir.1971).

[2] Justice White wrote an opinion concurring in the judgment, which Justice Black joined. Justice Goldberg wrote an opinion concurring in part and dissenting in part, which Chief Justice Warren and Justice Douglas joined.

℀AO91 (Rev. 8/01) Criminal Complaint

UNITED STATES DISTRICT COURT

_____ DISTRICT OF _____

UNITED STATES OF AMERICA
V.

CRIMINAL COMPLAINT

Case Number:

(Name and Address of Defendant)

I, the undersigned complainant state that the following is true and correct to the best of my

knowledge and belief. On or about _____ in _____ County, in
                                              (Date)
the _____ District of _____ defendant(s) did,

(Track Statutory Language of Offense)

in violation of Title _____ United States Code, Section(s) _____ .

I further state that I am a(n)_____ and that this complaint is based on the
                                                Official Title
following facts:

Continued on the attached sheet and made a part of this complaint: ☐ Yes   ☐ No

_____
Signature of Complainant

_____
Printed Name of Complainant

Sworn to before me and signed in my presence,

_____ at
Date

_____
City   State

_____   _____
Name of Judicial Officer   Title of Judicial Officer   Signature of Judicial Officer

Rules 3 and 4 require that the sworn support for an arrest warrant, whether the complaint or accompanying affidavits, be in writing. "It is clear that the Fourth Amendment permits the warrant-issuing magistrate to consider sworn oral testimony supplementing a duly executed affidavit to determine whether there is probable cause upon which to issue a search [and presumably an arrest] warrant." *Frazier*, 441 F.2d at 1226. Accord United States v. Clyburn, 24 F.3d 613, 617 (4th Cir.1994). Rule 41(d)(2)(B) provides for the issuance of a search warrant on the basis of sworn oral testimony "if doing so is reasonable under the circumstances." See p. 178 below.

In Stewart v. Abraham, 275 F.3d 220 (3d Cir.2001), the court held that the Fourth Amendment does not bar the immediate rearrest of a person on probable cause following a preliminary examination at which a magistrate dismissed a complaint charging the same offense for lack of probable cause and ordered the person released from custody. The court noted that the information on which the second complaint was based might be different from the evidence that was presented at the preliminary examination and that under the state law the standard of probable cause for issuance of a complaint was different from the standard for upholding a complaint at a preliminary examination.

4. Who issues a warrant? Rule 3 requires that the complaint be made before a magistrate judge or a state or local judicial officer. Rule 4(b)(1)(D) provides that an arrest warrant shall be "signed by a judge."

Magistrate judges are appointed by the judges of the United States district courts and are ordinarily to be members of the bar for at least five years. A full-time magistrate judge is appointed for a renewable term of eight years, a part-time magistrate judge for a renewable term of four years. 28 U.S.C. § 631. See generally 28 U.S.C. §§ 631–639.

Is the issuance of a warrant *constitutionally* a judicial function? In Coolidge v. New Hampshire, 403 U.S. 443 (1971), the Court held that the Fourth Amendment prohibited the Attorney General of the state from issuing a search warrant. The Court observed that at the time he issued the warrant, the Attorney General "was actively in charge of the investigation and later was to be chief prosecutor at the trial." Quoting language from Johnson v. United States, 333 U.S. 10, 13–14 (1948), the Court said that a prosecutor was not the "neutral and detached magistrate" that the Constitution requires. "Prosecutors and policemen simply cannot be asked to maintain the requisite neutrality with regard to their own investigations— the 'competitive enterprise [of ferreting out crime]' that must rightly engage their single-minded attention." *Coolidge*, 403 U.S. at 450. Under state law, the Attorney General was a justice of the peace and authorized to issue the warrant.

AO 442   (Rev. 10/03) Warrant for Arrest

UNITED STATES DISTRICT COURT

_____ District of _____

UNITED STATES OF AMERICA

V.

WARRANT FOR ARREST

Case Number:

To: The United States Marshal
    and any Authorized United States Officer

YOU ARE HEREBY COMMANDED to arrest _____

Name

and bring him or her forthwith to the nearest magistrate judge to answer a(n)

☐ Indictment   ☐ Information   ☐ Complaint   ☐ Order of court   ☐ Probation Violation Petition   ☐ Supervised Release Violation Petition   ☐ Violation Notice

charging him or her with   (brief description of offense)

in violation of Title _____ United States Code, Section(s) _____

_____
Name of Issuing Officer

_____
Signature of Issuing Officer

_____
Title of Issuing Officer

_____
Date and Location

RETURN		
This warrant was received and executed with the arrest of the above-named defendant at		
DATE RECEIVED	NAME AND TITLE OF ARRESTING OFFICER	SIGNATURE OF ARRESTING OFFICER
DATE OF ARREST		

AO 442   (Rev. 10/03) Warrant for Arrest

THE FOLLOWING IS FURNISHED FOR INFORMATION ONLY:

DEFENDANT'S NAME: _____

ALIAS: _____

LAST KNOWN RESIDENCE: _____

LAST KNOWN EMPLOYMENT: _____

PLACE OF BIRTH: _____

DATE OF BIRTH: _____

SOCIAL SECURITY NUMBER: _____

HEIGHT: _____   WEIGHT: _____

SEX: _____   RACE: _____

HAIR: _____   EYES: _____

SCARS, TATTOOS, OTHER DISTINGUISHING MARKS: _____
_____
_____

FBI NUMBER: _____

COMPLETE DESCRIPTION OF AUTO: _____

INVESTIGATIVE AGENCY AND ADDRESS: _____
_____
_____
_____

While a warrant must be issued by someone "independent of the police or prosecution," he need not in all cases be a judge or a lawyer. In Shadwick v. City of Tampa, 407 U.S. 345 (1972), the Court upheld issuance by a clerk of the municipal court of an arrest warrant for "impaired driving" in violation of a municipal ordinance. The clerk was a civil servant; he was not a lawyer. The Court concluded that clerks of the municipal court met the two prongs of the test of authority to issue a warrant: the person who issues it "must be neutral and detached, and he must be capable of determining whether probable cause exists for the requested arrest or search." Reference in prior cases to a "magistrate" or "judicial officer" implied only that. Id. at 348. (The Court indicated that its holding did not necessarily extend to the issuance of warrants in more serious cases or to authorization of an official "entirely outside the sphere of the judicial branch" to issue warrants.) See generally Gerstein v. Pugh, 420 U.S. 103, 117–18 (1975), p. 522 below. In Connally v. Georgia, 429 U.S. 245 (1977), the Court held that an unsalaried justice of the peace who received a fee for each search warrant that he issued but no fee for rejecting an application for a warrant was not the "neutral and detached" officer required by the Constitution, because of the "element of personal financial gain" in the issuance of a warrant.

In State v. Ruotolo, 247 A.2d 1 (N.J.1968), the court said that a deputy court clerk could issue an arrest warrant on the basis of a complaint made before him by the defendant's wife charging the defendant with nonsupport, a misdemeanor. "By its very nature probable cause is a standard which can be applied by laymen, so long as they exercise reasonable caution. It is a practical, non-technical concept, not requiring the complex weighing of factual and legal considerations which is the judge's daily task." Id. at 5.

To the contrary, in State ex rel. Duhn v. Tahash, 147 N.W.2d 382 (Minn.1966), the Supreme Court of Minnesota (relying on *Giordenello*, p. 6 above) held that a deputy clerk could not issue a warrant based on a complaint charging a felony. In State v. Paulick, 151 N.W.2d 591 (Minn. 1967), the court extended *Duhn* to a prosecution for violation of a traffic ordinance:

> It occurs to us that in initiating and prosecuting charges which are misdemeanors the grave consequences to the accused resulting from a wrongful arrest far outweigh the potential harm to the community in requiring something more than the peremptory issuance of a warrant by a clerk untrained in the law. The harm to an accused arrested in his home or at his place of work, the humiliation and embarrassment to his family, and the fact he has a record of arrest, however unjust, are consequences difficult to measure. . . . However conscientious and impartial may be the clerk of Hennepin County Municipal Court who supervised the execution of the complaint and issued the warrant on behalf of the village of Minnetonka, his background and experience we can assume are not in the law. It is highly improbable that he was qualified to determine whether the complaint and warrant met consti-

tutional standards. It is with the greatest difficulty that we envision his refusing to issue a warrant upon the complaint of a state highway patrolman. These are functions which the judiciary cannot delegate, since they require both a knowledge of the law and the authority to grant or refuse the request of law-enforcement officers to initiate criminal procedures. . . .

Id. at 597–98.

To the same effect, see Caulk v. Municipal Court, 243 A.2d 707 (Del.1968). Whether those decisions survive *Shadwick*, above, may be doubted, but they have not been overruled.

5. Whether or not the approval of a prosecuting official is sufficient for the filing of a complaint and issuance of an arrest warrant, should his approval be *necessary*? An early draft of the American Law Institute's Model Code of Pre-Arraignment Procedure provided that, with some specific exceptions, a complaint shall be issued "only by a prosecuting attorney having jurisdiction over the prosecution of the offense and shall be filed only with his approval." ALI § 6.02(1) (Tent.Draft No. 1, 1966). The Draft provided also that a judicial officer might permit the filing of a complaint "if, after hearing the complainant and the prosecuting attorney, he finds there is reasonable cause to believe that the person named in the complaint has committed the offense charged." § 6.02(3). Procedures for the filing of a complaint are not included in the Model Code of Pre-Arraignment Procedure as finally adopted. See ALI, A Model Code of Pre-Arraignment Procedure § 130.2(1)(b), (6) (1975).

6. Whatever may be the requirements of the Constitution and the procedure formally prescribed by state law, in most cases "the prosecutor alone makes the effective warrant decision." Miller & Tiffany, "Prosecutor Dominance of the Warrant Decision: A Study of Current Practices," 1964 Wash. U. L.Q. 1, 4. The courts and magistrates have generally recognized the prosecutor's control of the prosecutorial function and his "greater capacity to make the initial decision correctly." Id. at 12. The result is a tacit division of labor by which the police (who, in the case of minor crimes, commonly also serve a prosecutorial role) and prosecutor have primary responsibility for the initiation of the criminal process, and the judiciary asserts its responsibility as the case develops for trial.

Whose judgment that a person should be charged with a crime is more likely to be correct, the magistrate's or the prosecutor's? Whose judgment that a person should not be charged is more likely to be correct?

How realistic is the Court's insistence on the judgment of a "neutral and detached magistrate," *Coolidge*, p. 15 above? Does the observable fact that the magistrate's judgment is commonly a perfunctory approval of the prosecutorial decision suggest that the current practice should be reformed or that the standard set by the Court is inappropriate to the functions being performed? Or does the procedure of applying for the magistrate's "rubber stamp" serve a purpose even if it is almost always given?

7. Does *Giordenello* require a magisterial judgment for issuance of a summons (as in *Jaben*) as well as an arrest warrant? In United States v. Greenberg, 320 F.2d 467 (9th Cir.1963), the court concluded that it does, at least under the scheme of the federal rules, which leaves the choice of warrant or summons to the attorney for the government. See Rule 4(a). "[I]nsofar as a defendant is concerned, there is but little distinction between the issuance of a warrant or a summons. If he fails to respond to a summons, a warrant of arrest may issue. If he appears in response to the summons, in most instances he is required to post bail or suffer arrest and detention until a determination has been made by the Commissioner in respect to the charges pending against him." 320 F.2d at 471.

8. Once an arrest warrant has been issued, how quickly must it be executed? "[O]rdinarily there is no legal requirement that a warrant of arrest must be executed immediately or at the first opportunity. . . . While its execution should not be unreasonably delayed there may be perfectly valid reasons why further investigation should be made before the drastic step is taken of arresting a citizen on a criminal charge. Certainly there is no constitutional right to be arrested promptly or otherwise." United States v. Joines, 258 F.2d 471, 472–73 (3d Cir.1958). Accord United States v. Drake, 655 F.2d 1025 (10th Cir.1981). See Hoffa v. United States, 385 U.S. 293, 310 (1966), in which the Court observed that "there is no constitutional right to be arrested." In what circumstances would it be appropriate for law enforcement officials to file a complaint and obtain issuance of an arrest warrant and then to delay execution of the warrant in order to investigate further?

"Police officials are required to use diligence in the execution of arrest warrants. They may not hold one unexecuted for an unreasonable period of time in the hope that they may ultimately find the defendant in a house or other building which they would like to search, but which they could not lawfully search except as an incident of a lawful arrest. Agents are not required to neglect all other investigatory and enforcement activity in order to execute every arrest warrant, however, and sixteen days' delay in executing an arrest warrant upon one whose residential address was not definitely known is far from unreasonable on its face. Moreover, such agents are entitled to proceed with some circumspection, so that the fact of their search for a defendant is not disclosed to him at a time when he may flee successfully." United States v. Weaver, 384 F.2d 879, 880–81 (4th Cir.1967).

AO 83 (Rev. 10/03) Summons in a Criminal Case

UNITED STATES DISTRICT COURT

DISTRICT OF _____

UNITED STATES OF AMERICA
V.

SUMMONS IN A CRIMINAL CASE

Case Number: _____

(Name and Address of Defendant)

YOU ARE HEREBY SUMMONED to appear before the United States District Court at the place, date and time set forth below.

Place	Room
	Date and Time
Before:	

To answer a(n)

☐ Indictment ☐ Information ☐ Complaint ☐ Probation Violation Petition ☐ Supervised Release Violation Petition ☐ Violation Notice

Charging you with a violation of Title _____ United States Code, Section(s) _____

Brief description of offense:

_____   _____
Signature of Issuing Officer   Date

_____
Name and Title of Issuing Officer

In Godfrey v. United States, 358 F.2d 850, 852 (D.C.Cir.1966), the court said that if there is delay in filing a complaint in order "to advance the public interest in effective law enforcement,"[3] there is a special obligation to make the arrest quickly after the arrest warrant is issued; "the disadvantage to the accused inherent in the deliberate preference accorded the public interest in the one period should not be compounded by a failure to exercise appropriate diligence in the other." "[E]very time there is delay in the making of the arrest and there is a search made as incidental to the arrest, the law enforcement officers take the risk that they will be charged with using the arrest as a mere pretext for the search. . . . In other words, the delay in making the arrest is one of the factors to be taken into consideration when the time comes for a judicial determination of the question of whether or not the search was 'reasonable.' " Carlo v. United States, 286 F.2d 841, 846 (2d Cir.1961).

9. An arrest made in good-faith reliance on an ordinance later declared unconstitutional is valid, and evidence seized in a search incident to the arrest should not be suppressed. Michigan v. DeFillippo, 443 U.S. 31 (1979) (6–3). "The enactment of a law forecloses speculation by enforcement officers concerning its constitutionality—with the possible exception of a law so grossly and flagrantly unconstitutional that any person of reasonable prudence would be bound to see its flaws." Id. at 38. See Sandul v. Larion, 119 F.3d 1250 (6th Cir.1997) (First Amendment rights; *DeFillippo* found not applicable).

Arrest Without a Warrant

United States v. Watson
423 U.S. 411, 96 S.Ct. 820, 46 L.Ed.2d 598 (1976)

■ Mr. Justice White delivered the opinion of the Court.

This case presents questions under the Fourth Amendment as to the legality of a warrantless arrest and of an ensuing search of the arrestee's automobile carried out with his purported consent.

I

The relevant events began on August 17, 1972, when an informant, one Khoury, telephoned a postal inspector informing him that respondent Watson was in possession of a stolen credit card and had asked Khoury to cooperate in using the card to their mutual advantage. On five to 10 previous occasions Khoury had provided the inspector with reliable infor-

---

3. For example, when an undercover agent has a basis for a complaint but is not ready to "surface." See Ross v. United States, 349 F.2d 210 (D.C.Cir.1965).

mation on postal inspection matters, some involving Watson. Later that day Khoury delivered the card to the inspector. On learning that Watson had agreed to furnish additional cards, the inspector asked Khoury to arrange to meet with Watson. Khoury did so, a meeting being scheduled for August 22. Watson canceled that engagement, but at noon on August 23, Khoury met with Watson at a restaurant designated by the latter. Khoury had been instructed that if Watson had additional stolen credit cards, Khoury was to give a designated signal. The signal was given, the officers closed in, and Watson was forthwith arrested. He was removed from the restaurant to the street where he was given the warnings required by Miranda v. Arizona, 384 U.S. 436 (1966). A search having revealed that Watson had no credit cards on his person, the inspector asked if he could look inside Watson's car, which was standing within view. Watson said, "Go ahead," and repeated these words when the inspector cautioned that "[i]f I find anything, it is going to go against you." Using keys furnished by Watson, the inspector entered the car and found under the floor mat an envelope containing two credit cards in the names of other persons. These cards were the basis for two counts of a four-count indictment charging Watson with possessing stolen mail in violation of 18 U.S.C. § 1708.

Prior to trial, Watson moved to suppress the cards, claiming that his arrest was illegal for want of probable cause and an arrest warrant and that his consent to search the car was involuntary and ineffective because he had not been told that he could withhold consent. The motion was denied, and Watson was convicted of illegally possessing the two cards seized from his car.

A divided panel of the Court of Appeals for the Ninth Circuit reversed . . . ruling that the admission in evidence of the two credit cards found in the car was prohibited by the Fourth Amendment. In reaching this judgment, the court decided two issues in Watson's favor. First, notwithstanding its agreement with the District Court that Khoury was reliable and that there was probable cause for arresting Watson, the court held the arrest unconstitutional because the postal inspector had failed to secure an arrest warrant although he concededly had time to do so. Second, based on the totality of the circumstances, one of which was the illegality of the arrest, the court held Watson's consent to search had been coerced and hence was not a valid ground for the warrantless search of the automobile. We granted certiorari. . . .

II

A major part of the Court of Appeals' opinion was its holding that Watson's warrantless arrest violated the Fourth Amendment. Although it did not expressly do so, it may have intended to overturn the conviction on the independent ground that the two credit cards were the inadmissible fruits of an unconstitutional arrest. . . . However that may be, the Court of Appeals treated the illegality of Watson's arrest as an important factor in determining the voluntariness of his consent to search his car. We therefore deal first with the arrest issue.

Contrary to the Court of Appeals' view, Watson's arrest was not invalid because executed without a warrant. Title 18 U.S.C. § 3061(a)(3) expressly empowers the Board of Governors of the Postal Service to authorize Postal Service officers and employees "performing duties related to the inspection of postal matters" to

> make arrests without warrant for felonies cognizable under the laws of the United States if they have reasonable grounds to believe that the person to be arrested has committed or is committing such a felony.

By regulation, 39 CFR § 232.5(a)(3) (1975), and in identical language, the Board of Governors has exercised that power and authorized warrantless arrests. Because there was probable cause in this case to believe that Watson had violated § 1708, the inspector and his subordinates, in arresting Watson, were acting strictly in accordance with the governing statute and regulations. The effect of the judgment of the Court of Appeals was to invalidate the statute as applied in this case and as applied to all the situations where a court fails to find exigent circumstances justifying a warrantless arrest. We reverse that judgment.

Under the Fourth Amendment, the people are to be "secure in their persons, houses, papers, and effects, against unreasonable searches and seizures . . . and no Warrants shall issue, but upon probable cause. . . ." Section 3061 represents a judgment by Congress that it is not unreasonable under the Fourth Amendment for postal inspectors to arrest without a warrant provided they have probable cause to do so. This was not an isolated or quixotic judgment of the legislative branch. Other federal law enforcement officers have been expressly authorized by statute for many years to make felony arrests on probable cause but without a warrant. This is true of United States marshals . . . and of agents of the Federal Bureau of Investigation . . . the Drug Enforcement Administration . . . the Secret Service . . . and the Customs Service. . . .

Because there is a "strong presumption of constitutionality due to an Act of Congress, especially when it turns on what is 'reasonable,'" "[o]bviously the Court should be reluctant to decide that a search thus authorized by Congress was unreasonable and that the Act was therefore unconstitutional." United States v. Di Re, 332 U.S. 581, 585 (1948). Moreover, there is nothing in the Court's prior cases indicating that under the Fourth Amendment a warrant is required to make a valid arrest for a felony. Indeed, the relevant prior decisions are uniformly to the contrary.

. . .

The cases construing the Fourth Amendment thus reflect the ancient common-law rule that a peace officer was permitted to arrest without a warrant for a misdemeanor or felony committed in his presence as well as for a felony not committed in his presence if there was reasonable ground for making the arrest. . . . This has also been the prevailing rule under state constitutions and statutes. . . .

The balance struck by the common law in generally authorizing felony arrests on probable cause, but without a warrant, has survived substantially intact. It appears in almost all of the States in the form of express statutory authorization. . . .

This is the rule Congress has long directed its principal law enforcement officers to follow. Congress has plainly decided against conditioning warrantless arrest power on proof of exigent circumstances. Law enforcement officers may find it wise to seek arrest warrants where practicable to do so, and their judgments about probable cause may be more readily accepted where backed by a warrant issued by a magistrate. . . . But we decline to transform this judicial preference into a constitutional rule when the judgment of the Nation and Congress has for so long been to authorize warrantless public arrests on probable cause rather than to encumber criminal prosecutions with endless litigation with respect to the existence of exigent circumstances, whether it was practicable to get a warrant, whether the suspect was about to flee, and the like.

Watson's arrest did not violate the Fourth Amendment, and the Court of Appeals erred in holding to the contrary.

. . .

[The Court concluded further that Watson's consent to the search was valid.]

. . . [4]

―――――

10. In United States v. Santana, 427 U.S. 38 (1976), police officers went to the defendant's house to arrest her. When they arrived, she was standing in the doorway. As they approached, she retreated into the vestibule, where they made the arrest. The Court held that the arrest without a warrant was lawful.

In Warden v. Hayden, 387 U.S. 294 (1967) [p. 242 note 134 below], we recognized the right of police, who had probable cause to believe that an armed robber had entered a house a few minutes before, to make a warrantless entry to arrest the robber and to search for weapons. This case, involving a true "hot pursuit," is clearly governed by *Warden*; the need to act quickly here is even greater than in that case while the intrusion is much less. . . .

We thus conclude that a suspect may not defeat an arrest which has been set in motion in a public place, and is therefore proper under *Watson*, by the expedient of escaping to a private place. . . .

427 U.S. at 42–43. See Fontenot v. Cormier, 56 F.3d 669 (5th Cir.1995) (*Santana* applied); cf. Joyce v. Town of Tewksbury, Mass., 112 F.3d 19 (1st Cir.1997) (police pursued person standing inside door of third person's house into house; *Santana* noted).

―――――

[4] Justice Powell wrote a concurring opinion. Justice Stewart concurred in the result. Justice Marshall wrote a dissenting opinion, which Justice Brennan joined.

Draper v. United States

358 U.S. 307, 79 S.Ct. 329, 3 L.Ed.2d 327 (1959)

[Petitioner was convicted of knowingly concealing and transporting narcotic drugs. Before trial he moved to suppress evidence seized from him at the time of his arrest. He contended that his arrest, without a warrant, was without probable cause and unlawful, and therefore that the search of his person and seizure of the evidence incident to the arrest were unlawful. The district court denied the motion and the evidence was used against him at the trial. The court of appeals affirmed his conviction.]

■ MR. JUSTICE WHITTAKER delivered the opinion of the Court.

. . .

The evidence offered at the hearing on the motion to suppress was not substantially disputed. It established that one Marsh, a federal narcotic agent with 29 years' experience, was stationed at Denver; that one Hereford had been engaged as a "special employee" of the Bureau of Narcotics at Denver for about six months, and from time to time gave information to Marsh regarding violations of the narcotic laws, for which Hereford was paid small sums of money, and that Marsh had always found the information given by Hereford to be accurate and reliable. On September 3, 1956, Hereford told Marsh that James Draper (petitioner) recently had taken up abode at a stated address in Denver and "was peddling narcotics to several addicts" in that city. Four days later, on September 7, Hereford told Marsh "that Draper had gone to Chicago the day before [September 6] by train [and] that he was going to bring back three ounces of heroin [and] that he would return to Denver either on the morning of the 8th of September or the morning of the 9th of September also by train." Hereford also gave Marsh a detailed physical description of Draper and of the clothing he was wearing,[5] and said that he would be carrying "a tan zipper bag," and that he habitually "walked real fast."

On the morning of September 8, Marsh and a Denver police officer went to the Denver Union Station and kept watch over all incoming trains from Chicago, but they did not see anyone fitting the description that Hereford had given. Repeating the process on the morning of September 9, they saw a person, having the exact physical attributes and wearing the precise clothing described by Hereford, alight from an incoming Chicago train and start walking "fast" toward the exit. He was carrying a tan zipper bag in his right hand and the left was thrust in his raincoat pocket. Marsh, accompanied by the police officer, overtook, stopped and arrested him. They then searched him and found the two "envelopes containing heroin" clutched in his left hand in his raincoat pocket, and found the syringe in the tan zipper bag. Marsh then took him (petitioner) into custody. Hereford died four days after the arrest and therefore did not testify at the hearing on the motion.

---

5. Hereford told Marsh that Draper was a Negro of light brown complexion, 27 years of age, 5 feet 8 inches tall, weighed about 160 pounds, and that he was wearing a light colored raincoat, brown slacks and black shoes.

26 U.S.C. (Supp. V) § 7607, added by § 104(a) of the Narcotic Control Act of 1956, 70 Stat. 570, provides, in pertinent part:

> The Commissioner . . . and agents, of the Bureau of Narcotics . . . may— . . .
>
> . . .
>
> (2) make arrests without warrant for violations of any law of the United States relating to narcotic drugs . . . where the violation is committed in the presence of the person making the arrest or where such person has reasonable grounds to believe that the person to be arrested has committed or is committing such violation.

The crucial question for us then is whether knowledge of the related facts and circumstances gave Marsh "probable cause" within the meaning of the Fourth Amendment, and "reasonable grounds" within the meaning of § 104(a), supra,[6] to believe that petitioner had committed or was committing a violation of the narcotic laws. If it did, the arrest, though without a warrant, was lawful and the subsequent search of petitioner's person and the seizure of the found heroin were validly made incident to a lawful arrest, and therefore the motion to suppress was properly overruled and the heroin was competently received in evidence at the trial. . . .

Petitioner does not dispute this analysis of the question for decision. Rather, he contends (1) that the information given by Hereford to Marsh was "hearsay" and, because hearsay is not legally competent evidence in a criminal trial, could not legally have been considered, but should have been put out of mind, by Marsh in assessing whether he had "probable cause" and "reasonable grounds" to arrest petitioner without a warrant, and (2) that, even if hearsay could lawfully have been considered, Marsh's information should be held insufficient to show "probable cause" and "reasonable grounds" to believe that petitioner had violated or was violating the narcotic laws and to justify his arrest without a warrant.

Considering the first contention, we find petitioner entirely in error. Brinegar v. United States, 338 U.S. 160, 172–73, has settled the question the other way. There, in a similar situation, the convict contended "that the factors relating to inadmissibility of the evidence [for] *purposes of proving guilt at the trial*, deprive[d] the evidence as a whole of sufficiency to show probable cause for the search. . . ." Id., at 172. (Emphasis added.) But this Court, rejecting that contention, said: "[T]he so-called distinction places a wholly unwarranted emphasis upon the criterion of admissibility in evidence, to prove the accused's guilt, of the facts relied upon to show probable cause. That emphasis, we think, goes much too far in confusing and disregarding the difference between what is required to prove guilt in a criminal case and what is required to show probable cause for arrest or search. It approaches requiring (if it does not in practical effect require) proof sufficient to establish guilt in order to substantiate the existence of

---

6. The terms "probable cause" as used in the Fourth Amendment and "reasonable grounds" as used in § 104(a) of the Narcotic Control Act, 70 Stat. 570, are substantial equivalents of the same meaning. . . .

probable cause. There is a large difference between the two things to be proved [guilt and probable cause], as well as between the tribunals which determine them, and therefore a like difference in the *quanta* and modes of proof required to establish them." 338 U.S., at 172–73.

Nor can we agree with petitioner's second contention that Marsh's information was insufficient to show probable cause and reasonable grounds to believe that petitioner had violated or was violating the narcotic laws and to justify his arrest without a warrant. The information given to narcotic agent Marsh by "special employee" Hereford may have been hearsay to Marsh, but coming from one employed for that purpose and whose information had always been found accurate and reliable, it is clear that Marsh would have been derelict in his duties had he not pursued it. And when, in pursuing that information, he saw a man, having the exact physical attributes and wearing the precise clothing and carrying the tan zipper bag that Hereford had described, alight from one of the very trains from the very place stated by Hereford and start to walk at a "fast" pace toward the station exit, Marsh had personally verified every facet of the information given him by Hereford except whether petitioner had accomplished his mission and had the three ounces of heroin on his person or in his bag. And surely, with every other bit of Hereford's information being thus personally verified, Marsh had "reasonable grounds" to believe that the remaining unverified bit of Hereford's information—that Draper would have the heroin with him—was likewise true.

"In dealing with probable cause, . . . as the very name implies, we deal with probabilities. These are not technical; they are the factual and practical considerations of everyday life on which reasonable and prudent men, not legal technicians, act." Brinegar v. United States, supra, at 175. Probable cause exists where "the facts and circumstances within [the arresting officers'] knowledge and of which they had reasonably trustworthy information [are] sufficient in themselves to warrant a man of reasonable caution in the belief that" an offense has been or is being committed. Carroll v. United States, 267 U.S. 132, 162.

We believe that, under the facts and circumstances here, Marsh had probable cause and reasonable grounds to believe that petitioner was committing a violation of the laws of the United States relating to narcotic drugs at the time he arrested him. The arrest was therefore lawful, and the subsequent search and seizure, having been made incident to that lawful arrest, were likewise valid. It follows that petitioner's motion to suppress was properly denied and that the seized heroin was competent evidence lawfully received at the trial.

■ MR. JUSTICE DOUGLAS, dissenting.

Decisions under the Fourth Amendment, taken in the long view, have not given the protection to the citizen which the letter and spirit of the Amendment would seem to require. One reason, I think, is that wherever a culprit is caught red-handed, as in leading Fourth Amendment cases, it is difficult to adopt and enforce a rule that would turn him loose. A rule protective of law-abiding citizens is not apt to flourish where its advocates are usually criminals. Yet the rule we fashion is for the innocent and guilty alike. If the word of the informer on which the present arrest was made is sufficient to make the arrest legal, his word would also protect the police who, acting on it, hauled the innocent citizen off to jail.

Of course, the education we receive from mystery stories and television shows teaches that what happened in this case is efficient police work. The police are tipped off that a man carrying narcotics will step off the morning train. A man meeting the precise description does alight from the train. No warrant for his arrest has been—or, as I see it, could then be—obtained. Yet he is arrested; and narcotics are found in his pocket and a syringe in the bag he carried. This is the familiar pattern of crime detection which has been dinned into public consciousness as the correct and efficient one. It is, however, a distorted reflection of the constitutional system under which we are supposed to live.

With all due deference, the arrest made here on the mere word of an informer violated the spirit of the Fourth Amendment and the requirement of the law, 26 U.S.C. (Supp. V) § 7607, governing arrests in narcotics cases. . . . The arresting officers did not have a bit of evidence, known to them and as to which they could take an oath had they gone to a magistrate for a warrant, that petitioner had committed any crime. The arresting officers did not know the grounds on which the informer based his conclusion; nor did they seek to find out what they were. They acted solely on the informer's word. In my view that was not enough.

The rule which permits arrest for felonies, as distinguished from misdemeanors, if there are reasonable grounds for believing a crime has been or is being committed . . . grew out of the need to protect the public safety by making prompt arrests. . . . Yet, apart from those cases where the crime is committed in the presence of the officer, arrests without warrants, like searches without warrants, are the exception, not the rule in our society. . . .

. . .

The Court is quite correct in saying that proof of "reasonable grounds" for believing a crime was being committed need not be proof admissible at the trial. It could be inferences from suspicious acts, e.g., consort with known peddlers, the surreptitious passing of a package, an intercepted message suggesting criminal activities, or any number of such events coming to the knowledge of the officer. . . . But, if he takes the law into his own hands and does not seek the protection of a warrant, he must act on some evidence known to him. The law goes far to protect the citizen. Even suspicious acts observed by the officers may be as consistent with innocence as with guilt. That is not enough, for even the guilty may not be implicated on suspicion alone. . . . The reason is, as I have said, that the standard set by the Constitution and by the statute is one that will protect both the officer and the citizen. For if the officer acts with "probable cause" or on "reasonable grounds," he is protected even though the citizen is innocent. . . .

Here the officers had no evidence—apart from the mere word of an informer—that petitioner was committing a crime. The fact that petitioner walked fast and carried a tan zipper bag was not evidence of any crime. The officers knew nothing except what they had been told by the informer. If they went to a magistrate to get a warrant of arrest and relied solely on the report of the informer, it is not conceivable to me that one would be granted. . . . For they could not present to the magistrate any of the facts which the informer may have had. They could swear only to the fact that the informer had made the accusation. They could swear to no evidence that lay in their own knowledge. They could present, on information and belief, no facts which the informer disclosed. No magistrate could issue a warrant on the mere word of an officer, without more. . . . We are not justified in lowering the standard when an arrest is made without a warrant and allowing the officers more leeway than we grant the magistrate.

With all deference I think we break with tradition when we sustain this arrest. We said in United States v. Di Re, [332 U.S. 581 (1948)], at 595, "a search is not to be made legal by what it turns up. In law it is good or bad when it starts and does not change character from its success." In this case it was only after the arrest and search were made that there was a shred of evidence known to the officers that a crime was in the process of being committed.

———

11. In Smith v. Ohio, 494 U.S. 541 (1990), the Court emphasized the point made by Justice Douglas at the end of his opinion in *Draper*: an arrest cannot be justified by what is found in a search incident to the arrest. "The exception for searches incident to arrest permits the police to search a lawfully arrested person and areas within his immediate control. . . . [I]t does not permit the police to search any citizen without a warrant or probable cause so long as an arrest immediately follows." Id. at 543.

12. "[T]here are at least two means by which the credibility of an informant may be established. One is by corroborating external circumstances occurring in the course of the very case that is at issue, as happened in the Draper case. . . . The other is the fact that on prior occasions in other cases the informant has given information which turned out to be reliable." Costello v. United States, 324 F.2d 260, 262 (9th Cir.1963). How significant were the "corroborating external circumstances" in *Draper*? See Illinois v. Gates, 462 U.S. 213 (1983), p. 180 below.

13.

It is notorious that the narcotics informer is often himself involved in the narcotics traffic and is often paid for his information in cash, narcotics, immunity from prosecution, or lenient punishment. . . .

The reliability of such persons is obviously suspect. The fact that their information may have produced convictions in the past does not justify taking their reports on faith. . . . [T]he present informer practice amounts to condoning felonies on condition that the confessed or suspected felon brings about the conviction of others. Under such stimulation it is to be expected that the informer will not infrequently reach for shadowy leads, or even seek to incriminate the innocent. The practice of paying fees to the informer for the cases he makes may also be expected, from time to time, to induce him to lure non-users into the drug habit and then entrap them into law violations.

For such reasons, the law has wisely circumscribed the use of informers' reports as a basis for making arrest. It has required a showing of reliability of the information and some corroboration by facts within the arresting officer's own knowledge. Such corroboration may be obtained by placing the suspect under surveillance and observing whether his behavior—e.g., making contact with persons known to be in the trade, or surreptitious passing of a package—tends to support the informer's story.

How much personal knowledge the policeman must have before making the arrest cannot be determined for all cases. Since circumstances vary, the rule must be stated in terms of what is reasonably inferable from the particular circumstances by a prudent police officer. . . . It would appear from *Draper* [v. United States, 358 U.S. 307 (1959)] that when a reliable informer tells an officer that an individual has left town to buy narcotics and is returning by train at a certain time, the policeman's observation of his return is enough to justify an arrest without a warrant.

When deprivation of liberty by arrest is justified by a combination of an informer's report and a policeman's own observations, the less the policeman is required to observe, the more significant becomes the informer's report. Since observation of so commonplace an act as coming home by train is enough, in combination with the report of an informer, to justify an arrest, the only significant limitation of the informer's power to cause an arrest is the requirement of reliability. The requirement that the informer be reliable stands as the only effective legal safeguard against false denunciations by irresponsible individuals who may be motivated by self-interest, spite, or even paranoia. The only other safeguard which remains rests not on law but on the good will of the police officer.

Jones v. United States, 266 F.2d 924, 928–29 (D.C.Cir.1959) (Bazelon, J.).

14. "We have discovered no case that extends this requirement [of evidence that an informant's information is credible or that he is reliable] to the identified bystander or victim-eyewitness to a crime, and now hold that no such requirement need be met. The rationale behind requiring a showing of credibility and reliability is to prevent searches based upon an unknown informant's tip that may not reflect anything more than idle rumor or irresponsible conjecture. Thus, without the establishment of the probability of reliability, a 'neutral and detached magistrate' could not adequately assess the probative value of the tip in exercising his judgment as to the existence of probable cause. Many informants are intimately involved with the persons informed upon and with the illegal conduct at hand, and this circumstance could also affect their credibility. None of

Boston Police Department
Arrest Booking Form

Report Date: 02/10/1997 11:55:19
Booking Status: COMPLETED
Printed By: Dahlbeck, Joseph W

District: 09   **Cell Number:** 5
Charges: Breaking And Entering (Residence)
Court: Boston Municipal   **UCR Code:**
Docket #: WA 123145-0000

Master Name: Pomeroy, Arnold, George   **DOB:** 03/17/1956
Location Of Arrest: 7 Warren Ave

Booking Name: Layfield, Robert, Arthur
Alias: Pomeroy, Raymond, Allen
Address: Apt 23, 312 Evergreen CR , Boston, MA.

Booking Number: 95-000316-04   **Incident Number:**   **CR Number:** 000001-80
Booking Date: 02/10/1997 11:25   **Arrest Date:** 03/17/1995 14:00   **RA Number:**

Sex: Male	**Height:** 5' 11"	**Occupation:** Welder
Race: White Non-Hispanic	**Weight:** 200 lbs	**Employer / School:**
Date Of Birth: 06/09/1942	**Build:** Medium	**Emp/School Address:**
Place Of Birth: Boston, MA, USA	**Eye Color:** Brown	**Social Sec. Number:** 100104100
Marital Status: Separated	**Hair Color:** Dark	**Operators License:** S02489647
Mother Name: Jones, Hazel K	**Complexion:** Medium	**State:**
Father Name: Layfield, Arthur		

Phone Used: YES   **Scars / Marks /:**
Examined at Hospital: NO   **Tattoos:**
Breathalizer Used: NO   **Clothing Desc:**

Arresting Officer: BPD	09566	Joseph W Dahlbeck		
Booking Officer: BPD	10127	Sean P Scannell	**Arresting Partner ID:**	10427
Informed Of Rights: BPD	09566	Joseph W Dahlbeck	**Unit:**	123
Placed In Cell By: BPD	10427	Claudio R McKenzie	**Transporting Unit:**	123
Searched By: BPD	10427	Claudio R McKenzie		

Cautions: **Booking Comments:** none   **Visible Injuries:** Any injuries would be listed in this area

JUVENILE INFORMATION

Person Notified: **Relationship:**   **Phone:**
Address: **Juv. Prob. Officer:**
Notified By: BPD   **Notified Date / Time:**

Ball Set By:
Balled By:
Amount:

I Selected the Bail Comm.

_____
Signature Of Prisoner

BOP Check:
Suicide Check:
BOP Warrant:
BOP Court:

_____
Signature of Duty Supervisor

these considerations is present in the eyewitness situation. . . . Such observers are seldom involved with the miscreants or the crime. Eyewitnesses by definition are not passing along idle rumor, for they either have been the victims of the crime or have otherwise seen some portion of it." United States v. Bell, 457 F.2d 1231, 1238–39 (5th Cir.1972).

15. "[T]he arresting officer testified that he was informed by a lieutenant from the Criminal Investigation Bureau that an anonymous phone call had been received informing the lieutenant that a described man named Bernie Horowitz was then shaping up for work at the mail room of the New York Times Building and had in his possession a brown paper bag containing stolen United States savings bonds and pornographic literature; that he found the defendant at the mail room of the Times Building, identified himself as a police officer, asked the defendant his name and obtained a brown paper bag which the defendant carried containing United States savings bonds in the name of Anthony Cardone which were later identified as having been stolen." The description that was given of Horowitz was that he "was over six feet tall, weighed more than 200 pounds, and was known as 'Mr. Clean' because of the lack of hair on his head." People v. Horowitz, 233 N.E.2d 453, 453–54 (N.Y.1967). Was Horowitz's arrest lawful?

16.

On September 22, 1961, at about 3:45 A.M., the defendant and two other men were stopped by two uniformed Baltimore City police officers while riding in a 1960 Oldsmobile, bearing Maryland license number AL29–32. The officers got out of the police car, drew their pistols, placed the defendant and the others under arrest, told them to put their hands on the dashboard, and held them in that position until their sergeant arrived. Then, the defendant and the other occupants were ordered out of the car and were subjected to a search, in the course of which the arresting officers discovered in the right jacket pocket of the defendant a small package wrapped in green paper, the contents of which were later identified as heroin. In a subsequent search at police headquarters, a similar package, the contents of which were also later identified as heroin, was found in the defendant's sock.

Officer Snead, one of the arresting officers, testified that the reason he stopped the vehicle the defendant was driving was that he had received a teletype message on his patrol car radio to stop a vehicle matching the description of the Oldsmobile, with Maryland tags number AL29–32, in which were two colored occupants who were suspected of illegally possessing narcotics, that he had not been informed of and did not know the defendant's name or his description, and that at no time did he see the defendant violate any law.

The instruction to stop the vehicle which the defendant was driving, on which the arresting officers relied in making their arrest, was placed on teletype at approximately 12:30 A.M. September 22, by the Maryland State Police at the request of one Greenfeld, a federal agent who was acting upon information which had been relayed to him in Baltimore by Federal narcotics agents in New York who had had the defendant under surveillance as a result of information passed on to them by a special employee (an informant). The New York agents both testified that they had not observed the defendant violate any law nor had their special employee, who merely had heard that the defendant had narcotics in his possession which he was taking back to Baltimore. Agent Greenfeld testified that based on the information he had received from New York, his evaluation thereof, and a conversation with Captain Carroll of the Baltimore Police Narcotics Squad as to the local narcotics activities of the defendant, he "believed" that the defendant was bringing narcotics to Baltimore.

Stanley v. State, 186 A.2d 478, 479–80 (Md.1962). Was the arrest constitutionally valid?

"The police department of a large metropolis does not and can not operate on a segmented basis with each officer acting separately and independently of each other and detached from the central headquarters. There must be cooperation, co-ordination and direction, with some central control and exchange of information." Miller v. United States, 356 F.2d 63, 67 (5th Cir.1966). When the basis of an arrest is "the collective information of the police rather than that of only the officer who performs the act of arresting," Smith v. United States, 358 F.2d 833, 835 (D.C.Cir.1966), what should be the test?

17. Whiteley v. Warden, 401 U.S. 560 (1971). Relying on a police bulletin, an officer arrested Whiteley. It turned out that the warrant for Whiteley's arrest on which the bulletin was based was invalid. The Court rejected the argument that the arresting officer nevertheless had probable cause for the arrest because he was entitled to rely on the bulletin. "Certainly police officers called upon to aid other officers in executing arrest warrants are entitled to assume that the officers requesting aid offered the magistrate the information requisite to support an independent judicial assessment of probable cause. Where, however, the contrary turns out to be true, an otherwise illegal arrest cannot be insulated from challenge by the decision of the instigating officer to rely on fellow officers to make the arrest." Id. at 568. The precedential value of Whiteley v. Warden, insofar as application of the exclusionary rule is concerned, was questioned in Arizona v. Evans, 514 U.S. 1 (1995) (6–3), p. 150 note 81 below. Cf. United States v. Hensley, 469 U.S. 221 (1985), p. 125 note 69 below.

———

Beck v. Ohio

379 U.S. 89, 85 S.Ct. 223, 13 L.Ed.2d 142 (1964)

■ MR. JUSTICE STEWART delivered the opinion of the Court.

On the afternoon of November 10, 1961, the petitioner, William Beck, was driving his automobile in the vicinity of East 115th Street and Beulah Avenue in Cleveland, Ohio. Cleveland police officers accosted him, identified themselves, and ordered him to pull over to the curb. The officers possessed neither an arrest warrant nor a search warrant. Placing him under arrest, they searched his car but found nothing of interest. They then took him to a nearby police station where they searched his person and found an envelope containing a number of clearing house slips "beneath the sock of his leg." The petitioner was subsequently charged in the Cleveland Municipal Court with possession of clearing house slips in violation of a state criminal statute. . . .

. . .

[Before trial, the petitioner moved to suppress the clearing house slips. The motion was denied. The slips were admitted in evidence at trial and he was convicted. The Ohio courts affirmed the conviction; admission of the slips was upheld on the ground that the search was incident to a lawful arrest and therefore valid.]

There are limits to the permissible scope of a warrantless search incident to a lawful arrest, but we proceed on the premise that, if the arrest itself was lawful, those limits were not exceeded here. . . . The constitutional validity of the search in this case, then, must depend upon the constitutional validity of the petitioner's arrest. Whether that arrest was constitutionally valid depends in turn upon whether, at the moment the arrest was made, the officers had probable cause to make it—whether at that moment the facts and circumstances within their knowledge and of which they had reasonably trustworthy information were sufficient to warrant a prudent man in believing that the petitioner had committed or was committing an offense. . . . "The rule of probable cause is a practical, nontechnical conception affording the best compromise that has been found for accommodating . . . often opposing interests. Requiring more would unduly hamper lawful enforcement. To allow less would be to leave law-abiding citizens at the mercy of the officers' whim or caprice." Brinegar v. United States, [338 U.S. 160 (1949)], at 176.

. . .

The record is meager, consisting only of the testimony of one of the arresting officers, given at the hearing on the motion to suppress. As to the officer's own knowledge of the petitioner before the arrest, the record shows no more than that the officer "had a police picture of him and knew what he looked like," and that the officer knew that the petitioner had "a record in connection with clearing house and scheme of chance." Beyond that, the officer testified only that he had "information" that he had "heard reports," that "someone specifically did relate that information," and that he "knew who that person was." There is nowhere in the record any indication of what "information" or "reports" the officer had received or, beyond what has been set out above, from what source the "information" and "reports" had come. The officer testified that when he left the station house, "I had in mind looking for [the petitioner] in the area of East 115th Street and Beulah, stopping him if I did see him make a stop in that area." But the officer testified to nothing that would indicate that any informer had said that the petitioner could be found at that time and place. . . . And the record does not show that the officers saw the petitioner "stop" before they arrested him, or that they saw, heard, smelled, or otherwise perceived anything else to give them ground for belief that the petitioner had acted or was then acting unlawfully.

No decision of this Court has upheld the constitutional validity of a warrantless arrest with support so scant as this record presents. The respondent relies upon Draper v. United States, 358 U.S. 307. But in that case the record showed that a named special employee of narcotics agents who had on numerous occasions given reliable information had told the arresting officer that the defendant, whom he described minutely, had taken up residence at a stated address and was selling narcotics to addicts in Denver. The informer further had told the officer that the defendant was going to Chicago to obtain narcotics and would be returning to Denver on one of two trains from Chicago, which event in fact took place. In complete contrast, the record in this case does not contain a single objective fact to support a belief by the officers that the petitioner was engaged in criminal activity at the time they arrested him.

An arrest without a warrant bypasses the safeguards provided by an objective predetermination of probable cause, and substitutes instead the far less reliable procedure of an after-the-event justification for the arrest or search, too likely to be subtly influenced by the familiar shortcomings of hindsight judgment. "Whether or not the requirements of reliability and particularity of the information on which an officer may act are more stringent where an arrest warrant is absent, they surely cannot be less stringent than where an arrest warrant is obtained. Otherwise, a principal incentive now existing for the procurement of arrest warrants would be destroyed." Wong Sun v. United States, 371 U.S. 471, 479–80. Yet even in cases where warrants were obtained, the Court has held that the Constitution demands a greater showing of probable cause than can be found in the present record. . . .

When the constitutional validity of an arrest is challenged, it is the function of a court to determine whether the facts available to the officers at the moment of the arrest would "warrant a man of reasonable caution in the belief" that an offense has been committed. Carroll v. United States, 267 U.S. 132, 162. If the court is not informed of the facts upon which the arresting officers acted, it cannot properly discharge that function. All that the trial court was told in this case was that the officers knew what the petitioner looked like and knew that he had a previous record of arrests or convictions for violations of the clearing house law. Beyond that, the arresting officer who testified said no more than that someone (he did not say who) had told him something (he did not say what) about the petitioner. We do not hold that the officer's knowledge of the petitioner's physical appearance and previous record was either inadmissible or entirely irrelevant upon the issue of probable cause. . . . But to hold that knowledge of either or both of these facts constituted probable cause would be to hold that anyone with a previous criminal record could be arrested at will.

It is possible that an informer did in fact relate information to the police officer in this case which constituted probable cause for the petitioner's arrest. But when the constitutional validity of that arrest was challenged, it was incumbent upon the prosecution to show with considerably more specificity than was shown in this case what the informer actually said, and why the officer thought the information was credible. We may assume that the officers acted in good faith in arresting the petitioner. But "good faith on the part of the arresting officers is not enough." Henry v. United States, 361 U.S. 98, 102. If subjective good faith alone were the test, the protections of the Fourth Amendment would evaporate, and the people would be "secure in their persons, houses, papers, and effects," only in the discretion of the police.

. . . [7]

————

18.

The pertinent circumstances are those of the moment, the actual ones. Officers patrolling the streets at night do not prearrange the setting. They do not schedule their steps in the calm of an office. Things just happen. They are required as a matter of duty to act as reasonably prudent men would act under the circumstances as those circumstances happen. . . .

Among the other pertinent circumstances is the qualification and function of the person making the arrest. The standard is a reasonable, cautious and prudent man. But the question is whether the person making the arrest had probable cause. Probable cause is not a philosophical concept existing in a vacuum; it is a practical and factual matter. A fact which spells reasonable cause to a doctor may make no impression on a carpenter, and vice versa. Did the person who made the arrest, if a reasonable and prudent man, have probable cause? An officer experienced in the narcotics traffic may find probable cause in the smell of drugs and the appearance of paraphernalia which to the lay eye is without significance. His action is not measured by what might be probable cause to an untrained civilian passerby. When a peace officer makes the arrest the standard means a reasonable, cautious and prudent peace officer. The question is what constituted probable cause in the eyes of a reasonable, cautious and prudent peace officer under the circumstances of the moment.

Bell v. United States, 254 F.2d 82, 85–86 (D.C.Cir.1958).

19.

Shortly after midnight on a February morning in 1966, Grady Johnson and Henry Ussery, while walking along a sidewalk, were attacked by several men. A wallet, a watch and a small sum of money were taken from Johnson, and a watch and a penknife from Ussery. Within a few minutes, police officers, responding to a reported shooting

[7] Justice Clark wrote a dissenting opinion, which Justice Black joined. Justice Harlan also wrote a dissenting opinion.

in the same block, arrived at the scene. Soon gathered there, too, were a number of spectators, among whom our appellant was standing.

Ussery, bruised and bleeding about his face, informed Officers Arthur G. Delaney and Rudolph Scipio of the attack, and pointed to appellant—a stranger to him—as one of the robbers. Though somewhat excited, and admittedly having been drinking prior to the incident, Ussery insisted that he was positive in his identification.

Officer Scipio then approached appellant and inquired as to what he was doing in the area. Appellant replied that he had just left a party, and was taking a walk to get some fresh air. The officer then informed appellant of Ussery's accusation, which appellant denied, and proceeded to arrest him. A concomitant search uncovered on appellant's person the watch taken from Johnson, and the watch and penknife stolen from Ussery.

Pendergrast v. United States, 416 F.2d 776 (D.C.Cir.1969). Were the arrest and search incident to it lawful?

20.

In essence, the testimony of the arresting officers was that they had been specially assigned to look for the perpetrator of a series of day-time housebreakings that had taken place in a particular area in Northeast Washington. They said that the Police Department had broadcast many descriptions of the suspect ("lookouts"), the latest having been issued on the day prior to the arrest. The lookouts—based on information received from complaining witnesses—described the suspect as a "brown-skinned" colored man about "five feet seven" or "five feet eight" in height, about 150 pounds in weight, "very neatly" dressed, wearing a "gray topcoat," sometimes said to have a "half-belt" in the back, or a "black topcoat," and a "brown" or "gray" hat. His age was variously described as "middle teens," "late teens," "19, 21, 22," or "22–24." The look-outs, issued from time to time over a period of months, referred to each of a series of crimes of common pattern, all having been committed by someone who forced open the front doors of houses, with some instrument, in the daylight hours.

On the day in question, shortly before noon, the officers, who were in plain clothes, were driving an unmarked car down one of the streets in the area where the crimes had occurred. They saw Ellis approach on foot from the opposite direction. They testified they were mindful of the descriptions given in the look-outs, and that Ellis appeared to them to be the wanted man: he was "brown-skinned," "around five seven or five eight" in height, from "a hundred forty-five to a hundred and fifty" pounds in weight, "very neatly dressed," wearing a "gray topcoat with a half-belt in the back," and a "brown" hat, and was estimated to be "between twenty-two and twenty-five" years old.

The officers drove on a short distance, turned their car around, and waited. They saw Ellis go up on the porch of a house, knock on the door, stand there looking "around the area" for a "few minutes," then return to the street and walk back toward the direction from which he had come. As Ellis approached, the officers hailed him and asked him to come to their car, saying that they were police officers. They got out of the car, and asked Ellis his name. He gave it. He was then asked, "Do you have any identification?" The answer was in the negative. Ellis appeared nervous; he "dropped his money . . . chewing gum, cigarettes, and so forth on the ground." The officers "asked him twice to take his hand out of his pocket." However, he "kept his right hand in his coat pocket and his arm close against his side." One of the officers "patted him and found a bulge in his inside pocket on the righthand side." The officers then searched him, and found certain items which were later used against him.

Ellis v. United States, 264 F.2d 372, 373–74 (D.C.Cir.1959). The use against Ellis of the items found on his person was permissible only if the search was incident to a lawful arrest. Were the items properly admitted in evidence?

21.

At 2:00 A.M. on November 9, 1962, the Old Hickory Barbecue Restaurant in Southeast Washington was robbed. A police lookout, based on descriptions of three robbers given by the witnesses at the restaurant, was broadcast. Private Fallin, the arresting officer, testified that the lookout contained "a general description of three colored males." Forty-five minutes after receiving the first lookout, Fallin testified, he received another call to respond to South Capitol and Howard Streets. There he found a taxi driver and more police. The cab driver told Fallin that a suspicious-acting person had fled from his cab as he drove into the Esso station on that corner. Fallin proceeded to track with his dog behind the Esso station in what appeared to be an abandoned area. After searching almost an hour, however, the dog was injured and the tracking operation was discontinued.

On returning to his cruiser, Fallin testified, he met his partner. His partner told him that a man had just come out of the general area where he was searching and was at that time walking down the highway. Fallin, with his partner, then approached this man, who turned out to be Gatlin, and arrested him at approximately 3:40 A.M.

Gatlin v. United States, 326 F.2d 666, 668–70 (D.C.Cir.1963). Was Gatlin arrested lawfully?

22. Although a reasonable mistake of fact may furnish an objective basis for reasonable suspicion or probable cause, a mistake of law, however reasonable, cannot. Furthermore, the good faith exception to the exclusionary rule, see p. 148 below, does not extend to a mistake of law. United States v. Chanthasouxat, 342 F.3d 1271 (11th Cir. 2003). Cf. Illinois v. Rodriguez, p. 169 below.

23. In Ornelas v. United States, 517 U.S. 690 (1996) (8–1), the Court considered the standard for appellate review of a determination that there is either reasonable suspicion (justifying an investigative stop, see pp. 100–117 below) or probable cause. It said:

> Articulating precisely what "reasonable suspicion" and "probable cause" mean is not possible. They are commonsense, nontechnical conceptions that deal with "the factual and practical considerations of everyday life on which reasonable and prudent men, not legal technicians, act." Illinois v. Gates, 462 U.S. 213, 231 (1983) (quoting Brinegar v. United States, 338 U.S. 160, 176 (1949)) . . . As such, the standards are "not readily, or even usefully, reduced to a neat set of legal rules." *Gates*, supra, at 232. We have described reasonable suspicion simply as "a particularized and objective basis" for suspecting the person stopped of criminal activity, United States v. Cortez, 449 U.S. 411, 417–18 (1981), and probable cause to search as existing where the known facts and circumstances are sufficient to warrant a man of reasonable prudence in the belief that contraband or evidence of a crime will be found. . . . We have cautioned that these two legal principles are not "finely-tuned standards," comparable to the standards of proof beyond a reasonable doubt or of proof by a preponderance of the evidence. *Gates*, supra, at 235. They are instead fluid concepts that take their substantive content from the particular contexts in which the standards are being assessed. . . .

> The principal components of a determination of reasonable suspicion or probable cause will be the events which occurred leading up to the stop or search, and then the decision whether these historical facts, viewed from the standpoint of an objectively reasonable police officer, amount to reasonable suspicion or to probable cause. The first part of the analysis involves only a determination of historical facts, but the second is a mixed question of law and fact: "[T]he historical facts are admitted or established, the rule of law is undisputed, and the issue is whether the facts satisfy the [relevant] statutory [or constitutional] standard, or to put it another way, whether the rule of law as applied to the established facts is or is not violated." Pullman-Standard v. Swint, 456 U.S. 273, 289, n.19 (1982).

> We think independent appellate review of these ultimate determinations of reasonable suspicion and probable cause is consistent with the position we have taken in past cases. We have never, when reviewing a probable-cause or reasonable-suspicion determination ourselves, expressly deferred to the trial court's determination. . . . A policy of sweeping deference would permit, "[i]n the absence of any significant difference in the facts," "the Fourth Amendment's incidence [to] tur[n] on whether different trial judges draw general conclusions that the facts are sufficient or insufficient to constitute probable cause." *Brinegar*, supra, at 171. Such varied results would be inconsistent with the idea of a unitary system of law. This, if a matter-of-course, would be unacceptable.

> In addition, the legal rules for probable cause and reasonable suspicion acquire content only through application. Independent re-

view is therefore necessary if appellate courts are to maintain control of, and to clarify the legal principles. . . .

Finally, de novo review tends to unify precedent and will come closer to providing law enforcement officers with a defined "set of rules which, in most instances, makes it possible to reach a correct determination beforehand as to whether an invasion of privacy is justified in the interest of law enforcement." New York v. Belton, 453 U.S. 454, 458 (1981). . . .

. . .

We therefore hold that as a general matter determinations of reasonable suspicion and probable cause should be reviewed de novo on appeal. Having said this, we hasten to point out that a reviewing court should take care both to review findings of historical fact only for clear error and to give due weight to inferences drawn from those facts by resident judges and local law enforcement officers.

A trial judge views the facts of a particular case in light of the distinctive features and events of the community; likewise a police officer views the facts through the lens of his police experience and expertise. The background facts provide a context for the historical facts, and when seen together yield inferences that deserve deference. . . . The background facts, though rarely the subject of explicit findings, inform the judge's assessment of the historical facts.

In a similar vein, our cases have recognized that a police officer may draw inferences based on his own experience in deciding whether probable cause exists. . . . An appeals court should give due weight to a trial court's finding that the officer was credible and the inference was reasonable.

517 U.S. at 696–700.

The Court revisited *Ornelas* in United States v. Arvizu, 534 U.S. 266 (2002), as it applies to reasonable suspicion. It said that a court should not reduce the "totality of the circumstances" test to a rigid formula and indicated considerable deference to the trained judgment of the officer who makes a stop.

24. The temporary detention of a motorist who the arresting officer has probable cause to believe has committed a civil traffic violation does not violate the Fourth Amendment even if the officer's reliance on the traffic violation was pretextual (the officer was seeking evidence of some unrelated crime) and the stop was not objectively reasonable (it deviated substantially from ordinary police practice). Having probable cause, the stop is reasonable under the Fourth Amendment, without more. Whren v. United States, 517 U.S. 806 (1996).

The Court extended the holding of *Whren* to a full custodial arrest, rather than a traffic stop, in Arkansas v. Sullivan, 532 U.S. 769 (2001) (per curiam). See United States v. Castro, 166 F.3d 728 (5th Cir. 1999) (en banc) (pretextual arrest for speeding and seat belt violations followed by impoundment and search of vehicle, at behest of narcotics investigators; *Whren* applied).

————

In the preceding cases, would the police officer who made the arrest have been derelict in his duty if he had *not* done so? If the officer in any of the cases should not have made the arrest, was there something else that he should have done?

————

25.   Probable cause. The Supreme Court has not developed the concept of probable cause significantly beyond its expression in Carroll v. United States, 267 U.S. 132 (1925), and Brinegar v. United States, 338 U.S. 160 (1949), the most important portions of which are quoted in the opinion in *Draper*, p. 26 above. The statements in those cases were restatements of existing law without much clarification. See, e.g., Husty v. United States, 282 U.S. 694, 700–701 (1931); Dumbra v. United States, 268 U.S. 435, 441 (1925); Stacey v. Emery, 97 U.S. 642, 645 (1878).

If the primary function of a formula which expresses the standard of "probable cause" is to advise law enforcement officials of the circumstances in which they may arrest (or search)—an assumption which is by no means apparent from the cases—can you do any better than the Court has done in framing a formula? Putting aside the adequacy of the Court's formulation of the standard, do you have a clear understanding of why the standard is what it is? Has the Court expressed and explained the values which led it to permit the arrest in *Draper* but not *Beck*?

26.   "Whether or not the requirements of reliability and particularity of the information on which an officer may act are more stringent where an arrest warrant is absent, they surely cannot be less stringent than where an arrest warrant is obtained. Otherwise, a principal incentive now existing for the procurement of arrest warrants would be destroyed." Wong Sun v. United States, 371 U.S. 471, 479–80 (1963).

Is the Court's statement in *Wong Sun*, above, persuasive? What might be the response to the argument that police would not obtain warrants if to do so they had to have stronger evidence than to arrest without a warrant? Consider United States v. Watson, 423 U.S. 411 (1976), p. 22 above.

Although the Court has often expressed a preference for an arrest or search pursuant to a warrant rather than without a warrant, e.g. Illinois v. Gates, 462 U.S. 213, 236 (1983); United States v. Ventresca, 380 U.S. 102 (1965), it has also emphasized in many cases that the Fourth Amendment requires only that an arrest or search be "reasonable" and that failure to obtain a warrant is not itself indicative of unreasonableness. E.g., Illinois v. Rodriguez, 497 U.S. 177 (1990); Chambers v. Maroney, 399 U.S. 42 (1970). One might conclude from such cases that the preference for a warrant is in practice not very strong.

————

The Requirement of a Warrant

———

A warrantless arrest is not invalid simply because the arresting officer failed to take advantage of an opportunity to obtain a warrant. In Trupiano v. United States, 334 U.S. 699, 705 (1948), the Court said: "The absence of a warrant of arrest, even though there was sufficient time to obtain one, does not destroy the validity of an arrest under these circumstances [felony committed in the presence of the arresting officer]. Warrants of arrest are designed to meet the dangers of unlimited and unreasonable arrests of persons who are not at the moment committing any crime. Those dangers, obviously, are not present where a felony plainly occurs before the eyes of an officer of the law at a place where he is lawfully present. Common sense then dictates that an arrest in that situation is valid despite the failure to obtain a warrant of arrest."

The same rule, that a warrant is not required to make an arrest, applies to a minor criminal offense. Atwater v. City of Lago Vista, 532 U.S. 318 (2001) (5–4) (misdemeanor seat belt violation punishable only by fine).

The intimation in *Trupiano* that if there is time a warrant must be obtained to arrest for a crime *not* being committed in the presence of the arresting officer has not been developed. See United States v. Watson, 423 U.S. 411 (1976). Should such a requirement be imposed? Why (not)? See generally the dissenting opinion of Justice White in Chimel v. California, 395 U.S. 752, 770 (1969), p. 215 note 122 below.

———

27. If an arrest is made pursuant to a warrant that is subsequently found to be invalid, can it be sustained as an arrest without a warrant, if there was probable cause to arrest? The answer generally has been that it is. See Chimel v. California, 395 U.S. 752 (1969), p. 205 below; Giordenello v. United States, 357 U.S. 480, 487–88 (1958). In light of this rule, how much force have the requirements of an arrest warrant other than the existence of probable cause? What reasons are there for or against upholding an arrest on this basis?

28. Shortly after he was advised by police radio to be on the lookout for two suspects in a holdup earlier that night, a police officer saw two people in a car parked in a private parking lot. The broadcast descriptions of the suspects and the car they were driving corresponded generally to the officer's observations. Suspecting that they were the wanted men but believing (as he testified later) that there was not probable cause for their arrest on the holdup charge, the officer arrested the two men for vagrancy. The facts known to the officer did furnish probable cause to arrest the men for the holdup. There was not probable cause for their arrest for vagrancy. Is evidence found in a search of the car incident to the arrest admissible against the two men? See Ricehill v. Brewer, 459 F.2d 537 (8th Cir.1972); Klingler v. United States, 409 F.2d 299 (8th Cir.1969). Is Whren v. United States, 517 U.S. 806 (1996), p. 41 note 24 above, controlling?

———

Payton v. New York
445 U.S. 573, 100 S.Ct. 1371, 63 L.Ed.2d 639 (1980)

■ Mr. Justice Stevens delivered the opinion of the Court.

These appeals challenge the constitutionality of New York statutes that authorize police officers to enter a private residence without a warrant and with force, if necessary, to make a routine felony arrest.

. . .

. . . We now . . . hold that the Fourth Amendment to the United States Constitution, made applicable to the States by the Fourteenth Amendment . . . prohibits the police from making a warrantless and nonconsensual entry into a suspect's home in order to make a routine felony arrest.

. . .

I

On January 14, 1970, after two days of intensive investigation, New York detectives had assembled evidence sufficient to establish probable cause to believe that Theodore Payton had murdered the manager of a gas station two days earlier. At about 7:30 a.m. on January 15, six officers went to Payton's apartment in the Bronx, intending to arrest him. They had not obtained a warrant. Although light and music emanated from the apartment, there was no response to their knock on the metal door. They summoned emergency assistance and, about 30 minutes later, used crowbars to break open the door and enter the apartment. No one was there. In plain view, however, was a .30-caliber shell casing that was seized and later admitted into evidence at Payton's murder trial.

In due course Payton surrendered to the police, was indicted for murder, and moved to suppress the evidence taken from his apartment. The trial judge held that the warrantless and forcible entry was authorized by the New York Code of Criminal Procedure, and that the evidence in plain view was properly seized. He found that exigent circumstances justified the officers' failure to announce their purpose before entering the apartment as required by the statute. He had no occasion, however, to decide whether those circumstances also would have justified the failure to obtain a warrant, because he concluded that the warrantless entry was adequately supported by the statute without regard to the circumstances. . . .

On March 14, 1974, Obie Riddick was arrested for the commission of two armed robberies that had occurred in 1971. He had been identified by the victims in June of 1973, and in January 1974 the police had learned his address. They did not obtain a warrant for his arrest. At about noon on March 14, a detective, accompanied by three other officers, knocked on the door of the Queens house where Riddick was living. When his young son opened the door, they could see Riddick sitting in bed covered by a sheet. They entered the house and placed him under arrest. Before permitting him to dress, they opened a chest of drawers two feet from the bed in search of weapons and found narcotics and related paraphernalia. Riddick was subsequently indicted on narcotics charges. At a suppression hearing, the trial judge held that the warrantless entry into his home was authorized by the revised New York statute, and that the search of the immediate area was reasonable under Chimel v. California, 395 U.S. 752. . . .

The New York Court of Appeals, in a single opinion, affirmed the convictions of both Payton and Riddick. . . .

. . .

Before addressing the narrow question presented by these appeals, we put to one side other related problems that are *not* presented today. Although it is arguable that the warrantless entry to effect Payton's arrest might have been justified by exigent circumstances, none of the New York courts relied on any such justification. The Court of Appeals majority treated both Payton's and Riddick's cases as involving routine arrests in which there was ample time to obtain a warrant, and we will do the same. Accordingly, we have no occasion to consider the sort of emergency or dangerous situation, described in our cases as "exigent circumstances," that would justify a warrantless entry into a home for the purpose of either arrest or search.

Nor do these cases raise any question concerning the authority of the police, without either a search or arrest warrant, to enter a third party's home to arrest a suspect. The police broke into Payton's apartment intending to arrest Payton and they arrested Riddick in his own dwelling. We also note that in neither case is it argued that the police lacked probable cause to believe that the suspect was at home when they entered. Finally, in both cases we are dealing with entries into homes made without the consent of any occupant. In *Payton*, the police used crowbars to break down the door and in *Riddick*, although his three-year-old son answered the door, the police entered before Riddick had an opportunity either to object or to consent.

II

It is familiar history that indiscriminate searches and seizures conducted under the authority of "general warrants" were the immediate evils that motivated the framing and adoption of the Fourth Amendment.

Indeed, as originally proposed in the House of Representatives, the draft contained only one clause, which directly imposed limitations on the issuance of warrants, but imposed no express restrictions on warrantless searches or seizures. As it was ultimately adopted, however, the Amendment contained two separate clauses, the first protecting the basic right to be free from unreasonable searches and seizures and the second requiring that warrants be particular and supported by probable cause. . . .

It is thus perfectly clear that the evil the Amendment was designed to prevent was broader than the abuse of a general warrant. Unreasonable searches or seizures conducted without any warrant at all are condemned by the plain language of the first clause of the Amendment. Almost a century ago the Court stated in resounding terms that the principles reflected in the Amendment "reached farther than the concrete form" of the specific cases that gave it birth, and "apply to all invasions on the part of the Government and its employés of the sanctity of a man's home and the privacies of life." Boyd v. United States, 116 U.S. 616, 630. Without pausing to consider whether that broad language may require some qualification, it is sufficient to note that the warrantless arrest of a person is a species of seizure required by the Amendment to be reasonable. . . .

The simple language of the Amendment applies equally to seizures of persons and to seizures of property. Our analysis in this case may therefore properly commence with rules that have been well established in Fourth Amendment litigation involving tangible items. As the Court reiterated just a few years ago, the "physical entry of the home is the chief evil against which the wording of the Fourth Amendment is directed." United States v. United States District Court, 407 U.S. 297, 313. And we have long adhered to the view that the warrant procedure minimizes the danger of needless intrusions of that sort.

It is a "basic principle of Fourth Amendment law" that searches and seizures inside a home without a warrant are presumptively unreasonable. Yet it is also well settled that objects such as weapons or contraband found in a public place may be seized by the police without a warrant. The seizure of property in plain view involves no invasion of privacy and is presumptively reasonable, assuming that there is probable cause to associate the property with criminal activity. . . .

. . .

The majority of the New York Court of Appeals, however, suggested that there is a substantial difference in the relative intrusiveness of an entry to search for property and an entry to search for a person. . . . It is true that the area that may legally be searched is broader when executing a search warrant than when executing an arrest warrant in the home. . . . This difference may be more theoretical than real, however, because the police may need to check the entire premises for safety reasons, and sometimes they ignore the restrictions on searches incident to arrest.

But the critical point is that any differences in the intrusiveness of entries to search and entries to arrest are merely ones of degree rather than kind. The two intrusions share this fundamental characteristic: the breach of the entrance to an individual's home. The Fourth Amendment protects the individual's privacy in a variety of settings. In none is the zone of privacy more clearly defined than when bounded by the unambiguous physical dimensions of an individual's home—a zone that finds its roots in clear and specific constitutional terms: "The right of the people to be secure in their . . . houses . . . shall not be violated." That language unequivocally establishes the proposition that "[a]t the very core [of the Fourth Amendment] stands the right of a man to retreat into his own home and there be free from unreasonable governmental intrusion." Silverman v. United States, 365 U.S. 505, 511. In terms that apply equally to seizures of property and to seizures of persons, the Fourth Amendment has drawn a firm line at the entrance to the house. Absent exigent circumstances, that threshold may not reasonably be crossed without a warrant.

III

Without contending that United States v. Watson, [423 U.S. 411 (1976)], decided the question presented by these appeals, New York argues that the reasons that support the Watson holding require a similar result here. In *Watson* the Court relied on (a) the well-settled common-law rule that a warrantless arrest in a public place is valid if the arresting officer had probable cause to believe the suspect is a felon; (b) the clear consensus among the States adhering to that well settled common-law rule; and (c) the expression of the judgment of Congress that such an arrest is "reasonable." We consider each of these reasons as it applies to a warrantless entry into a home for the purpose of making a routine felony arrest.

A

An examination of the common-law understanding of an officer's authority to arrest sheds light on the obviously relevant, if not entirely dispositive, consideration of what the Framers of the Amendment might have thought to be reasonable. . . .

A study of the common law on the question whether a constable had the authority to make warrantless arrests in the home on mere suspicion of a felony—as distinguished from an officer's right to arrest for a crime committed in his presence—reveals a surprising lack of judicial decisions and a deep divergence among scholars.

. . .

[T]he common-law rule on warrantless home arrests was not as clear as the rule on arrests in public places. . . . [T]he weight of authority as it appeared to the Framers was to the effect that a warrant was required, or at the minimum that there were substantial risks in proceeding without one. The common-law sources display a sensitivity to privacy interests that could not have been lost on the Framers. The zealous and frequent repetition of the adage that a "man's house is his castle," made it abundantly clear that both in England and in the Colonies "the freedom of one's house" was one of the most vital elements of English liberty.[8]

Thus, our study of the relevant common law does not provide the same guidance that was present in *Watson*. Whereas the rule concerning the validity of an arrest in a public place was supported by cases directly in point and by the unanimous views of the commentators, we have found no direct authority supporting forcible entries into a home to make a routine arrest and the weight of the scholarly opinion is somewhat to the contrary. Indeed, the absence of any 17th or 18th century English cases directly in point, together with the unequivocal endorsement of the tenet that "a man's house is his castle," strongly suggests that the prevailing practice was not to make such arrests except in hot pursuit or when authorized by a warrant. . . . In all events, the issue is not one that can be said to have been definitively settled by the common law at the time the Fourth Amendment was adopted.

B

A majority of the States that have taken a position on the question permit warrantless entry into the home to arrest even in the absence of exigent circumstances. At this time, 24 States permit such warrantless entries; 15 States clearly prohibit them, though 3 States do so on federal constitutional grounds alone; and 11 States have apparently taken no position on the question.

But these current figures reflect a significant decline during the last decade in the number of States permitting warrantless entries for arrest. . . .

A longstanding, widespread practice is not immune from constitutional scrutiny. But neither is it to be lightly brushed aside. This is particularly so when the constitutional standard is as amorphous as the word "reasonable," and when custom and contemporary norms necessarily play such a large role in the constitutional analysis. In this case, although the weight of state-law authority is clear, there is by no means the kind of virtual unanimity on this question that was present in United States v. Watson, with regard to warrantless arrests in public places. . . . Only 24 of the 50 States currently sanction warrantless entries into the home to arrest . . . and there is an obvious declining trend. . . .

C

No congressional determination that warrantless entries into the home are "reasonable" has been called to our attention. None of the federal statutes cited in the *Watson* opinion reflects any such legislative judgment. Thus, that support for the *Watson* holding finds no counterpart in this case. . . .

---

8. . . . 2 Legal Papers of John Adams 142 (L. Wroth and H. Zobel ed. 1965).

[N]either history nor this Nation's experience requires us to disregard the overriding respect for the sanctity of the home that has been embedded in our traditions since the origins of the Republic.

IV

The parties have argued at some length about the practical consequences of a warrant requirement as a precondition to a felony arrest in the home. In the absence of any evidence that effective law enforcement has suffered in those States that already have such a requirement . . . we are inclined to view such arguments with skepticism. More fundamentally, however, such arguments of policy must give way to a constitutional command that we consider to be unequivocal.

Finally, we note the State's suggestion that only a search warrant based on probable cause to believe the suspect is at home at a given time can adequately protect the privacy interests at stake, and since such a warrant requirement is manifestly impractical, there need be no warrant of any kind. We find this ingenious argument unpersuasive. It is true that an arrest warrant requirement may afford less protection than a search warrant requirement, but it will suffice to interpose the magistrate's determination of probable cause between the zealous officer and the citizen. If there is sufficient evidence of a citizen's participation in a felony to persuade a judicial officer that his arrest is justified, it is constitutionally reasonable to require him to open his doors to the officers of the law. Thus, for Fourth Amendment purposes, an arrest warrant founded on probable cause implicitly carries with it the limited authority to enter a dwelling in which the suspect lives when there is reason to believe the suspect is within.

Because no arrest warrant was obtained in either of these cases, the judgments must be reversed. . . .

. . . [9]

———

29. *Payton* is applied in Kirk v. Louisiana, 536 U.S. 635 (2002) (per curiam). See Valdez v. McPheters, 172 F.3d 1220 (10th Cir.1999), holding that an arrest warrant is sufficient to authorize entry of a house in order to make an arrest only if the arresting officers reasonably believe that the person resides there and is within.

30. In Welsh v. Wisconsin, 466 U.S. 740 (1984) (6–2), the Supreme Court gave a partial answer to the question left open in *Payton*: What exigent circumstances justify a warrantless entry into a home to make an arrest? Police, having probable cause to believe that the defendant had been driving while drunk, arrested him in his home without a warrant. A

[9] Justice Blackmun wrote a concurring opinion. Justice White wrote a dissenting opinion, which Chief Justice Burger and Justice Rehnquist joined. Justice Rehnquist also wrote a dissenting opinion.

first offense of drunk driving was a noncriminal violation. The Court held
that the Fourth Amendment prohibited an entry to arrest in those circumstances. It said that "it is difficult to conceive of a warrantless home arrest
that would not be unreasonable under the Fourth Amendment when the
underlying offense is extremely minor."

In view of the nature of the offense, the Court said, it was immaterial
that evidence, the alcohol content of the defendant's blood, might imminently be lost. "[A]n important factor to be considered when determining
whether any exigency exists is the gravity of the underlying offense for
which the arrest is being made. Moreover, although no exigency is created
simply because there is probable cause to believe that a serious crime has
been committed . . . application of the exigent-circumstances exception in
the context of a home entry should rarely be sanctioned when there is
probable cause to believe that only a minor offense . . . has been committed." Id. at 753.

See United States v. Gray, 626 F.2d 102 (9th Cir.1980) (drug offenses;
warrantless entry to arrest in exigent circumstances upheld); United States
v. Campbell, 581 F.2d 22 (2d Cir.1978) (armed robbery; same). Compare
United States v. Santana, 427 U.S. 38 (1976), p. 25 note 10 above.

See New York v. Harris, 495 U.S. 14 (1990), p. 81 below.

31.   Premises of third persons. In the absence of an emergency or
consent to the entry, the Fourth Amendment requires a *search* warrant to
enter the home of a third person in order to arrest a person for whom the
police have an arrest warrant. Steagald v. United States, 451 U.S. 204
(1981) (7–2).

> [W]hile an arrest warrant and a search warrant both serve to subject
> the probable cause determination of the police to judicial review, the
> interests protected by the two warrants differ. An arrest warrant is
> issued by a magistrate upon a showing that probable cause exists to
> believe that the subject of the warrant has committed an offense and
> thus the warrant primarily serves to protect an individual from an
> unreasonable seizure. A search warrant, in contrast, is issued upon a
> showing of probable cause to believe that the legitimate object of a
> search is located in a particular place and therefore safeguards an
> individual's interest in the privacy of his home and possessions against
> the unjustified intrusion of the police.
>
>   . . . Because an arrest warrant authorizes the police to deprive a
> person of his liberty, it necessarily also authorizes a limited invasion of
> that person's privacy interest when it is necessary to arrest him in his
> home. This analysis, however, is plainly inapplicable when the police
> seek to use an arrest warrant as legal authority to enter the home of a
> third party to conduct a search. Such a warrant embodies no judicial
> determination whatsoever regarding the person whose home is to be
> searched. Because it does not authorize the police to deprive the third
> person of his liberty, it cannot embody any derivative authority to
> deprive this person of his interest in the privacy of his home. Such a

deprivation must instead be based on an independent showing that a legitimate object of a search is located in the third party's home. We have consistently held however, that such a determination is the province of the magistrate, and not that of the police officer.

Id. at 212–13, 214–15 n.7.

In United States v. Underwood, 717 F.2d 482 (9th Cir.1983), the defendant was arrested in the home of another person, where he was an overnight guest. Having a warrant for his arrest and information that he was in the house, officers entered the house without a search warrant and arrested him. Upholding the arrest, the court said that *Payton* rather than *Steagald* controlled. It reasoned that the person arrested had no greater rights in the home of a third person than in his own, so that if an arrest warrant sufficed in the latter case it sufficed also in the former. *Steagald* was distinguished on the ground that there it was the third person whose home was entered who objected to the search. Accord United States v. Buckner, 717 F.2d 297 (6th Cir.1983).

32. Is Lewis v. United States, p. 304 below, consistent with *Payton*? See United States v. White, 660 F.2d 1178 (7th Cir.1981). Consider note 172, following the opinion in *Lewis*, p. 307 below.

"Arrest"

Rios v. United States

364 U.S. 253, 80 S.Ct. 1431, 4 L.Ed.2d 1688 (1960)

■ MR. JUSTICE STEWART delivered the opinion of the Court.

An indictment filed in the United States District Court for the Southern District of California charged the petitioner with unlawful receipt and concealment of narcotics in violation of 21 U.S.C. § 174. . . .

At about ten o'clock on the night of February 18, 1957, two Los Angeles police officers, dressed in plain clothes and riding in an unmarked car, observed a taxicab standing in a parking lot next to an apartment house at the corner of First and Flower Streets in Los Angeles. The neighborhood had a reputation for "narcotics activity." The officers saw the petitioner look up and down the street, walk across the lot, and get into the cab. Neither officer had ever before seen the petitioner, and neither of them had any idea of his identity. Except for the reputation of the neighborhood, neither officer had received information of any kind to suggest that someone might be engaged in criminal activity at that time and place. They were not searching for a participant in any previous crime. They were in possession of no arrest or search warrants.

The taxicab drove away, and the officers followed it in their car for a distance of about two miles through the city. At the intersection of First and State Streets the cab stopped for a traffic light. The two officers alighted from their car and approached on foot to opposite sides of the cab. One of the officers identified himself as a policeman. In the next minute there occurred a rapid succession of events. The cab door was opened; the petitioner dropped a recognizable package of narcotics to the floor of the vehicle; one of the officers grabbed the petitioner as he alighted from the cab; the other officer retrieved the package; and the first officer drew his revolver.

The precise chronology of all that happened is not clear in the record. In their original arrest report the police stated that the petitioner dropped the package only after one of the officers had opened the cab door. In testifying later, this officer said that he saw the defendant drop the package before the door of the cab was opened. The taxi driver gave a substantially different version of what occurred. He stated that one of the officers drew his revolver and "took hold of the defendant's arm while he was still in the cab."

. . .

[The package of narcotics was turned over to federal authorities and was admitted in evidence at the petitioner's trial.]

. . . The seizure can survive constitutional inhibition only upon a showing that the surrounding facts brought it within one of the exceptions to the rule that a search must rest upon a search warrant. . . . Here justification is primarily sought upon the claim that the search was an incident to a lawful arrest. Yet upon no possible view of the circumstances revealed in the testimony of the Los Angeles officers could it be said that there existed probable cause for an arrest at the time the officers decided to alight from their car and approach the taxi in which the petitioner was riding. . . . This the Government concedes.

If, therefore, the arrest occurred when the officers took their positions at the doors of the taxicab, then nothing that happened thereafter could make that arrest lawful, or justify a search as its incident. . . . But the Government argues that the policemen approached the standing taxi only for the purpose of routine interrogation, and that they had no intent to detain the petitioner beyond the momentary requirements of such a mission. If the petitioner thereafter voluntarily revealed the package of narcotics to the officers' view, a lawful arrest could then have been supported by their reasonable cause to believe that a felony was being committed in their presence. The validity of the search thus turns upon the narrow question of when the arrest occurred, and the answer to that question depends upon an evaluation of the conflicting testimony of those who were there that night.

The judgment is vacated, and the case is remanded to the District Court for further proceedings consistent with this opinion.

. . . [10]

---

192 F.Supp. 888 (S.D.Cal.1961)

■ HALL, CHIEF JUDGE.

. . .

Without extended discussion I now resolve such conflicts in the testimony as there are, and find the facts concerning the arrest and the seizure of the narcotics to be as follows:

(1) That Officers Beckman and Grace were lawfully making a routine surveillance of the taxicab and its occupants, and for the purpose of making a routine interrogation, they approached the taxicab but did not stop or detain it until after the commission of a crime by the defendant in the officers' sight and presence;

(2) That the taxicab in which the defendant was riding was not stopped by the officers;

(3) That it stopped for a traffic light at a brightly-lighted intersection;

(4) That while the taxicab was thus stopped, Officer Beckman approached the taxicab on the right side and Officer Grace approached it on the left;

(5) That Officer Beckman flashed his flashlight on his badge, exhibiting it to the driver and to the defendant who was sitting in the back seat, to identify himself, and he did identify himself orally as a police officer;

(6) That after, and almost simultaneous with, such identification, the officer saw the defendant, and the defendant did, voluntarily take from his pocket a rubber contraceptive of a light color which appeared to the officer to be filled with a light powder, and defendant voluntarily dropped it to the floor of the cab;

(7) That immediately thereafter the defendant and Officer Beckman simultaneously reached for the door of the taxicab, and both opened the door;

(8) That defendant alighted from the cab, and he was not pulled or forced out of it by either officer; and that thereupon, and not before, Officer Beckman announced that defendant was under arrest on suspicion of narcotics; and thereupon, and not before, the defendant was under arrest;

(9) That the time transpiring between the time Officer Beckman identified himself as above set forth and the time when defendant was out of the cab was about one minute;

[10] Justice Frankfurter wrote a dissenting opinion which Justice Clark, Justice Harlan, and Justice Whittaker joined. Justice Harlan wrote a memorandum which Justice Clark and Justice Whittaker joined.

(10) That within seconds after defendant got out of the taxicab, Officer Grace retrieved the contraceptive containing the heroin from the floor of the taxicab where the defendant had placed it by dropping it there;

(11) That by voluntarily dropping the package of narcotics to the floor and getting out of the cab, the defendant voluntarily gave up possession thereof;

(12) That Officer Beckman had had more than four years experience working the Narcotic Detail in Los Angeles, and had made over 400 arrests;

(13) That it was known to him that a common method of carrying heroin is to carry it in a rubber contraceptive;

(14) That under those circumstances and the "testimony of the officer's own senses," (Burks v. United States, 9 Cir., 287 F.2d 117, and cases therein cited), in light of his experience, when he saw defendant take a contraceptive from his pocket and drop it to the floor of the taxicab, and when he observed the nature of the object, he had reasonable cause to believe that contraceptive contained heroin, and reasonable cause to, in good faith, believe that defendant had committed a felony in his presence, viz.: violation of the State and Federal Penal Statutes relating to narcotics.

From the foregoing, I conclude as a matter of law, that the arrest was lawful, the search and seizure were reasonable and lawful, and if conducted by federal officers, the arrest and search and seizure would have been reasonable and lawful, and the arrest and search and seizure did not violate the defendant's immunity from unreasonable searches and seizures under the Fourth Amendment, and would not have done so if conducted by federal officers.

The motion of the defendant to suppress the evidence is denied. . . .

. . .

---

33.   In a footnote in *Rios*, above, the Court noted: "The petitioner later broke free from the policeman's grasp and ran into an alley. There the officer apprehended him after shooting him in the back." 364 U.S. at 256 n.1.[11]

---

11.   See also Abel v. United States, 362 U.S. 217 (1960), in which the Court carefully treated the seizure of evidence as an incident to the petitioner's arrest and mentioned only in passing the facts that following his arrest in New York he was "taken by airplane to a detention center for aliens in Texas" and kept there "for several weeks until arrested upon the charge of conspiracy to commit espionage for which he was brought to trial," id. at 225. The Court's studious attention to the precise moment when an arrest occurs and comparative disregard of other more substantial interferences with the person in some situations has led one commentator to observe that "by focusing judicial attention upon the search and seizure aspects of police procedures, the rule [requiring the exclusion of evidence obtained unlawfully] tends to create an impression that other forms of police

When a police officer believes that he has the authority to make an arrest and exercises (or, if he is mistaken, purports to exercise) his authority, there is ordinarily no difficulty in concluding that an "arrest" has been made. Difficulty arises when the officer intends not to arrest but to take action having some, but (necessarily, since the intention is lacking) not all, the characteristics of the paradigm. In such cases, one can try to draw the line between arrests and nonarrests more and more precisely, and then attribute to all the instances labeled "arrest" the significance and consequences of the paradigm. Or one can proceed by comparing the paradigm and a particular instance and noting the similarities and differences, and then noting what consequences are at stake and what it is about the paradigm that leads to that consequence and why, and finally deciding whether the particular instance sufficiently resembles the paradigm in the relevant respect. One may answer the question, "Is this an arrest?" with the question, "Why do you want to know?" or with the answer, equally incomplete, "It all depends," or "It is and it isn't." Once the difficulty is presented as raising the question, "Is this an arrest?" however, there may be pressure to avoid incomplete answers in favor of an answer which tends to construct a platonic ideal against which actual instances can be measured.

Even if one can assert with confidence that there is no ideal "arrest," and that "really" at stake is a complex of related acts, it is not clear that the second of the two approaches is the best one for the law. The law may have to deal with some "givens," such as language of special significance and historically fixed meaning, in this case the language of the Fourth Amendment. Also, the law is not the process or product of intellectual inquiry wherever it may lead; it is intended to help us to accomplish certain objectives. In this case, one might ask whether relatively simple rules reflected in simple, direct language (or even the appearance of simple rules) might not achieve the objectives of arrest practice better than a more subtle analysis.

———

34. In the following cases, when did the arrest occur?

(i)

At 5:30 A.M., on July 22, 1959, a uniformed police officer was walking his beat when he observed the defendant attempting to flag a taxicab. The defendant was carrying what appeared to be a sack and from it an electrical cord was dragging on the ground. The officer stopped the defendant, asked him where he was coming from and what his name was. The defendant replied that he was coming from a party and stated his name. Upon the request of the officer, the defendant

illegality, however seriously they may invade personal rights and liberty, are of lesser importance." Barrett, "Personal Rights, Property Rights, and the Fourth Amendment," 1960 Sup. Ct. Rev. 46, 55–56.

took from his wallet a selective service card which corroborated the defendant's oral identification. The officer testified that, "walking my beat all night long, I did not observe any party anywhere." However, at this point, no crime had been reported to the officer and he had observed none. No warrant for the arrest of the defendant was outstanding.

The officer then asked the defendant to accompany him to a police call box which was about one block away. When the defendant inquired whether he was under arrest, the officer replied, "No, you are just being detained." At the call box, the defendant seated himself on the record player contained in the sack (a pillow case) and the officer put in his call. He inquired whether there had been any reported housebreakings (up to that time he was not aware that a crime had been committed) and was told there had not been. He then requested the dispatch of a scout car to the area, when, by coincidence, a scout car appeared. At this point, the defendant fled from the scene, leaving the property behind. He was apprehended one week later. . . .

United States v. Mitchell, 179 F.Supp. 636, 637 (D.D.C.1959).

(ii)

On March 26, 1959, around 10 a.m., Officers Dorrell and Fesler went to a warehouse where defendant was employed. After speaking to the foreman, the latter called defendant from a box car which had been pulled up alongside of the building. Defendant walked over to the officers where he was shown their identification cards and told "[W]e are police officers. We would like to talk to you." Defendant then said "[J]ust a minute," turned and started to walk back toward the box car. Officer Dorrell took hold of defendant's arm and said, "[W]e would like to talk to you now." The officer did not pull or shove the defendant who then turned back around; the officer let go of his arm. Defendant then walked towards the door, together with the two officers, through the warehouse, outside under a roofed portion of a platform. Although Sergeant Fesler thought that as defendant turned around Officer Dorrell suggested to him that they go outside "to get away from the other people inside there," the officers did not "walk" him outside the warehouse, did not in any way physically touch him as they walked out together, did not tell him to go outside, and said nothing to him while walking before they reached the outside of the warehouse. Standing on the outside platform, Officer Dorrell asked him if he was using narcotics, which defendant denied; then if he was selling them, and defendant said "no." The officer then said to him, "[W]ell, then, you don't mind if we look through your pockets, do you?" and defendant answered "[N]o, go ahead and search me if you want to. I don't have anything on me." Whereupon Officer Dorrell searched him and found in defendant's right hand shirt pocket three capsules of heroin. Defendant told the officers the capsules contained heroin and he had bought them for his own use for $20; but denied having an outfit. They then told him he was under arrest and handcuffed him.

People v. Zavaleta, 6 Cal.Rptr. 166, 167 (Dist.Ct.App.1960). See People v. Haven, 381 P.2d 927 (Cal.1963) (*Zavaleta* disapproved).

(iii)

Harry Hobson, a policeman of the Santa Barbara police force, was informed by a man named Pembleton that he had been the victim of a robbery and that the robber drove a " '49 or '50 Chevy two-door dropped down in the back end"; that the robber was about 5 feet 10 inches tall, weighed about 150 pounds, was dark complexioned and had dark curly hair. Pembleton told Officer Hobson that the man, later identified by Pembleton, struck him, knocked him down, struck him several times while he was on the ground, and that while he was in the latter position he felt his wallet being pulled out of his pocket and that the robber then ran away.

The next day Officer Hobson, in ordinary street clothes, saw the defendant through a porch screen at an address on Haley Street in Santa Barbara and asked him to come out. When the defendant complied with the request Hobson then identified himself as being from the police department and asked the defendant if he would go to the police station with him and "be checked out on a robbery case." The defendant stated that he would do so and Hobson asked him if he would drive his own car. Defendant stated that he had no driver's license, but that Hobson could drive defendant's car and that he would go with him. Hobson then drove the defendant's automobile with defendant riding therein to the police station.

At the police station parking lot Hobson asked the defendant if he could search defendant's car and defendant answered, "Yes, go ahead." Hobson opened the door on the driver's side of the automobile and upon looking under the front seat found a 14-inch billy club with a wooden handle and a leather thong attached thereto, used for wrapping around the wrist. Hobson then asked defendant, "What is this?" and defendant answered that it was a billy club and said further, "I was hoping you wouldn't find that." Hobson inquired as to how long it had been in the automobile and was told by the defendant, "It's been in there about five months." The defendant was then arrested. . . .

People v. Hood, 309 P.2d 135, 136 (Cal.Dist.Ct.App.1957).

Would your answer to the question when the arrest occurred in any of the cases be different if the issue to be decided was not whether evidence obtained pursuant to the arrest could be used against the defendant but rather (1) whether the defendant was entitled to use force to resist the arrest; (2) whether the police officer was entitled to use force to effect the arrest; (3) whether the police officer was liable for false arrest; (4) whether the police officer was required to file an arrest report; (5) whether the police officer was required to carry out a directive that all persons who are arrested shall be brought to the station house for fingerprinting and then brought before a magistrate?

———

California v. Hodari D.
499 U.S. 621, 111 S.Ct. 1547, 113 L.Ed.2d 690 (1991)

■ JUSTICE SCALIA delivered the opinion of the Court.

Late one evening in April 1988, Officers Brian McColgin and Jerry Pertoso were on patrol in a high-crime area of Oakland, California. They were dressed in street clothes but wearing jackets with "Police" embossed on both front and back. Their unmarked car proceeded west on Foothill Boulevard, and turned south onto 63rd Avenue. As they rounded the corner, they saw four or five youths huddled around a small red car parked at the curb. When the youths saw the officers' car approaching they apparently panicked, and took flight. The respondent here, Hodari D., and one companion ran west through an alley; the others fled south. The red car also headed south, at a high rate of speed.

The officers were suspicious and gave chase. McColgin remained in the car and continued south on 63rd Avenue; Pertoso left the car, ran back north along 63rd, then west on Foothill Boulevard, and turned south onto 62nd Avenue. Hodari, meanwhile, emerged from the alley onto 62nd and ran north. Looking behind as he ran, he did not turn and see Pertoso until the officer was almost upon him, whereupon he tossed away what appeared to be a small rock. A moment later, Pertoso tackled Hodari, handcuffed him, and radioed for assistance. Hodari was found to be carrying $130 in cash and a pager; and the rock he had discarded was found to be crack cocaine.

In the juvenile proceeding brought against him, Hodari moved to suppress the evidence relating to the cocaine. The court denied the motion without opinion. The California Court of Appeal reversed, holding that Hodari had been "seized" when he saw Officer Pertoso running towards him, that this seizure was unreasonable under the Fourth Amendment, and that the evidence of cocaine had to be suppressed as the fruit of that illegal seizure. The California Supreme Court denied the State's application for review. We granted certiorari. . . .

As this case comes to us, the only issue presented is whether, at the time he dropped the drugs, Hodari had been "seized" within the meaning of the Fourth Amendment.[12] If so, respondent argues, the drugs were the

---

12. California conceded below that Officer Pertoso did not have the "reasonable suspicion" required to justify stopping Hodari, see Terry v. Ohio, 392 U.S. 1 (1968). That it would be unreasonable to stop, for brief inquiry, young men who scatter in panic upon the mere sighting of the police is not self-evident, and arguably contradicts proverbial common sense. See Proverbs 28:1 ("The wicked flee when no man pursueth"). We do not decide that point here, but rely entirely upon the State's concession.

fruit of that seizure and the evidence concerning them was properly excluded. If not, the drugs were abandoned by Hodari and lawfully recovered by the police, and the evidence should have been admitted. (In addition, of course, Pertoso's seeing the rock of cocaine, at least if he recognized it as such, would provide reasonable suspicion for the unquestioned seizure that occurred when he tackled Hodari. . . .)

We have long understood that the Fourth Amendment's protection against "unreasonable . . . seizures" includes seizure of the person. . . . From the time of the founding to the present, the word "seizure" has meant a "taking possession," 2 N. Webster, An American Dictionary of the English Language 67 (1828). . . . For most purposes at common law, the word connoted not merely grasping, or applying physical force to, the animate or inanimate object in question, but actually bringing it within physical control. . . . To constitute an arrest, however—the quintessential "seizure of the person" under our Fourth Amendment jurisprudence—the mere grasping or application of physical force with lawful authority, whether or not it succeeded in subduing the arrestee, was sufficient. . . .

To say that an arrest is effected by the slightest application of physical force, despite the arrestee's escape, is not to say that for Fourth Amendment purposes there is a *continuing* arrest during the period of fugitivity. If, for example, Pertoso had laid his hands upon Hodari to arrest him, but Hodari had broken away and had *then* cast away the cocaine, it would hardly be realistic to say that that disclosure had been made during the course of an arrest. . . . The present case, however, is even one step further removed. It does not involve the application of any physical force; Hodari was untouched by Officer Pertoso at the time he discarded the cocaine. His defense relies instead upon the proposition that a seizure occurs "when the officer, by means of physical force *or show of authority*, has in some way restrained the liberty of a citizen." Terry v. Ohio, 392 U.S. 1, 19, n.16 (1968) (emphasis added). Hodari contends (and we accept as true for purposes of this decision) that Pertoso's pursuit qualified as a "show of authority" calling upon Hodari to halt. The narrow question before us is whether, with respect to a show of authority as with respect to application of physical force, a seizure occurs even though the subject does not yield. We hold that it does not.

The language of the Fourth Amendment, of course, cannot sustain respondent's contention. The word "seizure" readily bears the meaning of a laying on of hands or application of physical force to restrain movement, even when it is ultimately unsuccessful. ("She seized the purse-snatcher, but he broke out of her grasp.") It does not remotely apply, however, to the prospect of a policeman yelling "Stop, in the name of the law!" at a fleeing form that continues to flee. That is no seizure. Nor can the result respondent wishes to achieve be produced—indirectly, as it were—by suggesting that Pertoso's uncomplied-with show of authority was a common-law arrest, and then appealing to the principle that all common-law arrests are seizures. An arrest requires *either* physical force (as described above) or, where that is absent, *submission* to the assertion of authority. . . .

We do not think it desirable, even as a policy matter, to stretch the Fourth Amendment beyond its words and beyond the meaning of arrest, as respondent urges. Street pursuits always place the public at some risk, and compliance with police orders to stop should therefore be encouraged. Only a few of those orders, we must presume, will be without adequate basis, and since the addressee has no ready means of identifying the deficient ones it almost invariably is the responsible course to comply. Unlawful orders will not be deterred, moreover, by sanctioning through the exclusionary rule those of them that are *not* obeyed. Since policemen do not command "Stop!" expecting to be ignored, or give chase hoping to be outrun, it fully suffices to apply the deterrent to their genuine, successful seizures.

Respondent contends that his position is sustained by the so-called *Mendenhall* test, formulated by Justice Stewart's opinion in United States v. Mendenhall, 446 U.S. 544, 554 (1980), and adopted by the Court in later cases . . . : "A person has been 'seized' within the meaning of the Fourth Amendment only if, in view of all the circumstances surrounding the incident, a reasonable person would have believed that he was not free to leave." 446 U.S., at 554. . . . In seeking to rely upon that test here, respondent fails to read it carefully. It says that a person has been seized "only if," not that he has been seized "whenever"; it states a *necessary*, but not a *sufficient* condition for seizure—or, more precisely, for seizure effected through a "show of authority." *Mendenhall* establishes that the test for existence of a "show of authority" is an objective one: not whether the citizen perceived that he was being ordered to restrict his movement, but whether the officer's words and actions would have conveyed that to a reasonable person. Application of this objective test was the basis for our decision in the other case principally relied upon by respondent, [Michigan v.] *Chesternut*, [486 U.S. 567 (1988)], where we concluded that the police cruiser's slow following of the defendant did not convey the message that he was not free to disregard the police and go about his business. We did not address in *Chesternut*, however, the question whether, if the *Mendenhall* test was met—if the message that the defendant was not free to leave *had* been conveyed—a Fourth Amendment seizure would have occurred. . . .

. . .

In sum, assuming that Pertoso's pursuit in the present case constituted a "show of authority" enjoining Hodari to halt, since Hodari did not comply with that injunction he was not seized until he was tackled. The cocaine abandoned while he was running was in this case not the fruit of a seizure, and his motion to exclude evidence of it was properly denied. . . .

. . . [13]

---

[13] Justice Stevens wrote a dissenting opinion, which Justice Marshall joined.

35. Applying Terry v. Ohio, p. 100 below, the Court held that a person's "unprovoked flight" from approaching police officers in an area known for narcotics activity furnished reasonable suspicion justifying a *Terry* stop. Illinois v. Wardlow, 528 U.S. 119, 124 (2000) (5–4).

36. Rejecting the analysis of the Court in *Hodari D.*, the Supreme Court of New Jersey observed: "We are not satisfied as the Supreme Court was . . . that the biblical observation that '[t]he wicked flee when no man pursueth' " [p. 58 n.12 above] "is a satisfactory explanation of why a young man in a contemporary urban setting might run at the sight of the police." State v. Tucker, 642 A.2d 401, 407 (N.J.1994).

In State v. Young, 957 P.2d 681 (Wash.1998), the Supreme Court of Washington rejected *Hodari D.* and said that under state law the test was not whether a person has actually been seized but whether a reasonable person would have felt that he was free to leave. Other state cases following or rejecting *Hodari D.* are cited.

The Manner of Arrest

Tennessee v. Garner
471 U.S. 1, 105 S.Ct. 1694, 85 L.Ed.2d 1 (1985)

■ JUSTICE WHITE delivered the opinion of the Court.

This case requires us to determine the constitutionality of the use of deadly force to prevent the escape of an apparently unarmed suspected felon. We conclude that such force may not be used unless it is necessary to prevent the escape and the officer has probable cause to believe that the suspect poses a significant threat of death or serious physical injury to the officer or others.

I

At about 10:45 p.m. on October 3, 1974, Memphis Police Officers Elton Hymon and Leslie Wright were dispatched to answer a "prowler inside call." Upon arriving at the scene they saw a woman standing on her porch and gesturing toward the adjacent house. She told them she had heard glass breaking and that "they" or "someone" was breaking in next door. While Wright radioed the dispatcher to say that they were on the scene, Hymon went behind the house. He heard a door slam and saw someone run across the backyard. The fleeing suspect, who was appellee-respondent's decedent, Edward Garner, stopped at a 6-feet-high chain link fence at the edge of the yard. With the aid of a flashlight, Hymon was able to see Garner's face and hands. He saw no sign of a weapon, and, though not certain, was "reasonably sure" and "figured" that Garner was unarmed.

App. 41, 56; Record 219. He thought Garner was 17 or 18 years old and about 5′5″ or 5′7″ tall. While Garner was crouched at the base of the fence, Hymon called out "police, halt" and took a few steps toward him. Garner then began to climb over the fence. Convinced that if Garner made it over the fence he would elude capture, Hymon shot him. The bullet hit Garner in the back of the head. Garner was taken by ambulance to a hospital, where he died on the operating table. Ten dollars and a purse taken from the house were found on his body.

In using deadly force to prevent the escape, Hymon was acting under the authority of a Tennessee statute and pursuant to Police Department policy. The statute provides that "[i]f, after notice of the intention to arrest the defendant, he either flee or forcibly resist, the officer may use all the necessary means to effect the arrest." Tenn.Code Ann. § 40–7–108 (1982).[14] The Department policy was slightly more restrictive than the statute, but still allowed the use of deadly force in cases of burglary. . . . The incident was reviewed by the Memphis Police Firearms Review Board and presented to a grand jury. Neither took any action. . . .

Garner's father then brought this action in the Federal District Court for the Western District of Tennessee, seeking damages under 42 U.S.C. § 1983 for asserted violations of Garner's constitutional rights. The complaint . . . named as defendants Officer Hymon, the Police Department, its Director, and the Mayor and city of Memphis. After a 3-day bench trial, the District Court entered judgment for all defendants. . . . It . . . concluded that Hymon's actions were authorized by the Tennessee statute, which in turn was constitutional. Hymon had employed the only reasonable and practicable means of preventing Garner's escape. Garner had "recklessly and heedlessly attempted to vault over the fence to escape, thereby assuming the risk of being fired upon." App. to Pet. for Cert. A10.

. . .

The Court of Appeals reversed and remanded. 710 F.2d 240 (1983). It reasoned that the killing of a fleeing suspect is a "seizure" under the Fourth Amendment, and is therefore constitutional only if "reasonable." The Tennessee statute failed as applied to this case because it did not adequately limit the use of deadly force by distinguishing between felonies of different magnitudes—"the facts, as found, did not justify the use of deadly force under the Fourth Amendment." Id., at 246. Officers cannot resort to deadly force unless they "have probable cause . . . to believe that the suspect [has committed a felony and] poses a threat to the safety of the officers or a danger to the community if left at large." Ibid.

The State of Tennessee, which had intervened to defend the statute, see 28 U.S.C. § 2403(b), appealed to this Court. The city filed a petition for certiorari. We noted probable jurisdiction in the appeal and granted the petition. . . .

---

14. Although the statute does not say so explicitly, Tennessee law forbids the use of deadly force in the arrest of a misdemeanant. See Johnson v. State, 114 S.W.2d 819 (1938).

II

Whenever an officer restrains the freedom of a person to walk away, he has seized that person. . . . While it is not always clear just when minimal police interference becomes a seizure . . . there can be no question that apprehension by the use of deadly force is a seizure subject to the reasonableness requirement of the Fourth Amendment.

A

A police officer may arrest a person if he has probable cause to believe that person committed a crime. . . . Petitioners and appellant argue that if this requirement is satisfied the Fourth Amendment has nothing to say about how that seizure is made. This submission ignores the many cases in which this Court, by balancing the extent of the intrusion against the need for it, has examined the reasonableness of the manner in which a search or seizure is conducted. To determine the constitutionality of a seizure "[w]e must balance the nature and quality of the intrusion on the individual's Fourth Amendment interests against the importance of the governmental interests alleged to justify the intrusion." United States v. Place, 462 U.S. 696, 703 (1983). . . . Because one of the factors is the extent of the intrusion, it is plain that reasonableness depends on not only when a seizure is made, but also how it is carried out. . . .

. . .

B

The . . . balancing process . . . demonstrates that, notwithstanding probable cause to seize a suspect, an officer may not always do so by killing him. The intrusiveness of a seizure by means of deadly force is unmatched. The suspect's fundamental interest in his own life need not be elaborated upon. The use of deadly force also frustrates the interest of the individual, and of society, in judicial determination of guilt and punishment. Against these interests are ranged governmental interests in effective law enforcement. It is argued that overall violence will be reduced by encouraging the peaceful submission of suspects who know that they may be shot if they flee. Effectiveness in making arrests requires the resort to deadly force, or at least the meaningful threat thereof. "Being able to arrest such individuals is a condition precedent to the state's entire system of law enforcement." Brief for Petitioners 14.

Without in any way disparaging the importance of these goals, we are not convinced that the use of deadly force is a sufficiently productive means of accomplishing them to justify the killing of nonviolent suspects. . . . The use of deadly force is a self-defeating way of apprehending a suspect and so setting the criminal justice mechanism in motion. If successful, it guarantees that that mechanism will not be set in motion. And while the meaningful threat of deadly force might be thought to lead to the arrest of more live suspects by discouraging escape attempts, the presently available evidence does not support this thesis. The fact is that a majority of police departments in this country have forbidden the use of deadly force against nonviolent suspects. . . . If those charged with the enforcement of the criminal law have abjured the use of deadly force in arresting nondangerous felons, there is a substantial basis for doubting that the use of such force is an essential attribute of the arrest power in all felony cases. . . . Petitioners and appellant have not persuaded us that shooting nondangerous fleeing suspects is so vital as to outweigh the suspect's interest in his own life.

The use of deadly force to prevent the escape of all felony suspects, whatever the circumstances, is constitutionally unreasonable. It is not better that all felony suspects die than that they escape. Where the suspect poses no immediate threat to the officer and no threat to others, the harm resulting from failing to apprehend him does not justify the use of deadly force to do so. It is no doubt unfortunate when a suspect who is in sight escapes, but the fact that the police arrive a little late or are a little slower afoot does not always justify killing the suspect. A police officer may not seize an unarmed, nondangerous suspect by shooting him dead. The Tennessee statute is unconstitutional insofar as it authorizes the use of deadly force against such fleeing suspects.

It is not, however, unconstitutional on its face. Where the officer has probable cause to believe that the suspect poses a threat of serious physical harm, either to the officer or to others, it is not constitutionally unreasonable to prevent escape by using deadly force. Thus, if the suspect threatens the officer with a weapon or there is probable cause to believe that he has committed a crime involving the infliction or threatened infliction of serious physical harm, deadly force may be used if necessary to prevent escape, and if, where feasible, some warning has been given. As applied in such circumstances, the Tennessee statute would pass constitutional muster.

III

A

It is insisted that the Fourth Amendment must be construed in light of the common-law rule, which allowed the use of whatever force was necessary to effect the arrest of a fleeing felon, though not a misdemeanant. . . . Most American jurisdictions also imposed a flat prohibition against the use of deadly force to stop a fleeing misdemeanant, coupled with a general privilege to use such force to stop a fleeing felon. . . .

The State and city argue that because this was the prevailing rule at the time of the adoption of the Fourth Amendment and for some time thereafter, and is still in force in some States, use of deadly force against a fleeing felon must be "reasonable." It is true that this Court has often looked to the common law in evaluating the reasonableness, for Fourth Amendment purposes, of police activity. . . . On the other hand, it "has not simply frozen into constitutional law those law enforcement practices that existed at the time of the Fourth Amendment's passage." Payton v. New York, 445 U.S. 573, 591, n.33 (1980). Because of sweeping change in the legal and technological context, reliance on the common-law rule in this case would be a mistaken literalism that ignores the purposes of a historical inquiry.

B

It has been pointed out many times that the common-law rule is best understood in light of the fact that it arose at a time when virtually all felonies were punishable by death. . . . Courts have also justified the common-law rule by emphasizing the relative dangerousness of felons. . . .

Neither of these justifications makes sense today. Almost all crimes formerly punishable by death no longer are or can be. . . . And while in earlier times "the gulf between the felonies and the minor offences was broad and deep," 2 [F.] Pollock & [F.] Maitland [The History of English Law (2d ed. 1909)] 467, n.3 . . . today the distinction is minor and often arbitrary. Many crimes classified as misdemeanors, or nonexistent, at common law are now felonies. . . . These changes have undermined the concept, which was questionable to begin with, that use of deadly force against a fleeing felon is merely a speedier execution of someone who has already forfeited his life. They have also made the assumption that a "felon" is more dangerous than a misdemeanant untenable. Indeed, numerous misdemeanors involve conduct more dangerous than many felonies.

There is an additional reason why the common-law rule cannot be directly translated to the present day. The common-law rule developed at a time when weapons were rudimentary. Deadly force could be inflicted almost solely in a hand-to-hand struggle during which, necessarily, the safety of the arresting officer was at risk. Handguns were not carried by police officers until the latter half of the last century. . . . Only then did it become possible to use deadly force from a distance as a means of apprehension. As a practical matter, the use of deadly force under the standard articulation of the common-law rule has an altogether different meaning—and harsher consequences—now than in past centuries. . . .

One other aspect of the common-law rule bears emphasis. It forbids the use of deadly force to apprehend a misdemeanant, condemning such action as disproportionately severe. . . .

In short, though the common law pedigree of Tennessee's rule is pure on its face, changes in the legal and technological context mean the rule is distorted almost beyond recognition when literally applied.

C

In evaluating the reasonableness of police procedures under the Fourth Amendment, we have also looked to prevailing rules in individual jurisdictions. . . . The rules in the States are varied. . . .

It cannot be said that there is a constant or overwhelming trend away from the common-law rule. . . . Nonetheless, the long-term movement has been away from the rule that deadly force may be used against any fleeing felon, and that remains the rule in less than half the States.

This trend is more evident and impressive when viewed in light of the policies adopted by the police departments themselves. Overwhelmingly, these are more restrictive than the common-law rule. . . . A 1974 study reported that the police department regulations in a majority of the large cities of the United States allowed the firing of a weapon only when a felon presented a threat of death or serious bodily harm. . . . Overall, only 7.5% of departmental and municipal policies explicitly permit the use of deadly force against any felon; 86.8% explicitly do not. . . . In light of the rules adopted by those who must actually administer them, the older and fading common-law view is a dubious indicium of the constitutionality of the Tennessee statute now before us.

D

Actual departmental policies are important for an additional reason. We would hesitate to declare a police practice of long standing "unreasonable" if doing so would severely hamper effective law enforcement. But the indications are to the contrary. There has been no suggestion that crime has worsened in any way in jurisdictions that have adopted, by legislation or departmental policy, rules similar to that announced today. . . . [T]he obvious state interests in apprehension are not sufficiently served to warrant the use of lethal weapons against all fleeing felons. . . .

Nor do we agree with petitioners and appellant that the rule we have adopted requires the police to make impossible, split-second evaluations of unknowable facts. . . . We do not deny the practical difficulties of attempting to assess the suspect's dangerousness. However, similarly difficult judgments must be made by the police in equally uncertain circumstances. . . . Nor is there any indication that in States that allow the use of deadly force only against dangerous suspects . . . the standard has been difficult to apply or has led to a rash of litigation involving inappropriate second-guessing of police officers' split-second decisions. Moreover, the highly technical felony/misdemeanor distinction is equally, if not more, difficult to apply in the field. An officer is in no position to know, for example, the precise value of property stolen, or whether the crime was a first or second offense. Finally, as noted above, this claim must be viewed with suspicion in light of the similar self-imposed limitations of so many police departments.

IV

. . .

[T]he Court of Appeals . . . held that "the facts, as found, did not justify the use of deadly force." 710 F.2d, at 246. We agree. Officer Hymon could not reasonably have believed that Garner—young, slight, and unarmed—posed any threat. Indeed, Hymon never attempted to justify his actions on any basis other than the need to prevent an escape. The District Court stated in passing that "[t]he facts of this case did not indicate to Officer Hymon that Garner was 'nondangerous.'" App. to Pet. for Cert. A34. This conclusion is not explained, and seems to be based solely on the fact that Garner had broken into a house at night. However, the fact that Garner was a suspected burglar could not, without regard to the other circumstances, automatically justify the use of deadly force. Hymon did not have probable cause to believe that Garner, whom he correctly believed to be unarmed, posed any physical danger to himself or others.

. . . While we agree that burglary is a serious crime, we cannot agree that it is so dangerous as automatically to justify the use of deadly force. The FBI classifies burglary as a "property" rather than a "violent" crime. . . . Although the armed burglar would present a different situation, the fact that an unarmed suspect has broken into a dwelling at night does not automatically mean he is physically dangerous. This case demonstrates as much. . . . In fact, the available statistics demonstrate that burglaries only rarely involve physical violence. During the 10-year period from 1973–1982, only 3.8% of all burglaries involved violent crime. . . .

V

. . . We hold that the statute is invalid insofar as it purported to give Hymon the authority to act as he did. . . .

. . . [15]

––––––

37. *Garner* was applied in Pruitt v. City of Montgomery, Alabama, 771 F.2d 1475 (11th Cir.1985) (use of deadly force not justified). Compare Ryder v. City of Topeka, 814 F.2d 1412, 1419 n.16 (10th Cir.1987) (use of deadly force justified), in which the court rejected the suggestion in *Pruitt* that an officer has probable cause to believe a suspect poses a serious threat to his person *only* if the suspect displays a weapon. See generally City of Los Angeles v. Lyons, 461 U.S. 95 (1983) (5–4), in which the defendant sought an injunction restraining Los Angeles police officers from using a "chokehold" on arrested persons who do not appear to be threatening the immediate use of deadly force. A majority of the Court concluded that the federal courts lacked jurisdiction to grant the injunction in the circumstances of the case.

A police officer's high-speed automobile chase to apprehend a suspected offender which results in the latter's death does not violate his substantive right not to be deprived of life without due process, even if the officer's pursuit is deliberately or recklessly indifferent to life. Such a claim would be substantiated only if the officer had "a purpose to cause harm unrelated to the legitimate object of arrest." County of Sacramento v. Lewis, 523 U.S. 833 (1998).

––––––

[15] Justice O'Connor wrote a dissenting opinion, which Chief Justice Burger and Justice Rehnquist joined.

Wilson v. Arkansas

514 U.S. 927, 115 S.Ct. 1914, 131 L.Ed.2d 976 (1995)

■ JUSTICE THOMAS delivered the opinion of the Court.

At the time of the framing, the common law of search and seizure recognized a law enforcement officer's authority to break open the doors of a dwelling, but generally indicated that he first ought to announce his presence and authority. In this case, we hold that this common-law "knock and announce" principle forms a part of the reasonableness inquiry under the Fourth Amendment.

I

During November and December 1992, petitioner Sharlene Wilson made a series of narcotics sales to an informant acting at the direction of the Arkansas State Police. In late November, the informant purchased marijuana and methamphetamine at the home that petitioner shared with Bryson Jacobs. On December 30, the informant telephoned petitioner at her home and arranged to meet her at a local store to buy some marijuana. According to testimony presented below, petitioner produced a semiautomatic pistol at this meeting and waved it in the informant's face, threatening to kill her if she turned out to be working for the police. Petitioner then sold the informant a bag of marijuana.

The next day, police officers applied for and obtained warrants to search petitioner's home and to arrest both petitioner and Jacobs. Affidavits filed in support of the warrants set forth the details of the narcotics transactions and stated that Jacobs had previously been convicted of arson and firebombing. The search was conducted later that afternoon. Police officers found the main door to petitioner's home open. While opening an unlocked screen door and entering the residence, they identified themselves as police officers and stated that they had a warrant. Once inside the home, the officers seized marijuana, methamphetamine, valium, narcotics paraphernalia, a gun, and ammunition. They also found petitioner in the bathroom, flushing marijuana down the toilet. Petitioner and Jacobs were arrested and charged with delivery of marijuana, delivery of methamphetamine, possession of drug paraphernalia, and possession of marijuana.

Before trial, petitioner filed a motion to suppress the evidence seized during the search. Petitioner asserted that the search was invalid on various grounds, including that the officers had failed to "knock and announce" before entering her home. The trial court summarily denied the suppression motion. After a jury trial, petitioner was convicted of all charges and sentenced to 32 years in prison.

The Arkansas Supreme Court affirmed petitioner's conviction on appeal. . . .

We granted certiorari to resolve the conflict among the lower courts as to whether the common-law knock-and-announce principle forms a part of the Fourth Amendment reasonableness inquiry. . . . We hold that it does, and accordingly reverse and remand.

II

The Fourth Amendment to the Constitution protects "[t]he right of the people to be secure in their persons, houses, papers, and effects, against unreasonable searches and seizures." In evaluating the scope of this right, we have looked to the traditional protections against unreasonable searches and seizures afforded by the common law at the time of the framing. . . . "Although the underlying command of the Fourth Amendment is always that searches and seizures be reasonable," New Jersey v. T.L.O., 469 U.S. 325, 337 (1985), our effort to give content to this term may be guided by the meaning ascribed to it by the Framers of the Amendment. An examination of the common law of search and seizure leaves no doubt that the reasonableness of a search of a dwelling may depend in part on whether law enforcement officers announced their presence and authority prior to entering.

Although the common law generally protected a man's house as "his castle of defence and asylum," 3 W. Blackstone, Commentaries *288 (hereinafter Blackstone), common-law courts long have held that "when the King is party, the sheriff (if the doors be not open) may break the party's house, either to arrest him, or to do other execution of the K[ing]'s process, if otherwise he cannot enter." Semayne's Case, 5 Co.Rep. 91a, 91b, 77 Eng.Rep. 194, 195 (K.B. 1603). To this rule, however, common-law courts appended an important qualification:

> But before he breaks it, he ought to signify the cause of his coming, and to make request to open doors . . . for the law without a default in the owner abhors the destruction or breaking of any house (which is for the habitation and safety of man) by which great damage and inconvenience might ensue to the party, when no default is in him; for perhaps he did not know of the process, of which, if he had notice, it is to be presumed that he would obey it. . . .

Ibid., 77 Eng.Rep., at 195–96.

. . .

Several prominent founding-era commentators agreed on this basic principle. . . .

The common-law knock-and-announce principle was woven quickly into the fabric of early American law. Most of the States that ratified the Fourth Amendment had enacted constitutional provisions or statutes generally incorporating English common law . . . and a few States had enacted statutes specifically embracing the common-law view that the breaking of the door of a dwelling was permitted once admittance was refused. . . . Early American courts similarly embraced the common-law knock-and-announce principle. . . .

Our own cases have acknowledged that the common-law principle of announcement is "embedded in Anglo–American law," Miller v. United States, 357 U.S. 301, 313 (1958), but we have never squarely held that this principle is an element of the reasonableness inquiry under the Fourth Amendment. We now so hold. Given the longstanding common-law endorsement of the practice of announcement, we have little doubt that the Framers of the Fourth Amendment thought that the method of an officer's entry into a dwelling was among the factors to be considered in assessing the reasonableness of a search or seizure. Contrary to the decision below, we hold that in some circumstances an officer's unannounced entry into a home might be unreasonable under the Fourth Amendment.

This is not to say, of course, that every entry must be preceded by an announcement. The Fourth Amendment's flexible requirement of reasonableness should not be read to mandate a rigid rule of announcement that ignores countervailing law enforcement interests. As even petitioner concedes, the common-law principle of announcement was never stated as an inflexible rule requiring announcement under all circumstances. . . .

. . .

Thus, because the common-law rule was justified in part by the belief that announcement generally would avoid "the destruction or breaking of any house . . . by which great damage and inconvenience might ensue," Semayne's Case, supra, at 91b, 77 Eng.Rep., at 196, courts acknowledged that the presumption in favor of announcement would yield under circumstances presenting a threat of physical violence. . . . Similarly, courts held that an officer may dispense with announcement in cases where a prisoner escapes from him and retreats to his dwelling. . . . Proof of "demand and refusal" was deemed unnecessary in such cases because it would be a "senseless ceremony" to require an officer in pursuit of a recently escaped arrestee to make an announcement prior to breaking the door to retake him. . . . Finally, courts have indicated that unannounced entry may be justified where police officers have reason to believe that evidence would likely be destroyed if advance notice were given. . . .

We need not attempt a comprehensive catalog of the relevant countervailing factors here. For now, we leave to the lower courts the task of determining the circumstances under which an unannounced entry is reasonable under the Fourth Amendment. We simply hold that although a search or seizure of a dwelling might be constitutionally defective if police officers enter without prior announcement, law enforcement interests may also establish the reasonableness of an unannounced entry.

III

Respondent contends that the judgment below should be affirmed because the unannounced entry in this case was justified for two reasons. First, respondent argues that police officers reasonably believed that a prior announcement would have placed them in peril, given their knowledge that petitioner had threatened a government informant with a semiautomatic weapon and that Mr. Jacobs had previously been convicted of arson and firebombing. Second, respondent suggests that prior announcement would have produced an unreasonable risk that petitioner would destroy easily disposable narcotics evidence.

These considerations may well provide the necessary justification for the unannounced entry in this case. Because the Arkansas Supreme Court did not address their sufficiency, however, we remand to allow the state courts to make any necessary findings of fact and to make the determination of reasonableness in the first instance. . . .

. . .

———

38. Applying Wilson v. Arkansas, in Richards v. Wisconsin, 520 U.S. 385 (1997), the Court held that the Fourth Amendment does not permit a blanket exception to the knock-and-announce rule for a category of crimes (narcotics felonies). The Court concluded nevertheless that a no-knock entry was justified by the particular circumstances. See Ingram v. City of Columbus, 185 F.3d 579 (6th Cir.1999) (circumstances did not justify exception to knock-and-announce rule).

39. In United States v. Banks, 540 U.S. ___ (2003), the Court held that a 15–20 second wait after the police knocked and announced their authority was long enough to permit a forcible entry, in the circumstances of the case. The police had gone to the defendant's apartment with a warrant to search for drugs. After waiting 15–20 seconds, they broke open the front door. The defendant testified that he was in the shower and had heard nothing before the door was broken open. The Court said that the critical inquiry was whether the police had reason to fear the destruction of evidence on the basis of what they knew, not whether the person inside had in fact heard them or whether there was time for him to get to the door. Since someone wanting to dispose of drugs could do so by flushing them down the toilet or sink within as little as 15–20 seconds, the police acted reasonably in not waiting longer.

40. "An unannounced intrusion into a dwelling . . . is no less an unannounced intrusion whether officers break down a door, force open a chain lock or a partially open door, open a locked door by use of a passkey, or . . . open a closed but unlocked door." Sabbath v. United States, 391 U.S. 585, 590 (1968). In United States v. Beale, 445 F.2d 977 (5th Cir.1971), the court observed that *Sabbath* applied only where at least minimal force was used "in the sense of physical action by the officer to remove the barrier that prevents his entry," and "left undisturbed the existent distinction between entry where some force is employed and entry where force is not an element at all." On that basis, the court concluded that the requirement of notice of authority and purpose did not apply to an entry by deception. Accord, e.g., United States v. Raines, 536 F.2d 796, 800 (8th Cir.1976): "A police entry into a private home by invitation without force, though the invitation be obtained by ruse, is not a breaking and does not invoke the common law requirement of prior announcement of authority and purpose, codified in § 3109." See United States v. Lopez, 475 F.2d 537 (7th Cir.1973), in which federal agents waited outside the defendant's motel room until the door was opened and immediately entered to arrest the occupants.

We raised the hue and cry and chased the Shire,
but he seems to have disappeared into thin eyre.

41.   Police officials were admitted to the defendant's home by his young son; they told him they were gas inspectors and asked to wait for his father's return. About twenty minutes later the defendant came home and was arrested on the back porch. The defendant was believed to have participated in an armed robbery in the course of which a policeman had been shot; news that an accomplice had been arrested a short time before had been broadcast on the radio. Was the arrest lawful? See People v. Macias, 234 N.E.2d 783 (Ill.1968).

42.   If there would have been no necessity to break and enter in order to arrest but for the police officers' deliberate failure to arrest the defendant before he entered his home, does the necessity justify the entry? Does the reason why the police failed to arrest earlier make a difference? See McKnight v. United States, 183 F.2d 977 (D.C.Cir.1950), with which compare United States v. Drake, 655 F.2d 1025 (10th Cir.1981). See note 8, p. 20 above.

43.   Is the requirement of notice applicable to an entry for a purpose other than to make an arrest?

> [T]he police officer on radio patrol duty received a "radio run" to the effect that there was a "disorderly man at 404 West 115th Street." He proceeded to a rooming (converted apartment) house at this address where he was met by the night manager. The officer heard "shouting, screaming, clapping of hands" and the manager stated "that that had been going on for several evenings."

The manager then directed the police officer and a fellow officer to a fifth floor "apartment," evidently a division of the converted apartment house. The noise was coming from this apartment. As the officer knocked on the door, the shouting stopped, and a male voice inside said three times: "Wait a minute. Wait a minute, I'm not dressed." After a minute's wait, the officer directed the manager to open the door with his passkey. Upon opening the door they saw defendant standing in the middle of the room, stripped to the waist, and wet with perspiration. He was holding "a syringe, an eye dropper, with a needle on the end of it, in his right hand." When defendant saw the three men, he threw the contraband under a bed and the officer placed him under arrest.

People v. Gallmon, 227 N.E.2d 284, 285–86 (N.Y.1967). If "the officer did not come to the premises or to the apartment to make an arrest . . . [but] had responded to a call from the manager of a rooming house to investigate an unusual, noisy disturbance," id. at 286, was the arrest lawful?

44. Federal law and state law. To what extent can the states determine for themselves when and how an arrest should be made? In Ker v. California, 374 U.S. 23, 31 (1963), the Supreme Court said that the Constitution required "no total obliteration of state laws relating to arrests and searches in favor of federal law."

"This Court's long-established recognition that standards of reasonableness under the Fourth Amendment are not susceptible of Procrustean application is carried forward when that Amendment's proscriptions are enforced against the States through the Fourteenth Amendment. . . . The States are not . . . precluded from developing workable rules governing arrests, searches and seizures to meet 'the practical demands of effective criminal investigation and law enforcement' in the States, provided that those rules do not violate the constitutional proscription of unreasonable searches and seizures and the concomitant command that evidence so seized is inadmissible against one who has standing to complain. . . . Such a standard implies no derogation of uniformity in applying federal constitutional guarantees but is only a recognition that conditions and circumstances vary just as do investigative and enforcement techniques." Id. at 33–34.

While a state may not allow an arrest based on less than probable cause, it may require more. The usual rule, derived from the common law, is that a police officer can arrest a person without a warrant if he has reasonable grounds (in effect, probable cause) to believe that the person has committed a felony or if the person has committed a misdemeanor in the officer's presence. In the absence of applicable federal law, the law of the state in which an arrest occurs determines the validity of the arrest for federal law. United States v. Di Re, 332 U.S. 581, 589 (1948). See, e.g., United States v. Thompson, 356 F.2d 216, 223–24 (2d Cir.1965); cf. Sabbath v. United States, 380 F.2d 108 (9th Cir.1967) (method of entry to arrest by federal officers for federal offense is a matter of federal law), rev'd on other grounds, 391 U.S. 585 (1968). See also United States v. Mahoney, 712 F.2d 956 (5th Cir.1983) (application, in federal court, of good-faith exception to exclusionary rule to evidence obtained by state officers is a matter of federal law).

If evidence is obtained pursuant to an arrest that is unlawful under state law but not unconstitutional—i.e., an arrest that the state could constitutionally have authorized—is the Fourth Amendment's prohibition against *unreasonable* searches and seizures violated, so that the rule requiring exclusion of evidence obtained in violation of the defendant's constitutional rights is applicable? If state law determines the lawfulness of the arrest, does a violation of the law make the arrest constitutionally unreasonable? In *Di Re*, above, the Court indicated that, at least in a federal court, the answer is that it does. See United States v. Mota, 982 F.2d 1384 (9th Cir.1993) (*Di Re* applied). Some other cases, however, have held otherwise. See, e.g., United States v. Walker, 960 F.2d 409 (5th Cir.1992).

Cases generally hold that a nonconstitutional violation of a state law affecting some matter other than the amount of evidence needed to make an arrest does not call for application of the *Di Re* principle. E.g., United States v. Hall, 543 F.2d 1229 (9th Cir.1976) (arrest based on wiretap lawful under federal law but not state law, which would have required suppression of evidence); United States v. Dudek, 530 F.2d 684 (6th Cir.1976) (failure to comply with state requirement of prompt return and verified inventory following search).

See State v. Bridges, 925 P.2d 357 (1996). In that case, Hawaii police obtained the cooperation of California police in the investigation of a drug conspiracy, because some of the events involved in the conspiracy occurred in California. The California police used audio and video recording equipment to obtain evidence against the defendants that was relevant to their prosecution in Hawaii. The equipment did not violate the federal Constitution or the law of California but would have violated the law of Hawaii if it had occurred there. In an opinion thoroughly discussing the reasons for the exclusion of illegally obtained evidence and citing cases in other jurisdictions, the court held that the evidence should not be excluded in the Hawaii prosecution.

Consequences of an Unlawful Arrest

Ker v. Illinois
119 U.S. 436, 7 S.Ct. 225, 30 L.Ed. 421 (1886)

[Ker was convicted of larceny in the Illinois courts. He alleged that he had been in Lima, Peru and that a warrant for his extradition had been issued, but that, without presenting the warrant, the person who was directed to receive him into custody from the Peruvian authorities had forcibly arrested him and transported him to Illinois.]

■ MR. JUSTICE MILLER delivered the opinion of the court.

. . .

. . . It is contended . . . that the proceedings in the arrest in Peru, and the extradition and delivery to the authorities of Cook County, were not "due process of law," and we may suppose, although it is not so alleged, that this reference is to that clause of Article XIV of the Amendments to the Constitution of the United States which declares that no State shall deprive any person of life, liberty, or property "without due process of law." The "due process of law" here guaranteed is complied with when the party is regularly indicted by the proper grand jury in the State court, has a trial according to the forms and modes prescribed for such trials, and when, in that trial and proceedings, he is deprived of no rights to which he is lawfully entitled. We do not intend to say that there may not be proceedings previous to the trial, in regard to which the prisoner could invoke in some manner the provisions of this clause of the Constitution, but, for mere irregularities in the manner in which he may be brought into the custody of the law, we do not think he is entitled to say that he should not be tried at all for the crime with which he is charged in a regular indictment. He may be arrested for a very heinous offence by persons without any warrant, or without any previous complaint, and brought before a proper officer, and this may be in some sense said to be "without due process of law." But it would hardly be claimed, that after the case had been investigated and the defendant held by the proper authorities to answer for the crime, he could plead that he was first arrested "without due process of law." So here, when found within the jurisdiction of the State of Illinois and liable to answer for a crime against the laws of that State, unless there was some positive provision of the Constitution or of the laws of this country violated in bringing him into court, it is not easy to see how he can say that he is there "without due process of law," within the meaning of the constitutional provision.

. . .

The question of how far his forcible seizure in another country, and transfer by violence, force, or fraud, to this country, could be made available to resist trial in the State court, for the offence now charged upon him, is one which we do not feel called upon to decide, for in that transaction we do not see that the Constitution, or laws, or treaties, of the United States guarantee him any protection. There are authorities of the highest respectability which hold that such forcible abduction is no sufficient reason why the party should not answer when brought within the jurisdiction of the court which has the right to try him for such an offence, and presents no valid objection to his trial in such court. . . .

. . .

45. In Frisbie v. Collins, 342 U.S. 519 (1952), Collins sought his release by a petition for habeas corpus from a Michigan state prison, where he was serving a life sentence for murder. He alleged that "while he was living in Chicago, Michigan officers forcibly seized, handcuffed, blackjacked and took him to Michigan." He claimed that his trial and conviction in such circumstances denied him due process of law and violated the Federal Kidnapping Act, 18 U.S.C. § 1201, and that the conviction was therefore a nullity. The claim was rejected.

"This Court has never departed from the rule announced in Ker v. Illinois, 119 U.S. 436, 444, that the power of a court to try a person for crime is not impaired by the fact that he had been brought within the court's jurisdiction by reason of a 'forcible abduction.' No persuasive reasons are now presented to justify overruling this line of cases. They rest on the sound basis that due process of law is satisfied when one present in court is convicted of crime after having been fairly apprized of the charges against him and after a fair trial in accordance with constitutional procedural safeguards. There is nothing in the Constitution that requires a court to permit a guilty person rightfully convicted to escape justice because he was brought to trial against his will." Frisbie v. Collins, 342 U.S. at 522. The Court noted the severe penalties prescribed for kidnapping and concluded that the statute did not include "a sanction barring a state from prosecuting persons wrongfully brought to it by its officers." Id. at 523.

The Court applied *Ker* in United States v. Alvarez-Machain, 504 U.S. 655 (1992) (6–3). The defendant, a citizen and resident of Mexico, was indicted in the United States for the kidnapping and murder of a federal narcotics agent. Federal agents abducted him in Mexico and brought him into the United States, where he was arrested. He claimed that the federal court lacked jurisdiction to try him because his abduction violated an extradition treaty between the United States and Mexico. The Court held that although the treaty established procedures for extradition, it did not prohibit other methods of obtaining a wanted person's presence and that the treaty had not been violated.

46. Some inroad on *Ker* and Frisbie v. Collins was made in United States v. Toscanino, 500 F.2d 267 (2d Cir.1974). The defendant, who was convicted of a narcotics offense in New York, alleged that American agents kidnapped him in Uruguay, brought him to Brazil and tortured him there, and finally brought him to the United States to be prosecuted.

Observing that cases decided since Frisbie v. Collins had "eroded" its holding, the court said: "[W]e view due process as now requiring a court to divest itself of jurisdiction over the person of a defendant where it has been acquired as the result of the government's deliberate, unnecessary and unreasonable invasion of the accused's constitutional rights. This conclusion represents but an extension of the well-recognized power of federal courts in the civil context to decline to exercise jurisdiction over a defendant whose presence has been secured by force or fraud." Id. at 275. The case on which the court relied primarily is Rochin v. California, 342 U.S. 165 (1952), p. 351 below. Those cases, it said, indicated that due process was concerned not only with a fair trial but also with the conduct of law enforcement authorities before trial. In the end, however, the court appeared to rely not (or not only) on a constitutional ruling but on its "supervisory power over the administration of criminal justice in the district courts within our jurisdiction," 500 F.2d at 276. (*Ker* and Frisbie v. Collins were distinguished further on the ground that those cases did not involve violation of a treaty, as *Toscanino* did.)

The case was remanded with instructions to conduct an evidentiary hearing if, in response to the government's denial, the defendant was able to offer "some credible supporting evidence" of his allegations, 500 F.2d at 281. On remand, the district court concluded that the defendant did not submit any credible evidence to support his claim that United States officials were involved in his abduction or torture, and declined to hold an evidentiary hearing. 398 F.Supp. 916 (E.D.N.Y.1975).

Toscanino was limited in United States ex rel. Lujan v. Gengler, 510 F.2d 62 (2d Cir.1975), in which the defendant was abducted in Bolivia and brought to the United States where he was arrested: "[I]n recognizing that *Ker* and *Frisbie* no longer provided a carte blanche to government agents bringing defendants from abroad to the United States by the use of torture, brutality and similar outrageous conduct, we did not intend to suggest that *any* irregularity in the circumstances of a defendant's arrival in the jurisdiction would vitiate the proceedings of the criminal court. In holding that *Ker* and *Frisbie* must yield to the extent they were inconsistent with the Supreme Court's more recent pronouncements we scarcely could have meant to eviscerate the *Ker–Frisbie* rule, which the Supreme Court has never felt impelled to disavow." 510 F.2d at 65.

"[A]bsent a set of incidents like that in *Toscanino*, not every violation by prosecution or police is so egregious that *Rochin* and its progeny require nullification of the indictment." Id. at 65, 66. The court noted also the absence of a violation of international law in this case, since there was no allegation of a protest by another nation.

Except for *Toscanino*, the courts of appeals have regularly applied the *Ker–Frisbie* rule. E.g., United States v. Matta-Ballesteros, 71 F.3d 754 (9th Cir.1995); Matta-Ballesteros v. Henman, 896 F.2d 255 (7th Cir.1990) (additional cases cited). Frisbie v. Collins was cited with approval in *Alvarez-Machain*, note 45 above. Also, in Gerstein v. Pugh, 420 U.S. 103, 119 (1975), the Court declared that its ruling, see p. 522 below, marked no "retreat from the established rule that illegal arrest or detention does not void a subsequent conviction," id. at 525.

47. As Frisbie v. Collins, note 45 above, indicates, a person illegally arrested is not entitled to be released on habeas corpus if there is legal cause for his detention. "Where it appears that sufficient ground for detention exists a prisoner will not be discharged for defects in the original arrest or commitment." Stallings v. Splain, 253 U.S. 339, 343 (1920). "The invalidity of [an arrest] warrant is not comparable to the invalidity of an indictment. A person may not be punished for a crime without a formal and sufficient accusation even if he voluntarily submits to the jurisdiction of the court. . . . But a false arrest does not necessarily deprive the court of jurisdiction of the proceeding in which it was made." Albrecht v. United States, 273 U.S. 1, 8 (1927). In Kelly v. Griffin, 241 U.S. 6 (1916), Chicago police arrested the defendant. On the following day, a complaint was made before the U.S. commissioner, a warrant was issued, and the defendant was turned over to the U.S. marshal. The Court rejected the defendant's claim that if his arrest were illegal, he was entitled to be released before the federal warrant could be executed. "[H]owever illegal the arrest by the Chicago police it does not follow that the taking of the appellant's body by the marshal under the warrant . . . was void. The action of the officers of the State or city did not affect the jurisdiction of the Commissioner of the United States. . . . [T]he appellant came within reach of the Commissioner's warrant by his own choice, and the most that can be said is that the effective exercise of authority was made easier by what had been done. It was not even argued that the appellant was entitled to a chance to escape before either of the warrants could be executed. This proceeding is not a fox hunt. But merely to be declared free in a room with the marshal standing at the door having another warrant in his hand would be an empty form." Id. at 12–13.

48. How does the rule that a court's jurisdiction over a defendant does not depend at all on the manner in which he was brought before the court comport with the result in Rochin v. California, 342 U.S. 165 (1952), p. 351 below, in which, relying on the Due Process Clause, the Court reversed a conviction based in part on indubitably reliable evidence (morphine capsules recovered from the defendant's stomach by "stomach pumping") because the evidence had been obtained by conduct that "shocks the conscience," id. at 172. *Rochin* was one of the cases on which the court relied in *Toscanino*, see note 46, p. 76 above. See United States v. Hart, 409

F.2d 221 (10th Cir.1969) (brutality by police is not itself a bar to prosecution).

––––––

Evidence Obtained as the Result of an Unlawful Arrest (Wong Sun v. United States)

––––––

49. In Wong Sun v. United States, 371 U.S. 471 (1963), the Court made it clear that the rule excluding from use at trial evidence that was obtained in violation of the defendant's constitutional rights, see p. 145 below, applies to evidence of all kinds that is the "fruit" of an unlawful (i.e. unconstitutional) arrest.

> The exclusionary rule has traditionally barred from trial physical, tangible materials obtained either during or as a direct result of an unlawful invasion. It follows from our holding in Silverman v. United States, 365 U.S. 505, that the Fourth Amendment may protect against the overhearing of verbal statements as well as against the more traditional seizure of "papers and effects." Similarly, testimony as to matters observed during an unlawful invasion has been excluded in order to enforce the basic constitutional policies. . . . Thus, verbal evidence which derives . . . immediately from an unlawful entry and an unauthorized arrest . . . is no less the "fruit" of official illegality than the more common tangible fruits of the unwarranted intrusion. . . . Nor do the policies underlying the exclusionary rule invite any logical distinction between physical and verbal evidence. Either in terms of deterring lawless conduct by federal officers . . . or of closing the doors of the federal courts to any use of evidence unconstitutionally obtained . . . the danger in relaxing the exclusionary rules in the case of verbal evidence would seem too great to warrant introducing such a distinction.

371 U.S. at 485–86.

The Court declined to hold that any evidence which would not have been discovered *but for* an illegal arrest must be suppressed. It said that "the more apt question in such a case is 'whether, granting establishment of the primary illegality, the evidence to which instant objection is made has been come at by exploitation of that illegality or instead by means sufficiently distinguishable to be purged of the primary taint,' Maguire, Evidence of Guilt 221 (1959)." On that basis it concluded that a confession made several days after a defendant had been unlawfully arrested, been released and lawfully arraigned, when he returned voluntarily to make the statement, was not "tainted" by the illegality of the arrest and was admissible at trial. Id. at 488, 491.

The courts have generally asked two questions to determine whether evidence is tainted by an unlawful arrest. One is whether, despite the arrest, the evidence was the product of "a clear act of free will on the part of the defendant," Rogers v. United States, 330 F.2d 535, 541 (5th Cir. 1964). See United States v. Hoffman, 385 F.2d 501, 504 (7th Cir.1967), in which the court referred to "the exercise of those attributes of will, perception, memory and volition unique to the individual human personality which serve to distinguish the evidentiary character of a witness from the relative immutability of inanimate evidence."

The Court relied on the "free will" test in Brown v. Illinois, 422 U.S. 590 (1975), in which, following an illegal arrest, the defendant was given the *Miranda* warnings (see Miranda v. Arizona, p. 417 below) and subsequently made incriminating statements. The Court rejected the conclusion that the giving of the warnings automatically broke the connection between the illegal arrest and the statements. Otherwise, it said, illegal arrests for investigation "would be encouraged by the knowledge that evidence derived therefrom could well be made admissible at trial by the simple expedient of giving *Miranda* warnings." 422 U.S. at 602. It said further: "The question whether a confession is the product of a free will under *Wong Sun* must be answered on the facts of each case. No single fact is dispositive. The workings of the human mind are too complex, and the possibilities of misconduct too diverse, to permit protection of the Fourth Amendment to turn on such a talismanic test. The *Miranda* warnings are an important factor, to be sure, in determining whether the confession is obtained by exploitation of an illegal arrest. But they are not the only factor to be considered. The temporal proximity of the arrest and the confession, the presence of intervening circumstances . . . and, particularly, the purpose and flagrancy of the official misconduct are all relevant." Id. at 603–604. Compare the suggestion in Collins v. Beto, 348 F.2d 823, 828 (5th Cir. 1965), that "the best and perhaps the only way" to purge the taint of an illegal arrest and render admissible statements made during the ensuing detention is "to afford the suspect an effective opportunity to obtain the assistance of counsel." See Rawlings v. Kentucky, 448 U.S. 98, 106–10 (1980). Cf. United States v. Bailey, 691 F.2d 1009 (11th Cir.1982) (unlawful arrest provoked criminal response furnishing basis for second lawful arrest; search pursuant to latter arrest upheld).

The other question that is asked is whether the evidence was the product of "deliberate exploitation" by the police of the primary illegality. Copeland v. United States, 343 F.2d 287, 291 (D.C.Cir.1964) (evidence admissible); see United States v. Pimental, 645 F.2d 85 (1st Cir.1981) (evidence admissible); United States ex rel. Gockley v. Myers, 450 F.2d 232 (3d Cir.1971) (evidence inadmissible). In that connection, see Nix v. Williams, p. 147 note 77 below, holding that evidence that the police would inevitably have discovered without any illegal conduct on their part need not be excluded because the police were in fact led to it by such conduct.

In United States v. Ceccolini, 435 U.S. 268 (1978), the Court reversed a judgment that a witness's testimony be excluded under *Wong Sun* because the government was led to the witness by an illegal search. A police officer had looked into an envelope in a shop operated by the defendant, where the officer was taking a "break," and had discovered policy slips. He asked the witness, who worked in the store, who owned the envelope; she told him that the defendant owned it and had instructed her to give it to someone.

The officer reported this fact to an FBI agent investigating gambling operations in the area. Four months later, the agent interviewed the witness. She spoke willingly, incriminating the defendant, and she later testified against him at trial. The Court said that the witness's willingness to testify had a bearing on the connection required by *Wong Sun* between the illegality and the evidence to be excluded: "[E]valuated properly, the degree of free will necessary to dissipate the taint will very likely be found more often in the case of live-witness testimony than other kinds of evidence." Furthermore, were the *Wong Sun* rule applied to exclude the testimony of a witness whenever the government was led to him by an illegal act, the exclusion "would perpetually disable a witness from testifying about relevant and material facts, regardless of how unrelated such testimony might be to the purpose of the originally illegal search or the evidence discovered thereby. . . . [S]ince the cost of excluding live-witness testimony often will be greater [than the cost of excluding particular tangible evidence], a closer, more direct link between the illegality and that kind of testimony is required." The Court concluded that "the exclusionary rule should be invoked with much greater reluctance where the claim is based on a causal relationship between a constitutional violation and the discovery of a live witness than when a similar claim is advanced to support suppression of an inanimate object." Id. at 276–78, 280.

See United States v. Leonardi, 623 F.2d 746 (2d Cir.1980) (*Ceccolini* applied). *Ceccolini* is distinguished in United States v. Scios, 590 F.2d 956 (D.C.Cir.1978); the majority opinion and especially the dissenting opinion of Judge Wilkey contain extended discussions of the "taint" issue.

In New York v. Harris, 495 U.S. 14 (1990) (5–4), the Court held that a person's arrest in his home without a warrant, in violation of *Payton*, p. 44 above, did not require the exclusion of a statement he made while in custody following the arrest. Although Harris's statement was the product of his arrest, it was not the product of unlawful custody, since there was probable cause for his arrest; nor was it a product of his having been arrested in his home rather than elsewhere. *Payton*, the Court said, "was designed to protect the physical integrity of the home; it was not intended to grant criminal suspects, like Harris, protection for statements made outside their premises where the police have probable cause to arrest the suspect for committing a crime." Id. at 17. See also United States v. Crews, 445 U.S. 463 (1980), in which the Court held that a witness's courtroom identification of the defendant was independent of the defendant's illegal arrest, so that exclusion of the identification was not required.

50. Consider the following cases:

(i) The defendant was arrested unlawfully on a charge of robbery. Clothing that he was wearing at the time of his arrest was used in a lineup at which he was identified by the victim of the robbery.

(ii) The defendants were arrested during the night and detained unlawfully. At noon the next day the body of a man was discovered. From that point the police had probable cause to arrest the defendants on a charge of murder. Several hours later the defendants' clothing was taken from them for laboratory examinations, which disclosed blood and other incriminating matter on the clothing. The results of the examinations were introduced in evidence against them.

(iii) The police received information that the defendant had committed a rape. They unlawfully entered his house in his absence and found his work badge, by which they discovered where he worked. They then went to his place of work and arrested him. They examined his clothing, and the clothing and the results of the examination were introduced in evidence against him. The defendant claimed that at the time of his arrest he was about to destroy the clothing.

(iv) The defendants parked a car which they were driving in a motel parking lot. A security officer of the motel became suspicious; unlawfully, he arrested and detained them in their automobile for investigation, and called the police. Within a few minutes the police obtained a report on the license number of the car, the license plate being in plain view, and learned that the car was stolen. Testimony that the defendants were driving a stolen car was introduced at their trial for unlawful interstate transportation of a stolen motor vehicle.

(v) The defendant was arrested unlawfully. While he was being driven to the station house in a police car, he stuffed some papers under the back seat. They were retrieved and introduced in evidence against him.

Was the use of the evidence in these cases consistent with Wong Sun? See (i) Miller v. Eklund, 364 F.2d 976 (9th Cir.1966); (ii) Hancock v. Nelson, 363 F.2d 249 (1st Cir.1966); (iii) Leek v. Maryland, 353 F.2d 526 (4th Cir.1965); (iv) United States v. Ruffin, 389 F.2d 76 (7th Cir.1968); also, United States v. Kennedy, 457 F.2d 63 (10th Cir.1972); (v) United States v. Barber, 557 F.2d 628 (8th Cir.1977).

51. The *"McNabb–Mallory* rule." Rule 5(a), Fed.R.Crim.P., provides that a person who is arrested shall be taken "without unnecessary delay" before a magistrate judge or a state or local judicial officer. In McNabb v. United States, 318 U.S. 332 (1943), decided before promulgation of the rules, the Court held that incriminating statements made by a defendant during a period of unlawful detention between his arrest and presentation before a magistrate could not be used against him at trial. It said that the detention of arrested persons for questioning before presenting them for commitment is "a procedure which is wholly incompatible with the vital but very restricted duties of the investigating and arresting officers of the Government." Id. at 342. The Court's holding was not constitutionally based; rather, it was an exercise of the Court's "supervision of the administration of justice in the federal courts." Id. at 340.

In Mallory v. United States, 354 U.S. 449 (1957), the Court reaffirmed this ruling, basing it this time on Rule 5(a). It said that, although the duty to bring arrested persons before a committing magistrate "without unnecessary delay" did not call for "mechanical or automatic obedience," it allowed "arresting officers little more leeway than the interval between arrest and the ordinary administrative steps required to bring a suspect before the nearest available magistrate." Id. at 453, 455. Since neither *McNabb* nor *Mallory* was a constitutional holding, it has been assumed that the states are not obliged to follow the rule there announced. E.g., State v. Stubbs, 407 P.2d 215 (Kan.1965).

In *Mallory*, the Court said: "Circumstances may justify a brief delay between arrest and arraignment, as for instance, where the story volunteered by the accused is susceptible of quick verification through third parties." 354 U.S. at 455. A delay of 26 hours between arrest and arraignment was found not to be "unnecessary" for purposes of the *McNabb–Mallory* rule, in United States v. Collins, 462 F.2d 792 (2d Cir.1972): "We have consistently held that delays for purposes of routine processing—here a total of 3 hours and 15 minutes spent at the 105th Precinct, FBI headquarters and Assistant United States Attorney Puccio's office—or for overnight lodging—here the 11½ hours in the Manhattan House of Detention—do not constitute unnecessary delay within the *McNabb–Mallory* rule. . . . Of the remaining 9½ hours, 3½ hours, the time spent in transit, was clearly necessary to move Collins through the complexities of the combined federal-state system, ½ hour was necessary to establish his identity and 5½ hours were consumed in particularizing a voluntarily given confession. No part of these detention periods was unnecessary. The conduct of the FBI and the New York City Police Department was at all times directed to processing Collins as expeditiously as possible for arraignment." *Collins*, 462 F.2d at 795–96. See also United States v. Marrero, 450 F.2d 373 (2d Cir.1971) (delay from 8:00 p.m. until noon on following day was not unreasonable); Pettyjohn v. United States, 419 F.2d 651 (D.C.Cir. 1969) (seven hours delay after defendant's arrest late at night was not unreasonable). Rule 5(a) does not prevent federal authorities from questioning a person in state custody before he is presented to a federal magistrate, so long as the state custody is not at the instance of the federal authorities. E.g., Barnett v. United States, 384 F.2d 848 (5th Cir.1967).

In *Pettyjohn*, the defendant gave the police a confession after being advised of his Miranda rights (see p. 417 below). The court said that by agreeing to speak after being advised of his rights to silence and to consult an attorney the defendant had also waived his right to be brought before a magistrate as soon as possible. "Surely the law does not allow a person to voluntarily discuss the crime to which he has just confessed for a period of some twenty minutes and then claim on appeal that the twenty minute period during which they spoke constituted a prejudicial delay in violation of his right to rapid arraignment." 419 F.2d at 656. *Pettyjohn* was followed (over a dissent) in United States v. Poole, 495 F.2d 115 (D.C.Cir.1974); the relationship between *McNabb–Mallory* and *Miranda* is thoroughly discussed in the several opinions. See also United States v. Salamanca, 990 F.2d 629 (D.C.Cir.1993); United States v. Duvall, 537 F.2d 15, 23–26 (2d Cir.1976).

A federal statute enacted in 1968 provides in effect that a delay of six hours before a person is brought before a magistrate does not by itself require exclusion of a confession obtained during that period. 18 U.S.C. § 3501(c). In United States v. Alvarez-Sanchez, 511 U.S. 350 (1994), the Court said that this provision has no application to a detention by state

Boston Police Department
Prisoner Booking Form

Report Date: 05/09/1997 13:12:49
Booking Status: COMPLETED
Printed By: Dahlbeck, Joseph W

Booking Name: Layfield
First: Robert
Middle: Arthur
Address: Apt 23, 312 Evergreen CR , Boston, MA.
Sex: Male
Race: White Non-Hispanic
Date of Birth: 06/09/1942

District: 09
Booking Number: 95-000316-04
Incident Number: 95-1000000
Charges: Breaking & Entering N/T, Poss cl B

Arrest Date: 03/17/1995   14:00
Booking Date: 02/10/1997   11:25

Miranda Warning

Before asking you any questions, it is my duty to advise you of your rights:

- You have the right to remain silent;
- If you choose to speak, anything you say may be used against you in a court of law or other proceeding;
- You have the right to consult with a lawyer before answering any questions and you may have him present with you during questioning;
- If you cannot afford a lawyer and you want one, a lawyer will be provided for you by the Commonwealth without cost to you;
- You may also waive the right to counsel and your right to remain silent and you may answer any question or make any statement you wish. If you decide to answer any questions you may stop any time to consult with a lawyer.

Do you understand what I have told you?

Yes, I understand

Informed of Rights By Officer:

09566	Joseph W Dahlbeck

Signature of Prisoner   _Signature of Officer_

Prisoner Property
Money: $ 36.25   **Property Storage Number:** 5
Property: timex watch, gold ring, pocket knife,

Telephone Used: YES
Breathalyzer Used: NO
Examined at Hospital: NO

Visible Injuries:
   Any injuries would be listed in this area

Acknowledgement of property items being held

Signature of Prisoner

officials for a violation of state law, so long as there is no collusion with federal officials. It declined to consider whether the effect of § 3501(c), when it applied, is to require exclusion on grounds of delay of incriminating statements made outside the six-hour "safe harbor" or only to prohibit suppression on such grounds of incriminating statements made within that period. See United States v. Perez, 733 F.2d 1026 (2d Cir.1984) (court has discretion to exclude confession solely on ground of delay of more than six hours, if unreasonable).

Even if there is unreasonable delay before a person is brought before a magistrate, a statement need not be excluded if it is made within the period while the delay is not unreasonable. United States v. Martinez-Gallegos, 807 F.2d 868 (9th Cir.1987). See generally United States v. Rubio, 709 F.2d 146 (2d Cir.1983).

Although a violation of *McNabb–Mallory* is not itself a violation of the person's constitutional rights, a prolonged detention after arrest may be. See Coleman v. Frantz, 754 F.2d 719 (7th Cir.1985) (detention for 18 days). See generally Sanders v. City of Houston, 543 F.Supp. 694 (S.D.Tex.1982); Dommer v. Hatcher, 427 F.Supp. 1040 (N.D.Ind.1975), rev'd in part, 653 F.2d 289 (7th Cir.1981); Lively v. Cullinane, 451 F.Supp. 1000 (D.D.C. 1978), all discussing the time that police are allowed to complete booking and investigative procedures.

If a person is arrested without a warrant or indictment, the Fourth Amendment requires that he be brought promptly before a judicial officer for a determination of probable cause. Gerstein v. Pugh, 420 U.S. 103 (1975), p. 522 below. This requirement is ordinarily satisfied if the determination is made within 48 hours. County of Riverside v. McLaughlin, 500 U.S. 44 (1991), p. 527 below. This constitutional requirement is distinct from the *McNabb–Mallory* rule, which is nonconstitutional and applies to arrests on a warrant as well as arrests without a warrant, but the two are closely related.

Civil Remedies

52. In Ker v. Illinois, 119 U.S. 436 (1886), p. 74 above, the Court noted that its conclusion did not leave Ker or the Peruvian government "without remedy for his unauthorized seizure within its territory." Peru could seek extradition of Ker's abductor and try him for violation of its laws. Ker could sue his abductor "in an action of trespass and false imprisonment, and the facts [alleged] . . . would without doubt sustain the action. Whether he could recover a sum sufficient to justify the action would probably depend on moral aspects of the case," which the Court did not consider. 119 U.S. at 444.[16]

16. In Mulligan v. Schlachter, 389 F.2d 231 (6th Cir.1968), the complainant sought damages under the Civil Rights Act, see note 53 below, for an alleged arrest and seizure of his property without probable cause, on a charge of murder for which he was subsequently tried and convicted. The court said: "[A] trial does not necessarily provide adequate recompense for constitutional depriva-

The "moral aspects" of such cases have not often been favorable to civil recovery. Persons arrested illegally typically are not "respectable citizens" and find it difficult to prove significant injury to their reputation, which would be the basis for recovery of substantial damages. Juries do not readily favor a person who has been arrested, albeit unlawfully, over a policeman who was "only doing his duty." It has been suggested that tort liability might be an effective means of controlling police illegality, if there were (1) government liability for the illegal acts of individual police officers,[17] (2) minimum liquidated damages, and (3) restriction of defenses based on reputation, etc. which keep potential plaintiffs out of court. Foote, "Tort Remedies for Police Violations of Individual Rights," 39 Minn. L. Rev. 493, 514–16 (1955).

53.   42 U.S.C. § 1983. In Monroe v. Pape, 365 U.S. 167 (1961), the petitioners brought an action for violation of their constitutional rights, in which they claimed damages under the Civil Rights Act of 1871, R.S. § 1979, 42 U.S.C. § 1983: "Every person who, under color of any statute, ordinance, regulation, custom, or usage, of any State or Territory, subjects, or causes to be subjected, any citizen of the United States or other person within the jurisdiction thereof to the deprivation of any rights, privileges, or immunities secured by the Constitution and laws, shall be liable to the party injured in an action at law, suit in equity, or other proper proceeding for redress." The complaint alleged that without an arrest or search warrant "13 Chicago police officers broke into petitioners' home in the early morning, routed them from bed, made them stand naked in the living room, and ransacked every room, emptying drawers and ripping mattress covers"; "that Mr. Monroe was then taken to the police station and detained on 'open' charges for 10 hours, while he was interrogated about a two-day-old murder, that he was not taken before a magistrate, though one was accessible, that he was not permitted to call his family or attorney, [and] that he was subsequently released without criminal charges being preferred against him." 365 U.S. at 169.

The Court held that the complaint stated a cause of action, since there were alleged "facts constituting a deprivation under color of state authority of a right guaranteed by the Fourteenth Amendment." A purpose of the statute was "to provide a federal remedy where the state remedy, though adequate in theory, was not available in practice"; it was, therefore, irrelevant that the petitioners might also have a remedy under state tort law and that the state remedy had not been sought first and refused. Id. at 171, 174.

Aside from the observation in another context that § 1983 "should be read against the background of tort liability that makes a man responsible for the natural consequences of his actions," id. at 187, the Court left unclear what were the elements of the legal wrong that the plaintiffs had

tions. . . . While considerations of state-federal comity and judicial efficiency may dictate that a civil rights action be dismissed when the alleged deprivation has been examined fully during a state criminal trial or has been waived by the complainant, the simple fact of an unreversed state conviction cannot by itself require dismissal." Id. at 232–33.

17. Some states have provisions for indemnification of police officers who are held liable for damages arising out of the performance of their duties. E.g., Wis.Stat. § 895.46(1)(a).

suffered and what was the measure of damages that they should recover. With respect both to liability and to defenses to liability, the courts have, for the most part, applied the law of torts of the state in which the wrong occurred. But there are qualifications to that general approach.

Summarizing case law since Monroe v. Pape, the Court has said: "Our general approach to questions of immunity under § 1983 is by now well established. Although the statute on its face admits of no immunities, we have read it 'in harmony with general principles of tort immunities and defenses rather than in derogation of them.' Imbler v. Pachtman, 424 U.S. 409, 418 (1976). Our initial inquiry is whether an official claiming immunity under § 1983 can point to a common-law counterpart to the privilege he asserts. Tower v. Glover, 467 U.S. 914 (1984). If 'an official was accorded immunity from tort actions at common law when the Civil Rights Act was enacted in 1871, the Court next considers whether § 1983's history or purposes nonetheless counsel against recognizing the same immunity in § 1983 actions.' Id., at 920. Thus, while we look to the common law for guidance, we do not assume that Congress intended to incorporate every common-law immunity into § 1983 in unaltered form." Malley v. Briggs, 475 U.S. 335, 338 (1986).

Concerning the statute of limitations applicable to § 1983 actions, see Garcia v. Wilson, 731 F.2d 640 (10th Cir.1984), aff'd, 471 U.S. 261 (1985), concluding that "every section 1983 claim is in essence an action for injury to personal rights" and holding that all such claims will be so characterized for purposes of the statute of limitations. The opinion reviews cases in other circuits.

The liability of police officers for an unlawful arrest and actions taken in the wake of an arrest is a major issue under § 1983. In Pierson v. Ray, 386 U.S. 547 (1967), the Court held that police officers are not liable under § 1983 for making an illegal arrest if "they acted in good faith and with probable cause"; "a policeman's lot is not so unhappy that he must choose between being charged with dereliction of duty if he does not arrest when he has probable cause, and being mulcted in damages if he does." Id. at 555. Since the policemen who were defendants claimed to have acted in good faith with probable cause pursuant to a statute later found to be invalid, the Court was not called upon to decide whether a policeman was liable if he acted in good faith *without* probable cause. Subsequent cases, however, have established that an officer who acts reasonably and in good faith with respect to probable cause does have immunity. In Anderson v. Creighton, 483 U.S. 635, 641 (1987) (6–3), the Court said: "[I]t is inevitable that law enforcement officials will in some cases reasonably but mistakenly conclude that probable cause is present, and . . . in such cases those officials—like other officials who act in ways they reasonably believe to be lawful—should not be held personally liable." To the same effect, see Hunter v. Bryant, 502 U.S. 224 (1991) (6–2).

It is generally held that a police officer who negligently but in good faith seeks and obtains a search warrant on an insufficient affidavit is not liable under § 1983. E.g., Stadium Films, Inc. v. Baillargeon, 542 F.2d 577, 578 (1st Cir.1976): "Under the prevailing view in this country, a peace officer may not be held liable in damages for making negligent errors of law in seeking or executing a search warrant." On the other hand, the issuance of a warrant does not by itself preclude liability of the officer who applied for the warrant. The officer is liable despite the magistrate's issuance of the warrant "if, on an objective basis, it is obvious that no reasonably competent officer would have concluded that a warrant should issue." Malley v. Briggs, 475 U.S. 335, 341 (1986) (7–2).

A claim that police officers used excessive force in making an arrest or other seizure of the person is tested by a standard of objective reasonableness under the Fourth Amendment rather than a standard of substantive due process. Graham v. Connor, 490 U.S. 386 (1989). See Saucier v. Katz, 533 U.S. 194 (2001). In Jenkins v. Averett, 424 F.2d 1228 (4th Cir.1970), the plaintiff had been chased by the police for six blocks and was then shot in the leg. He was not subsequently charged with any crime. The court held that the plaintiff was entitled to recover under § 1983, even if the shot was not intentionally fired. It said that the plaintiff had been subjected "to the reckless use of excessive force" amounting to "gross and culpable conduct." Since that was sufficient to support a claim for assault and battery under state law, it was sufficient under federal law also: "if intent is required, it may be supplied, for federal purposes, by gross and culpable negligence, just as it was supplied in the common law cause of action." The court went on to say that "bad motive or evil intent" was not generally a necessary element of a claim under § 1983. Id. at 1232. The court held also that damages of $448, covering the plaintiff's out-of-pocket expenses, were inadequate and that he should be compensated for pain and suffering.

In Baker v. McCollan, 443 U.S. 137 (1979) (6–3), the plaintiff alleged that he had been arrested pursuant to a warrant intended for another person and was detained for several days before the mistake was discovered and he was released. The warrant itself was facially valid. Observing that the plaintiff might have a tort action for false imprisonment under state law, the Court held that, there having been no violation of a constitutional right, he did not have a cause of action under § 1983. Compare Coleman v. Frantz, p. 85 above. To the same effect as Baker v. McCollan, see Street v. Surdyka, 492 F.2d 368 (4th Cir.1974). The plaintiff was arrested without a warrant for a misdemeanor not committed in the arresting officer's presence. Assuming that the arrest violated state law and might give rise to an action for false arrest under common law but that the arrest was not unconstitutional (there having been probable cause), the court held that the plaintiff had no cause of action under § 1983. See also Allen v. Eicher, 295 F.Supp. 1184, 1185 (D.Md.1969), holding that an interrogation in violation of Miranda v. Arizona, p. 417 below, and the subsequent trial use in the complainant's criminal trial of his statements during the interrogation did not constitute a cause of action under the Civil Rights Act: "*Miranda* does not per se make an interrogation which violates its precepts into an actionable tort. Unlike an illegal arrest, or an illegal search or seizure, an improper interrogation is not itself a tort." 295 F.Supp. at 1185–86.

In Pritchard v. Perry, 508 F.2d 423 (4th Cir.1975), the court rejected the defendant's claim that the plaintiff could not recover under § 1983, because his arrest and detention had been brief and without injury to him.

It said: "That an infringement of personal liberty such as follows from an unconstitutional arrest has resulted in but a short period of restraint or has involved no physical injury may go in mitigation of damages but it manifestly cannot immunize the constitutional deprivation or abort an aggrieved plaintiff's right of action under Section 1983. The enabling statute was not so considered at the time of its enactment nor has it since been authoritatively construed. There is no justification for the incorporation of a *de minimis* rule by way of a limitation on the right of action by an individual for an admitted violation of constitutional rights. There is no warrant for any separation of constitutional rights into redressable rights and non-redressable rights, of major and minor unconstitutional deprivations, and Section 1983 makes no such distinction and authorizes no such separation." Id. at 425.

In Monroe v. Pape, above, the Court held that Congress had not intended to make municipalities liable for their officers' violations of the Civil Rights Act, and upheld the dismissal of the complaint against the City of Chicago. That holding was overruled in Monell v. Department of Social Services of the City of New York, 436 U.S. 658 (1978) (7–2). The Court concluded that local governing bodies can be sued directly for relief, where the allegedly unconstitutional action executes or implements official policy adopted by the body or governmental "custom." Liability cannot, however, be based solely on the tortious conduct of an employee under a doctrine of *respondeat superior*.

"Proof of a single incident of unconstitutional activity is not sufficient to impose liability under *Monell*, unless proof of the incident includes proof that it was caused by an existing, unconstitutional municipal policy, which policy can be attributed to a municipal policymaker. Otherwise the existence of the unconstitutional policy, and its origin, must be separately proved." City of Oklahoma City v. Tuttle, 471 U.S. 808, 823 (1985) (7–1). The question, when there is a policy and when an independent action by an employee, is discussed in City of St. Louis v. Praprotnik, 485 U.S. 112 (1988) (7–1). Compare Grandstaff v. City of Borger, 767 F.2d 161 (5th Cir.1985) (municipality liable), with Carter v. District of Columbia, 795 F.2d 116 (D.C.Cir.1986) (municipality not liable), and Vippolis v. Village of Haverstraw, 768 F.2d 40 (2d Cir.1985) (same).

In City of Canton v. Harris, 489 U.S. 378 (1989) (6–3), the Court held that a municipality might be liable under § 1983 for an injury due to inadequate police training, but only if the failure to train reflected a deliberate or conscious choice that amounted to a municipal policy. See Parker v. District of Columbia, 850 F.2d 708 (D.C.Cir.1988) (inadequate police training; municipal liability upheld); Spell v. McDaniel, 824 F.2d 1380 (4th Cir.1987) (same).

Municipalities do not have a "qualified immunity" from liability based on the good faith of the officials involved. Owen v. City of Independence, 445 U.S. 622 (1980) (5–4). They are, however, immune from punitive damages under § 1983. City of Newport v. Fact Concerts, Inc., 453 U.S. 247 (1981) (6–3). *Monell* notwithstanding, it remains the law that neither a state nor state officials acting in their official capacity are "persons" who may be sued under § 1983. Will v. Michigan Department of State Police, 491 U.S. 58 (1989) (5–4).

In Pierson v. Ray, above, the Court said also that § 1983 did not remove judges' traditional immunity for acts within their office, 386 U.S. at 553–55, as it had held earlier that legislators retained immunity under the statute for acts within their office, Tenney v. Brandhove, 341 U.S. 367 (1951). A court reporter does not share judges' absolute immunity for performance of the judicial function and has only qualified immunity for failing to produce a transcript for a federal criminal trial. Antoine v. Byers & Anderson, Inc., 508 U.S. 429 (1993).

A prosecutor's absolute immunity from liability under § 1983 for actions taken in his prosecutorial role was affirmed in Imbler v. Pachtman, 424 U.S. 409 (1976). The Court noted that under the common law a prosecutor had absolute immunity from suits for malicious prosecution. It said further:

> A prosecutor is duty bound to exercise his best judgment both in deciding which suits to bring and in conducting them in court. The public trust of the prosecutor's office would suffer if he were constrained in making every decision by the consequences in terms of his own potential liability in a suit for damages. Such suits could be expected with some frequency, for a defendant often will transform his resentment at being prosecuted into the ascription of improper and malicious actions to the State's advocate. . . . Further, if the prosecutor could be made to answer in court each time such a person charged him with wrongdoing, his energy and attention would be diverted from the pressing duty of enforcing the criminal law.

> Moreover, suits that survived the pleadings would pose substantial danger of liability even to the honest prosecutor. The prosecutor's possible knowledge of a witness' falsehoods, the materiality of evidence not revealed to the defense, the propriety of a closing argument, and—ultimately in every case—the likelihood that prosecutorial misconduct so infected a trial as to deny due process, are typical of issues with which judges struggle in actions for post-trial relief, sometimes to differing conclusions. The presentation of such issues in a § 1983 action often would require a virtual retrial of the criminal offense in a new forum, and the resolution of some technical issues by the lay jury. It is fair to say, we think, that the honest prosecutor would face greater difficulty in meeting the standards of qualified immunity than other executive or administrative officials. Frequently acting under serious constraints of time and even information, a prosecutor inevitably makes many decisions that could engender colorable claims of constitutional deprivation. Defending these decisions, often years after they were made, could impose unique and intolerable burdens upon a prosecutor responsible annually for hundreds of indictments and trials. . . .

The affording of only a qualified immunity to the prosecutor also could have an adverse effect upon the functioning of the criminal justice system. Attaining the system's goal of accurately determining guilt or innocence requires that both the prosecution and the defense have wide discretion in the conduct of the trial and the presentation of evidence. The veracity of witnesses in criminal cases frequently is subject to doubt before and after they testify, as is illustrated by the history of this case. If prosecutors were hampered in exercising their judgment as to the use of such witnesses by concern about resulting personal liability, the triers of fact in criminal cases often would be denied relevant evidence.

The ultimate fairness of the operation of the system itself could be weakened by subjecting prosecutors to § 1983 liability. Various post-trial procedures are available to determine whether an accused has received a fair trial. These procedures include the remedial powers of the trial judge, appellate review, and state and federal post-conviction collateral remedies. In all of these the attention of the reviewing judge or tribunal is focused primarily on whether there was a fair trial under law. This focus should not be blurred by even the subconscious knowledge that a post-trial decision in favor of the accused might result in the prosecutor's being called upon to respond in damages for his error or mistaken judgment.

We conclude that the considerations outlined above dictate the same absolute immunity under § 1983 that the prosecutor enjoys at common law. To be sure, this immunity does leave the genuinely wronged defendant without civil redress against a prosecutor whose malicious or dishonest action deprives him of liberty. But the alternative of qualifying a prosecutor's immunity would disserve the broader public interest. It would prevent the vigorous and fearless performance of the prosecutor's duty that is essential to the proper functioning of the criminal justice system. Moreover, it often would prejudice defendants in criminal cases by skewing post-conviction judicial decisions that should be made with the sole purpose of insuring justice.

424 U.S. at 424–28.

The Court confined its holding to the prosecutor's prosecutorial functions ("initiating a prosecution and . . . presenting the State's case") and declined to consider "whether like or similar reasons require immunity for those aspects of the prosecutor's responsibility that cast him in the role of an administrator or investigative officer rather than that of an advocate." Id. at 430–31.

Following *Imbler*, the Court held that a prosecutor's participation as lawyer for the state in a hearing to determine whether there is probable cause for issuance of a search warrant is covered by absolute prosecutorial immunity, but that such immunity does not extend to the function of giving legal advice to the police in the investigative stage of a criminal proceeding; with respect to the latter, a prosecutor has only qualified (good faith) immunity. Burns v. Reed, 500 U.S. 478 (1991). Nor does a prosecutor have absolute immunity if he makes an affidavit to support an application for an arrest warrant, because he is there functioning not as an advocate but as a complaining witness, Kalina v. Fletcher, 522 U.S. 118 (1997). Prosecutors were held not to have absolute immunity from liability for alleged preindictment fabrication of false evidence, inasmuch as the alleged acts occurred while the prosecutors were acting as investigators rather than as advocates. Buckley v. Fitzsimmons, 509 U.S. 259 (1993) (5–4). Similarly, in Briggs v. Goodwin, 569 F.2d 10 (D.C.Cir.1977), the court held that a prosecutor who was presenting witnesses to a grand jury as part of an investigation of certain violations of federal law was functioning in an "investigative" capacity rather than as an advocate, and therefore did not have the absolute immunity granted by *Imbler*. Nor are a prosecutor's allegedly false statements to the press covered by absolute immunity. "Comments to the media," the Court said, "have no functional tie to the judicial process just because they are made by a prosecutor." *Buckley*, above, 509 U.S. at 277.

Prosecutors who withheld exculpatory evidence that was discovered following the defendants' convictions for murder but while direct appeals were pending did not have absolute immunity. The prosecutors were not personally involved in the post-conviction proceedings and were not then acting as prosecutors. Houston v. Partee, 978 F.2d 362 (7th Cir.1992).

In Scheuer v. Rhodes, 416 U.S. 232 (1974), the estates of three students killed during the disturbance at Kent State University in 1970 sought damages under § 1983 against the Governor and other officers of the State of Ohio, officers and members of the National Guard, and the president of the university. The court held that the defendants did not have absolute executive immunity from suit, but had an immunity that is "qualified or limited," so that their liability depended on all the circumstances. "[I]n varying scope, a qualified immunity is available to officers of the executive branch of government, the variation being dependent upon the scope of discretion and responsibilities of the office and all the circumstances as they reasonably appeared at the time of the action on which liability is sought to be based. It is the existence of reasonable grounds for the belief formed at the time and in light of all the circumstances, coupled with good-faith belief, that affords a basis for qualified immunity of executive officers for acts performed in the course of official conduct." Id. at 239, 247–48.

The rationale of *Scheuer* was applied in Apton v. Wilson, 506 F.2d 83 (D.C.Cir.1974), an action for alleged violations of constitutional rights occurring during the "Mayday Demonstrations" in Washington in 1970; the named defendants included the Attorney General and other high officials in the Department of Justice, the Chief of Police, and other police officers. In both cases, the disposition was to remand for further proceedings; the courts did not have facts before them with which to decide whether the defendants did have immunity in the circumstances of the case.

Relying on *Scheuer* and related cases, the court, in Bryan v. Jones, 530 F.2d 1210 (5th Cir.1976), held that in a § 1983 action for false imprisonment, the defense of official immunity is available to a jailer acting in reasonable good faith. Qualified immunity of prison officials is not available for unconstitutional acts if officials had fair warning that the acts were unconstitutional, even in a novel factual situation. Hope v. Pelzer, 536 U.S. 730 (2002) (6–3). "[P]rivate prison guards, unlike those who work directly for the government, do not enjoy immunity from suit in a § 1983 case." Richardson v. McKnight, 521 U.S. 399 (1997) (5–4).

It has been held that court-appointed defense counsel and public defenders acting in their capacity as lawyers also have absolute immunity from suit under § 1983. E.g., Robinson v. Bergstrom, 579 F.2d 401 (7th Cir.1978); Minns v. Paul, 542 F.2d 899 (4th Cir.1976). In *Minns*, the court said that there were two reasons for such immunity: "(a) the need to recruit and hold able lawyers to represent indigents—both full and part-time public defenders, as well as private practitioners appointed by courts to represent individual defendants or litigants, and (b) the need to encourage counsel in the full exercise of professionalism, i.e., the unfettered discretion, in the light of their training and experience, to decline to press the frivolous, to assign priorities between indigent litigants, and to make strategic decisions with regard to a single litigant as to how best his interests may be advanced." Id. at 901. The court added that the latter consideration was particularly compelling when counsel is supplied by the state, since the lawyer may have no control over which clients he will accept and "the client has no economic incentive for eschewing frivolous claims." Id. at 902. That conclusion is considerably undermined by Ferri v. Ackerman, 444 U.S. 193, 204 (1979), below, in which the Court said that since "a defense counsel's principal responsibility is to serve the individual interests of his client," it was not necessary to insulate him entirely from the risk of a claim against him by the client. See White v. Bloom, 621 F.2d 276, 280 (8th Cir.1980), stating that after Ferri v. Ackerman, the position taken in *Robinson* and *Minns* is "no longer tenable."

In any event, it is generally held that defense counsel, whether appointed or retained, is not acting under color of state law, as required by § 1983, but is acting as a private attorney. E.g., United States ex rel. Simmons v. Zibilich, 542 F.2d 259 (5th Cir.1976). "The lack of state action for volunteer court-appointed counsel follows from the nature of the attorney-client relationship. . . . The court-appointed attorney, like any retained counsel, serves his client. He represents the client, not the state. The ancillary facts that the court has a hand in providing counsel, and that the attorney selection board in Orleans Parish obtains its authority from statute, do not alter the attorney-client relationship. That relationship is our concern here." Id. at 261. The Court has held also that a public defender who represents an indigent defendant in a state criminal proceeding does not act "under color of state law." Polk County v. Dodson, 454 U.S. 312 (1981) (8–1). The Court said that a public defender's function rather than his employment relationship with the state is determinative. A public defender's function is defined by "the same standards of competence and integrity as a private lawyer" and requires the "exercise of independent judgment on behalf of the client." Id. at 321.

Public defenders have no immunity from liability under § 1983, however, for intentional misconduct such as a conspiracy with state officials to violate federal constitutional rights. Tower v. Glover, 467 U.S. 914 (1984). (With respect to the holding of Polk County v. Dodson, above, an otherwise private person acts "under color of state law" if he engages in a conspiracy with state officials to violate federal rights. Dennis v. Sparks, 449 U.S. 24 (1980).) See also Ferri v. Ackerman, 444 U.S. 193 (1979), holding that an attorney appointed to represent an indigent defendant in a federal criminal trial does not, as a matter of federal law, have absolute immunity in a state malpractice suit brought against him by his former client.

Government witnesses, like other witnesses, have an absolute immunity from a convicted defendant's suit under § 1983 for damages for having given perjured testimony at the defendant's trial. Briscoe v. LaHue, 460 U.S. 325 (1983) (6–3). The witnesses in question were police officers. The Court observed that the principle of Pierson v. Ray (judges) and Imbler v. Pachtman (prosecutors), above, applied also to witnesses, "who perform a somewhat different function in the trial process but whose participation in bringing the litigation to a just—or possibly unjust—conclusion is equally indispensable." 460 U.S. at 345.

54. "[A] jury may be permitted to assess punitive damages in an action under § 1983 when the defendant's conduct is shown to be motivated by evil motive or intent, or when it involves reckless or callous indifference to the federally protected rights of others." Smith v. Wade, 461 U.S. 30, 56 (1983) (5–4).

55. In an action under § 1983 charging that the defendant police officers made an unlawful entry into the plaintiff's apartment and assaulted him, the district judge found that there had been an unlawful entry but not an assault, and that the plaintiff did not suffer physical or emotional damage. The judge awarded damages of $500 which he described as "nominal damages." On appeal, the court said that the award was improper. "If a compensable injury has been shown, compensatory damages must be given; if not, nominal damages should not be used to compensate plaintiff in any substantial manner, since he has shown no right to such compensation. We do not accept those decisions that have awarded as nominal damages more than a token amount. Five hundred dollars charged against an individual police officer is no mere token." The court went on to say that substantial damages could be awarded as compensation "for actual, though wholly impalpable injuries," such as "an intangible loss of civil rights or purely mental suffering." Magnett v. Pelletier, 488 F.2d 33 (1st Cir.1973).

"[I]n order to recover damages for allegedly unconstitutional conviction or imprisonment, or for other harm caused by actions whose unlawfulness would render a conviction or sentence invalid, a § 1983 plaintiff must prove that the conviction or sentence has been reversed on direct appeal, expunged by executive order, declared invalid by a state tribunal authorized to make such determination, or called into question by a federal court's issuance of a writ of habeas corpus, 28 U.S.C. § 2254. A claim for damages bearing that relationship to a conviction or sentence that has *not* been so invalidated is not cognizable under § 1983. Thus, when a state prisoner seeks damages in a § 1983 suit, the district court must consider whether a judgment in favor of the plaintiff would necessarily imply the invalidity of his conviction or sentence; if it would, the complaint must be dismissed unless the plaintiff can demonstrate that the conviction or sentence has already been invalidated. But if the district court determines that the plaintiff's action, even if successful, will *not* demonstrate the invalidity of any outstanding criminal judgment against the plaintiff, the action should be allowed to proceed, in the absence of some other bar to the suit." Heck v. Humphrey, 512 U.S. 477, 486–87 (1994).

56. Bivens v. Six Unknown Named Agents of Federal Bureau of Narcotics, 403 U.S. 388 (1971). Section 1983 provides no remedy for violation of constitutional rights by federal officials. In *Bivens*, the Supreme Court held that the violation of rights protected by the Fourth Amendment by a federal agent acting under color of his authority gives rise to a federal cause of action. The person whose rights are violated is entitled to recover money damages for any injuries he suffered as a result of the violation.

On remand, the court of appeals held that federal police officers, such as FBI agents, have no immunity from actions for damages based on a violation of constitutional rights. With respect to liability, the court said: "[T]o prevail the police officer need not allege and prove probable cause in the constitutional sense. The standard governing police conduct is composed of two elements, the first is subjective and the second is objective. Thus the officer must allege and prove not only that he believed, in good faith, that his conduct was lawful, but also that his belief was reasonable. And so we hold that it is a defense to allege and prove good faith and reasonable belief in the validity of the arrest and search and in the necessity for carrying out the arrest and search in the way the arrest was made and the search was conducted. We think, as a matter of constitutional law and as a matter of common sense, a law enforcement officer is entitled to protection." 456 F.2d 1339, 1348 (2d Cir.1972).

As a general matter, the rules applicable to actions under § 1983, p. 86 note 53 above, are applicable also to actions against federal officers under *Bivens*. See, e.g., Brawer v. Horowitz, 535 F.2d 830 (3d Cir.1976) (federal prosecutors have the same immunity as state prosecutors).

57. Arrest records. Can a person who is arrested and subsequently released without charges being filed or following dismissal of the charges or an acquittal have his arrest record and fingerprints and photographs made at the time of his arrest suppressed? The FBI maintains an elaborate system for the accumulation and retrieval of arrest records and fingerprints of persons arrested on federal or state charges. See Utz v. Cullinane, 520 F.2d 467, 480–82 (D.C.Cir.1975); Menard v. Saxbe, 498 F.2d 1017, 1020–22 (D.C.Cir.1974). Local and state police departments maintain their own files.

In *Menard*, the appellant sued to compel removal from the FBI files of an arrest record including his fingerprints. He had been arrested and detained by the California police, who later released him without charges. The district court found that there had been probable cause for the arrest. Expungement of the record was denied. On appeal from the district court's

order the court of appeals held that Menard was entitled to an order
directing the FBI to remove his record from its criminal files. The court
noted the variety of disabilities that may flow from an arrest record.

> There is an undoubted "social stigma" involved in an arrest record.
> "[I]t is common knowledge that a man with an arrest record is much
> more apt to be subject to police scrutiny—the first to be questioned
> and the last eliminated as a suspect to an investigation."[18] Existence of
> a record may burden a decision whether to testify at trial. And records
> of arrest are used by judges in making decisions as to sentencing,
> whether to grant bail, or whether to release pending appeal.

> The arrest record is used outside the field of criminal justice. Most
> significant is its use in connection with subsequent inquiries on appli-
> cations for employment and licenses to engage in certain fields of work.
> An arrest record often proves to be a substantial barrier to employ-
> ment.

498 F.2d at 1024.

The court said that ordinarily an action to expunge an arrest record
should be brought against the local police agency that made the arrest.
With respect to the FBI, the court said that "the FBI's function of
maintaining and disseminating criminal identification records and files
carries with it as a corollary the responsibility to discharge this function
reliably and responsibly and without unnecessary harm to individuals
whose rights have been invaded. The FBI cannot take the position that it is
a mere passive recipient of records received from others, when it in fact
energizes those records by maintaining a system of criminal files and
disseminating the criminal records widely, acting in effect as a step-up
transformer that puts into the system a capacity for both good and harm."
Id. at 1026. Having been informed by the local police that there was no
basis for Menard's arrest, the FBI had no authority to retain his record in
its criminal files along with arrest records. The court's decision was based
on its interpretation of the statute (28 U.S.C. § 534) authorizing the FBI to
maintain identification files.

In Tarlton v. Saxbe, 507 F.2d 1116 (D.C.Cir.1974), the court of appeals
indicated that the FBI's duty went beyond expungement of arrest records
later reported to it as incorrect and included some more general duty to
prevent dissemination of inaccurate arrest and conviction records. The
court recognized the practical difficulties that such an affirmative duty
might impose on the FBI, and remanded to the district court for an inquiry
into its appropriate nature and scope. The court noted that the FBI could
not reasonably be required to resolve a factual or legal conflict between
arresting authorities and the person arrested, nor to guarantee the accuracy of its files. The district court's findings and orders, which include a
description of the FBI's practices, appear at 407 F.Supp. 1083 (D.D.C.1976).
See generally Utz v. Cullinane, above (transmission of local arrest records
to FBI).

The rulings in *Menard* and *Tarlton* are unusual. Where there is no
claim that the police conduct in making the arrest was abusive or that

18. Davidson v. Dill, 503 P.2d 157, 159
(Colo.1972).

Boston Police Department
Mugshot Form

Report Date: 05/09/1997 12:57:24
Booking Status: COMPLETED
Printed By: Dahlbeck, Joseph W

Master Name: Pomeroy, Arnold, George
Booking Name: Layfield, Robert, Arthur
Address: Apt 23, 312 Evergreen CR , Boston, MA.
Charges: Breaking & Entering N/T, Poss cl B

Sex: Male
Date of Birth: 06/09/1942
Height: 5' 11"
Weight: 200   lbs
Eye Color: Brown
Hair Color: Dark Brown
Race: White Non-Hispanic
Booking No: 95-000316-04
Booking Date: 02/10/1997 11:25
Incident Number: 95-1000000
BPD CR No: 000001-80
State Tracking No: 1234567890123
FBI No: 1234567890

Boston Police Department
Mugshot Form

Report Date: 05/09/1997 12:57:24
Booking Status: COMPLETED
Printed By: Dahlbeck, Joseph W

Master Name: Pomeroy, Arnold, George
Booking Name: Layfield, Robert, Arthur
Address: Apt 23, 312 Evergreen CR , Boston, MA.
Charges: Breaking & Entering N/T, Poss cl B

Sex: Male
Date of Birth: 06/09/1942
Height: 5' 11"
Weight: 200   lbs
Eye Color: Brown
Hair Color: Dark Brown
Race: White Non-Hispanic
Booking No: 95-000316-04
Booking Date: 02/10/1997 11:25
Incident Number: 95-1000000
BPD CR No: 000001-80
State Tracking No: 1234567890123
FBI No: 1234567890

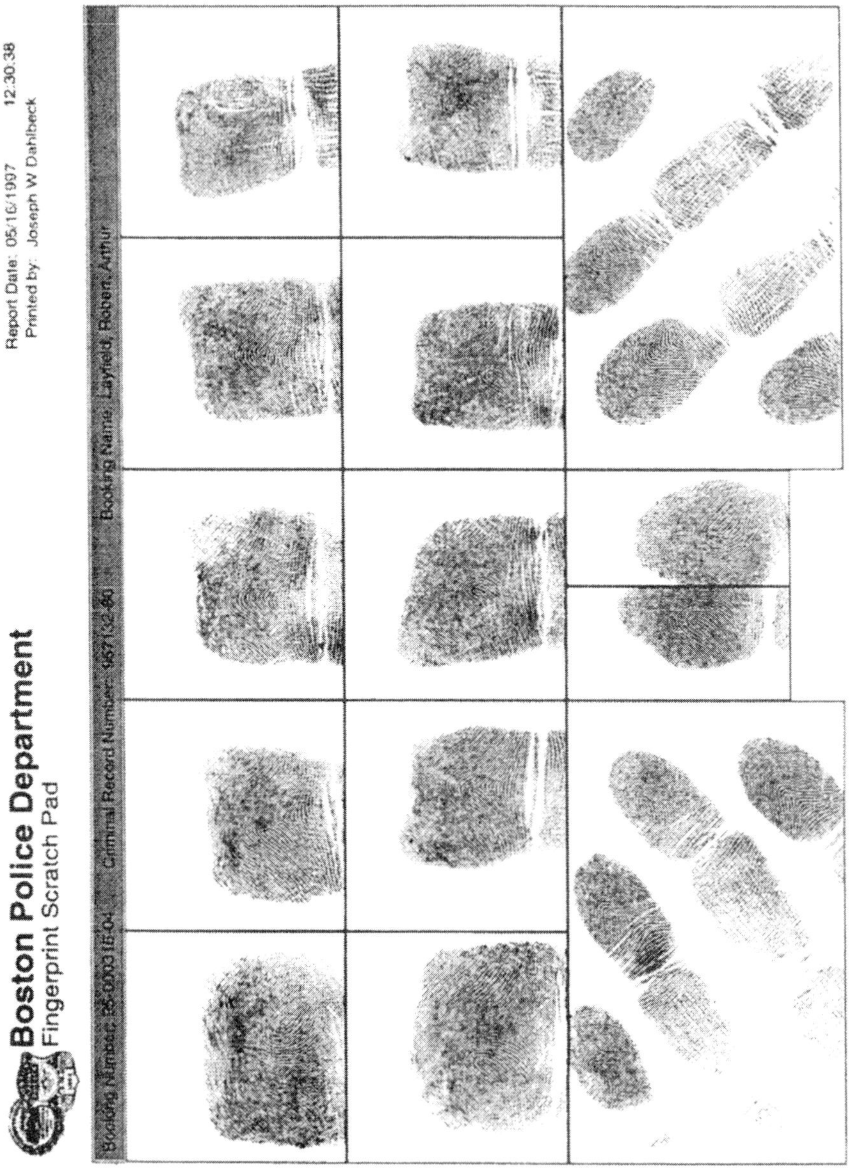
Boston Police Department
Fingerprint Scratch Pad
Report Date: 05/16/1997 12:30:38
Printed by: Joseph W Dahlbeck
Booking Number:
Criminal Record Number:
Booking Name: Layfield, Robert, Arthur

there was an intention to make improper use of the arrest record, expungement has generally not been ordered. "[A]n acquittal, standing alone, is not in itself sufficient to warrant an expunction of an arrest record." United States v. Linn, 513 F.2d 925, 927–28 (10th Cir.1975). In Herschel v. Dyra, 365 F.2d 17, 20 (7th Cir.1966), the court said: "We think that under the obligations which the Chicago Police Department has in maintaining the public safety and welfare in Chicago, the Superintendent of Police is justified and, indeed, duty-bound to compile and retain arrest records of all persons arrested, and that the execution of that policy does not violate plaintiff's right of privacy." To the same effect, see, e.g., United States v. Schnitzer, 567 F.2d 536 (2d Cir.1977). But see Kowall v. United States, 53 F.R.D. 211 (W.D.Mich.1971) (expungement order upheld). For an example of a case in which improper conduct in making the arrests was the basis of the demand for expungement, see Sullivan v. Murphy, 478 F.2d 938 (D.C.Cir.1973) (case remanded to district court for fashioning of remedy). See also Bilick v. Dudley, 356 F.Supp. 945 (S.D.N.Y.1973) (arrests without probable cause and in violation of First Amendment rights; expungement ordered).

The subject of expungement of records maintained by the executive branch of government is discussed thoroughly in Sealed Appellant v. Sealed Appellee, 130 F.3d 695 (5th Cir.1997). The appellee had been convicted of wire fraud and conspiracy. The conviction was subsequently set aside because of error in the jury instructions, and he was not retried. Six years later, alleging that records of his conviction interfered with his professional law-enforcement activities, he filed a petition for expungement of all records of his convictions. The court said that "[t]here is no constitutional basis for a 'right to expungement.'" Id. at 699. "To have standing, a party claiming expungement of executive branch records must make a showing of more than mere burden. Unlike a person asking for expungement of judicial records—over which the court has supervisory powers—the claimant must show an affirmative rights violation by executive branch officers or agencies to justify the intrusion into the executive's affairs. This injury must be such that no other remedy would afford relief." Id. at 697. The court concluded that the district court's expungement order was an abuse of discretion.

In United States v. Doe, 730 F.2d 1529 (D.C.Cir.1984), the court held that the provision of the Federal Youth Corrections Act for setting aside a conviction requires that court records disclosing a conviction be sealed and available only to judicial, administrative, and law enforcement officials in the performance of their duties. But see United States v. Doe, 732 F.2d 229 (1st Cir.1984).

Compare Paul v. Davis, 424 U.S. 693 (1976) (5–3), in which the plaintiff's name and photograph appeared on a flyer describing "active shoplifters" that the police distributed to local merchants. He had been charged with shoplifting, but the case had been filed without a disposition. Observing that the plaintiff might well have a claim for defamation under state law, the Court concluded that he nevertheless did not have any claim under 42 U.S.C. § 1983 for deprivation of a constitutional right, in particular a denial of due process of law.

———

CHAPTER 2

STOP (AND FRISK)

Terry v. Ohio

392 U.S. 1, 88 S.Ct. 1868, 20 L.Ed.2d 889 (1968)

■ MR. CHIEF JUSTICE WARREN delivered the opinion of the Court.

This case presents serious questions concerning the role of the Fourth Amendment in the confrontation on the street between the citizen and the policeman investigating suspicious circumstances.

Petitioner Terry was convicted of carrying a concealed weapon and sentenced to the statutorily prescribed term of one to three years in the penitentiary. Following the denial of a pretrial motion to suppress, the prosecution introduced in evidence two revolvers and a number of bullets seized from Terry and a codefendant, Richard Chilton, by Cleveland Police Detective Martin McFadden. At the hearing on the motion to suppress this evidence, Officer McFadden testified that while he was patrolling in plain clothes in downtown Cleveland at approximately 2:30 in the afternoon of October 31, 1963, his attention was attracted by two men, Chilton and Terry, standing on the corner of Huron Road and Euclid Avenue. He had never seen the two men before, and he was unable to say precisely what first drew his eye to them. However, he testified that he had been a policeman for 39 years and a detective for 35 and that he had been assigned to patrol this vicinity of downtown Cleveland for shoplifters and pickpockets for 30 years. He explained that he had developed routine habits of observation over the years and that he would "stand and watch people or walk and watch people at many intervals of the day." He added: "Now, in this case when I looked over they didn't look right to me at the time."

His interest aroused, Officer McFadden took up a post of observation in the entrance to a store 300 to 400 feet away from the two men. "I get more purpose to watch them when I seen their movements," he testified. He saw one of the men leave the other one and walk southwest on Huron Road, past some stores. The man paused for a moment and looked in a store window, then walked on a short distance, turned around and walked back toward the corner, pausing once again to look in the same store window. He rejoined his companion at the corner, and the two conferred briefly. Then the second man went through the same series of motions, strolling down Huron Road, looking in the same window, walking on a short distance, turning back, peering in the store window again, and returning to confer with the first man at the corner. The two men repeated this ritual alternately between five and six times apiece—in all, roughly a dozen trips. At one point, while the two were standing together on the corner, a third man approached them and engaged them briefly in conversation. This man then left the two others and walked west on Euclid Avenue. Chilton and Terry resumed their measured pacing, peering, and conferring. After this had gone on for 10 to 12 minutes, the two men walked off together, heading west on Euclid Avenue, following the path taken earlier by the third man.

By this time Officer McFadden had become thoroughly suspicious. He testified that after observing their elaborately casual and oft-repeated reconnaissance of the store window on Huron Road, he suspected the two men of "casing a job, a stick-up," and that he considered it his duty as a police officer to investigate further. He added that he feared "they may have a gun." Thus, Officer McFadden followed Chilton and Terry and saw them stop in front of Zucker's store to talk to the same man who had conferred with them earlier on the street corner. Deciding that the situation was ripe for direct action, Officer McFadden approached the three men, identified himself as a police officer and asked for their names. At this point his knowledge was confined to what he had observed. He was not acquainted with any of the three men by name or by sight, and he had received no information concerning them from any other source. When the men "mumbled something" in response to his inquiries, Officer McFadden grabbed petitioner Terry, spun him around so that they were facing the other two, with Terry between McFadden and the others, and patted down the outside of his clothing. In the left breast pocket of Terry's overcoat Officer McFadden felt a pistol. He reached inside the overcoat pocket, but was unable to remove the gun. At this point, keeping Terry between himself and the others, the officer ordered all three men to enter Zucker's store. As they went in, he removed Terry's overcoat completely, removed a .38-caliber revolver from the pocket and ordered all three men to face the wall with their hands raised. Officer McFadden proceeded to pat down the outer clothing of Chilton and the third man, Katz. He discovered another revolver in the outer pocket of Chilton's overcoat, but no weapons were found on Katz. The officer testified that he only patted the men down to see whether they had weapons, and that he did not put his hands beneath the outer garments of either Terry or Chilton until he felt their guns. So far as appears from the record, he never placed his hands beneath Katz' outer garments. Officer McFadden seized Chilton's gun, asked the proprietor of the store to call a police wagon, and took all three men to the station, where Chilton and Terry were formally charged with carrying concealed weapons.

On the motion to suppress the guns the prosecution took the position that they had been seized following a search incident to a lawful arrest. The trial court rejected this theory, stating that it "would be stretching the facts beyond reasonable comprehension" to find that Officer McFadden had had probable cause to arrest the men before he patted them down for weapons. However, the court denied the defendants' motion on the ground that Officer McFadden, on the basis of his experience, "had reasonable cause to believe . . . that the defendants were conducting themselves suspiciously, and some interrogation should be made of their action." Purely for his own protection, the court held, the officer had the right to pat down the outer clothing of these men, who he had reasonable cause to believe might be armed. The court distinguished between an investigatory "stop" and an arrest, and between a "frisk" of the outer clothing for weapons and a full-blown search for evidence of crime. The frisk, it held, was essential to the proper performance of the officer's investigatory duties, for without it "the answer to the police officer may be a bullet, and a loaded pistol discovered during the frisk is admissible."

After the court denied their motion to suppress, Chilton and Terry waived jury trial and pleaded not guilty. The court adjudged them guilty, and the Court of Appeals for the Eighth Judicial District, Cuyahoga County, affirmed. . . . The Supreme Court of Ohio dismissed their appeal on the ground that no "substantial constitutional question" was involved. We granted certiorari . . . to determine whether the admission of the revolvers in evidence violated petitioner's rights under the Fourth Amendment, made applicable to the States by the Fourteenth. . . . We affirm the conviction.

I

The Fourth Amendment provides that "the right of the people to be secure in their persons, houses, papers, and effects, against unreasonable searches and seizures, shall not be violated. . . ." This inestimable right of personal security belongs as much to the citizen on the streets of our cities as to the homeowner closeted in his study to dispose of his secret affairs. . . . We have recently held that "the Fourth Amendment protects people, not places," Katz v. United States, 389 U.S. 347, 351 (1967), and whenever an individual may harbor a reasonable "expectation of privacy," id., at 361 (Mr. Justice Harlan, concurring), he is entitled to be free from unreasonable governmental intrusion. Of course, the specific content and incidents of this right must be shaped by the context in which it is asserted. For "what the Constitution forbids is not all searches and seizures, but unreasonable searches and seizures." Elkins v. United States, 364 U.S. 206, 222 (1960). Unquestionably petitioner was entitled to the protection of the Fourth Amendment as he walked down the street in Cleveland. . . . The question is whether in all the circumstances of this on-the-street encounter, his right to personal security was violated by an unreasonable search and seizure.

We would be less than candid if we did not acknowledge that this question thrusts to the fore difficult and troublesome issues regarding a sensitive area of police activity—issues which have never before been squarely presented to this Court. Reflective of the tensions involved are the practical and constitutional arguments pressed with great vigor on both sides of the public debate over the power of the police to "stop and frisk"—as it is sometimes euphemistically termed—suspicious persons.

On the one hand, it is frequently argued that in dealing with the rapidly unfolding and often dangerous situations on city streets the police are in need of an escalating set of flexible responses, graduated in relation to the amount of information they possess. For this purpose it is urged that distinctions should be made between a "stop" and an "arrest" (or a "seizure" of a person), and between a "frisk" and a "search." Thus, it is argued, the police should be allowed to "stop" a person and detain him briefly for questioning upon suspicion that he may be connected with criminal activity. Upon suspicion that the person may be armed, the police should have the power to "frisk" him for weapons. If the "stop" and the "frisk" give rise to probable cause to believe that the suspect has committed a crime, then the police should be empowered to make a formal "arrest," and a full incident "search" of the person. This scheme is justified in part upon the notion that a "stop" and a "frisk" amount to a mere "minor inconvenience and petty indignity," which can properly be imposed upon the citizen in the interest of effective law enforcement on the basis of a police officer's suspicion.

On the other side the argument is made that the authority of the police must be strictly circumscribed by the law of arrest and search as it has developed to date in the traditional jurisprudence of the Fourth Amendment. It is contended with some force that there is not—and cannot be—a variety of police activity which does not depend solely upon the voluntary cooperation of the citizen and yet which stops short of an arrest based upon probable cause to make such an arrest. The heart of the Fourth Amendment, the argument runs, is a severe requirement of specific justification for any intrusion upon protected personal security, coupled with a highly developed system of judicial controls to enforce upon the agents of the State the commands of the Constitution. Acquiescence by the courts in the compulsion inherent in the field interrogation practices at issue here, it is urged, would constitute an abdication of judicial control over, and indeed an encouragement of, substantial interference with liberty and personal security by police officers whose judgment is necessarily colored by their primary involvement in "the often competitive enterprise of ferreting out crime." Johnson v. United States, 333 U.S. 10, 14 (1948). This, it is argued, can only serve to exacerbate police-community tensions in the crowded centers of our Nation's cities.

In this context we approach the issues in this case mindful of the limitations of the judicial function in controlling the myriad daily situations in which policemen and citizens confront each other on the street. The State has characterized the issue here as "the right of a police officer . . . to make an on-the-street stop, interrogate and pat down for weapons (known in street vernacular as 'stop and frisk')." But this is only partly accurate. For the issue is not the abstract propriety of the police conduct, but the admissibility against petitioner of the evidence uncovered by the search and seizure. Ever since its inception, the rule excluding evidence seized in violation of the Fourth Amendment has been recognized as a principal mode of discouraging lawless police conduct. . . . Thus its major thrust is a deterrent one . . . and experience has taught that it is the only effective deterrent to police misconduct in the criminal context, and that without it the constitutional guarantee against unreasonable searches and seizures would be a mere "form of words." Mapp v. Ohio, 367 U.S. 643, 655 (1961). The rule also serves another vital function—"the imperative of judicial integrity." Elkins v. United States, 364 U.S. 206, 222 (1960). Courts which sit under our Constitution cannot and will not be made party to lawless invasions of the constitutional rights of citizens by permitting unhindered governmental use of the fruits of such invasions. Thus in our system evidentiary rulings provide the context in which the judicial process of inclusion and exclusion approves some conduct as comporting with constitutional guarantees and disapproves other actions by state agents. A ruling admitting evidence in a criminal trial, we recognize, has the necessary effect of legitimizing the conduct which produced the evidence, while an application of the exclusionary rule withholds the constitutional imprimatur.

The exclusionary rule has its limitations, however, as a tool of judicial control. It cannot properly be invoked to exclude the products of legitimate police investigative techniques on the ground that much conduct which is closely similar involves unwarranted intrusions upon constitutional protections. Moreover, in some contexts the rule is ineffective as a deterrent. Street encounters between citizens and police officers are incredibly rich in diversity. They range from wholly friendly exchanges of pleasantries or mutually useful information to hostile confrontations of armed men involving arrests, or injuries, or loss of life. Moreover, hostile confrontations are not all of a piece. Some of them begin in a friendly enough manner, only to take a different turn upon the injection of some unexpected element into the conversation. Encounters are initiated by the police for a wide variety of purposes, some of which are wholly unrelated to a desire to prosecute for crime. Doubtless some police "field interrogation" conduct violates the Fourth Amendment. But a stern refusal by this Court to condone such activity does not necessarily render it responsive to the exclusionary rule. Regardless of how effective the rule may be where obtaining convictions is an important objective of the police, it is powerless to deter invasions of constitutionally guaranteed rights where the police either have no interest in prosecuting or are willing to forgo successful prosecution in the interest of serving some other goal.

Proper adjudication of cases in which the exclusionary rule is invoked demands a constant awareness of these limitations. The wholesale harassment by certain elements of the police community, of which minority groups, particularly Negroes, frequently complain, will not be stopped by the exclusion of any evidence from any criminal trial. Yet a rigid and unthinking application of the exclusionary rule, in futile protest against practices which it can never be used effectively to control, may exact a high toll in human injury and frustration of efforts to prevent crime. No judicial opinion can comprehend the protean variety of the street encounter, and we can only judge the facts of the case before us. Nothing we say today is to be taken as indicating approval of police conduct outside the legitimate investigative sphere. Under our decision, courts still retain their traditional responsibility to guard against police conduct which is overbearing or harassing, or which trenches upon personal security without the objective evidentiary justification which the Constitution requires. When such conduct is identified, it must be condemned by the judiciary and its fruits must be excluded from evidence in criminal trials. And, of course, our approval of legitimate and restrained investigative conduct undertaken on the basis of ample factual justification should in no way discourage the employment of other remedies than the exclusionary rule to curtail abuses for which that sanction may prove inappropriate.

Having thus roughly sketched the perimeters of the constitutional debate over the limits on police investigative conduct in general and the background against which this case presents itself, we turn our attention to the quite narrow question posed by the facts before us: whether it is always unreasonable for a policeman to seize a person and subject him to a limited search for weapons unless there is probable cause for an arrest. Given the narrowness of this question, we have no occasion to canvass in detail the constitutional limitations upon the scope of a policeman's power when he confronts a citizen without probable cause to arrest him.

II

Our first task is to establish at what point in this encounter the Fourth Amendment becomes relevant. That is, we must decide whether and when Officer McFadden "seized" Terry and whether and when he conducted a "search." There is some suggestion in the use of such terms as "stop" and "frisk" that such police conduct is outside the purview of the Fourth Amendment because neither action rises to the level of a "search" or "seizure" within the meaning of the Constitution. We emphatically reject this notion. It is quite plain that the Fourth Amendment governs "seizures" of the person which do not eventuate in a trip to the station house and prosecution for crime—"arrests" in traditional terminology. It must be recognized that whenever a police officer accosts an individual and restrains his freedom to walk away, he has "seized" that person. And it is nothing less than sheer torture of the English language to suggest that a careful exploration of the outer surfaces of a person's clothing all over his or her body in an attempt to find weapons is not a "search." Moreover, it is simply fantastic to urge that such a procedure performed in public by a policeman while the citizen stands helpless, perhaps facing a wall with his hands raised, is a "petty indignity." It is a serious intrusion upon the sanctity of the person, which may inflict great indignity and arouse strong resentment, and it is not to be undertaken lightly.

The danger in the logic which proceeds upon distinctions between a "stop" and an "arrest," or "seizure" of the person, and between a "frisk" and a "search" is twofold. It seeks to isolate from constitutional scrutiny the initial stages of the contact between the policeman and the citizen. And by suggesting a rigid all-or-nothing model of justification and regulation under the Amendment, it obscures the utility of limitations upon the scope, as well as the initiation, of police action as a means of constitutional regulation. This Court has held in the past that a search which is reasonable at its inception may violate the Fourth Amendment by virtue of its intolerable intensity and scope. . . . The scope of the search must be "strictly tied to and justified by" the circumstances which rendered its initiation permissible. Warden v. Hayden, 387 U.S. 294, 310 (1967) (Mr. Justice Fortas, concurring). . . .

The distinctions of classical "stop-and-frisk" theory thus serve to divert attention from the central inquiry under the Fourth Amendment—the reasonableness in all the circumstances of the particular governmental invasion of a citizen's personal security. "Search" and "seizure" are not talismans. We therefore reject the notions that the Fourth Amendment does not come into play at all as a limitation upon police conduct if the officers stop short of something called a "technical arrest" or a "full-blown search."

In this case there can be no question, then, that Officer McFadden "seized" petitioner and subjected him to a "search" when he took hold of him and patted down the outer surfaces of his clothing. We must decide whether at that point it was reasonable for Officer McFadden to have interfered with petitioner's personal security as he did.[1] And in determining whether the seizure and search were "unreasonable" our inquiry is a dual one—whether the officer's action was justified at its inception, and whether it was reasonably related in scope to the circumstances which justified the interference in the first place.

III

If this case involved police conduct subject to the Warrant Clause of the Fourth Amendment, we would have to ascertain whether "probable cause" existed to justify the search and seizure which took place. However, that is not the case. We do not retreat from our holdings that the police must, whenever practicable, obtain advance judicial approval of searches and seizures through the warrant procedure . . . or that in most instances failure to comply with the warrant requirement can only be excused by exigent circumstances. . . . But we deal here with an entire rubric of police conduct—necessarily swift action predicated upon the on-the-spot observations of the officer on the beat—which historically has not been, and as a practical matter could not be, subjected to the warrant procedure. Instead, the conduct involved in this case must be tested by the Fourth Amendment's general proscription against unreasonable searches and seizures.

Nonetheless, the notions which underlie both the warrant procedure and the requirement of probable cause remain fully relevant in this context. In order to assess the reasonableness of Officer McFadden's

---

1. We thus decide nothing today concerning the constitutional propriety of an investigative "seizure" upon less than probable cause for purposes of "detention" and/or interrogation. Obviously, not all personal intercourse between policemen and citizens involves "seizures" of persons. Only when the officer, by means of physical force or show of authority, has in some way restrained the liberty of a citizen may we conclude that a "seizure" has occurred. We cannot tell with any certainty upon this record whether any such "seizure" took place here prior to Officer McFadden's initiation of physical contact for purposes of searching Terry for weapons, and we thus may assume that up to that point no intrusion upon constitutionally protected rights had occurred.

conduct as a general proposition, it is necessary "first to focus upon the governmental interest which allegedly justifies official intrusion upon the constitutionally protected interests of the private citizen," for there is "no ready test for determining reasonableness other than by balancing the need to search [or seize] against the invasion which the search [or seizure] entails." Camara v. Municipal Court, 387 U.S. 523, 534–35, 536–37 (1967). And in justifying the particular intrusion the police officer must be able to point to specific and articulable facts which, taken together with rational inferences from those facts, reasonably warrant that intrusion. The scheme of the Fourth Amendment becomes meaningful only when it is assured that at some point the conduct of those charged with enforcing the laws can be subjected to the more detached, neutral scrutiny of a judge who must evaluate the reasonableness of a particular search or seizure in light of the particular circumstances. And in making that assessment it is imperative that the facts be judged against an objective standard: would the facts available to the officer at the moment of the seizure or the search "warrant a man of reasonable caution in the belief" that the action taken was appropriate? . . . Anything less would invite intrusions upon constitutionally guaranteed rights based on nothing more substantial than inarticulate hunches, a result this Court has consistently refused to sanction. . . . And simple " 'good faith on the part of the arresting officer is not enough.' . . . If subjective good faith alone were the test, the protections of the Fourth Amendment would evaporate, and the people would be 'secure in their persons, houses, papers, and effects,' only in the discretion of the police." Beck v. Ohio [379 U.S. 89 (1964)], at 97.

Applying these principles to this case, we consider first the nature and extent of the governmental interests involved. One general interest is of course that of effective crime prevention and detection; it is this interest which underlies the recognition that a police officer may in appropriate circumstances and in an appropriate manner approach a person for purposes of investigating possibly criminal behavior even though there is no probable cause to make an arrest. It was this legitimate investigative function officer McFadden was discharging when he decided to approach petitioner and his companions. He had observed Terry, Chilton, and Katz go through a series of acts, each of them perhaps innocent in itself, but which taken together warranted further investigation. There is nothing unusual in two men standing together on a street corner, perhaps waiting for someone. Nor is there anything suspicious about people in such circumstances strolling up and down the street, singly or in pairs. Store windows, moreover, are made to be looked in. But the story is quite different where, as here, two men hover about a street corner for an extended period of time, at the end of which it becomes apparent that they are not waiting for anyone or anything; where these men pace alternately along an identical route, pausing to stare in the same store window roughly 24 times; where each completion of this route is followed immediately by a conference between the two men on the corner; where they are joined in one of these conferences by a third man who leaves swiftly; and where the two men finally follow the third and rejoin him a couple of blocks away. It would have been poor police work indeed for an officer of 30 years' experience in the detection of thievery from stores in this same neighborhood to have failed to investigate this behavior further.

The crux of this case, however, is not the propriety of Officer McFadden's taking steps to investigate petitioner's suspicious behavior, but rather, whether there was justification for McFadden's invasion of Terry's personal security by searching him for weapons in the course of that investigation. We are now concerned with more than the governmental interest in investigating crime; in addition, there is the more immediate interest of the police officer in taking steps to assure himself that the person with whom he is dealing is not armed with a weapon that could unexpectedly and fatally be used against him. Certainly it would be unreasonable to require that police officers take unnecessary risks in the performance of their duties. American criminals have a long tradition of armed violence, and every year in this country many law enforcement officers are killed in the line of duty, and thousands more are wounded. Virtually all of these deaths and a substantial portion of the injuries are inflicted with guns and knives.

In view of these facts, we cannot blind ourselves to the need for law enforcement officers to protect themselves and other prospective victims of violence in situations where they may lack probable cause for an arrest. When an officer is justified in believing that the individual whose suspicious behavior he is investigating at close range is armed and presently dangerous to the officer or to others, it would appear to be clearly unreasonable to deny the officer the power to take necessary measures to determine whether the person is in fact carrying a weapon and to neutralize the threat of physical harm.

We must still consider, however, the nature and quality of the intrusion on individual rights which must be accepted if police officers are to be conceded the right to search for weapons in situations where probable cause to arrest for crime is lacking. Even a limited search of the outer clothing for weapons constitutes a severe, though brief, intrusion upon cherished personal security, and it must surely be an annoying, frightening, and perhaps humiliating experience. Petitioner contends that such an intrusion is permissible only incident to a lawful arrest, either for a crime involving the possession of weapons or for a crime the commission of which led the officer to investigate in the first place. However, this argument must be closely examined.

Petitioner does not argue that a police officer should refrain from making any investigation of suspicious circumstances until such time as he has probable cause to make an arrest; nor does he deny that police officers in properly discharging their investigative function may find themselves confronting persons who might well be armed and dangerous. Moreover, he does not say that an officer is always unjustified in searching a suspect to discover weapons. Rather, he says it is unreasonable for the policeman to take that step until such time as the situation evolves to a point where there is probable cause to make an arrest. When that point has been

reached, petitioner would concede the officer's right to conduct a search of
the suspect for weapons, fruits or instrumentalities of the crime, or "mere"
evidence, incident to the arrest.

There are two weaknesses in this line of reasoning, however. First, it
fails to take account of traditional limitations upon the scope of searches,
and thus recognizes no distinction in purpose, character, and extent between a search incident to an arrest and a limited search for weapons. The
former, although justified in part by the acknowledged necessity to protect
the arresting officer from assault with a concealed weapon . . . is also
justified on other grounds . . . and can therefore involve a relatively
extensive exploration of the person. A search for weapons in the absence of
probable cause to arrest, however, must, like any other search, be strictly
circumscribed by the exigencies which justify its initiation. . . . Thus it
must be limited to that which is necessary for the discovery of weapons
which might be used to harm the officer or others nearby, and may
realistically be characterized as something less than a "full" search, even
though it remains a serious intrusion.

A second, and related, objection to petitioner's argument is that it
assumes that the law of arrest has already worked out the balance between
the particular interests involved here—the neutralization of danger to the
policeman in the investigative circumstance and the sanctity of the individual. But this is not so. An arrest is a wholly different kind of intrusion upon
individual freedom from a limited search for weapons, and the interests
each is designed to serve are likewise quite different. An arrest is the initial
stage of a criminal prosecution. It is intended to vindicate society's interest
in having its laws obeyed, and it is inevitably accompanied by future
interference with the individual's freedom of movement, whether or not
trial or conviction ultimately follows. The protective search for weapons, on
the other hand, constitutes a brief, though far from inconsiderable, intrusion upon the sanctity of the person. It does not follow that because an
officer may lawfully arrest a person only when he is apprised of facts
sufficient to warrant a belief that the person has committed or is committing a crime, the officer is equally unjustified, absent that kind of evidence,
in making any intrusions short of an arrest. Moreover, a perfectly reasonable apprehension of danger may arise long before the officer is possessed
of adequate information to justify taking a person into custody for the
purpose of prosecuting him for a crime. Petitioner's reliance on cases which
have worked out standards of reasonableness with regard to "seizures"
constituting arrests and searches incident thereto is thus misplaced. It
assumes that the interests sought to be vindicated and the invasions of
personal security may be equated in the two cases, and thereby ignores a
vital aspect of the analysis of the reasonableness of particular types of
conduct under the Fourth Amendment. . . .

Our evaluation of the proper balance that has to be struck in this type
of case leads us to conclude that there must be a narrowly drawn authority
to permit a reasonable search for weapons for the protection of the police
officer, where he has reason to believe that he is dealing with an armed and

dangerous individual, regardless of whether he has probable cause to arrest the individual for a crime. The officer need not be absolutely certain that the individual is armed; the issue is whether a reasonably prudent man in the circumstances would be warranted in the belief that his safety or that of others was in danger. . . . And in determining whether the officer acted reasonably in such circumstances, due weight must be given, not to his inchoate and unparticularized suspicion or "hunch," but to the specific reasonable inferences which he is entitled to draw from the facts in light of his experience. . . .

IV

We must now examine the conduct of Officer McFadden in this case to determine whether his search and seizure of petitioner were reasonable, both at their inception and as conducted. He had observed Terry, together with Chilton and another man, acting in a manner he took to be preface to a "stick-up." We think on the facts and circumstances Officer McFadden detailed before the trial judge a reasonably prudent man would have been warranted in believing petitioner was armed and thus presented a threat to the officer's safety while he was investigating his suspicious behavior. The actions of Terry and Chilton were consistent with McFadden's hypothesis that these men were contemplating a daylight robbery—which, it is reasonable to assume, would be likely to involve the use of weapons—and nothing in their conduct from the time he first noticed them until the time he confronted them and identified himself as a police officer gave him sufficient reason to negate that hypothesis. Although the trio had departed the original scene, there was nothing to indicate abandonment of an intent to commit a robbery at some point. Thus, when Officer McFadden approached the three men gathered before the display window at Zucker's store he had observed enough to make it quite reasonable to fear that they were armed; nothing in their response to his hailing them, identifying himself as a police officer, and asking their names served to dispel that reasonable belief. We cannot say his decision at that point to seize Terry and pat his clothing for weapons was the product of a volatile or inventive imagination, or was undertaken simply as an act of harassment; the record evidences the tempered act of a policeman who in the course of an investigation had to make a quick decision as to how to protect himself and others from possible danger, and took limited steps to do so.

The manner in which the seizure and search were conducted is, of course, as vital a part of the inquiry as whether they were warranted at all. The Fourth Amendment proceeds as much by limitations upon the scope of governmental action as by imposing preconditions upon its initiation. . . . The entire deterrent purpose of the rule excluding evidence seized in violation of the Fourth Amendment rests on the assumption that "limitations upon the fruit to be gathered tend to limit the quest itself." United States v. Poller, 43 F.2d 911, 914 (C.A.2d Cir.1930). . . . Thus, evidence may not be introduced if it was discovered by means of a seizure and search which were not reasonably related in scope to the justification for their initiation. . . .

We need not develop at length in this case, however, the limitations which the Fourth Amendment places upon a protective seizure and search for weapons. These limitations will have to be developed in the concrete factual circumstances of individual cases. . . . Suffice it to note that such a search, unlike a search without a warrant incident to a lawful arrest, is not justified by any need to prevent the disappearance or destruction of evidence of crime. . . . The sole justification of the search in the present situation is the protection of the police officer and others nearby, and it must therefore be confined in scope to an intrusion reasonably designed to discover guns, knives, clubs, or other hidden instruments for the assault of the police officer.

The scope of the search in this case presents no serious problem in light of these standards. Officer McFadden patted down the outer clothing of petitioner and his two companions. He did not place his hands in their pockets or under the outer surface of their garments until he had felt weapons, and then he merely reached for and removed the guns. He never did invade Katz' person beyond the outer surfaces of his clothes, since he discovered nothing in his pat-down which might have been a weapon. Officer McFadden confined his search strictly to what was minimally necessary to learn whether the men were armed and to disarm them once he discovered the weapons. He did not conduct a general exploratory search for whatever evidence of criminal activity he might find.

V

We conclude that the revolver seized from Terry was properly admitted in evidence against him. At the time he seized petitioner and searched him for weapons, Officer McFadden had reasonable grounds to believe that petitioner was armed and dangerous, and it was necessary for the protection of himself and others to take swift measures to discover the true facts and neutralize the threat of harm if it materialized. The policeman carefully restricted his search to what was appropriate to the discovery of the particular items which he sought. Each case of this sort will, of course, have to be decided on its own facts. We merely hold today that where a police officer observes unusual conduct which leads him reasonably to conclude in light of his experience that criminal activity may be afoot and that the persons with whom he is dealing may be armed and presently dangerous; where in the course of investigating this behavior he identifies himself as a policeman and makes reasonable inquiries; and where nothing in the initial stages of the encounter serves to dispel his reasonable fear for his own or others' safety, he is entitled for the protection of himself and others in the area to conduct a carefully limited search of the outer clothing of such persons in an attempt to discover weapons which might be used to assault him. Such a search is a reasonable search under the Fourth Amendment, and any weapons seized may properly be introduced in evidence against the person from whom they were taken.

■ Mr. Justice Harlan, concurring.

While I unreservedly agree with the Court's ultimate holding in this case, I am constrained to fill in a few gaps, as I see them, in its opinion. I do this because what is said by this Court today will serve as initial guidelines for law enforcement authorities and courts throughout the land as this important new field of law develops.

A police officer's right to make an on-the-street "stop" and an accompanying "frisk" for weapons is of course bounded by the protections afforded by the Fourth and Fourteenth Amendments. The Court holds, and I agree, that while the right does not depend upon possession by the officer of a valid warrant, nor upon the existence of probable cause, such activities must be reasonable under the circumstances as the officer credibly relates them in court. Since the question in this and most cases is whether evidence produced by a frisk is admissible, the problem is to determine what makes a frisk reasonable.

If the State of Ohio were to provide that police officers could, on articulable suspicion less than probable cause, forcibly frisk and disarm persons thought to be carrying concealed weapons, I would have little doubt that action taken pursuant to such authority could be constitutionally reasonable. Concealed weapons create an immediate and severe danger to the public, and though that danger might not warrant routine general weapons checks, it could well warrant action on less than a "probability." I mention this line of analysis because I think it vital to point out that it cannot be applied in this case. On the record before us Ohio has not clothed its policemen with routine authority to frisk and disarm on suspicion; in the absence of state authority, policemen have no more right to "pat down" the outer clothing of passers-by, or of persons to whom they address casual questions, than does any other citizen. Consequently, the Ohio courts did not rest the constitutionality of this frisk upon any general authority in Officer McFadden to take reasonable steps to protect the citizenry, including himself, from dangerous weapons.

The state courts held, instead, that when an officer is lawfully confronting a possibly hostile person in the line of duty he has a right, springing only from the necessity of the situation and not from any broader right to disarm, to frisk for his own protection. This holding, with which I agree and with which I think the Court agrees, offers the only satisfactory basis I can think of for affirming this conviction. The holding has, however, two logical corollaries that I do not think the Court has fully expressed.

In the first place, if the frisk is justified in order to protect the officer during an encounter with a citizen, the officer must first have constitutional grounds to insist on an encounter, to make a *forcible* stop. Any person, including a policeman, is at liberty to avoid a person he considers dangerous. If and when a policeman has a right instead to disarm such a person for his own protection, he must first have a right not to avoid him but to be in his presence. That right must be more than the liberty (again, possessed by every citizen) to address questions to other persons, for ordinarily the person addressed has an equal right to ignore his interrogator and walk away; he certainly need not submit to a frisk for the questioner's protection. I would make it perfectly clear that the right to frisk in this case depends upon the reasonableness of a forcible stop to investigate a suspected crime.

Where such a stop is reasonable, however, the right to frisk must be immediate and automatic if the reason for the stop is, as here, an articulable suspicion of a crime of violence. Just as a full search incident to a lawful arrest requires no additional justification, a limited frisk incident to a lawful stop must often be rapid and routine. There is no reason why an officer, rightfully but forcibly confronting a person suspected of a serious crime, should have to ask one question and take the risk that the answer might be a bullet.

The facts of this case are illustrative of a proper stop and an incident frisk. Officer McFadden had no probable cause to arrest Terry for anything, but he had observed circumstances that would reasonably lead an experienced, prudent policeman to suspect that Terry was about to engage in burglary or robbery. His justifiable suspicion afforded a proper constitutional basis for accosting Terry, restraining his liberty of movement briefly, and addressing questions to him, and Officer McFadden did so. When he did, he had no reason whatever to suppose that Terry might be armed, apart from the fact that he suspected him of planning a violent crime. McFadden asked Terry his name, to which Terry "mumbled something." Whereupon McFadden, without asking Terry to speak louder and without giving him any chance to explain his presence or his actions, forcibly frisked him.

I would affirm this conviction for what I believe to be the same reasons the Court relies on. I would, however, make explicit what I think is implicit in affirmance on the present facts. Officer McFadden's right to interrupt Terry's freedom of movement and invade his privacy arose only because circumstances warranted forcing an encounter with Terry in an effort to prevent or investigate a crime. Once that forced encounter was justified, however, the officer's right to take suitable measures for his own safety followed automatically.

Upon the foregoing premises, I join the opinion of the Court.[2]

———

Adams v. Williams

407 U.S. 143, 92 S.Ct. 1921, 32 L.Ed.2d 612 (1972)

■ MR. JUSTICE REHNQUIST delivered the opinion of the Court.

Respondent Robert Williams was convicted in a Connecticut state court of illegal possession of a handgun found during a "stop and frisk," as well

[2] Justice White also wrote a concurring opinion. Justice Black noted his concurrence in the opinion of the Court with specific reservations. Justice Douglas wrote a dissenting opinion.

as of possession of heroin that was found during a full search incident to his weapons arrest. After respondent's conviction was affirmed by the Supreme Court of Connecticut . . . this Court denied certiorari. . . . Williams' petition for federal habeas corpus relief was denied by the District Court and by a divided panel of the Second Circuit . . . but on rehearing en banc the Court of Appeals granted relief. . . . That court held that evidence introduced at Williams' trial had been obtained by an unlawful search of his person and car, and thus the state court judgments of conviction should be set aside. Since we conclude that the policeman's actions here conformed to the standards this Court laid down in Terry v. Ohio, 392 U.S. 1 (1968), we reverse.

Police Sgt. John Connolly was alone early in the morning on car patrol duty in a high-crime area of Bridgeport, Connecticut. At approximately 2:15 a.m. a person known to Sgt. Connolly approached his cruiser and informed him that an individual seated in a nearby vehicle was carrying narcotics and had a gun at his waist.

After calling for assistance on his car radio, Sgt. Connolly approached the vehicle to investigate the informant's report. Connolly tapped on the car window and asked the occupant, Robert Williams, to open the door. When Williams rolled down the window instead, the sergeant reached into the car and removed a fully loaded revolver from Williams' waistband. The gun had not been visible to Connolly from outside the car, but it was in precisely the place indicated by the informant. Williams was then arrested by Connolly for unlawful possession of the pistol. A search incident to that arrest was conducted after other officers arrived. They found substantial quantities of heroin on Williams' person and in the car, and they found a machete and a second revolver hidden in the automobile.

Respondent contends that the initial seizure of his pistol, upon which rested the later search and seizure of other weapons and narcotics, was not justified by the informant's tip to Sgt. Connolly. He claims that absent a more reliable informant, or some corroboration of the tip, the policeman's actions were unreasonable under the standards set forth in Terry v. Ohio, supra.

In *Terry* this Court recognized that "a police officer may in appropriate circumstances and in an appropriate manner approach a person for purposes of investigating possibly criminal behavior even though there is no probable cause to make an arrest." Id., at 22. The Fourth Amendment does not require a policeman who lacks the precise level of information necessary for probable cause to arrest to simply shrug his shoulders and allow a crime to occur or a criminal to escape. On the contrary, *Terry* recognizes that it may be the essence of good police work to adopt an intermediate response. See id., at 23. A brief stop of a suspicious individual, in order to determine his identity or to maintain the status quo momentarily while obtaining more information, may be most reasonable in light of the facts known to the officer at the time. Id., at 21–22. . . .

The Court recognized in *Terry* that the policeman making a reasonable investigatory stop should not be denied the opportunity to protect himself from attack by a hostile suspect. "When an officer is justified in believing that the individual whose suspicious behavior he is investigating at close range is armed and presently dangerous to the officer or to others," he may conduct a limited protective search for concealed weapons. 392 U.S., at 24. The purpose of this limited search is not to discover evidence of crime, but to allow the officer to pursue his investigation without fear of violence, and thus the frisk for weapons might be equally necessary and reasonable, whether or not carrying a concealed weapon violated any applicable state law. So long as the officer is entitled to make a forcible stop,[3] and has reason to believe that the suspect is armed and dangerous, he may conduct a weapons search limited in scope to this protective purpose. Id., at 30.

Applying these principles to the present case, we believe that Sgt. Connolly acted justifiably in responding to his informant's tip. The informant was known to him personally and had provided him with information in the past. This is a stronger case than obtains in the case of an anonymous telephone tip. The informant here came forward personally to give information that was immediately verifiable at the scene. Indeed, under Connecticut law, the informant might have been subject to immediate arrest for making a false complaint had Sgt. Connolly's investigation proved the tip incorrect. Thus, while the Court's decisions indicate that this informant's unverified tip may have been insufficient for a narcotics arrest or search warrant . . . the information carried enough indicia of reliability to justify the officer's forcible stop of Williams.

In reaching this conclusion, we reject respondent's argument that reasonable cause for a stop and frisk can only be based on the officer's personal observation, rather than on information supplied by another person. Informants' tips, like all other clues and evidence coming to a policeman on the scene, may vary greatly in their value and reliability. One simple rule will not cover every situation. Some tips, completely lacking in indicia of reliability, would either warrant no police response or require further investigation before a forcible stop of a suspect would be authorized. But in some situations—for example, when the victim of a street crime seeks immediate police aid and gives a description of his assailant, or when a credible informant warns of a specific impending crime—the subtleties of the hearsay rule should not thwart an appropriate police response.

While properly investigating the activity of a person who was reported to be carrying narcotics and a concealed weapon and who was sitting alone in a car in a high-crime area at 2:15 in the morning, Sgt. Connolly had ample reason to fear for his safety. When Williams rolled down his window, rather than complying with the policeman's request to step out of the car so that his movements could more easily be seen, the revolver allegedly at Williams' waist became an even greater threat. Under these circumstances the policeman's action in reaching to the spot where the gun was thought

---

3. Petitioner does not contend that Williams acted voluntarily in rolling down the window of his car.

to be hidden constituted a limited intrusion designed to insure his safety, and we conclude that it was reasonable. The loaded gun seized as a result of this intrusion was therefore admissible at Williams' trial. Terry v. Ohio, 392 U.S., at 30.

Once Sgt. Connolly had found the gun precisely where the informant had predicted, probable cause existed to arrest Williams for unlawful possession of the weapon. Probable cause to arrest depends "upon whether, at the moment the arrest was made . . . the facts and circumstances within [the arresting officers'] knowledge and of which they had reasonably trustworthy information were sufficient to warrant a prudent man in believing that the [suspect] had committed or was committing an offense." Beck v. Ohio, 379 U.S. 89, 91 (1964). In the present case the policeman found Williams in possession of a gun in precisely the place predicted by the informant. This tended to corroborate the reliability of the informant's further report of narcotics and, together with the surrounding circumstances, certainly suggested no lawful explanation for possession of the gun. Probable cause does not require the same type of specific evidence of each element of the offense as would be needed to support a conviction. . . . Rather, the court will evaluate generally the circumstances at the time of the arrest to decide if the officer had probable cause for his action. . . .

Under the circumstances surrounding Williams' possession of the gun seized by Sgt. Connolly, the arrest on the weapons charge was supported by probable cause, and the search of his person and of the car incident to that arrest was lawful. . . . The fruits of the search were therefore properly admitted at Williams' trial, and the Court of Appeals erred in reaching a contrary conclusion.

. . . [4]

---

58. An anonymous tip was held to provide sufficient basis for a stop of a person driving in a car in Alabama v. White, 496 U.S. 325 (1990) (6–3). The Court said:

> Reasonable suspicion is a less demanding standard than probable cause not only in the sense that reasonable suspicion can be established with information that is different in quantity or content than that required to establish probable cause, but also in the sense that reasonable suspicion can arise from information that is less reliable than that required to show probable cause.

Id. at 330. In this case, the Court said, "under the totality of the circumstances the anonymous tip, as corroborated, exhibited sufficient indicia of reliability to justify the investigatory stop of the respondent's car." Id. at 338.

---

[4] Justice Douglas wrote a dissenting opinion, which Justice Marshall joined. Justice Brennan wrote a dissenting opinion. Justice Marshall wrote a dissenting opinion, which Justice Douglas joined.

White is distinguished in Florida v. J.L., 529 U.S. 266 (2000), in which the Court held that an anonymous tip that a person is carrying a gun is not by itself sufficient to justify a stop and frisk. The Court declined to adopt a "firearm exception" that would authorize a stop and frisk if a tip alleged that a person was illegally carrying a gun, even if the tip would otherwise be insufficient.

59. In *Terry*, the Court said that "whenever a police officer accosts an individual and restrains his freedom to walk away, he has 'seized' that person," p. 105 above. Whether or not a seizure has occurred depends on all the circumstances of the particular case. Michigan v. Chesternut, 486 U.S. 567 (1988). In *Chesternut*, the Court concluded that the police conduct—accelerating a patrol car to catch up with the defendant, who was on foot, and then briefly driving alongside him, in a city neighborhood—did not constitute a seizure. See also California v. Hodari D., p. 58 above.

The question has arisen often in the context of a stop of an airline passenger suspected of carrying narcotics. See the various opinions in Florida v. Royer, 460 U.S. 491 (1983) (5–4), and United States v. Mendenhall, 446 U.S. 544 (1980) (5–4). In *Mendenhall*, the police actions were upheld; in *Royer*, they were not. For additional cases involving the stop of an airline passenger, see, e.g., United States v. Borys, 766 F.2d 304 (7th Cir.1985) (brief stop of defendant at airport and 75-minute seizure of his luggage upheld); United States v. Wilson, 953 F.2d 116 (4th Cir.1991) (prolonged, persistent questioning of disembarking airline passenger who had plainly indicated unwillingness to engage in further conversation was seizure under Fourth Amendment); United States v. Moore, 675 F.2d 802 (6th Cir.1982); United States v. Black, 675 F.2d 129 (7th Cir.1982). In United States v. Wylie, 569 F.2d 62 (D.C.Cir.1977), distinguishing between a "contact," which leaves the person accosted by a policeman free to walk away, and a "stop," the court said that the crucial consideration when there is no explicit show of force is whether the person reasonably believed he was not free to walk away. See United States v. Jordan, 958 F.2d 1085 (D.C.Cir.1992) (defendant was seized within meaning of Fourth Amendment when officer took and retained his driver's license and thereby prevented him from going about his business).

Terry also requires courts to distinguish between an investigative stop, which does not require probable cause, and an arrest, which does. The distinction is discussed in the majority and dissenting opinions in United States v. White, 648 F.2d 29 (D.C.Cir.1981), in which officers stopped an automobile and with guns drawn ordered the occupants to get out. The majority concluded that the police action was an investigative stop. See also, to the same effect, United States v. Merritt, 695 F.2d 1263 (10th Cir.1982), and United States v. Jackson, 652 F.2d 244 (2d Cir.1981). But see United States v. Morin, 665 F.2d 765 (5th Cir.1982) (successive stops of airline passenger based on same information "strongly indicate" an arrest); United States v. Ceballos, 654 F.2d 177 (2d Cir.1981) (arrest). See also United States v. Chaidez, 919 F.2d 1193 (7th Cir.1990) (police actions falling between stop and arrest upheld as reasonable, albeit without probable cause).

Brief questioning during a temporary detention not amounting to an arrest is not custodial interrogation and does not have to be preceded by *Miranda* warnings, see p. 417 below, even if there is probable cause for an arrest. United States v. Woods, 720 F.2d 1022 (9th Cir.1983).

60. *Terry* was extended to the search of a car for dangerous weapons after the driver has stepped out of the car, in Michigan v. Long, 463 U.S. 1032 (1983) (6–3). The same test that is applied to the protective frisk of the person under *Terry* may authorize a protective search of the interior of the car.

The New York Court of Appeals disapproved the reasoning of *Long* and reached a different rule under the state constitution in People v. Torres, 543 N.E.2d 61 (N.Y.1989). The court observed that "it is unrealistic to assume . . . that having been stopped and questioned without incident, a suspect who is about to be released and permitted to proceed on his way would, upon reentry into his vehicle, reach for a concealed weapon and threaten the departing police officer's safety." Id. at 65. See also United States v. Barlin, 686 F.2d 81 (2d Cir.1982) (search of handbag).

Cf. Ybarra v. Illinois, 444 U.S. 85 (1979) (6–3), in which the Court declined to uphold a frisk of the patron of a tavern that police were searching pursuant to a valid search warrant; the Court noted that there were no specific facts indicating that the patron was connected with criminal activity or might be inclined to assault the police. But see generally United States v. Bonds, 829 F.2d 1072 (11th Cir.1987) (stop and frisk distinguished; frisk upheld).

61. In United States v. Place, 462 U.S. 696 (1983), the Court relied on the principles of *Terry* and succeeding cases to uphold the authority of law enforcement personnel briefly to detain personal luggage for exposure to a trained narcotic detection dog on the basis of reasonable suspicion, not amounting to probable cause, that the luggage contains narcotics. The very limited nature of the intrusion on privacy, the Court said, justifies the lessened requirement for the procedure. With respect to the nature of the intrusion, "the canine sniff is sui generis. We are aware of no other investigative procedure that is so limited both in the manner in which the information is obtained and in the content of the information revealed by the procedure." Id. at 707. In the actual case, however, the Court concluded that the duration and circumstances of the detention exceeded what was permitted.

Place is distinguished in B.C. v. Plumas Unified School District, 192 F.3d 1260 (9th Cir.1999), in which school authorities required students to pass in front of a dog trained to sniff for drugs. Saying that a dog sniff of one's person is offensive, the court held that the sniff violated the plaintiff's reasonable expectation of privacy and constituted a search. *Place* is distinguished also in United States v. Thomas, 757 F.2d 1359 (2d Cir.1985) (using trained dog to sniff contents of private premises). See also Bond v.

United States, 529 U.S. 334 (2000) (7–2) (law officer's manipulation of luggage of bus passenger, which passenger had placed on rack above his seat, was a search that violated the passenger's rights under the Fourth Amendment).

62.

On September 5, 1975, New York City Policeman Saverio Alesi was patrolling in uniform on Eighth Avenue between 42d and 45th Streets. At approximately 3:00 P.M. he observed appellee Magda talking with another man on the north side of 43d Street just west of Eighth Avenue. They were about thirty to thirty-five feet from Alesi, who was standing on the southwest corner of the intersection.

As Alesi watched the two men, he saw them exchange something. Although he could not see exactly what had changed hands, he did see that each man gave and received something simultaneously. After the exchange, the unidentified participant looked in the officer's direction. Immediately after doing so, he turned away in a "rapid motion" and proceeded west on 43d Street. Meanwhile, Magda crossed 43d Street at an angle and started down Eighth Avenue toward 42d Street. As he passed, Alesi tapped him on the shoulder and asked him to stop. Magda turned to face Alesi and slowed his pace but continued down Eighth Avenue, walking backwards. The two men proceeded in this fashion for several steps, covering about ten feet before they both stopped.

Alesi inquired about what had taken place on 43d Street, and at first Magda said that nothing had happened. When asked a second time, Magda replied, "All right. I bought a marijuana cigarette for a dollar," and produced the cigarette from his inside coat pocket. Alesi placed him under arrest and walked him back to 43d Street in a vain attempt to find the other man. Alesi then searched Magda and, upon discovering an unloaded handgun and a robbery demand note, took him to the police station and booked him on gun and drug charges. Subsequent investigation by the FBI linked the note with a robbery at the United Mutual Savings Bank in New York City and resulted in the instant indictment.

The area in which Alesi first observed Magda had "a high incidence of narcotics dealing." United States v. Magda, 547 F.2d 756, 757 (2d Cir. 1976). Alesi had been a policeman for 11 years, a foot patrolman for about three and thereafter a motorcycle policeman. He had been a foot patrolman in the area of the stop for six months, during which he had witnessed two narcotics arrests. Was his conduct lawful?

63.

About 2:50 A.M. on July 2, 1966, Sergeant Bergin, while in the vicinity of Commonwealth Avenue, Brookline, observed the defendant walking on Crowninshield Road to Commonwealth Avenue. There had been several breaking and entering incidents in the neighborhood, but none had been reported that night. The officer stopped the defendant and inquired about his identity and purpose for being abroad. The defendant identified himself and stated that he was walking from Boston to visit a friend who lived on Commonwealth Avenue in Brookline. When questioned as to the route he was taking, the defendant replied that "he had felt like taking a walk." Observing that the defendant was carrying a paper bag with the name of "Mal's Department Store" on the outside, the officer asked if he might examine its contents, and the defendant readily assented. The bag contained new articles of clothing, consisting of underwear and socks, and a sales slip bearing the date of June 28. The defendant informed the officer that he had purchased the articles on the preceding day, July 1. Because the items of clothing were apparently not of the defendant's size, the officer became suspicious and frisked him to determine if he was carrying any weapons. The frisk consisted of the officer quickly running his hands over the defendant's clothing. He discovered, in the small of the defendant's back and tucked under his shirt and belt, a screwdriver, the shaft of which was seven inches long; it was not new and had paint marks on both the shaft and handle. The defendant said he had bought the screwdriver along with the clothing at Mal's Department Store. The defendant was thereupon arrested and taken to the police station where a thorough search was made. He was charged with possession of burglarious instruments.

Commonwealth v. Matthews, 244 N.E.2d 908, 909 (Mass.1969). Is the screwdriver admissible in evidence against the defendant?

64.

At 12:15 a.m. on the morning of October 15, 1972, Kenneth Steck, a police officer assigned to the Tactical Patrol Force of the New York Police Department, was working the 6:00 p.m. to 2:00 a.m. tour of duty, assigned to patrol by foot a certain section of Brooklyn. While walking his beat on a street illuminated by ordinary street lamps and devoid of pedestrian traffic, he and his partner noticed someone walking on the same side of the street in their direction. When the solitary figure of the defendant, Louis De Bour, was within 30 or 40 feet of the uniformed officers he crossed the street. The two policemen followed suit and when De Bour reached them Officer Steck inquired as to what he was doing in the neighborhood. De Bour, clearly but nervously, answered that he had just parked his car and was going to a friend's house.

The patrolman then asked De Bour for identification. As he was answering that he had none, Officer Steck noticed a slight waist-high bulge in defendant's jacket. At this point the policeman asked De Bour to unzipper his coat. When De Bour complied with this request Officer Steck observed a revolver protruding from his waistband. The loaded weapon was removed from behind his waistband and he was arrested for possession of the gun.

At the suppression hearing Officer Steck testified to the above facts noting that the encounter lasted "a few minutes." On cross-examination, Officer Steck stated that at the time he believed defendant might have been involved with narcotics and crossed the street to avoid apprehension. On the other hand the defendant testified that he never saw the police until they crossed the street in front of him and that he continued walking straight ahead. He stated that the police asked him where he was going and also whether he had any dope in his pockets. He answered that he had been visiting at his mother's home with relatives. De Bour further testified that during this encounter, Steck's partner proceeded to pat his clothing and two or three minutes later Steck found the gun and fired it in order to see whether it was operable.

People v. De Bour, 352 N.E.2d 562, 565 (N.Y.1976). Were the police officers' stop of De Bour and subsequent actions lawful?

65. "On September 10, 1968, Seattle police officers were alerted by police broadcast to pick up two men in a 1964 Pontiac convertible. A warrant had been issued for the arrest of one of the men, Bobby Ray Bush. Officers apprehended the car and, as they did not know which man was Bush, they arrested both Bush and his companion, appellant. The officers in the course of the arrest patted down appellant and, finding a pistol and ammunition, arrested him for carrying a concealed weapon." Hurst v. United States, 425 F.2d 177 (9th Cir.1970). Was the police conduct lawful?

66.

Part of the difficulty in developing a rule for frisks is that the policeman, assuming his good faith, will be acting on a subjective standard—his own immediate sense of risk to himself—while the court testing his action for purposes of admissibility will be acting on an objective standard—what a reasonably prudent policeman in his position would do after weighing the risks of harm from possible hidden weapons presented by the particular known circumstances against our society's aversion to physical intrusions on the person of a free man.

. . . Where the standard of action—necessarily almost unreflective and reflexive—is to be tested after the event by a non-congruent rational test, the deterrent effect of the rule must perforce become less than complete. . . .

Yet the objective rule does have some useful prophylactic effect. . . . At the very least it provides some insurance against dishonesty by the policeman who does not in fact have reason to suspect that the subject is armed, but who would be willing to fabricate his remembered emotions to validate a productive frisk. . . . And guarding against this danger becomes particularly important if, as we believe, a proper frisk permits seizure of nonweapon contraband. Moreover, the objective rule signals to the public at large that, to the extent possible, courts do what they can to maintain constitutional protections as more than mere verbal symbols.

The standard of probability which is required to justify intrusions at the "frisk" level has been variously stated. . . .

. . .

We need not now determine which verbal formulation of the standard is correct. For our purposes there is a common denominator. A reviewing court must: (1) determine the objective evidence then available to the law enforcement officer and (2) decide what level of probability existed that the individual was armed and about to engage in dangerous conduct; it must then rule whether that level of probability justified the "frisk" in light of (3) the manner in which the frisk was conducted as bearing on the resentment it might justifiably arouse in the person frisked (assuming he is not about to engage in criminal conduct) and the community and (4) the risk to the officer and the community of not disarming the individual at once.

United States v. Lopez, 328 F.Supp. 1077, 1095–97 (E.D.N.Y.1971). See United States v. Sigmond-Ballesteros, 285 F.3d 1117 (9th Cir.2002) (rejecting various alleged grounds for reasonable suspicion justifying stop of motor vehicle).

67. The "plain feel" rule, analogous to the plain view doctrine, see Horton v. California, 496 U.S. 128 (1990), p. 197 below, is upheld in Minnesota v. Dickerson, 508 U.S. 366, 375–76 (1993): "If a police officer lawfully pats down a suspect's outer clothing and feels an object whose contour or mass makes its identity immediately apparent, there has been no invasion of the suspect's privacy beyond that already authorized by the officer's search for weapons; if the object is contraband, its warrantless seizure would be justified by the same practical considerations that inhere in the plain view context."

———

Brown v. Texas

443 U.S. 47, 99 S.Ct. 2637, 61 L.Ed.2d 357 (1979)

■ MR. CHIEF JUSTICE BURGER delivered the opinion of the Court.

This appeal presents the question whether appellant was validly convicted for refusing to comply with a policeman's demand that he identify himself pursuant to a provision of the Texas Penal Code which makes it a crime to refuse such identification on request.

I

At 12:45 on the afternoon of December 9, 1977, officers Venegas and Sotelo of the El Paso Police Department were cruising in a patrol car. They observed appellant and another man walking in opposite directions away from one another in an alley. Although the two men were a few feet apart when they first were seen, officer Venegas later testified that both officers believed the two had been together or were about to meet until the patrol car appeared.

The car entered the alley, and officer Venegas got out and asked appellant to identify himself and explain what he was doing there. The other man was not questioned or detained. The officer testified that he stopped appellant because the situation "looked suspicious and we had never seen that subject in that area before." The area of El Paso where appellant was stopped has a high incidence of drug traffic. However, the officers did not claim to suspect appellant of any specific misconduct, nor did they have any reason to believe that he was armed.

Appellant refused to identify himself and angrily asserted that the officers had no right to stop him. Officer Venegas replied that he was in a "high drug problem area"; officer Sotelo then "frisked" appellant, but found nothing.

When appellant continued to refuse to identify himself, he was arrested for violation of Texas Penal Code Ann. § 38.02(a), which makes it a criminal act for a person to refuse to give his name and address to an officer "who has lawfully stopped him and requested the information." Following the arrest the officers searched appellant; nothing untoward was found.

While being taken to the El Paso County Jail appellant identified himself. Nonetheless, he was held in custody and charged with violating § 38.02(a). When he was booked he was routinely searched a third time. Appellant was convicted in the El Paso Municipal Court and fined $20 plus court costs for violation of § 38.02. He then exercised his right under Texas law to a trial *de novo* in the El Paso County Court. There, he moved to set aside the information on the ground that § 38.02(a) of the Texas Penal Code violated the First, Fourth, and Fifth Amendments and was unconstitutionally vague in violation of the Fourteenth Amendment. The motion was denied. Appellant waived jury, and the court convicted him and imposed a fine of $45 plus court costs.

. . . On appeal here we noted probable jurisdiction. . . . We reverse.

II

When the officers detained appellant for the purpose of requiring him to identify himself, they performed a seizure of his person subject to the requirements of the Fourth Amendment. In convicting appellant, the County Court necessarily found as a matter of fact that the officers "lawfully stopped" appellant. . . . The Fourth Amendment, of course, "applies to all seizures of the person, including seizures that involve only a brief detention short of traditional arrest." Davis v. Mississippi, 394 U.S. 721 (1969); Terry v. Ohio, 392 U.S. 1, 16–19 (1968). "[W]henever a police officer accosts an individual and restrains his freedom to walk away, he has 'seized' that person," id., at 16, and the Fourth Amendment requires that the seizure be "reasonable." United States v. Brignoni-Ponce, 422 U.S. 873, 878 (1975).

The reasonableness of seizures that are less intrusive than a traditional arrest . . . depends "on a balance between the public interest and the individual's right to personal security free from arbitrary interference by law officers." Pennsylvania v. Mimms, 434 U.S. 106, 109 (1977). . . . Consideration of the constitutionality of such seizures involves a weighing of the gravity of the public concerns served by the seizure, the degree to which the seizure advances the public interest, and the severity of the interference with individual liberty. . . .

A central concern in balancing these competing considerations in a variety of settings has been to assure that an individual's reasonable expectation of privacy is not subject to arbitrary invasions solely at the unfettered discretion of officers in the field. . . . To this end, the Fourth Amendment requires that a seizure must be based on specific, objective facts indicating that society's legitimate interests require the seizure of the particular individual, or that the seizure must be carried out pursuant to a plan embodying explicit, neutral limitations on the conduct of individual officers. . . .

The State does not contend that appellant was stopped pursuant to a practice embodying neutral criteria, but rather maintains that the officers were justified in stopping appellant because they had a "reasonable, articulable suspicion that a crime had just been, was being, or was about to be committed." We have recognized that in some circumstances an officer may detain a suspect briefly for questioning although he does not have "probable cause" to believe that the suspect is involved in criminal activity, as is required for a traditional arrest. . . . However, we have required the officers to have a reasonable suspicion, based on objective facts, that the individual is involved in criminal activity. . . .

The flaw in the State's case is that none of the circumstances preceding the officers' detention of appellant justified a reasonable suspicion that he was involved in criminal conduct. Officer Venegas testified at appellant's trial that the situation in the alley "looked suspicious," but he was unable to point to any facts supporting that conclusion.[5] There is no indication in the record that it was unusual for people to be in the alley. The fact that appellant was in a neighborhood frequented by drug users, standing alone, is not a basis for concluding that appellant himself was engaged in criminal conduct. In short, the appellant's activity was no different from the activity of other pedestrians in that neighborhood. When pressed, officer Venegas acknowledged that the only reason he stopped appellant was to ascertain his identity. The record suggests an understandable desire to assert a police presence; however that purpose does not negate Fourth Amendment guarantees.

In the absence of any basis for suspecting appellant of misconduct, the balance between the public interest and appellant's right to personal security and privacy tilts in favor of freedom from police interference. The Texas statute under which appellant was stopped and required to identify

5. This situation is to be distinguished from the observations of a trained, experienced police officer who is able to perceive and articulate meaning in given conduct which would be wholly innocent to the untrained observer. . . .

himself is designed to advance a weighty social objective in large metropolitan centers: prevention of crime. But even assuming that purpose is served to some degree by stopping and demanding identification from an individual without any specific basis for believing he is involved in criminal activity, the guarantees of the Fourth Amendment do not allow it. When such a stop is not based on objective criteria, the risk of arbitrary and abusive police practices exceeds tolerable limits. . . .

The application of Texas Penal Code Ann. § 38.02 to detain appellant and require him to identify himself violated the Fourth Amendment because the officers lacked any reasonable suspicion to believe appellant was engaged or had engaged in criminal conduct. Accordingly, appellant may not be punished for refusing to identify himself, and the conviction is reversed.

> . . .

----

68. The investigative stop of a vehicle for 20 minutes, on the basis of a reasonable and articulable suspicion that the occupants were engaged in transporting marijuana is permissible under the Fourth Amendment. United States v. Sharpe, 470 U.S. 675 (1985) (7–2). The Court declined to say what period of time would be too long to count as an investigative stop. It is necessary "to consider the law enforcement purposes to be served by the stop as well as the time reasonably needed to effectuate those purposes. . . . Much as a 'bright line' rule would be desirable, in evaluating whether an investigative detention is unreasonable, common sense and ordinary human experience must govern over rigid criteria." Id. at 685.

In United States v. Brigham, 343 F.3d 490 (5th Cir. 2003), the court held that questioning the driver and passengers of a vehicle for eight minutes after a valid traffic stop about matters unrelated to the stop violated their rights under the Fourth Amendment. The court observed that a computer check on a driver's license and registration is permissible and that questioning while the computer check is carried out is permissible, if it does not prolong the detention. Here, however, the questioning preceded a computer check and, therefore, prolonged the detention.

69. A brief stop and detention of a person who is suspected of having been involved in a completed crime may be lawful even though there is not probable cause for his arrest. In United States v. Hensley, 469 U.S. 221 (1985), a police department issued a "flyer" asking that the defendant be held for investigation of a robbery, if he were located. The flyer was distributed to other nearby police departments in the area. An officer in another department who was aware of the flyer stopped the defendant and called headquarters to determine whether a warrant for his arrest had been issued. During the brief detention that followed, evidence was discovered that furnished an independent basis for his arrest.

The Court held that, even though the department issuing the flyer lacked probable cause for the defendant's arrest, the brief stop was lawful. It acknowledged that the situation was different from one like *Terry*, in

Boston Police DEPARTMENT CIRCULAR #:
POSTER GENERATED BY: Dahlbeck, Joseph W

WANTED

FOR DEMONSTRATION ONLY

Pomeroy, Arnold, George

LAST KNOWN ADDRESS:	Apt 23, 312 Evergreen CR , Boston, MA.
DOB:	03/17/1956
HEIGHT:	5' 11"
WEIGHT:	200
BUILD:	Medium
RACE:	White Non-Hispanic
COMPLEXION:	Medium
SEX:	Male
EYES:	Brown
HAIR:	Dark Brown
CAUTION FLAGS:	ARMED
COURT:	Boston Municipal Ct
DOCKET #:	95cr87469
INCIDENT #:	953258933

ALIASES: Raymond Allen Pomeroy, Rocko

Right Thumb
0 9 ʊ 000 12
22 19 ʊ 000 14

ARMED

Please Contact Area A-1 Detectives 343-0000

YOU CAN HELP THE BOSTON POLICE DEPARTMENT BY
CALLING THE CRIME STOPPERS UNIT. IF YOUR
INFORMATION LEADS TO THE ARREST AND INDICTMENT
OF ANY VIOLENT FELONY OFFENDER YOU CAN
RECEIVE A REWARD UP TO $1,000.00

1-(800) 494-TIPS

CALLERS REMAIN ANONYMOUS

which the stop is for investigation of suspected ongoing criminal activity. Nevertheless,

> where police have been unable to locate a person suspected of involvement in a past crime, the ability to briefly stop that person, ask questions, or check identification in the absence of probable cause promotes the strong government interest in solving crimes and bringing offenders to justice. Restraining police action until after probable cause is obtained would not only hinder the investigation, but might also enable the suspect to flee in the interim and to remain at large. Particularly in the context of felonies or crimes involving a threat to public safety, it is in the public interest that the crime be solved and the suspect detained as promptly as possible. The law enforcement interests at stake in these circumstances outweigh the individual's interest to be free of a stop and detention that is no more extensive than permissible in the investigation of imminent or ongoing crimes.
>
> [I]f police have a reasonable suspicion, grounded in specific and articulable facts that a person they encounter was involved in or is wanted in connection with a completed felony, then a *Terry* stop may be made to investigate that suspicion.

Id. at 229. The Court added that the officer who stopped the defendant was entitled to rely on the flyer issued by the other department and was not required himself to have knowledge of facts justifying the stop. It is enough if the police who issue such a flyer have a basis justifying the action taken.

Florida v. Bostick

501 U.S. 429, 111 S.Ct. 2382, 115 L.Ed.2d 389 (1991)

■ JUSTICE O'CONNOR delivered the opinion of the Court.

We have held that the Fourth Amendment permits police officers to approach individuals at random in airport lobbies and other public places to ask them questions and to request consent to search their luggage, so long as a reasonable person would understand that he or she could refuse to cooperate. This case requires us to determine whether the same rule applies to police encounters that take place on a bus.

I

Drug interdiction efforts have led to the use of police surveillance at airports, train stations, and bus depots. Law enforcement officers stationed at such locations routinely approach individuals, either randomly or because they suspect in some vague way that the individuals may be engaged in criminal activity, and ask them potentially incriminating questions. Broward County has adopted such a program. County Sheriff's Department officers routinely board buses at scheduled stops and ask passengers for permission to search their luggage.

In this case, two officers discovered cocaine when they searched a suitcase belonging to Terrance Bostick. The underlying facts of the search are in dispute, but the Florida Supreme Court, whose decision we review here, stated explicitly the factual premise for its decision:

> Two officers, complete with badges, insignia and one of them holding a recognizable zipper pouch, containing a pistol, boarded a bus bound from Miami to Atlanta during a stopover in Fort Lauderdale. Eyeing the passengers, the officers admittedly without articulable suspicion, picked out the defendant passenger and asked to inspect his ticket and identification. The ticket, from Miami to Atlanta, matched the defendant's identification and both were immediately returned to him as unremarkable. However, the two police officers persisted and explained their presence as narcotics agents on the lookout for illegal drugs. In pursuit of that aim, they then requested the defendant's consent to search his luggage. Needless to say, there is a conflict in the evidence about whether the defendant consented to the search of the second bag in which the contraband was found and as to whether he was informed of his right to refuse consent. However, any conflict must be resolved in favor of the state, it being a question of fact decided by the trial judge.

554 So.2d 1153, 1154–55 (1989), quoting 510 So.2d 321, 322 (Fla.App.1987) (Letts, J., dissenting in part).

Two facts are particularly worth noting. First, the police specifically advised Bostick that he had the right to refuse consent. Bostick appears to have disputed the point, but, as the Florida Supreme Court noted explicitly, the trial court resolved this evidentiary conflict in the State's favor. Second, at no time did the officers threaten Bostick with a gun. The Florida Supreme Court indicated that one officer carried a zipper pouch containing a pistol—the equivalent of carrying a gun in a holster—but the court did not suggest that the gun was ever removed from its pouch, pointed at Bostick, or otherwise used in a threatening manner. The dissent's characterization of the officers as "gun-wielding inquisitor[s]," post, at 9, is colorful, but lacks any basis in fact.

Bostick was arrested and charged with trafficking in cocaine. He moved to suppress the cocaine on the grounds that it had been seized in violation of his Fourth Amendment rights. The trial court denied the motion but made no factual findings. Bostick subsequently entered a plea of guilty, but reserved the right to appeal the denial of the motion to suppress.

The Florida District Court of Appeal affirmed, but considered the issue sufficiently important that it certified a question to the Florida Supreme Court. 510 So.2d, at 322. The Supreme Court reasoned that Bostick had been seized because a reasonable passenger in his situation would not have felt free to leave the bus to avoid questioning by the police. . . . It rephrased and answered the certified question so as to make the bus setting dispositive in every case. It ruled categorically that " 'an impermissible seizure result[s] when police mount a drug search on buses during scheduled stops and question boarded passengers without articulable reasons for doing so, thereby obtaining consent to search the passengers' luggage.' " Ibid. The Florida Supreme Court thus adopted a per se rule that the Broward County Sheriff's practice of "working the buses" is unconstitutional. The result of this decision is that police in Florida, as elsewhere, may approach persons at random in most public places, ask them questions and seek consent to a search . . . but they may not engage in the same behavior on a bus. . . . We granted certiorari . . . to determine whether the Florida Supreme Court's per se rule is consistent with our Fourth Amendment jurisprudence.

II

The sole issue presented for our review is whether a police encounter on a bus of the type described above necessarily constitutes a "seizure" within the meaning of the Fourth Amendment. The State concedes, and we accept for purposes of this decision, that the officers lacked the reasonable suspicion required to justify a seizure and that, if a seizure took place, the drugs found in Bostick's suitcase must be suppressed as tainted fruit.

Our cases make it clear that a seizure does not occur simply because a police officer approaches an individual and asks a few questions. So long as a reasonable person would feel free "to disregard the police and go about his business," California v. Hodari D., 499 U.S. 621, 628 (1991), the encounter is consensual and no reasonable suspicion is required. The encounter will not trigger Fourth Amendment scrutiny unless it loses its consensual nature. . . .

[W]e have held repeatedly that mere police questioning does not constitute a seizure. . . .

There is no doubt that if this same encounter had taken place before Bostick boarded the bus or in the lobby of the bus terminal, it would not rise to the level of a seizure. The Court has dealt with similar encounters in airports and has found them to be "the sort of consensual encounter[s] that implicat[e] no Fourth Amendment interest." Florida v. Rodriguez, 469 U.S. 1, 5–6 (1984). We have stated that even when officers have no basis for suspecting a particular individual, they may generally ask questions of that individual . . . ask to examine the individual's identification . . . and request consent to search his or her luggage . . . as long as the police do not convey a message that compliance with their requests is required.

Bostick insists that this case is different because it took place in the cramped confines of a bus. A police encounter is much more intimidating in this setting, he argues, because police tower over a seated passenger and there is little room to move around. Bostick claims to find support in language from Michigan v. Chesternut, 486 U.S. 567, 573 (1988), and other cases, indicating that a seizure occurs when a reasonable person would believe that he or she is not "free to leave." Bostick maintains that a reasonable bus passenger would not have felt free to leave under the circumstances of this case because there is nowhere to go on a bus. Also, the bus was about to depart. Had Bostick disembarked, he would have risked being stranded and losing whatever baggage he had locked away in the luggage compartment.

The Florida Supreme Court found this argument persuasive, so much so that it adopted a per se rule prohibiting the police from randomly boarding buses as a means of drug interdiction. The state court erred, however, in focusing on whether Bostick was "free to leave" rather than on the principle that those words were intended to capture. When police attempt to question a person who is walking down the street or through an airport lobby, it makes sense to inquire whether a reasonable person would feel free to continue walking. But when the person is seated on a bus and has no desire to leave, the degree to which a reasonable person would feel that he or she could leave is not an accurate measure of the coercive effect of the encounter.

Here, for example, the mere fact that Bostick did not feel free to leave the bus does not mean that the police seized him. Bostick was a passenger on a bus that was scheduled to depart. He would not have felt free to leave the bus even if the police had not been present. Bostick's movements were "confined" in a sense, but this was the natural result of his decision to take the bus; it says nothing about whether or not the police conduct at issue was coercive.

   . . .

. . . Bostick's freedom of movement was restricted by a factor independent of police conduct—i.e., by his being a passenger on a bus. Accordingly, the "free to leave" analysis on which Bostick relies is inapplicable. In such a situation, the appropriate inquiry is whether a reasonable person would feel free to decline the officers' requests or otherwise terminate the encounter. This formulation follows logically from prior cases and breaks no new ground. We have said before that the crucial test is whether, taking into account all of the circumstances surrounding the encounter, the police conduct would "have communicated to a reasonable person that he was not at liberty to ignore the police presence and go about his business." *Chesternut*, supra, at 569. . . . Where the encounter takes place is one factor, but it is not the only one. And, as the Solicitor General correctly observes, an individual may decline an officer's request without fearing prosecution. . . . We have consistently held that a refusal to cooperate, without more, does not furnish the minimal level of objective justification needed for a detention or seizure. . . .

The facts of this case, as described by the Florida Supreme Court, leave some doubt whether a seizure occurred. Two officers walked up to Bostick on the bus, asked him a few questions, and asked if they could search his bags. As we have explained, no seizure occurs when police ask questions of an individual, ask to examine the individual's identification, and request consent to search his or her luggage—so long as the officers do not convey a message that compliance with their requests is required. Here, the facts recited by the Florida Supreme Court indicate that the officers did not point guns at Bostick or otherwise threaten him and that they specifically advised Bostick that he could refuse consent.

Nevertheless, we refrain from deciding whether or not a seizure occurred in this case. The trial court made no express findings of fact, and the Florida Supreme Court rested its decision on a single fact—that the encounter took place on a bus—rather than on the totality of the circumstances. We remand so that the Florida courts may evaluate the seizure question under the correct legal standard. . . .

. . .

We adhere to the rule that, in order to determine whether a particular encounter constitutes a seizure, a court must consider all the circumstances surrounding the encounter to determine whether the police conduct would have communicated to a reasonable person that the person was not free to decline the officers' requests or otherwise terminate the encounter. That rule applies to encounters that take place on a city street or in an airport lobby, and it applies equally to encounters on a bus. The Florida Supreme Court erred in adopting a per se rule.

. . .

■ JUSTICE MARSHALL, with whom JUSTICE BLACKMUN and JUSTICE STEVENS join, dissenting.

. . .

I

At issue in this case is a "new and increasingly common tactic in the war on drugs": the suspicionless police sweep of buses in interstate or intrastate travel. . . . Typically under this technique, a group of state or federal officers will board a bus while it is stopped at an intermediate point on its route. Often displaying badges, weapons or other indicia of authority, the officers identify themselves and announce their purpose to intercept drug traffickers. They proceed to approach individual passengers, requesting them to show identification, produce their tickets, and explain the purpose of their travels. Never do the officers advise the passengers that they are free not to speak with the officers. An "interview" of this type ordinarily culminates in a request for consent to search the passenger's luggage. . . .

These sweeps are conducted in "dragnet" style. The police admittedly act without an "articulable suspicion" in deciding which buses to board and which passengers to approach for interviewing. By proceeding systematically in this fashion, the police are able to engage in a tremendously high volume of searches. . . . The percentage of successful drug interdictions is low. . . .

To put it mildly, these sweeps "are inconvenient, intrusive, and intimidating." United States v. Chandler, 744 F.Supp. [333 (D.D.C.1990)], at 335. They occur within cramped confines, with officers typically placing themselves in between the passenger selected for an interview and the exit of the bus. . . . Because the bus is only temporarily stationed at a point short of its destination, the passengers are in no position to leave as a means of evading the officers' questioning. Undoubtedly, such a sweep holds up the progress of the bus. . . . Thus, this "new and increasingly common tactic," United States v. Lewis, 921 F.2d [1294 (D.C.App. 1990)], at 1295, burdens the experience of traveling by bus with a degree of governmental interference to which, until now, our society has been proudly unaccustomed. . . .

. . .

The question for this Court, then, is whether the suspicionless, dragnet-style sweep of buses in intrastate and interstate travel is consistent with the Fourth Amendment. The majority suggests that this latest tactic in the drug war is perfectly compatible with the Constitution. I disagree.

II

. . .

[The facts in this case] exhibit all of the elements of coercion associated with a typical bus sweep. Two officers boarded the Greyhound bus on which respondent was a passenger while the bus, en route from Miami to Atlanta, was on a brief stop to pick up passengers in Fort Lauderdale. The officers made a visible display of their badges and wore bright green "raid" jackets bearing the insignia of the Broward County Sheriff's Department; one held a gun in a recognizable weapons pouch. . . . These facts alone constitute an intimidating "show of authority." See Michigan v. Chesternut, 486 U.S. 567, 575 (1988). . . . Once on board, the officers approached respondent, who was sitting in the back of the bus, identified themselves as narcotics officers and began to question him. . . . One officer stood in front of respondent's seat, partially blocking the narrow aisle through which respondent would have been required to pass to reach the exit of the bus. . . .

. . .

. . . Apart from trying to accommodate the officers, respondent had only two options. First, he could have remained seated while obstinately refusing to respond to the officers' questioning. But in light of the intimidating show of authority that the officers made upon boarding the bus, respondent reasonably could have believed that such behavior would only arouse the officers' suspicions and intensify their interrogation. Indeed, officers who carry out bus sweeps like the one at issue here frequently admit that this is the effect of a passenger's refusal to cooperate. . . . The majority's observation that a mere refusal to answer questions, "without more," does not give rise to a reasonable basis for seizing a passenger, ante, at 437, is utterly beside the point, because a passenger unadvised of his rights and otherwise unversed in constitutional law *has no reason to know* that the police cannot hold his refusal to cooperate against him.

Second, respondent could have tried to escape the officers' presence by leaving the bus altogether. But because doing so would have required respondent to squeeze past the gun-wielding inquisitor who was blocking the aisle of the bus, this hardly seems like a course that respondent reasonably would have viewed as available to him. . . . Our decisions recognize the obvious point . . . that the choice of the police to "display" their weapons during an encounter exerts significant coercive pressure on the confronted citizen. . . . We have never suggested that the police must go so far as to put a citizen in immediate apprehension of *being shot* before a court can take account of the intimidating effect of being questioned by an officer with weapon in hand.

Even if respondent had perceived that the officers would *let* him leave the bus, moreover, he could not reasonably have been expected to resort to this means of evading their intrusive questioning. For so far as respondent knew, the bus' departure from the terminal was imminent. Unlike a person approached by the police on the street . . . or at a bus or airport terminal after reaching his destination . . . a passenger approached by the police at an intermediate point in a long bus journey cannot simply leave the scene and repair to a safe haven to avoid unwanted probing by law-enforcement officials. The vulnerability that an intrastate or interstate traveler experiences when confronted by the police outside of his "own familiar territory" surely aggravates the coercive quality of such an encounter. . . .

. . .

Rather than requiring the police to justify the coercive tactics employed here, the majority blames respondent for his own sensation of constraint. The majority concedes that respondent "did not feel free to leave the bus" as a means of breaking off the interrogation by the Broward County officers. Ante, at 436. But this experience of confinement, the majority explains, "was the natural result of *his* decision to take the bus." Ibid. (emphasis added). Thus, in the majority's view, because respondent's "freedom of movement was restricted by a factor independent of police conduct—i.e., by his being a passenger on a bus," ante, at 436, respondent was not seized for purposes of the Fourth Amendment.

This reasoning borders on sophism and trivializes the values that underlie the Fourth Amendment. Obviously, a person's "voluntary decision" to place himself in a room with only one exit does not authorize the police to force an encounter upon him by placing themselves in front of the exit. It is no more acceptable for the police to force an encounter on a person by exploiting his "voluntary decision" to expose himself to perfectly legitimate personal or social constraints. By consciously deciding to single out persons who have undertaken interstate or intrastate travel, officers who conduct suspicionless, dragnet-style sweeps put passengers to the choice of cooperating or of exiting their buses and possibly being stranded in unfamiliar locations. It is exactly because this "choice" is no "choice" at all that police engage in this technique.

In my view, the Fourth Amendment clearly condemns the suspicionless, dragnet-style sweep of intrastate or interstate buses. Withdrawing this particular weapon from the government's drug-war arsenal would hardly leave the police without any means of combatting the use of buses as instrumentalities of the drug trade. The police would remain free, for example, to approach passengers whom they have a reasonable, articulable basis to suspect of criminal wrongdoing. Alternatively, they could continue to confront passengers without suspicion so long as they took simple stops, like advising the passengers confronted of their right to decline to be questioned, to dispel the aura of coercion and intimidation that pervades such encounters. There is no reason to expect that such requirements would render the Nation's buses law-enforcement-free zones.

. . .

———

70. When police officers approach a passenger on a bus to ask questions and request his consent to a search, the failure to advise him that he does not need to cooperate does not of itself require the suppression of his responses and any evidence found in the search. Rather, whether the passenger was seized before answering the questions and whether he consented to the search depends on all the circumstances. United States v. Drayton, 536 U.S. 194 (2002) (6–3) (admission of evidence upheld).

In United States v. Stephens, 206 F.3d 914 (9th Cir. 2000), narcotics agents became suspicious of the defendant when they observed him in a bus terminal and watched as he boarded a bus and placed his bag in an overhead compartment. When the bus was scheduled to depart, they boarded the bus and announced that they were conducting a routine narcotics investigation and would like to talk to the passengers but that anyone was free to leave. In response to a question, the defendant said that he had no carry-on baggage. The agents removed the bag that he had carried on and asked if anyone owned it. When the bag was not claimed, they removed it and opened it. It contained narcotics. The court concluded that the defendant had abandoned the bag but that the abandonment was involuntary and the result of an unlawful seizure. It said that the agents' announcement and conduct indicated to passengers that they had only two choices: to cooperate with the agents or to get off the bus, which would itself have created suspicion. In view of all the circumstances, the court concluded that the defendant had been seized.

71.

One has an undoubted right to resist an unlawful arrest, and courts will uphold the right of resistance in proper cases. But courts will hardly penalize failure to display a spirit of resistance or to hold futile debates on legal issues in the public highway with an officer of the law. A layman may not find it expedient to hazard resistance on his own judgment of the law at a time when he cannot know what information, correct or incorrect, the officers may be acting upon. It is likely to end in fruitless and unseemly controversy in a public street, if not in an additional charge of resisting an officer. . . .

It is the right of one placed under arrest to submit to custody and to reserve his defenses for the neutral tribunals erected by the law for the purpose of judging his case. An inference of probable cause from a failure to engage in discussion of the merits of the charge with arresting officers is unwarranted. Probable cause cannot be found from submissiveness, and the presumption of innocence is not lost or impaired by neglect to argue with a policeman. It is the officer's responsibility to know what he is arresting for, and why, and one in the unhappy plight of being taken into custody is not required to test the legality of the arrest before the officer who is making it.

United States v. Di Re, 332 U.S. 581, 594–95 (1948).

Does the same reasoning apply to a person who is stopped but not arrested by a police officer? To what extent can an officer rely on a person's unresponsiveness or uncooperativeness as a basis for determining that he should be detained further or arrested? Does it make any difference in this connection whether the person is required to stop if told to do so by an officer or can only be asked to stop by the officer?

72. In Immigration and Naturalization Service v. Delgado, 466 U.S. 210 (1984) (7–2), the Court upheld an INS practice of "factory surveys," pursuant to which agents of the INS enter a factory, briefly question workers about their status in this country, and, if the questions arouse no suspicion, move on. If a worker acknowledges that he is an alien or his responses to the questions are unsatisfactory, he is asked to produce immigration papers. The INS conducted the surveys in question pursuant to warrants obtained on probable cause to believe that illegally resident aliens were employed in the factories, and in one case without a warrant but with the employer's consent. During the survey, workers were free to move around the factory. Agents were posted at the exits to the factories; otherwise there was no indication that workers were not free to leave after answering questions or without answering them.

The Court said:

Although we have yet to rule directly on whether mere questioning of an individual by a police official, without more, can amount to a seizure under the Fourth Amendment . . . interrogation relating to one's identity or a request for identification by the police does not, by itself, constitute a Fourth Amendment seizure. . . .

[P]olice questioning, by itself, is unlikely to result in a Fourth Amendment violation. While most citizens will respond to a police request, the fact that people do so, and do so without being told they are free not to respond, hardly eliminates the consensual nature of the response. . . . Unless the circumstances of the encounter are so intimidating as to demonstrate that a reasonable person would have believed he was not free to leave if he had not responded, one cannot say that the questioning resulted in a detention under the Fourth Amendment. But if the person refuses to answer and the police take additional steps . . . to obtain an answer, then the Fourth Amendment imposes some minimal level of objective justification to validate the detention or seizure.

466 U.S. at 216–17. The Court relied on *Delgado* in *Bostick*, p. 127 above, 501 U.S. at 436.

73. Should a policeman have authority to stop (and frisk) a person for questioning if he has no reason to believe that the person has himself committed a crime but believes that he has information concerning a crime? Suppose, for example, that a witness to a street holdup is anxious to leave the scene of the crime. Should a police officer be able to require him to remain? Or to give his name and address? Or to answer questions? If so, what should be the consequences of the person's refusal to do so?

Roadblock

Michigan Department of State Police v. Sitz

496 U.S. 444, 110 S.Ct. 2481, 110 L.Ed.2d 412 (1990)

■ Chief Justice Rehnquist delivered the opinion of the Court.

This case poses the question whether a State's use of highway sobriety checkpoints violates the Fourth and Fourteenth Amendments to the United States Constitution. We hold that it does not and therefore reverse the contrary holding of the Court of Appeals of Michigan.

Petitioners, the Michigan Department of State Police and its director, established a sobriety checkpoint pilot program in early 1986. The director appointed a Sobriety Checkpoint Advisory Committee comprising representatives of the State Police force, local police forces, state prosecutors, and the University of Michigan Transportation Research Institute. Pursuant to its charge, the advisory committee created guidelines setting forth procedures governing checkpoint operations, site selection, and publicity.

Under the guidelines, checkpoints would be set up at selected sites along state roads. All vehicles passing through a checkpoint would be stopped and their drivers briefly examined for signs of intoxication. In cases where a checkpoint officer detected signs of intoxication, the motorist would be directed to a location out of the traffic flow where an officer would check the motorist's driver's license and car registration and, if warranted, conduct further sobriety tests. Should the field tests and the officer's observations suggest that the driver was intoxicated, an arrest would be made. All other drivers would be permitted to resume their journey immediately.

The first—and to date the only—sobriety checkpoint operated under the program was conducted in Saginaw County with the assistance of the Saginaw County Sheriff's Department. During the 75-minute duration of the checkpoint's operation, 126 vehicles passed through the checkpoint. The average delay for each vehicle was approximately 25 seconds. Two drivers were detained for field sobriety testing, and one of the two was arrested for driving under the influence of alcohol. A third driver who drove through without stopping was pulled over by an officer in an observation vehicle and arrested for driving under the influence.

On the day before the operation of the Saginaw County checkpoint, respondents filed a complaint in the Circuit Court of Wayne County seeking declaratory and injunctive relief from potential subjection to the checkpoints. Each of the respondents "is a licensed driver in the State of Michigan . . . who regularly travels throughout the State in his automobile." See Complaint, App. 3a–4a. During pretrial proceedings, petitioners agreed to delay further implementation of the checkpoint program pending the outcome of this litigation.

After the trial, at which the court heard extensive testimony concerning, inter alia, the "effectiveness" of highway sobriety checkpoint programs, the court ruled that the Michigan program violated the Fourth Amendment and Art. 1, § 11, of the Michigan Constitution. . . . On appeal, the Michigan Court of Appeals affirmed the holding that the program violated the Fourth Amendment. . . . [W]e granted certiorari. . . .

To decide this case, the trial court performed a balancing test derived from our opinion in Brown v. Texas, 443 U.S. 47 (1979). . . .

. . .

Petitioners concede, correctly in our view, that a Fourth Amendment "seizure" occurs when a vehicle is stopped at a checkpoint. . . . The question thus becomes whether such seizures are "reasonable" under the Fourth Amendment.

It is important to recognize what our inquiry is *not* about. No allegations are before us of unreasonable treatment of any person after an actual detention at a particular checkpoint. . . . As pursued in the lower courts, the instant action challenges only the use of sobriety checkpoints generally. We address only the initial stop of each motorist passing through a checkpoint and the associated preliminary questioning and observation by checkpoint officers. Detention of particular motorists for more extensive field sobriety testing may require satisfaction of an individualized suspicion standard. . . .

No one can seriously dispute the magnitude of the drunken driving problem or the States' interest in eradicating it. Media reports of alcohol-related death and mutilation on the Nation's roads are legion. The anecdotal is confirmed by the statistical. . . .

Conversely, the weight bearing on the other scale—the measure of the intrusion on motorists stopped briefly at sobriety checkpoints—is slight. . . . The trial court and the Court of Appeals, thus, accurately gauged the "objective" intrusion, measured by the duration of the seizure and the intensity of the investigation, as minimal. . . .

With respect to what it perceived to be the "subjective" intrusion on motorists, however, the Court of Appeals found such intrusion substantial. . . . The court first affirmed the trial court's finding that the guidelines governing checkpoint operation minimize the discretion of the officers on the scene. But the court also agreed with the trial court's conclusion that the checkpoints have the potential to generate fear and surprise in motorists. This was so because the record failed to demonstrate that approaching motorists would be aware of their option to make U-turns or turnoffs to avoid the checkpoints. On that basis, the court deemed the subjective intrusion from the checkpoints unreasonable. . . .

We believe the Michigan courts misread our cases concerning the degree of "subjective intrusion" and the potential for generating fear and surprise. The "fear and surprise" to be considered are not the natural fear of one who has been drinking over the prospect of being stopped at a sobriety checkpoint but, rather, the fear and surprise engendered in law abiding motorists by the nature of the stop. . . . Here, checkpoints are selected pursuant to the guidelines, and uniformed police officers stop every approaching vehicle. . . .

The Court of Appeals went on to consider as part of the balancing analysis the "effectiveness" of the proposed checkpoint program. Based on extensive testimony in the trial record, the court concluded that the checkpoint program failed the "effectiveness" part of the test, and that this failure materially discounted petitioners' strong interest in implementing the program. We think the Court of Appeals was wrong on this point as well.

The actual language from Brown v. Texas, upon which the Michigan courts based their evaluation of "effectiveness," describes the balancing factor as "the degree to which the seizure advances the public interest." 443 U.S., at 51. This passage from *Brown* was not meant to transfer from politically accountable officials to the courts the decision as to which among reasonable alternative law enforcement techniques should be employed to deal with a serious public danger. Experts in police science might disagree over which of several methods of apprehending drunken drivers is preferable as an ideal. But for purposes of Fourth Amendment analysis, the choice among such reasonable alternatives remains with the governmental officials who have a unique understanding of, and a responsibility for, limited public resources, including a finite number of police officers. . . .

In Delaware v. Prouse, [440 U.S. 648 (1979)], we disapproved random stops made by Delaware Highway Patrol officers in an effort to apprehend unlicensed drivers and unsafe vehicles. We observed that *no* empirical evidence indicated that such stops would be an effective means of promoting roadway safety and said that "[i]t seems common sense that the percentage of all drivers on the road who are driving without a license is very small and that the number of licensed drivers who will be stopped in order to find one unlicensed operator will be large indeed." Id., at 659–660. We observed that the random stops involved the "kind of standardless and unconstrained discretion [which] is the evil the Court has discerned when in previous cases it has insisted that the discretion of the official in the field be circumscribed, at least to some extent." Id., at 661. We went on to state that our holding did not "cast doubt on the permissibility of roadside truck weigh-stations and inspection checkpoints, at which some vehicles may be subject to further detention for safety and regulatory inspection than are others." Id., at 663, n.26.

Unlike *Prouse*, this case involves neither a complete absence of empirical data nor a challenge to random highway stops. During the operation of the Saginaw County checkpoint, the detention of the 126 vehicles that entered the checkpoint resulted in the arrest of two drunken drivers. Stated as a percentage, approximately 1.6 percent of the drivers passing through the checkpoint were arrested for alcohol impairment. In addition, an expert witness testified at the trial that experience in other States demonstrated that, on the whole, sobriety checkpoints resulted in drunken driving arrests of around 1 percent of all motorists stopped. . . .

In sum, the balance of the State's interest in preventing drunken driving, the extent to which this system can reasonably be said to advance that interest, and the degree of intrusion upon individual motorists who are briefly stopped, weighs in favor of the state program. We therefore hold that it is consistent with the Fourth Amendment. The judgment of the Michigan Court of Appeals is accordingly reversed, and the cause is remanded for further proceedings not inconsistent with this opinion.

. . . [6]

---

74. Distinguishing *Sitz*, the Court held that a highway checkpoint program, the primary purpose of which was narcotics interdiction, violated the Fourth Amendment. City of Indianapolis v. Edmond, 531 U.S. 32 (2000) (6–3). It said:

Of course, there are circumstances that may justify a law enforcement checkpoint, where the primary purpose would otherwise, but for some emergency, relate to ordinary crime control. For example, as the Court of Appeals noted, the Fourth Amendment would almost certainly permit an appropriately tailored roadblock set up to thwart an imminent terrorist attack or to catch a dangerous criminal who is likely to flee by way of a particular route. . . . The exigencies created by these scenarios are far removed from the circumstances under which authorities might simply stop cars as a matter of course to see if there just happens to be a felon leaving the jurisdiction. While we do not limit the purposes that may justify a checkpoint program to any rigid set of categories, we decline to approve a program whose primary purpose is ultimately indistinguishable from the general interest in crime control.

. . .

Our holding also does not affect the validity of border searches or searches at places like airports and government buildings, where the

---

[6] Justice Blackmun wrote an opinion concurring in the judgment. Justice Brennan wrote a dissenting opinion, which Justice Marshall joined. Justice Stevens also wrote a dissenting opinion, part of which Justice Brennan and Justice Marshall joined.

On remand, the Michigan Court of Appeals held that the roadblock violated the state constitution's prohibition against unreasonable seizures. Sitz v. Department of State Police, 485 N.W. 2d 135 (Mich.App. 1992).

> need for such measures to ensure public safety can be particularly acute. Nor does our opinion speak to other intrusions aimed primarily at purposes beyond the general interest in crime control. Our holding also does not impair the ability of police officers to act appropriately upon information that they properly learn during a checkpoint stop justified by a lawful primary purpose, even where such action may result in the arrest of a motorist for an offense unrelated to that purpose. Finally, we caution that the purpose inquiry in this context is to be conducted only at the programmatic level and is not an invitation to probe the minds of individual officers acting at the scene.

Id. at 44, 47–48.

Edmond was distinguished in Illinois v. Lidster, 540 U.S. ___ (2004). In *Lidster*, the police set up a traffic checkpoint near the scene of a hit-and-run accident, in order to ask persons in the cars whether they had any information about the accident. Such "information seeking" highway stops are not presumptively unconstitutional, the Court said. Rather, their reasonableness under the Fourth Amendment must be judged on the basis of the particular circumstances. On that basis, the Court said that the brief stops in this case were constitutional.

75. In United States v. Brignoni-Ponce, 422 U.S. 873 (1975), two officers of the Border Patrol pursued the car driven by Brignoni-Ponce and stopped it near the Mexican border in Southern California; their only reason for doing so was that the three occupants appeared to be of Mexican descent. They questioned him and his passengers about their citizenship and arrested all three when they learned that the passengers were aliens who had entered illegally. On appeal from their convictions, the government claimed that the stop was pursuant to the Border Patrol's statutory authority, since in the border area "a person's apparent Mexican ancestry alone justifies belief that he or she is an alien," id. at 877. While conceding the importance and difficulty of enforcing the immigration law, the Court denied the broad authority sought:

> [B]ecause of the importance of the governmental interest at stake, the minimal intrusion of a brief stop, and the absence of practical alternatives for policing the border, we hold that when an officer's observations lead him reasonably to suspect that a particular vehicle may contain aliens who are illegally in the country, he may stop the car briefly and investigate the circumstances that provoke suspicion. As in *Terry* [v. Ohio, 392 U.S. 1 (1968)], the stop and inquiry must be "reasonably related in scope to the justification for their initiation." 392 U.S., at 29. The officer may question the driver and passengers about their citizenship and immigration status, and he may ask them to explain suspicious circumstances, but any further detention or search must be based on consent or probable cause.

We are unwilling to let the Border Patrol dispense entirely with the requirement that officers must have a reasonable suspicion to justify roving-patrol stops. In the context of border area stops, the reasonableness requirement of the Fourth Amendment demands something more than the broad and unlimited discretion sought by the Government. Roads near the border carry not only aliens seeking to enter the country illegally, but a large volume of legitimate traffic as well. . . . To approve roving-patrol stops of all vehicles in the border area, without any suspicion that a particular vehicle is carrying illegal immigrants, would subject the residents of these and other areas to potentially unlimited interference with their use of the highways, solely at the discretion of Border Patrol officers. . . .

We are not convinced that the legitimate needs of law enforcement require this degree of interference with lawful traffic. . . . [T]he nature of illegal alien traffic and the characteristics of smuggling operations tend to generate articulable grounds for identifying violators. Consequently, a requirement of reasonable suspicion for stops allows the Government adequate means of guarding the public interest and also protects residents of the border areas from indiscriminate official interference. Under the circumstances, and even though the intrusion incident to a stop is modest, we conclude that it is not "reasonable" under the Fourth Amendment to make such stops on a random basis.

Brignoni-Ponce, 422 U.S. at 881–83.

Brief, routine stops at a permanent checkpoint away from the border were upheld in United States v. Martinez-Fuerte, 428 U.S. 543 (1976) (7–2). The Court said that a brief stop for questioning was permissible even in the absence of any basis for stopping a particular car and that some cars could be directed to a secondary inspection area for further brief inquiry into the residence status of the occupants without the "reasonable suspicion" required for a roving-patrol stop; such further inquiry could be made "largely on the basis of apparent Mexican ancestry," id. at 563. The Court balanced the minimal invasion of private interests against the strong public interest in controlling unlawful immigration and the success of the checkpoint at serving that objective. See also United States v. Cortez, 449 U.S. 411 (1981) (stop of vehicle reasonably believed to be carrying illegal aliens upheld).

In Delaware v. Prouse, 440 U.S. 648 (1979) (8–1), a police officer stopped a car for what he called a "routine" stop; he said that he had observed no violation or suspicious activity but, being on patrol and not "answering any complaints," decided to pull the car over for a license and registration check. When the car was stopped, the officer smelled marijuana smoke and seized marijuana in plain view on the floor of the car. The Court emphasized the entire lack of standards regulating the stop and observed: "When there is not probable cause to believe that a driver is violating any one of the multitude of applicable traffic and equipment regulations—or other articulable basis amounting to reasonable suspicion that the driver is unlicensed or his vehicle unregistered—we cannot conceive of any legitimate basis upon which a patrolman could decide that stopping a particular driver for a spot check would be more productive than stopping any other driver." Id. at 661.

The Court held: "Except in those situations in which there is at least articulable and reasonable suspicion that a motorist is unlicensed or that an automobile is not registered, or that either the vehicle or an occupant is otherwise subject to seizure for violation of law, stopping an automobile and detaining the driver in order to check his driver's license and the registration of the automobile are unreasonable under the Fourth Amendment. This holding does not preclude the . . . States from developing methods for spot checks that involve less intrusion or that do not involve the unconstrained exercise of discretion. Questioning of all oncoming traffic at roadblock-type stops is one possible alternative. We hold only that persons in automobiles on public roadways may not for that reason alone have their travel and privacy interfered with at the unbridled discretion of police officers." Id. at 663.

In Pennsylvania v. Mimms, 434 U.S. 106 (1977) (per curiam; 6–3), the Court held that a police officer who has lawfully directed a driver to stop his automobile, in this case because the license plate had expired, needs no additional basis of suspicion before ordering the driver to get out of the car. The Court said that the potential danger to the officer, both from armed drivers and from oncoming traffic, outweighs the "de minimis" additional intrusion on the driver's personal liberty.

The Court extended its reasoning in *Mimms* to passengers in a car that has been lawfully stopped, in Maryland v. Wilson, 519 U.S. 408 (1997) (7–2). It said: "[D]anger to an officer from a traffic stop is likely to be greater when there are passengers in addition to the driver in the stopped car. While there is not the same basis for ordering the passengers out of the car as there is for ordering the driver out, the additional intrusion on the passenger is minimal. We therefore hold that an officer making a traffic stop may order passengers to get out of the car pending completion of the stop." Id. at 414–15. Cf. Michigan v. Summers, 452 U.S. 692 (1981), p. 195 note 108 below.

———

CHAPTER 3

SEARCH

"The right of the people to be secure in their persons, houses, papers, and effects, against unreasonable searches and seizures, shall not be violated, and no warrants shall issue, but upon probable cause, supported by oath or affirmation, and particularly describing the place to be searched, and the persons or things to be seized." U.S. Constitution amend. IV.

[The Amendment] took its origin in the determination of the framers of the Amendments to the Federal Constitution to provide for that instrument a Bill of Rights, securing to the American people, among other things, those safeguards which had grown up in England to protect the people from unreasonable searches and seizures, such as were permitted under the general warrants issued under authority of the Government by which there had been invasions of the home and privacy of the citizens and the seizure of their private papers in support of charges, real or imaginary, made against them. Such practices had also received sanction under warrants and seizures under the so-called writs of assistance, issued in the American colonies. . . . Resistance to these practices had established the principle which was enacted into the fundamental law in the Fourth Amendment, that a man's house was his castle and not to be invaded by any general authority to search and seize his goods and papers. . . .

The effect of the Fourth Amendment is to put the courts of the United States and Federal officials, in the exercise of their power and authority, under limitations and restraints as to the exercise of such power and authority, and to forever secure the people, their persons, houses, papers and effects against all unreasonable searches and seizures under the guise of law. This protection reaches all alike, whether accused of crime or not, and the duty of giving to it force and effect is obligatory upon all entrusted under our Federal system with the enforcement of the laws. The tendency of those who execute the criminal laws of the country to obtain conviction by means of unlawful seizures and enforced confessions, the latter often obtained after subjecting accused persons to unwarranted practices destructive of rights secured by the Federal Constitution, should find no sanction in the judgments of the courts which are charged at all times with the support of the Constitution and to which people of all conditions have a right to appeal for the maintenance of such fundamental rights.

Weeks v. United States, 232 U.S. 383, 390, 391–92 (1914). The Court held that evidence obtained by a search and seizure which violated the defendant's rights under the Fourth Amendment was inadmissible in evidence against him in a federal court.

———

The security of one's privacy against arbitrary intrusion by the police—which is at the core of the Fourth Amendment—is basic to a free society. It is therefore implicit in "the concept of ordered liberty" and as such enforceable against the States through the Due Process Clause. The knock at the door, whether by day or by night, as a prelude to a search, without authority of law but solely on the authority of the police, did not need the commentary of recent history to be condemned as inconsistent with the conception of human rights enshrined in the history and the basic constitutional documents of English-speaking peoples.

Accordingly, we have no hesitation in saying that were a State affirmatively to sanction such police incursion into privacy it would run counter to the guaranty of the Fourteenth Amendment. But the ways of enforcing such a basic right raise questions of a different order. How such arbitrary conduct should be checked, what remedies against it should be afforded, the means by which the right should be made effective, are all questions that are not to be so dogmatically answered as to preclude the varying solutions which spring from an allowable range of judgment on issues not susceptible of quantitative solution.

In Weeks v. United States, [232 U.S. 383 (1914)], this Court held that in a federal prosecution the Fourth Amendment barred the use of evidence secured through an illegal search and seizure. This ruling was made for the first time in 1914. It was not derived from the explicit requirements of the Fourth Amendment; it was not based on legislation expressing Congressional policy in the enforcement of the Constitution. The decision was a matter of judicial implication. Since then it has been frequently applied and we stoutly adhere to it. But the immediate question is whether the basic right to protection against arbitrary intrusion by the police demands the exclusion of logically relevant evidence obtained by an unreasonable search and seizure because, in a federal prosecution for a federal crime, it would be excluded. As a matter of inherent reason, one would suppose this to be an issue as to which men with complete devotion to the protection of the right of privacy might give different answers. When we find that in fact most of the English-speaking world does not regard as vital to such protection the exclusion of evidence thus obtained, we must hesitate to treat this remedy as an essential ingredient of the right. The contrariety of views of the States is particularly impressive in view of the careful reconsideration which they have given the problem in the light of the *Weeks* decision.[1]

. . .

The jurisdictions which have rejected the *Weeks* doctrine have not left the right to privacy without other means of protection. Indeed, the exclusion of evidence is a remedy which directly serves only to protect those upon whose person or premises something incriminating has been found. We cannot, therefore, regard it as a departure from basic standards to remand such persons, together with those who emerge scatheless from a search, to the remedies of private action and such protection as the internal discipline of the police, under the eyes of an alert public opinion, may afford. Granting that in practice the exclusion of evidence may be an effective way of deterring unreasonable searches, it is not for this Court to condemn as falling below the minimal standards assured by the Due Process Clause a State's reliance upon other methods which, if consistently enforced, would be equally effective. . . . We cannot brush aside the experience of States which deem the incidence of such conduct by the police too slight to call for a deterrent remedy not by way of disciplinary measures but by overriding the relevant rules of evidence. There are, moreover, reasons for excluding evidence unreasonably obtained by the federal police which are less compelling in the case of police under State or local authority. The public opinion of a community can far more effectively be exerted against oppressive conduct on the part of police directly responsible to the community itself than can local opinion, sporadically aroused, be brought to bear upon remote authority pervasively exerted throughout the country.

We hold, therefore, that in a prosecution in a State court for a State crime the Fourteenth Amendment does not forbid the admission of evidence obtained by an unreasonable search and seizure.

Wolf v. Colorado, 338 U.S. 25, 27–33 (1949).

———

Today we once again examine *Wolf*'s constitutional documentation of the right to privacy free from unreasonable state intrusion, and, after its dozen years on our books, are led by it to close the only courtroom door remaining open to evidence secured by official lawlessness in flagrant abuse of that basic right, reserved to all persons as a specific guarantee against that very same unlawful conduct. We hold that all evidence obtained by searches and seizures in violation of the Constitution is, by that same authority, inadmissible in a state court.

Since the Fourth Amendment's right of privacy has been declared enforceable against the States through the Due Process Clause of the

[1] The Court's analysis of state cases indicated that 47 states had considered the *Weeks* doctrine since the decision of that case, and that 31 states rejected the doctrine and 16 accepted it. The analysis of state cases is detailed in an appendix to the Court's opinion, 338 U.S. at 33.

"Nice weather we're having, eh Mulligan?"

Fourteenth, it is enforceable against them by the same sanction of exclusion as is used against the Federal Government. Were it otherwise, then just as without the *Weeks* [v. United States, 232 U.S. 383 (1914)] rule the assurance against unreasonable federal searches and seizures would be "a form of words," valueless and undeserving of mention in a perpetual charter of inestimable human liberties, so too, without that rule the freedom from state invasions of privacy would be so ephemeral and so neatly severed from its conceptual nexus with the freedom from all brutish means of coercing evidence as not to merit this Court's high regard as a freedom "implicit in the concept of ordered liberty." At the time that the Court held in *Wolf* that the Amendment was applicable to the States through the Due Process Clause, the cases of this Court, as we have seen, had steadfastly held that as to federal officers the Fourth Amendment included the exclusion of the evidence seized in violation of its provisions. Even *Wolf* "stoutly adhered" to that proposition. The right to privacy, when conceded operatively enforceable against the States, was not susceptible of destruction by avulsion of the sanction upon which its protection and enjoyment had always been deemed dependent under the *Boyd* [v. United States, 116 U.S. 616 (1886)], *Weeks* and *Silverthorne* [Lumber Co. v. United States, 251 U.S. 385 (1920)] cases. Therefore, in extending the substantive protections of due process to all constitutionally unreasonable searches—state or federal—it was logically and constitutionally necessary that the exclusion doctrine—an essential part of the right to privacy—be also insisted upon as an essential ingredient of the right newly recognized by the *Wolf* case. In short, the admission of the new constitutional right by *Wolf* could not consistently tolerate denial of its most important constitutional privilege, namely, the exclusion of the evidence which an accused had been forced to give by reason of the unlawful seizure. To hold otherwise is to grant the right but in reality to withhold its privilege and enjoyment.

Mapp v. Ohio, 367 U.S. 643, 654–56 (1961). See Bivens v. Six Unknown Named Agents of Federal Bureau of Narcotics, 403 U.S. 388 (1971), p. 95 note 56 above.[2]

---

76. In Walder v. United States, 347 U.S. 62 (1954), the Court held that illegally obtained evidence can be used by the prosecution to impeach the credibility of the defendant's own testimony. The defendant had testified that he had never possessed narcotics. The prosecution was permitted to introduce into evidence narcotics obtained by an illegal search.

(Never let criminal defendant testify!)

Walder was applied in United States v. Havens, 446 U.S. 620, 627–28 (1980) (5–4), in which the Court held that "a defendant's statements made in response to proper cross-examination reasonably suggested by the defendant's direct examination are subject to otherwise proper impeachment by the government, albeit by evidence that has been illegally obtained that is inadmissible on the government's direct case, or otherwise, as substantive evidence of guilt." The majority in *Havens* emphasized the importance of "arriving at the truth" in a criminal trial and concluded that that interest outweighed the incremental furthering of the ends served by the exclusionary rule if evidence were excluded in these circumstances. Id. at 626–27. The dissenting Justices argued that the majority's rule allowed the prosecutor to lay the basis for admission of otherwise excluded evidence by structuring his questions on cross-examination accordingly.

In James v. Illinois, 493 U.S. 307 (1990) (5–4), however, the Court held that the *Walder* exception to the exclusionary rule does not extend to the use of illegally obtained evidence to impeach testimony of a defense witness other than the defendant. In *James*, the evidence in question was statements of the defendant that he made while he was unlawfully arrested.

77. Inevitable discovery. In Nix v. Williams, 467 U.S. 431 (1984) (7–2), drawing on the rule that police illegality does not require the exclusion of evidence that has been obtained "by means wholly indepen-

---

2. In a civil drug forfeiture proceeding (pursuant to 21 U.S.C § 881(a)(7)), the Due Process Clause requires that before real property is seized, the property owner be given notice and an opportunity to be heard, unless there are exigent circumstances establishing a need for immediate seizure. United States v. James Daniel Good Real Property, 510 U.S. 43 (1993) (5–4). The Court observed: "While the Fourth Amendment places limits on the Government's power to seize property for purposes of forfeiture, it does not provide the sole measure of constitutional protection that must be afforded property owners in forfeiture proceedings." Id. at 495–96.

dent of any constitutional violation," id. at 443, the Court held that evidence to which the police are led by such a violation need not be excluded if "it would ultimately or inevitably have been discovered even if no violation of any constitutional or statutory provision had taken place," id. at 434. In Nix v. Williams, the police were led to the body of a murder victim by the defendant, in response to police conduct that violated his right to counsel under the Sixth Amendment. Finding that teams searching for the body were closing in on the location where it was concealed and would inevitably have found it in the same condition in which it was actually found, the Court held that evidence obtained thereby was properly admitted.

Nix v. Williams was applied in United States v. Cherry, 759 F.2d 1196 (5th Cir.1985) (some evidence admitted, some excluded). The court said that in order for the "inevitable discovery" exception to apply, "the prosecution must demonstrate both a reasonable probability that the evidence would have been discovered in the absence of police misconduct and that the government was actively pursuing a substantial alternate line of investigation at the time of the constitutional violation." Id. at 1205–1206. Otherwise, the court said, the exception would encourage the police to engage in illegal conduct. "In certain circumstances, however, such as when the hypothetical independent source comes into being only after the misconduct, the absence of a strong deterrent interest may warrant the application of the inevitable discovery exception without a showing of active pursuit by the government in order to ensure that the government is not unjustifiably disadvantaged by the police misconduct." Id. at 1206.

See United States v. Silvestri, 787 F.2d 736 (1st Cir.1986), discussing *Cherry* and other cases, and concluding: "Our review of these cases reveals that there are three basic concerns which surface in an inevitable discovery analysis: are the legal means truly independent; are both the use of the legal means and the discovery by that means truly inevitable; and does the application of the inevitable discovery exception either provide an incentive for police misconduct or significantly weaken fourth amendment protection?" Id. at 774. In *Silvestri*, the court considered cases in which police make a search and seize items prior to obtaining a warrant that authorized the search and seizure. It concluded that the warrant application process need not have been initiated at the time the search occurs but that there must have been probable cause for the issuance of a warrant at that time.

See Murray v. United States, 487 U.S. 533 (1988) (4–3), p. 190 note 104 below.

————

78. Good-faith exception. In United States v. Leon, 468 U.S. 897, 900 (1984) (6–3), the Court held that the exclusionary rule does not "bar the use in the prosecution's case in chief of evidence obtained by officers acting in reasonable reliance on a search warrant issued by a detached and neutral magistrate but ultimately found to be unsupported by probable cause."

The Court first repeated prior statements that the use of evidence obtained in violation of the Fourth Amendment is not itself a violation of the Amendment and that the exclusion of such evidence is not a cure for the violation itself but rather a judicial measure to deter violations. Therefore, it said, application of the exclusionary rule depends on "weighing the costs and benefits." The principle cost of excluding "inherently trustworthy tangible evidence" is that it interferes "with the criminal justice system's truth-finding function," with the result "that some guilty defendants may go free or receive reduced sentences as a result of favorable plea bargains." Id. at 907. The Court referred to prior cases, see note 83 p. 151 below, in which it had found that the costs of applying the exclusionary rule exceeded the benefits.

The Court considered the benefit that might be derived from evidence obtained pursuant to a warrant and concluded "that the marginal or nonexistent benefits produced by suppressing evidence obtained in objectively reasonable reliance on a subsequently invalidated search warrant cannot justify the substantial cost of exclusion," id. at 922. The exclusion of evidence, it said, remained "an appropriate remedy if the magistrate or judge issuing a warrant was misled by information in an affidavit that the affiant knew was false or would have known was false except for his reckless disregard of the truth," or "where the issuing magistrate wholly abandoned his judicial role," or if a warrant were altogether lacking in indicia of probable cause or were "facially deficient." Id. at 923. In such cases, an officer relying on the warrant would not be acting in an objectively reasonable manner.

In a dissenting opinion, which Justice Marshall joined, Justice Brennan said that the majority's ruling was the *"pièce de résistance"* of "the Court's gradual but determined strangulation of the [exclusionary] rule." Id. at 928–29. The majority's cost/benefit analysis, he said, gave "an illusion of technical precision and ineluctability," id. at 929, but was a product of "inherently unstable compounds of intuition, hunches, and occasional pieces of partial and often inconclusive data," id. at 942. "[T]he entire enterprise of attempting to assess the benefits and costs of the exclusionary rule in various contexts is a virtually impossible task for the judiciary to perform honestly or accurately." Id.

Justice Brennan rejected the majority's view of the exclusionary rule as a deterrent measure separate from the Fourth Amendment itself. "Because seizures are executed principally to secure evidence, and because such evidence generally has utility in our legal system only in the context of a trial supervised by a judge, it is apparent that the admission of illegally obtained evidence implicates the same constitutional concerns as the initial seizure of that evidence." Id. at 933.

The good-faith exception was applied also in a companion case to *Leon*, Massachusetts v. Sheppard, 468 U.S. 981 (1984) (7–2).

79. With respect to probable cause for issuance of a warrant, does the Court's test of objective reasonableness have the effect that there is a "discount" on the amount of evidence that is required for issuance of a warrant? For cases applying *Leon*, see, e.g., United States v. Thomas, 263 F.3d 805 (8th Cir.2001) (warrant invalid because it contained incorrect address; exclusion not required); United States v. Weaver, 99 F.3d 1372 (6th Cir.1996) (reasonably prudent officer would have sought more corroboration of probable cause, and officer did not, therefore, rely on warrant in good faith); United States v. Merida, 765 F.2d 1205 (5th Cir.1985) ("inadequate showing of nexus between items sought and location to be searched"; exclusion not required); United States v. Savoca, 761 F.2d 292 (6th Cir. 1985) (no probable cause; exclusion not required); United States v. Strand, 761 F.2d 449 (8th Cir.1985) (seized items not included in warrant; exclusion required); United States v. Merchant, 760 F.2d 963 (9th Cir.1985) (warrantless search based on subterfuge that person was on probation; exclusion required).

The good-faith exception to the exclusionary rule was extended to a warrantless administrative search pursuant to a statute subsequently declared invalid under the Fourth Amendment, in Illinois v. Krull, 480 U.S. 340 (1987) (5–4).

80. After the decision in *Leon*, it was feared by those who agreed with the dissenting opinion that the good-faith exception would be extended to searches without a warrant, e.g., a search incident to an arrest, see Chimel v. California, 395 U.S. 752 (1969), p. 205 below. That has not happened. But cf. Illinois v. Rodriguez, 497 U.S. 177 (1990), p. 169 below.

81. The exclusionary rule does not apply to "evidence seized in violation of the Fourth Amendment by an officer who acted in reliance on a police record indicating the existence of an outstanding arrest warrant—a record that is later determined to be erroneous," if the source of the error is a clerical error of a court employee and not the fault of the police. Arizona v. Evans, 514 U.S. 1 (1995) (7–2).

82. Observing that "the grant of motions to suppress evidence obtained pursuant to defective search warrants is relatively uncommon and apparently poses no significant obstacle to law-enforcement efforts" and stating its view that "the good-faith exception will ultimately reduce respect for and compliance with the probable-cause standard," the New Jersey Supreme Court rejected the *Leon* rule as inapplicable to the State constitution's provision against unreasonable search and seizure. State v. Novembrino, 519 A.2d 820 (N.J.1987). The good-faith exception is rejected also in State v. Marsala, 579 A.2d 58 (Conn.1990); State v. Gutierrez, 863 P.2d 1052 (N.M.1993); Commonwealth v. Edmunds, 586 A.2d 887 (Pa. 1991); and State v. Oakes, 598 A.2d 119 (Vt.1991). In *Gutierrez*, the court noted that seven other states had rejected the exception, including, in addition to those mentioned, Idaho, New York, and North Carolina. 863 P.2d at 1068 n.10.

83. In United States v. Calandra, 414 U.S. 338 (1974) (6–3), the Supreme Court held that the exclusionary rule announced in *Mapp*, p. 145 above, does not apply to evidence presented to a grand jury. It said:

> The exclusionary rule was adopted to effectuate the Fourth Amendment right of all citizens "to be secure in their houses, papers, and effects, against unreasonable searches and seizures. . . ." Under this rule, evidence obtained in violation of the Fourth Amendment cannot be used in a criminal proceeding against the victim of the illegal search and seizure. . . . This prohibition applies as well to the fruits of the illegally seized evidence. . . .
>
> The purpose of the exclusionary rule is not to redress the injury to the privacy of the search victim. . . . Instead, the rule's prime purpose is to deter future unlawful police conduct and thereby effectuate the guarantee of the Fourth Amendment against unreasonable search and seizures. . . . In sum, the rule is a judicially-created remedy designed to safeguard Fourth Amendment rights generally through its deterrent effect, rather than a personal constitutional right of the party aggrieved.
>
> Despite its broad deterrent purpose, the exclusionary rule has never been interpreted to proscribe the use of illegally-seized evidence in all proceedings or against all persons. As with any remedial device, the application of the rule has been restricted to those areas where its remedial objectives are thought most efficaciously served.

Id. at 347.

The Court concluded that application of the exclusionary rule "would seriously impede the grand jury" and that "any incremental deterrent effect which might be achieved by extending the rule to grand jury proceedings is uncertain at best." Id. at 349, 351. In a dissenting opinion joined by Justice Douglas and Justice Marshall, Justice Brennan observed: "For the first time, the Court today discounts to the point of extinction the vital function of the [exclusionary] rule to insure that the judiciary avoids even the slightest appearance of sanctioning illegal government conduct." Id. at 360.

Extending *Calandra*, in United States v. Puglia, 8 F.3d 478 (7th Cir.1993), the court of appeals held that the use in a grand jury proceeding of evidence that had previously been suppressed does not require dismissal of an indictment.

The application of the exclusionary rule was limited again, in United States v. Janis, 428 U.S. 433 (1976) (5–3). The Court there ruled that evidence unlawfully obtained (in good faith) by state criminal law enforcement officials and turned over to federal officials need not be excluded in a federal tax proceeding. Concluding that whatever deterrent effect such an application of the rule might have was outweighed by the social costs of excluding the evidence, the Court held that "the judicially created exclusionary rule should not be extended to forbid the use in the civil proceeding of one sovereign of evidence seized by a criminal law enforcement agent of another sovereign," id. at 459–60. See Wolf v. Commissioner of Internal Revenue, 13 F.3d 189 (6th Cir.1993) (*Janis* applied). The exclusionary rule does not apply in civil deportation hearings, Immigration and Naturalization Service v. Lopez-Mendoza, 468 U.S. 1032 (1984) (5–4), or in parole revocation hearings, Pennsylvania Board of Probation and Parole v. Scott, 524 U.S. 357 (1998) (5–4).

84. In Stone v. Powell, 428 U.S. 465 (1976), the Court limited the availability of collateral federal proceedings to contest the validity of a state criminal conviction on the ground that unconstitutionally obtained evidence was introduced at the trial. See note 434, p. 877 below.

85. The Fourth Amendment does not apply to a search and seizure by United States officials of property owned by a nonresident alien and located in a foreign country. United States v. Verdugo-Urquidez, 494 U.S. 259 (1990) (6–3). See also United States v. Mount, 757 F.2d 1315 (D.C.Cir.1985) (exclusionary rule not applicable to search conducted abroad by foreign officials; additional cases cited).

Consent

Stoner v. California
376 U.S. 483, 84 S.Ct. 889, 11 L.Ed.2d 856 (1964)

■ MR. JUSTICE STEWART delivered the opinion of the Court.

The petitioner was convicted of armed robbery after a jury trial in the Superior Court of Los Angeles County, California. At the trial several articles which had been found by police officers in a search of the petitioner's hotel room during his absence were admitted into evidence over his objection. A District Court of Appeal of California affirmed the conviction, and the Supreme Court of California denied further review. We granted certiorari, limiting review "to the question of whether evidence was admitted which had been obtained by an unlawful search and seizure." 374 U.S. 826. For the reasons which follow, we conclude that the petitioner's conviction must be set aside.

The essential facts are not in dispute. On the night of October 25, 1960, the Budget Town Food Market in Monrovia, California, was robbed by two men, one of whom was described by eyewitnesses as carrying a gun and wearing horn-rimmed glasses and a grey jacket. Soon after the robbery a checkbook belonging to the petitioner was found in an adjacent parking lot and turned over to the police. Two of the stubs in the checkbook indicated that checks had been drawn to the order of the Mayfair Hotel in Pomona, California. Pursuing this lead, the officers learned from the Police Department of Pomona that the petitioner had a previous criminal record, and they obtained from the Pomona police a photograph of the petitioner. They showed the photograph to the two eyewitnesses to the robbery, who both stated that the picture looked like the man who had carried the gun. On the basis of this information the officers went to the Mayfair Hotel in Pomona at about 10 o'clock on the night of October 27. They had neither search nor arrest warrants. There then transpired the following events, as later recounted by one of the officers:

> We approached the desk, the night clerk, and asked him if there was a party by the name of Joey L. Stoner living at the hotel. He checked his records and stated "Yes, there is." And we asked him what room he was in. He stated he was in Room 404 but he was out at this time.

> We asked him how he knew that he was out. He stated that the hotel regulations required that the key to the room would be placed in the mail box each time they left the hotel. The key was in the mail box, that he therefore knew he was out of the room.

> We asked him if he would give us permission to enter the room, explaining our reasons for this.

> Q.   What reasons did you explain to the clerk?

> A.   We explained that we were there to make an arrest of a man who had possibly committed a robbery in the City of Monrovia, and that we were concerned about the fact that he had a weapon. He stated "In this case, I will be more than happy to give you permission and I will take you directly to the room."

> Q.   Is that what the clerk told you?

> A.   Yes, sir.

> Q.   What else happened?

> A.   We left one detective in the lobby, and Detective Oliver, Officer Collins, and myself, along with the night clerk, got on the elevator and proceeded to the fourth floor, and went to Room 404. The night clerk placed a key in the lock, unlocked the door, and says, "Be my guest."

The officers entered and made a thorough search of the room and its contents. They found a pair of horn-rimmed glasses and a grey jacket in the room, and a .45-caliber automatic pistol with a clip and several cartridges in the bottom of a bureau drawer. The petitioner was arrested two days later in Las Vegas, Nevada. He waived extradition and was returned to California for trial on the charge of armed robbery. The gun, the cartridges and clip, the horn-rimmed glasses, and the grey jacket were all used as evidence against him at his trial.

The search of the petitioner's room by the police officers was conducted without a warrant of any kind, and it therefore "can survive constitutional inhibition only upon a showing that the surrounding facts brought it within one of the exceptions to the rule that a search must rest upon a search warrant. [...]" Rios v. United States, 364 U.S. 253, 261. . . .

[T]he respondent has made no argument that the search can be justified as an incident to the petitioner's arrest. Instead, the argument is made that the search of the hotel room, although conducted without the petitioner's consent, was lawful because it was conducted with the consent of the hotel clerk. We find this argument unpersuasive.

Even if it be assumed that a state law which gave a hotel proprietor blanket authority to authorize the police to search the rooms of the hotel's guests could survive constitutional challenge, there is no intimation in the California cases cited by the respondent that California has any such law. Nor is there any substance to the claim that the search was reasonable because the police, relying upon the night clerk's expressions of consent, had a reasonable basis for the belief that the clerk had authority to consent to the search. Our decisions make clear that the rights protected by the Fourth Amendment are not to be eroded by strained applications of the law of agency or by unrealistic doctrines of "apparent authority." . . .

It is important to bear in mind that it was the petitioner's constitutional right which was at stake here, and not the night clerk's nor the hotel's. It was a right, therefore, which only the petitioner could waive by word or deed, either directly or through an agent. It is true that the night clerk clearly and unambiguously consented to the search. But there is nothing in the record to indicate that the police had any basis whatsoever to believe that the night clerk had been authorized by the petitioner to permit the police to search the petitioner's room.

At least twice this Court has explicitly refused to permit an otherwise unlawful police search of a hotel room to rest upon consent of the hotel proprietor. Lustig v. United States, 338 U.S. 74; United States v. Jeffers, 342 U.S. 48. In *Lustig* the manager of a hotel allowed police to enter and search a room without a warrant in the occupant's absence, and the search was held unconstitutional. In *Jeffers* the assistant manager allowed a similar search, and that search was likewise held unconstitutional.

It is true, as was said in *Jeffers*, that when a person engages a hotel room he undoubtedly gives "implied or express permission" to "such persons as maids, janitors or repairmen" to enter his room "in the performance of their duties." 342 U.S., at 51. But the conduct of the night clerk and the police in the present case was of an entirely different order. In a closely analogous situation the Court has held that a search by police officers of a house occupied by a tenant invaded the tenant's constitutional right, even though the search was authorized by the owner of the house, who presumably had not only apparent but actual authority to enter the house for some purposes, such as to "view waste." Chapman v. United States, 365 U.S. 610. The Court pointed out that the officers' purpose in entering was not to view waste but to search for distilling equipment, and concluded that to uphold such a search without a warrant would leave tenants' homes secure only in the discretion of their landlords.

No less than a tenant of a house, or the occupant of a room in a boarding house . . . a guest in a hotel room is entitled to constitutional protection against unreasonable searches and seizures. . . . That protection would disappear if it were left to depend upon the unfettered discretion of an employee of the hotel. It follows that this search without a warrant was unlawful. Since evidence obtained through the search was admitted at the trial, the judgment must be reversed. . . .

. . . [3]

Schneckloth v. Bustamonte
412 U.S. 218, 93 S.Ct. 2041, 36 L.Ed.2d 854 (1973)

■ MR. JUSTICE STEWART delivered the opinion of the Court.

It is well settled under the Fourth and Fourteenth Amendments that a search conducted without a warrant issued upon probable cause is "per se unreasonable . . . subject only to a few specifically established and well-delineated exceptions." Katz v. United States, 389 U.S. 347, 357. . . . It is equally well settled that one of the specifically established exceptions to the requirements of both a warrant and probable cause is a search that is conducted pursuant to consent. . . . The constitutional question in the present case concerns the definition of "consent" in this Fourth and Fourteenth Amendment context.

I

The respondent was brought to trial in a California court upon a charge of possessing a check with intent to defraud. He moved to suppress the introduction of certain material as evidence against him on the ground that the material had been acquired through an unconstitutional search and seizure. In response to the motion, the trial judge conducted an evidentiary hearing where it was established that the material in question had been acquired by the State under the following circumstances:

While on routine patrol in Sunnyvale, California, at approximately 2:40 in the morning, Police Officer James Rand stopped an automobile when he observed that one headlight and its license plate light were burned out. Six men were in the vehicle. Joe Alcala and the respondent, Robert Bustamonte, were in the front seat with Joe Gonzales, the driver. Three older men were seated in the rear. When, in response to the policeman's question, Gonzales could not produce a driver's license, Officer Rand asked if any of the other five had any evidence of identification. Only Alcala produced a license, and he explained that the car was his brother's. After the six occupants had stepped out of the car at the officer's request and after two additional policemen had arrived, Officer Rand asked Alcala if he could search the car. Alcala replied, "Sure, go ahead." Prior to the search no one was threatened with arrest and, according to Officer Rand's uncontradicted testimony, it "was all very congenial at this time." Gonzales testified that Alcala actually helped in the search of the car, by opening the

---

[3] Justice Harlan wrote an opinion concurring in part and dissenting in part.

trunk and glove compartment. In Gonzales' words: "[T]he police officer asked Joe [Alcala], he goes, 'Does the trunk open?' And Joe said, 'Yes.' He went to the car and got the keys and opened up the trunk." Wadded up under the left rear seat, the police officers found three checks that had previously been stolen from a car wash.

The trial judge denied the motion to suppress, and the checks in question were admitted in evidence at Bustamonte's trial. On the basis of this and other evidence he was convicted. . . .

Thereafter, the respondent sought a writ of habeas corpus in a federal district court. It was denied. On appeal, the Court of Appeals for the Ninth Circuit . . . set aside the District Court's order. . . . The appellate court reasoned that a consent was a waiver of a person's Fourth and Fourteenth Amendment rights, and that the State was under an obligation to demonstrate, not only that the consent had been uncoerced, but that it had been given with an understanding that it could be freely and effectively withheld. Consent could not be found, the court held, solely from the absence of coercion and a verbal expression of assent. Since the District Court had not determined that Alcala had known that his consent could have been withheld and that he could have refused to have his vehicle searched, the Court of Appeals vacated the order denying the writ and remanded the case for further proceedings. We granted certiorari to determine whether the Fourth and Fourteenth Amendments require the showing thought necessary by the Court of Appeals. . . .

II

It is important to make it clear at the outset what is not involved in this case. The respondent concedes that a search conducted pursuant to a valid consent is constitutionally permissible. . . . And similarly the State concedes that "[w]hen a prosecutor seeks to rely upon consent to justify the lawfulness of a search, he has the burden of proving that the consent was, in fact, freely and voluntarily given." Bumper v. North Carolina, 391 U.S. 543, 548. . . .

The precise question in this case, then, is what must the prosecution prove to demonstrate that a consent was "voluntarily" given. And upon that question there is a square conflict of views between the state and federal courts that have reviewed the search involved in the case before us. The Court of Appeals for the Ninth Circuit concluded that it is an essential part of the State's initial burden to prove that a person knows he has a right to refuse consent. The California courts have followed the rule that voluntariness is a question of fact to be determined from the totality of all the circumstances, and that the state of a defendant's knowledge is only one factor to be taken into account in assessing the voluntariness of a consent. . . .

A

The most extensive judicial exposition of the meaning of "voluntariness" has been developed in those cases in which the Court has had to determine the "voluntariness" of a defendant's confession for purposes of the Fourteenth Amendment. . . . It is to that body of case law to which we turn for initial guidance on the meaning of "voluntariness" in the present context.

Those cases yield no talismanic definition of "voluntariness," mechanically applicable to the host of situations where the question has arisen. . . . [N]either linguistics nor epistemology will provide a ready definition of the meaning of "voluntariness."

Rather, "voluntariness" has reflected an accommodation of the complex of values implicated in police questioning of a suspect. At one end of the spectrum is the acknowledged need for police questioning as a tool for the effective enforcement of criminal laws. . . . Without such investigation, those who were innocent might be falsely accused, those who were guilty might wholly escape prosecution, and many crimes would go unsolved. In short, the security of all would be diminished. . . . At the other end of the spectrum is the set of values reflecting society's deeply felt belief that the criminal law cannot be used as an instrument of unfairness, and that the possibility of unfair and even brutal police tactics poses a real and serious threat to civilized notions of justice. "[I]n cases involving involuntary confessions, this Court enforces the strongly felt attitude of our society that important human values are sacrificed where an agency of the government, in the course of securing a conviction, wrings a confession out of an accused against his will." Blackburn v. Alabama, 361 U.S. 199, 206–207. . . .

This Court's decisions reflect a frank recognition that the Constitution requires the sacrifice of neither security nor liberty. The Due Process Clause does not mandate that the police forgo all questioning, nor that they be given carte blanche to extract what they can from a suspect. "The ultimate test remains that which has been the only clearly established test in Anglo–American courts for two hundred years: the test of voluntariness. Is the confession the product of an essentially free and unconstrained choice by its maker? If it is, if he has willed to confess, it may be used against him. If it is not, if his will has been overborne and his capacity for self-determination critically impaired, the use of his confession offends due process." Culombe v. Connecticut, [367 U.S. 568 (1961)], at 602.

In determining whether a defendant's will was overborne in a particular case, the Court has assessed the totality of all the surrounding circumstances—both the characteristics of the accused and the details of the interrogation. Some of the factors taken into account have included the youth of the accused . . . his lack of education . . . or his low intelligence . . . the lack of any advice to the accused of his constitutional rights . . . the length of detention . . . the repeated and prolonged nature of the questioning . . . and the use of physical punishment such as the deprivation of food or sleep. . . . In all of these cases, the Court determined the factual circumstances surrounding the confession, assessed the psychological impact on the accused, and evaluated the legal significance of how the accused reacted. . . .

The significant fact about all of these decisions is that none of them turned on the presence or absence of a single controlling criterion; each reflected a careful scrutiny of all the surrounding circumstances. . . . In none of them did the Court rule that the Due Process Clause required the prosecution to prove as part of its initial burden that the defendant knew he had a right to refuse to answer the questions that were put. While the state of the accused's mind, and the failure of the police to advise the accused of his rights, were certainly factors to be evaluated in assessing the "voluntariness" of an accused's responses, they were not in and of themselves determinative. . . .

B

Similar considerations lead us to agree with the courts of California that the question whether a consent to a search was in fact "voluntary" or was the product of duress or coercion, express or implied, is a question of fact to be determined from the totality of all the circumstances. While knowledge of the right to refuse consent is one factor to be taken into account, the government need not establish such knowledge as the sine qua non of an effective consent. As with police questioning, two competing concerns must be accommodated in determining the meaning of a "voluntary" consent—the legitimate need for such searches and the equally important requirement of assuring the absence of coercion.

In situations where the police have some evidence of illicit activity, but lack probable cause to arrest or search, a search authorized by a valid consent may be the only means of obtaining important and reliable evidence. In the present case for example, while the police had reason to stop the car for traffic violations, the State does not contend that there was probable cause to search the vehicle or that the search was incident to a valid arrest of any of the occupants. Yet, the search yielded tangible evidence that served as a basis for a prosecution, and provided some assurance that others, wholly innocent of the crime, were not mistakenly brought to trial. And in those cases where there is probable cause to arrest or search, but where the police lack a warrant, a consent search may still be valuable. If the search is conducted and proves fruitless, that in itself may convince the police that an arrest with its possible stigma and embarrassment is unnecessary, or that a far more extensive search pursuant to a warrant is not justified. In short, a search pursuant to consent may result in considerably less inconvenience for the subject of the search, and, properly conducted, is a constitutionally permissible and wholly legitimate aspect of effective police activity.

But the Fourth and Fourteenth Amendments require that a consent not be coerced, by explicit or implicit means, by implied threat or covert force. For, no matter how subtly the coercion were applied, the resulting "consent" would be no more than a pretext for the unjustified police intrusion against which the Fourth Amendment is directed. . . .

The problem of reconciling the recognized legitimacy of consent searches with the requirement that they be free from any aspect of official coercion cannot be resolved by any infallible touchstone. To approve such searches without the most careful scrutiny would sanction the possibility of official coercion; to place artificial restrictions upon such searches would jeopardize their basic validity. Just as was true with confessions, the requirement of a "voluntary" consent reflects a fair accommodation of the constitutional requirements involved. In examining all the surrounding circumstances to determine if in fact the consent to search was coerced, account must be taken of subtly coercive police questions, as well as the possibly vulnerable subjective state of the person who consents. Those searches that are the product of police coercion can thus be filtered out without undermining the continuing validity of consent searches. In sum, there is no reason for us to depart in the area of consent searches, from the traditional definition of "voluntariness."

The approach of the Court of Appeals for the Ninth Circuit finds no support in any of our decisions that have attempted to define the meaning of "voluntariness." Its ruling, that the State must affirmatively prove that the subject of the search knew that he had a right to refuse consent, would, in practice, create serious doubt whether consent searches could continue to be conducted. . . . [W]here there was no evidence of any coercion, explicit or implicit, the prosecution would nevertheless be unable to demonstrate that the subject of the search in fact had known of his right to refuse consent.

The very object of the inquiry—the nature of a person's subjective understanding—underlines the difficulty of the prosecution's burden under the rule applied by the Court of Appeals in this case. Any defendant who was the subject of a search authorized solely by his consent could effectively frustrate the introduction into evidence of the fruits of that search by simply failing to testify that he in fact knew he could refuse to consent. . . .

One alternative that would go far toward proving that the subject of a search did know he had a right to refuse consent would be to advise him of that right before eliciting his consent. That, however, is a suggestion that has been almost universally repudiated by both federal and state courts, and, we think, rightly so. For it would be thoroughly impractical to impose on the normal consent search the detailed requirements of an effective warning. Consent searches are part of the standard investigatory techniques of law enforcement agencies. They normally occur on the highway, or in a person's home or office, and under informal and unstructured conditions. The circumstances that prompt the initial request to search may develop quickly or be a logical extension of investigative police questioning. The police may seek to investigate further suspicious circumstances or to follow up leads developed in questioning persons at the scene of a crime. These situations are a far cry from the structured atmosphere of a trial where, assisted by counsel if he chooses, a defendant is informed of his trial rights. . . . And, while surely a closer question, these situations are still immeasurably far removed from "custodial interrogation" where, in Miranda v. Arizona [384 U.S. 436 (1966)] we found that the Constitution required certain now familiar warnings as a prerequisite to police interrogation. . . .

Consequently, we cannot accept the position of the Court of Appeals in this case that proof of knowledge of the right to refuse consent is a necessary prerequisite to demonstrating a "voluntary" consent. Rather, it is only by analyzing all the circumstances of an individual consent that it can be ascertained whether in fact it was voluntary or coerced. It is this careful sifting of the unique facts and circumstances of each case that is evidenced in our prior decisions involving consent searches.

. . .

[I]f under all the circumstances it has appeared that the consent was not given voluntarily—that it was coerced by threats or force, or granted only in submission to a claim of lawful authority—then we have found the consent invalid and the search unreasonable. . . .

. . .

In short, neither this Court's prior cases, nor the traditional definition of "voluntariness" requires proof of knowledge of a right to refuse as the sine qua non of an effective consent to a search.

. . .

D

Much of what has already been said disposes of the argument that the Court's decision in the *Miranda* case requires the conclusion that knowledge of a right to refuse is an indispensable element of a valid consent. The considerations that informed the Court's holding in *Miranda* are simply inapplicable in the present case. In *Miranda* the Court found that the techniques of police questioning and the nature of custodial surroundings produce an inherently coercive situation. . . .

In this case, there is no evidence of any inherently coercive tactics—either from the nature of the police questioning or the environment in which it took place. Indeed, since consent searches will normally occur on a person's own familiar territory, the specter of incommunicado police interrogation in some remote station house is simply inapposite. There is no reason to believe, under circumstances such as are present here, that the response to a policeman's question is presumptively coerced; and there is, therefore, no reason to reject the traditional test for determining the voluntariness of a person's response. . . .

It is also argued that the failure to require the Government to establish knowledge as a prerequisite to a valid consent, will relegate the Fourth Amendment to the special province of "the sophisticated, the knowledgeable and the privileged." We cannot agree. The traditional definition of voluntariness we accept today has always taken into account evidence of minimal schooling, low intelligence, and the lack of any effective warnings to a person of his rights; and the voluntariness of any statement taken under those conditions has been carefully scrutinized to determine whether it was in fact voluntarily given.

E

Our decision today is a narrow one. We hold only that when the subject of a search is not in custody and the State attempts to justify a search on the basis of his consent, the Fourth and Fourteenth Amendments require that it demonstrate that the consent was in fact voluntarily given, and not the result of duress or coercion, express or implied. Voluntariness is a question of fact to be determined from all the circumstances, and while the subject's knowledge of a right to refuse is a factor to be taken into account, the prosecution is not required to demonstrate such knowledge as a prerequisite to establishing a voluntary consent. Because the California courts followed these principles in affirming the respondent's conviction, and because the Court of Appeals for the Ninth Circuit in remanding for an evidentiary hearing required more, its judgment must be reversed.

. . . [4]

---

86. The test of whether consent to a search is voluntary that the Court elaborated in Schneckloth v. Bustamonte, above, is applied in United States v. Watson, 423 U.S. 411 (1976), the facts of which are given above, p. 22. Holding that the consent was given voluntarily, the Court said: "There were no promises made to . . . [Watson] and no indication of more subtle forms of coercion that might flaw his judgment. He had been arrested and was in custody, but his consent was given while on a public street, not in the confines of the police station. Moreover, the fact of custody alone has never been enough in itself to demonstrate a coerced confession or consent to search. Similarly, under *Schneckloth*, the absence of proof that Watson knew he could withhold his consent, though it may be a factor in the overall judgment, is not to be given controlling significance. There is no indication in this record that Watson was a newcomer to the law, mentally deficient, or unable in the face of a custodial arrest to exercise a free choice. He was given *Miranda* warnings and was further cautioned that the results of the search of his car could be used against him. He persisted in his consent." Id. at 424–25. See Ohio v. Robinette, 519 U.S. 33 (1996) (8–1).

87. A person's general consent to a search of his car may extend to closed containers within the car. "A suspect may of course delimit as he chooses the scope of the search to which he consents. But if his consent would reasonably be understood to extend to a particular container, the Fourth Amendment provides no grounds for requiring a more explicit authorization." Florida v. Jimeno, 500 U.S. 248 (1991) (7–2).

[4] Justice Blackmun wrote a concurring opinion. Justice Powell also wrote a concurring opinion, which Chief Justice Burger and Justice Rehnquist joined. Justice Douglas, Justice Brennan, and Justice Marshall wrote dissenting opinions.

In Schneckloth v. Bustamonte, consent to the search of the car was held to include a search "under the left rear seat" where three wadded checks were found. Even if the conclusion that Alcala's consent was voluntarily given is accepted, does it follow that his answer, "Sure, go ahead," in response to the officer's asking if he could search the car included the place where the checks were found? If so, on what basis? Compare United States v. Ibarra, 948 F.2d 903 (5th Cir.1991), in which consent to the search of a house was held to include search of an attic, the entrance to which was inside a bedroom closet and was boarded up; police knocked out the boards with a sledgehammer.

––––––––

Why is it that a man who truly consents, in the fullest sense, to a search of premises cannot later complain that the search violates his rights under the Fourth Amendment? Is it enough to say simply that he has "waived" his rights? If the search turns out to be against the man's interest, *why* does his consent constitute a "waiver"?

––––––––

88. "[N]o sane man who denies his guilt would actually be willing that policemen search his room for contraband which is certain to be discovered. It follows that when police identify themselves as such, search a room, and find contraband in it, the occupant's words or signs of acquiescence in the search, accompanied by denial of guilt, do not show consent; at least in the absence of some extraordinary circumstance, such as ignorance that contraband is present." Higgins v. United States, 209 F.2d 819, 820 (D.C.Cir.1954). To the same effect, that it "defies ordinary common sense" that a person who is carrying incriminating evidence would consent to a search of his person, see United States v. Viale, 312 F.2d 595, 601 (2d Cir.1963).

On the other hand:

> [The defendant] argues that since it is incredible he would freely have consented to a search which he knew would disclose incriminating evidence, his words of consent should be considered an involuntary submission to authority and therefore insufficient to waive a constitutional right. Acceptance of this contention would mean that expressions of consent could relieve officers of the need of obtaining a warrant only when the speaker was not aware that the search would disclose damaging evidence—a fact usually not within the officers' knowledge. Such a ruling not only would almost destroy the principle permitting a search on consent but would enable experienced criminals to lay traps for officers who, relying on the words of consent, failed to secure a search warrant that would have been theirs for the asking. Where . . . no force or deception was either used or threatened, we see no reason why a court should disregard a suspect's expression of

consent simply because efficient and lawful investigation and his own attempt to avoid apprehension had produced a situation where he could hardly avoid giving it.

United States v. Gorman, 355 F.2d 151, 158–59 (2d Cir.1965). "Bowing to events, even if one is not happy about them, is not the same thing as being coerced." Robbins v. MacKenzie, 364 F.2d 45, 50 (1st Cir.1966). See United States v. Lace, 669 F.2d 46, 52–53 (2d Cir.1982): "The consent to a search by one who realizes that the jig is up and a search warrant will issue in any event is similar to a plea of guilty by one who believes that he will be convicted if he stands trial. . . . His act does not become involuntary simply because the consequences would have been the same if he refused."

––––––––

The issue whether a defendant's own (alleged) consent to a search was effective arises only if he later contests the use of evidence discovered during the search. Would it be a sound rule of constitutional law that consent is never an effective basis for a search without a warrant if there is time to obtain a warrant? Why (not)? Would it be a sound rule of police practice that police should never ask for consent to search without a warrant unless there is no time to obtain one?

––––––––

89. A state regulation authorizing a probation officer to search a probationer's home without a warrant, if there are reasonable grounds to believe that he has contraband on the premises, including items prohibited by the terms of probation, does not violate the Fourth Amendment. The special needs of the probation system justify departure from the requirements of a warrant and probable cause. The regulation authorizing the search satisfies the requirement of reasonableness. Griffin v. Wisconsin, 483 U.S. 868 (1987) (5–4).

A warrantless search (supported by reasonable suspicion) of the premises of a person sentenced to probation for a drug offense, whose probation was expressly conditional on his submission to a search by a law enforcement officer at any time, is valid. United States v. Knights, 534 U.S. 112 (2001). The Court said that, viewing the totality of the circumstances, the fact that a person is on probation alters the balance by which the reasonableness of the search is assessed. It both increases the likelihood that the person is violating the law and, as a form of criminal punishment, somewhat reduces the person's liberty and, therefore, his expectation of privacy. See United States v. Reyes, 283 F.3d 446 (2d Cir.2002), stating that a person on probation has a "significantly diminished" expectation of privacy with respect to supervision by a probation officer and rejecting the "stalking horse" theory that if a probation officer acts at the behest of law enforcement authorities, the usual Fourth Amendment standards apply.

––––––––

Consent of Another

---

90. In *Stoner*, p. 152 above, the Court concluded that the hotel clerk's consent did not authorize the police to search the defendant's hotel room. Further, as noted in the opinion, although the owner of premises who has leased them to another may have authority to enter the premises for a variety of purposes, he does not generally have authority to consent to a search by police for evidence that incriminates his tenant. Chapman v. United States, 365 U.S. 610 (1961). So also, an employer does not have authority to consent to a search of a desk that has been assigned for the exclusive use of an employee. United States v. Blok, 188 F.2d 1019 (D.C.Cir.1951). Could an employer retain such authority by advising each employee that although his desk was otherwise for his exclusive use, the employer retained authority at will to search it himself or allow others to search it?

In what circumstances *does* the consent of one person authorize a search of premises and the evidentiary use against another person of items found in the search?

Suppose Stoner had hidden his pistol in a flower pot in the hotel lobby. If the police had searched the lobby with the consent of the hotel management and found the pistol, could it have been used in evidence against Stoner? Why (not)?

---

91. The defendant rented a small wooden shack from Stein. He arranged with Stein that Stein would receive deliveries for him and gave Stein a key to the shack so that deliveries could be stored inside. Postal authorities became suspicious of the defendant's activities, and inspectors questioned Stein, who unlocked the shack and invited the inspectors to examine its contents. The search led to evidence that incriminated the defendant, who was prosecuted for mail fraud. Did Stein's possession of a key and unwitting involvement in the defendant's unlawful activity give him authority to allow the postal inspectors to enter and search the shack? For a similar case, see United States v. Diggs, 544 F.2d 116 (3d Cir.1976), in which the defendant's wife gave a locked metal box to her uncle for safekeeping. He became suspicious and asked FBI agents to open it. They did so and found money taken in a recent bank robbery.

92. A person's consent to a general search of a computer does not authorize a search of the files of another joint user of the computer, whose files are protected by a password to which the consenting person does not have access. Trulock v. Freeh, 275 F.3d 391 (4th Cir.2001). The court likened the protected files to a locked footlocker.

93. If one person who shares the use of premises with another consents to a search of a portion of the premises used in common by both and the search reveals evidence that incriminates the other person, can the evidence be seized and used against him?

In United States v. Matlock, 415 U.S. 164 (1974), the Court upheld the validity of a woman's consent to the search of a room in which she had been living together with the defendant. The Court said that "the consent of one who possesses common authority over premises or effects is valid as against the absent, nonconsenting person with whom that authority is shared." Id. at 170.

On what does "common authority" depend?

"Common authority is, of course, not to be implied from the mere property interest a third party has in the property. The authority which justifies the third-party consent does not rest upon the law of property, with its attendant historical and legal refinements . . . but rests rather on mutual use of the property by persons generally having joint access or control for most purposes, so that it is reasonable to recognize that any of the co-inhabitants has the right to permit the inspection in his own right and that the others have assumed the risk that one of their number might permit the common area to be searched." Id. at 171 n.7.

See Frazier v. Cupp, 394 U.S. 731 (1969), upholding the authority of a "joint user" of a duffel bag to consent to a search that revealed evidence against the defendant, the other user.

For a variety of situations in which the courts found authority to consent by someone other than the defendant, see United States v. Buettner-Janusch, 646 F.2d 759 (2d Cir.1981) (research assistant and professional colleague with access to premises); United States v. Gargiso, 456 F.2d 584 (2d Cir.1972) (highest officer of company at scene of search); United States v. Cataldo, 433 F.2d 38 (2d Cir.1970) (roommate's consent effective as to defendant's separate bedroom); Drummond v. United States, 350 F.2d 983 (8th Cir.1965) (coconspirator using premises in common with owner); Burge v. United States, 342 F.2d 408 (9th Cir.1965) (owner's consent effective against house guest); United States v. Sferas, 210 F.2d 69 (7th Cir.1954) (consent of one partner to search of partnership premises effective against other partner); Calhoun v. United States, 172 F.2d 457, 458 (5th Cir.1949) (consent of "owner and master of the house" effective against one who has only permission to use a room "whenever he happened to be there").

Matlock has been applied to the search of a suitcase belonging to the defendant and being carried by her companion while they boarded an airplane; the court said that the defendant "granted her companion sufficient control over the suitcase so that it is reasonable to conclude that she assumed the risk that he might permit it to be searched at the airport check point." United States v. Canada, 527 F.2d 1374, 1379 (9th Cir.1975).

In United States v. Heisman, 503 F.2d 1284 (8th Cir.1974), the court held that a cotenant who had a legal right to enter a portion of premises used by the defendant but not a factual "possessory right" could not validly consent to a search there. See also United States v. Harris, 534 F.2d 95 (7th Cir.1976) (consent of occasional visitor inadequate).

94.

The right of one party to consent to a search which affects the interest of another derives from the consenting party's equal right of possession or control of the same premises or property as the other. Such cases fall into three classes. In one class a party having a joint right of control consents to a search directed only at himself and not at the other, but it discloses evidence harmful to the other. A second class consists of those cases in which one having a joint right of control consents to a search which he knows is directed at the other although he does so in the independent exercise of his right of joint control. The justification of the search in both these classes of cases results from the impossibility of severing the joint right of control and the undesirability of permitting the exercise of the right of one to be limited by the right of the other. . . .

A new and intruding element which has not been isolated heretofore may be said to distinguish a third class of cases. This element is the consenting party's agreement to the search out of motives of hostility to the other, made with the intent to harm him by an antagonistic consent. Where it is possible to identify this element a serious question would arise whether the right to consent is not spent when it reaches this point of deliberate antagonistic intrusion on the rights of the other who has an equal right to possession or control. This would be especially true where a wife intentionally acts against her husband's interest, since she would not be acting in harmony with the marital relationship from which her joint right of ownership or control is derived, but in antagonism to it.

United States ex rel. Cabey v. Mazurkiewicz, 431 F.2d 839, 842–43 (3d Cir.1970).

———

In *Matlock*, above, the court referred to the "*absent*, nonconsenting person" (emphasis added). Suppose joint occupants of premises are both present when the police ask to make a search. If the occupants have "equal rights" in the premises, is the consent of one of the occupants sufficient to authorize the search despite the objection of the other? In United States v. Sumlin, 567 F.2d 684 (6th Cir.1977), the court said yes. The defendant was arrested at an apartment in which he was a joint occupant with one Alexander, in whose name the apartment was leased. After the arrest, the defendant was asked for permission to search the apartment, which he refused. The arresting officers then obtained permission to search from Alexander. The defendant did not ask Alexander to withhold her consent.

The court said that the defendant's presence while the search was made without his consent was not constitutionally significant. It noted that in *Matlock* the defendant had just been arrested in the yard of the place that was searched pursuant to the consent of a third person. United States v. Morning, 64 F.3d 531 (9th Cir.1995), is to the same effect. "[T]he primary factor is the defendant's reasonable expectations under the circumstances. Those expectations must include the risk that a co-occupant will allow someone to enter, even if the defendant does not approve of the entry. The risks to property or privacy interests are not substantially lessened because of the defendant's own lack of consent. Although there is always the fond hope that a co-occupant will follow one's known wishes, the risks remain. A defendant cannot expect sole exclusionary authority unless he lives alone, or at least has a special and private space within the joint residence." Id. at 536. Accord United States v. Flores, 172 F.3d 695 (9th Cir.1999); United States v. Rith, 164 F.3d 1323 (10th Cir.1999); J.L. Foti Construction Co. v. Donovan, 786 F.2d 714 (6th Cir.1986) (administrative search).

Other courts have taken a different view. In State v. Leach, 782 P.2d 1035, 1040 (Wash.1989), the Washington Supreme Court said: "Where the police have obtained consent to search from an individual possessing, at best, equal control over the premises, that consent remains valid against a cohabitant, who also possesses equal control, only while the cohabitant is absent. However, should the cohabitant be present and able to object, the police must also obtain the cohabitant's consent. Any other rule exalts expediency over an individual's Fourth Amendment guarantees." Similarly, in Randolph v. State, 590 S.E.2d 834 (Ga.Ct.App.2003), the court said: "*Matlock* and its progeny stand for the proposition that, in the absence of evidence to the contrary, there is a presumption that a co-occupant has waived his right of privacy as to other co-occupants. However, when police are confronted with an unequivocal assertion of that co-occupant's Fourth Amendment right, such presumption cannot stand. After all, the right involved is the right to be free from police intrusion, not the right to invite police into one's home." Id. at 838. See United States v. Impink, 728 F.2d 1228, 1234 (9th Cir.1984).

In view of the facts that the defendant in *Matlock* had just been arrested in the yard and the officers knew that he lived in the house, was the rule about absent nonconsenting persons, on which the Court relied, really dispositive?

Is there a basis in the Fourth Amendment for the principle that the consent of one joint occupant to a search is effective against other occupants if they are absent but not if they are present? If so, could a joint occupant avoid that principle by expressly stating to other joint occupants (with "equal rights" in the premises) that he did not consent to any searches without a warrant? Why (not)?

95. The family home. It is generally the rule that the consent of one spouse to a search of the family home is effective against the other, absent spouse. E.g., United States v. Duran, 957 F.2d 499, 505 (7th Cir.1992): "[A] spouse presumptively has authority to consent to a search of all areas of the homestead; the nonconsenting spouse may rebut this presumption only by showing that the consenting spouse was denied access to the particular area searched." Do you agree with the statement in *Cabey*, p. 166 note 94 above, that if spouses are antagonistic to one another, the authority of either to consent to a search of joint premises is affected? In Kelley v. State, 197 S.W.2d 545 (Tenn.1946), for example, a woman asked the police to come to her house to arrest her husband for assaulting her and when they arrived led them to contraband which he had concealed in the house. Applying the theory that the validity of the woman's consent depended on an agency relationship with her husband, the court created an "angry wife" exception to the rule upholding third-party consent and invalidated the search. Fifty years later, in State v. Bartram, 925 S.W.2d 227 (1996), the court overruled *Kelley*. It said that the agency theory was no longer regarded as the basis for a spouse's consent, which rested simply on the spouse's common, independent authority over the premises.

Is the consent of a parent in whose home a child is living effective against the child? In State v. Kinderman, 136 N.W.2d 577 (Minn.1965), shortly after the defendant had been arrested on a charge of robbery and while he was still in custody, police officers went to his home and obtained his father's permission to make a search. The house was owned by the father; the defendant, who was 22 years old, occupied a bedroom on the second floor. The court upheld the admission in evidence of a gun found in a closet in the defendant's bedroom and items of defendant's clothing found in the basement. It said: "We can agree that the father's 'house' may also be that of the child, but if a man's house is still his castle in which his rights are superior to the state, those rights should also be superior to the rights of children who live in his house. We cannot agree that a child, whether he be dependent or emancipated (defendant was 22 years of age at the time of his arrest), has the same constitutional rights of privacy in the family home which he might have in a rented hotel room." Id. at 580. To the same effect, relying on the parent's "proprietary interest in the house . . . undiminished by any kind of a less-than-fee interest" of the defendant, see Maxwell v. Stephens, 348 F.2d 325, 336–37 (8th Cir.1965). Accord, e.g., United States v. Rith, 164 F.3d 1323 (10th Cir.1999); United States v. Peterson, 524 F.2d 167, 178–81 (4th Cir.1975). Would the same reasoning be applicable if the defendant were at home and objected to the search?

Contrary to the above cases, in People v. Nunn, 304 N.E.2d 81 (Ill.1973), the court held that the 19-year-old defendant had a reasonable expectation of privacy in a room in his mother's house that he kept locked, and that her consent to a search of the room was not effective. See State v. Kieffer, 577 N.W.2d 352 (Wis.1998) (father-in-law, who owned house, lacked authority to consent). Compare United States v. Block, 590 F.2d 535 (4th Cir.1978) (mother's consent authorized search of son's room in her house but not of locked trunk in room).

Suppose the defendant and his mother live as tenants or guests in a house owned by his sister. Does the mother have authority to consent to a search of the defendant's room (and a bureau used by the defendant)? See Reeves v. Warden, 346 F.2d 915 (4th Cir.1965). In Holzhey v. United States, 223 F.2d 823 (5th Cir.1955), the defendant lived in the home of her son-in-law and daughter. Did they have authority to consent to a search of a part of the home used primarily by the defendant? Is it relevant that the defendant made "occasional" small payments of rent?

Does a housekeeper who is alone in the house when police arrive have authority to consent to a search of parts of the house which she regularly enters for housekeeping purposes? See Cunningham v. Heinze, 352 F.2d 1 (9th Cir.1965). See also United States v. Dearing, 9 F.3d 1428 (9th Cir.1993) (live-in caretaker of handicapped child lacked actual or apparent authority to authorize search of homeowner's bedroom); People v. Misquez, 313 P.2d 206 (Cal.Dist.Ct.App.1957) (babysitter); People v. Carswell, 308 P.2d 852 (Cal.Dist.Ct.App.1957) (housepainter). In United States v. Jones, 335 F.3d 527 (6th Cir.2003), after having arrested the defendant in his car and asked him for and been refused permission to search his residence, police went to the residence and asked a handyman who was there for permission to search, which he gave. The court held that the handyman's consent was not effective. "Although . . . an employee does in some instances have sufficient authority to consent to entry into or a search of the employer's residence, the lesser, and necessarily derivative, interest of the employee cannot override the greater interest of the owner. When the primary occupant has denied permission to enter and conduct a search, his employee does not have the authority to override that denial." Id. at 531.

---

96. The defendant loaned his automobile to a friend who wanted to "take his young daughter . . . for a ride around town." Does his friend, while still in possession of the car, have authority to consent to a search of the automobile for evidence that incriminates the defendant? Does the extent of the search make a difference? See United States v. Eldridge, 302 F.2d 463 (4th Cir.1962). If the defendant leaves a locked briefcase in the home of a friend and the friend turns it over to the police, may they, without a warrant, force it open and search it if they have probable cause to believe that it contains narcotics? See Sartain v. United States, 303 F.2d 859 (9th Cir.1962). Compare Corngold v. United States, 367 F.2d 1 (9th Cir.1966) (package delivered to airline for transportation).

Illinois v. Rodriguez
497 U.S. 177, 110 S.Ct. 2793, 111 L.Ed.2d 148 (1990)

■ JUSTICE SCALIA delivered the opinion of the Court.

In United States v. Matlock, 415 U.S. 164 (1974), this Court reaffirmed that a warrantless entry and search by law enforcement officers does not violate the Fourth Amendment's proscription of "unreasonable searches and seizures" if the officers have obtained the consent of a third party who possesses common authority over the premises. The present case presents an issue we expressly reserved in *Matlock*, see id., at 177, n.14: whether a warrantless entry is valid when based upon the consent of a third party whom the police, at the time of the entry, reasonably believe to possess common authority over the premises, but who in fact does not do so.

I

Respondent Edward Rodriguez was arrested in his apartment by law enforcement officers and charged with possession of illegal drugs. The police gained entry to the apartment with the consent and assistance of Gail Fischer, who had lived there with respondent for several months. The relevant facts leading to the arrest are as follows.

On July 26, 1985, police were summoned to the residence of Dorothy Jackson on South Wolcott in Chicago. They were met by Ms. Jackson's daughter, Gail Fischer, who showed signs of a severe beating. She told the officers that she had been assaulted by respondent Edward Rodriguez earlier that day in an apartment on South California. Fischer stated that Rodriguez was then asleep in the apartment, and she consented to travel there with the police in order to unlock the door with her key so that the officers could enter and arrest him. During this conversation, Fischer several times referred to the apartment on South California as "our" apartment, and said that she had clothes and furniture there. It is unclear whether she indicated that she currently lived at the apartment, or only that she used to live there.

The police officers drove to the apartment on South California, accompanied by Fischer. They did not obtain an arrest warrant for Rodriguez, nor did they seek a search warrant for the apartment. At the apartment, Fischer unlocked the door with her key and gave the officers permission to enter. They moved through the door into the living room, where they observed in plain view drug paraphernalia and containers filled with white powder that they believed (correctly, as later analysis showed) to be cocaine. They proceeded to the bedroom, where they found Rodriguez asleep and discovered additional containers of white powder in two open attaché cases. The officers arrested Rodriguez and seized the drugs and related paraphernalia.

Rodriguez was charged with possession of a controlled substance with intent to deliver. He moved to suppress all evidence seized at the time of his arrest, claiming that Fischer had vacated the apartment several weeks earlier and had no authority to consent to the entry. The Cook County Circuit Court granted the motion, holding that at the time she consented to the entry Fischer did not have common authority over the apartment. The Court concluded that Fischer was not a "usual resident" but rather an "infrequent visitor" at the apartment on South California, based upon its findings that Fischer's name was not on the lease, that she did not contribute to the rent, that she was not allowed to invite others to the apartment on her own, that she did not have access to the apartment when respondent was away, and that she had moved some of her possessions from the apartment. The Circuit Court also rejected the State's contention that, even if Fischer did not possess common authority over the premises, there was no Fourth Amendment violation if the police *reasonably believed* at the time of their entry that Fischer possessed the authority to consent.

The Appellate Court of Illinois affirmed the Circuit Court in all respects. . . . [W]e granted certiorari. . . .

II

The Fourth Amendment generally prohibits the warrantless entry of a person's home, whether to make an arrest or to search for specific objects. . . . The prohibition does not apply, however, to situations in which voluntary consent has been obtained, either from the individual whose property is searched . . . or from a third party who possesses common authority over the premises. . . . The State of Illinois contends that that exception applies in the present case.

As we stated in *Matlock*, 415 U.S., at 171, n.7, "[c]ommon authority" rests "on mutual use of the property by persons generally having joint access or control for most purposes. . . ." The burden of establishing that common authority rests upon the State. On the basis of this record, it is clear that burden was not sustained. . . . To the contrary, the Appellate Court's determination of no common authority over the apartment was obviously correct.

III

A

The State contends that, even if Fischer did not in fact have authority to give consent, it suffices to validate the entry that the law enforcement officers reasonably believed she did. . . .

. . .

B

On the merits of the issue, respondent asserts that permitting a reasonable belief of common authority to validate an entry would cause a defendant's Fourth Amendment rights to be "vicariously waived." Brief for Respondent 32. We disagree.

We have been unyielding in our insistence that a defendant's waiver of his trial rights cannot be given effect unless it is "knowing" and "intelligent." Colorado v. Spring, 479 U.S. 564, 574–75 (1987). . . . But one must make a distinction between, on the one hand, trial rights that *derive* from the violation of constitutional guarantees and, on the other hand, the nature of those constitutional guarantees themselves. . . .

What Rodriguez is assured by the trial right of the exclusionary rule, where it applies, is that no evidence seized in violation of the Fourth Amendment will be introduced at his trial unless he consents. What he is assured by the Fourth Amendment itself, however, is not that no government search of his house will occur unless he consents; but that no such search will occur that is "unreasonable." U.S. Const., Amdt. 4. There are various elements, of course, that can make a search of a person's house "reasonable"—one of which is the consent of the person or his cotenant. The essence of respondent's argument is that we should impose upon this element a requirement that we have not imposed upon other elements that regularly compel government officers to exercise judgment regarding the facts: namely, the requirement that their judgment be not only responsible but correct.

The fundamental objective that alone validates all unconsented governmental searches is, of course, the seizure of persons who have committed or are about to commit crimes, or of evidence related to crimes. But "reasonableness," with respect to this necessary element, does not demand that the government be factually correct in its assessment that that is what a search will produce. Warrants need only be supported by "probable cause," which demands no more than a proper "assessment of probabilities in particular factual contexts...." Illinois v. Gates, 462 U.S. 213, 232 (1983). . . .

Another element often, though not invariably, required in order to render an unconsented search "reasonable" is, of course, that the officer be authorized by a valid warrant. Here also we have not held that "reasonableness" precludes error with respect to those factual judgments that law enforcement officials are expected to make. . . .

. . .

. . . It is apparent that in order to satisfy the "reasonableness" requirement of the Fourth Amendment, what is generally demanded of the many factual determinations that must regularly be made by agents of the government—whether the magistrate issuing a warrant, the police officer executing a warrant, or the police officer conducting a search or seizure under one of the exceptions to the warrant requirement—is not that they always be correct, but that they always be reasonable. . . .

We see no reason to depart from this general rule with respect to facts bearing upon the authority to consent to a search. Whether the basis for such authority exists is the sort of recurring factual question to which law enforcement officials must be expected to apply their judgment; and all the Fourth Amendment requires is that they answer it reasonably. The Constitution is no more violated when officers enter without a warrant because they reasonably (though erroneously) believe that the person who has consented to their entry is a resident of the premises, than it is violated when they enter without a warrant because they reasonably (though erroneously) believe they are in pursuit of a violent felon who is about to escape. . . .

. . .

[W]hat we hold today does not suggest that law enforcement officers may always accept a person's invitation to enter premises. Even when the invitation is accompanied by an explicit assertion that the person lives there, the surrounding circumstances could conceivably be such that a reasonable person would doubt its truth and not act upon it without further inquiry. As with other factual determinations bearing upon search and seizure, determination of consent to enter must "be judged against an objective standard: would the facts available to the officer at the moment . . . 'warrant a man of reasonable caution in the belief?'" that the consenting party had authority over the premises? Terry v. Ohio, 392 U.S. 1, 21–22 (1968). If not, then warrantless entry without further inquiry is unlawful unless authority actually exists. But if so, the search is valid.

■ JUSTICE MARSHALL, with whom JUSTICE BRENNAN and JUSTICE STEVENS join, dissenting.

. . .

The baseline for the reasonableness of a search or seizure in the home is the presence of a warrant. . . . Because the sole law enforcement purpose underlying third-party consent searches is avoiding the inconvenience of securing a warrant, a departure from the warrant requirement is not justified simply because an officer reasonably believes a third party has consented to a search of the defendant's home. . . .

. . .

Unlike searches conducted pursuant to the recognized exceptions to the warrant requirement . . . third-party consent searches are not based on an exigency and therefore serve no compelling social goal. Police officers, when faced with the choice of relying on consent by a third party or securing a warrant, should secure a warrant, and must therefore accept the risk of error should they instead choose to rely on consent.

. . .

A search conducted pursuant to an officer's reasonable but mistaken belief that a third party had authority to consent is . . . on an entirely different constitutional footing from one based on the consent of a third party who in fact has such authority. Even if the officers reasonably believed that Fischer had authority to consent, she did not, and Rodriguez's expectation of privacy was therefore undiminished. Rodriguez accordingly can challenge the warrantless intrusion into his home as a violation of the Fourth Amendment. . . .

. . .

Acknowledging that the third party in this case lacked authority to consent, the majority seeks to rely on cases suggesting that reasonable but mistaken factual judgments by police will not invalidate otherwise reasonable searches. . . .

[T]he possibility of factual error is built into the probable cause standard, and such a standard, by its very definition, will in some cases result in the arrest of a suspect who has not actually committed a crime. Because probable cause defines the reasonableness of searches and seizures outside of the home, a search is reasonable under the Fourth Amendment whenever that standard is met, notwithstanding the possibility of "mistakes" on the part of police. . . . In contrast, our cases have already struck the balance against warrantless home intrusions in the absence of an exigency. . . . Because reasonable factual errors by law enforcement officers will not validate unreasonable searches, the reasonableness of the officer's mistaken belief that the third party had authority to consent is irrelevant.

. . .

───────

97. Would "a state law which gave a hotel proprietor blanket authority to authorize the police to search the rooms of the hotel's guests . . . survive constitutional challenge," *Stoner*, p. 152 above? If so, could state law also give the manager of an apartment building such authority? The manager of a public housing project? If not, why not? Compare United States v. Biswell, 406 U.S. 311 (1972), in which the Court upheld the warrantless search, authorized by federal statute, of a gun dealer's storeroom.

98.

On the morning of February 28, 1968, the Dean of Men of Troy State University was called to the office of the Chief of Police of Troy, Alabama, to discuss "the drug problem" at the University. Two State narcotic agents and two student informers from Troy State University were also present. Later on that same day, the Dean of Men was called to the city police station for another meeting; at this time he was informed by the officers that they had sufficient evidence that marijuana was in the dormitory rooms of certain Troy State students and that they desired the cooperation of University officials in searching these rooms. The police officers were advised by the Dean of Men that they would receive the full cooperation of the University officials in searching for the marijuana. The informers, whose identities have not yet been disclosed, provided the police officers with names of students whose rooms were to be searched. Still later on that same day (which was during the week of final examinations at the University and was to be followed by a week-long holiday) the law enforcement officers, accompanied by some of the University officials, searched six or seven dormitory rooms located in two separate residence halls. The rooms of both Piazzola and Marinshaw were searched without search warrants and without their consent. Present during the search of the room occupied by Marinshaw were two State narcotic agents, the University security officer, and a counselor of the residence hall where Marinshaw's room was located. Piazzola's room was searched twice. Present during the first search were two State narcotic agents and a University official; no evidence was found at this time. The second search of Piazzola's room, which disclosed the incriminating evidence, was conducted solely by the State and City police officials.

At the time of the seizure the University had in effect the following regulation: "The college reserves the right to enter rooms for inspection purposes. If the administration deems it necessary, the room may be searched and the occupant required to open his personal baggage and any other personal material which is sealed." Each of the petitioners was familiar with this regulation. After the search of the petitioners' rooms and the discovery of the marijuana, they were arrested, and the State criminal prosecutions and convictions ensued.

Piazzola v. Watkins, 442 F.2d 284, 286 (5th Cir.1971). Were the searches lawful?

99. The Fourth Amendment's prohibition against unreasonable searches and seizures applies to searches of students conducted by school officials. New Jersey v. T.L.O., 469 U.S. 325 (1985) (6–3). However, the standard of reasonableness is not as stringent as the standard applied to law enforcement officers in the conduct of criminal investigations. The Court said:

> How, then, should we strike the balance between the schoolchild's legitimate expectations of privacy and the school's equally legitimate need to maintain an environment in which learning can take place? It is evident that the school setting requires some easing of the restrictions to which searches by public authorities are ordinarily subject. The warrant requirement, in particular, is unsuited to the school environment: requiring a teacher to obtain a warrant before searching a child suspected of an infraction of school rules (or of the criminal law) would unduly interfere with the maintenance of the swift and informal disciplinary procedures needed in the schools. Just as we have in other cases dispensed with the warrant requirement when "the burden of obtaining a warrant is likely to frustrate the governmental purpose behind the search," Camara v. Municipal Court, 387 U.S. [523 (1967)], at 532–33, we hold today that school officials need not obtain a warrant before searching a student who is under their authority.

> The school setting also requires some modification of the level of suspicion of illicit activity needed to justify a search. Ordinarily, a search—even one that may permissibly be carried out without a warrant—must be based upon "probable cause" to believe that a violation of the law has occurred. . . . However, "probable cause" is not an irreducible requirement of a valid search. . . . Where a careful balancing of governmental and private interests suggests that the public interest is best served by a Fourth Amendment standard of reasonableness that stops short of probable cause, we have not hesitated to adopt such a standard.

We join the majority of courts that have examined this issue in concluding that the accommodation of the privacy interests of schoolchildren with the substantial need of teachers and administrators for freedom to maintain order in the schools does not require strict adherence to the requirement that searches be based on probable cause to believe that the subject of the search has violated or is violating the law. Rather, the legality of a search of a student should depend simply on the reasonableness, under all the circumstances, of the search. Determining the reasonableness of any search involves a twofold inquiry: first, one must consider "whether the . . . action was justified at its inception," Terry v. Ohio, 392 U.S. [1 (1968)], at 20; second, one must determine whether the search as actually conducted "was reasonably related in scope to the circumstances which justified the interference in the first place," ibid. Under ordinary circumstances, a search of a student by a teacher or other school official will be "justified at its inception" when there are reasonable grounds for suspecting that the search will turn up evidence that the student has violated or is violating either the law or the rules of the school. Such a search will be permissible in its scope when the measures adopted are reasonably related to the objectives of the search and not excessively intrusive in light of the age and sex of the student and the nature of the infraction.

This standard will, we trust, neither unduly burden the efforts of school authorities to maintain order in their schools nor authorize unrestrained intrusions upon the privacy of schoolchildren. By focusing attention on the question of reasonableness, the standard will spare teachers and school administrators the necessity of schooling themselves in the niceties of probable cause and permit them to regulate their conduct according to the dictates of reason and common sense. At the same time, the reasonableness standard should ensure that the interests of students will be invaded no more than is necessary to achieve the legitimate end of preserving order in the school.

469 U.S. at 340–43.

In an opinion concurring in part and dissenting in part, Justice Brennan argued that, although the warrant requirement was not applicable, the standard of probable cause should be retained. In an opinion concurring in part and dissenting in part, Justice Stevens argued that a warrantless search of students by school officials should be restricted to cases in which there is reason to believe that the search will uncover *"evidence that the student is violating the law or engaging in conduct that is seriously disruptive of school order, or the educational process."* Id. at 378. The Court's rule, he urged, would unnecessarily allow school officials to search for evidence of violation of minor school regulations. (Justice Marshall joined both opinions.)

The Fourth Amendment does not prohibit a program of random testing for drugs by urinalysis of public school students who participate voluntarily in interscholastic athletics. Vernonia School District 47J v. Acton, 515 U.S. 646 (1995) (6–3).

Search Warrant

FEDERAL RULES OF CRIMINAL PROCEDURE

Rule 41

SEARCH AND SEIZURE

(a) Scope and Definitions.

(1) *Scope.* This rule does not modify any statute regulating search or seizure, or the issuance and execution of a search warrant in special circumstances.

(2) *Definitions.* The following definitions apply under this rule:

(A) "Property" includes documents, books, papers, any other tangible objects, and information.

(B) "Daytime" means the hours between 6:00 a.m. and 10:00 p.m. according to local time.

(C) "Federal law enforcement officer" means a government agent (other than an attorney for the government) who is engaged in enforcing the criminal laws and is within any category of officers authorized by the Attorney General to request a search warrant.

(b) Authority to Issue a Warrant. At the request of a federal law enforcement officer or an attorney for the government:

(1) a magistrate judge with authority in the district—or if none is reasonably available, a judge of a state court of record in the district—has authority to issue a warrant to search for and seize a person or property located within the district;

(2) a magistrate judge with authority in the district has authority to issue a warrant for a person or property outside the district if the person or property is located within the district when the warrant is issued but might move or be moved outside the district before the warrant is executed; and

(3) a magistrate judge—in an investigation of domestic terrorism or international terrorism (as defined in 18 U.S.C. § 2331)—having authority in any district in which activities related to the terrorism may have occurred, may issue a warrant for a person or property within or outside that district.

(c) Persons or Property Subject to Search or Seizure. A warrant may be issued for any of the following:

(1) evidence of a crime;

(2) contraband, fruits of crime, or other items illegally possessed;

(3) property designed for use, intended for use, or used in committing a crime; or

(4) a person to be arrested or a person who is unlawfully restrained.

(d) Obtaining a Warrant.

(1) *Probable Cause.* After receiving an affidavit or other information, a magistrate judge or a judge of a state court of record must issue the warrant if there is probable cause to search for and seize a person or property under Rule 41(c).

(2) *Requesting a Warrant in the Presence of a Judge.*

(A) *Warrant on an Affidavit.* When a federal law enforcement officer or an attorney for the government presents an affidavit in support of a warrant, the judge may require the affiant to appear personally and may examine under oath the affiant and any witness the affiant produces.

(B) *Warrant on Sworn Testimony.* The judge may wholly or partially dispense with a written affidavit and base a warrant on sworn testimony if doing so is reasonable under the circumstances.

(C) *Recording Testimony.* Testimony taken in support of a warrant must be recorded by a court reporter or by a suitable recording device, and the judge must file the transcript or recording with the clerk, along with any affidavit.

(3) *Requesting a Warrant by Telephonic or Other Means.*

(A) *In General.* A magistrate judge may issue a warrant based on information communicated by telephone or other appropriate means, including facsimile transmission.

(B) *Recording Testimony.* Upon learning that an applicant is requesting a warrant, a magistrate judge must:

(i) place under oath the applicant and any person on whose testimony the application is based; and

(ii) make a verbatim record of the conversation with a suitable recording device, if available, or by a court reporter, or in writing.

(C) *Certifying Testimony.* The magistrate judge must have any recording or court reporter's notes transcribed, certify the transcription's accuracy, and file a copy of the record and the transcription with the clerk. Any written verbatim record must be signed by the magistrate judge and filed with the clerk.

(D) *Suppression Limited.* Absent a finding of bad faith, evidence obtained from a warrant issued under Rule 41(d)(3)(A) is not subject to suppression on the ground that issuing the warrant in that manner was unreasonable under the circumstances.

(e) Issuing the Warrant.

(1) *In General.* The magistrate judge or a judge of a state court of record must issue the warrant to an officer authorized to execute it.

(2) *Contents of the Warrant.* The warrant must identify the person or property to be searched, identify any person or property to be seized, and designate the magistrate judge to whom it must be returned. The warrant must command the officer to:

(A) execute the warrant within a specified time no longer than 10 days;

(B) execute the warrant during the daytime, unless the judge for good cause expressly authorizes execution at another time; and

(C) return the warrant to the magistrate judge designated in the warrant.

(3) *Warrant by Telephonic or Other Means.* If a magistrate judge decides to proceed under Rule 41(d)(3)(A), the following additional procedures apply:

(A) *Preparing a Proposed Duplicate Original Warrant.* The applicant must prepare a "proposed duplicate original warrant" and must read or otherwise transmit the contents of that document verbatim to the magistrate judge.

(B) *Preparing an Original Warrant.* The magistrate judge must enter the contents of the proposed duplicate original warrant into an original warrant.

(C) *Modifications.* The magistrate judge may direct the applicant to modify the proposed duplicate original warrant. In that case, the judge must also modify the original warrant.

(D) *Signing the Original Warrant and the Duplicate Original Warrant.* Upon determining to issue the warrant, the magistrate judge must immediately sign the original warrant, enter on its face the exact time it issued, and direct the applicant to sign the judge's name on the duplicate original warrant.

(f) Executing and Returning the Warrant.

(1) *Noting the Time.* The officer executing the warrant must enter on its face the exact date and time it is executed.

(2) *Inventory.* An officer present during the execution of the warrant must prepare and verify an inventory of any property seized. The officer must do so in the presence of another officer and the person from whom, or from whose premises, the property was taken. If either one is not present, the officer must prepare and verify the inventory in the presence of at least one other credible person.

(3) *Receipt.* The officer executing the warrant must:

(A) give a copy of the warrant and a receipt for the property taken to the person from whom, or from whose premises, the property was taken; or

(B) leave a copy of the warrant and receipt at the place where the officer took the property.

(4) *Return*. The officer executing the warrant must promptly return it—together with a copy of the inventory—to the magistrate judge designated on the warrant. The judge must, on request, give a copy of the inventory to the person from whom, or from whose premises, the property was taken and to the applicant for the warrant.

(g) Motion to Return Property. A person aggrieved by an unlawful search and seizure of property or by the deprivation of property may move for the property's return. The motion must be filed in the district where the property was seized. The court must receive evidence on any factual issue necessary to decide the motion. If it grants the motion, the court must return the property to the movant, but may impose reasonable conditions to protect access to the property and its use in later proceedings.

(h) Motion to Suppress. A defendant may move to suppress evidence in the court where the trial will occur, as Rule 12 provides.

(i) Forwarding Papers to the Clerk. The magistrate judge to whom the warrant is returned must attach to the warrant a copy of the return, of the inventory, and of all other related papers and must deliver them to the clerk in the district where the property was seized.

———

100. In the absence of special circumstances, Rule 41(d) requires an officer executing a warrant to give a copy of the warrant to the person whose premises are to be searched, if present, before the search is executed. United States v. Gantt, 194 F.3d 987 (9th Cir.1999) (deliberate violation of Rule 41(d) required suppression of evidence).

It is a violation of the Fourth Amendment for police who are executing a search warrant to allow members of the media or other persons to accompany them into the premises to be searched, if their presence is not in aid of execution of the warrant. Wilson v. Layne, 526 U.S. 603 (1999). (The Court (8–1) held also, however, that since the law was not clearly established at the time of the search, police officers who permitted members of the media to accompany them were entitled to qualified immunity as defendants in a lawsuit under 42 U.S.C. § 1983, charging them with a violation of the rights of the persons whose home was searched.)

———

Illinois v. Gates

462 U.S. 213, 103 S.Ct. 2317, 76 L.Ed.2d 527 (1983)

■ JUSTICE REHNQUIST delivered the opinion of the Court.

Respondents Lance and Susan Gates were indicted for violation of state drug laws after police officers, executing a search warrant, discovered marihuana and other contraband in their automobile and home. Prior to trial the Gateses moved to suppress evidence seized during this search. The

Illinois Supreme Court affirmed the decisions of lower state courts granting the motion. . . . It held that the affidavit submitted in support of the State's application for a warrant to search the Gateses' property was inadequate under this Court's decisions in Aguilar v. Texas, 378 U.S. 108 (1964) and Spinelli v. United States, 393 U.S. 410 (1969).

We granted certiorari to consider the application of the Fourth Amendment to a magistrate's issuance of a search warrant on the basis of a partially corroborated anonymous informant's tip. . . .

. . .

. . . A chronological statement of events usefully introduces the issues at stake. Bloomingdale, Ill., is a suburb of Chicago located in Du Page County. On May 3, 1978, the Bloomingdale Police Department received by mail an anonymous handwritten letter which read as follows:

This letter is to inform you that you have a couple in your town who strictly make their living on selling drugs. They are Sue and Lance Gates, they live on Greenway, off Bloomingdale Rd. in the condominiums. Most of their buys are done in Florida. Sue his wife drives their car to Florida, where she leaves it to be loaded up with drugs, then Lance flys down and drives it back. Sue flys back after she drops the car off in Florida. May 3 she is driving down there again and Lance will be flying down in a few days to drive it back. At the time Lance drives the car back he has the trunk loaded with over $100,000.00 in drugs. Presently they have over $100,000.00 worth of drugs in their basement.

They brag about the fact they never have to work, and make their entire living on pushers.

I guarantee if you watch them carefully you will make a big catch. They are friends with some big drugs dealers, who visit their house often.

Lance & Susan Gates

Greenway

in Condominiums

The letter was referred by the Chief of Police of the Bloomingdale Police Department to Detective Mader, who decided to pursue the tip. Mader learned, from the office of the Illinois Secretary of State, that an Illinois driver's license had been issued to one Lance Gates, residing at a stated address in Bloomingdale. He contacted a confidential informant, whose examination of certain financial records revealed a more recent address for the Gateses, and he also learned from a police officer assigned to O'Hare Airport that "L. Gates" had made a reservation on Eastern Airlines flight 245 to West Palm Beach, Fla., scheduled to depart from Chicago on May 5 at 4:15 p.m.

Mader then made arrangements with an agent of the Drug Enforcement Administration for surveillance of the May 5 Eastern Airlines flight. The agent later reported to Mader that Gates had boarded the flight, and that federal agents in Florida had observed him arrive in West Palm Beach and take a taxi to the nearby Holiday Inn. They also reported that Gates went to a room registered to one Susan Gates and that, at 7:00 o'clock the next morning, Gates and an unidentified woman left the motel in a Mercury bearing Illinois license plates and drove northbound on an interstate frequently used by travelers to the Chicago area. In addition, the DEA agent informed Mader that the license plate number on the Mercury was registered to a Hornet station wagon owned by Gates. The agent also advised Mader that the driving time between West Palm Beach and Bloomingdale was approximately 22 to 24 hours.

Mader signed an affidavit setting forth the foregoing facts, and submitted it to a judge of the Circuit Court of Du Page County, together with a copy of the anonymous letter. The judge of that court thereupon issued a search warrant for the Gateses' residence and for their automobile. The judge, in deciding to issue the warrant, could have determined that the *modus operandi* of the Gateses had been substantially corroborated. As the anonymous letter predicted, Lance Gates had flown from Chicago to West Palm Beach late in the afternoon of May 5th, had checked into a hotel room registered in the name of his wife, and, at 7:00 o'clock the following morning, had headed north, accompanied by an unidentified woman, out of West Palm Beach on an interstate highway used by travelers from South Florida to Chicago in an automobile bearing a license plate issued to him.

At 5:15 a.m. on March 7th, only 36 hours after he had flown out of Chicago, Lance Gates, and his wife, returned to their home in Bloomingdale, driving the car in which they had left West Palm Beach some 22 hours earlier. The Bloomingdale police were awaiting them, searched the trunk of the Mercury, and uncovered approximately 350 pounds of marihuana. A search of the Gateses' home revealed marihuana, weapons, and other contraband. The Illinois Circuit Court ordered suppression of all these items, on the ground that the affidavit submitted to the Circuit Judge failed to support the necessary determination of probable cause to believe that the Gateses' automobile and home contained the contraband in question. This decision was affirmed in turn by the Illinois Appellate Court . . . and by a divided vote of the Supreme Court of Illinois. . . .

The Illinois Supreme Court concluded—and we are inclined to agree—that, standing alone, the anonymous letter sent to the Bloomingdale Police Department would not provide the basis for a magistrate's determination that there was probable cause to believe contraband would be found in the Gateses' car and home. The letter provides virtually nothing from which one might conclude that its author is either honest or his information reliable; likewise, the letter gives absolutely no indication of the basis for the writer's predictions regarding the Gateses' criminal activities. Something more was required, then, before a magistrate could conclude that there was probable cause to believe that contraband would be found in the Gateses' home and car. . . .

The Illinois Supreme Court also properly recognized that Detective Mader's affidavit might be capable of supplementing the anonymous letter with information sufficient to permit a determination of probable cause. . . . In holding that the affidavit in fact did not contain sufficient additional information to sustain a determination of probable cause, the

Illinois court applied a "two-pronged test," derived from our decision in Spinelli v. United States, 393 U.S. 410 (1969). The Illinois Supreme Court, like some others, apparently understood *Spinelli* as requiring that the anonymous letter satisfy each of two independent requirements before it could be relied on. . . . According to this view, the letter, as supplemented by Mader's affidavit, first had to adequately reveal the "basis of knowledge" of the letterwriter—the particular means by which he came by the information given in his report. Second, it had to provide facts sufficiently establishing either the "veracity" of the affiant's informant, or, alternatively, the "reliability" of the informant's report in this particular case.

The Illinois court, alluding to an elaborate set of legal rules that have developed among various lower courts to enforce the "two-pronged test," found that the test had not been satisfied. First, the "veracity" prong was not satisfied because, "[t]here was simply no basis [for] conclud[ing] that the anonymous person [who wrote the letter to the Bloomingdale Police Department] was credible." . . . The court indicated that corroboration by police of details contained in the letter might never satisfy the "veracity" prong, and in any event, could not do so if, as in the present case, only "innocent" details are corroborated. . . . In addition, the letter gave no indication of the basis of its writer's knowledge of the Gateses' activities. The Illinois court understood *Spinelli* as permitting the detail contained in a tip to be used to infer that the informant had a reliable basis for his statements, but it thought that the anonymous letter failed to provide sufficient detail to permit such an inference. Thus, it concluded that no showing of probable cause had been made.

We agree with the Illinois Supreme Court that an informant's "veracity," "reliability," and "basis of knowledge" are all highly relevant in determining the value of his report. We do not agree, however, that these elements should be understood as entirely separate and independent requirements to be rigidly exacted in every case, which the opinion of the Supreme Court of Illinois would imply. Rather, as detailed below, they should be understood simply as closely intertwined issues that may usefully illuminate the common-sense, practical question whether there is "probable cause" to believe that contraband or evidence is located in a particular place.

III

This totality-of-the-circumstances approach is far more consistent with our prior treatment of probable cause than is any rigid demand that specific "tests" be satisfied by every informant's tip. Perhaps the central teaching of our decisions bearing on the probable cause standard is that it is a "practical, nontechnical conception." Brinegar v. United States, 338 U.S. 160, 176 (1949). "In dealing with probable cause . . . as the very name implies, we deal with probabilities. These are not technical; they are the factual and practical considerations of everyday life on which reasonable and prudent men, not legal technicians, act." Id., at 175. . . .

[P]robable cause is a fluid concept—turning on the assessment of probabilities in particular factual contexts—not readily, or even usefully, reduced to a neat set of legal rules. Informants' tips doubtless come in many shapes and sizes from many different types of persons. . . . Rigid legal rules are ill-suited to an area of such diversity. . . .

Moreover, the "two-pronged test" directs analysis into two largely independent channels—the informant's "veracity" or "reliability" and his "basis of knowledge." . . . There are persuasive arguments against according these two elements such independent status. Instead, they are better understood as relevant considerations in the totality-of-the-circumstances analysis that traditionally has guided probable cause determinations: a deficiency in one may be compensated for, in determining the overall reliability of a tip, by a strong showing as to the other, or by some other indicia of reliability. . . .

If, for example, a particular informant is known for the unusual reliability of his predictions of certain types of criminal activities in a locality, his failure, in a particular case, to thoroughly set forth the basis of his knowledge surely should not serve as an absolute bar to a finding of probable cause based on his tip. . . . Likewise, if an unquestionably honest citizen comes forward with a report of criminal activity—which if fabricated would subject him to criminal liability—we have found rigorous scrutiny of the basis of his knowledge unnecessary. . . . Conversely, even if we entertain some doubt as to an informant's motives, his explicit and detailed description of alleged wrongdoing, along with a statement that the event was observed first-hand, entitles his tip to greater weight than might otherwise be the case. Unlike a totality-of-the-circumstances analysis, which permits a balanced assessment of the relative weights of all the various indicia of reliability (and unreliability) attending an informant's tip, the "two-pronged test" has encouraged an excessively technical dissection of informants' tips, with undue attention being focused on isolated issues that cannot sensibly be divorced from the other facts presented to the magistrate.

. . .

We also have recognized that affidavits "are normally drafted by non-lawyers in the midst and haste of a criminal investigation. Technical requirements of elaborate specificity once exacted under common law pleading have no proper place in this area." United States v. Ventresca, supra, 380 U.S. 102, 108 (1965). Likewise, search and arrest warrants long have been issued by persons who are neither lawyers nor judges, and who certainly do not remain abreast of each judicial refinement of the nature of "probable cause." . . . The rigorous inquiry into the *Spinelli* prongs and the complex superstructure of evidentiary and analytical rules that some have seen implicit in our *Spinelli* decision, cannot be reconciled with the fact that many warrants are—quite properly . . . issued on the basis of nontechnical, common-sense judgments of laymen applying a standard less demanding than those used in more formal legal proceedings. Likewise, given the informal, often hurried context in which it must be applied, the "built-in subtleties," Stanley v. State, 313 A.2d 847, 860 (1974), of the "two-pronged test" are particularly unlikely to assist magistrates in determining probable cause.

Similarly, we have repeatedly said that after-the-fact scrutiny by courts of the sufficiency of an affidavit should not take the form of de novo review. A magistrate's "determination of probable cause should be paid great deference by reviewing courts." *Spinelli*, supra, at 419. "A grudging or negative attitude by reviewing courts toward warrants," *Ventresca*, 380 U.S., at 108, is inconsistent with the Fourth Amendment's strong preference for searches conducted pursuant to a warrant; "courts should not invalidate warrant[s] by interpreting affidavit[s] in a hypertechnical, rather than a commonsense, manner." Id., at 109.

If the affidavits submitted by police officers are subjected to the type of scrutiny some courts have deemed appropriate, police might well resort to warrantless searches, with the hope of relying on consent or some other exception to the Warrant Clause that might develop at the time of the search. In addition, the possession of a warrant by officers conducting an arrest or search greatly reduces the perception of unlawful or intrusive police conduct, by assuring "the individual whose property is searched or seized of the lawful authority of the executing officer, his need to search, and the limits of his power to search." United States v. Chadwick, 433 U.S. 1, 9 (1977). . . .

. . . The strictures that inevitably accompany the "two-pronged test" cannot avoid seriously impeding the task of law enforcement. . . . If, as the Illinois Supreme Court apparently thought, that test must be rigorously applied in every case, anonymous tips would be of greatly diminished value in police work. Ordinary citizens, like ordinary witnesses . . . generally do not provide extensive recitations of the basis of their everyday observations. Likewise, as the Illinois Supreme Court observed in this case, the veracity of persons supplying anonymous tips is by hypothesis largely unknown, and unknowable. As a result, anonymous tips seldom could survive a rigorous application of either of the *Spinelli* prongs. Yet, such tips, particularly when supplemented by independent police investigation, frequently contribute to the solution of otherwise "perfect crimes." While a conscientious assessment of the basis for crediting such tips is required by the Fourth Amendment, a standard that leaves virtually no place for anonymous citizen informants is not.

For all these reasons, we conclude that it is wiser to abandon the "two-pronged test" established by our decisions in *Aguilar* and *Spinelli*. In its place we reaffirm the totality-of-the-circumstances analysis that traditionally has informed probable cause determinations. . . . The task of the issuing magistrate is simply to make a practical, common-sense decision whether, given all the circumstances set forth in the affidavit before him, including the "veracity" and "basis of knowledge" of persons supplying hearsay information, there is a fair probability that contraband or evidence of a crime will be found in a particular place. And the duty of a reviewing court is simply to ensure that the magistrate had a "substantial basis for . . . conclud[ing]" that probable cause existed. Jones v. United States, 362 U.S. [257 (1960)], at 271. We are convinced that this flexible, easily applied standard will better achieve the accommodation of public and private interests that the Fourth Amendment requires than does the approach that has developed from *Aguilar* and *Spinelli*.

. . .

IV

Our decisions applying the totality-of-the-circumstances analysis outlined above have consistently recognized the value of corroboration of details of an informant's tip by independent police work. In Jones v. United States, 362 U.S., at 269, we held that an affidavit relying on hearsay "is not to be deemed insufficient on that score, so long as a substantial basis for crediting the hearsay is presented." We went on to say that even in making a warrantless arrest an officer "may rely upon information received through an informant, rather than upon his direct observations, so long as the informant's statement is reasonably corroborated by other matters within the officer's knowledge." Ibid. Likewise, we recognized the probative value of corroborative efforts of police officials in *Aguilar*—the source of the "two-pronged test"—by observing that if the police had made some effort to corroborate the informant's report at issue, "an entirely different case" would have been presented. *Aguilar*, 378 U.S., at 109, n.1.

Our decision in Draper v. United States, 358 U.S. 307 (1959), however, is the classic case on the value of corroborative efforts of police officials. There, an informant named Hereford reported that Draper would arrive in Denver on a train from Chicago on one of two days, and that he would be carrying a quantity of heroin. The informant also supplied a fairly detailed physical description of Draper, and predicted that he would be wearing a light colored raincoat, brown slacks and black shoes, and would be walking "real fast." Id. at 309. Hereford gave no indication of the basis for his information.

On one of the stated dates police officers observed a man matching this description exit a train arriving from Chicago; his attire and luggage matched Hereford's report and he was walking rapidly. We explained in *Draper* that, by this point in his investigation, the arresting officer "had personally verified every facet of the information given him by Hereford except whether petitioner had accomplished his mission and had the three ounces of heroin on his person or in his bag. And surely, with every other bit of Hereford's information being thus personally verified, [the officer] had 'reasonable grounds' to believe that the remaining unverified bit of Hereford's information—that Draper would have the heroin with him—was likewise true," id., at 313.

The showing of probable cause in the present case was fully as compelling as that in *Draper*. Even standing alone, the facts obtained through the independent investigation of Mader and the DEA at least suggested that the Gateses were involved in drug trafficking. In addition to being a popular vacation site, Florida is well-known as a source of narcotics and other illegal drugs. . . . Lance Gates' flight to Palm Beach, his brief, overnight stay in a motel, and apparent immediate return north to Chicago in the family car, conveniently awaiting him in West Palm Beach, is as suggestive of a prearranged drug run, as it is of an ordinary vacation trip.

In addition, the magistrate could rely on the anonymous letter, which had been corroborated in major part by Mader's efforts—just as had occurred in *Draper*.[5] The Supreme Court of Illinois reasoned that *Draper* involved an informant who had given reliable information on previous occasions, while the honesty and reliability of the anonymous informant in this case were unknown to the Bloomingdale police. While this distinction might be an apt one at the time the Police Department received the anonymous letter, it became far less significant after Mader's independent investigative work occurred. The corroboration of the letter's predictions that the Gates' car would be in Florida, that Lance Gates would fly to Florida in the next day or so, and that he would drive the car north toward Bloomingdale all indicated, albeit not with certainty, that the informant's other assertions also were true. "[B]ecause an informant is right about some things, he is more probably right about other facts," *Spinelli*, 393 U.S., at 427 (White, J., concurring)—including the claim regarding the Gateses' illegal activity. This may well not be the type of "reliability" or "veracity" necessary to satisfy some views of the "veracity prong" of *Spinelli*, but we think it suffices for the practical, common-sense judgment called for in making a probable-cause determination. It is enough, for purposes of assessing probable cause, that "[c]orroboration through other sources of information reduced the chances of a reckless or prevaricating tale," thus providing "a substantial basis for crediting the hearsay." Jones v. United States, 362 U.S., at 269, 271.

Finally, the anonymous letter contained a range of details relating not just to easily obtained facts and conditions existing at the time of the tip, but to future actions of third parties ordinarily not easily predicted. The letterwriter's accurate information as to the travel plans of each of the Gateses was of a character likely obtained only from the Gateses themselves, or from someone familiar with their not entirely ordinary travel

5. The Illinois Supreme Court thought that the verification of details contained in the anonymous letter in this case amounted only to "[t]he corroboration of innocent activity," 423 N.E.2d 887, 893 (1981), and that this was insufficient to support a finding of probable cause. We are inclined to agree, however, with the observation of Justice Moran in his dissenting opinion that "[i]n this case, just as in *Draper*, seemingly innocent activity became suspicious in the light of the initial tip." 423 N.E.2d, at 896. And it bears noting that *all* of the corroborating detail established in *Draper*, supra, was of entirely innocent activity—a fact later pointed out by the Court. . . .

This is perfectly reasonable. As discussed previously, probable cause requires only a probability or substantial chance of criminal activity, not an actual showing of such activity. By hypothesis, therefore, innocent behavior frequently will provide the basis for a showing of probable cause; to require otherwise would be to *sub silentio* impose a drastically more rigorous definition of probable cause than the security of our citizens demands. We think the Illinois court attempted a too rigid classification of the types of conduct that may be relied upon in seeking to demonstrate probable cause. . . . In making a determination of probable cause the relevant inquiry is not whether particular conduct is "innocent" or "guilty," but the degree of suspicion that attaches to particular types of non-criminal acts.

plans. If the informant had access to accurate information of this type a magistrate could properly conclude that it was not unlikely that he also had access to reliable information of the Gateses' alleged illegal activities. Of course, the Gateses' travel plans might have been learned from a talkative neighbor or travel agent; under the "two-pronged test" developed from *Spinelli*, the character of the details in the anonymous letter might well not permit a sufficiently clear inference regarding the letterwriter's "basis of knowledge." But, as discussed previously, supra, at 235, probable cause does not demand the certainty we associate with formal trials. It is enough that there was a fair probability that the writer of the anonymous letter had obtained his entire story either from the Gateses or someone they trusted. And corroboration of major portions of the letter's predictions provides just this probability. It is apparent, therefore, that the judge issuing the warrant had a "substantial basis for . . . conclud[ing]" that probable cause to search the Gateses' home and car existed. The judgment of the Supreme Court of Illinois therefore must be reversed.[6]

―――――

101.

Probable cause—the area between bare suspicion and virtual certainty—describes not a point but a zone, within which the graver the crime the more latitude the police must be allowed. The shooting of seven persons (four fatally) by a team of criminals in the space of two hours is about as grave a crisis as a local police department will encounter. The police must be allowed more leeway in resolving it than when they are investigating the theft of a bicycle. Especially when a multiple murderer is at large in circumstances suggesting that he may be about to kill again, the interest in public safety is paramount.

It is true that the gravity of the crime and the threat of its imminent repetition usually are discussed in relation to the existence of an emergency justifying a search or arrest without a warrant . . . rather than in relation to probable cause for the search or arrest. But there is some judicial recognition of the latter relation. . . . The amount of information that prudent police will collect before deciding to make a search or an arrest, and hence the amount of probable cause they will have, is a function of the gravity of the crime, and especially the danger of its imminent repetition. If a multiple murderer is at large, the police must compress their investigation and make the decision to search or arrest on less information than if they could investigate at their leisure.

Llaguno v. Mingey, 763 F.2d 1560, 1565–66 (7th Cir.1985).

102. It is generally assumed that the standards of "probable cause" for an arrest and for a search are alike. The Court has cited search cases to explain the meaning of probable cause in arrest cases, see, e.g., Beck v.

―――――

[6] Justice White wrote an opinion concurring in the judgment. Justice Brennan wrote a dissenting opinion, which Justice Marshall joined. Justice Stevens wrote a dissenting opinion, which Justice Brennan joined.

℀AO106 (Rev. 7/87) Affidavit for Search Warrant

UNITED STATES DISTRICT COURT

DISTRICT OF _____

In the Matter of the Search of
(Name, address or brief description of person, property or premises to be searched)

**APPLICATION AND AFFIDAVIT
FOR SEARCH WARRANT**

Case Number: _____

I, _____ being duly sworn depose and say:

I am a(n) _____ and have reason to believe
                                    Official Title

that   ☐ on the person of or   ☐ on the property or premises known as (name, description and/or location)

in the _____ District of _____

there is now concealed a certain person or property, namely (describe the person or property to be seized)

which is (state one or more bases for search and seizure set forth under Rule 41(b) of the Federal Rules of Criminal Procedure)

concerning a violation of Title _____ United States code, Section(s) _____

The facts to support a finding of Probable Cause are as follows:

Continued on the attached sheet and made a part hereof: ☐ Yes   ☐ No

_____
Signature of Affiant

Sworn to before me and subscribed in my presence,

_____ at _____
Date   City   State

_____   _____
Name of Judicial Officer   Title of Judicial Officer   Signature of Judicial Officer

Ohio, 379 U.S. 89 (1964), and the reverse, see, e.g., Aguilar v. Texas, 378 U.S. 108 (1964). (But see Johnson v. United States, 333 U.S. 10 (1948), in which the Court suggested that evidence that might have justified a search was insufficient to justify an arrest.) Is it a sufficient explanation for the convergence of these standards that "the language of the Fourth Amendment, that '. . . no Warrants shall issue, but upon probable cause, supported by Oath or affirmation, and particularly describing . . . the persons or things to be seized,' of course applies to arrest as well as search warrants," Giordenello v. United States, 357 U.S. 480, 485–86 (1958)? Or that a lawful arrest may permit an otherwise unlawful search, see pp. 205–228 below? Or that it is often not clear whether the police conduct being evaluated is "really" a search or an arrest? See, e.g., Brinegar v. United States, 338 U.S. 160 (1949). Are there relevant differences between an arrest and a search which suggest that a different amount and/or kind of information should be required to authorize each? If so, are the differences such that a different standard for each can meaningfully and usefully be expressed?

103.   In Commonwealth v. White, 371 N.E.2d 777 (Mass.1977), the court held that statements obtained in violation of the *Miranda* requirements cannot be used as the basis of probable cause for issuance of a search warrant. The court relied on earlier cases holding that evidence obtained in violation of the Fourth Amendment cannot be used as the basis for a search warrant and that statements obtained in violation of *Miranda* cannot be considered in determining whether there is probable cause for an arrest. *White* was affirmed without opinion, by an equally divided Court. 439 U.S. 280 (1978).

104.   Evidence obtained in the course of a search pursuant to a valid search warrant is not inadmissible because the same evidence had been discovered in the course of a prior illegal search, provided that the warrant was obtained on the basis of information wholly independent of the prior illegality. Murray v. United States, 487 U.S. 533 (1988) (4–3).

105.   Premises of a third person. In Zurcher v. Stanford Daily, 436 U.S. 547 (1978) (5–3), police secured a warrant to search the offices of a student newspaper for photographs that might be evidence of a crime. There was no claim that the newspaper staff was at all involved in the crime. In an action under 42 U.S.C. § 1983, the lower court held that a warrant to search for materials in the possession of one who is not himself suspected of a crime could not be issued unless there was probable cause to believe that a subpoena *duces tecum* would be impracticable and that the possessor would not obey a court order that the material be preserved. The court also held that where the innocent possessor is a newspaper, special First Amendment interests are involved and require a clear showing that the warrant is necessary.

The Supreme Court reversed. Referring to past cases, it held that the fact that the possessor of seizable material was himself innocent is immaterial to the issuance of a warrant. Nor does the fact that the possessor is a newspaper require more than scrupulous observance of the Fourth Amendment's requirements.

The Justice Department has issued guidelines for federal agents' use of search warrants to obtain documentary evidence from innocent third parties. These guidelines allow use of a warrant only if less intrusive means like a subpoena would jeopardize the availability or usefulness of the materials sought. Special, stricter limitations are placed on use of a warrant that might intrude on a confidential relationship, for example when the third party is a lawyer or physician.

106. The Fourth Amendment authorizes the issuance only of search warrants "particularly describing the place to be searched." How particular must the description be?

The "place to be searched" is usually regarded as one premises or residential unit, however large or small, whether it is composed of multiple buildings, on one hand, or several units are contained within a single building, on the other. "For purposes of the Fourth Amendment, two or more apartments in the same building stand on the same footing as two or more houses. A single warrant cannot describe an entire building when cause is shown for searching only one apartment." Moore v. United States, 461 F.2d 1236, 1238 (D.C.Cir.1972). Accord United States v. Busk, 693 F.2d 28 (3d Cir.1982). See generally United States v. Votteller, 544 F.2d 1355, 1362–64 (6th Cir.1976), and cases cited.

A warrant authorizing the search of the apartment on the third floor of a building did not violate the particularity requirement of the Warrant Clause because it turned out that, unknown to the officers at the time the warrant was issued, there were two apartments on the floor and the officers had probable cause to search only one. Since the officers acted in accordance with the warrant and the facts as they believed them to be and ceased to search the second apartment when they realized that it was a separate unit, their presence in the latter was not a violation of the occupant's rights. Maryland v. Garrison, 480 U.S. 79 (1987) (6–3). See also United States v. Williams, 917 F.2d 1088 (8th Cir.1990) (officers obtained search warrant for rooming house reasonably believing it was a single family dwelling; search upheld).

107. Government agents obtained a warrant to search the premises of the Hillside Press, which was owned by the appellant and his brother. During the search, they found on the floor under a desk a briefcase that they had seen the appellant carry into the office a short while before. They searched the briefcase and found evidence incriminating the appellant. He moved to suppress the evidence on the ground that the briefcase was his personal property and was not covered by the warrant. The motion was denied. On appeal, the judgment was affirmed. United States v. Micheli, 487 F.2d 429 (1st Cir.1973). The court said:

> [W]e do not mean to suggest that anything found on the premises would necessarily fall within the scope of a warrant to search premises. Nor would we imply that the result would be different if, when the officers entered, appellant was physically holding the briefcase. To allow our decision to be interpreted as giving carte blanche to seize any objects reposing within premises covered by a warrant would be a disservice to law enforcement officials, individuals who may find their personal privacy invaded by a premises search warrant, and courts which must rule on suppression motions. Without attempting to write in black letters, we think some confusion may be spared by setting forth our rationale in deciding this case.

AO 93   (Rev. 8/98) Search Warrant

UNITED STATES DISTRICT COURT

District of _____

In the Matter of the Search of
(Name, address or brief description of person or property to be searched)

SEARCH WARRANT

Case Number: _____

TO: _____ and any Authorized Officer of the United States

Affidavit(s) having been made before me by _____ who has reason to believe
                                                                     Affiant

that   ☐   on the person of,   or   ☐   on the premises known as (name, description and/or location)

in the _____ District of _____ there is now
concealed a certain person or property, namely (describe the person or property)

I am satisfied that the affidavit(s) and any record testimony establish probable cause to believe that the person or property so described is now concealed on the person or premises above-described and establish grounds for the issuance of this warrant.

            YOU ARE HEREBY COMMANDED to search on or before _____
                                                                   Date
(not to exceed 10 days) the person or place named above for the person or property specified, serving this warrant and making the search   ☐   in the daytime — 6:00 AM to 10:00 P.M.   ☐   at anytime in the day or night as I find reasonable cause has been established and if the person or property be found there to seize same, leaving a copy of this warrant and receipt for the person or property taken, and prepare a written inventory of the person or property seized and promptly return this warrant to
_____ as required by law.
                                U.S. Judge or Magistrate

_____ at _____
Date and Time Issued   City and State

_____   _____
Name and Title of Judicial Officer   Signature of Judicial Officer

AO 93   (Rev. 8/98) Search Warrant (Reverse)

RETURN	**Case Number:**	
DATE WARRANT RECEIVED	DATE AND TIME WARRANT EXECUTED	COPY OF WARRANT AND RECEIPT FOR ITEMS LEFT WITH

INVENTORY MADE IN THE PRESENCE OF

INVENTORY OF PERSON OR PROPERTY TAKEN PURSUANT TO THE WARRANT

CERTIFICATION

I swear that this inventory is a true and detailed account of the person or property taken by me on the warrant.

_____

Subscribed, sworn to, and returned before me this date.

_____   _____
U.S. Judge or Magistrate   Date

Had appellant been a doctor on call at the Press and had the agents reason to know that the briefcase belonged to him, we would not reach the result we do here. We are not helped, in distinguishing these two situations, by the general proposition that a warrant to search premises does not permit a personal search of one who merely happens to be present at the time. For the question is: what is a personal search? A search of clothing currently worn is plainly within the ambit of a personal search and outside the scope of a warrant to search the premises. But a personal effect such as a briefcase, carried on to the premises and then tucked under a desk, does not clearly fall either within the realm of a personal search or a search of the premises. While the articulation of guiding principle may result in a line drawn with a stub of chalk rather than with a draftsman's pen, we nevertheless think principle exists.

Some courts approach the quest for principle by immunizing from a search under sanction of a premises warrant any item within the physical possession of an individual on the premises. . . . This has the virtue of precision but suffers from being at once too broad and too narrow. It is too broad in that a search warrant could be frustrated to the extent that there are hands inside the premises to pick up objects before the door is opened by the police. . . .

A focus on actual physical possession is too narrow, however, in that it would leave vulnerable many personal effects, such as wallets, purses, cases, or overcoats, which are often set down upon chairs or counters, hung on racks, or checked for convenient storage. The Fourth Amendment's basic interest in protecting privacy . . . and avoiding unreasonable governmental intrusions . . . is hardly furthered by making its applicability hinge upon whether the individual happens to be holding or wearing his personal belongings after he chances into a place where a search is underway. . . .

In determining to what extent a recognizable personal effect not currently worn, but apparently temporarily put down, such as a briefcase, falls outside the scope of a warrant to search the premises, we would be better advised to examine the relationship between the person and the place. . . . It should not be assumed that whatever is found on the premises described in the warrant necessarily falls within the proper scope of the search; rather, it is necessary to examine why a person's belongings happen to be on the premises. . . . [T]he protective boundary established by requiring a search warrant should encompass those extensions of a person which he reasonably seeks to preserve as private, regardless of where he may be.

[T]he problem we are discussing is a narrow one, falling between two primary rules, one permitting searches of premises, the other prohibiting searches of person. In this interstitial area where the literal application of either primary rule would frustrate the legitimate interests of either the police or the individual, we think it more consistent with the Fourth Amendment that searches of the personal effects of visitors to premises be appraised by reference to the reasonable expectations of privacy which visitors bring to premises rather than by attributing significance to a literal coup de main.

Our basic rationale for deciding that appellant's briefcase fell within the scope of the warrant to search the premises does not, therefore, rest upon the fact that at the time of the search his briefcase was out of his physical possession. Rather, we base our decision on the fact that, as co-owner of the Hillside Press, appellant was not in the position of a mere visitor or passerby who suddenly found his belongings vulnerable to a search of the premises. He had a special relation to the place, which meant that it could reasonably be expected that some of his personal belongings would be there. Thus, the showing of probable cause and necessity which was required prior to the initial intrusion into his office reasonably comprehended within its scope those personal articles, such as his briefcase, which might be lying about the office. The search of the briefcase, under these circumstances, was properly carried out within the scope of the warrant.

487 F.2d at 430–32. Compare Commonwealth v. Snow, 298 N.E.2d 804 (Mass.1973) (search of customer's coat on rack in barber shop).

108. Persons on the premises. In Ybarra v. Illinois, 444 U.S. 85 (1979) (6–3), police executed a valid warrant to search a tavern for evidence of narcotics offenses. During the search, the police frisked about a dozen patrons who were present. Narcotics were found on the person of the defendant. The Court held that the warrant to search the premises did not allow a search of the person of those who were present, who had "individualized [constitutional] protection . . . separate and distinct from the Fourth and Fourteenth Amendment protection possessed by the proprietor of the tavern." Id. at 91–92. The Court apparently allowed the possibility of a warrant to search premises as well as unnamed persons found on the premises, provided there was probable cause for such a search. Id. at 92 n.4. Compare United States v. Barlin, 686 F.2d 81 (2d Cir.1982) (search of handbag of person present while search is conducted upheld).

The Court has held, however, that officers executing a valid warrant to search for contraband have authority to detain the occupants of the premises while a proper search is conducted. Michigan v. Summers, 452 U.S. 692 (1981) (6–3). Referring to "stop" cases like Terry v. Ohio, p. 100 above, the Court said that these are "such limited intrusions on the personal security of those detained and are justified by such substantial law enforcement interests that they may be made on less than probable cause, so long as police have an articulable basis for suspecting criminal activity." 452 U.S. at 699. Among the "law enforcement interests" that the Court mentioned are "preventing flight in the event that incriminating evidence is found," "minimizing the risk of harm to the officers," and facilitating "the orderly completion of the search." Id. at 702–703.

The Court concluded: "If the evidence that a citizen's residence is harboring contraband is sufficient to persuade a judicial officer that an invasion of the citizen's privacy is justified, it is constitutionally reasonable to require that citizen to remain while officers of the law execute a valid warrant to search his home. Thus, for Fourth Amendment purposes, we hold that a warrant to search for contraband founded on probable cause implicitly carries with it the limited authority to detain the occupants of the premises while a proper search is conducted." Id. at 704–705. The Court observed that it did not decide whether the same result would be reached if a warrant authorized a search only for evidence.

Applying Michigan v. Summers, in Burchett v. Kiefer, 310 F.3d 937 (6th Cir.2002), the court held that police executing a search warrant may detain a person who approaches but does not go on the property and flees when the police tell him to get on the ground, for the duration of the search.

109. The Fourth Amendment requires that warrants "particularly" describe "the persons or things to be seized." In Marron v. United States, 275 U.S. 192, 196 (1927), the Court said: "The requirement that warrants shall particularly describe the things to be seized makes general searches under them impossible and prevents the seizure of one thing under a warrant describing another. As to what is to be taken, nothing is left to the discretion of the officer executing the warrant."

A warrant that fails to describe the things to be seized is invalid and is not saved by the fact that the application for the warrant described the things to be seized. Groh v. Ramirez, 540 U.S. ___ (2004) (7–2). The Court indicated that a warrant might incorporate some other document by reference, but the warrant in this case did not do so. A search pursuant to such a warrant is unconstitutional even if, in fact, the officers who conducted the search confined it to the items that were listed in the application.

See Lo-Ji Sales, Inc. v. New York, 442 U.S. 319 (1979) (warrant to search generally for obscene materials too broad); Stanford v. Texas, 379 U.S. 476 (1965) (warrant to search for books, records and other written material "concerning the Communist Party of Texas" too broad); United States v. Cardwell, 680 F.2d 75 (9th Cir.1982) (warrant to search for business records too broad); United States v. Klein, 565 F.2d 183 (1st Cir.1977) (generic description of sound tapes, which failed to distinguish ones to be seized from others, was too broad); United States v. Jarvis, 560 F.2d 494 (2d Cir.1977) ("John Doe" arrest warrant invalid even though person identified by "extrinsic evidence"); VonderAhe v. Howland, 508 F.2d 364 (9th Cir.1974) (warrant to seize "fiscal records" too broad).

See generally Andresen v. Maryland, 427 U.S. 463, 479–82 (1976), in which the Court observed: "We recognize that there are grave dangers inherent in executing a warrant authorizing a search and seizure of a person's papers that are not necessarily present in executing a warrant to search for physical objects whose relevance is more easily ascertainable. In searches for papers, it is certain that some innocuous documents will be examined, at least cursorily, in order to determine whether they are, in fact, among those papers authorized to be seized. Similar dangers, of course, are present in executing a warrant for the 'seizure' of telephone conversations. In both kinds of searches, responsible officials, including judicial officials, must take care to assure that they are conducted in a manner that minimizes unwarranted intrusions upon privacy." Id. at 482 n.11.

The good-faith exception to the exclusionary rule, see note 78, p. 148 above, was applied to an overbroad warrant in United States v. Maxwell, 920 F.2d 1028 (D.C.Cir.1990). But see United States v. George, 975 F.2d 72 (2d Cir.1992).

In United States v. Stefonek, 179 F.3d 1030 (7th Cir.1999), the court concluded that a warrant specifying the things to be seized as "evidence of crime" did not meet the particularity requirement, but that since the affidavit accompanying the application for the warrant contained an adequate specification and the agents executing the warrant knew the specification and complied with it, suppression of the evidence seized was not necessary. The court said that advising the person whose premises are searched of the scope of the search was a secondary purpose of the particularity requirement.

———

Horton v. California
496 U.S. 128, 110 S.Ct. 2301, 110 L.Ed.2d 112 (1990)

■ JUSTICE STEVENS delivered the opinion of the Court.

In this case we revisit an issue that was considered, but not conclusively resolved, in Coolidge v. New Hampshire, 403 U.S. 443 (1971): Whether the warrantless seizure of evidence of crime in plain view is prohibited by the Fourth Amendment if the discovery of the evidence was not inadvertent. We conclude that even though inadvertence is a characteristic of most legitimate "plain view" seizures, it is not a necessary condition.

I

Petitioner was convicted of the armed robbery of Erwin Wallaker, the treasurer of the San Jose Coin Club. When Wallaker returned to his home after the Club's annual show, he entered his garage and was accosted by two masked men, one armed with a machine gun and the other with an electrical shocking device, sometimes referred to as a "stun gun." The two men shocked Wallaker, bound and handcuffed him, and robbed him of jewelry and cash. During the encounter sufficient conversation took place to enable Wallaker subsequently to identify petitioner's distinctive voice. His identification was partially corroborated by a witness who saw the robbers leaving the scene and by evidence that petitioner had attended the coin show.

Sergeant LaRault, an experienced police officer, investigated the crime and determined that there was probable cause to search petitioner's home for the proceeds of the robbery and for the weapons used by the robbers. His affidavit for a search warrant referred to police reports that described the weapons as well as the proceeds, but the warrant issued by the Magistrate only authorized a search for the proceeds, including three specifically described rings.

Pursuant to the warrant, LaRault searched petitioner's residence, but he did not find the stolen property. During the course of the search, however, he discovered the weapons in plain view and seized them. Specifically, he seized an Uzi machine gun, a .38-caliber revolver, two stun guns, a handcuff key, a San Jose Coin Club advertising brochure, and a few items of clothing identified by the victim. LaRault testified that while he was searching for the rings, he also was interested in finding other evidence connecting petitioner to the robbery. Thus, the seized evidence was not discovered "inadvertently."

The trial court refused to suppress the evidence found in petitioner's home and, after a jury trial, petitioner was found guilty and sentenced to prison. The California Court of Appeal affirmed. . . . It rejected petitioner's argument that our decision in *Coolidge* required suppression of the seized evidence that had not been listed in the warrant because its discovery was not inadvertent. . . . The California Supreme Court denied petitioner's request for review. . . .

Because the California courts' interpretation of the "plain view" doctrine conflicts with the view of other courts, and because the unresolved issue is important, we granted certiorari. . . .

II

. . .

The right to security in person and property protected by the Fourth Amendment may be invaded in quite different ways by searches and seizures. A search compromises the individual interest in privacy; a seizure deprives the individual of dominion over his or her person or property. . . . The "plain-view" doctrine is often considered an exception to the general rule that warrantless searches are presumptively unreasonable, but this characterization overlooks the important difference between searches and seizures. If an article is already in plain view, neither its observation nor its seizure would involve any invasion of privacy. . . . A seizure of the article, however, would obviously invade the owner's possessory interest. . . . If "plain view" justifies an exception from an otherwise applicable warrant requirement, therefore, it must be an exception that is addressed to the concerns that are implicated by seizures rather than by searches.

The criteria that generally guide "plain view" seizures were set forth in Coolidge v. New Hampshire, 403 U.S. 443 (1971). The Court held that the police, in seizing two automobiles parked in plain view on the defendant's driveway in the course of arresting the defendant, violated the Fourth Amendment. Accordingly, particles of gun powder that had been subsequently found in vacuum sweepings from one of the cars could not be introduced in evidence against the defendant. The State endeavored to justify the seizure of the automobiles, and their subsequent search at the police station, on four different grounds, including the "plain-view" doctrine. The scope of that doctrine as it had developed in earlier cases was fairly summarized in these three paragraphs from Justice Stewart's opinion:

It is well established that under certain circumstances the police may seize evidence in plain view without a warrant. But it is important to keep in mind that, in the vast majority of cases, *any* evidence seized by the police will be in plain-view, at least at the moment of seizure. The problem with the "plain-view" doctrine has been to identify the circumstances in which plain view has legal significance rather than being simply the normal concomitant of any search, legal or illegal.

An example of the applicability of the "plain-view" doctrine is the situation in which the police have a warrant to search a given area for specified objects, and in the course of the search come across some other article of incriminating character. [. . .] Where the initial intrusion that brings the police within plain view of such an article is supported, not by a warrant, but by one of the recognized exceptions to the warrant requirement, the seizure is also legitimate. Thus the police may inadvertently come across evidence while in "hot pursuit" of a fleeing suspect. [. . .] And an object that comes into view during a search incident to arrest that is appropriately limited in scope under existing law may be seized without a warrant. [. . .] Finally, the "plain-view" doctrine has been applied where a police officer is not searching for evidence against the accused, but nonetheless inadvertently comes across an incriminating object. [. . .]

What the "plain-view" cases have in common is that the police officer in each of them had a prior justification for an intrusion in the course of which he came inadvertently across a piece of evidence incriminating the accused. The doctrine serves to supplement the prior justification—whether it be a warrant for another object, hot pursuit, search incident to lawful arrest, to some other legitimate reason for being present unconnected with a search directed against the accused—and permits the warrantless seizure. Of course, the extension of the original justification is legitimate only where it is immediately apparent to the police that they have evidence before them; the "plain-view" doctrine may not be used to extend a general exploratory search from one object to another until something incriminating at last emerges.

Id., at 465–66 (footnote omitted). Justice Stewart then described the two limitations on the doctrine that he found implicit in its rationale: First, "that plain view *alone* is never enough to justify the warrantless seizure of evidence, id., at 468; and second, that 'the discovery of evidence in plain view must be inadvertent.'" Id., at 469.

Justice Stewart's analysis of the "plain-view" doctrine did not command a majority, and a plurality of the Court has since made clear that the discussion is "not a binding precedent." Texas v. Brown, 460 U.S. 730, 737 (1983) (opinion of Rehnquist, J.). . . .

   . . .

II

Justice Stewart concluded that the inadvertence requirement was necessary to avoid a violation of the express constitutional requirement that a valid warrant must particularly describe the things to be seized. He explained:

The rationale of the exception to the warrant requirement, as just stated, is that a plain-view seizure will not turn an initially valid (and therefore limited) search into a "general" one, while the inconvenience of procuring a warrant to cover an inadvertent discovery is great. But where the discovery is anticipated, where the police know in advance the location of the evidence and intend to seize it, the situation is altogether different. The requirement of a warrant to seize imposes no inconvenience whatever, or at least none which is constitutionally cognizable in a legal system that regards warrantless searches as "per se unreasonable" in the absence of "exigent circumstances."

If the initial intrusion is bottomed upon a warrant that fails to mention a particular object, though the police know its location and intend to seize it, then there is a violation of the express constitutional requirement of "Warrants . . . particularly describing . . . [the] things to be seized."

403 U.S., at 469–71.

We find two flaws in this reasoning. First, evenhanded law enforcement is best achieved by the application of objective standards of conduct, rather than standards that depend upon the subjective state of mind of the officer. The fact that an officer is interested in an item of evidence and fully expects to find it in the course of a search should not invalidate its seizure if the search is confined in area and duration by the terms of a warrant or a valid exception to the warrant requirement. If the officer has knowledge approaching certainty that the item will be found, we see no reason why he or she would deliberately omit a particular description of the item to be seized from the application for a search warrant. Specification of the additional item could only permit the officer to expand the scope of the search. On the other hand, if he or she has a valid warrant to search for one item and merely a suspicion concerning the second, whether or not it amounts to probable cause, we fail to see why that suspicion should immunize the second item from seizure if it is found during a lawful search for the first. The hypothetical case put by Justice White in his dissenting opinion in *Coolidge* is instructive:

Let us suppose officers secure a warrant to search a house for a rifle. While staying well within the range of a rifle search, they discover two photographs of the murder victim, both in plain sight in the bedroom. Assume also that the discovery of the one photograph was inadvertent but finding the other was anticipated. The Court would permit the seizure of only one of the photographs. But in terms of the "minor" peril to Fourth Amendment values there is surely no difference between these two photographs: the interference with possession is the same in each case and the officers' appraisal of the photograph they expected to see is no less reliable than their judgment about the other. And in both situations the actual inconvenience and danger to evidence remain identical if the officers must depart and secure a warrant.

Id., at 516.

Second, the suggestion that the inadvertence requirement is necessary to prevent the police from conducting general searches, or from converting specific warrants into general warrants, is not persuasive because that interest is already served by the requirements that no warrant issue unless it "particularly describ[es] the place to be searched and the persons or things to be seized," . . . and that a warrantless search be circumscribed by the exigencies which justify its initiation. . . . Scrupulous adherence to these requirements serves the interests in limiting the area and duration of the search that the inadvertence requirement inadequately protects. Once those commands have been satisfied and the officer has a lawful right of access, however, no additional Fourth Amendment interest is furthered by requiring that the discovery of evidence be inadvertent. If the scope of the search exceeds that permitted by the terms of a validly issued warrant or the character of the relevant exception from the warrant requirement, the subsequent seizure is unconstitutional without more. . . .

In this case, the scope of the search was not enlarged in the slightest by the omission of any reference to the weapons in the warrant. Indeed, if the three rings and other items named in the warrant had been found at the outset—or if petitioner had them in his possession and had responded to the warrant by producing them immediately—no search for weapons could have taken place. . . .

As we have already suggested, by hypothesis the seizure of an object in plain view does not involve an intrusion on privacy. If the interest in privacy has been invaded, the violation must have occurred before the object came into plain view and there is no need for an inadvertence limitation on seizures to condemn it. The prohibition against general searches and general warrants serves primarily as a protection against unjustified intrusions on privacy. But reliance on privacy concerns that support that prohibition is misplaced when the inquiry concerns the scope of an exception that merely authorizes an officer with a lawful right of access to an item to seize it without a warrant.

In this case the items seized from petitioner's home were discovered during a lawful search authorized by a valid warrant. When they were discovered, it was immediately apparent to the officer that they constituted incriminating evidence. He had probable cause, not only to obtain a warrant to search for the stolen property, but also to believe that the weapons and handguns had been used in the crime he was investigating. The search was authorized by the warrant; the seizure was authorized by the "plain-view" doctrine. The judgment is affirmed.

. . . [7]

---

110. In Arizona v. Hicks, 480 U.S. 321 (1987) (6–3), the Court rejected the argument that the plain-view doctrine authorized police to *move* an object in order to examine it more closely. The Court said: "[T]aking action, unrelated to the objectives of the authorized intrusion, which exposed to view concealed portions of the apartment or its contents, did produce a new invasion of respondent's privacy unjustified by the

[7] Justice Brennan wrote a dissenting opinion, which Justice Marshall joined.

©AO 93A   (Rev. 5/85) Search Warrant Upon Oral Testimony

UNITED STATES DISTRICT COURT

District of _____

In the Matter of the Search of
(Name, address or brief description of person or property to be searched)

SEARCH WARRANT UPON ORAL TESTIMONY

Case Number: _____

TO: _____ and any Authorized Officer of the United States

Sworn oral testimony has been communicated to me by _____
Affiant

that ☐ on the person of, or ☐ on the premises known as (name, description and/or location)

in the _____ District of _____ there is now
concealed a certain person or property, namely (describe the person or property)

I am satisfied that the circumstances are such as to make it reasonable to dispense with a written affidavit and that there is probable cause to believe that the property or person so described is concealed on the person or premises above described and that grounds for application for issuance of the search warrant exist as communicated orally to me in a sworn statement which has been recorded electronically, stenographically, or in long-hand and upon the return of the warrant, will be transcribed, certified as accurate and attached hereto.

YOU ARE HEREBY COMMANDED to search on or before _____
Date

the person or place named above for the person or property specified, serving this warrant and making the search ☐ in the day-time — 6:00 AM to 10:00 PM   ☐ at anytime in the day or night as I find reasonable cause has been established and if the person or property be found there to seize same, leaving a copy of this warrant and receipt for the person or property taken, and prepare a written inventory of the person or property seized and promptly return this warrant to _____
U.S. Judge or Magistrate Judge

as required by law.

_____   at   _____
Date and Time Issued   City and State

_____   _____
Name and Title of Judicial Officer   Signature of Judicial Officer

I certify that on _____ at _____
Date Time

_____ orally authorized the
U.S. Judge or Magistrate Judge

issuance and execution of a search warrant conforming to all the foregoing terms.

_____   _____   _____
Name of affiant   Signature of affiant   Exact time warrant

exigent circumstance that validated the entry." Id. at 325. The police had moved stereo equipment, which they suspected, but did not have probable cause to believe, was stolen, in order to read its serial numbers.

111. Rule 41(e)(2)(A) provides that a warrant "must command the officer to . . . execute the warrant within a specified time no longer than 10 days." So long as the warrant is executed within that period, the officer may presumably choose a time that will facilitate an arrest. See note 8, p. 20 above.

112. Rule 41(e)(1) provides that a warrant must be issued "to an officer authorized to execute it." Referring to a comparable provision in an earlier version of the rule, in United States v. Soriano, 482 F.2d 469, 478 (5th Cir.1973), the court said that the requirement protected "several important interests. . . . [O]ne of its functions is to fix responsibility in the event the warrant is not executed. Also, it enables the magistrate to make a presearch determination that an appropriate officer will serve the warrant. It assists the person whose premises are to be searched in ensuring that the search will be made by an authorized officer and not by an imposter. And it provides a record so that, if necessary, the judicial processes can make a post-search determination that the search was conducted by an authorized officer." Where, however, there was only "technical noncompliance" with the requirement and "the magistrate knew in advance who was to serve the warrant, and the designated officer indeed served it," id. at 479, the search was not invalid.

113. Rule 41(e)(2)(B) provides that a warrant must ordinarily be executed during the daytime. Is there any requirement that a warrant be executed, if practicable, while the occupant of the premises is at home? See United States v. Gervato, 474 F.2d 40 (3d Cir.1973), concluding that there is not. In Payne v. United States, 508 F.2d 1391, 1394 (5th Cir.1975), the court followed *Gervato*, saying that notwithstanding the "knock-and-announce" requirement, see Wilson v. Arkansas p. 68 above, "forcible entry pursuant to a search warrant of unoccupied premises is not per se a violation of the Fourth Amendment." "The statutory requirements of judicial supervision based on probable cause, the requisites of specificity in describing the premises and the items to be seized, and the delivery of a written inventory of the items taken to the occupant or other competent person provide adequate safeguards against potential abuse and sufficiently limit police discretion."

114. Rule 41(f)(4) provides that "[t]he officer executing the warrant must promptly return it—together with a copy of the inventory—to the magistrate judge designated on the warrant." The failure to make a prompt return was held not to be "constitutionally significant" and, therefore, not to require suppression of evidence obtained pursuant to a valid warrant, in United States v. Hall, 505 F.2d 961 (3d Cir.1974). To the same effect, see United States v. Dudek, 530 F.2d 684 (6th Cir.1976) (cases cited). In *Hall*, the court said that suppression was required only if the defendant showed prejudice from the violation of the rule.

115. Suppose a defendant attacks a search warrant on the ground that the affidavits supporting the warrant are false. The Court considered the procedure for making such an attack and the circumstances in which an affidavit's falsity invalidates a warrant in Franks v. Delaware, 438 U.S.

154 (1978) (7–2). It concluded that, in order to avoid having to conduct a hearing without sufficient cause, a "substantial preliminary showing" of falsity is required.

> [W]here the defendant makes a substantial preliminary showing that a false statement knowingly and intentionally, or with reckless disregard for the truth, was included by the affiant in the warrant affidavit, and if the allegedly false statement is necessary to the finding of probable cause, the Fourth Amendment requires that a hearing be held at the defendant's request. In the event that at that hearing the allegation of perjury or reckless disregard is established by the defendant by a preponderance of the evidence, and, with the affidavit's false material set to one side, the affidavit's remaining content is insufficient to establish probable cause, the search warrant must be voided and the fruits of the search excluded to the same extent as if probable cause was lacking on the face of the affidavit.

> . . .

> . . . There is, of course, a presumption of validity with respect to the affidavit supporting the search warrant. To mandate an evidentiary hearing, the challenger's attack must be more than conclusory and must be supported by more than a mere desire to cross-examine. There must be allegations of deliberate falsehood or of reckless disregard for the truth, and those allegations must be accompanied by an offer of proof. They should point out specifically the portion of the warrant affidavit that is claimed to be false; and they should be accompanied by a statement of supporting reasons. Affidavits or sworn or otherwise reliable statements of witnesses should be furnished, or their absence satisfactorily explained. Allegations of negligence or innocent mistake are insufficient. The deliberate falsity or reckless disregard whose impeachment is permitted today is only that of the affiant, not of any nongovernmental informant. Finally, if these requirements are met, and if, when material that is the subject of the alleged falsity or reckless disregard is set to one side, there remains sufficient content in the warrant affidavit to support a finding of probable cause, no hearing is required. On the other hand, if the remaining content is insufficient, the defendant is entitled, under the Fourth and Fourteenth Amendments, to his hearing. Whether he will prevail at that hearing is, of course, another issue.

Id. at 155–56, 171–72.

Franks was applied in United States v. Stanert, 762 F.2d 775 (9th Cir.1985) (defendant's preliminary showing required evidentiary hearing); United States v. Namer, 680 F.2d 1088 (5th Cir.1982) (search warrant invalid); United States v. Cortina, 630 F.2d 1207 (7th Cir.1980) (same).

Without a Warrant

Chimel v. California

395 U.S. 752, 89 S.Ct. 2034, 23 L.Ed.2d 685 (1969)

■ MR. JUSTICE STEWART delivered the opinion of the Court.

This case raises basic questions concerning the permissible scope under the Fourth Amendment of a search incident to a lawful arrest.

The relevant facts are essentially undisputed. Late in the afternoon of September 13, 1965, three police officers arrived at the Santa Ana, California, home of the petitioner with a warrant authorizing his arrest for the burglary of a coin shop. The officers knocked on the door, identified themselves to the petitioner's wife, and asked if they might come inside. She ushered them into the house, where they waited 10 or 15 minutes until the petitioner returned home from work. When the petitioner entered the house, one of the officers handed him the arrest warrant and asked for permission to "look around." The petitioner objected, but was advised that "on the basis of the lawful arrest," the officers would nonetheless conduct a search. No search warrant had been issued.

Accompanied by the petitioner's wife, the officers then looked through the entire three-bedroom house, including the attic, the garage, and a small workshop. In some rooms the search was relatively cursory. In the master bedroom and sewing room, however, the officers directed the petitioner's wife to open drawers and "to physically move contents of the drawers from side to side so that [they] might view any items that would have come from [the] burglary." After completing the search, they seized numerous items—primarily coins, but also several medals, tokens, and a few other objects. The entire search took between 45 minutes and an hour.

At the petitioner's subsequent state trial on two charges of burglary, the items taken from his house were admitted into evidence against him, over his objection that they had been unconstitutionally seized. He was convicted, and the judgments of conviction were affirmed by both the California District Court of Appeal . . . and the California Supreme Court. . . . Both courts accepted the petitioner's contention that the arrest warrant was invalid because the supporting affidavit was set out in conclusory terms, but held that since the arresting officers had procured the warrant "in good faith," and since in any event they had had sufficient information to constitute probable cause for the petitioner's arrest, that arrest had been lawful. From this conclusion the appellate courts went on to hold that the search of the petitioner's home had been justified, despite the absence of a search warrant, on the ground that it had been incident to a valid arrest. We granted certiorari in order to consider the petitioner's substantial constitutional claims. . . .

Without deciding the question, we proceed on the hypothesis that the California courts were correct in holding that the arrest of the petitioner was valid under the Constitution. This brings us directly to the question whether the warrantless search of the petitioner's entire house can be constitutionally justified as incident to that arrest. The decisions of this

Court bearing upon that question have been far from consistent, as even the most cursory review makes evident.

. . .

[I]n Harris v. United States, 331 U.S. 145, decided in 1947 . . . officers had obtained a warrant for Harris' arrest on the basis of his alleged involvement with the cashing and interstate transportation of a forged check. He was arrested in the living room of his four-room apartment, and in an attempt to recover two canceled checks thought to have been used in effecting the forgery, the officers undertook a thorough search of the entire apartment. Inside a desk drawer they found a sealed envelope marked "George Harris, personal papers." The envelope, which was then torn open, was found to contain altered selective service documents, and those documents were used to secure Harris' conviction for violating the Selective Training and Service Act of 1940. The Court rejected Harris' Fourth Amendment claim, sustaining the search as "incident to arrest." Id., at 151.

Only a year after *Harris*, however, the pendulum swung again. In Trupiano v. United States, 334 U.S. 699, agents raided the site of an illicit distillery, saw one of several conspirators operating the still, and arrested him, contemporaneously "seiz[ing] the illicit distillery." Id., at 702. The Court held that the arrest and others made subsequently had been valid, but that the unexplained failure of the agents to procure a search warrant—in spite of the fact that they had had more than enough time before the raid to do so—rendered the search unlawful. The opinion stated:

> It is a cardinal rule that, in seizing goods and articles, law enforcement agents must secure and use search warrants wherever reasonably practicable. . . . This rule rests upon the desirability of having magistrates rather than police officers determine when searches and seizures are permissible and what limitations should be placed upon such activities. . . . To provide the necessary security against unreasonable intrusions upon the private lives of individuals, the framers of the Fourth Amendment required adherence to judicial processes wherever possible. And subsequent history has confirmed the wisdom of that requirement.

> . . .

> A search or seizure without a warrant as an incident to a lawful arrest has always been considered to be a strictly limited right. It grows out of the inherent necessities of the situation at the time of the arrest. But there must be something more in the way of necessity than merely a lawful arrest.

Id., at 705, 708.

In 1950, two years after *Trupiano*, came United States v. Rabinowitz, 339 U.S. 56, the decision upon which California primarily relies in the case now before us. In *Rabinowitz*, federal authorities had been informed that the defendant was dealing in stamps bearing forged overprints. On the basis of that information they secured a warrant for his arrest, which they executed at his one-room business office. At the time of the arrest, the officers "searched the desk, safe, and file cabinets in the office for about an hour and a half," id., at 59, and seized 573 stamps with forged overprints. The stamps were admitted into evidence at the defendant's trial, and this Court affirmed his conviction, rejecting the contention that the warrantless search had been unlawful. The Court held that the search in its entirety fell within the principle giving law enforcement authorities "[t]he right 'to search the place where the arrest is made in order to find and seize things connected with the crime....'" Id., at 61. *Harris* was regarded as "ample authority" for that conclusion. Id., at 63. The opinion rejected the rule of *Trupiano* that "in seizing goods and articles, law enforcement agents must secure and use search warrants wherever reasonably practicable." The test, said the Court, "is not whether it is reasonable to procure a search warrant, but whether the search was reasonable." Id., at 66.

Rabinowitz has come to stand for the proposition, inter alia, that a warrantless search "incident to a lawful arrest" may generally extend to the area that is considered to be in the "possession" or under the "control" of the person arrested. And it was on the basis of that proposition that the California courts upheld the search of the petitioner's entire house in this case. That doctrine, however, at least in the broad sense in which it was applied by the California courts in this case, can withstand neither historical nor rational analysis.

Even limited to its own facts, the *Rabinowitz* decision was, as we have seen, hardly founded on an unimpeachable line of authority. . . .

Nor is the rationale by which the State seeks here to sustain the search of the petitioner's house supported by a reasoned view of the background and purpose of the Fourth Amendment. Mr. Justice Frankfurter wisely pointed out in his *Rabinowitz* dissent that the Amendment's proscription of "unreasonable searches and seizures" must be read in light of "the history that gave rise to the words"—a history of "abuses so deeply felt by the Colonies as to be one of the potent causes of the Revolution...." 339 U.S., at 69. The Amendment was in large part a reaction to the general warrants and warrantless searches that had so alienated the colonists and had helped speed the movement for independence. In the scheme of the Amendment, therefore, the requirement that "no Warrants shall issue, but upon probable cause," plays a crucial part. As the Court put it in McDonald v. United States, 335 U.S. 451:

> We are not dealing with formalities. The presence of a search warrant serves a high function. Absent some grave emergency, the Fourth Amendment has interposed a magistrate between the citizen and the police. This was done not to shield criminals nor to make the home a safe haven for illegal activities. It was done so that an objective mind might weigh the need to invade that privacy in order to enforce the law. The right of privacy was deemed too precious to entrust to the discretion of those whose job is the detection of crime and the arrest of criminals. . . . And so the Constitution requires a magistrate to pass on the desires of the police before they violate the privacy of the home.

We cannot be true to that constitutional requirement and excuse the absence of a search warrant without a showing by those who seek exemption from the constitutional mandate that the exigencies of the situation made that course imperative.

Id., at 455–56. . . . Clearly, the general requirement that a search warrant be obtained is not lightly to be dispensed with, and "the burden is on those seeking [an] exemption [from the requirement] to show the need for it. . . ." United States v. Jeffers, 342 U.S. 48, 51.

Only last Term in Terry v. Ohio, 392 U.S. 1, we emphasized that "the police must, whenever practicable, obtain advance judicial approval of searches and seizures through the warrant procedure," id., at 20, and that "[t]he scope of [a] search must be 'strictly tied to and justified by' the circumstances which rendered its initiation permissible." Id., at 19. . . .

A similar analysis underlies the "search incident to arrest" principle, and marks its proper extent. When an arrest is made, it is reasonable for the arresting officer to search the person arrested in order to remove any weapons that the latter might seek to use in order to resist arrest or effect his escape. Otherwise, the officer's safety might well be endangered, and the arrest itself frustrated. In addition, it is entirely reasonable for the arresting officer to search for and seize any evidence on the arrestee's person in order to prevent its concealment or destruction. And the area into which an arrestee might reach in order to grab a weapon or evidentiary items must, of course, be governed by a like rule. A gun on a table or in a drawer in front of one who is arrested can be as dangerous to the arresting officer as one concealed in the clothing of the person arrested. There is ample justification, therefore, for a search of the arrestee's person and the area "within his immediate control"—construing that phrase to mean the area from within which he might gain possession of a weapon or destructible evidence.

There is no comparable justification, however, for routinely searching rooms other than that in which an arrest occurs—or, for that matter, for searching through all the desk drawers or other closed or concealed areas in that room itself. Such searches, in the absence of well-recognized exceptions, may be made only under the authority of a search warrant. The "adherence to judicial processes" mandated by the Fourth Amendment requires no less.

     . . .

It is argued in the present case that it is "reasonable" to search a man's house when he is arrested in it. But that argument is founded on little more than a subjective view regarding the acceptability of certain sorts of police conduct, and not on considerations relevant to Fourth Amendment interests. Under such an unconfined analysis, Fourth Amendment protection in this area would approach the evaporation point. It is not easy to explain why, for instance, it is less subjectively "reasonable" to search a man's house when he is arrested on his front lawn—or just down the street—than it is when he happens to be in the house at the time of arrest. As Mr. Justice Frankfurter put it:

> To say that the search must be reasonable is to require some criterion of reason. It is no guide at all either for a jury or for district judges or the police to say that an "unreasonable search" is forbidden—that the search must be reasonable. What is the test of reason which makes a search reasonable? The test is the reason underlying and expressed by the Fourth Amendment: the history and the experience which it embodies and the safeguards afforded by it against the evils to which it was a response.

United States v. Rabinowitz, 339 U.S., at 83 (dissenting opinion). Thus, although "[t]he recurring questions of the reasonableness of searches" depend upon "the facts and circumstances—the total atmosphere of the case," id., at 63, 66 (opinion of the Court), those facts and circumstances must be viewed in the light of established Fourth Amendment principles.

It would be possible, of course, to draw a line between *Rabinowitz* and *Harris* on the one hand, and this case on the other. For *Rabinowitz* involved a single room, and *Harris* a four-room apartment, while in the case before us an entire house was searched. But such a distinction would be highly artificial. The rationale that allowed the searches and seizures in *Rabinowitz* and *Harris* would allow the searches and seizures in this case. No consideration relevant to the Fourth Amendment suggests any point of rational limitation, once the search is allowed to go beyond the area from which the person arrested might obtain weapons or evidentiary items. The only reasoned distinction is one between a search of the person arrested and the area within his reach on the one hand, and more extensive searches on the other.

The petitioner correctly points out that one result of decisions such as *Rabinowitz* and *Harris* is to give law enforcement officials the opportunity to engage in searches not justified by probable cause, by the simple expedient of arranging to arrest suspects at home rather than elsewhere. We do not suggest that the petitioner is necessarily correct in his assertion that such a strategy was utilized here, but the fact remains that had he been arrested earlier in the day, at his place of employment rather than at home, no search of his house could have been made without a search warrant. In any event, even apart from the possibility of such police tactics, the general point so forcefully made by Judge Learned Hand in United States v. Kirschenblatt, 16 F.2d 202, remains:

> After arresting a man in his house, to rummage at will among his papers in search of whatever will convict him, appears to us to be indistinguishable from what might be done under a general warrant; indeed, the warrant would give more protection, for presumably it must be issued by a magistrate. True, by hypothesis the power would not exist if the supposed offender were not found on the premises; but it is small consolation to know that one's papers are safe only so long as one is not at home.

Id., at 203.

Rabinowitz and *Harris* have been the subject of critical commentary for many years, and have been relied upon less and less in our own decisions. It is time, for the reasons we have stated, to hold that on their own facts, and insofar as the principles they stand for are inconsistent with those that we have endorsed today, they are no longer to be followed.

Application of sound Fourth Amendment principles to the facts of this case produces a clear result. The search here went far beyond the petitioner's person and the area from within which he might have obtained either a weapon or something that could have been used as evidence against him. There was no constitutional justification, in the absence of a search warrant, for extending the search beyond that area. The scope of the search was, therefore, "unreasonable" under the Fourth and Fourteenth Amendments, and the petitioner's conviction cannot stand.[8]

---

116. As the Court acknowledged in *Chimel,* above, the course of decisions concerning the scope of a valid search "incident to an arrest" has not been unwavering. In addition to the cases cited, see Weeks v. United States, 232 U.S. 383 (1914); Carroll v. United States, 267 U.S. 132 (1925); Agnello v. United States, 269 U.S. 20 (1925); Marron v. United States, 275 U.S. 192 (1927); Go-Bart Importing Co. v. United States, 282 U.S. 344 (1931); United States v. Lefkowitz, 285 U.S. 452 (1932), all discussed elsewhere in the Court's opinion in *Chimel.* See also Kremen v. United States, 353 U.S. 346 (1957); Abel v. United States, 362 U.S. 217 (1960).

117. How should *Chimel* be applied to items on the defendant's person at the time of his arrest that are themselves containers of other items? Such things include small containers carried by almost everyone, like a wallet or pocketbook, as well as large containers, like a briefcase or suitcase.

In United States v. Simpson, 453 F.2d 1028 (10th Cir.1972), for example, the defendant was arrested on a warrant charging him with possession and transportation of explosives. At the time of his arrest his wallet, found in his pocket, was searched and someone else's selective service documents were found. Simpson was prosecuted for the unlawful possession of the documents. His motion to suppress the documents was denied. The court said:

> The general rule is that incident to a lawful arrest, a search without a warrant may be made of portable personal effects in the immediate possession of the person arrested. The discovery during a search of a totally unrelated object which provides grounds for prosecution of a crime different than that which the accused was arrested for does not render the search invalid. . . . We observe that although the

[8] Justice Harlan wrote a concurring opinion. Justice White wrote a dissenting opinion, see note 122, p. 215 below, which Justice Black joined.

general rule approved here does not require specific justification on a case-to-case basis, we take notice that knives and other small weapons can be secreted in wallets and that cards and addresses may disclose names of those who may have conspired with the person searched in the commission of the crime charged.

Id. at 1031. The reference to "personal property not immediately associated with the person," in *Chadwick*, p. 212 note 119 below, is evidently intended to refer to cases of this kind.

See, e.g., United States v. Harrison, 461 F.2d 1127 (5th Cir.1972). The defendant was arrested pursuant to a warrant charging him with parole violations. He was found lying on a mattress in his apartment. After arresting him, FBI agents found a wallet inside a cigar box on a table next to the mattress. There were documents in the wallet linking the defendant to new crimes. Relying on *Chimel*, the court upheld the use of the documents against him.

Is there any reason why the police should not remove a wallet and similar containers without searching them? Does *Chimel* on its own terms authorize the search of a wallet of an arrested person after it has been taken from his possession?

118. A group of about eight narcotics agents arrested the appellant Becker in his apartment at around midnight.

Appellant was sitting on a couch in the living-dining room area of his apartment watching television. He was directed to stand next to a wall with his hands up against it. This location was approximately 12 feet from the corner of the couch where Becker was first seen, and was the nearest wall space free of furniture or openings. The arresting agent testified that he had no handcuffs and finally secured Becker with a belt. He stated that appellant kept turning around and "wasn't being real cooperative." Some four or five minutes elapsed before the prisoner was secured. Another agent who was in the same room said that Becker refused to follow orders—that he continued to turn around, kept his hands down instead of up and was constantly moving in a direction other than where he was told to remain. He described appellant's conduct as "resisting" and said it was almost five minutes before the resistance ended.

There was a desk-type table three to five feet from where appellant was standing and the L.S.D. tablets were found in one of its drawers which had been closed. The agent who discovered the drugs stated, "There was a time when I secured the chest to make sure there were no weapons." He said that when Becker had been subdued the other agent searched the prisoner while he checked the surrounding area for weapons. This witness testified that he had put his gun away before he began his search for weapons and that he was "no longer threatened by the situation." However, since Becker had not been tied with the belt at that time, he considered that there was "still a potential danger." It was admitted that Becker never tried to use physical force on any agent. . . . [T]he agent who subdued Becker stated that he was searching him when the pills were found and that he did not believe he had put the belt on appellant's arms at that time.

United States v. Becker, 485 F.2d 51, 53 (6th Cir.1973).

Was the search of the table drawer permitted under *Chimel*?

In United States v. Myers, 308 F.3d 251 (3d Cir.2002), the court considered at length the permissible scope of a search incident to an arrest. Distinguishing the search of the passenger compartment of an automobile after the driver's arrest, which is governed by the *Belton* rule (p. 214 note 121) the court said that a search incident to an arrest is "reasonable" under the Fourth Amendment only "when it is confined to, and controlled by, the circumstances that warrant the intrusion," 308 F.3d at 266. Noting that the defendant, who was handcuffed behind his back, lying face down, and watched by two armed police officers, would have to have been an acrobat or Houdini to gain access to a school bag lying a few feet from him, the court held that a search of the bag by a third police officer was not permissible. See United States v. Griffith, 537 F.2d 900, 904 (7th Cir.1976), in which the court said: "Once a suspect is under the control of arresting officers, the area of permissible search under *Chimel* is narrowed accordingly." The area which the officers could search was not enlarged by the fact that they allowed the person whom they arrested to move freely about the room while getting dressed. "They did not have the right to create a situation which gave them a pretext for searching beyond the area of defendant's immediate control."

In People v. Fitzpatrick, 300 N.E.2d 139 (N.Y.1973), however, the court held that "the authorized 'grabbable' area" under *Chimel* included a closet in which the defendant had been hiding, so that the police could search the closet after the defendant had been removed from the closet, handcuffed, and taken out of the room into the hall, where the police advised him of his rights and questioned him briefly before returning to the closet to search it. In a ruling similar to *Fitzpatrick*, the court held that a search incident to an arrest could be conducted after the defendant had been handcuffed and removed from the room, in United States v. Turner, 926 F.2d 883 (9th Cir.1991). The court said that since the area searched was under the arrested person's immediate control at the moment of arrest and could have been searched then, it was reasonable to delay the search for a few minutes for the officers' safety. Does the reasoning of *Chimel* support that conclusion? See, to the same effect, United States v. Abdul-Saboor, 85 F.3d 664, 668 (D.C.Cir.1996) (area subject to "incident" search is not literally area within defendant's control but turns on "whether the arrest and search are so separated in time or by intervening events that the latter cannot fairly be said to have been incident to the former").

119. In United States v. Chadwick, 433 U.S. 1 (1977), the Court upheld a ruling that federal agents could not make a warrantless search of a heavy, locked footlocker that the defendants had placed in the trunk of a car just before their arrest. "Once law enforcement officers have reduced luggage or other personal property not immediately associated with the person of the arrestee to their exclusive control, and there is no longer any danger that the arrestee might gain access to the property to seize a weapon or destroy evidence, a search of that property is no longer an incident of the arrest." Id. at 15.

In United States v. Eatherton, 519 F.2d 603 (1st Cir.1975), decided before *Chadwick*, the court upheld the search of a briefcase carried by the defendant, who was arrested on the street and dropped the briefcase to the ground, as he was ordered; before searching the briefcase, the arresting officers handcuffed the defendant behind his back and placed him in their car. The court said that while "a briefcase may be a different order of container from a cigarette box, it is not easy to rest a principled articulation of the reach of the fourth amendment upon the distinction." Declining to rely on such "gossamer distinctions," the court concluded also that the cases indicated no difference between searching such a container if it were removed from the defendant's person and searching it after it had been dropped to the ground in response to a command. Id. at 610. In United States v. Schleis, 582 F.2d 1166 (8th Cir.1978), however, the court applied *Chadwick* and invalidated the stationhouse search of a locked briefcase taken from the defendant at the time of his arrest.

In United States v. Burnette, 698 F.2d 1038 (9th Cir.1983), a police officer seized and searched the defendant's purse at the time of her arrest. The search was lawful as an incident of the arrest. Later, at the station the purse was searched more thoroughly and incriminating evidence was found. Reasoning that the initial search reduced the defendant's expectation of privacy, the court concluded that the subsequent search was lawful. "[O]nce an item in an individual's possession has been lawfully seized and searched, subsequent searches of that item, so long as it remains in the legitimate uninterrupted possession of the police, may be conducted without a warrant." Id. at 1038. Cf. United States v. Edwards, 415 U.S. 800 (1974), p. 221 below. With *Burnette*, compare United States v. Monclavo-Cruz, 662 F.2d 1285 (9th Cir.1981), in which the court held that the warrantless search of a woman's purse an hour after the woman had been arrested and the purse had been seized from the car in which she had been riding was not lawful.

Chadwick evidently distinguishes between "personal property . . . immediately associated with the person" and other kinds of containers in the possession of a person who is arrested, the former being subject to a full search incident to the arrest and the latter not. What does the quoted phrase mean? Is it equivalent to the common distinction in ordinary language between things carried "on the person" and things carried "by the person"? What justification is there, under *Chimel* or otherwise, for such a distinction?

120. Customs officials opened a large, locked metal container that was shipped to the United States from abroad. Marijuana was found inside. Following the practice of "controlled delivery" in order to determine the owner of the container, the officials resealed the container and delivered it to the addressee. After the delivery, they maintained close but imperfect surveillance over the container. Before they could obtain a warrant to seize the container, the person to whom delivery was made left his apartment with it. The officials arrested him, seized the container, and reopened it at the police station. The marijuana inside was seized.

The Court held that the second warrantless seizure and search were lawful, since there was not a "substantial likelihood" that the contents of the container had been changed between the first and second searches. "It is obvious that the privacy interest in the contents of a container diminishes with respect to a container that law enforcement authorities have already lawfully opened and found to contain illicit drugs. No protected privacy interest remains in contraband in a container once government officers lawfully have opened that container and identified its contents as illegal. The simple act of resealing the container to enable the police to make a controlled delivery does not operate to revive or restore the lawfully invaded privacy rights." Illinois v. Andreas, 463 U.S. 765, 771 (1983) (7–2).

Compare Walter v. United States, 447 U.S. 649 (1980) (5–4), holding that government agents, having lawfully obtained possession of films that they believed to be obscene, were required to obtain a warrant before screening the films. With *Walter*, compare United States v. Passaro, 624 F.2d 938 (9th Cir.1980), upholding the search of an arrested person's wallet and photocopying of a document found in the wallet unrelated to the crime for which he was arrested.

121. In New York v. Belton, 453 U.S. 454 (1981) (6–3), the Court held that a search incident to a lawful custodial arrest of the occupant of an automobile can extend to the entire passenger compartment of the automobile, including all containers, closed or open, within it. "Container," the Court said, includes "any object capable of holding another object," including the glove compartment, luggage, boxes, clothing, etc. Id. at 460 n.4. Quoting *Chimel*, the Court based its conclusion on "the generalization that articles inside the relatively narrow compass of the passenger compartment of an automobile are in fact generally, even if not inevitably, within 'the area into which an arrestee might reach in order to grab a weapon or evidentiary item.' " Id. at 460.

Belton authorizes a search of the passenger compartment of a vehicle after the occupant has been ordered out and arrested, handcuffed, and placed in the back of a police car. E.g., United States v. McLaughlin, 170 F.3d 889 (9th Cir.1999) (search lawful although driver had already been removed from scene); United States v. Doward, 41 F.3d 789 (1st Cir.1994). Generally confirming this line of reasoning, the Court held that a *Belton* search is lawful if the police officer does not initiate contact until the occupant of an automobile has left it, provided that he left it "recently" and is still in close proximity to it. Thornton v. United States, 541 U.S. ___ (2004) (7–2). The Court said that in those circumstances the justifications for a warrantless arrest that were stated in *Chimel*—"to remove any weapon the arrestee might seek to use to resist arrest or to escape, and . . . to prevent the concealment or destruction of evidence," id. at ___—remains applicable. In a separate opinion, Justice Scalia argued that the rationale of *Chimel* does not justify a search in those circumstances. Rather, he said, if the officer has reasonable grounds to believe that evidence relevant to the crime for which the person has been arrested will be found in the automobile, a search is justified under the pre-*Chimel* rationale of United States v. Rabinowitz, p. 206 above. 541 U.S. at ___ (opinion concurring in the judgment).

Belton evidently sets up a potential conflict with *Chadwick*, p. ___ note 119 above. Why should a container be more subject to search if it is found as an incident of the arrest of the occupant of a car than if a person is arrested while carrying it? See note 129, p. 235 below.

122. In a dissenting opinion in *Chimel*, above, Justice White argued: "An arrest itself may often create an emergency situation making it impracticable to obtain a warrant before embarking on a related search. Again assuming that there is probable cause to search premises at the spot where a suspect is arrested, it seems to me unreasonable to require the police to leave the scene in order to obtain a search warrant when they are already legally there to make a valid arrest, and when there must almost always be a strong possibility that confederates of the arrested man will in the meanwhile remove the items for which the police have probable cause to search. This must so often be the case that it seems to me as unreasonable to require a warrant for a search of the premises as to require a warrant for search of the person and his very immediate surroundings." 395 U.S. at 773–74.

Assuming, as the majority in *Chimel* concluded, that Justice White's factual assertions are an insufficient basis for a rule generally allowing searches of premises where an arrest occurs, does *Chimel* allow justification of a warrantless search of premises in particular cases if the police have special reason to believe that evidence (or, more particularly, contraband or stolen goods) is on the premises and will be removed before a warrant can be obtained? If not, what action can the police take in such cases to prevent removal of the items in question?

In a footnote to its opinion in *Chimel*, the Court said: "Our holding today is of course entirely consistent with the recognized principle that, assuming the existence of probable cause, automobiles and other vehicles may be searched without warrants 'where it is not practicable to secure a warrant because the vehicle can be quickly moved out of the locality or jurisdiction in which the warrant must be sought.' Carroll v. United States, 267 U.S. 132, 153 ...'" 395 U.S. at 764 n.9. In view of the Court's rejection of Justice White's argument, are *Chimel* and *Carroll* "entirely consistent"?

Compare Vale v. Louisiana, 399 U.S. 30 (1970), p. 226 below, with Chambers v. Maroney, 399 U.S. 42 (1970), p. 228 below, which the Court decided on the same day.

123. A police officer arrested the defendant's roommate and accompanied him to his room for him to get identification. Waiting at the door of the room, the officer saw what appeared to be marijuana inside. He entered

the room, confirmed that what he had seen was marijuana, and seized it.
The defendant was subsequently prosecuted for possession of the marijuana. Holding that the entry into the room was lawful, the Court said:

> [I]t is not "unreasonable" under the Fourth Amendment for a
> police officer, as a matter of routine, to monitor the movements of an
> arrested person, as his judgment dictates, following the arrest. The
> officer's need to ensure his own safety—as well as the integrity of the
> arrest—is compelling. Such surveillance is not an impermissible inva-
> sion of the privacy or personal liberty of an individual who has been
> arrested.

Washington v. Chrisman, 455 U.S. 1, 7 (1982) (6–3).

124. A search of the person incident to an arrest for a traffic offense,
for which the arrestee is taken into custody, was upheld in United States v.
Robinson, 414 U.S. 218 (1973) (6–3). Robinson was stopped and arrested
for driving without a license. The arresting officer patted him down and felt
an object in Robinson's coat pocket. He reached into the pocket and
removed the object, which turned out to be a crumpled cigarette packet. He
opened the packet and found narcotics, for possession of which Robinson
was prosecuted. The Court distinguished a search of the person from a
search of the area surrounding the person. The former, the Court said, as
an incident of a lawful arrest, had never been questioned. In particular, a
search of the person is not limited to the "frisk" authorized by Terry v.
Ohio, p. 100 above.

> The justification or reason for the authority to search incident to a
> lawful arrest rests quite as much on the need to disarm the suspect in
> order to take him into custody as it does on the need to preserve
> evidence on his person for later use at trial. . . . The standards
> traditionally governing a search incident to lawful arrest are not,
> therefore, commuted to the stricter *Terry* standards by the absence of
> probable fruits or further evidence of the particular crime for which
> the arrest is made.

> Nor are we inclined, on the basis of what seems to us to be a
> rather speculative judgment, to qualify the breadth of the general
> authority to search incident to a lawful custodial arrest on an assump-
> tion that persons arrested for the offense of driving while their license
> has been revoked are less likely to be possessed of dangerous weapons
> than are those arrested for other crimes. It is scarcely open to doubt
> that the danger to an officer is far greater in the case of the extended
> exposure which follows the taking of a suspect into custody and
> transporting him to the police station than in the case of the relatively
> fleeting contact resulting from the typical *Terry*-type stop. This is an
> adequate basis for treating all custodial arrests alike for purposes of
> search justification.

> But quite apart from these distinctions . . . [we do not agree] that
> there must be litigated in each case the issue of whether or not there
> was present one of the reasons supporting the authority for a search of

the person incident to a lawful arrest. We do not think the long line of authorities of this Court dating back to *Weeks* [v. United States, 232 U.S. 383 (1914)], nor what we can glean from the history of practice in this country and in England, requires such a case by case adjudication. A police officer's determination as to how and where to search the person of a suspect whom he has arrested is necessarily a quick ad hoc judgment which the Fourth Amendment does not require to be broken down in each instance into an analysis of each step in the search. The authority to search the person incident to a lawful custodial arrest, while based upon the need to disarm and to discover evidence, does not depend on what a court may later decide was the probability in a particular arrest situation that weapons or evidence would in fact be found upon the person of the suspect. A custodial arrest of a suspect based on probable cause is a reasonable intrusion under the Fourth Amendment; that intrusion being lawful, a search incident to the arrest requires no additional justification. It is the fact of the lawful arrest which establishes the authority to search, and we hold that in the case of a lawful custodial arrest a full search of the person is not only an exception to the warrant requirement of the Fourth Amendment, but is also a "reasonable" search under that Amendment.
414 U.S. at 234–35.

In Knowles v. Iowa, 525 U.S. 113 (1998), the Court apparently regarded *Robinson* as authorizing a search not only of the person of someone who is arrested for a traffic offense but also of the car, as an incident of the arrest. See id. at 118. However, in *Knowles* the Court declined to apply that rule if a person is stopped for a traffic offense and issued a citation, instead of being arrested. The Court said that in such a case the risk to the officer is less and there is no concern about the destruction of evidence, so a general "bright-line rule" as in *Robinson* was inapt.

The courts in several states have rejected the reasoning of *Robinson*, on the basis of the state constitution. In Zehrung v. State, 569 P.2d 189, 199–200 (Alaska 1977), for example, the court said: "[A]bsent specific articulable facts justifying the intrusion . . . a warrantless search incident to an arrest, other than for weapons, is unreasonable and therefore violative of the Alaska Constitution if the charge on which the arrest is made is not one, evidence of which could be concealed on the person." (On a petition for rehearing, the ruling was later qualified.) The court said that the stated rule "should normally be followed unless exigencies demand a different course of action." 573 P.2d 858 (Alaska 1978). To the same effect, see People v. Brisendine, 531 P.2d 1099 (Cal.1975); People v. Clyne, 541 P.2d 71 (Colo.1975); State v. Kaluna, 520 P.2d 51 (Haw.1974).

125. Protective sweep. In Maryland v. Buie, 494 U.S. 325, 327 (1990) (7–2), the Court upheld the practice of a "protective sweep": "a quick and limited search of premises, incident to an arrest and conducted to protect the safety of police officers or others . . . narrowly confined to a cursory visual inspection of those places in which a person might be hiding." The Court said that the reasoning that justified a frisk on the street in Terry v. Ohio, p. 100 above, and the search of a car in Michigan v. Long, p. 118 note 60 above, also justified a protective sweep. "In the instant case, there is an analogous interest of the officers in taking steps to assure themselves that the house in which a suspect is being or has just been arrested is not harboring other persons who are dangerous and who could unexpectedly launch an attack. The risk of danger in the context of an arrest in the home is as great as, if not greater than, it is in an on-the-street or roadside investigatory encounter. A *Terry* or *Long* frisk occurs before a police-citizen confrontation has escalated to the point of arrest. A protective sweep, in contrast, occurs as an adjunct to the serious step of taking a person into custody for the purpose of prosecuting him for a crime. Moreover, unlike an encounter on the street or along a highway, an in-home arrest puts the officer at the disadvantage of being on his adversary's 'turf.' An ambush in a confined setting of unknown configuration is more to be feared than it is in open, more familiar surroundings." 494 U.S. at 333.

The Court held that when an arrest is made inside a house or other premises, the arresting officers can

> as a precautionary matter and without probable cause or reasonable suspicion, look in closets and other spaces immediately adjoining the place of arrest from which an attack could be immediately launched. Beyond that . . . there must be articulable facts which, taken together with the rational inferences from those facts, would warrant a reasonably prudent officer in believing that the area to be swept harbors an individual posing a danger to those on the arrest scene. . . .

> [S]uch a protective sweep, aimed at protecting the arresting officers, if justified by the circumstances, is nevertheless not a full search of the premises, but may extend only to a cursory inspection of those spaces where a person may be found. The sweep lasts no longer than is necessary to dispel the reasonable suspicion of danger and in any event no longer than it takes to complete the arrest and depart the premises.

Id. at 334–36.

Justice Brennan, dissenting, observed that the Court for the first time had dispensed with the requirement of a warrant and probable cause inside private premises. Id. at 339.

Compare the majority and dissenting opinions in Vale v. Louisiana, p. 226 below.

See United States v. Biggs, 70 F.3d 913 (6th Cir.1995) (arrest of defendant in parking lot justified protective sweep of motel room); United States v. Ford, 56 F.3d 265 (D.C.Cir.1995) (search under mattress and behind window shades exceeded permissible scope of protective sweep).

Cupp v. Murphy

412 U.S. 291, 93 S.Ct. 2000, 36 L.Ed.2d 900 (1973)

■ MR. JUSTICE STEWART delivered the opinion of the Court.

The respondent, Daniel Murphy, was convicted by a jury in an Oregon court of the second-degree murder of his wife. The victim died by strangulation in her home in the city of Portland, and abrasions and lacerations were found on her throat. There was no sign of a break-in or robbery. Word of the murder was sent to the respondent, who was not then living with his wife. Upon receiving the message, Murphy promptly telephoned the Portland police and voluntarily came into Portland for questioning. Shortly after the respondent's arrival at the station house, where he was met by retained counsel, the police noticed a dark spot on the respondent's finger. Suspecting that the spot might be dried blood and knowing that evidence of strangulation is often found under the assailant's fingernails, the police asked Murphy if they could take a sample of scrapings from his fingernails. He refused. Under protest and without a warrant, the police proceeded to take the samples, which turned out to contain traces of skin and blood cells, and fabric from the victim's nightgown. This incriminating evidence was admitted at the trial.

The respondent appealed his conviction, claiming that the fingernail scrapings were the product of an unconstitutional search under the Fourth and Fourteenth Amendments. The Oregon Court of Appeals affirmed the conviction . . . and we denied certiorari. . . . Murphy then commenced the present action for federal habeas corpus relief. The District Court, in an unreported decision, denied the habeas petition, and the Court of Appeals for the Ninth Circuit reversed. . . . The Court of Appeals assumed the presence of probable cause to search or arrest, but held that in the absence of an arrest or other exigent circumstances, the search was unconstitutional. . . . We granted certiorari . . . to consider the constitutional question presented.

. . .

It is . . . undisputed that the police did not obtain an arrest warrant or formally "arrest" the respondent, as that term is understood under Oregon law. The respondent was detained only long enough to take the fingernail scrapings, and was not formally "arrested" until approximately one month later. Nevertheless, the detention of the respondent against his will constituted a seizure of his person, and the Fourth Amendment guarantee of freedom from "unreasonable searches and seizures" is clearly implicated. . . . As the Court said in Davis v. Mississippi, 394 U.S. 721, 726–27, "Nothing is more clear than that the Fourth Amendment was meant to prevent wholesale intrusions upon the personal security of our citizenry, whether these intrusions be termed 'arrests' or 'investigatory detentions.'"

In *Davis*, the Court held that fingerprints obtained during the brief detention of persons seized in a police dragnet procedure, without probable cause, were inadmissible in evidence. Though the Court recognized that fingerprinting "involves none of the probing into an individual's private life and thoughts that marks an interrogation or search," 394 U.S., at 727, the Court held the stationhouse detention in that case to be violative of the Fourth and Fourteenth Amendments. "Investigatory seizures would subject unlimited numbers of innocent persons to the harassment and ignominy incident to involuntary detention," id., at 726.

The respondent in this case, like Davis, was briefly detained at the station house. Yet here, there was . . . probable cause to believe that the respondent had committed the murder. The vice of the detention in *Davis* is therefore absent in the case before us. . . .

The inquiry does not end here, however, because Murphy was subjected to a search as well as a seizure of his person. Unlike the fingerprinting in *Davis*, the voice exemplar obtained in United States v. Dionisio, [410 U.S. 1 (1973)], or the handwriting exemplar obtained in United States v. Mara, 410 U.S. 19, the search of the respondent's fingernails went beyond mere "physical characteristics . . . constantly exposed to the public," United States v. Dionisio, supra, at 14, and constituted the type of "severe, though brief, intrusion upon cherished personal security" that is subject to constitutional scrutiny. Terry v. Ohio, [392 U.S. 1 (1968)], at 24–25.

We believe this search was constitutionally permissible under the principles of Chimel v. California, 395 U.S. 752. *Chimel* stands in a long line of cases recognizing an exception to the warrant requirement when a search is incident to a valid arrest. . . . The basis for this exception is that when an arrest is made, it is reasonable for a police officer to expect the arrestee to use any weapons he may have and to attempt to destroy any incriminating evidence then in his possession. . . . The Court recognized in *Chimel* that the scope of a warrantless search must be commensurate with the rationale that excepts the search from the warrant requirement. Thus, a warrantless search incident to arrest, the Court held in *Chimel*, must be limited to the area "into which an arrestee might reach." 395 U.S., at 763.

Where there is no formal arrest, as in the case before us, a person might well be less hostile to the police and less likely to take conspicuous, immediate steps to destroy incriminating evidence on his person. Since he knows he is going to be released, he might be likely instead to be concerned with diverting attention away from himself. Accordingly, we do not hold that a full *Chimel* search would have been justified in this case without a formal arrest and without a warrant. But the respondent was not subjected to such a search.

At the time Murphy was being detained at the station house, he was obviously aware of the detectives' suspicions. Though he did not have the full warning of official suspicion that a formal arrest provides, Murphy was sufficiently apprised of his suspected role in the crime to motivate him to attempt to destroy what evidence he could without attracting further attention. Testimony at trial indicated that after he refused to consent to the taking of fingernail samples, he put his hands behind his back and appeared to rub them together. He then put his hands in his pockets, and a "metallic sound, such as keys or change rattling" was heard. The rationale of *Chimel*, in these circumstances, justified the police in subjecting him to the very limited search necessary to preserve the highly evanescent evidence they found under his fingernails. . . .

On the facts of this case, considering the existence of probable cause, the very limited intrusion undertaken incident to the station house detention, and the ready destructibility of the evidence, we cannot say that this search violated the Fourth and Fourteenth Amendments. Accordingly, the judgment of the Court of Appeals is reversed.[9]

————

United States v. Edwards

415 U.S. 800, 94 S.Ct. 1234, 39 L.Ed.2d 771 (1974)

■ MR. JUSTICE WHITE delivered the opinion of the Court.

The question here is whether the Fourth Amendment should be extended to exclude from evidence certain clothing taken from respondent Edwards while he was in custody at the city jail approximately 10 hours after his arrest.

Shortly after 11 p.m. on May 31, 1970, respondent Edwards was lawfully arrested on the streets of Lebanon, Ohio, and charged with attempting to break into that city's Post Office. He was taken to the local jail and placed in a cell. Contemporaneously or shortly thereafter, investigation at the scene revealed that the attempted entry had been made through a wooden window which apparently had been pried up with a pry bar, leaving paint chips on the window sill and wire mesh screen. The next morning, trousers and a T-shirt were purchased for Edwards to substitute for the clothing which he had been wearing at the time of and since his arrest. His clothing was then taken from him and held as evidence. Examination of the clothing revealed paint chips matching the samples that had been taken from the window. This evidence and his clothing were received at trial over Edwards' objection that neither the clothing nor the results of its examination were admissible because the warrantless seizure of his clothing was invalid under the Fourth Amendment.

The Court of Appeals reversed. Expressly disagreeing with two other courts of appeals, it held that although the arrest was lawful and probable cause existed to believe that paint chips would be discovered on petitioner's clothing, the warrantless seizure of the clothing carried out "after the administrative process and mechanics of arrest have come to a halt" was nevertheless unconstitutional under the Fourth Amendment. United States v. Edwards, 474 F.2d 1206, 1211 (CA6 1973). We granted certiorari . . .

[9] Justice Marshall wrote a concurring opinion. Justice Blackmun wrote a brief concurring opinion which Chief Justice Burger joined. Justice Powell wrote a brief concurring opinion which Chief Justice Burger and Justice Rehnquist joined. Justice White noted that he thought the issue of probable cause remained open on remand. Justice Douglas and Justice Brennan wrote opinions dissenting in part.

and now conclude that the Fourth Amendment should not be extended to invalidate the search and seizure in the circumstances of this case.

The prevailing rule under the Fourth Amendment that searches and seizures may not be made without a warrant is subject to various exceptions. One of them permits warrantless searches incident to custodial arrests . . . and has traditionally been justified by the reasonableness of searching for weapons, instruments of escape and evidence of crime when a person is taken into official custody and lawfully detained. . . .

It is also plain that searches and seizures that could be made on the spot at the time of arrest may legally be conducted later when the accused arrives at the place of detention. If need be, Abel v. United States, 362 U.S. 217 (1960), settled this question. There the defendant was arrested at his hotel, but the belongings taken with him to the place of detention were searched there. In sustaining the search, the Court noted that a valid search of the property could have been made at the place of arrest and perceived little difference

> when the accused decides to take the property with him, for the search of it to occur instead at the first place of detention when the accused arrives there, especially as the search of the property carried by the accused to the place of detention has additional justification, similar to those which justify search of the person of one who is arrested.

Id., at 239. The Courts of Appeals have followed this same rule, holding that both the person and the property in his immediate possession may be searched at the station house after the arrest has occurred at another place and if evidence of crime is discovered, it may be seized and admitted in evidence. Nor is there any doubt that clothing or other belongings may be seized upon arrival of the accused at the place of detention and later subjected to laboratory analysis or that the test results are admissible at trial.

Conceding all this, the Court of Appeals in this case nevertheless held that a warrant is required where the search occurs after the administrative mechanics of arrest have been completed and the prisoner is incarcerated. But even on these terms, it seems to us that the normal processes incident to arrest and custody had not been completed when Edwards was placed in his cell on the night of May 31. With or without probable cause, the authorities were entitled at that point in time not only to search Edwards' clothing but also to take it from him and keep it in official custody. There was testimony that this was the standard practice in this city. The police were also entitled to take from Edwards any evidence of the crime in his immediate possession, including his clothing. And the Court of Appeals acknowledged that contemporaneously with or shortly after the time Edwards went to his cell, the police had probable cause to believe that the articles of clothing he wore were themselves material evidence of the crime for which he had been arrested. . . . But it was late at night; no substitute clothing was then available for Edwards to wear, and it would certainly have been unreasonable for the police to have stripped petitioner of his clothing and left him exposed in his cell throughout the night. . . . When the substitutes were purchased the next morning, the clothing he had been wearing at the time of arrest was taken from him and subjected to laboratory analysis. This was no more than taking from petitioner the effects in his immediate possession that constituted evidence of crime. This was and is a normal incident of a custodial arrest, and reasonable delay in effectuating it does not change the fact that Edwards was no more imposed upon than he could have been at the time and place of the arrest or immediately upon arrival at the place of detention. The police did no more on June 1 than they were entitled to do incident to the usual custodial arrest and incarceration.

Other closely related considerations sustain the examination of the clothing in this case. It must be remembered that on both May 31 and June 1 the police had lawful custody of Edwards and necessarily of the clothing he wore. When it became apparent that the articles of clothing were evidence of the crime for which Edwards was being held, the police were entitled to take, examine, and preserve them for use as evidence, just as they are normally permitted to seize evidence of crime when it is lawfully encountered. . . . Surely, the clothes could have been brushed down and vacuumed while Edwards had them on in the cell, and it was similarly reasonable to take and examine them as the police did, particularly in view of the existence of probable cause linking the clothes to the crime. Indeed, it is difficult to perceive what is unreasonable about the police examining and holding as evidence those personal effects of the accused that they already have in their lawful custody as the result of a lawful arrest.

. . .

[O]nce the defendant is lawfully arrested and is in custody, the effects in his possession at the place of detention that were subject to search at the time and place of his arrest may lawfully be searched and seized without a warrant even though a substantial period of time has elapsed between the arrest and subsequent administrative processing on the one hand and the taking of the property for use as evidence on the other. This is true where the clothing or effects are immediately seized upon arrival at the jail, held under the defendant's name in the "property room" of the jail and at a later time searched and taken for use at the subsequent criminal trial. The result is the same where the property is not physically taken from the defendant until sometime after his incarceration.

In upholding this search and seizure, we do not conclude that the warrant clause of the Fourth Amendment is never applicable to post-arrest seizures of the effects of an arrestee.[10] But we do think that the Court of

---

10. Holding the Warrant Clause inapplicable in the circumstances present here does not leave law enforcement officials subject to no restraints. This type of police conduct "must [still] be tested by the Fourth Amendment's general proscription against unreasonable searches and seizures." Terry v. Ohio, 392 U.S. 1, 20 (1968). But the Court of Appeals here conceded that probable cause existed for the search and seizure of petitioner's clothing, and petitioner complains only that a warrant should have been secured. We thus have no occasion to express a view concerning those circumstances surrounding custodial searches incident to incarceration which might "violate the dictates of reason

Appeals for the First Circuit captured the essence of situations like these when it said in United States v. DeLeo, 422 F.2d [487 (1st Cir.1970)] at 493 (footnote omitted):

> While the legal arrest of a person should not destroy the privacy of his premises, it does—for at least a reasonable time and to a reasonable extent—take his own privacy out of the realm of protection from police interest in weapons, means of escape and evidence.

The judgment of the Court of Appeals is reversed.

So ordered.

■ MR. JUSTICE STEWART, with whom MR. JUSTICE DOUGLAS, MR. JUSTICE BRENNAN, and MR. JUSTICE MARSHALL join, dissenting.

The Court says that the question before us "is whether the Fourth Amendment should be extended" to prohibit the warrantless seizure of Edwards' clothing. I think, on the contrary, that the real question in this case is whether the Fourth Amendment is to be ignored. For in my view the judgment of the Court of Appeals can be reversed only by disregarding established Fourth Amendment principles firmly embodied in many previous decisions of this Court.

As the Court has repeatedly emphasized in the past, "the most basic constitutional rule in this area is that 'searches conducted outside the judicial process, without prior approval by judge or magistrate, are per se unreasonable under the Fourth Amendment—subject only to a few specifically established and well-delineated exceptions.'" Coolidge v. New Hampshire, 403 U.S. 443, 454–55. . . . Since it is conceded here that the seizure of Edwards' clothing was not made pursuant to a warrant, the question becomes whether the Government has met its burden of showing that the circumstances of this seizure brought it within one of the "jealously and carefully drawn"[11] exceptions to the warrant requirement.

The Court finds a warrant unnecessary in this case because of the custodial arrest of the respondent. It is of course well-settled that the Fourth Amendment permits a warrantless search or seizure incident to a constitutionally valid custodial arrest. . . . But the mere fact of an arrest does not allow the police to engage in warrantless searches of unlimited geographic or temporal scope. Rather, the search must be spatially limited to the person of the arrestee and the area within his reach . . . and must, as to time, be "substantially contemporaneous with the arrest," Stoner v. California, 376 U.S. 483, 486. . . .

Under the facts of this case, I am unable to agree with the Court's holding that the search was "incident" to Edwards' custodial arrest. The search here occurred fully 10 hours after he was arrested, at a time when the administrative processing and mechanics of arrest had long since come

---

either because of their number or their manner of perpetration." Charles v. United States, 278 F.2d 386, 389 (9th Cir. 1960). . . .

11. Jones v. United States, 357 U.S. 493, 499.

to an end. His clothes were not seized as part of an "inventory" of a prisoner's effects, nor were they taken pursuant to a routine exchange of civilian clothes for jail garb. And the considerations that typically justify a warrantless search incident to a lawful arrest were wholly absent here.
. . .

Accordingly, I see no justification for dispensing with the warrant requirement here. The police had ample time to seek a warrant, and no exigent circumstances were present to excuse their failure to do so. Unless the exceptions to the warrant requirement are to be "enthroned into the rule," United States v. Rabinowitz, 339 U.S. 56, 80 (Frankfurter, J., dissenting), this is precisely the sort of situation where the Fourth Amendment requires a magistrate's prior approval for a search.

The Court says that the relevant question is "not whether it was reasonable to procure a search warrant, but whether the search itself was reasonable." Ante, at 807. Precisely such a view, however, was explicitly rejected in Chimel v. California, 395 U.S. [752 (1969)], at 764–65, where the Court characterized the argument as "founded on little more than a subjective view regarding the acceptability of certain sorts of police conduct, and not on considerations relevant to Fourth Amendment interests." . . .

The intrusion here was hardly a shocking one, and it cannot be said that the police acted in bad faith. The Fourth Amendment, however, was not designed to apply only to situations where the intrusion is massive and the violation of privacy shockingly flagrant. . . .

Because I believe that the Court today unjustifiably departs from well-settled constitutional principles, I respectfully dissent.

––––––

126. An inventory search of "property found on the person or in the possession of an arrested person who is to be jailed" was upheld in Illinois v. Lafayette, 462 U.S. 640 (1983). The Court mentioned the risks that a person's property would be stolen, that he would make a false claim that property was missing, and that he would injure himself or others. "Examining all the items removed from the arrestee's person or possession and listing or inventorying them is an entirely reasonable administrative procedure. It is immaterial whether the police actually fear any particular package or container; the need to protect against such risks arises independent of a particular officer's subjective concerns." Id. at 646. Responding to the suggestion that the interests of the police could be protected in a less intrusive way, such as allowing an arrested person to place his belongings in a secure locker, the Court said: "Perhaps so, but the real question is not what 'could have been achieved,' but whether the Fourth Amendment *requires* such steps; it is not our function to write a manual on administering routine, neutral procedures of the station house. Our role is to assure against violations of the Constitution." Id. at 647.

In Zehrung v. State, 569 P.2d 189 (Alaska 1977), modified, 573 P.2d 858 (1978), the court limited the authority to make an "inventory search" of a person who is taken into custody: "[W]hen one is arrested and brought to a jail for a minor offense for which bail has already been set in a bail schedule, he should be allowed a reasonable opportunity to attempt to raise bail before being subjected to the remand and booking procedures and the incident inventory search." 569 P.2d at 195.

See Mary Beth G. v. City of Chicago, 723 F.2d 1263 (7th Cir.1983) (policy of conducting strip search of all women arrested for misdemeanors prior to detention in city lockup is unconstitutional).

―――――

Vale v. Louisiana

399 U.S. 30, 90 S.Ct. 1969, 26 L.Ed.2d 409 (1970)

■ MR. JUSTICE STEWART delivered the opinion of the Court.

The appellant, Donald Vale, was convicted in a Louisiana court on a charge of possessing heroin and was sentenced as a multiple offender to 15 years' imprisonment at hard labor. The Louisiana Supreme Court affirmed the conviction, rejecting the claim that evidence introduced at the trial was the product of an unlawful search and seizure. . . .

The evidence adduced at the pretrial hearing on a motion to suppress showed that on April 24, 1967, officers possessing two warrants for Vale's arrest and having information that he was residing at a specified address proceeded there in an unmarked car and set up a surveillance of the house. The evidence of what then took place was summarized by the Louisiana Supreme Court as follows:

> After approximately 15 minutes the officers observed a green 1958 Chevrolet drive up and sound the horn and after backing into a parking place, again blew the horn. At this juncture Donald Vale, who was well known to Officer Brady, having arrested him twice in the previous month, was seen coming out of the house and walk up to the passenger side of the Chevrolet where he had a close brief conversation with the driver; and after looking up and down the street returned inside of the house. Within a few minutes he reappeared on the porch, and again cautiously looked up and down the street before proceeding to the passenger side of the Chevrolet, leaning through the window. From this the officers were convinced a narcotics sale had taken place. They returned to their car and immediately drove toward Donald Vale, and as they reached within approximately three cars lengths from the accused, (Donald Vale) he looked up and, obviously recognizing the officers, turned around, walking quickly toward the house. At the same time the driver of the Chevrolet started to make his getaway when the car was blocked by the police vehicle. The three officers promptly alighted from the car, whereupon Officers Soule and Laumann called

to Donald Vale to stop as he reached the front steps of the house, telling him he was under arrest. Officer Brady at the same time, seeing the driver of the Chevrolet, Arizzio Saucier, whom the officers knew to be a narcotic addict, place something hurriedly in his mouth, immediately placed him under arrest and joined his co-officers. Because of the transaction they had just observed they informed Donald Vale they were going to search the house, and thereupon advised him of his constitutional rights. After they all entered the front room, Officer Laumann made a cursory inspection of the house to ascertain if anyone else was present and within about three minutes Mrs. Vale and James Vale, mother and brother of Donald Vale, returned home carrying groceries and were informed of the arrest and impending search.

215 So.2d, at 815 (footnote omitted). The search of a rear bedroom revealed a quantity of narcotics.

The Louisiana Supreme Court held that the search of the house did not violate the Fourth Amendment because it occurred "in the immediate vicinity of the arrest" of Donald Vale and was "substantially contemporaneous therewith...." 215 So.2d, at 816. We cannot agree. Last Term in Chimel v. California, 395 U.S. 752, we held that when the search of a dwelling is sought to be justified as incident to a lawful arrest, it must constitutionally be confined to the area within the arrestee's reach at the time of his arrest—"the area from within which he might gain possession of a weapon or destructible evidence." 395 U.S., at 763. But even if *Chimel* is not accorded retroactive effect—a question on which we do not now express an opinion—no precedent of this Court can sustain the constitutional validity of the search in the case before us.

A search may be incident to an arrest " 'only if it is substantially contemporaneous with the arrest and is confined to the *immediate* vicinity of the arrest.' " Shipley v. California, 395 U.S. 818, 819. . . . If a search of a house is to be upheld as incident to an arrest, that arrest must take place *inside* the house . . . not somewhere outside—whether two blocks away . . . twenty feet away . . . or on the sidewalk near the front steps. "Belief, however well founded, that an article sought is concealed in a dwelling house furnishes no justification for a search of that place without a warrant." Agnello v. United States [269 U.S. 20 (1925)], at 33. That basic rule "has never been questioned in this Court." Stoner v. California [376 U.S. 483 (1964)], at 487 n.5.

The Louisiana Supreme Court thought the search independently supportable because it involved narcotics, which are easily removed, hidden, or destroyed. It would be unreasonable, the Louisiana court concluded, "to require the officers under the facts of the case to first secure a search warrant before searching the premises, as time is of the essence inasmuch as the officers never know whether there is anyone on the premises to be searched who could very easily destroy the evidence." 215 So.2d, at 816. Such a rationale could not apply to the present case, since by their own account the arresting officers satisfied themselves that no one else was in the house when they first entered the premises. But entirely apart from that point, our past decisions make clear that only in "a few specifically established and well-delineated" situations, Katz v. United States, 389 U.S. 347, 357, may a warrantless search of a dwelling withstand constitutional scrutiny, even though the authorities have probable cause to conduct it. The burden rests on the State to show the existence of such an exceptional situation. . . . And the record before us discloses none.

. . .

The officers were able to procure two warrants for Vale's arrest. They also had information that he was residing at the address where they found him. There is thus no reason, so far as anything before us appears, to suppose that it was impracticable for them to obtain a search warrant as well. . . . We decline to hold that an arrest on the street can provide its own "exigent circumstance" so as to justify a warrantless search of the arrestee's house.

The Louisiana courts committed constitutional error in admitting into evidence the fruits of the illegal search. . . .

. . . [12]

———

127. Having accompanied the defendant's wife to their trailer home, police officers were told by her that he had drugs inside. They asked him if they could search, and he said no. An officer then went to get a search warrant. The defendant having by then come onto the porch, the other officer allowed him to reenter the trailer only under the officer's observation. The former officer returned with a search warrant within two hours. A search uncovered marijuana. The Court held that in light of the circumstances and the need to prevent the destruction of evidence, the police conduct was reasonable and not a violation of the Fourth Amendment. Illinois v. McArthur, 531 U.S. 326 (2001) (8–1).

———

Chambers v. Maroney
399 U.S. 42, 90 S.Ct. 1975, 26 L.Ed.2d 419 (1970)

■ MR. JUSTICE WHITE delivered the opinion of the Court.

The principal question in this case concerns the admissibility of evidence seized from an automobile, in which petitioner was riding at the time of his arrest, after the automobile was taken to a police station and was there thoroughly searched without a warrant. The Court of Appeals for the Third Circuit found no violation of petitioner's Fourth Amendment rights. We affirm.

[12] Justice Black wrote a dissenting opinion, which Chief Justice Burger joined.

I

During the night of May 20, 1963, a Gulf service station in North Braddock, Pennsylvania, was robbed by two men, each of whom carried and displayed a gun. The robbers took the currency from the cash register; the service station attendant, one Stephen Kovacich, was directed to place the coins in his right-hand glove, which was then taken by the robbers. Two teen-agers, who had earlier noticed a blue compact station wagon circling the block in the vicinity of the Gulf station, then saw the station wagon speed away from a parking lot close to the Gulf station. About the same time, they learned that the Gulf station had been robbed. They reported to police, who arrived immediately, that four men were in the station wagon and one was wearing a green sweater. Kovacich told the police that one of the men who robbed him was wearing a green sweater and the other was wearing a trench coat. A description of the car and the two robbers was broadcast over the police radio. Within an hour, a light blue compact station wagon answering the description and carrying four men was stopped by the police about two miles from the Gulf station. Petitioner was one of the men in the station wagon. He was wearing a green sweater and there was a trench coat in the car. The occupants were arrested and the car was driven to the police station. In the course of a thorough search of the car at the station, the police found concealed in a compartment under the dashboard two .38-caliber revolvers (one loaded with dumdum bullets), a right-hand glove containing small change, and certain cards bearing the name of Raymond Havicon, the attendant at a Boron service station in McKeesport, Pennsylvania, who had been robbed at gunpoint on May 13, 1963. In the course of a warrant-authorized search of petitioner's home the day after petitioner's arrest, police found and seized certain .38-caliber ammunition, including some dumdum bullets similar to those found in one of the guns taken from the station wagon.

Petitioner was indicted for both robberies. His first trial ended in a mistrial but he was convicted of both robberies at the second trial. Both Kovacich and Havicon identified petitioner as one of the robbers. The materials taken from the station wagon were introduced into evidence, Kovacich identifying his glove and Havicon the cards taken in the May 13 robbery. The bullets seized at petitioner's house were also introduced over objections of petitioner's counsel. Petitioner was sentenced to a term of four to eight years' imprisonment for the May 13 robbery and to a term of two to seven years' imprisonment for the May 20 robbery, the sentences to run consecutively. Petitioner did not take a direct appeal from these convictions. In 1965, petitioner sought a writ of habeas corpus in the state court, which denied the writ after a brief evidentiary hearing; the denial of the writ was affirmed on appeal in the Pennsylvania appellate courts. Habeas corpus proceedings were then commenced in the United States District Court for the Western District of Pennsylvania. An order to show cause was issued. Based on the State's response and the state court record, the petition for habeas corpus was denied without a hearing. The Court of Appeals for the Third Circuit affirmed . . . and we granted certiorari. . . .

II

We pass quickly the claim that the search of the automobile was the fruit of an unlawful arrest. Both the courts below thought the arresting officers had probable cause to make the arrest. We agree. Having talked to the teen-age observers and to the victim Kovacich, the police had ample cause to stop a light blue compact station wagon carrying four men and to arrest the occupants, one of whom was wearing a green sweater and one of whom had a trench coat with him in the car.[13]

Even so, the search that produced the incriminating evidence was made at the police station some time after the arrest and cannot be justified as a search incident to an arrest: "Once an accused is under arrest and in custody, then a search made at another place, without a warrant, is simply not incident to the arrest." Preston v. United States, 376 U.S. 364, 367 (1964). . . . [T]he reasons that have been thought sufficient to justify warrantless searches carried out in connection with an arrest no longer obtain when the accused is safely in custody at the station house.

There are, however, alternative grounds arguably justifying the search of the car in this case. . . . Here . . . the police had probable cause to believe that the robbers, carrying guns and the fruits of the crime, had fled the scene in a light blue compact station wagon which would be carrying four men, one wearing a green sweater and another wearing a trench coat. As the state courts correctly held, there was probable cause to arrest the occupants of the station wagon that the officers stopped; just as obviously was there probable cause to search the car for guns and stolen money.

In terms of the circumstances justifying a warrantless search, the Court has long distinguished between an automobile and a home or office. In Carroll v. United States, 267 U.S. 132 (1925), the issue was the admissibility in evidence of contraband liquor seized in a warrantless search of a car on the highway. After surveying the law from the time of the adoption of the Fourth Amendment onward, the Court held that automobiles and other conveyances may be searched without a warrant in circumstances that would not justify the search without a warrant of a house or an office, provided that there is probable cause to believe that the car contains articles that the officers are entitled to seize. The Court expressed its holding as follows:

> We have made a somewhat extended reference to these statutes to show that the guaranty of freedom from unreasonable searches and seizures by the Fourth Amendment has been construed, practically since the beginning of the Government, as recognizing a necessary difference between a search of a store, dwelling house or other structure in respect of which a proper official warrant readily may be obtained, and a search of a ship, motor boat, wagon or automobile, for

---

13. In any event, as we point out below, the validity of an arrest is not necessarily determinative of the right to search a car if there is probable cause to make the search. Here, as will be true in many cases, the circumstances justifying the arrest are also those furnishing probable cause for the search.

contraband goods, where it is not practicable to secure a warrant because the vehicle can be quickly moved out of the locality or jurisdiction in which the warrant must be sought.

Having thus established that contraband goods concealed and illegally transported in an automobile or other vehicle may be searched for without a warrant, we come now to consider under what circumstances such search may be made. . . . [T]hose lawfully within the country, entitled to use the public highways, have a right to free passage without interruption or search unless there is known to a competent official authorized to search, probable cause for believing that their vehicles are carrying contraband or illegal merchandise. . . .

. . .

The measure of legality of such a seizure is, therefore, that the seizing officer shall have reasonable or probable cause for believing that the automobile which he stops and seizes has contraband liquor therein which is being illegally transported.

267 U.S., at 153–54, 155–56. The Court also noted that the search of an auto on probable cause proceeds on a theory wholly different from that justifying the search incident to an arrest:

The right to search and the validity of the seizure are not dependent on the right to arrest. They are dependent on the reasonable cause the seizing officer has for belief that the contents of the automobile offend against the law.

267 U.S., at 158–59. Finding that there was probable cause for the search and seizure at issue before it, the Court affirmed the convictions.

. . .

Neither *Carroll*, supra, nor other cases in this Court require or suggest that in every conceivable circumstance the search of an auto even with probable cause may be made without the extra protection for privacy that a warrant affords. But the circumstances that furnish probable cause to search a particular auto for particular articles are most often unforeseeable; moreover, the opportunity to search is fleeting since a car is readily movable. Where this is true, as in *Carroll* and the case before us now, if an effective search is to be made at any time, either the search must be made immediately without a warrant or the car itself must be seized and held without a warrant for whatever period is necessary to obtain a warrant for the search.[14]

In enforcing the Fourth Amendment's prohibition against unreasonable searches and seizures, the Court has insisted upon probable cause as a minimum requirement for a reasonable search permitted by the Constitu-

14. Following the car until a warrant can be obtained seems an impractical alternative since, among other things, the car may be taken out of the jurisdiction. Tracing the car and searching it hours or days later would of course permit instruments or fruits of crime to be removed from the car before the search.

tion. As a general rule, it has also required the judgment of a magistrate on the probable-cause issue and the issuance of a warrant before a search is made. Only in exigent circumstances will the judgment of the police as to probable cause serve as a sufficient authorization for a search. *Carroll*, supra, holds a search warrant unnecessary where there is probable cause to search an automobile stopped on the highway; the car is movable, the occupants are alerted, and the car's contents may never be found again if a warrant must be obtained. Hence an immediate search is constitutionally permissible.

Arguably, because of the preference for a magistrate's judgment, only the immobilization of the car should be permitted until a search warrant is obtained; arguably, only the "lesser" intrusion is permissible until the magistrate authorizes the "greater." But which is the "greater" and which the "lesser" intrusion is itself a debatable question and the answer may depend on a variety of circumstances. For constitutional purposes, we see no difference between on the one hand seizing and holding a car before presenting the probable cause issue to a magistrate and on the other hand carrying out an immediate search without a warrant. Given probable cause to search, either course is reasonable under the Fourth Amendment.

On the facts before us, the blue station wagon could have been searched on the spot when it was stopped since there was probable cause to search and it was a fleeting target for a search. The probable-cause factor still obtained at the station house and so did the mobility of the car unless the Fourth Amendment permits a warrantless seizure of the car and the denial of its use to anyone until a warrant is secured. In that event there is little to choose in terms of practical consequences between an immediate search without a warrant and the car's immobilization until a warrant is obtained.[15] The same consequences may not follow where there is unforeseeable cause to search a house. Compare Vale v. Louisiana, ante, p. 30. But as *Carroll*, supra, held, for the purposes of the Fourth Amendment there is a constitutional difference between houses and cars.

. . .

■ MR. JUSTICE HARLAN, concurring in part and dissenting in part.

. . .

In sustaining the search of the automobile I believe the Court ignores the framework of our past decisions circumscribing the scope of permissible search without a warrant. The Court has long read the Fourth Amendment's proscription of "unreasonable" searches as imposing a general principle that a search without a warrant is not justified by the mere knowledge by the searching officers of facts showing probable cause. The "general requirement that a search warrant be obtained" is basic to the

---

15. It was not unreasonable in this case to take the car to the station house. All occupants in the car were arrested in a dark parking lot in the middle of the night. A careful search at that point was impractical and perhaps not safe for the officers, and it would serve the owner's convenience and the safety of his car to have the vehicle and the keys together at the station house.

Amendment's protection of privacy, and " 'the burden is on those seeking [an] exemption . . . to show the need for it.' " E.g., Chimel v. California, 395 U.S. 752, 762 (1969). . . .

Fidelity to this established principle requires that, where exceptions are made to accommodate the exigencies of particular situations, those exceptions be no broader than necessitated by the circumstances presented. For example, the Court has recognized that an arrest creates an emergency situation justifying a warrantless search of the arrestee's person and of "the area from within which he might gain possession of a weapon or destructible evidence"; however, because the exigency giving rise to this exception extends only that far, the search may go no further. . . . Similarly we held in Terry v. Ohio, 392 U.S. 1 (1968), that a warrantless search in a "stop and frisk" situation must "be strictly circumscribed by the exigencies which justify its initiation." Id., at 26. Any intrusion beyond what is necessary for the personal safety of the officer or others nearby is forbidden.

Where officers have probable cause to search a vehicle on a public way, a further limited exception to the warrant requirement is reasonable because "the vehicle can be quickly moved out of the locality or jurisdiction in which the warrant must be sought." Carroll v. United States, 267 U.S. 132, 153 (1925). Because the officers might be deprived of valuable evidence if required to obtain a warrant before effecting any search or seizure, I agree with the Court that they should be permitted to take the steps necessary to preserve evidence and to make a search possible. . . . The Court holds that those steps include making a warrantless search of the entire vehicle on the highway—a conclusion reached by the Court in *Carroll* without discussion—and indeed appears to go further and to condone the removal of the car to the police station for a warrantless search there at the convenience of the police. I cannot agree that this result is consistent with our insistence in other areas that departures from the warrant requirement strictly conform to the exigency presented.

The Court concedes that the police could prevent removal of the evidence by temporarily seizing the car for the time necessary to obtain a warrant. It does not dispute that such a course would fully protect the interests of effective law enforcement; rather it states that whether temporary seizure is a "lesser" intrusion than warrantless search "is itself a debatable question and the answer may depend on a variety of circumstances." Ante, at 51–52.[16] I believe it clear that a warrantless search involves the greater sacrifice of Fourth Amendment values.

---

16. The Court, unable to decide whether search or temporary seizure is the "lesser" intrusion, in this case authorizes both. The Court concludes that it was reasonable for the police to take the car to the station, where they searched it once to no avail. The searching officers then entered the station, interrogated petitioner and the car's owner, and returned later for another search of the car—this one successful. At all times the car and its contents were secure against removal or destruction. Nevertheless, the Court approves the searches without even an inquiry into the officers' ability promptly to take their case before a magistrate.

The Fourth Amendment proscribes, to be sure, unreasonable "seizures" as well as "searches." However, in the circumstances in which this problem is likely to occur, the lesser intrusion will almost always be the simple seizure of the car for the period—perhaps a day—necessary to enable the officers to obtain a search warrant. In the first place, as this case shows, the very facts establishing probable cause to search will often also justify arrest of the occupants of the vehicle. Since the occupants themselves are to be taken into custody, they will suffer minimal further inconvenience from the temporary immobilization of their vehicle. Even where no arrests are made, persons who wish to avoid a search—either to protect their privacy or to conceal incriminating evidence—will almost certainly prefer a brief loss of the use of the vehicle in exchange for the opportunity to have a magistrate pass upon the justification for the search. To be sure, one can conceive of instances in which the occupant, having nothing to hide and lacking concern for the privacy of the automobile, would be more deeply offended by a temporary immobilization of his vehicle than by a prompt search of it. However, such a person always remains free to consent to an immediate search, thus avoiding any delay. Where consent is not forthcoming, the occupants of the car have an interest in privacy that is protected by the Fourth Amendment even where the circumstances justify a temporary seizure. . . . The Court's endorsement of a warrantless invasion of that privacy where another course would suffice is simply inconsistent with our repeated stress on the Fourth Amendment's mandate of " 'adherence to judicial processes.' " E.g., Katz v. United States, 389 U.S. [347 (1967)], at 357.[17]

　　. . . [18]

－－－－－－－

128. The Court has confirmed the rule of *Chambers*, that probable cause alone authorizes the search of a car and that a warrant need not be obtained, even if there is time to do so, on several occasions. E.g., Maryland v. Dyson, 527 U.S. 465 (1999) (per curiam); Pennsylvania v. Labron, 518 U.S. 938 (1996) (7–2); Texas v. White, 423 U.S. 67 (1975) (7–2).

The Supreme Court of Connecticut has rejected the rule of *Chambers*. "In light of our demonstrated constitutional preference for warrants and our concomitant obligation narrowly to describe exceptions to the state constitutional warrant requirement, we conclude that a warrantless automobile search supported by probable cause, but conducted after the auto-

---

17. Circumstances might arise in which it would be impracticable to immobilize the car for the time required to obtain a warrant—for example, where a single police officer must take arrested suspects to the station, and has no way of protecting the suspects' car during his absence. In such situations it might be wholly reasonable to per- form an on-the-spot search based on probable cause. However, where nothing in the situation makes impracticable the obtaining of a warrant, I cannot joint the Court in shunting aside that vital Fourth Amendment safeguard.

[18] Justice Stewart wrote a brief concurring opinion.

mobile has been impounded at the police station, violates article first, § 7, of the Connecticut constitution." State v. Miller, 630 A.2d 1315, 1326 (Conn.1993).

129. If the police have authority to search an automobile without a search warrant under the rationale of *Chambers*, the search can be as broad as a search pursuant to a warrant. United States v. Ross, 456 U.S. 798 (1982) (6–3). "The scope of a warrantless search based on probable cause is no narrower—and no broader—than the scope of a search authorized by a warrant supported by probable cause. Only the prior approval of the magistrate is waived; the search otherwise is as the magistrate could authorize." Id. at 823. More particularly, the Court said that containers within the automobile that might hold the items to be seized can be opened and searched. "When a legitimate search is under way, and when its purpose and its limits have been precisely defined, nice distinctions between closets, drawers, and containers, in the case of a home, or between glove compartments, upholstered seats, trunks, and wrapped packages, in the case of a vehicle, must give way to the interest in the prompt and efficient completion of the task at hand." Id. at 821. However, the Court noted its statement in *Chadwick*, p. 212 note 119 above, that the "automobile exception" could not be extended to other movable containers, like luggage, found in a public place. Id. at 811–12.

The search authorized by *Ross* includes containers that belong to a passenger or to someone not present in the car when it is stopped. Wyoming v. Houghton, 526 U.S. 295 (1999) (6–3).

For a time after *Ross* was decided, the Court distinguished between probable cause to search a car and probable cause to search a container within a car. In the latter situation, the Court said, not *Ross* but *Chadwick* prevailed. Yet, if the basis of the search was not *Chambers* but *Belton*, p. 214 note 121 above, *Chadwick* was inapplicable. The confusion that resulted is described in California v. Acevedo, 500 U.S. 565 (1991). Concluding that a uniform rule was desirable, the Court held in *Acevedo* that (the rule of *Belton* aside) whether there is probable cause to search a car or probable cause to search a container within a car, if the container is lawfully seized, it may be searched without a warrant. (It remains true, however, that if the police have probable cause to search only the container and not the car, *Ross* does not authorize a search of the car beyond what is necessary to find the container.) Aside from opting for a clear rule in the case of containers found in a car, *Acevedo* does little to resolve the tension between *Chadwick*, on one hand, and *Belton* and *Ross*, on the other.

If police officials remove containers from a vehicle pursuant to *Ross*, the search of the containers authorized by *Ross* need not take place immediately; in the absence of any particular claim that the delay affected the defendant's privacy interests, a warrantless search of the containers three days after their removal from the searched vehicles is not unreasonable. United States v. Johns, 469 U.S. 478 (1985) (7–2).

130. The "automobile exception" to the requirement of a search warrant was applied to a "Dodge Mini Motor Home" parked in a city lot, in California v. Carney, 471 U.S. 386 (1985) (6–3). Summarizing the rationale for the exception, the Court said:

> In short, the pervasive schemes of regulation, which necessarily lead to reduced expectations of privacy, and the exigencies attendant to ready mobility justify searches without prior recourse to the authority of a magistrate so long as the overriding standard of probable cause is met.
>
> When a vehicle is being used on the highways, or if it is readily capable of such use and is found stationary in a place not regularly used for residential purposes—temporary or otherwise—the two justifications for the vehicle exception come into play. First, the vehicle is obviously readily mobile by the turn of a switch key, if not actually moving. Second, there is a reduced expectation of privacy stemming from its use as a licensed motor vehicle subject to a range of police regulation inapplicable to a fixed dwelling. At least in these circumstances, the overriding societal interests in effective law enforcement justify an immediate search before the vehicle and its occupants become unavailable.

Id. at 392–93.

That was so, the Court concluded, even though the defendant's vehicle "possessed some, if not many of the attributes of a home." Id. at 393. The Court added that it did "not pass on the application of the vehicle exception to a motor home that is situated in a way or place that objectively indicates that it is being used as a residence. Among the factors that might be relevant in determining whether a warrant would be required in such a circumstance is its location, whether the vehicle is readily mobile or instead, for instance, elevated on blocks, whether the vehicle is licensed, whether it is connected to utilities, and whether it has convenient access to a public road." Id. at 394 n.3.

Carney was applied to an unattended motor home parked in a driveway, in United States v. Markham, 844 F.2d 366 (6th Cir.1988).

131. The Court held that there was not a violation of the Fourth Amendment when a police officer opened a car door to move papers obstructing his view of the Vehicle Identification Number on the dashboard, in New York v. Class, 475 U.S. 106 (5–4). The officer stopped the driver of the car for a traffic offense. After the driver got out of the car, the officer opened the car door to look for the VIN on the door jamb. He found none. Federal law requires that the VIN be either on the door jamb or on the dashboard, visible from outside the car. The officer reached into the car to move papers from the area of the dashboard where the VIN is located. Doing so, he saw a gun hidden under the seat. The Court upheld the seizure of the gun. The Court said that in the circumstances—the requirement that the VIN be visible from the outside, the minimal intrusion, the basis for stopping the driver initially, and the possible risk to the officer if he had asked the driver to re-enter the car to expose the VIN—the officer's action was reasonable. Cf. Arizona v. Hicks, 480 U.S. 321 (1987), p. 201 note 110 above.

————

South Dakota v. Opperman
428 U.S. 364, 96 S.Ct. 3092, 49 L.Ed.2d 1000 (1976)

■ Mr. Chief Justice Burger delivered the opinion of the Court.

We review the judgment of the Supreme Court of South Dakota, holding that local police violated the Fourth Amendment to the Federal Constitution, as applicable to the States under the Fourteenth Amendment, when they conducted a routine inventory search of an automobile lawfully impounded by police for violations of municipal parking ordinances.

(1)

Local ordinances prohibit parking in certain areas of downtown Vermillion, S.D., between the hours of 2 a.m. and 6 a.m. During the early morning hours of December 10, 1973, a Vermillion police officer observed respondent's unoccupied vehicle illegally parked in the restricted zone. At approximately 3 a.m., the officer issued an overtime parking ticket and placed it on the car's windshield. The citation warned:

"Vehicles in violation of any parking ordinance may be towed from the area."

At approximately 10 o'clock on the same morning, another officer issued a second ticket for an overtime parking violation. These circumstances were routinely reported to police headquarters, and after the vehicle was inspected, the car was towed to the city impound lot.

From outside the car at the impound lot, a police officer observed a watch on the dashboard and other items of personal property located on the back seat and back floorboard. At the officer's direction, the car door was then unlocked and, using a standard inventory form pursuant to standard police procedures, the officer inventoried the contents of the car, including the contents of the glove compartment, which was unlocked. There he found marihuana contained in a plastic bag. All items, including the contraband, were removed to the police department for safekeeping. During the late afternoon of December 10, respondent appeared at the police department to claim his property. The marihuana was retained by police.

Respondent was subsequently arrested on charges of possession of marihuana. His motion to suppress the evidence yielded by the inventory search was denied; he was convicted after a jury trial and sentenced to a fine of $100 and 14 days' incarceration in the county jail. On appeal, the Supreme Court of South Dakota reversed the conviction. The court concluded that the evidence had been obtained in violation of the Fourth Amendment prohibition against unreasonable searches and seizures. We granted certiorari . . . and we reverse.

(2)

This Court has traditionally drawn a distinction between automobiles and homes or offices in relation to the Fourth Amendment. Although automobiles are "effects" and thus within the reach of the Fourth Amendment . . . warrantless examinations of automobiles have been upheld in circumstances in which a search of a home or office would not. . . .

The reason for this well-settled distinction is twofold. First, the inherent mobility of automobiles creates circumstances of such exigency that, as a practical necessity, rigorous enforcement of the warrant requirement is impossible. . . . But the Court has also upheld warrantless searches where no immediate danger was presented that the car would be removed from the jurisdiction. . . . Besides the element of mobility, less rigorous warrant requirements govern because the expectation of privacy with respect to one's automobile is significantly less than that relating to one's home or office. In discharging their varied responsibilities for ensuring the public safety, law enforcement officials are necessarily brought into frequent contact with automobiles. Most of this contact is distinctly noncriminal in nature. . . . Automobiles, unlike homes, are subjected to pervasive and continuing governmental regulation and controls, including periodic inspection and licensing requirements. As an everyday occurrence, police stop and examine vehicles when license plates or inspection stickers have expired, or if other violations, such as exhaust fumes or excessive noise, are noted, or if headlights or other safety equipment are not in proper working order.

The expectation of privacy as to automobiles is further diminished by the obviously public nature of automobile travel. . . .

In the interests of public safety and as part of what the Court has called "community caretaking functions," Cady v. Dombrowski, [413 U.S. 433 (1973)] at 441, automobiles are frequently taken into police custody. Vehicle accidents present one such occasion. To permit the uninterrupted flow of traffic and in some circumstances to preserve evidence, disabled or damaged vehicles will often be removed from the highways or streets at the behest of police engaged solely in caretaking and traffic-control activities. Police will also frequently remove and impound automobiles which violate parking ordinances and which thereby jeopardize both the public safety and the efficient movement of vehicular traffic. The authority of police to seize and remove from the streets vehicles impeding traffic or threatening public safety and convenience is beyond challenge.

When vehicles are impounded, local police departments generally follow a routine practice of securing and inventorying the automobiles' contents. These procedures developed in response to three distinct needs: the protection of the owner's property while it remains in police custody . . . the protection of the police against claims or disputes over lost or stolen property . . . and the protection of the police from potential danger. . . . The practice has been viewed as essential to respond to incidents of theft or vandalism. . . . In addition, police frequently attempt to determine whether a vehicle has been stolen and thereafter abandoned.

These caretaking procedures have almost uniformly been upheld by the state courts, which by virtue of the localized nature of traffic regulation have had considerable occasion to deal with the issue. Applying the Fourth Amendment standard of "reasonableness," the state courts have overwhelmingly concluded that, even if an inventory is characterized as a "search," the intrusion is constitutionally permissible. . . .

The majority of the Federal Courts of Appeals have likewise sustained inventory procedures as reasonable police intrusions. . . . These cases have recognized that standard inventories often include an examination of the glove compartment, since it is a customary place for documents of ownership and registration . . . as well as a place for the temporary storage of valuables.

(3)

The decisions of this Court point unmistakably to the conclusion reached by both federal and state courts that inventories pursuant to standard police procedures are reasonable. . . .

In applying the reasonableness standard adopted by the Framers, this Court has consistently sustained police intrusions into automobiles impounded or otherwise in lawful police custody where the process is aimed at securing or protecting the car and its contents. In Cooper v. California [386 U.S. 58 (1967)], the Court upheld the inventory of a car impounded under the authority of a state forfeiture statute. Even though the inventory was conducted in a distinctly criminal setting and carried out a week after the car had been impounded, the Court nonetheless found that the car search, including examination of the glove compartment where contraband was found, was reasonable under the circumstances. This conclusion was reached despite the fact that no warrant had issued and probable cause to search for the contraband in the vehicle had not been established. The Court said in language explicitly applicable here:

> It would be unreasonable to hold that the police, having to retain the car in their custody for such a length of time, had no right, even for their own protection, to search it.

386 U.S., at 61–62.

In the following Term, the Court in Harris v. United States, 390 U.S. 234 (1968), upheld the introduction of evidence, seized by an officer who, after conducting an inventory search of a car and while taking means to safeguard it, observed a car registration card lying on the metal stripping of the car door. Rejecting the argument that a warrant was necessary, the Court held that the intrusion was justifiable since it was "taken to protect the car while it was in police custody." Id., at 236.

Finally, in Cady v. Dombrowski, supra, the Court upheld a warrantless search of an automobile towed to a private garage even though no probable cause existed to believe that the vehicle contained fruits of a crime. The sole justification for the warrantless incursion was that it was incident to the caretaking function of the local police to protect the community's safety. Indeed, the protective search was instituted solely because local police "were under the impression" that the incapacitated driver, a Chicago police officer, was required to carry his service revolver at all times; the police had reasonable grounds to believe a weapon might be in the car, and thus available to vandals. 413 U.S., at 436. The Court carefully noted that the protective search was carried out in accordance with *standard procedures* in the local police department, ibid., a factor tending to ensure that the intrusion would be limited in scope to the extent necessary to carry out the caretaking function. . . .

The holdings in *Cooper*, *Harris*, and *Cady* point the way to the correct resolution of this case. None of the three cases, of course, involves the precise situation presented here; but, as in all Fourth Amendment cases, we are obliged to look to all the facts and circumstances of this case in light of the principles set forth in these prior decisions. . . .

The Vermillion police were indisputably engaged in a caretaking search of a lawfully impounded automobile. . . . The inventory was conducted only after the car had been impounded for multiple parking violations. The owner, having left his car illegally parked for an extended period, and thus subject to impoundment, was not present to make other arrangements for the safekeeping of his belongings. The inventory itself was prompted by the presence in plain view of a number of valuables inside the car. As in *Cady*, there is no suggestion whatever that this standard procedure, essentially like that followed throughout the country, was a pretext concealing an investigatory police motive.

On this record we conclude that in following standard police procedures, prevailing throughout the country and approved by the overwhelming majority of courts, the conduct of the police was not "unreasonable" under the Fourth Amendment.

The judgment of the South Dakota Supreme Court is therefore reversed, and the case is remanded for further proceedings not inconsistent with this opinion.[19]

---

132. "[A]n inventory search must not be a ruse for a general rummaging in order to discover incriminating evidence. The policy or practice governing inventory searches should be designed to produce an inventory."

[19] Justice Powell wrote a concurring opinion. Justice Marshall wrote a dissenting opinion, which Justice Brennan and Justice Stewart joined. Justice White also dissented, and filed a brief statement indicating his agreement with most of the "analysis and conclusions" of Justice Marshall.

On remand, the South Dakota Supreme Court concluded that the search had violated a provision of the state constitution "almost identical" to the Fourth Amendment and, therefore, that the evidence should have been suppressed. State v. Opperman, 247 N.W.2d 673 (S.D.1976). Subsequently, in State v. Flittie, 425 N.W.2d 1 (S.D.1988), although adhering to its own view in the *Opperman* case itself, the South Dakota court reviewed with considerable approval the Supreme Court's rulings about inventory searches.

Although police officers conducting an inventory cannot have "uncanalized discretion," they need not be required to conduct the inventory "in a totally mechanical 'all or nothing' fashion. . . . The allowance of the exercise of judgment based on concerns related to the purpose of an inventory search does not violate the Fourth Amendment." Florida v. Wells, 495 U.S. 1, 4 (1990). See United States v. Castro, 129 F.3d 752 (5th Cir.1997) (purported inventory search following stop for traffic offense was not routine but was for investigative purpose; evidence suppressed).

(i.e. a checklist)

The Court relied on *Opperman* and Illinois v. Lafayette, p. 225 note 126 above, to uphold an on-site inventory search of a van, after the driver was arrested for drunk driving. In the course of the search, an officer opened a closed backpack behind the front seat, removed a nylon bag containing metal canisters, and opened the canisters, in which he found drugs, drug paraphernalia, and cash. In an outside zippered pouch of the backpack, he found a sealed envelope containing cash. The Court held that the seizure of the above items was lawful, as part of a "reasonable" inventory search carried out in good faith pursuant to police regulations, whether or not another procedure might equally have served the functions of the search with less invasion of privacy. Colorado v. Bertine, 479 U.S. 367 (1987) (7–2). In United States v. Andrews, 22 F.3d 1328, 1335 (5th Cir.1994), the court held that a page-by-page examination of a notebook as part of an inventory search, "to determine whether valuables might be found between its pages," was permissible. See also United States v. Khoury, 901 F.2d 948 (11th Cir.1990), holding that as part of the inventory search of a car, police officers could flip through a spiral notebook found in a briefcase in the trunk of the car in order to determine if it was valuable or contained anything of value, without examining it further.

Inventory searches that deviate from standard procedures have been invalidated. After the defendant's car was involved in a collision, he was taken into custody for traffic offenses, including driving without a proper license. The truck was impounded and searched at a service station away from the scene of the collision. During an inventory search, cocaine was found behind a door panel. The court held that searching behind a door panel was not standard procedure and could not be justified as an inventory search. Nor could the search, conducted away from the scene of the arrest, be justified as incident to it, or as performance of a "community caretaking" function. United States v. Lugo, 978 F.2d 631 (10th Cir.1992). See also United States v. Duguay, 93 F.3d 346 (7th Cir.1996) (inventory search invalid because not pursuant to standard procedure).

133. "[W]here police assumed custody of defendant's automobile for no legitimate state purpose other than safekeeping, and where defendant had arranged for alternative means, not shown to be unreasonable, for the safekeeping of his property, impoundment of defendant's automobile was unreasonable and, therefore, the concomitant inventory was an unreasonable search under the Fourth Amendment." State v. Goodrich, 256 N.W.2d 506, 507 (Minn.1977).

"[C]ontraband discovered in the course of an inventory conducted without first permitting vehicle occupants to utilize available alternative means of safeguarding their property is inadmissible as evidence in a criminal prosecution. Such police conduct amounts to an unreasonable and unwarranted intrusion into the privacy interests of occupants in contravention of the Fourth Amendment. . . ." State v. Mangold, 414 A.2d 1312, 1313 (N.J.1980). In *Mangold*, the inventory was made of a vehicle at the scene of an accident in which it was involved, while the occupants were still present.

134. Hot pursuit.

About 8 a.m. on March 17, 1962, an armed robber entered the business premises of the Diamond Cab Company in Baltimore, Maryland. He took some $363 and ran. Two cab drivers in the vicinity, attracted by shouts of "Holdup," followed the man to 2111 Cocoa Lane. One driver notified the company dispatcher by radio that the man was a Negro about 5′8″ tall, wearing a light cap and dark jacket, and that he had entered the house on Cocoa Lane. The dispatcher relayed the information to police who were proceeding to the scene of the robbery. Within minutes, police arrived at the house in a number of patrol cars. An officer knocked and announced their presence. Mrs. Hayden answered, and the officers told her they believed that a robber had entered the house, and asked to search the house. She offered no objection.

The officers spread out through the first and second floors and the cellar in search of the robber. Hayden was found in an upstairs bedroom feigning sleep. He was arrested when the officers on the first floor and in the cellar reported that no other man was in the house. Meanwhile an officer was attracted to an adjoining bathroom by the noise of running water, and discovered a shotgun and a pistol in a flush tank; another officer who, according to the District Court, "was searching the cellar for a man or the money" found in a washing machine a jacket and trousers of the type the fleeing man was said to have worn. A clip of ammunition for the pistol and a cap were found under the mattress of Hayden's bed, and ammunition for the shotgun was found in a bureau drawer in Hayden's room. All these items of evidence were introduced against respondent at his trial.

. . .

We agree with the Court of Appeals that neither the entry without warrant to search for the robber, nor the search for him without warrant was invalid. Under the circumstances of this case, "the exigencies of the situation made that course imperative." McDonald v. United States, 335 U.S. 451, 456. The police were informed that an armed robbery had taken place, and that the suspect had entered 2111 Cocoa Lane less than five minutes before they reached it. They acted reasonably when they entered the house and began to search for a man of the description they had been given and for weapons which he had used in the robbery or might use against them. The Fourth Amendment does not require police officers to delay in the course of an investigation if to do so would gravely endanger their lives or the lives of others. Speed here was essential, and only a thorough search of the house for persons and weapons could have insured that Hayden was the only man present and that the police had control of all weapons which could be used against them or to effect an escape.

We do not rely upon Harris v. United States, [331 U.S. 145 (1947)], in sustaining the validity of the search. The principal issue in *Harris* was whether the search there could properly be regarded as incident to the lawful arrest, since Harris was in custody before the search was made and the evidence seized. Here, the seizures occurred prior to or immediately contemporaneous with Hayden's arrest, as part of an effort to find a suspected felon, armed, within the house into which he had run only minutes before the police arrived. The permissible scope of search must, therefore, at the least, be as broad as may reasonably be necessary to prevent the dangers that the suspect at large in the house may resist or escape.

It is argued that, while the weapons, ammunition, and cap may have been seized in the course of a search for weapons, the officer who seized the clothing was searching neither for the suspect nor for weapons when he looked into the washing machine in which he found the clothing. But even if we assume, although we do not decide, that the exigent circumstances in this case made lawful a search without warrant only for the suspect or his weapons, it cannot be said on this record that the officer who found the clothes in the washing machine was not searching for weapons. He testified that he was searching for the man or the money, but his failure to state explicitly that he was searching for weapons, in the absence of a specific question to that effect, can hardly be accorded controlling weight. He knew that the robber was armed and he did not know that some weapons had been found at the time he opened the machine. In these circumstances the inference that he was in fact also looking for weapons is fully justified.

Warden, Maryland Penitentiary v. Hayden, 387 U.S. 294, 297–300 (1967).[20]

135. The "hot pursuit" that justified an entry to search without a warrant in Warden v. Hayden, p. 242 note 134 above, is an example of the general rule that the requirement of a warrant does not apply in an emergency ("exigent circumstances") provided that the emergency was not created or readily avoidable by official action. See, e.g., Llaguno v. Mingey, 763 F.2d 1560 (7th Cir.1985) (search for killer); United States v. McEachin, 670 F.2d 1139 (D.C.Cir.1981) (entry to prevent removal or destruction of evidence); United States v. Robinson, 533 F.2d 578 (D.C.Cir.1975) (search of unoccupied parked car believed to have been used in robbery an hour earlier, to obtain information to apprehend robbers); United States v. Goldenstein, 456 F.2d 1006 (8th Cir.1972) (person needing assistance). In United States v. Beltran, 917 F.2d 641 (1st Cir.1990) the Court said that

---

20. For another aspect of this case, see p. 246 below.

the emergency requiring an entry without a warrant was due to the failure of police to obtain a warrant while there was time and held that the search was unlawful.

See also United States v. Hand, 516 F.2d 472 (5th Cir.1975), in which "exigent circumstances" were held to authorize a search of the defendant's handbags, which she had left in her employer's office, for evidence of embezzlement. The defendant was not under arrest and was not present in the office when the bags were searched, but she had indicated that she was going to remove them. The court relied primarily on Chambers v. Maroney, p. 228 above. Accord United States v. De La Fuente, 548 F.2d 528 (5th Cir.1977) (suitcase carried by airline passenger could be searched after he checked it and was allowed to board, as alternative to detaining it until warrant was obtained). Are such decisions consistent with United States v. Chadwick, 433 U.S. 1 (1977), p. 212 note 119 above? In Ingram v. City of Columbus, 185 F.3d 579 (6th Cir.1999), the court said that officers entering premises pursuant to exigent circumstances do not have general authority to handcuff occupants and detain them at gunpoint.

The "exigent circumstances" rule is not without limits. In Mincey v. Arizona, 437 U.S. 385 (1978), the Court rejected its application to create a general "murder-scene exception" to requirements of the Fourth Amendment. *Mincey* was confirmed in Flippo v. West Virginia, 528 U.S. 11 (1999) (per curiam). *Mincey* was applied in Thompson v. Louisiana, 469 U.S. 17 (1984) (per curiam). See also Welsh v. Wisconsin, 466 U.S. 740 (1984), p. 49 note 30 above.

136. Postal authorities having a basis for suspicion may temporarily detain packages (first class mail) to investigate and to obtain a warrant for a search of the packages. United States v. Van Leeuwen, 397 U.S. 249 (1970). See United States v. Martell, 654 F.2d 1356 (9th Cir.1981) (brief detention of luggage; *Van Leeuwen* applied).

Van Leeuwen is distinguished in United States v. Hunt, 496 F.2d 888 (5th Cir.1974), in which the court held that the temporary removal of allegedly obscene materials and their delivery to a magistrate for a hearing on obscenity constituted a seizure within the meaning of the Fourth Amendment. The court noted that in *Van Leeuwen*, the packages were "merely removed . . . from the normal flow of the mails" and later replaced "to proceed on to their destination," while in *Hunt* the seizure involved items in the defendant's possession. Id. at 893.

137. Administrative searches. Commercial premises in a closely regulated industry may be subject to administrative searches without a search warrant. In New York v. Burger, 482 U.S. 691 (1987) (6–3), the Court upheld a statute authorizing the warrantless search of automobile junkyards. The administrative search was permissible, the Court said, even though the ultimate purpose of the regulatory scheme was prevention of crime and searches under it might disclose evidence of crime; nor was it significant that police officers rather than administrative officials conducted the search.

"Searches and seizures by government employers or supervisors of the private property of their employees . . . are subject to the restraints of the Fourth Amendment." O'Connor v. Ortega, 480 U.S. 709, 715 (1987) (5–4). *Ortega* involved a search by state hospital officials of the office of a physician employed by the hospital. The search was conducted in the wake of an investigation of alleged misconduct by the physician. Although all members of the Court agreed that the Fourth Amendment applies in this general context, there was no clear majority view about what the Amendment requires. The extent of an employee's "reasonable expectation of privacy" is affected by "the operational realities of the workplace," id. at 717, as well as the actual practices at the workplace. A majority of the Court concluded that a warrant is not required to search for a "work-related purpose," id. at 722; nor does the requirement of probable cause apply. Four members of the Court concluded that "public employer intrusions on the constitutionally protected privacy interests of government employees for noninvestigatory, work-related purposes, as well as for investigation of work-related misconduct, should be judged by the standard of reasonableness under all the circumstances." Id. at 725–26. A fifth Justice (Justice Scalia) concluded that "government searches to retrieve work-related materials or to investigate violations of workplace rules—searches of the sort that are regarded as reasonable and normal in the private-employer context—do not violate the Fourth Amendment." Id. at 732 (opinion concurring in the judgment). Four dissenting Justices concluded that in the absence of "special need" dictated by the purpose to be achieved, id. at 741–43, the ordinary requirements of a warrant and probable cause should apply. See Schowengerdt v. General Dynamics Corp., 823 F.2d 1328 (9th Cir.1987) (*Ortega* applied).

Federal regulations requiring blood and urine tests of railroad employees who are involved in certain train accidents and authorizing railroads to administer breath and urine tests to employees who violate certain safety rules were upheld in Skinner v. Railway Labor Executives' Association, 489 U.S. 602 (1989) (7–2). The regulations were promulgated to control widespread alcohol and drug abuse among the employees. The Court noted that the regulations were a safety measure and not intended to aid prosecution of the employees. It said that imposing a warrant requirement would significantly hinder the objectives of the testing program without adding to the protection afforded by the regulations themselves. In a companion case, National Treasury Employees Union v. Von Raab, 489 U.S. 656 (1989) (5–4), the Court upheld the U.S. Customs Service's program requiring drug tests by urinalysis of employees seeking assignment to positions involving the interdiction of drugs or the carrying of firearms. The Court remanded the case for determination whether, as applied to employees seeking assignment to positions involving the handling of classified information, the program identified the category of employees covered so as to include only employees likely to gain access to sensitive material.

A state statute authorizing a blood alcohol test of any motorist who is in an accident involving death or serious injury was declared invalid in Commonwealth v. Kohl, 615 A.2d 308 (Pa.1992), because, the court said, there was no special need to dispense with the warrant and probable cause requirements, as there was in *Skinner*; the test program involved here was solely to help the state prosecute drunk drivers.

See United States v. Attson, 900 F.2d 1427 (9th Cir.1990), holding that a doctor employed by the federal government in a public hospital was not subject to the requirements for search and seizure under the Fourth Amendment when he took a blood sample for medical reasons from a patient who was a criminal suspect.

Seizure

Warden, Maryland Penitentiary v. Hayden
387 U.S. 294, 87 S.Ct. 1642, 18 L.Ed.2d 782 (1967)

■ MR. JUSTICE BRENNAN delivered the opinion of the Court.

We review in this case the validity of the proposition that there is under the Fourth Amendment a "distinction between merely evidentiary materials, on the one hand, which may not be seized either under the authority of a search warrant or during the course of a search incident to arrest, and on the other hand, those objects which may validly be seized including the instrumentalities and means by which a crime is committed, the fruits of crime such as stolen property, weapons by which escape of the person arrested might be effected, and property the possession of which is a crime."[21]

A Maryland court sitting without a jury convicted respondent of armed robbery. Items of his clothing, a cap, jacket, and trousers, among other things, were seized during a search of his home, and were admitted in evidence without objection. After unsuccessful state court proceedings, he sought and was denied federal habeas corpus relief in the District Court for Maryland. A divided panel of the Court of Appeals believed that Harris v. United States, 331 U.S. 145, 154, sustained the validity of the search, but held that respondent was correct in his contention that the clothing seized was improperly admitted in evidence because the items had "evidential value only" and therefore were not lawfully subject to seizure. We granted certiorari. . . . We reverse.

. . .

[The facts and the first part of the Court's opinion, in which the Court concluded that the search of the defendant's home was lawful, are given in note 134, p. 242 above.]

---

21. Harris v. United States, 331 U.S. 145, 154 [(1947)].

We come, then, to the question whether, even though the search was lawful, the Court of Appeals was correct in holding that the seizure and introduction of the items of clothing violated the Fourth Amendment because they are "mere evidence." The distinction made by some of our cases between seizure of items of evidential value only and seizure of instrumentalities, fruits, or contraband has been criticized by courts and commentators. . . . We today reject the distinction as based on premises no longer accepted as rules governing the application of the Fourth Amendment.

. . .

Nothing in the language of the Fourth Amendment supports the distinction between "mere evidence" and instrumentalities, fruits of crime, or contraband. On its face, the provision assures the "right of the people to be secure in their persons, houses, papers, and effects . . ." without regard to the use to which any of these things are applied. This "right of the people" is certainly unrelated to the "mere evidence" limitation. Privacy is disturbed no more by a search directed to a purely evidentiary object than it is by a search directed to an instrumentality, fruit, or contraband. A magistrate can intervene in both situations, and the requirements of probable cause and specificity can be preserved intact. Moreover, nothing in the nature of property seized as evidence renders it more private than property seized, for example, as an instrumentality; quite the opposite may be true. Indeed, the distinction is wholly irrational, since, depending on the circumstances, the same "papers and effects" may be "mere evidence" in one case and "instrumentality" in another. . . .

In Gouled v. United States, 255 U.S. 298, 309, the Court said that search warrants "may not be used as a means of gaining access to a man's house or office and papers solely for the purpose of making search to secure evidence to be used against him in a criminal or penal proceeding. . . ." The Court derived from Boyd v. United States, [116 U.S. 616 (1886)], the proposition that warrants "may be resorted to only when a primary right to such search and seizure may be found in the interest which the public or the complainant may have in the property to be seized, or in the right to the possession of it, or when a valid exercise of the police power renders possession of the property by the accused unlawful and provides that it may be taken," 255 U.S., at 309; that is, when the property is an instrumentality or fruit of crime, or contraband. Since it was "impossible to say, on the record . . . that the Government had any interest" in the papers involved "other than as evidence against the accused . . ." "to permit them to be used in evidence would be, in effect, as ruled in the *Boyd* case, to compel the defendant to become a witness against himself." Id., at 311.

The items of clothing involved in this case are not "testimonial" or "communicative" in nature, and their introduction therefore did not compel respondent to become a witness against himself in violation of the Fifth Amendment. Schmerber v. California, 384 U.S. 757. This case thus does not require that we consider whether there are items of evidential value whose very nature precludes them from being the object of a reasonable search and seizure.

The Fourth Amendment ruling in *Gouled* was based upon the dual, related premises that historically the right to search for and seize property depended upon the assertion by the Government of a valid claim of superior interest, and that it was not enough that the purpose of the search and seizure was to obtain evidence to use in apprehending and convicting criminals. . . . Thus stolen property—the fruits of crime—was always subject to seizure. And the power to search for stolen property was gradually extended to cover "any property which the private citizen was not permitted to possess," which included instrumentalities of crime (because of the early notion that items used in crime were forfeited to the State) and contraband. Kaplan, "Search and Seizure: A No-Man's Land in the Criminal Law," 49 Calif. L. Rev. 474, 475. No separate governmental interest in seizing evidence to apprehend and convict criminals was recognized; it was required that some property interest be asserted. The remedial structure also reflected these dual premises. Trespass, replevin, and the other means of redress for persons aggrieved by searches and seizures, depended upon proof of a superior property interest. And since a lawful seizure presupposed a superior claim, it was inconceivable that a person could recover property lawfully seized. . . .

The premise that property interests control the right of the Government to search and seize has been discredited. Searches and seizures may be "unreasonable" within the Fourth Amendment even though the Government asserts a superior property interest at common law. We have recognized that the principal object of the Fourth Amendment is the protection of privacy rather than property, and have increasingly discarded fictional and procedural barriers rested on property concepts. . . .

The development of search and seizure law . . . is replete with examples of the transformation in substantive law brought about through the interaction of the felt need to protect privacy from unreasonable invasions and the flexibility in rulemaking made possible by the remedy of exclusion. . . .

The premise in *Gouled* that government may not seize evidence simply for the purpose of proving crime has likewise been discredited. The requirement that the Government assert in addition some property interest in material it seizes has long been a fiction, obscuring the reality that government has an interest in solving crime. *Schmerber* settled the proposition that it is reasonable, within the terms of the Fourth Amendment, to conduct otherwise permissible searches for the purpose of obtaining evidence which would aid in apprehending and convicting criminals. The requirements of the Fourth Amendment can secure the same protection of privacy whether the search is for "mere evidence" or for fruits, instrumentalities or contraband. There must, of course, be a nexus—automatically provided in the case of fruits, instrumentalities or contraband—between the item to be seized and criminal behavior. Thus in the case of "mere evidence," probable cause must be examined in terms of cause to believe that the evidence sought will aid in a particular apprehension or conviction. In so doing, consideration of police purposes will be required. . . . But no such problem is presented in this case. The clothes found in the washing machine matched the description of those worn by the robber and the police therefore could reasonably believe that the items would aid in the identification of the culprit.

The remedy of suppression, moreover, which made possible protection of privacy from unreasonable searches without regard to proof of a superior property interest, likewise provides the procedural device necessary for allowing otherwise permissible searches and seizures conducted solely to obtain evidence of crime. For just as the suppression of evidence does not entail a declaration of superior property interest in the person aggrieved, thereby enabling him to suppress evidence unlawfully seized despite his inability to demonstrate such an interest (as with fruits, instrumentalities, contraband), the refusal to suppress evidence carries no declaration of superior property interest in the State, and should thereby enable the State to introduce evidence lawfully seized despite its inability to demonstrate such an interest. And, unlike the situation at common law, the owner of property would not be rendered remediless if "mere evidence" could lawfully be seized to prove crime. For just as the suppression of evidence does not in itself necessarily entitle the aggrieved person to its return (as, for example, contraband), the introduction of "mere evidence" does not in itself entitle the State to its retention. Where public officials "unlawfully seize or *hold* a citizen's realty or chattels, recoverable by appropriate action at law or in equity . . ." the true owner may "bring his possessory action to reclaim that which is wrongfully withheld." Land v. Dollar, 330 U.S. 731, 738. (Emphasis added.)

The survival of the *Gouled* distinction is attributable more to chance than considered judgment. Legislation has helped perpetuate it. Thus, Congress has never authorized the issuance of search warrants for the seizure of mere evidence of crime. . . . *Gouled* concluded, needlessly it appears, that the Constitution virtually limited searches and seizures to these categories. After *Gouled*, pressure to test this conclusion was slow to mount. Rule 41(b) of the Federal Rules of Criminal Procedure incorporated the *Gouled* categories as limitations on federal authorities to issue warrants and Mapp v. Ohio, 367 U.S. 643, only recently made the "mere evidence" rule a problem in the state courts. Pressure against the rule in the federal courts has taken the form rather of broadening the categories of evidence subject to seizure, thereby creating considerable confusion in the law. . . .

The rationale most frequently suggested for the rule preventing the seizure of evidence is that "limitations upon the fruit to be gathered tend to limit the quest itself." United States v. Poller, 43 F.2d 911, 914 (C.A.2d Cir.1930). But privacy "would be just as well served by a restriction on search to the even-numbered days of the month. . . . And it would have the extra advantage of avoiding hair-splitting questions. . . ." *Kaplan*, at 479. The "mere evidence" limitation has spawned exceptions so numerous and confusion so great, in fact, that it is questionable whether it affords meaningful protection. But if its rejection does enlarge the area of permissible searches, the intrusions are nevertheless made after fulfilling the probable cause and particularity requirements of the Fourth Amendment and after the intervention of "a neutral and detached magistrate. . . ." Johnson v. United States, 333 U.S. 10, 14. The Fourth Amendment allows intrusions upon privacy under these circumstances, and there is no viable reason to distinguish intrusions to secure "mere evidence" from intrusions to secure fruits, instrumentalities, or contraband.

The judgment of the Court of Appeals is

Reversed.[22]

————

138.   In 1968 Congress implemented the decision in Warden v. Hayden, above, in the Omnibus Crime Control & Safe Streets Act, § 1401(a), 82 Stat. 238, which amended Title 18 U.S.C. by adding § 3103a: "Additional grounds for issuing warrant. . . . [A] warrant may be issued to search for and seize any property that constitutes evidence of a criminal offense in violation of the laws of the United States." A similar provision has been incorporated in Rule 41(c)(1), see p. 177 above.

Was the ruling in *Gouled* concerned with seizures or the scope of a search? Or was it concerned with the *occasion* for a search? Is it so obviously true that from a privacy perspective there is no reason to distinguish a search for evidence from a search for the fruits or instrumentalities of a crime or contraband?

139.   If police officials intend to use recovered stolen property in evidence against the thief and retain it pending the trial over the objection of the victim of the theft (who, aside from destroying the chain of custody, wants to use it in a way that will make it unavailable as evidence) is the property " 'wrongfully withheld,' " p. 249 above? If so, is the Court's

[22] Justice Fortas wrote a concurring opinion which Chief Justice Warren joined. Justice Black concurred in the result. Justice Douglas wrote a dissenting opinion.

observation that there is a "possessory action," id., to recover the property sufficient? Is the situation different if the owner of the property who wants its return (and is entitled to its return) is the thief? Suppose Hayden had demanded the return of his cap, jacket and trousers before trial?

Rule 41(g) provides for a "motion to return property," to be filed in the district where the property was seized. If, following a hearing on any factual issues, the motion is granted, the property must be returned to the movant, but the court "may impose reasonable conditions to protect access to the property and its use in later proceedings." See United States v. Wilson, 540 F.2d 1100, 1103–1104 (D.C.Cir.1976): "[I]t is fundamental to the integrity of the criminal justice process that property . . . against which no Government claim lies, be returned promptly to its rightful owner"; "the district court, once its need for the property has terminated, has both the jurisdiction and the duty to return the contested property here regardless and independently of the validity or invalidity of the underlying search and seizure." In United States v. Palmer, 565 F.2d 1063 (9th Cir.1977), the court ordered that money seized from a convicted bank robber, which the government offered in evidence at trial, should be returned to him rather than to the government, absent any claim of ownership adverse to his.

The warrantless seizure from a public place of a car that the police have probable cause to believe is forfeitable contraband is not a violation of the Fourth Amendment. Florida v. White, 526 U.S. 559 (1999) (7–2). The car was subject to forfeiture under a state statute because it had been used in drug transactions.

140. Andresen v. Maryland, 427 U.S. 463 (1976) (7–2). The question left open in Warden v. Hayden, see p. 248 above, whether the privilege against self-incrimination may inhibit the seizure of items if the seizure is lawful under the Fourth Amendment has been answered in the negative. In Andresen v. Maryland, investigators made a search on a warrant of the defendant's offices. The Court held that the privilege against self-incrimination did not require the suppression of incriminating records containing statements made by the defendant that were seized during the search.

> [I]n this case, petitioner was not asked to say or to do anything. The records seized contained statements that petitioner had voluntarily committed to writing. The search for and seizure of these records were conducted by law enforcement personnel. Finally, when these records were introduced at trial, they were authenticated by a handwriting expert, not by petitioner. Any compulsion of petitioner to speak, other than the inherent psychological pressure to respond at trial to unfavorable evidence, was not present.

> This case thus falls within the principle stated by Mr. Justice Holmes: "A party is privileged from producing the evidence but not

℗℈ AO 109 (Rev. 2/90) Seizure Warrant

UNITED STATES DISTRICT COURT

District of _____

In the Matter of the Seizure of
(Address or brief description of property or premises to be seized)

SEIZURE WARRANT

CASE NUMBER:

TO: _____ and any Authorized Officer of the United States

Affidavit(s) having been made before me by _____ who has reason to
Affiant

believe that in the _____ District of _____ there is now
certain property which is subject to forfeiture to the United States, namely (describe the property to be seized)

I am satisfied that the affidavit(s) and any recorded testimony establish probable cause to believe that the property so described is subject to seizure and that grounds exist for the issuance of this seizure warrant.

YOU ARE HEREBY COMMANDED to seize within 10 days the property specified, serving this warrant and making the seizure ☐ (in the daytime—6:00 A.M. to 10:00 P.M.)   ☐ (at any time in the day or night as I find reasonable cause has been established), leaving a copy of this warrant and receipt for the property seized, and prepare a written inventory of the property seized and promptly return this warrant to _____
U.S. Judge or Magistrate

as required by law.

_____ at _____
Date and Time Issued   City   State

_____ _____ _____
Name of Judicial Officer   Title of Judicial Officer   Signature of Judicial Officer

from its production." Johnson v. United States, 228 U.S. 457, 458 (1913). This principle recognizes that the protection afforded by the Self-Incrimination Clause of the Fifth Amendment "adheres basically to the person, not to information that may incriminate him." Couch v. United States, 409 U.S. [322 (1973)], at 328. Thus, although the Fifth Amendment may protect an individual from complying with a subpoena for the production of his personal records in his possession because the very act of protection may constitute a compulsory authentication of incriminating information . . . a seizure of the same materials by law enforcement officers differs in a crucial respect—the individual against whom the search is directed is not required to aid in the discovery, production, or authentication of incriminating evidence.

. . .

[A] contrary determination would prohibit the admission of evidence traditionally used in criminal cases and traditionally admissible despite the Fifth Amendment. For example, it would bar the admission of an accused's gambling records in a prosecution for gambling; a note given temporarily to a bank teller during a robbery and subsequently seized in the accused's automobile or home in a prosecution for bank robbery; and incriminating notes prepared, but not sent, by an accused in a kidnaping or blackmail prosecution.

We find a useful analogy to the Fifth Amendment question in those cases that deal with the "seizure" of oral communications. As the Court has explained, "[t]he constitutional privilege against self-incrimination . . . is designed to prevent the use of legal process to force from the lips of the accused individual the evidence necessary to convict him or to force him to produce and authenticate any personal documents or effects that might incriminate him." Bellis v. United States, 417 U.S. [85 (1974)], at 88, quoting United States v. White, 322 U.S. [694 (1944)] at 698. The significant aspect of this principle was apparent and applied in Hoffa v. United States, 385 U.S. 293 (1966), where the Court rejected the contention that an informant's "seizure" of the accused's conversation with him, and his subsequent testimony at trial concerning that conversation, violated the Fifth Amendment. The rationale was that, although the accused's statements may have been elicited by the informant for the purpose of gathering evidence against him, they were made voluntarily. We see no reasoned distinction to be made between the compulsion upon the accused in that case and the compulsion in this one. In each, the communication, whether oral or written, was made voluntarily. The fact that seizure was contemporaneous with the communication in *Hoffa* but subsequent to the communication here does not affect the question whether the accused was compelled to speak.

Finally, we do not believe that permitting the introduction into evidence of a person's business records seized during an otherwise lawful search would offend or undermine any of the policies undergirding the privilege. Murphy v. Waterfront Commission, 378 U.S. 52, 55 (1964).

In this case, petitioner, at the time he recorded his communication, at the time of the search, and at the time the records were admitted at trial, was not subjected to "the cruel trilemma of self-accusation, perjury or contempt." Ibid. Indeed, he was never required to say or to do anything under penalty of sanction. Similarly, permitting the admission of the records in question does not convert our accusatorial system of justice into an inquisitorial system. . . . Further, the search for and seizure of business records pose no danger greater than that inherent in every search that evidence will be "elicited by inhumane treatment and abuses." 378 U.S., at 55. In this case, the statements seized were voluntarily committed to paper before the police arrived to search for them, and petitioner was not treated discourteously during the search. Also, the "good cause" to "disturb," ibid., petitioner was independently determined by the judge who issued the warrants; and the State bore the burden of executing them. Finally, there is no chance, in this case, of petitioner's statements being self-deprecatory and untrustworthy because they were extracted from him—they were already in existence and had been made voluntarily.

427 U.S. at 473–77.

141. While the defendant was in police custody, police officers visited his home to speak to his wife about the crime of which he was suspected. During the course of the interview, she gave the officers guns and clothing belonging to her husband. Coolidge v. New Hampshire, 403 U.S. 443 (1971). The Court rejected his claim that their receiving the items without his permission constituted an unlawful search and seizure:

The first branch of the petitioner's argument is that when Mrs. Coolidge brought out the guns and clothing, and then handed them over to the police, she was acting as an "instrument" of the officials, complying with a "demand" made by them. Consequently, it is argued, Coolidge was the victim of a search and seizure within the constitutional meaning of those terms. Since we cannot accept this interpretation of the facts, we need not consider the petitioner's further argument that Mrs. Coolidge could not or did not "waive" her husband's constitutional protection against unreasonable searches and seizures.

Had Mrs. Coolidge, wholly on her own initiative, sought out her husband's guns and clothing and then taken them to the police station to be used as evidence against him, there can be no doubt under existing law that the articles would later have been admissible in evidence. . . . The question presented here is whether the conduct of the police officers at the Coolidge house was such as to make her actions their actions for purposes of the Fourth and Fourteenth Amendments and their attendant exclusionary rules. The test, as the petitioner's argument suggests, is whether Mrs. Coolidge, in light of all the circumstances of the case, must be regarded as having acted as an "instrument" or agent of the state when she produced her husband's belongings. . . .

In a situation like the one before us there no doubt always exist forces pushing the spouse to cooperate with the police. Among these are the simple but often powerful convention of openness and honesty, the fear that secretive behavior will intensify suspicion, and uncertainty as to what course is most likely to be helpful to the absent spouse. But there is nothing constitutionally suspect in the existence, without more, of these incentives to full disclosure or active cooperation with the police. The exclusionary rules were fashioned "to prevent, not to repair," and their target is official misconduct. They are "to compel respect for the constitutional guaranty in the only effectively available way—by removing the incentive to disregard it." Elkins v. United States, 364 U.S. 206, 217. But it is no part of the policy underlying the Fourth and Fourteenth Amendments to discourage citizens from aiding to the utmost of their ability in the apprehension of criminals. If, then, the exclusionary rule is properly applicable to the evidence taken from the Coolidge house on the night of February 2, it must be upon the basis that some type of unconstitutional police conduct occurred.

Yet it cannot be said that the police should have obtained a warrant for the guns and clothing before they set out to visit Mrs. Coolidge, since they had no intention of rummaging around among Coolidge's effects or of dispossessing him of any of his property. Nor can it be said that they should have obtained Coolidge's permission for a seizure they did not intend to make. There was nothing to compel them to announce to the suspect that they intended to question his wife about his movements on the night of the disappearance or about the theft from his employer. Once Mrs. Coolidge had admitted them, the policemen were surely acting normally and properly when they asked her, as they had asked those questioned earlier in the investigation, including Coolidge himself, about any guns there might be in the house. The question concerning the clothes Coolidge had been wearing on the night of the disappearance was logical and in no way coercive. Indeed, one might doubt the competence of the officers involved had they not asked exactly the questions they did ask. And surely when Mrs. Coolidge of her own accord produced the guns and clothes for inspection, rather than simply describing them, it was not incumbent on the police to stop her or avert their eyes.

The crux of the petitioner's argument must be that when Mrs. Coolidge asked the policemen whether they wanted the guns, they should have replied that they could not take them, or have first telephoned Coolidge at the police station and asked his permission to take them, or have asked her whether she had been authorized by her husband to release them. Instead, after one policeman had declined the offer, the other turned and said, "We might as well take them," to which Mrs. Coolidge replied, "If you would like them, you may take them."

In assessing the claim that this course of conduct amounted to a search and seizure, it is well to keep in mind that Mrs. Coolidge described her own motive as that of clearing her husband, and that she believed that she had nothing to hide. She had seen her husband himself produce his guns for two other policemen earlier in the week, and there is nothing to indicate that she realized that he had offered only three of them for inspection on that occasion. The two officers who questioned her behaved, as her own testimony shows, with perfect courtesy. There is not the slightest implication of an attempt on their part to coerce or dominate her, or, for that matter, to direct her actions by the more subtle techniques of suggestion that are available to officials in circumstances like these. To hold that the conduct of the police here was a search and seizure would be to hold, in effect, that a criminal suspect has constitutional protection against the adverse consequences of a spontaneous, good-faith effort by his wife to clear him of suspicion.

Coolidge, 403 U.S. at 487–90.

In United States v. Sherwin, 539 F.2d 1 (9th Cir.1976), the manager of a trucking company turned over to the FBI books contained in a shipment that he believed to be obscene. Following the reasoning in *Coolidge*, above, the court said that in a case of this kind "only the fact of consent is relevant, not whether it was properly authorized." Further, "the private person's legal authority to approve a transfer of objects found in a private search has no bearing on whether his relinquishment of those objects to the government is coerced or voluntary. . . . If a transfer is voluntary, then it is not a seizure and the fourth amendment's reasonableness standard is simply inapplicable." Id. at 7–8. See also United States v. Black, 767 F.2d 1334 (9th Cir. 1985) (surrender of business records by former employee and friend).

142. Employees of a private freight carrier opened a damaged package and found plastic bags containing a white powder concealed inside a tube. They notified federal narcotics agents. An agent removed the bags from the tube, opened them, and took a trace of the powder. He performed a field test on the powder, which was cocaine. The Court held that the agent's actions did not violate the Fourth Amendment. The inspection and removal of the plastic bags only confirmed information he had already obtained from the carrier's employees, whose action was a private search; they violated no additional expectation of privacy. The seizure of the bags without a warrant was lawful, since there was probable cause to believe that they contained contraband. The test was permissible since it could disclose only one further fact, whether or not the powder was cocaine, and did not invade any legitimate interest in privacy. United States v. Jacobsen, 466 U.S. 109 (1984) (7–2). Cf. Walter v. United States, 447 U.S. 649 (1980) (5–4), p. 214 above.

143. After the defendant had been taken into custody on a charge of murder, the police learned that he had left a suit of clothes at the cleaners shortly after the murder occurred. At their request, the proprietor of the cleaning establishment turned the suit over to them. It revealed evidence incriminating the defendant. The police had no warrant, nor did they have the defendant's permission to seize the suit. Clarke v. Neil, 427 F.2d 1322 (6th Cir.1970). Was the evidence admissible?

Standing

Rakas v. Illinois

439 U.S. 128, 99 S.Ct. 421, 58 L.Ed.2d 387 (1978)

■ MR. JUSTICE REHNQUIST delivered the opinion of the Court.

Petitioners were convicted of armed robbery in the Circuit Court of Kankakee County, Ill., and their convictions were affirmed on appeal. At their trial, the prosecution offered into evidence a sawed-off rifle and rifle shells that had been seized by police during a search of an automobile in which petitioners had been passengers. Neither petitioner is the owner of the automobile and neither has ever asserted that he owned the rifle or shells seized. The Illinois Appellate Court held that petitioners lacked standing to object to the allegedly unlawful search and seizure and denied their motion to suppress the evidence. We granted certiorari in light of the obvious importance of the issues raised to the administration of criminal justice . . . and now affirm.

I

Because we are not here concerned with the issue of probable cause, a brief description of the events leading to the search of the automobile will suffice. A police officer on a routine patrol received a radio call notifying him of a robbery of a clothing store in Bourbonnais, Ill., and describing the getaway car. Shortly thereafter, the officer spotted an automobile which he thought might be the getaway car. After following the car for some time and after the arrival of assistance, he and several other officers stopped the vehicle. The occupants of the automobile, petitioners and two female companions, were ordered out of the car and after the occupants had left the car, two officers searched the interior of the vehicle. They discovered a box of rifle shells in the glove compartment, which had been locked, and a sawed-off rifle under the front passenger seat. . . . After discovering the rifle and the shells, the officers took petitioners to the station and placed them under arrest.

Before trial petitioners moved to suppress the rifle and shells seized from the car on the ground that the search violated the Fourth and Fourteenth Amendments. They conceded that they did not own the automobile and were simply passengers; the owner of the car had been the driver of the vehicle at the time of the search. Nor did they assert that they owned the rifle or the shells seized. The prosecutor challenged petitioners' standing to object to the lawfulness of the search of the car because neither the car, the shells nor the rifle belonged to them. The trial court agreed that petitioners lacked standing and denied the motion to suppress the evidence. . . . In view of this holding, the court did not determine whether there was probable cause for the search and seizure. On appeal after petitioners' conviction, the Appellate Court of Illinois, Third Judicial District, affirmed the trial court's denial of petitioners' motion to suppress because it held that "without a proprietary or other similar interest in an automobile, a mere passenger therein lacks standing to challenge the legality of the search of the vehicle." 360 N.E.2d 1252, 1253 (1977). . . .

The Illinois Supreme Court denied petitioners leave to appeal.

II

Petitioners first urge us to relax or broaden the rule of standing enunciated in Jones v. United States, 362 U.S. 257 (1960), so that any criminal defendant at whom a search was "directed" would have standing to contest the legality of that search and object to the admission at trial of evidence obtained as a result of the search. Alternatively, petitioners argue that they have standing to object to the search under *Jones* because they were "legitimately on [the] premises" at the time of the search.

The concept of standing discussed in *Jones* focuses on whether the person seeking to challenge the legality of a search as a basis for suppressing evidence was himself the "victim" of the search or seizure. Id., at 261. Adoption of the so-called "target" theory advanced by petitioners would in effect permit a defendant to assert that a violation of the Fourth Amendment rights of a third party entitled him to have evidence suppressed at his trial. If we reject petitioners' request for a broadened rule of standing such as this, and reaffirm the holding of *Jones* and other cases that Fourth Amendment rights are personal rights that may not be asserted vicariously, we will have occasion to re-examine the "standing" terminology emphasized in *Jones*. For we are not at all sure that the determination of a motion to suppress is materially aided by labeling the inquiry identified in *Jones* as one of standing, rather than simply recognizing it as one involving the substantive question of whether or not the proponent of the motion to suppress has had his own Fourth Amendment rights infringed by the search and seizure which he seeks to challenge. We shall therefore consider in turn petitioners' target theory, the necessity for continued adherence to the notion of standing discussed in *Jones* as a concept that is theoretically distinct from the merits of a defendant's Fourth Amendment claim, and finally, the proper disposition of petitioners' ultimate claim in this case.

A

We decline to extend the rule of standing in Fourth Amendment cases in the manner suggested by petitioners. As we stated in Alderman v. United States, 394 U.S. 165 (1969), "Fourth Amendment rights are personal rights which, like some other constitutional rights, may not be vicariously asserted." Id., at 174. . . . A person who is aggrieved by an illegal search and seizure only through the introduction of damaging evidence secured by a search of a third person's premises or property has not had any of his Fourth Amendment rights infringed. . . . And since the exclusionary rule is an attempt to effectuate the guaranties of the Fourth Amendment . . . it is proper to permit only defendants whose Fourth Amendment rights have been violated to benefit from the rule's protections. . . . There is no reason to think that a party whose rights have been infringed will not, if evidence is used against him, have ample motivation to move to suppress it. . . . Even if such a person is not a defendant in the action, he may be able to recover damages for the violation of his Fourth Amendment rights . . . or seek redress under state law for invasion of privacy or trespass.

. . .

Conferring standing to raise vicarious Fourth Amendment claims would necessarily mean a more widespread invocation of the exclusionary rule during criminal trials. The Court's opinion in *Alderman* counseled against such an extension of the exclusionary rule:

> The deterrent values of preventing the incrimination of those whose rights the police have violated have been considered sufficient to justify the suppression of probative evidence even though the case against the defendant is weakened or destroyed. We adhere to that judgment. But we are not convinced that the additional benefits of extending the exclusionary rule to other defendants would justify further encroachment upon the public interest in prosecuting those accused of crime and having them acquitted or convicted on the basis of all the evidence which exposes the truth.

394 U.S., at 174–75. Each time the exclusionary rule is applied it exacts a substantial social cost for the vindication of Fourth Amendment rights. Relevant and reliable evidence is kept from the trier of fact and the search for truth at trial is deflected. . . . Since our cases generally have held that one whose Fourth Amendment rights are violated may successfully suppress evidence obtained in the course of an illegal search and seizure, misgivings as to the benefit of enlarging the class of persons who may invoke that rule are properly considered when deciding whether to expand standing to assert Fourth Amendment violations.

B

Had we accepted petitioners' request to allow persons other than those whose own Fourth Amendment rights were violated by a challenged search and seizure to suppress evidence obtained in the course of such police activity, it would be appropriate to retain *Jones'* use of standing in Fourth Amendment analysis. Under petitioners' target theory, a court could determine that a defendant had standing to invoke the exclusionary rule without having to inquire into the substantive question of whether the challenged search or seizure violated the Fourth Amendment rights of that particular defendant. However, having rejected petitioners' target theory and reaffirmed the principle that the "rights assured by the Fourth Amendment are personal rights, [which] . . . may be enforced by exclusion of evidence only at the instance of one whose own protection was infringed by the search and seizure," Simmons v. United States, 390 U.S. [377 (1968)], at 389, the question necessarily arises whether it serves any useful analytical purpose to consider this principle a matter of standing, distinct from the merits of a defendant's Fourth Amendment claim. We can think of no decided cases from this Court that would have come out differently had we concluded, as we do now, that the type of standing requirement discussed in *Jones* and reaffirmed today is more properly subsumed under substantive Fourth Amendment doctrine. Rigorous application of the principle that the rights secured by this Amendment are personal, in place of a notion of "standing," will produce no additional situations in which evidence must be excluded. The inquiry under either approach is the same. But we think the better analysis forthrightly focuses on the extent of a particular defendant's rights under the Fourth Amendment, rather than on any theoretically separate, but invariably intertwined concept of standing. . . .

It should be emphasized that nothing we say here casts the least doubt on cases which recognize that, as a general proposition, the issue of standing involves two inquiries: first, whether the proponent of a particular legal right has alleged "injury in fact," and, second, whether the proponent is asserting his own legal rights and interests rather than basing his claim for relief upon the rights of third parties. . . . But this Court's long history of insistence that Fourth Amendment rights are personal in nature has already answered many of these traditional standing inquiries, and we think that definition of those rights is more properly placed within the purview of substantive Fourth Amendment law than within that of standing. . . .

Analyzed in these terms, the question is whether the challenged search or seizure violated the Fourth Amendment rights of a criminal defendant who seeks to exclude the evidence obtained during it. That inquiry in turn requires a determination of whether the disputed search and seizure has infringed an interest of the defendant which the Fourth Amendment was designed to protect. We are under no illusion that by dispensing with the rubric of standing used in *Jones* we have rendered any simpler the determination of whether the proponent of a motion to suppress is entitled to contest the legality of a search and seizure. But by frankly recognizing that this aspect of the analysis belongs more properly under the heading of substantive Fourth Amendment doctrine than under the heading of standing, we think the decision of this issue will rest on sounder logical footing.

C

Here petitioners, who were passengers occupying a car which they neither owned nor leased, seek to analogize their position to that of the defendant in Jones v. United States, 362 U.S. 257 (1960). In *Jones*, petitioner was present at the time of the search of an apartment which was owned by a friend. The friend had given Jones permission to use the apartment and a key to it, with which Jones had admitted himself on the day of the search. He had a suit and shirt at the apartment and had slept there "maybe a night," but his home was elsewhere. At the time of the search, Jones was the only occupant of the apartment because the lessee was away for a period of several days. Id., at 259. Under these circumstances, this Court stated that while one wrongfully on the premises could not move to suppress evidence obtained as a result of searching them,[23] "anyone legitimately on premises where a search occurs may challenge its legality." 362 U.S., at 267. Petitioners argue that their occupancy of the automobile in question was comparable to that of Jones in the apartment and that they therefore have standing to contest the legality of the search— or as we have rephrased the inquiry, that they, like Jones, had their Fourth Amendment rights violated by the search.

We do not question the conclusion in *Jones* that the defendant in that case suffered a violation of his personal Fourth Amendment rights if the search in question was unlawful. Nonetheless, we believe that the phrase "legitimately on premises" coined in *Jones* creates too broad a gauge for measurement of Fourth Amendment rights. For example, applied literally, this statement would permit a casual visitor who has never seen, or been permitted to visit, the basement of another's house to object to a search of the basement if the visitor happened to be in the kitchen of the house at the time of the search. Likewise, a casual visitor who walks into a house one minute before a search of the house commences and leaves one minute after the search ends would be able to contest the legality of the search.

---

23. The Court in Jones was quite careful to note that "wrongful" presence at the scene of a search would not enable a defendant to object to the legality of the search. 362 U.S., at 267. . . . Despite this clear statement in *Jones*, several lower courts inexplicably have held that a person present in a stolen automobile at the time of a search may object to the lawfulness of the search of the automobile. . . .

The first visitor would have absolutely no interest or legitimate expectation of privacy in the basement, the second would have none in the house, and it advances no purpose served by the Fourth Amendment to permit either of them to object to the lawfulness of the search.[24]

We think that *Jones* on its facts merely stands for the unremarkable proposition that a person can have a legally sufficient interest in a place other than his own home so that the Fourth Amendment protects him from unreasonable governmental intrusion into that place. . . . In defining the scope of that interest, we adhere to the view expressed in *Jones* and echoed in later cases that arcane distinctions developed in property and tort law between guests, licensees, invitees, and the like, ought not to control. . . . But the *Jones* statement that a person need only be "legitimately on premises" in order to challenge the validity of the search of a dwelling place cannot be taken in its full sweep beyond the facts of that case.

Katz v. United States, 389 U.S. 347 (1967), provides guidance in defining the scope of the interest protected by the Fourth Amendment. In the course of repudiating the doctrine . . . that if police officers had not been guilty of a common-law trespass they were not prohibited by the Fourth Amendment from eavesdropping, the Court in *Katz* held that capacity to claim the protection of the Fourth Amendment depends not upon a property right in the invaded place but upon whether the person who claims the protection of the Amendment has a legitimate expectation of privacy in the invaded place. . . . Viewed in this manner, the holding in *Jones* can best be explained by the fact that Jones had a legitimate expectation of privacy in the premises he was using and therefore could claim the protection of the Fourth Amendment with respect to a governmental invasion of those premises, even though his "interest" in those premises might not have been a recognized property interest at common law.[25] . . .

24. This is not to say that such visitors could not contest the lawfulness of the seizure of evidence or the search if their own property were seized during the search.

25. Obviously, however, a "legitimate" expectation of privacy by definition means more than a subjective expectation of not being discovered. A burglar plying his trade in a summer cabin during the off season may have a thoroughly justified subjective expectation of privacy, but it is not one which the law recognizes as "legitimate." His presence, in the words of *Jones*, 362 U.S., at 267, is "wrongful"; his expectation is not "one that society is prepared to recognize as 'reasonable.'" Katz v. United States, 389 U.S. 347, 361 (1967) (Harlan, J., concurring). And it would, of course, be merely tautological to fall back on the notion that those expectations of privacy which are legit-imate depend primarily on cases deciding exclusionary rule issues in criminal cases. Legitimation of expectations of privacy by law must have a source outside of the Fourth Amendment, either by reference to concepts of real or personal property law or to understandings that are recognized and permitted by society. One of the main rights attaching to property is the right to exclude others . . . and one who owns or lawfully possesses or controls property will in all likelihood have a legitimate expectation of privacy by virtue of this right to exclude. Expectations of privacy protected by the Fourth Amendment, of course, need not be based on a common-law interest in real or personal property, or on the invasion of such an interest. These ideas were rejected both in *Jones*, supra, and *Katz*, supra. But by focusing on legitimate expectations of privacy in Fourth Amendment jurisprudence, the Court

Our Brother White in dissent expresses the view that by rejecting the phrase "legitimately on [the] premises" as the appropriate measure of Fourth Amendment rights, we are abandoning a thoroughly workable, "bright line" test in favor of a less certain analysis of whether the facts of a particular case give rise to a legitimate expectation of privacy. Post, at 168. If "legitimately on premises" were the successful litmus test of Fourth Amendment rights that he assumes it is, his approach would have at least the merit of easy application, whatever it lacked in fidelity to the history and purposes of the Fourth Amendment. But a reading of lower court cases that have applied the phrase "legitimately on premises," and of the dissent itself, reveals that this expression is not a shorthand summary for a bright line rule which somehow encapsulates the "core" of the Fourth Amendment's protections.

. . .

. . . In abandoning "legitimately on premises" for the doctrine that we announce today, we are not forsaking a time-tested and workable rule, which has produced consistent results when applied, solely for the sake of fidelity to the values underlying the Fourth Amendment. We also are rejecting blind adherence to a phrase which at most has superficial clarity and which conceals underneath that thin veneer all of the problems of line drawing which must be faced in any conscientious effort to apply the Fourth Amendment. Where the factual premises for a rule are so generally prevalent that little would be lost and much would be gained by abandoning case-by-case analysis, we have not hesitated to do so. . . . But the phrase "legitimately on premises" has not shown to be an easily applicable measure of Fourth Amendment rights so much as it has proved to be simply a label placed by the courts on results which have not been subjected to careful analysis. We would not wish to be understood as saying that legitimate presence on the premises is irrelevant to one's expectation of privacy, but it cannot be deemed controlling.

D

Judged by the foregoing analysis, petitioners' claims must fail. They asserted neither a property nor a possessory interest in the automobile, nor an interest in the property seized. And as we have previously indicated, the fact that they were "legitimately on [the] premises" in the sense that they were in the car with the permission of its owner is not determinative of whether they had a legitimate expectation of privacy in the particular areas of the automobile searched. It is unnecessary for us to decide here whether

has not altogether abandoned use of property concepts in determining the presence or absence of the privacy interests protected by that Amendment. No better demonstration of this proposition exists than the decision in Alderman v. United States, 394 U.S. 165 (1969), where the Court held that an individual's property interest in his own home was so great as to allow him to object to electronic surveillance of conversations emanating from his home, even though he himself was not a party to the conversations. On the other hand, even a property interest in premises may not be sufficient to establish a legitimate expectation of privacy with respect to particular items located on the premises or activity conducted thereon. . . .

the same expectations of privacy are warranted in a car as would be justified in a dwelling place in analogous circumstances. We have on numerous occasions pointed out that cars are not to be treated identically with houses or apartments for Fourth Amendment purposes. . . . But here petitioners' claim is one which would fail even in an analogous situation in a dwelling place since they made no showing that they had any legitimate expectation of privacy in the glove compartment or area under the seat of the car in which they were merely passengers. Like the trunk of an automobile, these are areas in which a passenger *qua* passenger simply would not normally have a legitimate expectation of privacy. . . .

Jones v. United States, 362 U.S. 257 (1960) and Katz v. United States, 389 U.S. 347 (1967), involved significantly different factual circumstances. Jones not only had permission to use the apartment of his friend, but had a key to the apartment with which he admitted himself on the day of the search and kept possessions in the apartment. Except with respect to his friend, Jones had complete dominion and control over the apartment and could exclude others from it. Likewise in *Katz*, the defendant occupied the telephone booth, shut the door behind him to exclude all others and paid the toll, which "entitled [him] to assume that the words he utter[ed] into the mouthpiece would not be broadcast to the world." 389 U.S., at 352. Katz and Jones could legitimately expect privacy in the areas which were the subject of the search and seizure they sought to contest. No such showing was made by these petitioners with respect to those portions of the automobile which were searched and from which incriminating evidence was seized.

III

The Illinois courts were therefore correct in concluding that it was unnecessary to decide whether the search of the car might have violated the rights secured to someone else by the Fourth and Fourteenth Amendments to the United States Constitution. Since it did not violate any rights of these petitioners their judgment of conviction is

Affirmed.[26]

---

144. *Rakas* is applied in United States v. Lochan, 674 F.2d 960 (1st Cir.1982), in which the defendant was driving a friend's car on a long trip, in the company of the friend. The court concluded that the defendant lacked standing to object to a search of the car. To the same effect, see United States v. Jefferson, 925 F.2d 1242 (10th Cir.1991) (nonowner driver and nonowner passenger lack standing, when owner also present as passenger). See also United States v. Carter, 14 F.3d 1150 (6th Cir. 1994) (evidence suppressed against owner of vehicle but not against passenger).

[26] Justice Powell wrote a concurring opinion, which Chief Justice Burger joined. Justice White wrote a dissenting opinion, which Justice Brennan, Justice Marshall, and Justice Stevens joined.

In United States v. Twilley, 222 F.3d 1092 (9th Cir.2000), the court said that although the defendant, as a passenger in a car, had no standing to challenge the search of the car, he had standing to challenge the initial stop. Furthermore, because the initial stop violated the Fourth Amendment, the items seized would be suppressed as fruit of the poisonous tree. Accord, United States v. Kimball, 25 F.3d 1 (1st Cir.1994).

In United States v. Dall, 608 F.2d 910 (1st Cir.1979), the defendant loaned his pickup truck, which was fitted with a "camper cap," to someone else, who was stopped for speeding in another state. The driver produced the out-of-state registration for the car and identified its owner, but did not have a driver's license. For that reason, the police impounded the vehicle; they called the owner, who confirmed the driver's story, and told him that he would have to come to pick up the truck, which he later did. Pursuant to established practice for impounded vehicles, the police opened the locked camper cap and inventoried the contents. Evidence found in the truck was later used against the defendant. Upholding admission of the evidence, the court of appeals said that the defendant's ownership of the truck was "not enough to establish a reasonable and legitimate expectation of privacy" in the circumstances, and that he therefore lacked standing to challenge the search. The expectation of privacy, it said, attached to the driver's possession and not the owner's title.

Minnesota v. Olson

495 U.S. 91, 110 S.Ct. 1684, 109 L.Ed.2d 85 (1990)

■ JUSTICE WHITE delivered the opinion of the Court.

The police in this case made a warrantless, nonconsensual entry into a house where respondent Robert Olson was an overnight guest and arrested him. The issue is whether the arrest violated Olson's Fourth Amendment rights. We hold that it did.

I

Shortly before 6 a.m. on Saturday, July 18, 1987, a lone gunman robbed an Amoco gasoline station in Minneapolis, Minnesota, and fatally shot the station manager. A police officer heard the police dispatcher report and suspected Joseph Ecker. The officer and his partner drove immediately to Ecker's home, arriving at about the same time that an Oldsmobile arrived. The driver of the Oldsmobile took evasive action, and the car spun out of control and came to a stop. Two men fled the car on foot. Ecker, who was later identified as the gunman, was captured shortly thereafter inside his home. The second man escaped.

Inside the abandoned Oldsmobile, police found a sack of money and the murder weapon. They also found a title certificate with the name Rob Olson crossed out as a secured party, a letter addressed to a Roger R. Olson of 3151 Johnson Street, and a videotape rental receipt made out to Rob Olson and dated two days earlier. The police verified that a Robert Olson lived at 3151 Johnson Street.

The next morning, Sunday, July 19, a woman identifying herself as Dianna Murphy called the police and said that a man by the name of Rob drove the car in which the gas-station killer left the scene and that Rob was planning to leave town by bus. About noon, the same woman called again, gave her address and phone number, and said that a man named Rob had told a Maria and two other women, Louanne and Julie, that he was the driver in the Amoco robbery. The caller stated that Louanne was Julie's mother and that the two women lived at 2406 Fillmore Northeast. The detective-in-charge who took the second phone call sent police officers to 2406 Fillmore to check out Louanne and Julie. When police arrived they determined that the dwelling was a duplex and that Louanne Bergstrom and her daughter Julie lived in the upper unit but were not home. Police spoke to Louanne's mother, Helen Niederhoffer, who lived in the lower unit. She confirmed that a Rob Olson had been staying upstairs but was not then in the unit. She promised to call the police when Olson returned. At 2 p.m., a pickup order, or "probable cause arrest bulletin," was issued for Olson's arrest. The police were instructed to stay away from the duplex.

At approximately 2:45 p.m., Niederhoffer called police and said Olson had returned. The detective-in-charge instructed police officers to go to the house and surround it. He then telephoned Julie from headquarters and told her Rob should come out of the house. The detective heard a male voice say "tell them I left." Julie stated that Rob had left, whereupon at 3 p.m. the detective ordered the police to enter the house. Without seeking permission and with weapons drawn, the police entered the upper unit and found respondent hiding in a closet. Less than an hour after his arrest, respondent made an inculpatory statement at police headquarters.

The Hennepin County trial court held a hearing and denied respondent's motion to suppress his statement. . . . The statement was admitted into evidence at Olson's trial, and he was convicted on one count of first-degree murder, three counts of armed robbery, and three counts of second-degree assault. On appeal, the Minnesota Supreme Court reversed. . . . The court ruled that respondent had a sufficient interest in the Bergstrom home to challenge the legality of his warrantless arrest there, that the arrest was illegal because there were no exigent circumstances to justify a warrantless entry, and that respondent's statement was tainted by that illegality and should have been suppressed. Because the admission of the statement was not harmless beyond reasonable doubt, the court reversed Olson's conviction and remanded for a new trial.

We granted the State's petition for certiorari . . . and now affirm.

II

It was held in Payton v. New York, 445 U.S. 573 (1980), that a suspect should not be arrested in his house without an arrest warrant, even though there is probable cause to arrest him. The purpose of the decision was not to protect the person of the suspect but to protect his home from entry in the absence of a magistrate's finding of probable cause. In this case, the court below held that Olson's warrantless arrest was illegal because he had a sufficient connection with the premises to be treated like a householder. The State challenges that conclusion.

Since the decision in Katz v. United States, 389 U.S. 347 (1967), it has been the law that "capacity to claim the protection of the Fourth Amendment depends . . . upon whether the person who claims the protection of the Amendment has a legitimate expectation of privacy in the invaded place." Rakas v. Illinois, 439 U.S. 128, 143 (1978). A subjective expectation of privacy is legitimate if it is " 'one that society is prepared to recognize as "reasonable," ' " id., at 143–44, n.12, quoting Katz, supra, at 361 (Harlan, J., concurring).

The State argues that Olson's relationship to the premises does not satisfy the 12 factors which in its view determine whether a dwelling is a "home."[27] Aside from the fact that it is based on the mistaken premise that a place must be one's "home" in order for one to have a legitimate expectation of privacy there, the State's proposed test is needlessly complex. We need go no further than to conclude, as we do, that Olson's status as an overnight guest is alone enough to show that he had an expectation of privacy in the home that society is prepared to recognize as reasonable.

As recognized by the Minnesota Supreme Court, the facts of this case are similar to those in Jones v. United States, 362 U.S. 257 (1960). In *Jones*, the defendant was arrested in a friend's apartment during the execution of a search warrant and sought to challenge the warrant as not supported by probable cause.

> [Jones] testified that the apartment belonged to a friend, Evans, who had given him the use of it, and a key, with which [Jones] had admitted himself on the day of the arrest. On cross-examination [Jones] testified that he had a suit and shirt at the apartment, that his home was elsewhere, that he paid nothing for the use of the apart-

---

27. The 12 factors are:

(1) the visitor has some property rights in the dwelling;

(2) the visitor is related by blood or marriage to the owner or lessor of the dwelling;

(3) the visitor receives mail at the dwelling or has his name on the door;

(4) the visitor has a key to the dwelling;

(5) the visitor maintains regular or continuous presence in the dwelling, especially sleeping there regularly;

(6) the visitor contributes to the upkeep of the dwelling, either monetarily or otherwise;

(7) the visitor has been present at the dwelling for a substantial length of time prior to the arrest;

(8) the visitor stores his clothes or other possessions in the dwelling;

(9) the visitor has been granted by the owner exclusive use of a particular area of the dwelling;

(10) the visitor has the right to exclude other persons from the dwelling;

(11) the visitor is allowed to remain in the dwelling when the owner is absent;

(12) the visitor has taken precautions to develop and maintain his privacy in the dwelling.

Brief for Petitioner 21.

ment, that Evans had let him use it "as a friend," that he had slept there "maybe a night," and that at the time of the search Evans had been away in Philadelphia for about five days.

Id., at 259.[28]

The Court ruled that Jones could challenge the search of the apartment because he was "legitimately on [the] premises," id., at 267. Although the "legitimately on [the] premises" standard was rejected in *Rakas* as too broad, 439 U.S., at 142–48, the *Rakas* Court explicitly reaffirmed the factual holding in *Jones*. . . . *Rakas* thus recognized that, as an overnight guest, Jones was much more than just legitimately on the premises.

The distinctions relied on by the State between this case and *Jones* are not legally determinative. The State emphasizes that in this case Olson was never left alone in the duplex or given a key, whereas in *Jones* the owner of the apartment was away and Jones had a key with which he could come and go and admit and exclude others. . . . We do not understand *Rakas*, however, to hold that an overnight guest can never have a legitimate expectation of privacy except when his host is away and he has a key, or that only when those facts are present may an overnight guest assert the "unremarkable proposition," id., at 142, that a person may have a sufficient interest in a place other than his home to enable him to be free in that place from unreasonable searches and seizures.

To hold that an overnight guest has a legitimate expectation of privacy in his host's home merely recognizes the everyday expectations of privacy that we all share. Staying overnight in another's home is a longstanding social custom that serves functions recognized as valuable by society. We stay in others' homes when we travel to a strange city for business or pleasure, when we visit our parents, children, or more distant relatives out of town, when we are in between jobs or homes, or when we house-sit for a friend. We will all be hosts and we will all be guests many times in our lives. From either perspective, we think that society recognizes that a houseguest has a legitimate expectation of privacy in his host's home.

From the overnight guest's perspective, he seeks shelter in another's home precisely because it provides him with privacy, a place where he and his possessions will not be disturbed by anyone but his host and those his host allows inside. We are at our most vulnerable when we are asleep because we cannot monitor our own safety or the security of our belongings. It is for this reason that, although we may spend all day in public places, when we cannot sleep in our own home we seek out another private place to sleep, whether it be a hotel room, or the home of a friend. Society expects at least as much privacy in these places as in a telephone booth—"a temporarily private place whose momentary occupants' expectations of freedom from intrusion are recognized as reasonable," *Katz*, 389 U.S., at 361 (Harlan, J., concurring).

---

28. Olson, who had been staying at Ecker's home for several days before the robbery, spent the night of the robbery on the floor of the Bergstroms' home with their permission. He had a change of clothes with him at the duplex.

That the guest has a host who has ultimate control of the house is not inconsistent with the guest having a legitimate expectation of privacy. The houseguest is there with the permission of his host, who is willing to share his house and his privacy with his guest. It is unlikely that the guest will be confined to a restricted area of the house; and when the host is away or asleep, the guest will have a measure of control over the premises. The host may admit or exclude from the house as he prefers, but it is unlikely that he will admit someone who wants to see or meet with the guest over the objection of the guest. On the other hand, few houseguests will invite others to visit them while they are guests without consulting their hosts; but the latter, who have the authority to exclude despite the wishes of the guest, will often be accommodating. The point is that hosts will more likely than not respect the privacy interests of their guests, who are entitled to a legitimate expectation of privacy despite the fact that they have no legal interest in the premises and do not have the legal authority to determine who may or may not enter the household. If the untrammeled power to admit and exclude were essential to Fourth Amendment protection, an adult daughter temporarily living in the home of her parents would have no legitimate expectation of privacy because her right to admit or exclude would be subject to her parents' veto.

Because respondent's expectation of privacy in the Bergstrom home was rooted in "understandings that are recognized and permitted by society," *Rakas*, supra, at 144, n.12, it was legitimate, and respondent can claim the protection of the Fourth Amendment.

. . .

[The Court upheld the "fact-specific" finding that there were not exigent circumstances justifying the warrantless entry.]

We therefore affirm the judgment of the Minnesota Supreme Court. [29]

. . .

---

145. In United States v. Haydel, 649 F.2d 1152, modified 664 F.2d 84 (5th Cir.1981), the court, applying *Rakas*, concluded that the defendant had a legitimate expectation of privacy in his parents' home, where he kept papers and clothing, and occasionally remained overnight, and that he had standing to contest a search. Supposing that, if his parents had consented to the search while he was absent, the search would have been lawful, see note 95, p. 168 above, does that have a bearing on the question of standing?

In People v. Moreno, 3 Cal.Rptr.2d 66, 69 (Ct.App.1992), the court concluded that since a babysitter "as a general rule . . . is in exclusive charge of the child and the premises," a babysitter has standing to challenge a search of the premises while sitting. If that is correct, is it for

[29] Justice Stevens wrote a concurring opinion. Justice Kennedy wrote a brief concurring opinion. Chief Justice Rehnquist and Justice Blackmun dissented.

the reason given by the court? Does the babysitter have authority to consent to a search of the premises?

In United States v. Padilla, 508 U.S. 77 (1993) (per curiam), the Court rejected a rule developed in the Ninth Circuit that a co-conspirator who, in virtue of the conspiracy has joint control and supervision over a searched place, has standing to contest the search. Co-conspirators, the Court said, may have standing based on their expectations and interests, but the fact of the conspiracy by itself makes no difference.

In State v. Stott, 794 A.2d 120 (N.J.2002), the court held that a patient in a psychiatric hospital has a reasonable expectation of privacy in the portion of a shared room occupied by him.

146. A federal agent posing as a dealer in narcotics arranged to purchase narcotics from the defendant. The transaction took place in a motel room rented by the agent. According to plan, while the transaction was in progress, other agents entered the room with a key and by breaking the night latch that the defendant had fastened. The agents seized the narcotics and arrested the defendant. Are the narcotics admissible in evidence against him? See Garza-Fuentes v. United States, 400 F.2d 219 (5th Cir.1968).

147. Before *Rakas* was decided, in United States v. Carriger, 541 F.2d 545, 549 (6th Cir.1976) (other cases cited), the court held that the tenant of an apartment building has "a reasonable expectation of privacy in the common areas of the building not open to the general public," and therefore has standing to object to an entry into the building by stealth. Cf. United States v. Fluker, 543 F.2d 709 (9th Cir.1976). But see, e.g., United States v. Cruz Pagan, 537 F.2d 554 (1st Cir.1976) (persons residing in multidwelling apartment house or condominium do not have a reasonable expectation of privacy in "well traveled common areas" such as a common garage; entry into garage involved no Fourth Amendment right of such persons). Cf. United States v. Kelly, 551 F.2d 760 (8th Cir.1977). Are such cases affected by *Rakas*?

148. In United States v. Gamez-Orduño, 235 F.3d 453 (9th Cir.2000), the defendants, who were smuggling drugs, stayed overnight in a trailer at the invitation of the occupant. The court held that, as overnight guests, they had standing under *Olson* to contest the search of the trailer, notwithstanding their illegal business. Compare Minnesota v. Carter, below.

149. The defendant was employed in a federal agency. He had his own office and a computer with internet access. His employer announced a policy that the internet was to be used only for official business and specifically prohibiting viewing unlawful materials. Employees were told that "electronic audits" would be conducted to ensure compliance, which would include inspection of employees' internet activity. Suspecting that the defendant was viewing and downloading pornographic material, the employer examined his computer files. The court held that in view of the announced policy, the defendant did not have a legitimate expectation of privacy in the search of his computer. United States v. Simons, 206 F.3d 392 (4th Cir.2000).

Minnesota v. Carter

525 U.S. 83, 119 S.Ct. 469, 142 L.Ed.2d 373 (1998)

■ CHIEF JUSTICE REHNQUIST delivered the opinion of the Court.

Respondents and the lessee of an apartment were sitting in one of its rooms, bagging cocaine. While so engaged they were observed by a police officer, who looked through a drawn window blind. The Supreme Court of Minnesota held that the officer's viewing was a search which violated respondents' Fourth Amendment rights. We hold that no such violation occurred.

James Thielen, a police officer in the Twin Cities suburb of Eagan, Minnesota, went to an apartment building to investigate a tip from a confidential informant. The informant said that he had walked by the window of a ground-floor apartment and had seen people putting a white powder into bags. The officer looked in the same window through a gap in the closed blind and observed the bagging operation for several minutes. He then notified headquarters, which began preparing affidavits for a search warrant while he returned to the apartment building. When two men left the building in a previously identified Cadillac, the police stopped the car. Inside were respondents Carter and Johns. As the police opened the door of the car to let Johns out, the observed a black zippered pouch and a handgun, later determined to be loaded, on the vehicle's floor. Carter and Johns were arrested, and a later police search of the vehicle the next day discovered pagers, a scale, and 47 grams of cocaine in plastic sandwich bags.

After seizing the car, the police returned to Apartment 103 and arrested the occupant, Kimberly Thompson, who is not a party to this appeal. A search of the apartment pursuant to a warrant revealed cocaine residue on the kitchen table and plastic baggies similar to those found in the Cadillac. Thielen identified Carter, Johns, and Thompson as the three people he had observed placing the powder into baggies. The police later learned that while Thompson was the lessee of the apartment, Carter and Johns lived in Chicago and had come to the apartment for the sole purpose of packaging the cocaine. Carter and Johns had never been to the apartment before and were only in the apartment for approximately 2½ hours. In return for the use of the apartment, Carter and Johns had given Thompson one-eighth of an ounce of the cocaine.

Carter and Johns were charged with conspiracy to commit controlled substance crime in the first degree and aiding and abetting in a controlled substance crime in the first degree. . . . They moved to suppress all evidence obtained from the apartment and the Cadillac, as well as to suppress several post-arrest incriminating statements they had made. They argued that Thielen's initial observation of their drug packaging activities was an unreasonable search in violation of the Fourth Amendment and that all evidence obtained as a result of this unreasonable search was inadmissible as fruit of the poisonous tree. The Minnesota trial court held that since, unlike the defendant in Minnesota v. Olson, 495 U.S. 91 (1990), Carter and Johns were not overnight social guests but temporary out-of-state visitors, they were not entitled to claim the protection of the Fourth Amendment against the government intrusion into the apartment. The trial court also concluded that Thielen's observation was not a search within the meaning of the Fourth Amendment. After a trial, Carter and Johns were each convicted of both offenses. . . .

A divided Minnesota Supreme Court reversed, holding that respondents had "standing" to claim the protection of the Fourth Amendment because they had " 'a legitimate expectation of privacy in the invaded place.' " 569 N.W.2d 169, 174 (1997) (quoting Rakas v. Illinois, 439 U.S. 128, 143 (1978)). The court noted that even though "society does not recognize as valuable the task of bagging cocaine, we conclude that society does recognize as valuable the right of property owners or leaseholders to invite persons into the privacy of their homes to conduct a common task, be it legal or illegal activity. We, therefore, hold that [respondents] had standing to bring [their] motion to suppress the evidence gathered as a result of Thielen's observations." 569 N.W.2d, at 176. . . . Based upon its conclusion that the respondents had "standing" to raise their Fourth Amendment claims, the court went on to hold that Thielen's observation constituted a search of the apartment under the Fourth Amendment, and that the search was unreasonable. Id., at 176–79. We granted certiorari . . . and now reverse.

The Minnesota courts analyzed whether respondents had a legitimate expectation of privacy under the rubric of "standing" doctrine, an analysis which this Court expressly rejected 20 years ago in *Rakas*. 439 U.S., at 139–40. In that case, we held that automobile passengers could not assert the protection of the Fourth Amendment against the seizure of incriminating evidence from a vehicle where they owned neither the vehicle nor the evidence. Ibid. Central to our analysis was the idea that in determining whether a defendant is able to show the violation of his (and not someone else's) Fourth Amendment rights, the "definition of those rights is more than within that of standing." 439 U.S., at 140. Thus, we held that in order to claim the protection of the Fourth Amendment, a defendant must demonstrate that he personally has an expectation of privacy in the place searched, and that his expectation is reasonable; i.e., one which has "a source outside of the Fourth Amendment, either by reference to concepts of real or personal property law or to understandings that are recognized and permitted by society." Id., at 143–44, and n.12. . . .

The Fourth Amendment . . . protects persons against unreasonable searches of "their persons [and] houses" and thus indicates that the Fourth Amendment is a personal right that must be invoked by an individual. See Katz v. United States, 389 U.S. 347, 351 (1967) ("[T]he Fourth Amendment protects people, not places"). But the extent to which the Fourth Amendment protects people may depend upon where those people are. We have held that "capacity to claim the protection of the Fourth Amendment depends . . . upon whether the person who claims the protection of the Amendment has a legitimate expectation of privacy in the invaded place." *Rakas*, supra, at 143. . . .

The text of the Amendment suggest that its protections extend only to people in "their" houses. But we have held that in some circumstances a person may have a legitimate expectation of privacy in the house of someone else. In Minnesota v. Olson, 495 U.S. 91 (1990), for example, we decided that an overnight guest in a house had the sort of expectation of privacy that the Fourth Amendment protects. . . .

. . . Thus an overnight guest in a home may claim the protection of the Fourth Amendment, but one who is merely present with the consent of the householder may not.

Respondents here were obviously not overnight guests, but were essentially present for a business transaction and were only in the home a matters of hours. There is no suggestion that they had a previous relationship with Thompson, or that there was any other purpose to their visit. Nor was there anything similar to the overnight guest relationship in *Olson* to suggest a degree of acceptance into the household. While the apartment was a dwelling place for Thompson, it was for these respondents simply a place to do business.

Property used for commercial purposes is treated differently for Fourth Amendment purposes than residential property. "An expectation of privacy in commercial premises, however, is different from, and indeed less than, a similar expectation in an individual's home." New York v. Burger, 482 U.S. 691, 700 (1987). And while it was a "home" in which respondents were present, it was not their home. Similarly, the Court has held that in some circumstances a worker can claim Fourth Amendment protection over his own workplace. See, e.g., O'Connor v. Ortega, 480 U.S. 709 (1987). But there is no indication that respondents in this case had nearly as significant a connection to Thompson's apartment as the worker in *O'Connor* had to his own private office. See id. at 716–17.

If we regard the overnight guest in Minnesota v. Olson as typifying those who may claim the protection of the Fourth Amendment in the home of another, and one merely "legitimately on the premises" as typifying those who may not do so, the present case is obviously somewhere in between. But the purely commercial nature of the transaction engaged in here, the relatively short period of time on the premises, and the lack of any previous connection between respondents and the householder, all lead us to conclude that respondents' situation is closer to that of one simply permitted on the premises. We therefore hold that any search which may have occurred did not violate their Fourth Amendment rights.

Because we conclude that respondents had no legitimate expectation of privacy in the apartment, we need not decide whether the police officer's observation constituted a "search." The judgment of the Supreme Court of Minnesota is accordingly reversed, and the cause is remanded for proceedings not inconsistent with this opinion.

■ JUSTICE SCALIA, with whom JUSTICE THOMAS joins, concurring.

I join the opinion of the Court because I believe it accurately applies our recent case law, including Minnesota v. Olson, 495 U.S. 91 (1990). I write separately to express my view that case law—like the submissions of the parties in this case—gives short shrift to the text of the Fourth Amendment, and to the well and long understood meaning of that text. Specifically, it leaps to apply the fuzzy standard of "legitimate expectation of privacy"—a consideration that is often relevant to whether a search or seizure covered by the Fourth Amendment is "unreasonable"—to the threshold question whether a search or seizure covered by the Fourth Amendment *has occurred*. If that latter question is addressed first and analyzed under the text of the Constitution as traditionally understood, the present case is not remotely difficult.

The Fourth Amendment protects "[t]he right of the people to be secure in *their* persons, houses, papers, and effects, against unreasonable searches and seizures...." U.S. Const., Amdt 4 (emphasis added). It must be acknowledged that the phrase "their . . . houses" in this provision is, in isolation, ambiguous. It could mean "their respective houses," so that the protection extends to each person only in his own house. But it could also mean "their respective and each other's houses," so that each person would be protected even when visiting the house of someone else. As today's opinion for the Court suggests, however, ante, at 88–90, it is not linguistically possible to give the provision the latter, expansive interpretation with respect to "houses" without giving it the same interpretation with respect to the nouns that are parallel to "houses"—"persons, . . . papers, and effects"—which would give me a constitutional right not to have your person unreasonably searched. This is so absurd that it has to my knowledge never been contemplated. The obvious meaning of the provision is that *each* person has the right to be secure against unreasonable searches and seizures in *his own* person, house, papers, and effects.

The Founding-era materials that I have examined confirm that this was the understood meaning. . . .

. . .

Of course this is not to say that the Fourth Amendment protects only the Lord of the Manor who holds his estate in fee simple. People call a house "their" home when legal title is in the bank, when they rent it, and even when they merely occupy it rent-free—*so long as they actually live there*. . . .

. . . [I]n deciding the question presented today we write upon a slate that is far from clean. . . . We went to the absolute limit of what text and tradition permit in Minnesota v. Olson, 495 U.S. 91 (1990), when we protected a mere overnight guest against an unreasonable search of his hosts' apartment. But whereas it is plausible to regard a person's overnight lodging as at least his "temporary" residence, it is entirely impossible to give that characterization to an apartment that he uses to package cocaine. Respondents here were not searched in "their . . . hous[e]" under any interpretation of the phrase that bears the remotest relationship to the well understood meaning of the Fourth Amendment.

. . .

■ Justice Kennedy, concurring.

I join the Court's opinion, for its reasoning is consistent with my view that almost all social guests have a legitimate expectation of privacy, and hence protection against unreasonable searches, in their host's home.

. . .

The homeowner's right to privacy is not at issue in this case. The Court does not reach the question whether the officer's unaided observations of Thompson's apartment constituted a search. If there was in fact a search, however, then Thompson had a right to object to the unlawful police surveillance of her apartment and the right to suppress any evidence disclosed by the search. Similarly, if the police had entered her home without a search warrant to arrest respondents, Thompson's own privacy interests would be violated and she could presumably bring an action under 42 U.S.C. § 1983 or an action for trespass. Our cases establish, however, that respondents have no independent privacy right, the violation of which results in exclusion of evidence against them, unless they can establish a meaningful connection to Thompson's apartment.

The settled rule is that the requisite connection is an expectation of privacy that society recognizes as reasonable. Katz v. United States, 389 U.S. 347, 361 (1967) (Harlan, J., concurring). The application of that rule involves consideration of the kind of place in which the individual claims the privacy interest and what expectations of privacy are traditional and well recognized. Ibid. I would expect that most, if not all, social guests legitimately expect that, in accordance with social custom, the homeowner will exercise her discretion to include or exclude others for the guests' benefit. As we recognized in Minnesota v. Olson, 495 U.S. 91 (1990), where these social expectations exist—as in the case of an overnight guest—they are sufficient to create a legitimate expectation of privacy, even in the absence of any property right to exclude others. In this respect, the dissent must be correct that the reasonable expectations of the owner are shared, to some extent, by the guest. This analysis suggests that, as a general rule, social guests will have an expectation of privacy in their host's home. That is not the case before us, however.

In this case respondents have established nothing more than a fleeting and insubstantial connection with Thompson's home. For all that appears in the record, respondents used Thompson's home simply as a convenient processing station, their purpose involving nothing more than the mechanical act of chopping and packaging a substance for distribution. There is no suggestion that respondents engaged in confidential communications with Thompson about their transaction. Respondents had not been to Thompson's apartment before, and they left it even before their arrest. The Minnesota Supreme Court, which overturned respondents' convictions, acknowledged that respondents could not be fairly characterized as Thompson's "guests." 569 N.W.2d 169, 175–76 (1997). . . .

If respondents here had been visiting homes, each for a minute or two, to drop off a bag of cocaine and were apprehended by a policeman wrongfully present in the nineteenth home; or if they had left the goods at a home where they were not staying and the police had seized the goods in their absence, we would have said that *Rakas* compels rejection of any privacy interest respondents might assert. So it does here, given that respondents have established no meaningful tie or connection to the owner, the owner's home, or the owner's expectation of privacy.

■ JUSTICE GINSBURG, with whom JUSTICE STEVENS and JUSTICE SOUTER join, dissenting.

The Court's decision undermines not only the security of short-term guests, but also the security of the home resident herself. In my view, when a homeowner or lessor personally invites a guest into her home to share in a common endeavor, whether it be for conversation, to engage in leisure activities, or for business purposes licit or illicit, that guest should share his host's shelter against unreasonable searches and seizures.

. . . I would here decide only the case of the homeowner who chooses to share the privacy of her home and her company with a guest, and would not reach classroom hypotheticals like the milkman or pizza deliverer.

My concern centers on an individual's choice to share her home and her associations there with persons she selects. Our decisions indicate that people have a reasonable expectation of privacy in their homes in part because they have the prerogative to exclude others. . . . The power to exclude implies the power to include. . . . Our Fourth Amendment decisions should reflect these complementary prerogatives.

A homedweller places her own privacy at risk, the Court's approach indicates, when she opens her home to others, uncertain whether the duration of their stay, their purpose, and their "acceptance into the household" will earn protection. Ante, at 90. . . . Human frailty suggests that today's decision will tempt police to pry into private dwellings without warrant, to find evidence incriminating guests who do not rest there through the night. . . . *Rakas* [v. Illinois, 439 U.S. 128 (1978)] tolerates that temptation with respect to automobile searches. . . . I see no impelling reason to extend this risk into the home. . . . As I see it, people are not genuinely "secure in their . . . houses . . . against unreasonable searches and seizures," U.S. Const., Amdt. 4, if their invitations to others increase the risk of unwarranted governmental peering and prying into their dwelling places.

Through the host's invitation, the guest gains a reasonable expectation of privacy in the home. Minnesota v. Olson, 495 U.S. 91 (1990), so held with respect to an overnight guest. The logic of that decision extends to shorter term guests as well. . . . Visiting the home of a friend, relative, or business associate, whatever the time of day, "serves functions recognized as valuable by society." *Olson*, 495 U.S., at 98. One need not remain overnight to anticipate privacy in another's home, "a place where [the guest] and his possessions will not be disturbed by anyone but his host and those his host allows inside." Id., at 99. In sum, when a homeowner chooses to share the privacy of her home and her company with a short-term guest, the twofold requirement "emerg[ing] from prior decisions" has been satisfied: Both host and guest "have exhibited an actual (subjective) expectation of privacy"; that "expectation [is] one [our] society is prepared to recognize as 'reasonable.' " Katz v. United States, 389 U.S. 347, 361 (1967) (Harlan, J., concurring).

As the Solicitor General acknowledged, the illegality of the host–guest conduct, the fact that they were partners in crime, would not alter the analysis. See Tr. of Oral Arg. 22–23. . . . Indeed, it must be this way. If the illegality of the activity made constitutional an otherwise unconstitutional search, such Fourth Amendment protection, reserved for the innocent only, would have little force in regulating police behavior toward either the innocent or the guilty.

Our leading decision in *Katz* is key to my view of this case. There, we ruled that the Government violated the petitioner's Fourth Amendment rights when it electronically recorded him transmitting wagering information while he was inside a public telephone booth. 389 U.S., at 353. . . .

The Court's decision in this case veers sharply from the path marked in *Katz*. I do not agree that we have a more reasonable expectation of privacy when we place a business call to a person's home from a public telephone booth on the side of the street . . . than when we actually enter that person's premises to engage in a common endeavor.

. . . [30]

------

150. The opinion in Jones v. United States, 362 U.S. 257 (1960), which was the principal discussion of standing by the Supreme Court before *Rakas*, had announced a rule of "automatic standing," to the effect that if possession of a seized item is the basis of the crime charged, the defendant had standing to contest the search and seizure without any further demonstration that a protected interest in privacy was affected by the search. Such a rule was necessary, the Court said, lest the government take contradictory positions by asserting the defendant's possession in its case in chief and contesting it in opposition to the motion to suppress.

------

[30] Justice Breyer wrote an opinion concurring in the judgment. He agreed with Justice Ginsburg, dissenting, that the defendants could claim the protection of the Fourth Amendment, but, on the basis of his own reading of the factual record, he concluded that the police officer's actions were not an unlawful search.

The dilemma that a defendant would otherwise have faced was alleviated in Simmons v. United States, 390 U.S. 377 (1968). The Court there held that "when a defendant testifies in support of a motion to suppress evidence on Fourth Amendment grounds, his testimony may not thereafter be admitted against him at trial on the issue of guilt unless he makes no objection." Id. at 394.[31] After *Simmons*, the *Jones* rule of automatic standing (which had commonly been applied if possession was a significant element, even if not an "essential" one, of the prosecution's case) was questioned. In a footnote in *Rakas*, 439 U.S. at 135 n.4, the Court noted that it had not decided whether the rule survived *Simmons*.

The Court decided the question and rejected the *Jones* rule, in United States v. Salvucci, 448 U.S. 83 (1980) (7–2). Noting the effect of *Simmons*, the Court said that the other aspect of *Jones*, that the government ought not take contradictory positions, was eliminated by recognition that possession of a seized good is not itself sufficient to establish a Fourth Amendment interest. Referring to its reasoning in *Rakas*, the Court said: "We simply decline to use possession of a seized good as a substitute for a factual finding that the owner of the good had a legitimate expectation of privacy in the area searched." Id. at 92.

Some state courts have disagreed with the Court's reasoning in *Rakas* and, relying on state constitutional provisions, have retained the rule of automatic standing. State v. Alston, 440 A.2d 1311 (N.J.1981); Commonwealth v. Sell, 470 A.2d 457 (Pa.1983). (In contrast, California, which had not required standing at all to contest an allegedly unlawful search, see People v. Martin, 290 P.2d 855 (Cal.1955), abrogated the *Martin* rule by an initiative measure providing that "relevant evidence shall not be excluded in any criminal proceeding." See In re Lance W., 694 P.2d 744 (Cal.1985).)

151. In Rawlings v. Kentucky, 448 U.S. 98 (1980) (5–2–2), the Court held that the defendant did not have a sufficient legitimate expectation of privacy to contest the legality of a search of his friend's purse, in which police found narcotics owned by him. Both the defendant and his friend were present when the purse was found and searched. The defendant had known his friend for only a few days and had not previously had access to her purse, he was aware that another person had access to the purse, and

---

31. *Simmons* was distinguished in United States v. Kahan, 415 U.S. 239 (1974), in which the Court rejected the defendant's claim that the admission at his criminal trial of false statements in his application for the appointment of counsel violated his privilege against self-incrimination and right to counsel. Citing Harris v. New York, 401 U.S. 222 (1971), p. 479 below, the Court said: "The protective shield of Simmons is not to be converted into a license for false representations on the issue of indigency free from the risk that the claimant will be held accountable for his falsehood." 415 U.S., at 243.

Simmons notwithstanding, "the government may call to testify at trial a third-party witness called by the defendant at a pretrial suppression hearing whose testimony at that hearing was favorable to the defendant's motion to establish standing and whose identity was not previously known to the government, but whose testimony to the same effect at trial inculpated the defendant." United States v. Boruff, 870 F.2d 316, 318 (5th Cir. 1989). The court reasoned that a defendant's privilege against self-incrimination is not involved when another person testifies in his behalf at a suppression hearing.

the circumstances of the transaction did not suggest that the defendant was taking precautions to maintain his privacy. His ownership of the seized items, while relevant, was insufficient by itself to create the necessary interest under the Fourth Amendment. Justice Marshall wrote a dissenting opinion, which Justice Brennan joined, in which he argued that a property interest in a seized item is enough to confer standing to challenge the legality of the search in which it was found and seized.

Many possessions are themselves containers, the opening and examining the contents of which may be a substantial invasion of privacy. After *Rakas*, are there any circumstances in which a property interest (possession or ownership) establishes rights under the Fourth Amendment without reference to any privacy interest? Or is a property interest significant only as an indication of a privacy interest? How ought Justice Rehnquist's allusion in *Rakas*, p. 262 n.24 above, to the seizure of a visitor's property be understood?

152.   In United States v. Kelly, 529 F.2d 1365 (8th Cir.1976), decided before *Rakas*, books and magazines were shipped to the defendant by United Parcel Service. While they were in the possession of UPS, they were seized by federal officials. The government argued that the defendant had no standing to contest the seizure, since he was not on the premises when the seizure occurred, alleged no interest in the premises, and was not charged with an offense of which possession of the seized evidence was an element. Upholding the defendant's standing, the court of appeals said:

> Logically, a person's protectible expectation of privacy must extend both to places *and objects*. A contrary conclusion would emasculate the plain language of the Fourth Amendment, which protects "papers" and "effects." . . .
>
> In the instant case, it is clear that Thomas Kelly was the sole victim of the government's investigation and the one against whom the search or seizure was directed. . . . The packages from which the books and magazines were taken were addressed to Century News. Appellant Kelly is the sole owner of Century News. . . . No other individuals, including employees of Sovereign News, the shipper and distributor of the materials, were prosecuted.
>
> Furthermore, Kelly maintained more than a marginal proprietary interest in the packages of books and magazines. . . . The packages were consigned to Century News, in other words Thomas Kelly; many of the books and magazines were ultimately delivered to Kelly; and Kelly wrote Sovereign News and obtained credit for shortages.
>
> These same facts support the conclusion that appellant was entitled to a reasonable expectation of privacy in the packages of books and magazines. . . . The government contends that appellant had no legitimate expectation of privacy since the packages were mailed C.O.D. to Century News and because a common carrier has a right to inspect packages. The government emphasizes that Kelly did not come into possession and had no right to possession until he had paid for the

shipments. The contentions of the government, however, are too firmly tied to concepts of traditional property law, and a defendant's expectation of privacy should not be deemed unreasonable merely because he had not yet paid postage nor because of a right of the UPS to inspect packages. . . .

The denial of standing to appellant would subject Kelly to contradictory assertions of power by the government. . . . Appellant has been convicted of the knowing *use* of an interstate carrier for the transportation of obscene materials. The government has attempted to show that Kelly exercised dominion and control over interstate shipments of purportedly obscene books at the time of their seizure and simultaneously has contended that Kelly does not have a sufficient interest to challenge the search or seizure of the same materials. Proper administration of criminal justice should not include such contradictory assertions of governmental power.

Id. at 1369–71.

Is the result in *Kelly* affected by *Rakas*?

153. The defendants employed a private detective agency to conduct electronic surveillance of various houses. Working with an electronics expert, the agency installed the necessary devices on telephone poles and in automobiles parked near the target houses. The agency edited the tape recordings that they obtained to exclude extraneous conversations and gave the master tapes to the defendants. The defendants paid all the expenses of the surveillance including the cost of the equipment. After the surveillance had been in operation for some time, one of the agency's employees was arrested in his car as he was leaving the location of the surveillance. In the back of the car the police found a tape recorder. At the police station, they played the tapes. Do the defendants have standing to challenge the seizure of the tapes or the playing of them? Does it make a difference who was the owner of the tapes, the defendants or the detective agency? See United States v. Hunt, 505 F.2d 931 (5th Cir.1974). See also United States v. Lisk, 522 F.2d 228 (7th Cir.1975), in which an explosive bomb belonging to the defendant was seized by police from the trunk of a friend's car; the defendant had no interest in the car but retained ownership of the bomb, which the friend was to return to him whenever the defendant asked for it. Assuming that the search of the car was unlawful, can the defendant obtain suppression of the bomb as evidence against him?

154. The importance of the standing requirement was reaffirmed in United States v. Payner, 447 U.S. 727 (1980) (6–3). There, the district court had suppressed evidence obtained in violation of a third person's constitutional rights, on the basis that, despite the defendant's lack of standing, the government's purposeful violation of the other person's constitutional rights required suppression of the evidence as an exercise of the court's inherent supervisory power. The Supreme Court reversed. It said that the balance of interests involved in the application of the exclusionary rule included the requirement of standing, and that the supervisory power should not be used to subvert that balance.

With *Payner,* compare Waring v. State, 670 P.2d 357, 363 (Alaska 1983), holding that under state law "a defendant has standing to assert the violation of a co-defendant's fourth amendment rights if he or she can show (1) that a police officer obtained the evidence as a result of gross or shocking misconduct, or (2) that the officer deliberately violated a co-defendant's rights."

155. United States v. Miller, 425 U.S. 435 (1976) (7–2). A grand jury subpoenaed from two banks records of the accounts of the defendant in connection with a tax investigation. The banks were required to maintain the records by federal law. The defendant was subsequently prosecuted and moved to suppress the records on the ground that they had been illegally seized, because the subpoenas were defective. The Court held that the defendant had no interest in the records that was protected by the Fourth Amendment and accordingly had no standing to challenge their production under the subpoenas. It said that a depositor's checks and deposit slips were not "confidential communications" but negotiable business instruments, and rejected the argument that the statutory requirement that the banks maintain the records gave the defendant a special constitutional claim. The records, it said, belonged to the banks and contained information voluntarily communicated by the defendant. "This Court has held repeatedly that the Fourth Amendment does not prohibit the obtaining of information revealed to a third party and conveyed by him to Government authorities, even if the information is revealed on the assumption that it will be used only for a limited purpose and the confidence placed in the third party will not be betrayed." Id. at 443.

Outer Boundaries of Search and Seizure

156.

Two police officers found appellant unconscious on a public street; they called an ambulance when they could not rouse him. One officer searched appellant in order to secure identification if possible and then to prepare a report for the hospital concerning the sick man. In the process, he examined the appellant's pockets, did not find identifying material, but found 15 cellophane envelopes containing a white powder which at the time appeared to the officer to be narcotics, packaged as he had observed contraband narcotics on other occasions.

After the arrival of the ambulance crew who attended the appellant, the latter regained consciousness and was taken to the police station where a capsule, containing a white powder similar to that in the cellophane envelopes, was found on his person. Subsequent laboratory analysis confirmed the officer's original tentative conclusion that the white substance was narcotics.

Vauss v. United States, 370 F.2d 250, 251 (D.C.Cir.1966). Can the narcotics be used in evidence against the appellant? If so, on what basis?

––––––––

Winston v. Lee
470 U.S. 753, 105 S.Ct. 1611, 84 L.Ed.2d 662 (1985)

■ JUSTICE BRENNAN delivered the opinion of the Court.

Schmerber v. California, 384 U.S. 757 (1966), held, inter alia, that a State may, over the suspect's protest, have a physician extract blood from a person suspected of drunken driving without violation of the suspect's right secured by the Fourth Amendment not to be subjected to unreasonable searches and seizures. However, *Schmerber* cautioned: "That we today hold that the Constitution does not forbid the States' minor intrusions into an individual's body under stringently limited conditions in no way indicates that it permits more substantial intrusions, or intrusions under other conditions." Id., at 772. In this case, the Commonwealth of Virginia seeks to compel the respondent Rudolph Lee, who is suspected of attempting to commit armed robbery, to undergo a surgical procedure under a general anesthetic for removal of a bullet lodged in his chest. Petitioners allege that the bullet will provide evidence of respondent's guilt or innocence. We conclude that the procedure sought here is an example of the "more substantial intrusion" cautioned against in *Schmerber*, and hold that to permit the procedure would violate respondent's right to be secure in his person guaranteed by the Fourth Amendment.

I

A

At approximately 1 a.m. on July 18, 1982, Ralph E. Watkinson was closing his shop for the night. As he was locking the door, he observed someone armed with a gun coming toward him from across the street. Watkinson was also armed and when he drew his gun, the other person told him to freeze. Watkinson then fired at the other person, who returned his fire. Watkinson was hit in the legs, while the other individual, who appeared to be wounded in his left side, ran from the scene. The police arrived on the scene shortly thereafter, and Watkinson was taken by ambulance to the emergency room of the Medical College of Virginia (MCV) Hospital.

Approximately 20 minutes later, police officers responding to another call found respondent eight blocks from where the earlier shooting occurred. Respondent was suffering from a gunshot wound to his left chest area and told the police that he had been shot when two individuals attempted to rob him. An ambulance took respondent to the MCV Hospital.

Watkinson was still in the MCV emergency room and, when respondent entered that room, said "[t]hat's the man that shot me." App. 14. After an investigation, the police decided that respondent's story of having been himself the victim of a robbery was untrue and charged respondent with attempted robbery, malicious wounding, and two counts of using a firearm in the commission of a felony.

B

The Commonwealth shortly thereafter moved in state court for an order directing respondent to undergo surgery to remove an object thought to be a bullet lodged under his left collarbone. . . .

. . .

[J]ust before the surgery was scheduled, the surgeon ordered that X rays be taken of respondent's chest. The X rays revealed that the bullet was in fact lodged two and one-half to three centimeters (approximately one inch) deep in muscular tissue in respondent's chest, substantially deeper than had been thought when the state court granted the motion to compel surgery. The surgeon now believed that a general anesthetic would be desirable for medical reasons.

. . . After an evidentiary hearing, the District Court enjoined the threatened surgery. . . . A divided panel of the Court of Appeals for the Fourth Circuit affirmed. . . . We granted certiorari . . . to consider whether a State may consistently with the Fourth Amendment compel a suspect to undergo surgery of this kind in a search for evidence of a crime.

II

The Fourth Amendment protects "expectations of privacy," see Katz v. United States, 389 U.S. 347 (1967)—the individual's legitimate expectations that in certain places and at certain times he has "the right to be let alone—the most comprehensive of rights and the right most valued by civilized men." Olmstead v. United States, 277 U.S. 438, 478 (1928) (Brandeis, J., dissenting). Putting to one side the procedural protections of the warrant requirement, the Fourth Amendment generally protects the "security" of "persons, houses, papers, and effects" against official intrusions up to the point where the community's need for evidence surmounts a specified standard, ordinarily "probable cause." Beyond this point, it is ordinarily justifiable for the community to demand that the individual give up some part of his interest in privacy and security to advance the community's vital interests in law enforcement; such a search is generally "reasonable" in the Amendment's terms.

A compelled surgical intrusion into an individual's body for evidence, however, implicates expectations of privacy and security of such magnitude that the intrusion may be "unreasonable" even if likely to produce evidence of a crime. In Schmerber v. California, 384 U.S. 757 (1966), we addressed a claim that the State had breached the Fourth Amendment's protection of the "right of the people to be secure in their *persons* . . . against unreasonable searches and seizures" (emphasis added) when it compelled an individual suspected of drunken driving to undergo a blood test. . . .

. . .

. . . The intrusion perhaps implicated Schmerber's most personal and deep-rooted expectations of privacy, and the Court recognized that Fourth Amendment analysis thus required a discerning inquiry into the facts and circumstances to determine whether the intrusion was justifiable. The Fourth Amendment neither forbids nor permits all such intrusions; rather, the Amendment's "proper function is to constrain, not against all intrusions as such, but against intrusions which are not justified in the circumstances, or which are made in an improper manner." Id., at 768.

The reasonableness of surgical intrusions beneath the skin depends on a case-by-case approach, in which the individual's interests in privacy and security are weighed against society's interests in conducting the procedure. In a given case, the question whether the community's need for evidence outweighs the substantial privacy interests at stake is a delicate one admitting of few categorical answers. We believe that *Schmerber*, however, provides the appropriate framework of analysis for such cases.

Schmerber recognized that the ordinary requirements of the Fourth Amendment would be the threshold requirements for conducting this kind of surgical search and seizure. We noted the importance of probable cause. . . . And we pointed out: "Search warrants are ordinarily required for searches of dwellings, and, absent an emergency, no less could be required where intrusions into the human body are concerned. . . . The importance of informed, detached and deliberate determinations of the issue whether or not to invade another's body in search of evidence of guilt is indisputable and great." Id., at 770.

Beyond these standards, *Schmerber*'s inquiry considered a number of other factors in determining the "reasonableness" of the blood test. A crucial factor in analyzing the magnitude of the intrusion in *Schmerber* is the extent to which the procedure may threaten the safety or health of the individual. . . . Notwithstanding the existence of probable cause, a search for evidence of a crime may be unjustifiable if it endangers the life or health of the suspect.

Another factor is the extent of intrusion upon the individual's dignitary interests in personal privacy and bodily integrity. . . .

Weighed against these individual interests is the community's interest in fairly and accurately determining guilt or innocence. This interest is of course of great importance. . . . In *Schmerber*, we concluded that this state interest was sufficient to justify the intrusion, and the compelled blood test was thus "reasonable" for Fourth Amendment purposes.

III

Applying the *Schmerber* balancing test in this case, we believe that the Court of Appeals reached the correct result. The Commonwealth plainly had probable cause to conduct the search. In addition, all parties apparently agree that respondent has had a full measure of procedural protections and has been able fully to litigate the difficult medical and legal questions necessarily involved in analyzing the reasonableness of a surgical incision of this magnitude. Our inquiry therefore must focus on the extent of the intrusion on respondent's privacy interests and on the State's need for the evidence.

The threats to the health or safety of respondent posed by the surgery are the subject of sharp dispute between the parties. Before the new revelations of October 18, the District Court found that the procedure could be carried out "with virtually no risk to [respondent]." 551 F.Supp., at 252. On rehearing, however, with new evidence before it, the District Court held that "the risks previously involved have increased in magnitude even as new risks are being added." Id., at 260.

The Court of Appeals examined the medical evidence in the record and found that respondent would suffer some risks associated with the surgical procedure. One surgeon had testified that the difficulty of discovering the exact location of the bullet "could require extensive probing and retracting of the muscle tissue," carrying with it "the concomitant risks of injury to the muscle as well as injury to the nerves, blood vessels and other tissue in the chest and pleural cavity." 717 F.2d at 900. The court further noted that "the greater intrusion and the larger incisions increase the risks of infection." Ibid. Moreover, there was conflict in the testimony concerning the nature and the scope of the operation. One surgeon stated that it would take 15–20 minutes, while another predicted the procedure could take up to two and one-half hours. . . . The court properly took the resulting uncertainty about the medical risks into account.

Both lower courts in this case believed that the proposed surgery, which for purely medical reasons required the use of a general anesthetic, would be an "extensive" intrusion on respondent's personal privacy and bodily integrity. . . . When conducted with the consent of the patient, surgery requiring general anesthesia is not necessarily demeaning or intrusive. In such a case, the surgeon is carrying out the patient's own will concerning the patient's body and the patient's right to privacy is therefore preserved. In this case, however, the Court of Appeals noted that the Commonwealth proposes to take control of respondent's body, to "drug this citizen—not yet convicted of a criminal offense—with narcotics and barbiturates into a state of unconsciousness," id., at 901, and then to search beneath his skin for evidence of a crime. This kind of surgery involves a virtually total divestment of respondent's ordinary control over surgical probing beneath his skin.

The other part of the balance concerns the Commonwealth's need to intrude into respondent's body to retrieve the bullet. The Commonwealth claims to need the bullet to demonstrate that it was fired from Watkinson's gun, which in turn would show that respondent was the robber who confronted Watkinson. However, although we recognize the difficulty of making determinations in advance as to the strength of the case against respondent, petitioners' assertions of a compelling need for the bullet are hardly persuasive. The very circumstances relied on in this case to demonstrate probable cause to believe that evidence will be found tend to vitiate the Commonwealth's need to compel respondent to undergo surgery. The Commonwealth has available substantial additional evidence that respondent was the individual who accosted Watkinson on the night of the robbery. No party in this case suggests that Watkinson's entirely spontaneous identification of respondent at the hospital would be inadmissible. In addition, petitioners can no doubt prove that Watkinson was found a few blocks from Watkinson's store shortly after the incident took place. And petitioners can certainly show that the location of the bullet (under respondent's left collarbone) seems to correlate with Watkinson's report that the robber "jerked" to the left. App. 13. The fact that the Commonwealth has available such substantial evidence of the origin of the bullet restricts the need for the Commonwealth to compel respondent to undergo the contemplated surgery.

In weighing the various factors in this case, we therefore reach the same conclusion as the courts below. The operation sought will intrude substantially on respondent's protected interests. The medical risks of the operation, although apparently not extremely severe, are a subject of considerable dispute; the very uncertainty militates against finding the operation to be "reasonable." In addition, the intrusion on respondent's privacy interests entailed by the operation can only be characterized as severe. On the other hand, although the bullet may turn out to be useful to the Commonwealth in prosecuting respondent, the Commonwealth has failed to demonstrate a compelling need for it. We believe that in these circumstances the Commonwealth has failed to demonstrate that it would be "reasonable" under the terms of the Fourth Amendment to search for evidence of this crime by means of the contemplated surgery.

IV

The Fourth Amendment is a vital safeguard of the right of the citizen to be free from unreasonable governmental intrusions into any area in which he has a reasonable expectation of privacy. Where the Court has found a lesser expectation of privacy . . . or where the search involves a minimal intrusion on privacy interests . . . the Court has held that the Fourth Amendment's protections are correspondingly less stringent. Conversely, however, the Fourth Amendment's command that searches be "reasonable" requires that when the State seeks to intrude upon an area in which our society recognizes a significantly heightened privacy interest, a more substantial justification is required to make the search "reasonable." Applying these principles, we hold that the proposed search in this case would be "unreasonable" under the Fourth Amendment.

Affirmed.[32]

---

[32] Chief Justice Burger wrote a brief concurring opinion. Justice Blackmun and Justice Rehnquist concurred in the judgment.

157. The defendant, accompanied by his brother and father, entered the Tucson Medical Center for treatment of a gunshot wound. A statute required medical personnel to notify the police of requests for treatment of wounds that might have resulted from criminal acts. The local police were notified of defendant's request for treatment. "The doctor removed a bullet from defendant's head and shortly thereafter he turned to a small group of men in the emergency room including policemen and detectives, held out the bullet which he had removed from defendant's head, and said something to the effect that 'I believe you want this object?' He then handed the bullet to the investigator from the Pima County Sheriff's office." The bullet proved to have been fired from the gun of a person who shot at an unknown assailant the night before. State v. Turner, 416 P.2d 409, 410 (Ariz.1966). Is the bullet admissible against the defendant over his objection at his trial for assault with intent to commit murder? See also People v. Capra, 216 N.E.2d 610 (N.Y.1966).

If after arresting a person the police take him to the hospital for treatment of wounds, may they, without a warrant, obtain from the hospital samples of blood extracted for typing purposes in preparation for a transfusion? May they arrange for a nurse to comb his hair and obtain hair samples for later use in evidence against him? See Commonwealth v. Gordon, 246 A.2d 325 (Pa.1968). See generally note 202, p. 363 below. If a person detained in jail is given a routine haircut as "an ordinary barbering incident" and, without the person's knowledge, at the request of the FBI the barber preserves hair clippings in an envelope and gives them to the FBI, can the clippings and laboratory analysis of them be used against him? See United States v. Cox, 428 F.2d 683 (7th Cir.1970).

158. "[A]n entry to fight a fire requires no warrant, and . . . once in the building, officials may remain there for a reasonable time to investigate the cause of the blaze. Thereafter, additional entries to investigate the cause of the fire must be made pursuant to the warrant procedures governing administrative searches." Michigan v. Tyler, 436 U.S. 499, 511 (1978) (7–1).

The holding of Michigan v. Tyler is elaborated in Michigan v. Clifford, 464 U.S. 287 (1984) (5–4):

> Except in certain carefully defined classes of cases, the nonconsensual entry and search of property are governed by the warrant requirement of the Fourth and Fourteenth Amendments. The constitutionality of warrantless and nonconsensual entries onto fire-damaged premises, therefore, normally turns on several factors: whether there are legitimate privacy interests in the fire-damaged property that are protected by the Fourth Amendment; whether exigent circumstances justify the government intrusion regardless of any reasonable expectations of privacy; and, whether the object of the search is to determine the cause of the fire or to gather evidence of criminal activity.

. . . Privacy expectations will vary with the type of property, the amount of fire damage, the prior and continued use of the premises, and in some cases the owner's efforts to secure it against intruders. Some fires may be so devastating that no reasonable privacy interests remain in the ash and ruins, regardless of the owner's subjective expectations. The test essentially is an objective one. . . . If reasonable privacy interests remain in the fire-damaged property, the warrant requirement applies, and any official entry must be made pursuant to a warrant in the absence of consent or exigent circumstances.

A burning building of course creates an exigency that justifies a warrantless entry by fire officials to fight the blaze. Moreover, in *Tyler* we held that once in the building, officials need no warrant to *remain* for "a reasonable time to investigate the cause of a blaze after it has been extinguished." 436 U.S., at 510. Where, however, reasonable expectations of privacy remain in the fire-damaged property, additional investigations begun after the fire has been extinguished and fire and police officials have left the scene, generally must be made pursuant to a warrant or the identification of some new exigency.

The aftermath of a fire often presents exigencies that will not tolerate the delay necessary to obtain a warrant or to secure the owner's consent to inspect fire-damaged premises. Because determining the cause and origin of a fire serves a compelling public interest, the warrant requirement does not apply in such cases.

If a warrant is necessary, the object of the search determines the type of warrant required. If the primary object is to determine the cause and origin of a recent fire, an administrative warrant will suffice. To obtain such a warrant, fire officials need show only that a fire of undetermined origin has occurred on the premises, that the scope of the proposed search is reasonable and will not intrude unnecessarily on the fire victim's privacy, and that the search will be executed at a reasonable and convenient time.

If the primary object of the search is to gather evidence of criminal activity, a criminal search warrant may be obtained only on a showing of probable cause to believe that relevant evidence will be found in the place to be searched. If evidence of criminal activity is discovered during the course of a valid administrative search, it may be seized under the "plain view" doctrine. . . . This evidence then may be used to establish probable cause to obtain a criminal search warrant. Fire officials may not, however, rely on this evidence to expand the scope of their administrative search without first making a successful showing of probable cause to an independent judicial officer.

The object of the search is important even if exigent circumstances exist. Circumstances that justify a warrantless search for the cause of a fire may not justify a search to gather evidence of criminal activity once that cause has been determined. If, for example, the administrative search is justified by the immediate need to ensure against rekindling, the scope of the search may be no broader than reasonably necessary to achieve its end. A search to gather evidence of criminal activity not in plain view must be made pursuant to a criminal warrant upon a traditional showing of probable cause.

464 U.S. at 291–95.

See Steigler v. Anderson, 496 F.2d 793 (3d Cir.1974) (investigation of the scene immediately after fire was extinguished was justified by exigent circumstances); State v. Hansen, 286 N.W.2d 163 (Iowa 1979) (investigation on day following fire, without warrant, not justified). See also Marshall v. Barlow's, Inc., 436 U.S. 307 (1978) (5–3) (holding unconstitutional a provision of the Occupational Safety and Health Act that authorized agents of the Secretary of Labor to inspect work areas for safety hazards and violations of OSHA regulations without a search warrant or comparable process).

159. Border search.

Both Congress and the courts have long appreciated the peculiar problems faced by customs officials in policing our extensive national borders and our numerous, large international port facilities. . . . Realization of customs officials' special problems has resulted not only in the courts' giving the broadest interpretation compatible with our constitutional principles in construing the statutory powers of customs officers . . . but also has resulted in the application of special standards when the legality of a stop, search, and seizure made by a customs official at or near our borders or international port facilities has been challenged. . . .

A customs officer has the unique power to stop a person at an international entry point and to conduct a "border search" without having a search warrant or even having a probable cause to believe the person has committed a crime. . . . Typically, mere suspicion of possible illegal activity within their jurisdiction is enough "cause" to permit a customs officer to stop and search a person. . . . This is not to say that the restrictions of the Fourth Amendment that searches and seizures may not be unreasonable are inapplicable to border stops and searches conducted by customs officials. On the contrary, border stops and searches, like all stops and searches by public officials, are restricted by the requirement that they be reasonable . . . but what is reasonable, of course, will depend on all the facts of a particular case. . . .

A customs officer's unique power to conduct a "border search" is coextensive with the limits of our international border areas, and a search and seizure within these areas by a customs officer, reasonable enough under these circumstances, could perhaps be challenged as violative of the Fourth Amendment if conducted by different officials elsewhere. The term "border area" in this context, is elastic . . . ; the precise limits of the border area depend on the particular factual situation presented by the case raising the issue. For our purposes, it need only be said that "border area" reasonably includes not only actual land border checkpoints but also the checkpoints at all international ports of entry and a reasonable extended geographic area in the immediate vicinity of any entry point.

United States v. Glaziou, 402 F.2d 8, 12–13 (2d Cir.1968).

In Almeida-Sanchez v. United States, 413 U.S. 266 (1973) (5–4), the government argued that a search of the defendant's car by a "roving patrol," about 25 miles from the border, constituted a border search and was therefore lawful despite the absence of consent or probable cause. The search was part of the Border Patrol's effort to prevent the illegal entry of aliens. Although conceding that a "routine border search" can be conducted not only at the border but also at its "functional equivalents," such as "an established station near the border, at a point marking the confluence of two or more roads that extend from the border," id. at 272–73, a majority of the Court held that the search was unlawful. *Almeida-Sanchez* was followed in United States v. Ortiz, 422 U.S. 891 (1975), in which the search was made at a traffic checkpoint 66 miles from the border on a main highway; the Border Patrol screened cars passing the checkpoint and stopped only a small number of them, those that aroused their suspicion. Cf. note 75, p. 140 above.

Applying the border exception to the usual requirements of the Fourth Amendment, the Supreme Court has upheld a federal statute authorizing customs officials to search incoming international mail, whether packages or letters, if they have "reasonable cause to suspect" that they contain illegally imported matter. United States v. Ramsey, 431 U.S. 606 (1977) (6–3). See also United States v. Montoya de Hernandez, 473 U.S. 531 (1985), discussed in note 195, p. 354 below.

160. Airline searches. In the wake of September 11, 2001, the inspection and search of passengers and their baggage before they board an airplane has been greatly intensified. Whether that change will be permanent or will be reversed when (and if) the danger of terrorist attacks diminishes remains to be seen. Even earlier, a number of less catastrophic hijackings had led airlines to adopt a variety of measures to prevent hijacking or danger to the occupants of a plane in flight. In United States v. Cyzewski, 484 F.2d 509 (5th Cir.1973), the defendants were identified as potential hijackers according to a confidential "Behavior Pattern Profile" of the Federal Aviation Agency. Federal marshals accosted them at the boarding area and asked for identification. When they said that their identification papers were in their luggage, the luggage was retrieved from the plane. Before the luggage was produced, the defendants produced identification from their pockets, which showed that they had purchased their tickets under false names. They refused to allow their luggage to be inspected but agreed to pass before a magnetometer which tested for metal objects. The magnetometer indicated that one of the defendants had a metal object in his suitcase. He said that the only metal objects were buckles on his shoes, and he placed his hand in the suitcase to remove the shoes. A marshal grabbed the bag at that point, opened it, and searched it. He found a bag of marijuana.

Was the seizure lawful? If so, on what basis?

In United States v. Edwards, 498 F.2d 496, 498 (2d Cir.1974), the court observed that "a consensus does seem to be emerging that an airport search is not to be condemned as violating the Fourth Amendment simply because it does not precisely fit into one of the previously recognized categories for dispensing with a search warrant, but only if the search is 'unreasonable' on the facts." The subject of airline searches is discussed extensively in United States v. Albarado, 495 F.2d 799 (2d Cir.1974), citing many additional cases, id. at 801 n.1. See generally note 59, p. 117 above.

161. The Fourth Amendment does not prohibit customs officials from boarding a vessel in waters leading to the open sea in order to check its documentation, pursuant to federal statutory authority; no specific, articulable suspicion is necessary. The difference in the circumstances between this situation and the stop of an automobile on a highway and the difference in the need for and the nature of documentation in the two situations justify the difference in outcome from cases involving a border check of an automobile. United States v. Villamonte-Marquez, 462 U.S. 579 (1983) (6–3).

162. Electronic tracking devices. In United States v. Knotts, 460 U.S. 276 (1983), the Court upheld the use of an electronic beeper placed inside a drum of chemicals to track a car containing the drum on public roads and to locate the drum on the defendant's premises. The beeper was placed in the drum with the consent of the company that sold it. The Court said that all that the investigating agents learned from the beeper could have been observed by ordinary visual surveillance and that all that the beeper did was to enhance their ordinary "sensory faculties." There was, therefore, no invasion of a legitimate expectation of privacy.

In United States v. Karo, 468 U.S. 705 (1984), the Court answered questions left unresolved by *Knotts*. First, the Court held (6–3) that the transfer of a container in which an electronic tracking device has been installed with the consent of the owner to a buyer having no knowledge of the device is not a search and seizure within the meaning of the Fourth Amendment. Second, the Court held that monitoring the device while it is on private premises not open to visual surveillance violates the Fourth Amendment rights of persons who have a justifiable interest in the privacy of the premises. (Justices O'Connor and Rehnquist would have limited the violation of Fourth Amendment rights to persons having a privacy interest in the container itself.) The usual requirement of a warrant is applicable.

For other similar cases, see United States v. McIver, 186 F.3d 1119 (9th Cir.1999) (device placed on underside of car); United States v. Michael, 645 F.2d 252 (5th Cir.1981) (device attached to van); United States v. Conroy, 589 F.2d 1258 (5th Cir.1979) (device placed on board ship by person with permission to be there); United States v. Pretzinger, 542 F.2d 517 (9th Cir.1976) (device attached to airplane); United States v. Emery, 541 F.2d 887 (1st Cir.1976) (device inserted in package of contraband before mail delivery).

163. Upholding the authority of prison officials to make random searches of prison cells and to seize "any articles, which, in their view, disserve legitimate institutional interests," the Court held that "the Fourth Amendment has no applicability to a prison cell." Hudson v. Palmer, 468 U.S. 517, 528 n.8, 536 (1984) (5–4). "[S]ociety is not prepared to recognize as legitimate any subjective expectation of privacy that a prisoner might have in his prison cell. . . . The recognition of privacy rights for prisoners in their individual cells simply cannot be reconciled with the concept of incarceration and the needs and objectives of penal institutions." Id. at 526.

In United States v. Cohen, 796 F.2d 20 (2d Cir.1986), the court held that, notwithstanding Hudson v. Palmer, a person detained pending trial is protected by the Fourth Amendment against a search of his cell initiated by the prosecution in an effort to obtain evidence. It said that in *Hudson*, the Court "did not contemplate a cell search intended solely to bolster the prosecution's case against a pre-trial detainee awaiting his day in court" and having nothing to do with security or other institutional concerns. Id. at 23.

Abandoned Property

After the defendant had vacated his hotel room, federal agents searched the room with the permission of the management. Their express purpose was to find evidence of crimes committed by the defendant. They found incriminating evidence in a wastepaper basket. Upholding the seizure and use of the evidence against the defendant, the Court said: "[P]etitioner had abandoned these articles. He had thrown them away. So far as he was concerned, they were *bona vacantia*. There can be nothing unlawful in the Government's appropriation of such abandoned property." Abel v. United States, 362 U.S. 217, 241 (1960).

California v. Greenwood

486 U.S. 35, 108 S.Ct. 1625, 100 L.Ed.2d 30 (1988)

■ JUSTICE WHITE delivered the opinion of the Court.

The issue here is whether the Fourth Amendment prohibits the warrantless search and seizure of garbage left for collection outside the curtilage of a home. We conclude, in accordance with the vast majority of lower courts that have addressed the issue, that it does not.

I

In early 1984, Investigator Jenny Stracner of the Laguna Beach Police Department received information indicating that respondent Greenwood might be engaged in narcotics trafficking. Stracner learned that a criminal suspect had informed a federal drug-enforcement agent in February 1984 that a truck filled with illegal drugs was en route to the Laguna Beach address at which Greenwood resided. In addition, a neighbor complained of heavy vehicular traffic late at night in front of Greenwood's single-family home. The neighbor reported that the vehicles remained at Greenwood's house for only a few minutes.

Stracner sought to investigate this information by conducting a surveillance of Greenwood's home. She observed several vehicles make brief stops at the house during the late-night and early-morning hours, and she followed a truck from the house to a residence that had previously been under investigation as a narcotics trafficking location.

On April 6, 1984, Stracner asked the neighborhood's regular trash collector to pick up the plastic garbage bags that Greenwood had left on the curb in front of his house and to turn the bags over to her without mixing their contents with garbage from other houses. The trash collector cleaned his truck bin of other refuse, collected the garbage bags from the street in front of Greenwood's house, and turned the bags over to Stracner. The officer searched through the rubbish and found items indicative of narcotics use. She recited the information that she had gleaned from the trash search in an affidavit in support of a warrant to search Greenwood's home.

Police officers encountered both respondents at the house later that day when they arrived to execute the warrant. The police discovered quantities of cocaine and hashish during their search of the house. Respondents were arrested on felony narcotics charges. They subsequently posted bail.

The police continued to receive reports of many late-night visitors to the Greenwood house. On May 4, Investigator Robert Rahaeuser obtained Greenwood's garbage from the regular trash collector in the same manner as had Stracner. The garbage again contained evidence of narcotics use.

Rahaeuser secured another search warrant for Greenwood's home based on the information from the second trash search. The police found more narcotics and evidence of narcotics trafficking when they executed the warrant. Greenwood was again arrested.

The Superior Court dismissed the charges against respondents. . . . The court found that the police would not have had probable cause to search the Greenwood home without the evidence obtained from the trash searches.

. . .

. . . We granted certiorari . . . and now reverse.

II

The warrantless search and seizure of the garbage bags left at the curb outside the Greenwood house would violate the Fourth Amendment only if respondents manifested a subjective expectation of privacy in their garbage that society accepts as objectively reasonable. . . . Respondents do not disagree with this standard.

They assert, however, that they had, and exhibited, an expectation of privacy with respect to the trash that was searched by the police: The trash, which was placed on the street for collection at a fixed time, was contained in opaque plastic bags, which the garbage collector was expected to pick up, mingle with the trash of others, and deposit at the garbage dump. The trash was only temporarily on the street, and there was little likelihood that it would be inspected by anyone.

It may well be that respondents did not expect that the contents of their garbage bags would become known to the police or other members of the public. An expectation of privacy does not give rise to Fourth Amendment protection, however, unless society is prepared to accept that expectation as objectively reasonable.

Here, we conclude that respondents exposed their garbage to the public sufficiently to defeat their claim to Fourth Amendment protection. It is common knowledge that plastic garbage bags left on or at the side of a public street are readily accessible to animals, children, scavengers, snoops, and other members of the public. . . . Moreover, respondents placed their refuse at the curb for the express purpose of conveying it to a third party, the trash collector, who might himself have sorted through respondents' trash or permitted others, such as the police, to do so. Accordingly, having deposited their garbage "in an area particularly suited for public inspection and, in a manner of speaking, public consumption, for the express purpose of having strangers take it," United States v. Reicherter, 647 F.2d 397, 399 (CA3 1981), respondents could have had no reasonable expectation of privacy in the inculpatory items that they discarded.

Furthermore, as we have held, the police cannot reasonably be expected to avert their eyes from evidence of criminal activity that could have been observed by any member of the public. . . .

. . .

Our conclusion that society would not accept as reasonable respondents' claim to an expectation of privacy in trash left for collection in an area accessible to the public is reinforced by the unanimous rejection of similar claims by the Federal Courts of Appeals. . . . In addition, of those state appellate courts that have considered the issue, the vast majority have held that the police may conduct warrantless searches and seizures of garbage discarded in public areas. . . .[33]

33. Given that the dissenters are among the tiny minority of judges whose views are contrary to ours, we are distinctly unimpressed with the dissent's prediction that "society will be shocked to learn" of today's decision. Post, at 46.

. . .

[The Court rejected the respondents' further arguments that their expectation of privacy in the trash should be deemed reasonable because a search of the trash was illegal under state law and that the Due Process Clause required California to apply the exclusionary rule to a search in violation of state law.]

The judgment of the California Court of Appeal is therefore reversed, and this case is remanded for further proceedings not inconsistent with this opinion.

. . .

■ JUSTICE BRENNAN, with whom JUSTICE MARSHALL joins, dissenting.

Every week for two months, and at least once more a month later, the Laguna Beach police clawed through the trash that respondent Greenwood left in opaque, sealed bags on the curb outside his home. . . . Complete strangers minutely scrutinized their bounty, undoubtedly dredging up intimate details of Greenwood's private life and habits. The intrusions proceeded without a warrant, and no court before or since has concluded that the police acted on probable cause to believe Greenwood was engaged in any criminal activity.

Scrutiny of another's trash is contrary to commonly accepted notions of civilized behavior. I suspect, therefore, that members of our society will be shocked to learn that the Court, the ultimate guarantor of liberty, deems unreasonable our expectation that the aspects of our private lives that are concealed safely in a trash bag will not become public.

. . .

A single bag of trash testifies eloquently to the eating, reading, and recreational habits of the person who produced it. A search of trash, like a search of the bedroom, can relate intimate details about sexual practices, health, and personal hygiene. Like rifling through desk drawers or intercepting phone calls, rummaging through trash can divulge the target's financial and professional status, political affiliations and inclinations, private thoughts, personal relationships, and romantic interests. It cannot be doubted that a sealed trash bag harbors telling evidence of the "intimate activity associated with the 'sanctity of a man's home and the privacies of life,'" which the Fourth Amendment is designed to protect. Oliver v. United States, 466 U.S. 170, 180 (1984) (quoting Boyd v. United States, 116 U.S. 616, 630 (1886)). . . .

The Court properly rejects the State's attempt to distinguish trash searches from other searches on the theory that trash is abandoned and therefore not entitled to an expectation of privacy. . . . In evaluating the reasonableness of Greenwood's expectation that his sealed trash bags would not be invaded, the Court has held that we must look to "understandings that are recognized and permitted by society."[34] Most of us, I believe, would

34. Rakas v. Illinois, 439 U.S. 128, 143–44, n.12 (1978). . . .

be incensed to discover a meddler—whether a neighbor, a reporter, or a detective—scrutinizing our sealed trash containers to discover some detail of our personal lives. . . .

. . .

Had Greenwood flaunted his intimate activity by strewing his trash all over the curb for all to see, or had some nongovernmental intruder invaded his privacy and done the same, I could accept the Court's conclusion that an expectation of privacy would have been unreasonable. Similarly, had police searching the city dump run across incriminating evidence that, despite commingling with the trash of others, still retained its identity as Greenwood's, we would have a different case. But all that Greenwood "exposed . . . to the public," ante, at 40, were the exteriors of several opaque, sealed containers. Until the bags were opened by police, they hid their contents from the public's view. . . . Faithful application of the warrant requirement does not require police to "avert their eyes from evidence of criminal activity that could have been observed by any member of the public." Rather, it only requires them to adhere to norms of privacy that members of the public plainly acknowledge.

The mere *possibility* that unwelcome meddlers *might* open and rummage through the containers does not negate the expectation of privacy in its contents any more than the possibility of a burglary negates an expectation of privacy in the home; or the possibility of a private intrusion negates an expectation of privacy in an unopened package; or the possibility that an operator will listen in on a telephone conversation negates an expectation of privacy in the words spoken on the telephone. . . .

Nor is it dispositive that "respondents placed their refuse at the curb for the express purpose of conveying it to a third party . . . who might himself have sorted through respondents' trash or permitted others, such as police, to do so." Ante, at 40. In the first place, Greenwood can hardly be faulted for leaving trash on his curb when a county ordinance commanded him to do so . . . and prohibited him from disposing of it in any other way. . . . Unlike in other circumstances where privacy is compromised, Greenwood could not "avoid exposing personal belongings . . . by simply leaving them at home." *O'Connor* [v. Ortega, 480 U.S. 709 (1987)], at 725. More importantly, even the voluntary relinquishment of possession or control over an effect does not necessarily amount to a relinquishment of a privacy expectation in it. Were it otherwise, a letter or package would lose all Fourth Amendment protection when placed in a mail box or other depository with the "express purpose" of entrusting it to the postal officer or a private carrier. . . .

III

In holding that the warrantless search of Greenwood's trash was consistent with the Fourth Amendment, the Court paints a grim picture of our society. It depicts a society in which local authorities may command their citizens to dispose of their personal effects in the manner least protective of the "sanctity of [the] home and the privacies of life," Boyd v.

United States, 116 U.S., at 630, and then monitor them arbitrarily and without judicial oversight—a society that is not prepared to recognize as reasonable an individual's expectation of privacy in the most private of personal effects sealed in an opaque container and disposed of in a manner designed to commingle it imminently and inextricably with the trash of others. . . .

———

164. In United States v. Hedrick, 922 F.2d 396 (7th Cir.1991), the court held that the defendant had no reasonable expectation of privacy in garbage cans left on the driveway within the curtilage for trash pickup. It observed: "As a general rule, the reasonableness of the expectation [of privacy] will increase as the garbage gets closer to the garage or house." Id. at 400. See United States v. Redmon, 117 F.3d 1036 (7th Cir.1997). See United States v. Long, 176 F.3d 1304 (10th Cir.1999) (same; trash bags placed on top of camper-trailer on defendant's property, near property line).

Greenwood was applied to shredded documents placed in trash bags, in United States v. Scott, 975 F.2d 927 (1st Cir.1992). The documents had been reduced to 5/32 inch strips, which IRS agents recovered from trash bags and "painstakingly pieced together," id. at 928. The court said:

> The fact that the abandoned property was partially destroyed by shredding, although constituting evidence of appellee's subjective desire or hope that the contents be unintelligible to third parties, does not change the fact that it is as a result of appellee's own actions that the shredded evidence was placed in the public domain. . . .

> What we have here is a failed attempt at secrecy by reason of underestimation of police resourcefulness, not invasion of constitutionally protected privacy. . . .

> Appellee here thought that reducing the documents to 5/32 inch pieces made them undecipherable. It turned out he was wrong. He is in no better position than the citizen who merely tears up a document by hand and discards the pieces onto the sidewalk. Can there be any doubt that the police are allowed to pick up the pieces from the sidewalk for use of the contents against that person? Should the mere use of more sophisticated "higher" technology in attempting destruction of the pieces of paper grant higher constitutional protection to this failed attempt at secrecy? We think not.

Id. at 929, 930.

165. The Supreme Court of the State of Washington declined to follow *Greenwood* and found that the warrantless search of defendant's trash violated the state constitution, in State v. Boland, 800 P.2d 1112 (Wash.1990). The Supreme Court of New Hampshire has ruled similarly, State v. Goss, 834 A.2d 316 (2003), as has the Supreme Court of New Jersey, State v. Hempele, 576 A.2d 793 (N.J.1990). Before *Greenwood* was decided, the Supreme Court of Hawaii had held that the state constitution prohibited the police from searching without a warrant trash placed in trash bags on private property. State v. Tanaka, 701 P.2d 1274 (Haw.1985).

166.

Defendant rented a room at the Eugene Hotel. The Eugene Police Department was informed by employees of the hotel that they suspected defendant of using narcotics. Detective Matoon of the Eugene Police Department went to the hotel and made inquiry of the manager of the hotel and other employees concerning defendant's activities. Matoon, learning that defendant was occupying room 705 went up to the seventh floor of the hotel where he enlisted the help of two maids who were in the process of cleaning and making ready the rooms on that floor. He asked them to keep the trash from room 705 separate from the trash collected from the other rooms. He explained to them that he thought that defendant was using narcotics and that he wanted to examine the trash taken from the room for narcotics. More specifically, he instructed them to look for "homemade cigarettes." During this time the hotel manager came up to the seventh floor and instructed the maids to commence cleaning room 705. The maids went into the room at approximately 2:30 p.m. and began cleaning the room. They deposited all items which they regarded as waste or trash and brought them out in a flat cardboard box to Matoon. If they had followed their usual procedure, they would have dumped the trash into a bag on their cleaning cart.

Matoon examined the contents of the receptacle brought to him while the maids returned to room 705 and resumed their cleaning. They then found on the floor between the bed and a chair a cigarette butt wrapped in a cardboard cover of a matchbook. They decided that this was what the officer was looking for so they brought it out to him. Matoon tentatively identified the butt as containing marijuana.

State v. Purvis, 438 P.2d 1002, 1002–1003 (Or.1968).

Assuming that Matoon asked the maids to remove, and they did remove, only what they would have removed in the customary course of their work, is the cigarette butt containing marijuana admissible in evidence against the defendant?

167. Open fields. In Hester v. United States, 265 U.S. 57, 59 (1924), the Supreme Court held that a trespass on open land did not itself constitute an unreasonable search or make a seizure unreasonable, and said: "[T]he special protection accorded by the Fourth Amendment to the people in their 'persons, houses, papers, and effects,' is not extended to the open fields. The distinction between the latter and the house is as old as the common law." In contrast to open fields, the "curtilage" of a dwelling is protected. *Hester* was reaffirmed in Oliver v. United States, 466 U.S. 170 (1984) (6–3). In *Oliver*, the Court said that "the curtilage is the area to which extends the intimate activity associated with the 'sanctity of a man's home and the privacies of life,' Boyd v. United States, 116 U.S. 616, 630

(1886), and therefore has been considered part of the home itself for Fourth Amendment purposes." 466 U.S. at 180. The curtilage is defined "by reference to the factors that determine whether an individual reasonably may expect that an area immediately adjacent to the home will remain private." Id.

No single factor determines whether an individual legitimately may claim under the Fourth Amendment that a place should be free of government intrusion not authorized by warrant. . . . In assessing the degree to which a search infringes upon individual privacy, the Court has given weight to such factors as the intention of the Framers of the Fourth Amendment . . . the uses to which the individual has put a location . . . and our societal understanding that certain areas deserve the most scrupulous protection from government invasion. . . . These factors are equally relevant to determining whether the government's intrusion upon open fields without a warrant or probable cause violates reasonable expectations of privacy and is therefore a search proscribed by the Amendment.

In this light, the rule of Hester v. United States . . . that we reaffirm today, may be understood as providing that an individual may not legitimately demand privacy for activities conducted out of doors in fields, except in the area immediately surrounding the home. . . . This rule is true to the conception of the right to privacy embodied in the Fourth Amendment. The Amendment reflects the recognition of the Founders that certain enclaves should be free from arbitrary government interference. For example, the Court since the enactment of the Fourth Amendment has stressed "the overriding respect for the sanctity of the home that has been embedded in our traditions since the origins of the Republic." Payton v. New York [445 U.S. 573 (1980)], at 601. . . .

In contrast, open fields do not provide the setting for those intimate activities that the Amendment is intended to shelter from government interference or surveillance. There is no societal interest in protecting the privacy of those activities, such as the cultivation of crops, that occur in open fields. Moreover, as a practical matter these lands usually are accessible to the public and the police in ways that a home, an office or commercial structure would not be. It is not generally true that fences or no trespassing signs effectively bar the public from viewing open fields in rural areas. And . . . the public and police lawfully may survey lands from the air. For these reasons, the asserted expectation of privacy in open fields is not an expectation that "society recognizes as reasonable."

466 U.S. at 177–79.

In United States v. Dunn, 480 U.S. 294, 301 (1987) (7–2), the Court said that the extent of a home's curtilage is based on four factors: "the proximity of the area claimed to be curtilage to the home, whether the area is included within an enclosure surrounding the home, the nature of the uses to which the area is put, and the steps taken by the resident to protect the area from observation by people passing by.'' Those factors, the Court said, do not yield a "finely tuned formula"; they "are useful analytical tools only to the degree that, in any given case, they bear upon the centrally relevant consideration—whether the area in question is so intimately tied to the home itself that it should be placed under the home's 'umbrella' of Fourth Amendment protection." Applying these factors, the Court concluded that a barn located 50 yards from a fence surrounding the defendant's house and 60 yards from the house itself was not within the curtilage. The Court held also that, under *Oliver*, the interior of the barn was not constitutionally protected, independently of the house, from being observed by police standing in the open fields outside it.

See Dow Chemical Co. v. United States, 476 U.S. 227 (1986) (5–4). The Environmental Protection Agency employed a commercial aerial photographer to fly over the defendant's industrial complex, which extended over 2000 acres, and to photograph equipment and installations open to view from above. The Court said that the area photographed "can perhaps be seen as falling somewhere between 'open fields' and curtilage, but lacking some of the critical characteristics of both." Id. at 236. It concluded that although the area might be protected from some forms of sophisticated technological surveillance, it was not protected from the aerial photography. See note 191, p. 342 below.

————

Unofficial Conduct

————

168. Burdeau v. McDowell, 256 U.S. 465, 475–76 (1921):

The Fourth Amendment gives protection against unlawful searches and seizures, and . . . its protection applies to governmental action. Its origin and history clearly show that it was intended as a restraint upon the activities of sovereign authority, and was not intended to be a limitation upon other than governmental agencies; as against such authority it was the purpose of the Fourth Amendment to secure the citizen in the right of unmolested occupation of his dwelling and the possession of his property, subject to the right of seizure by process duly issued.

[P]apers having come into the possession of the Government without a violation of petitioner's rights by governmental authority, we see no reason why the fact that individuals, unconnected with the Government, may have wrongfully taken them, should prevent them from being held for use in prosecuting an offense where the documents are of an incriminatory character.

Justice Brandeis dissented:

That the court would restore the papers to plaintiff if they were still in the thief's possession is not questioned. That it has power to control the disposition of these stolen papers, although they have passed into the possession of the law officer, is also not questioned. But it is said that no provision of the Constitution requires their surrender and that the papers could have been subpoenaed. This may be true. Still I cannot believe that action of a public official is necessarily lawful, because it does not violate constitutional prohibitions and because the same result might have been attained by other and proper means. At the foundation of our civil liberty lies the principle which denies to government officials an exceptional position before the law and which subjects them to the same rules of conduct that are commands to the citizen. And in the development of our liberty insistence upon procedural regularity has been a large factor. Respect for law will not be advanced by resort, in its enforcement, to means which shock the common man's sense of decency and fair play.

Id. at 477.

The principle of Burdeau v. McDowell has frequently been applied. E.g., United States v. Knoll, 16 F.3d 1313 (2d Cir.1994); Meister v. Commissioner, 504 F.2d 505 (3d Cir.1974) (taxpayer's records stolen by bookkeeper); Barnes v. United States, 373 F.2d 517 (5th Cir.1967) (motel owner).

"A private search in which the government is in no respect involved—either directly as a participant or indirectly as an encourager—is not subject to the Fourth Amendment because the private actor is motivated in whole or in part by a unilateral desire to aid in the enforcement of the law." United States v. Gumerlock, 590 F.2d 794, 800 (9th Cir.1979).

Searches of baggage by airline personnel have presented a recurring problem. "In the absence of the requisite government sanction—whether by explicit authorization or comparable degree of involvement—searches of cargo by common carriers resulting in the discovery and seizure of contraband which form the basis for subsequent criminal proceedings are private rather than governmental and thus not subject to the strictures of the Fourth Amendment. . . . Such searches, whether founded on common law right or conducted pursuant to tariff, do not differ for Fourth Amendment purposes from private searches: the evidence so obtained is not subject to exclusion under the Fourth Amendment because it was not discovered by government officers." United States v. Fannon, 556 F.2d 961, 963 (9th Cir.1977). Despite the principle enunciated, the court concluded that federal legislation authorizing airlines to condition transportation of persons or property on consent to searches for dangerous substances conferred on carriers "a governmental function sufficient to subject its conduct to constitutional limitations." Id. at 964. The court declined to say fully what was constitutionally required in these circumstances but said that at least "reasonable notice to the shipper that search is a condition of carriage" was required. Id. at 965.

For examples of cases in which the involvement of government agents was too great for the conduct in question to escape application of the Fourth Amendment, see United States v. Newton, 510 F.2d 1149 (7th Cir.1975); Corngold v. United States, 367 F.2d 1 (9th Cir.1966). See also United States v. Haes, 551 F.2d 767 (8th Cir.1977) (air freight); Knoll Associates, Inc. v. Federal Trade Commission, 397 F.2d 530 (7th Cir.1968) (corporate documents stolen by private person to aid government and with its approval).

In United States v. Bomengo, 580 F.2d 173 (5th Cir.1978), persons employed by an apartment complex entered the defendant's apartment in his absence to locate the source of a water leak. While they were inspecting, they saw guns with silencers attached in plain view and summoned the police. The police entered the apartment and saw the guns, then went away and obtained a search warrant for their seizure. The court said that "a police view subsequent to a search conducted by private citizens does not constitute a 'search' within the meaning of the Fourth Amendment so long as the view is confined to the scope and product of the initial search," id. at 175, and held that the initial view leading the police to obtain a warrant was not improper. See United States v. Runyan, 275 F.3d 449 (5th Cir.2001), appeal after remand, 290 F.3d 223 (2002), discussing the permissible scope of a warrantless police search following a private search, reported to the police, of the same premises or containers.

169.

In December 1982, defendant Lambert hired Diana Hall to be his housekeeper. Hall claims that Lambert and his friends openly used illegal drugs in the house. Beginning in May 1982, Hall approached the Federal Bureau of Investigation (FBI) and provided information about Lambert's drug activities. Hall concedes that the FBI paid her some expense money but she insists that her decision to go to the FBI was not motivated by money. Rather, she claims that she acted because of her concerns about the negative effects of drug use, particularly on young people, and her worry about Lambert's health. Over the course of the following year, Hall contacted the FBI approximately 25 times concerning Lambert's activities.

During several of her meetings with the FBI, Hall brought items which she had taken from the Lambert home. These items included test tubes, pills and other drug paraphernalia, as well as check stubs and phone bills which Hall thought might be related to Lambert's drug transactions. She insisted that these items had been discarded or abandoned by Lambert and that she had picked them up while performing her housekeeping duties.

Hall emphasized that the FBI never asked her to retrieve any items from Lambert's house or even suggested that this would be helpful to them. Agent Bill Welsh confirmed this during his testimony before the court. In fact, Hall and Welsh both testified that, after she had expressed a desire to search Lambert's closed safe and his garage, the FBI agents specifically told her *not* to do so.

In November 1982, defendant Block visited Lambert at his home and stayed for a few days in a basement bedroom. During that time, several other persons visited the home and a meeting took place in the basement. Hall, who was working upstairs, smelled chemical odors coming from the basement. She believed that the odors were caused by cocaine being cut or purified. The next day, as she was cleaning the basement, Hall went into a closet and discovered a small football-sized object. Next to it was a thermos. The thermos contained a white powder. Suspecting cocaine, Hall brought a sample from the thermos to the FBI. She emphasized that the FBI had not asked her to search for drugs or to bring this item to its office. The FBI analyzed the powder in its crime lab and determined that it was indeed cocaine.

United States v. Lambert, 771 F.2d 83, 86–87 (6th Cir.1985).

Lambert was prosecuted for drug offenses. Are the items taken from his home by Hall admissible in evidence against him?

170. Burglars entered the Genivivas' home and stole an amount of money. The burglars were arrested and the money was recovered and turned over to local police as evidence. If the police turn the money over to agents of the Internal Revenue Service, can it be used as evidence in a prosecution of the Genivivas for income tax evasion? See Geniviva v. Bingler, 206 F.Supp. 81 (W.D.Pa.1961).

171. In a divorce action, should evidence of the wife's adultery, which the husband obtained by an illegal forcible entry into her home in the company of private investigators, be admitted at the trial? See Sackler v. Sackler, 203 N.E.2d 481 (N.Y.1964), with which compare Williams v. Williams, 221 N.E.2d 622 (Ohio Ct.Com.Pl.1966). Compare Honeycutt v. Aetna Insurance Co., 510 F.2d 340 (7th Cir.1975), an action on an insurance claim in which the defendant insurance company introduced evidence of arson obtained during an unlawful search by state officials. The court of appeals concluded that "the Fourth and Fourteenth Amendments do *not* require in civil cases that the exclusionary rule be extended to situations where private parties seek to introduce evidence obtained through unauthorized searches made by state officials." Id. at 348.

CHAPTER 4

INFORMERS, EAVESDROPPING, WIRETAPPING

Lewis v. United States

385 U.S. 206, 87 S.Ct. 424, 17 L.Ed.2d 312 (1966)

▉ MR. CHIEF JUSTICE WARREN delivered the opinion of the Court.

The question for resolution here is whether the Fourth Amendment was violated when a federal narcotics agent, by misrepresenting his identity and stating his willingness to purchase narcotics, was invited into petitioner's home where an unlawful narcotics transaction was consummated and the narcotics were thereafter introduced at petitioner's criminal trial over his objection. We hold that under the facts of this case it was not. Those facts are not disputed and may be briefly stated as follows:

On December 3, 1964, Edward Cass, an undercover federal narcotics agent, telephoned petitioner's home to inquire about the possibility of purchasing marihuana. Cass, who previously had not met or dealt with petitioner, falsely identified himself as one "Jimmy the Pollack [sic]" and stated that a mutual friend had told him petitioner might be able to supply marihuana. In response, petitioner said, "Yes. I believe, Jimmy, I can take care of you," and then directed Cass to his home where, it was indicated, a sale of marihuana would occur. Cass drove to petitioner's home, knocked on the door, identified himself as "Jim," and was admitted. After discussing the possibility of regular future dealings at a discounted price, petitioner led Cass to a package located on the front porch of his home. Cass gave petitioner $50, took the package, and left the premises. The package contained five bags of marihuana. On December 17, 1964, a similar transaction took place, beginning with a phone conversation in which Cass identified himself as "Jimmy the Pollack" and ending with an invited visit by Cass to petitioner's home where a second sale of marihuana occurred. Once again, Cass paid petitioner $50, but this time he received in return a package containing six bags of marihuana.

Petitioner was arrested on April 27, 1965, and charged by a two-count indictment with violations of the narcotics laws relating to transfers of marihuana. 26 U.S.C. § 4742(a). A pretrial motion to suppress as evidence the marihuana and the conversations between petitioner and the agent was denied, and they were introduced at the trial. The District Court, sitting without a jury, convicted petitioner on both counts and imposed concurrent five-year penitentiary sentences. The Court of Appeals for the First Circuit affirmed . . . and we granted certiorari. . . .

Petitioner does not argue that he was entrapped, as he could not on the facts of this case; nor does he contend that a search of his home was made or that anything other than the purchased narcotics was taken away. His only contentions are that, in the absence of a warrant, any official intrusion upon the privacy of a home constitutes a Fourth Amendment violation and that the fact the suspect invited the intrusion cannot be held a waiver when the invitation was induced by fraud and deception.

Both petitioner and the Government recognize the necessity for some undercover police activity and both concede that the particular circumstances of each case govern the admissibility of evidence obtained by stratagem or deception. Indeed, it has long been acknowledged by the decisions of this Court . . . that, in the detection of many types of crime, the Government is entitled to use decoys and to conceal the identity of its agents. The various protections of the Bill of Rights, of course, provide checks upon such official deception for the protection of the individual. . . .

Petitioner argues that the Government overstepped the constitutional bounds in this case and places principal reliance on Gouled v. United States, 255 U.S. 298 (1921).[1] But a short statement of that case will demonstrate how misplaced his reliance is. There, a business acquaintance of the petitioner, acting under orders of federal officers, obtained entry into the petitioner's office by falsely representing that he intended only to pay a social visit. In the petitioner's absence, however, the intruder secretly ransacked the office and seized certain private papers of an incriminating nature. This Court had no difficulty concluding that the Fourth Amendment had been violated by the secret and general ransacking, notwithstanding that the initial intrusion was occasioned by a fraudulently obtained invitation rather than by force or stealth.

In the instant case, on the other hand, the petitioner invited the undercover agent to his home for the specific purpose of executing a felonious sale of narcotics. Petitioner's only concern was whether the agent was a willing purchaser who could pay the agreed price. Indeed, in order to convince the agent that his patronage at petitioner's home was desired, petitioner told him that if he became a regular customer there, he would in the future receive an extra bag of marihuana at no additional cost; and in fact petitioner did hand over an extra bag at a second sale which was consummated at the same place and in precisely the same manner. During neither of his visits to petitioner's home did the agent see, hear, or take anything that was not contemplated, and in fact intended, by petitioner as a necessary part of his illegal business. Were we to hold the deceptions of the agent in this case constitutionally prohibited, we would come near to a rule that the use of undercover agents in any manner is virtually unconsti-

---

[1] The aspect of *Gouled* discussed here is separate from that considered in connection with Warden v. Hayden, 387 U.S. 294 (1967), p. 246 above.

tutional per se. Such a rule would, for example, severely hamper the Government in ferreting out those organized criminal activities that are characterized by covert dealings with victims who either cannot or do not protest. A prime example is provided by the narcotics traffic.

The fact that the undercover agent entered petitioner's home does not compel a different conclusion. Without question, the home is accorded the full range of Fourth Amendment protections. . . . But when, as here, the home is converted into a commercial center to which outsiders are invited for purposes of transacting unlawful business, that business is entitled to no greater sanctity than if it were carried on in a store, a garage, a car, or on the street. A government agent, in the same manner as a private person, may accept an invitation to do business and may enter upon the premises for the very purposes contemplated by the occupant. Of course, this does not mean that, whenever entry is obtained by invitation and the locus is characterized as a place of business, an agent is authorized to conduct a general search for incriminating materials; a citation to the *Gouled* case, supra, is sufficient to dispose of that contention.

. . . The instant . . . case has been well summarized by the Government at the conclusion of its brief as follows:

> In short, this case involves the exercise of no governmental power to intrude upon protected premises; the visitor was invited and willingly admitted by the suspect. It concerns no design on the part of a government agent to observe or hear what was happening in the privacy of a home; the suspect chose the location where the transaction took place. It presents no question of the invasion of the privacy of a dwelling; the only statements repeated were those that were willingly made to the agent and the only things taken were the packets of marihuana voluntarily transferred to him. The pretense resulted in no breach of privacy; it merely encouraged the suspect to say things which he was willing and anxious to say to anyone who would be interested in purchasing marihuana.

Further elaboration is not necessary. The judgment is

Affirmed.

■ M<small>R</small>. J<small>USTICE</small> D<small>OUGLAS</small>, dissenting.

. . .

We are here concerned with the manner in which government agents enter private homes. In *Lewis* the undercover agent appeared as a prospective customer. Tomorrow he may be a policeman disguised as the grocery deliveryman or telephone repairman, or even a health inspector. . . .

. . .

Entering another's home in disguise to obtain evidence is a "search" that should bring into play all the protective features of the Fourth Amendment. When the agent in *Lewis* had reason for believing that petitioner possessed narcotics, a search warrant should have been obtained.

Almost every home is at times used for purposes other than eating, sleeping, and social activities. Are the sanctity of the home and its privacy stripped away whenever it is used for business? . . . I think not. A home is still a sanctuary, however the owner may use it. There is no reason why an owner's Fourth Amendment rights cannot include the right to open up his house to limited classes of people. And, when a homeowner invites a friend or business acquaintance into his home, he opens his house to a friend or acquaintance, not a government spy.

This does not mean he can make his sanctuary invasion-proof against government agents. The Constitution has provided a way whereby the home can lawfully be invaded, and that is with a search warrant. Where, as here, there is enough evidence to get a warrant to make a search I would not allow the Fourth Amendment to be short-circuited.

We downgrade the Fourth Amendment when we forgive noncompliance with its mandate and allow these easier methods of the police to thrive.

A householder who admits a government agent, knowing that he is such, waives of course any right of privacy. One who invites or admits an old "friend" takes, I think, the risk that the "friend" will tattle and disclose confidences or that the Government will wheedle them out of him. The case for me, however, is different when government plays an ignoble role of "planting" an agent in one's living room or uses fraud and deception in getting him there. These practices are at war with the constitutional standards of privacy which are parts of our choicest tradition.

. . . [2]

---

172. What precisely is the principle established by *Lewis*? Is any entry pursuant to an invitation permissible under the Fourth Amendment despite the official's concealment of his official capacity, provided that he does only what he was invited inside to do? How should the Court's phrase "the very purposes contemplated by the occupant," p. 306 above, be understood? (In one obvious sense, Cass's purpose in entering could not have been more opposed to the purpose for which Lewis invited him in.) In United States v. Guidry, 534 F.2d 1220 (6th Cir.1976), for example, a federal agent who suspected that the defendants were engaged in counterfeiting arranged to pose as the "helper" of a service representative of a printing company when the latter made a call at the defendants' house. The service representative told the defendants that he was there to look at the printing press, which they wanted to sell. While he was in the house, the agent observed the press and removed from it a piece of paper with green ink. Was the agent's observation of the press lawful? The removal of the paper? See also United States v. Ressler, 536 F.2d 208 (7th Cir.1976).

[2] Justice Brennan wrote a concurring opinion, which Justice Fortas joined.

How important in *Lewis* is the fact that the purpose for which Cass was invited to enter was itself illegal? Suppose, as Justice Douglas imagined, p. 306 above, a police officer posed as a telephone repairman and observed nothing except what a repairman would inevitably observe and would, therefore, be expected to observe. In *Guidry*, above, the purpose of the service representative's visit was entirely lawful. See also United States v. Wagner, 884 F.2d 1090 (8th Cir.1989), in which an officer posed as a UPS delivery man, and United States v. Alvarez, 812 F.2d 668 (11th Cir.1987), in which agents posed as bank representatives seeking information for a "merchant questionnaire." In United States v. Giraldo, 743 F.Supp. 152 (E.D.N.Y.1990), the court held that entry obtained by an agent's representation that she was a gas company worker checking for a gas leak was unlawful, because the purported purpose of the visit gave the defendant no effective choice to deny entry.

Does it make any difference that the purpose of the entry is a business transaction? Suppose Lewis had invited Cass to his house and told him that he was going to give him a gift of marijuana.

For an extreme application of *Lewis*, see U.S. v. Baldwin, 621 F.2d 251, 632 F.2d 1 (6th Cir.1980). In that case, an undercover agent obtained employment as handyman and chauffeur in the home of a person who was under investigation. The agent lived there for six months, during which period he found and removed material that was used as evidence against his employer.

173.   The defendant was convicted of tax offenses. The evidence against him included microfilms of records that the defendant voluntarily made available to an IRS agent who was conducting an audit of the defendant's returns at the request of the Organized Crime and Racketeering Section of the Department of Justice. The court of appeals found that "the agent's failure to apprise the appellant of the obvious criminal nature of this investigation was a sneaky deliberate deception." United States v. Tweel, 550 F.2d 297, 299 (5th Cir.1977). Should the evidence have been admitted? Compare United States v. Davis, 749 F.2d 292 (5th Cir.1985) ("mere failure to warn an individual that an investigation might result in criminal charges does not constitute fraud, deceit or trickery").

174.   The defendant was indicted for income tax evasion. Thereafter, on several occasions an accountant who had prepared the defendant's tax returns for many years and had prepared net worth schedules for the defendant at the request of his counsel came alone and voluntarily to the United States Attorney's office. He was interviewed by government counsel and agents of the Internal Revenue Service and voluntarily turned over to them his file on the defendant, which included the net worth schedules. The government had prepared its own net worth schedules for use at trial, with which it compared the schedules prepared for the defendant. Defense counsel was promptly advised of the disclosures. The matter was called to the court's attention before trial by the defendant's motion to suppress. United States v. Mancuso, 378 F.2d 612 (4th Cir.1967). Were any rights of the defendant infringed? If so, what action should the court have taken?

175. In Weatherford v. Bursey, 429 U.S. 545 (1977) (7–2), an under-cover government agent who, as an agent, had been involved in a crime with the defendant was arrested with him in order to maintain his cover. During the pretrial period, the agent met with the defendant and the defendant's lawyer on two occasions when the trial was discussed. The agent did not initiate the meetings, nor did he discuss what happened at them with the prosecutor. He appeared at the trial as a witness for the prosecution. The Court concluded that there had been no denial of the right to counsel in those circumstances. Nothing having been communicated to the prosecution, the defense was not hampered in any way. Furthermore, there was no purposeful intrusion into the attorney-client relationship, and the intrusion that took place was necessitated by the nature of undercover work. Compare Hoffa v. United States, 385 U.S. 293, 304–309 (1966); United States v. Valencia, 541 F.2d 618 (6th Cir.1976) (attorney's secretary was government informant; indictment dismissed).

See United States v. Mastroianni, 749 F.2d 900 (1st Cir.1984). A government informant was invited to attend a meeting of the defendants with defense counsel. The court of appeals upheld the district court's finding that the informant's attendance at the meeting was not a deliberate intrusion into the defense camp and was permissible to maintain the informant's "cover." After the meeting, the informant was "debriefed" by the government and revealed confidential matter that he had heard at the defense meeting. The court of appeals upheld the district court's finding that the government had met its high burden of showing that the defendants were not prejudiced by the informant's disclosures. See also United States v. Melvin, 650 F.2d 641 (5th Cir.1981) (inter alia, applying reasoning of *Morrison*, p. 1015 note 516 below).

176. Is it permissible for the government to employ informers on a "contingent fee" basis, the fee being based on a government agent's estimate of the value of their services? Does it matter whether the government is seeking evidence against a particular defendant? Or whether it has agreed to pay for evidence of a crime already committed rather than a crime expected to be committed? See United States v. Cervantes-Pacheco, 800 F.2d 452 (5th Cir.1986), overruling a prior decision to the contrary and stating the general rule that contingent fee arrangements are, within limits, permissible.

Katz v. United States

389 U.S. 347, 88 S.Ct. 507, 19 L.Ed.2d 576 (1967)

■ MR. JUSTICE STEWART delivered the opinion of the Court.

The petitioner was convicted in the District Court for the Southern District of California under an eight-count indictment charging him with transmitting wagering information by telephone from Los Angeles to

Miami and Boston, in violation of a federal statute. At trial the Government was permitted, over the petitioner's objection, to introduce evidence of the petitioner's end of telephone conversations, overheard by FBI agents who had attached an electronic listening and recording device to the outside of the public telephone booth from which he had placed his calls. In affirming his conviction, the Court of Appeals rejected the contention that the recordings had been obtained in violation of the Fourth Amendment, because "[t]here was no physical entrance into the area occupied by [the petitioner]."[3] We granted certiorari in order to consider the constitutional questions thus presented.

The petitioner has phrased those questions as follows:

A.   Whether a public telephone booth is a constitutionally protected area so that evidence obtained by attaching an electronic listening recording device to the top of such a booth is obtained in violation of the right to privacy of the user of the booth.

B.   Whether physical penetration of a constitutionally protected area is necessary before a search and seizure can be said to be violative of the Fourth Amendment to the United States Constitution.

We decline to adopt this formulation of the issues. In the first place, the correct solution of Fourth Amendment problems is not necessarily promoted by incantation of the phrase "constitutionally protected area." Secondly, the Fourth Amendment cannot be translated into a general constitutional "right to privacy." That Amendment protects individual privacy against certain kinds of governmental intrusion, but its protections go further, and often have nothing to do with privacy at all. Other provisions of the Constitution protect personal privacy from other forms of governmental invasion. But the protection of a person's *general* right to privacy—his right to be let alone by other people—is, like the protection of his property and of his very life, left largely to the law of the individual States.

Because of the misleading way the issues have been formulated, the parties have attached great significance to the characterization of the telephone booth from which the petitioner placed his calls. The petitioner has strenuously argued that the booth was a "constitutionally protected area." The Government has maintained with equal vigor that it was not. But this effort to decide whether or not a given "area," viewed in the abstract, is "constitutionally protected" deflects attention from the problem presented by this case. For the Fourth Amendment protects people, not places. What a person knowingly exposes to the public, even in his own home or office, is not a subject of Fourth Amendment protection. . . . But what he seeks to preserve as private, even in an area accessible to the public, may be constitutionally protected. . . .

The Government stresses the fact that the telephone booth from which the petitioner made his calls was constructed partly of glass, so that he was

3.   369 F.2d 130, 134.

as visible after he entered it as he would have been if he had remained outside. But what he sought to exclude when he entered the booth was not the intruding eye—it was the uninvited ear. He did not shed his right to do so simply because he made his calls from a place where he might be seen. No less than an individual in a business office, in a friend's apartment, or in a taxicab, a person in a telephone booth may rely upon the protection of the Fourth Amendment. One who occupies it, shuts the door behind him, and pays the toll that permits him to place a call is surely entitled to assume that the words he utters into the mouthpiece will not be broadcast to the world. To read the Constitution more narrowly is to ignore the vital role that the public telephone has come to play in private communication.

The Government contends, however, that the activities of its agents in this case should not be tested by Fourth Amendment requirements, for the surveillance technique they employed involved no physical penetration of the telephone booth from which the petitioner placed his calls. It is true that the absence of such penetration was at one time thought to foreclose further Fourth Amendment inquiry, Olmstead v. United States, 277 U.S. 438, 457, 464, 466; Goldman v. United States, 316 U.S. 129, 134–36, for that Amendment was thought to limit only searches and seizures of tangible property. But "[t]he premise that property interests control the right of the Government to search and seize has been discredited." Warden v. Hayden, 387 U.S. 294, 304. Thus, although a closely divided Court supposed in *Olmstead* that surveillance without any trespass and without the seizure of any material object fell outside the ambit of the Constitution, we have since departed from the narrow view on which that decision rested. Indeed, we have expressly held that the Fourth Amendment governs not only the seizure of tangible items, but extends as well to the recording of oral statements, overheard without any "technical trespass under . . . local property law." Silverman v. United States, 365 U.S. 505, 511. Once this much is acknowledged, and once it is recognized that the Fourth Amendment protects people—and not simply "areas"—against unreasonable searches and seizures, it becomes clear that the reach of that Amendment cannot turn upon the presence or absence of a physical intrusion into any given enclosure.

We conclude that the underpinnings of *Olmstead* and *Goldman* have been so eroded by our subsequent decisions that the "trespass" doctrine there enunciated can no longer be regarded as controlling. The Government's activities in electronically listening to and recording the petitioner's words violated the privacy upon which he justifiably relied while using the telephone booth and thus constituted a "search and seizure" within the meaning of the Fourth Amendment. The fact that the electronic device employed to achieve that end did not happen to penetrate the wall of the booth can have no constitutional significance.

The question remaining for decision, then, is whether the search and seizure conducted in this case complied with constitutional standards. In that regard, the Government's position is that its agents acted in an entirely defensible manner: They did not begin their electronic surveillance until investigation of the petitioner's activities had established a strong probability that he was using the telephone in question to transmit gambling information to persons in other States, in violation of federal law. Moreover, the surveillance was limited, both in scope and in duration, to the specific purpose of establishing the contents of the petitioner's unlawful telephonic communications. The agents confined their surveillance to the brief periods during which he used the telephone booth,[4] and they took great care to overhear only the conversations of the petitioner himself.

Accepting this account of the Government's actions as accurate, it is clear that this surveillance was so narrowly circumscribed that a duly authorized magistrate properly notified of the need for such investigation, specifically informed of the basis on which it was to proceed, and clearly apprised of the precise intrusion it would entail, could constitutionally have authorized, with appropriate safeguards, the very limited search and seizure that the Government asserts in fact took place. Only last Term we sustained the validity of such an authorization, holding that, under sufficiently "precise and discriminate circumstances," a federal court may empower government agents to employ a concealed electronic device "for the narrow and particularized purpose of ascertaining the truth of the . . . allegations" of a "detailed factual affidavit alleging the commission of a specific criminal offense." Osborn v. United States, 385 U.S. 323, 329–30. Discussing that holding, the Court in Berger v. New York, 388 U.S. 41, said that "the order authorizing the use of the electronic device" in *Osborn* "afforded similar protections to those . . . of conventional warrants authorizing the seizure of tangible evidence." Through those protections, "no greater invasion of privacy was permitted than was necessary under the circumstances." Id., at 57. Here, too, a similar judicial order could have accommodated "the legitimate needs of law enforcement"[5] by authorizing the carefully limited use of electronic surveillance.

The Government urges that, because its agents relied upon the decisions in *Olmstead* and *Goldman*, and because they did no more here than they might properly have done with prior judicial sanction, we should retroactively validate their conduct. That we cannot do. It is apparent that the agents in this case acted with restraint. Yet the inescapable fact is that this restraint was imposed by the agents themselves, not by a judicial officer. They were not required, before commencing the search, to present their estimate of probable cause for detached scrutiny by a neutral magistrate. They were not compelled, during the conduct of the search itself, to observe precise limits established in advance by a specific court order. Nor

---

4. Based upon their previous visual observations of the petitioner, the agents correctly predicted that he would use the telephone booth for several minutes at approximately the same time each morning. The petitioner was subjected to electronic surveillance only during this predetermined period. Six recordings, averaging some three minutes each, were obtained and admitted in evidence. They preserved the petitioner's end of conversations concerning the placing of bets and the receipt of wagering information.

5. Lopez v. United States, 373 U.S. 427, 464 (dissenting opinion of Mr. Justice Brennan).

were they directed, after the search had been completed, to notify the authorizing magistrate in detail of all that had been seized. In the absence of such safeguards, this Court has never sustained a search upon the sole ground that officers reasonably expected to find evidence of a particular crime and voluntarily confined their activities to the least intrusive means consistent with that end. Searches conducted without warrants have been held unlawful "notwithstanding facts unquestionably showing probable cause," Agnello v. United States, 269 U.S. 20, 33, for the Constitution requires "that the deliberate, impartial judgment of a judicial officer . . . be interposed between the citizen and the police. . . ." Wong Sun v. United States, 371 U.S. 471, 481–82. "Over and again this Court has emphasized that the mandate of the [Fourth] Amendment requires adherence to judicial processes," United States v. Jeffers, 342 U.S. 48, 51, and that searches conducted outside the judicial process, without prior approval by judge or magistrate, are per se unreasonable under the Fourth Amendment—subject only to a few specifically established and well-delineated exceptions.

It is difficult to imagine how any of those exceptions could ever apply to the sort of search and seizure involved in this case. Even electronic surveillance substantially contemporaneous with an individual's arrest could hardly be deemed an "incident" of that arrest. Nor could the use of electronic surveillance without prior authorization be justified on grounds of "hot pursuit." And, of course, the very nature of electronic surveillance precludes its use pursuant to the suspect's consent.

The Government does not question these basic principles. Rather, it urges the creation of a new exception to cover this case. It argues that surveillance of a telephone booth should be exempted from the usual requirement of advance authorization by a magistrate upon a showing of probable cause. We cannot agree. Omission of such authorization

> bypasses the safeguards provided by an objective predetermination of probable cause, and substitutes instead the far less reliable procedure of an after-the-event justification for the . . . search, too likely to be subtly influenced by the familiar shortcomings of hindsight judgment.

Beck v. Ohio, 379 U.S. 89, 96. And bypassing a neutral predetermination of the scope of a search leaves individuals secure from Fourth Amendment violations "only in the discretion of the police." Id., at 97.

These considerations do not vanish when the search in question is transferred from the setting of a home, an office, or a hotel room to that of a telephone booth. Wherever a man may be, he is entitled to know that he will remain free from unreasonable searches and seizures. The government agents here ignored "the procedure of antecedent justification . . . that is central to the Fourth Amendment,"[6] a procedure that we hold to be a

6. See Osborn v. United States, 385 U.S. 323, 330.

constitutional precondition of the kind of electronic surveillance involved in this case. Because the surveillance here failed to meet that condition, and because it led to the petitioner's conviction, the judgment must be reversed. . . . [7]

---

177. Observing that most people are aware that the telephone numbers dialed from a telephone may be recorded by the telephone company for a variety of purposes, the Supreme Court held that the use on a private telephone of a pen register, which mechanically records dialed numbers without overhearing conversations, was not a search within the meaning of the Fourth Amendment. Smith v. Maryland, 442 U.S. 735 (1979) (5–3).

Congress has enacted legislation regulating the installation and use of a pen register. The new provisions, with certain exceptions, prohibit installation or use of a pen register without a court order. An attorney for the government or a state investigative or law enforcement officer may apply to a court for an order authorizing the installation and use of a pen register, which order may be issued ex parte for not more than 60 days. 18 U.S.C. §§ 3121–3126.

178. In United States v. United States District Court for the Eastern District of Michigan, 407 U.S. 297 (1972), the Court rejected the government's claim that the need to investigate in order to protect domestic security allowed the Attorney General to authorize electronic surveillance without a warrant. The Court stated that its opinion was applicable to domestic security only and not to matters involving foreign nations. It noted also that different procedures might be reasonable in connection with domestic security matters than were used in ordinary criminal cases.

179. In Dalia v. United States, 441 U.S. 238 (1979) (5–4), the Court considered the problem of entries into private premises to install an electronic surveillance device pursuant to an order under 18 U.S.C. §§ 2510–2522, p. 326 below. The Court held that "the Fourth Amendment does not prohibit per se a covert entry performed for the purpose of installing otherwise legal electronic bugging equipment." 441 U.S. at 248. Further, the Court concluded that Congress had intended to include authorization to make such an entry within the power conferred on the courts by the statute and that a judicial order authorizing surveillance, which complied with the requirements for a search warrant under the Fourth Amendment, does not need to include explicit authorization for the entry. See United States v. Villegas, 899 F.2d 1324 (2d Cir.1990) (warrant for covert entry to take photographs without seizing any property upheld).

---

[7] Justice Douglas wrote a concurring opinion, which Justice Brennan joined. Justice Harlan and Justice White also wrote concurring opinions. Justice Black wrote a dissenting opinion.

United States v. White

401 U.S. 745, 91 S.Ct. 1122, 28 L.Ed.2d 453 (1971)

■ MR. JUSTICE WHITE announced the judgment of the Court and an opinion in which THE CHIEF JUSTICE, MR. JUSTICE STEWART, and MR. JUSTICE BLACKMUN join.

In 1966, respondent James A. White was tried and convicted under two consolidated indictments charging various illegal transactions in narcotics violative of 26 U.S.C. § 4705(a) and 21 U.S.C. § 174. He was fined and sentenced as a second offender to 25-year concurrent sentences. The issue before us is whether the Fourth Amendment bars from evidence the testimony of governmental agents who related certain conversations which had occurred between defendant White and a government informant, Harvey Jackson, and which the agents overheard by monitoring the frequency of a radio transmitter carried by Jackson and concealed on his person. On four occasions the conversations took place in Jackson's home; each of these conversations was overheard by an agent concealed in a kitchen closet with Jackson's consent and by a second agent outside the house using a radio receiver. Four other conversations—one in respondent's home, one in a restaurant, and two in Jackson's car—were overheard by the use of radio equipment. The prosecution was unable to locate and produce Jackson at the trial and the trial court overruled objections to the testimony of the agents who conducted the electronic surveillance. The jury returned a guilty verdict and defendant appealed.

The Court of Appeals read Katz v. United States, 389 U.S. 347 (1967), as . . . interpreting the Fourth Amendment to forbid the introduction of the agents' testimony in the circumstances of this case. Accordingly, the court reversed. . . . In our view, the Court of Appeals misinterpreted both the *Katz* case and the Fourth Amendment. . . .

I

Until Katz v. United States, neither wiretapping nor electronic eavesdropping violated a defendant's Fourth Amendment rights "unless there has been an official search and seizure of his person, or such a seizure of his papers or his tangible material effects, or an actual physical invasion of his house 'or curtilage' for the purpose of making a seizure." Olmstead v. United States, 277 U.S. 438, 466 (1928); Goldman v. United States, 316 U.S. 129, 135–36 (1942). But where "eavesdropping was accomplished by means of an unauthorized physical penetration into the premises occupied" by the defendant, although falling short of a "technical trespass under the local property law," the Fourth Amendment was violated and any evidence of what was seen and heard, as well as tangible objects seized, was considered the inadmissible fruit of an unlawful invasion. Silverman v. United States, 365 U.S. 505, 509, 511 (1961). . . .

Katz v. United States, however, finally swept away doctrines that electronic eavesdropping is permissible under the Fourth Amendment unless physical invasion of a constitutionally protected area produced the challenged evidence. In that case government agents, without petitioner's consent or knowledge, attached a listening device to the outside of a public telephone booth and recorded the defendant's end of his telephone conversations. In declaring the recordings inadmissible in evidence in the absence of a warrant authorizing the surveillance, the Court overruled *Olmstead* and *Goldman* and held that the absence of physical intrusion into the telephone booth did not justify using electronic devices in listening to and recording Katz' words, thereby violating the privacy on which he justifiably relied while using the telephone in those circumstances.

The Court of Appeals understood *Katz* to render inadmissible against White the agents' testimony concerning conversations that Jackson broadcast to them. We cannot agree. *Katz* involved no revelation to the Government by a party to conversations with the defendant nor did the Court indicate in any way that a defendant has a justifiable and constitutionally protected expectation that a person with whom he is conversing will not then or later reveal the conversation to the police.

Hoffa v. United States, 385 U.S. 293 (1966), which was left undisturbed by *Katz*, held that however strongly a defendant may trust an apparent colleague, his expectations in this respect are not protected by the Fourth Amendment when it turns out that the colleague is a government agent regularly communicating with the authorities. In these circumstances, "no interest legitimately protected by the Fourth Amendment is involved," for that amendment affords no protection to "a wrongdoer's misplaced belief that a person to whom he voluntarily confides his wrongdoing will not reveal it." Hoffa v. United States, at 302. No warrant to "search and seize" is required in such circumstances, nor is it when the Government sends to defendant's home a secret agent who conceals his identity and makes a purchase of narcotics from the accused, Lewis v. United States, 385 U.S. 206 (1966), or when the same agent, unbeknown to the defendant, carries electronic equipment to record the defendant's words and the evidence so gathered is later offered in evidence. Lopez v. United States, 373 U.S. 427 (1963).

Conceding that *Hoffa*, *Lewis*, and *Lopez* remained unaffected by *Katz*, the Court of Appeals nevertheless read both *Katz* and the Fourth Amendment to require a different result if the agent not only records his conversations with the defendant but instantaneously transmits them electronically to other agents equipped with radio receivers. Where this occurs, the Court of Appeals held, the Fourth Amendment is violated and the testimony of the listening agents must be excluded from evidence.

. . .

Concededly a police agent who conceals his police connections may write down for official use his conversations with a defendant and testify concerning them, without a warrant authorizing his encounters with the defendant and without otherwise violating the latter's Fourth Amendment rights. . . . For constitutional purposes, no different result is required if the agent instead of immediately reporting and transcribing his conversations with defendant, either (1) simultaneously records them with electronic equipment which he is carrying on his person . . . (2) or carries radio equipment which simultaneously transmits the conversations either to recording equipment located elsewhere or to other agents monitoring the transmitting frequency. . . . If the conduct and revelations of an agent operating without electronic equipment do not invade the defendant's constitutionally justifiable expectations of privacy, neither does a simultaneous recording of the same conversations made by the agent or by others from transmissions received from the agent to whom the defendant is talking and whose trustworthiness the defendant necessarily risks.

Our problem is not what the privacy expectations of particular defendants in particular situations may be or the extent to which they may in fact have relied on the discretion of their companions. Very probably, individual defendants neither know nor suspect that their colleagues have gone or will go to the police or are carrying recorders or transmitters. Otherwise, conversation would cease and our problem with these encounters would be nonexistent or far different from those now before us. Our problem, in terms of the principles announced in *Katz*, is what expectations of privacy are constitutionally "justifiable"—what expectations the Fourth Amendment will protect in the absence of a warrant. So far, the law permits the frustration of actual expectations of privacy by permitting authorities to use the testimony of those associates who for one reason or another have determined to turn to the police, as well as by authorizing the use of informants in the manner exemplified by *Hoffa* and *Lewis*. If the law gives no protection to the wrongdoer whose trusted accomplice is or becomes a police agent, neither should it protect him when that same agent has recorded or transmitted the conversations which are later offered in evidence to prove the State's case. . . .

Inescapably, one contemplating illegal activities must realize and risk that his companions may be reporting to the police. If he sufficiently doubts their trustworthiness, the association will very probably end or never materialize. But if he has no doubts, or allays them, or risks what doubt he has, the risk is his. In terms of what his course will be, what he will or will not do or say, we are unpersuaded that he would distinguish between probable informers on the one hand and probable informers with transmitters on the other. Given the possibility or probability that one of his colleagues is cooperating with the police, it is only speculation to assert that the defendant's utterances would be substantially different or his sense of security any less if he also thought it possible that the suspected colleague is wired for sound. At least there is no persuasive evidence that the difference in this respect between the electronically equipped and the unequipped agent is substantial enough to require discrete constitutional recognition, particularly under the Fourth Amendment which is ruled by fluid concepts of "reasonableness."

Nor should we be too ready to erect constitutional barriers to relevant and probative evidence which is also accurate and reliable. An electronic recording will many times produce a more reliable rendition of what a defendant has said than will the unaided memory of a police agent. It may also be that with the recording in existence it is less likely that the informant will change his mind, less chance that threat or injury will suppress unfavorable evidence and less chance that cross-examination will confound the testimony. Considerations like these obviously do not favor the defendant, but we are not prepared to hold that a defendant who has no constitutional right to exclude the informer's unaided testimony nevertheless has a Fourth Amendment privilege against a more accurate version of the events in question.

It is thus untenable to consider the activities and reports of the police agent himself, though acting without a warrant, to be a "reasonable" investigative effort and lawful under the Fourth Amendment but to view the same agent with a recorder or transmitter as conducting an "unreasonable" and unconstitutional search and seizure. Our opinion is currently shared by Congress and the Executive Branch, Title III, Omnibus Crime Control and Safe Streets Act of 1968, 82 Stat. 212, 18 U.S.C. § 2510 et seq. (1964 ed., Supp. V), and the American Bar Association. Project on Standards for Criminal Justice, Electronic Surveillance § 4.1 (Approved Draft 1971). It is also the result reached by prior cases in this Court. . . .

No different result should obtain where, as in . . . the instant case, the informer disappears and is unavailable at trial; for the issue of whether specified events on a certain day violate the Fourth Amendment should not be determined by what later happens to the informer. His unavailability at trial and proffering the testimony of other agents may raise evidentiary problems or pose issues of prosecutorial misconduct with respect to the informer's disappearance, but they do not appear critical to deciding whether prior events invaded the defendant's Fourth Amendment rights.

. . .

The judgment of the Court of Appeals is reversed.

. . .

■ MR. JUSTICE HARLAN, dissenting.

. . .

Before turning to matters of precedent and policy, several preliminary observations should be made. We deal here with the constitutional validity of instantaneous third-party electronic eavesdropping, conducted by federal law enforcement officers, without any prior judicial approval of the technique utilized, but with the consent and cooperation of a participant in the conversation, and where the substance of the matter electronically overheard is related in a federal criminal trial by those who eavesdropped as direct, not merely corroborative, evidence of the guilt of the nonconsenting party. The magnitude of the issue at hand is evidenced not simply by the obvious doctrinal difficulty of weighing such activity in the Fourth Amendment balance, but also, and more importantly, by the prevalence of police utilization of this technique. . . .

. . .

[T]he decisions of this Court . . . establish sound general principles for application of the Fourth Amendment. . . . I have already traced some of these principles . . . : that verbal communication is protected by the Fourth Amendment, that the reasonableness of a search does not depend on the presence or absence of a trespass, and that the Fourth Amendment is principally concerned with protecting interests of privacy, rather than property rights.

Especially when other recent Fourth Amendment decisions, not otherwise so immediately relevant, are read with those already discussed, the primacy of an additional general principle becomes equally evident: official investigatory action that impinges on privacy must typically, in order to be constitutionally permissible, be subjected to the warrant requirement. . . .

. . .

The impact of the practice of third-party bugging, must, I think, be considered such as to undermine that confidence and sense of security in dealing with one another that is characteristic of individual relationships between citizens in a free society. It goes beyond the impact on privacy occasioned by the ordinary type of "informer" investigation upheld in *Lewis* and *Hoffa*. The argument of the plurality opinion, to the effect that it is irrelevant whether secrets are revealed by the mere tattletale or the transistor, ignores the differences occasioned by third-party monitoring and recording which insures full and accurate disclosure of all that is said, free of the possibility of error and oversight that inheres in human reporting.

Authority is hardly required to support the proposition that words would be measured a good deal more carefully and communication inhibited if one expected his conversations were being transmitted and transcribed. Were third-party bugging a prevalent practice, it might well smother that spontaneity—reflected in frivolous, impetuous, sacrilegious, and defiant discourse—that liberates daily life. Much off-hand exchange is easily forgotten and one may count on the obscurity of his remarks, protected by the very fact of a limited audience, and the likelihood that the listener will either overlook or forget what is said, as well as the listener's inability to reformulate a conversation without having to contend with a documented record.[8] All these values are sacrificed by a rule of law that

---

8. From the same standpoint it may also be thought that electronic recording by an informer of a face-to-face conversation with a criminal suspect, as in *Lopez* [v. United States, 373 U.S. 427 (1963)], should be differentiated from third-party monitoring, as in . . . the case before us, in that the latter assures revelation to the Government by obviating the possibility that the informer may be tempted to renege in his undertaking to pass on to the Government all that he has learned. While the continuing vitality of *Lopez* is not drawn directly into question by this case, candor compels me to acknowledge that the views expressed in this opinion may impinge upon that part of the reasoning in *Lopez* which suggested that a suspect has no right to anticipate unreliable testimony. I am now persuaded that such an approach misconceives the basic issue, focusing, as it does, on the interests of a particular individual rather than evaluating the impact of a practice on the sense of security that is the true concern of the Fourth Amendment's protection of privacy. Distinctions do, however, exist between *Lopez*, where a known government agent uses a recording device, and this case which involves third-party overhearing.

permits official monitoring of private discourse limited only by the need to locate a willing assistant.

. . .

Finally, it is too easy to forget—and, hence, too often forgotten—that the issue here is whether to interpose a search warrant procedure between law enforcement agencies engaging in electronic eavesdropping and the public generally. By casting its "risk analysis" solely in terms of the expectations and risks that "wrongdoers" or "one contemplating illegal activities" ought to bear, the plurality opinion, I think, misses the mark entirely. . . . The interest . . . [that the majority] fails to protect is the expectation of the ordinary citizen, who has never engaged in illegal conduct in his life, that he may carry on his private discourse freely, openly, and spontaneously without measuring his every word against the connotations it might carry when instantaneously heard by others unknown to him and unfamiliar with his situation or analyzed in a cold, formal record played days, months, or years after the conversation. Interposition of a warrant requirement is designed not to shield "wrongdoers," but to secure a measure of privacy and a sense of personal security throughout our society.

The Fourth Amendment does, of course, leave room for the employment of modern technology in criminal law enforcement, but in the stream of current developments in Fourth Amendment law I think it must be held that third-party electronic monitoring, subject only to the self-restraint of law enforcement officials, has no place in our society.

. . . [9]

———

180. *White* and Lopez v. United States, 373 U.S. 427 (1963), which is discussed in *White*, are affirmed in United States v. Caceres, 440 U.S. 741 (1979) (7–2). There, an agent of the Internal Revenue Service secretly transmitted conversations with the defendant, without obtaining authorization as required by IRS regulations. Recordings of the conversations were offered in evidence against the defendant, but were excluded by the district court. The Court held that the failure to follow the regulations, which were not constitutionally required, did not require suppression of the evidence.

181. The reasoning in *White* was applied to telephonic eavesdropping and recording with the consent of one of the parties to the conversation, in United States v. Bonanno, 487 F.2d 654 (2d Cir.1973), and, over a strong

However unlikely that the participant recorder will not play his tapes, the fact of the matter is that in a third-party situation the intrusion is instantaneous. Moreover, differences in the prior relationship between the investigator and the suspect may provide a focus for future distinctions. . . .

[9] Justice Brennan wrote an opinion concurring in the result. Justice Black noted his concurrence in the result. Justice Douglas and Justice Marshall also wrote dissenting opinions.

dissent, in Holmes v. Burr, 486 F.2d 55 (9th Cir.1973). Suppose the person consenting to the tap owns the telephone but is not a party to the conversation. See United States v. San Martin, 469 F.2d 5 (2d Cir.1972) (question raised but not decided); cf. United States v. Pui Kan Lam, 483 F.2d 1202 (2d Cir.1973).

The Supreme Court of Vermont has held that a police officer's secret recording of a conversation he had with a person in the person's own home, without a judicially authorized warrant, violated the person's rights under the state constitution. State v. Geraw, 795 A.2d 1219 (2002). The court relied heavily on Justice Harlan's dissenting opinion in *White* and emphasized that the location of the recorded conversation may make a difference; the home, it said, is a place where the expectation of privacy is at its highest. The court observed further that the fact that the person spoke freely to the police officer does not indicate that he had no expectation of privacy so far as recording is concerned; otherwise the officer would not have recorded secretly. Relying on their state constitutions, Alaska and Massachusetts have also rejected *White*. State v. Glass, 583 P.2d 872 (Alaska 1978); Commonwealth v. Blood, 507 N.E.2d 1029 (Mass.1987).

182. United States v. Longoria, 177 F.3d 1179 (10th Cir.1999). The defendant conversed in Spanish with his codefendants while they were together with a government informant in the latter's shop. The informant secretly recorded the conversations, which were later introduced in evidence. The defendant believed that the informant did not understand Spanish. The defendant claimed that he had a "reasonable expectation of privacy" and therefore, that the conversations were "oral communications" protected from disclosure under 18 U.S.C. §§ 2510(2), 2515. The court held that, despite his belief that the informant did not speak Spanish, his expectation of privacy was not one that society is prepared to accept as reasonable.

183. Police officers installed audio and video recording equipment in the hotel suite of the defendant, with the cooperation of a person who rented the suite for the defendant's use. The equipment was installed before the defendant's arrival. The officers monitored conversations between the defendant and the other person, in which the defendant incriminated himself. The officers monitored activity in the corridor outside the suite and turned on the equipment only when the person cooperating with them was in the suite. United States v. Lee, 359 F.3d 194 (3d Cir.2004). In those circumstances, the court said, the rules applicable to monitoring a conversation between a consenting person and another apply. It made no difference that the equipment was installed in the room rather than being carried by the consenting person.

184. Who has standing to object to the introduction of evidence obtained by unlawful eavesdropping? In Alderman v. United States, 394 U.S. 165, 176 (1969) (5–2–1) the Court said: "[A]ny petitioner would be entitled to the suppression of government evidence originating in electronic surveillance violative of his own Fourth Amendment right to be free of unreasonable searches and seizures. Such violation would occur if the United States unlawfully overheard conversations of a petitioner himself or conversations occurring on his premises, whether or not he was present or participated in those conversations."

This was the conclusion of Chief Justice Warren and Justices White (who wrote the opinion) and Brennan. Justices Douglas and Fortas believed that standing should be extended also to "a person concerning whom an investigation involving illegal electronic surveillance has been conducted," 394 U.S. at 201, whether or not he participated in the monitored conversation or it occurred on his premises. (That position is rejected generally in the Court's discussion of the "target" theory of standing in Rakas v. Illinois, 439 U.S. 128 (1978), pp. 258–62 above.)

Justices Harlan and Stewart believed that a person should not have standing to object to introduction of an overheard conversation in which he did not participate even if the conversation occurred on his premises. In an opinion concurring in part and dissenting in part, Justice Harlan said:

> There is a very simple reason why the traditional law of standing permits the owner of the premises to exclude a tangible object illegally seized on his property, despite the fact that he does not own the particular object taken by the police. Even though he does not have title to the object, the owner of the premises is in possession of it—and we have held that a property interest of even less substance is a sufficient predicate for standing under the Fourth Amendment. . . . This simple rationale does not, however, justify granting standing to the property owner with regard to third-party conversations. The absent property owner does not have a property interest of any sort in a conversation in which he did not participate. The words that were spoken are gone beyond recall.

> Consequently, in order to justify the traditional rule, one must argue, as does the majority, that the owner of the premises should be granted standing because the bugged third-party conversations are "fruits" of the police's infringement of the owner's property rights. The "fruits" theory, however, does not necessarily fit when the police overhear private conversations in violation of the Fourth Amendment. As Katz v. United States, 389 U.S. 347, 352–53 (1967), squarely holds, the right to the privacy of one's conversation does not hinge on whether the Government has committed a technical trespass upon the premises on which the conversations took place. Olmstead v. New York, 277 U.S. 438 (1928), is no longer the law. If in fact there has been no trespass upon the premises, I do not understand how traditional theory permits the owner to complain if a conversation is overheard in which he did not participate. Certainly the owner cannot suppress records of such conversations on the ground that they are the "fruits" of an unconstitutional invasion of his property rights. . . .

> It is true, of course, that the "fruits" theory would require a different result if the police used a listening device which did physically trespass upon the accused's premises. But the fact that this theory

depends completely on the presence or absence of a technical trespass only serves to show that the entire theoretical basis of standing law must be reconsidered in the area of conversational privacy. For we have not buried *Olmstead*, so far as it dealt with the substance of Fourth Amendment rights, only to give it new life in the law of standing. Instead, we should reject traditional property concepts entirely, and reinterpret standing law in the light of the substantive principles developed in *Katz*. Standing should be granted to every person who participates in a conversation he legitimately expects will remain private—for it is such persons that *Katz* protects. On the other hand, property owners should not be permitted to assert a Fourth Amendment claim in this area if we are to respect the principle, whose vitality the Court has now once again reaffirmed, which establishes "the general rule that Fourth Amendment rights are personal rights which . . . may not be vicariously asserted." Ante, at 174. For granting property owners standing does not permit them to vindicate intrusions upon their *own* privacy, but simply permits criminal defendants to intrude into the private lives of others.

The following hypothetical suggests the paradoxical quality of the Court's rule. Imagine that I own an office building and permit a friend of mine, Smith, to use one of the vacant offices without charge. Smith uses the office to have a private talk with a third person, Jones. The next day, I ask my friend to tell me what Jones had said in the office I had given him. Smith replies that the conversation was private, and that what was said was "none of your business." Can it be that I could properly feel aggrieved because the conversation occurred on my property? It would make no sense if I were to reply to Smith: "*My privacy has been infringed if you do not tell me what was said, for I own the property!*" It is precisely the other way around—Smith is telling me that when he and Jones had talked together, they had a legitimate expectation that their conversation would remain secret, even from me as the property owner.

Now suppose that I had placed a listening device in the office I had given to Smith, without telling him. Could anyone doubt that I would be guilty of an outrageous violation of the privacy of Smith and Jones if I then listened to what they had said? It would be ludicrous to defend my conduct on the ground that I, after all, was the owner of the office building. The case does not stand differently if I am accused of a crime and demand the right to hear the Smith–Jones conversation which the police had monitored. The Government doubtless has violated the privacy of Smith and Jones, but their privacy would be violated *further* if the conversation were also made available to me.

In the field of conversational privacy, the Fourth Amendment protects persons, not places. . . . And a man can only be in one place at one time. If the privacy of his conversation is respected at that place, he may engage in all those activities for which that privacy is an essential prerequisite. His privacy is not at all disturbed by the fact that other people in other places cannot speak without the fear of being overheard. That fact may be profoundly disturbing to the man whose privacy remains intact. But it remains a fact about *other* people's privacy. . . .

. . .

The Court's response seems to be that the Fourth Amendment protects "houses" as well as "persons." But this is simply to treat private conversations as if they were pieces of tangible *property*. Since an individual cannot carry his possessions with him wherever he goes, the Fourth Amendment protects a person's "house" so that his personal possessions may be kept out of the Government's easy reach. In contrast, a man must necessarily carry his voice around with him, and cannot leave it at home even if he wished. When a man is not at home, he cannot converse there. There is thus no need to protect a man's "house" in order to protect *his* right to engage in private conversation. Consequently, the Court has not increased the scope of an accused's *personal* privacy by holding that the police have unconstitutionally invaded his "house" by putting a "bug" there. Houses don't speak; only people do. The police only have violated the *privacy* of those persons whose conversations are overheard.

I entirely agree, however, that if the police see a person's tangible property while committing their trespass, they may not constitutionally use this knowledge either to obtain a search warrant or to gain a conviction. Since a man has no choice but to leave the bulk of his physical possessions in his "house," the Fourth Amendment must protect his "house" in this way or else the immunity of his personal possessions from arbitrary search could not be assured. Thus if an individual's personal *possessions* are to be protected at all, they must be protected in his house; but a person's private *conversations* are protected as much as is possible when he can complain as to any conversation in which he personally participated. To go further and protect other conversations occurring on his property is simply to give the householder the right to complain as to the Government's treatment of others.

Alderman, 394 U.S. at 189–95.

Responding to Justice Harlan's argument, Justice White said:

If the police make an unwarranted search of a house and seize tangible property belonging to third parties—even a transcript of a third-party conversation—the homeowner may object to its use against him, not because he had any interest in the seized items as "effects" protected by the Fourth Amendment, but because they were the fruits of an unauthorized search of his house, which is itself expressly protected by the Fourth Amendment. Nothing seen or found on the premises may legally form the basis for an arrest or search warrant or for testimony at the homeowner's trial, since the prosecution would be using the fruits of a Fourth Amendment violation. . . .

The Court has characteristically applied the same rule where an unauthorized electronic surveillance is carried out by physical invasion of the premises. This much the dissent frankly concedes. Like physical evidence which might be seized, overheard conversations are fruits of an illegal entry and are inadmissible in evidence. . . .

Because the Court has now decided that the Fourth Amendment protects a person's private conversations as well as his private premises . . . the dissent would discard the concept that private conversations overheard through an illegal entry into a private place must be excluded as the fruits of a Fourth Amendment violation. Although officers without a valid warrant may not search a house for physical evidence or incriminating information, whether the owner is present or away, the dissent would permit them to enter that house without consent and without a warrant, install a listening device and use any overheard third-party conversations against the owner in a criminal case, in spite of the obvious violation of his Fourth Amendment right to be secure in his own dwelling. Even if the owner is present on his premises during the surveillance, he would have no complaint unless his own conversations were offered or used against him. Information from a telephone tap or from the microphone in the kitchen or in the rooms of guests or children would be freely usable as long as the homeowner's own conversations are not monitored and used against him. Indeed, if the police, instead of installing a device, secreted themselves on the premises, they could neither testify about nor use against the owner anything they saw or carried away, but would be free to use against him everything they overheard except his own conversations. And should police overhear third parties describing narcotics which they have discovered in the owner's desk drawer, the police could not then open the drawer and seize the narcotics, but they could secure a warrant on the basis of what they had heard and forthwith seize the narcotics pursuant to that warrant.

These views we do not accept. We adhere to the established view in this Court that the right to be secure in one's house against unauthorized intrusion is not limited to protection against a policeman viewing or seizing tangible property—"papers" and "effects." Otherwise, the express security for the home provided by the Fourth Amendment would approach redundancy. The rights of the owner of the premises are as clearly invaded when the police enter and install a listening device in his house as they are when the entry is made to undertake a warrantless search for tangible property; and the prosecution as surely employs the fruits of an illegal search of the home when it offers overheard third-party conversations as it does when it introduces tangible evidence belonging not to the homeowner but to others.

394 U.S. at 176–80.

185. What interest in the premises is necessary for standing to object to a conversation in which one did not participate? In *Alderman*, the Court expressed no opinion on that question, 394 U.S. at 168 n.1; see id. at 191–92 (opinion of Harlan, J.).

---

18 U.S.C. §§ 2510–2522

In 1968 as part of the Omnibus Crime Control and Safe Streets Act, Congress enacted very broad prohibitions against wiretapping and eavesdropping by the use of eavesdropping devices. The prohibitions cover the interception, disclosure, or other use of wire or oral communications, as well as the manufacture, distribution, possession and advertising of devices intended to be used for the unlawful interception of communications. Unlawfully intercepted communications and their fruits were declared inadmissible in all governmental proceedings. 18 U.S.C. § 2515. A civil cause of action was provided for persons whose communications were unlawfully intercepted, disclosed, or used. 18 U.S.C. §§ 2510–2515, 2520.

The prohibitions are subject to equally broad exceptions, which allow wiretapping and eavesdropping for the purpose of law enforcement. The provisions for authorization of wiretapping or eavesdropping and prescribing how it is to be carried out are given below.

---

§ **2516.** Authorization for interception of wire, oral, or electronic commuications

(1) The Attorney General, Deputy Attorney General, Associate Attorney General, or any Assistant Attorney General, any acting Assistant Attorney General, or any Deputy Assistant Attorney General or acting Deputy Assistant Attorney General in the Criminal Division specially designated by the Attorney General, may authorize an application to a Federal judge of competent jurisdiction for, and such judge may grant in conformity with section 2518 of this chapter an order authorizing or approving the interception of wire or oral communications by the Federal Bureau of Investigation, or a Federal agency having responsibility for the investigation of the offense as to which the application is made, when such interception may provide or has provided evidence of—

(a) any offense punishable by death or by imprisonment for more than one year under sections 2274 through 2277 of title 42 of the United States Code (relating to the enforcement of the Atomic Energy Act of 1954), section 2284 of title 42 of the United States Code (relating to sabotage of nuclear facilities or fuel), or under the following chapters of this title: chapter 37 (relating to espionage), chapter 55 (relating to kidnapping) chapter 90 (relating to protection of trade secrets), chapter 105 (relating to treason), chapter 102 (relating to riots), chapter 65 (relating to malicious mischief), chapter 111 (relating to destruction of vessels), or chapter 81 (relating to piracy);

(b) a violation of section 186 or section 501(c) of title 29, United States Code (dealing with restrictions on payments and loans to labor organizations), or any offense which involves murder, kidnapping, robbery, or extortion, and which is punishable under this title;

(c) any offense which is punishable under the following sections of this title: section 201 (bribery of public officials and witnesses), section 215 (relating to bribery of bank officials), section 224 (bribery in sporting contests), subsection (d), (e), (f), (g), (h), or (i) of section 844 (unlawful use of explosives), section 1032 (relating to concealment of assets), section 1084 (transmission of wagering information), section 751 (relating to escape), section 1014 (relating to loans and credit applications generally; renewals and discounts), sections 1503, 1512, and 1513 (influencing or injuring an officer, juror, or witness generally), section 1510 (obstruction of criminal investigations), section 1511 (obstruction of State or local law enforcement), section 1591 (sex trafficking of children by force, fraud, or coercion), section 1751 (Presidential and Presidential staff assassination, kidnapping, and assault), section 1951 (interference with commerce by threats or violence), section 1952 (interstate and foreign travel or transportation in aid of racketeering enterprises), section 1958 (relating to use of interstate commerce facilities in the commission of murder for hire), section 1959 (relating to violent crimes in aid of racketeering activity), section 1954 (offer, acceptance, or solicitation to influence operations of employee benefit plan), section 1955 (prohibition of business enterprises of gambling), section 1956 (laundering of monetary instruments), section 1957 (relating to engaging in monetary transactions in property derived from specified unlawful activity), section 659 (theft from interstate shipment), section 664 (embezzlement from pension and welfare funds), section 1343 (fraud by wire, radio, or television), section 1344 (relating to bank fraud), sections 2251 and 2252 (sexual exploitation of children), section 2251A (selling or buying of children), section 2252A (relating to material constituting or containing child pornography), section 1466A (relating to child obscenity), section 2260 (production of sexually explicit depictions of a minor for importation into the United States), sections 2421, 2422, 2433, and 2425 (relating to transportation for illegal sexual activity and related crimes), sections 2312, 2313, 2314, and 2315 (interstate transportation of stolen property), section 2321 (relating to trafficking in certain motor vehicles or motor vehicle parts), section 1203 (relating to hostage taking), section 1029 (relating to fraud and related activity in connection with access devices), section 3146 (relating to penalty for failure to appear), section 3521(b)(3) (relating to witness relocation and assistance), section 32 (relating to destruction of aircraft or aircraft facilities), section 1963 (violations with respect to racketeer influenced and corrupt organizations), section 115 (relating to threatening or retaliating against a Federal official), section 1341 (relating to mail fraud), a felony violation of section 1030 (relating to computer fraud and abuse), section 351 (violations with respect to congressional, Cabinet, or Supreme Court assassinations, kidnapping, and assault), section 831 (relating to prohibited transactions involving nuclear materials), section 33 (relating to destruction of motor vehicles or motor vehicle facilities), section 175 (relating to biological weapons), section 1992 (relating to wrecking trains), a felony violation of section 1028 (relating to production of false identification documentation), section 1425 (relating to the procurement of citizenship or nationalization unlawfully), section 1426 (relating to the reproduction of naturalization or citizenship papers), section 1427 (relating to the sale of naturalization or citizenship papers), section 1541 (relating to passport issuance without authority), section 1542 (relating to false statements in passport applications), section 1543 (relating to forgery or false use of passports), section 1544 (relating to misuse of passports), or section 1546 (relating to fraud and misuse of visas, permits, and other documents);

(d) any offense involving counterfeiting punishable under section 471, 472, or 473 of this title;

(e) any offense involving fraud connected with a case under title 11 or the manufacture, importation, receiving, concealment, buying, selling, or otherwise dealing in narcotic drugs, marihuana, or other dangerous drugs, punishable under any law of the United States;

(f) any offense including extortionate credit transactions under sections 892, 893, or 894 of this title;

(g) a violation of section 5322 of title 31, United States Code (dealing with the reporting of currency transactions);

(h) any felony violation of sections 2511 and 2512 (relating to interception and disclosure of certain communications and to certain intercepting devices) of this title;

(i) any felony violation of chapter 71 (relating to obscenity) of this title;

(j) any violation of section 60123(b) (relating to destruction of a natural gas pipeline) or section 46502 (relating to aircraft piracy) of title 49;

(k) any criminal violation of section 2778 of title 22 (relating to the Arms Export Control Act);

(l) the location of any fugitive from justice from an offense described in this section;

(m) a violation of section 274, 277, or 278 of the Immigration and Nationality Act (8 U.S.C. 1324, 1327, or 1328) (relating to the smuggling of aliens);

(n) any felony violation of sections 922 and 924 of title 18, United States Code (relating to firearms); or

(o) any violation of section 5861 of the Internal Revenue Code of 1986 (relating to firearms); or

(p) a felony violation of section 1028 (relating to production of false identification documents), section 1542 (relating to false statements in passport applications), section 1546 (relating to fraud and misuse of visas, permits, and other documents) of this title or a violation of section 274, 277, or 278 of the Immigration and Nationality Act (relating to the smuggling of aliens); or

(q) any criminal violation of section 229 (relating to chemical weapons); or sections 2332, 2332a, 2332b, 2332d, 2332f, 2339A, 2339B, or 2339C of this title (relating to terrorism); or

(r) any conspiracy to commit any offense described in any subparagraph of this paragraph.

(2) The principal prosecuting attorney of any State, or the principal prosecuting attorney of any political subdivision thereof, if such attorney is authorized by a statute of that State to make application to a State court judge of competent jurisdiction for an order authorizing or approving the interception of wire, oral, or electronic communications, may apply to such judge for, and such judge may grant in conformity with section 2518 of this chapter and with the applicable State statute an order authorizing, or approving the interception of wire, oral, or electronic communications by investigative or law enforcement officers having responsibility for the investigation of the offense as to which the application is made, when such interception may provide or has provided evidence of the commission of the offense of murder, kidnapping, gambling, robbery, bribery, extortion, or dealing in narcotic drugs, marihuana or other dangerous drugs, or other crime dangerous to life, limb, or property, and punishable by imprisonment for more than one year, designated in any applicable State statute authorizing such interception, or any conspiracy to commit any of the foregoing offenses.

(3) Any attorney for the Government (as such term is defined for the purposes of the Federal Rules of Criminal Procedure) may authorize an application to a Federal judge of competent jurisdiction for, and such judge may grant, in conformity with section 2518 of this title, an order authorizing or approving the interception of electronic communications by an investigative or law enforcement officer having responsibility for the investigation of the offense as to which the application is made, when such interception may provide or has provided evidence of any Federal felony.

§ 2517. Authorization for disclosure and use of intercepted wire, oral, or electronic communications

(1) Any investigative or law enforcement officer who, by any means authorized by this chapter, has obtained knowledge of the contents of any wire, oral, or electronic communication, or evidence derived therefrom, may disclose such contents to another investigative or law enforcement officer to

the extent that such disclosure is appropriate to the proper performance of the official duties of the officer making or receiving the disclosure.

(2) Any investigative or law enforcement officer who, by any means authorized by this chapter, has obtained knowledge of the contents of any wire, oral, or electronic communication or evidence derived therefrom may use such contents to the extent such use is appropriate to the proper performance of his official duties.

(3) Any person who has received, by any means authorized by this chapter, any information concerning a wire, oral, or electronic communication, or evidence derived therefrom intercepted in accordance with the provisions of this chapter may disclose the contents of that communication or such derivative evidence while giving testimony under oath or affirmation in any proceeding held under the authority of the United States or of any State or political subdivision thereof.

(4) No otherwise privileged wire, oral, or electronic communication intercepted in accordance with, or in violation of, the provisions of this chapter shall lose its privileged character.

(5) When an investigative or law enforcement officer, while engaged in intercepting wire, oral, or electronic communications in the manner authorized herein, intercepts wire, oral, or electronic communications relating to offenses other than those specified in the order of authorization or approval, the contents thereof, and evidence derived therefrom, may be disclosed or used as provided in subsections (1) and (2) of this section. Such contents and any evidence derived therefrom may be used under subsection (3) of this section when authorized or approved by a judge of competent jurisdiction where such judge finds on subsequent application that the contents were otherwise intercepted in accordance with the provisions of this chapter. Such application shall be made as soon as practicable.

(6) Any investigative or law enforcement officer, or attorney for the Government, who by any means authorized by this chapter, has obtained knowledge of the contents of any wire, oral, or electronic communication, or evidence derived therefrom, may disclose such contents to any other Federal law enforcement, intelligence, protective, immigration, national defense, or national security official to the extent that such contents include foreign intelligence or counterintelligence (as defined in section 3 of the National Security Act of 1947), or foreign intelligence information (as defined in subsection (19) of section 2510 of this title), to assist the official who is to receive that information in the performance of his official duties. Any Federal official who receives information pursuant to this provision may use that information only as necessary in the conduct of that person's official duties subject to any limitations on the unauthorized disclosure of such information.

(7) Any investigative or law enforcement officer, or other Federal official in carrying out official duties as such Federal official, who by any means authorized by this chapter, has obtained knowledge of the contents of any wire, oral, or electronic communication, or evidence derived there-

from, may disclose such contents or derivative evidence to a foreign investigative or law enforcement officer to the extent that such disclosure is appropriate to the proper performance of the official duties of the officer making or receiving the disclosure, and foreign investigative or law enforcement officers may use or disclose such contents or derivative evidence to the extent such use or disclosure is appropriate to the proper performance of their official duties.

(8) Any investigative or law enforcement officer, or other Federal official in carrying out official duties as such Federal official, who by any means authorized by this chapter, has obtained knowledge of the contents of any wire, oral, or electronic communication, or evidence derived therefrom, may disclose such contents or derivative evidence to any appropriate Federal, State, local, or foreign government official to the extent that such contents or derivative evidence reveals a threat of actual or potential attack or other grave hostile acts of a foreign power or an agent of a foreign power, domestic or international sabotage, domestic or international terrorism, or clandestine intelligence gathering activities by an intelligence service or network of a foreign power or by an agent of a foreign power, within the United States or elsewhere, for the purpose of preventing or responding to such a threat. Any official who receives information pursuant to this provision may use that information only as necessary in the conduct of that person's official duties subject to any limitations on the unauthorized disclosure of such information, and any State, local, or foreign official who receives information pursuant to this provision may use that information only consistent with such guidelines as the Attorney General and Director of Central Intelligence shall jointly issue.

§ 2518.   Procedure for interception of wire, oral, or electronic communications

(1) Each application for an order authorizing or approving the interception of a wire, oral, or electronic communication under this chapter shall be made in writing upon oath or affirmation to a judge of competent jurisdiction and shall state the applicant's authority to make such application. Each application shall include the following information:

(a) the identity of the investigative or law enforcement officer making the application, and the officer authorizing the application;

(b) a full and complete statement of the facts and circumstances relied upon by the applicant, to justify his belief that an order should be issued, including (i) details as to the particular offense that has been, is being, or is about to be committed, (ii) except as provided in subsection (11), a particular description of the nature and location of the facilities from which or the place where the communication is to be intercepted, (iii) a particular description of the type of communications sought to be intercepted, (iv) the identity of the person, if known, committing the offense and whose communications are to be intercepted;

(c) a full and complete statement as to whether or not other investigative procedures have been tried and failed or why they reasonably appear to be unlikely to succeed if tried or to be too dangerous;

(d) a statement of the period of time for which the interception is required to be maintained. If the nature of the investigation is such that the authorization for interception should not automatically terminate when the described type of communication has been first obtained, a particular description of facts establishing probable cause to believe that additional communications of the same type will occur thereafter;

(e) a full and complete statement of the facts concerning all previous applications known to the individual authorizing and making the application, made to any judge for authorization to intercept, or for approval of interceptions of, wire, oral, or electronic communications involving any of the same persons, facilities or places specified in the application, and the action taken by the judge on each such application; and

(f) where the application is for the extension of an order, a statement setting forth the results thus far obtained from the interception, or a reasonable explanation of the failure to obtain such results.

(2) The judge may require the applicant to furnish additional testimony or documentary evidence in support of the application.

(3) Upon such application the judge may enter an ex parte order, as requested or as modified, authorizing or approving interception of wire, oral, or electronic communications within the territorial jurisdiction of the court in which the judge is sitting (and outside that jurisdiction but within the United States in the case of a mobile interception device authorized by a Federal court within such jurisdiction), if the judge determines on the basis of the facts submitted by the applicant that—

(a) there is probable cause for belief that an individual is committing, has committed, or is about to commit a particular offense enumerated in section 2516 of this chapter;

(b) there is probable cause for belief that particular communications concerning that offense will be obtained through such interception;

(c) normal investigative procedures have been tried and have failed or reasonably appear to be unlikely to succeed if tried or to be too dangerous;

(d) except as provided in subsection (11), there is probable cause for belief that the facilities from which, or the place where, the wire, oral, or electronic communications are to be intercepted are being used, or are about to be used, in connection with the commission of such offense, or are leased to, listed in the name of, or commonly used by such person.

(4) Each order authorizing or approving the interception of any wire, oral, or electronic communication under this chapter shall specify—

(a) the identity of the person, if known, whose communications are to be intercepted;

(b) the nature and location of the communications facilities as to which, or the place where, authority to intercept is granted;

(c) a particular description of the type of communication sought to be intercepted, and a statement of the particular offense to which it relates;

(d) the identity of the agency authorized to intercept the communications, and of the person authorizing the application; and

(e) the period of time during which such interception is authorized, including a statement as to whether or not the interception shall automatically terminate when the described communication has been first obtained.

An order authorizing the interception of a wire, oral, or electronic communication under this chapter shall, upon request of the applicant, direct that a provider of wire or electronic communication service, landlord, custodian or other person shall furnish the applicant forthwith all information, facilities, and technical assistance necessary to accomplish the interception unobtrusively and with a minimum of interference with the services that such service provider, landlord, custodian, or person is according the person whose communications are to be intercepted. Any provider of wire or electronic communication service, landlord, custodian or other person furnishing such facilities or technical assistance shall be compensated therefor by the applicant for reasonable expenses incurred in providing such facilities or assistance. Pursuant to section 2522 of this chapter, an order may also be issued to enforce the assistance capability and capacity requirements under the Communications Assistance for Law Enforcement Act.

(5) No order entered under this section may authorize or approve the interception of any wire, oral, or electronic communication for any period longer than is necessary to achieve the objective of the authorization, nor in any event longer than thirty days. Such thirty-day period begins on the earlier of the day on which the investigative or law enforcement officer first begins to conduct an interception under the order or ten days after the order is entered. Extensions of an order may be granted, but only upon application for an extension made in accordance with subsection (1) of this section and the court making the findings required by subsection (3) of this section. The period of extension shall be no longer than the authorizing judge deems necessary to achieve the purposes for which it was granted and in no event for longer than thirty days. Every order and extension thereof shall contain a provision that the authorization to intercept shall be executed as soon as practicable, shall be conducted in such a way as to minimize the interception of communications not otherwise subject to interception under this chapter, and must terminate upon attainment of the authorized objective, or in any event in thirty days. In the event the

intercepted communication is in a code or foreign language, and an expert in that foreign language or code is not reasonably available during the interception period, minimization may be accomplished as soon as practicable after such interception. An interception under this chapter may be conducted in whole or in part by Government personnel, or by an individual operating under a contract with the Government, acting under the supervision of an investigative or law enforcement officer authorized to conduct the interception.

(6) Whenever an order authorizing interception is entered pursuant to this chapter, the order may require reports to be made to the judge who issued the order showing what progress has been made toward achievement of the authorized objective and the need for continued interception. Such reports shall be made at such intervals as the judge may require.

(7) Notwithstanding any other provision of this chapter, any investigative or law enforcement officer, specially designated by the Attorney General, the Deputy Attorney General, the Associate Attorney General or by the principal prosecuting attorney of any State or subdivision thereof acting pursuant to a statute of that State, who reasonably determines that—

(a) an emergency situation exists that involves—

(i) immediate danger of death or serious physical injury to any person,

(ii) conspiratorial activities threatening the national security interest, or

(iii) conspiratorial activities characteristic of organized crime,

that requires a wire, oral, or electronic communication to be intercepted before an order authorizing such interception can, with due diligence, be obtained, and

(b) there are grounds upon which an order could be entered under this chapter to authorize such interception,

may intercept such wire, oral, or electronic communication if an application for an order approving the interception is made in accordance with this section within forty-eight hours after the interception has occurred, or begins to occur. In the absence of an order, such interception shall immediately terminate when the communication sought is obtained or when the application for the order is denied, whichever is earlier. In the event such application for approval is denied, or in any other case where the interception is terminated without an order having been issued, the contents of any wire, oral, or electronic communication intercepted shall be treated as having been obtained in violation of this chapter, and an inventory shall be served as provided for in subsection (d) of this section on the person named in the application.

(8)(a) The contents of any wire, oral, or electronic communication intercepted by any means authorized by this chapter shall, if possible, be recorded on tape or wire or other comparable device. The recording of the contents of any wire, oral, or electronic communication under this subsection shall be done in such way as will protect the recording from editing or other alterations. Immediately upon the expiration of the period of the order, or extensions thereof, such recordings shall be made available to the judge issuing such order and sealed under his directions. Custody of the recordings shall be wherever the judge orders. They shall not be destroyed except upon an order of the issuing or denying judge and in any event shall be kept for ten years. Duplicate recordings may be made for use or disclosure pursuant to the provisions of subsections (1) and (2) of section 2517 of this chapter for investigations. The presence of the seal provided for by this subsection, or a satisfactory explanation for the absence thereof, shall be a prerequisite for the use or disclosure of the contents of any wire, oral, or electronic communication or evidence derived therefrom under subsection (3) of section 2517.

(b) Applications made and orders granted under this chapter shall be sealed by the judge. Custody of the applications and orders shall be wherever the judge directs. Such applications and orders shall be disclosed only upon a showing of good cause before a judge of competent jurisdiction and shall not be destroyed except on order of the issuing or denying judge, and in any event shall be kept for ten years.

(c) Any violation of the provisions of this subsection may be punished as contempt of the issuing or denying judge.

(d) Within a reasonable time but not later than ninety days after the filing of an application for an order of approval under section 2518(7)(b) which is denied or the termination of the period of an order or extensions thereof, the issuing or denying judge shall cause to be served, on the persons named in the order or the application, and such other parties to intercepted communications as the judge may determine in his discretion that is in the interest of justice, an inventory which shall include notice of—

(1) the fact of the entry of the order or the application;

(2) the date of the entry and the period of authorized, approved or disapproved interception, or the denial of the application; and

(3) the fact that during the period wire, oral, or electronic communications were or were not intercepted.

The judge, upon the filing of a motion, may in his discretion make available to such person or his counsel for inspection such portions of the intercepted communications, applications and orders as the judge determines to be in the interest of justice. On an ex parte showing of good cause to a judge of competent jurisdiction the serving of the inventory required by this subsection may be postponed.

(9) The contents of any wire, oral, or electronic communication intercepted pursuant to this chapter or evidence derived therefrom shall not be received in evidence or otherwise disclosed in any trial, hearing, or other proceeding in a Federal or State court unless each party, not less than ten days before the trial, hearing, or proceeding, has been furnished with a

copy of the court order, and accompanying application, under which the interception was authorized or approved. This ten-day period may be waived by the judge if he finds that it was not possible to furnish the party with the above information ten days before the trial, hearing, or proceeding and that the party will not be prejudiced by the delay in receiving such information.

(10)(a) Any aggrieved person in any trial, hearing, or proceeding in or before any court, department, officer, agency, regulatory body, or other authority of the United States, a State, or a political subdivision thereof, may move to suppress the contents of any wire or oral communication intercepted pursuant to this chapter, or evidence derived therefrom, on the grounds that—

(i) the communication was unlawfully intercepted;

(ii) the order of authorization or approval under which it was intercepted is insufficient on its face; or

(iii) the interception was not made in conformity with the order of authorization or approval.

Such motion shall be made before the trial, hearing, or proceeding unless there was no opportunity to make such motion or the person was not aware of the grounds of the motion. If the motion is granted, the contents of the intercepted wire or oral communication, or evidence derived therefrom, shall be treated as having been obtained in violation of this chapter. The judge, upon the filing of such motion by the aggrieved person, may in his discretion make available to the aggrieved person or his counsel for inspection such portions of the intercepted communication or evidence derived therefrom as the judge determines to be in the interests of justice.

(b) In addition to any other right to appeal, the United States shall have the right to appeal from an order granting a motion to suppress made under paragraph (a) of this subsection, or the denial of an application for an order of approval, if the United States attorney shall certify to the judge or other official granting such motion or denying such application that the appeal is not taken for purposes of delay. Such appeal shall be taken within thirty days after the date the order was entered and shall be diligently prosecuted.

(c) The remedies and sanctions described in this chapter with respect to the interception of electronic communications are the only judicial remedies and sanctions for nonconstitutional violations of this chapter involving such communications.

(11) The requirements of subsections (1)(b)(ii) and (3)(d) of this section relating to the specification of the facilities from which, or the place where, the communication is to be intercepted do not apply if—

(a) in the case of an application with respect to the interception of an oral communication—

(i) the application is by a Federal investigative or law enforcement officer and is approved by the Attorney General, the Deputy

Attorney General, the Associate Attorney General, an Assistant Attorney General, or an acting Assistant Attorney General;

(ii) the application contains a full and complete statement as to why such specification is not practical and identifies the person committing the offense and whose communications are to be intercepted; and

(iii) the judge finds that such specification is not practical; and

(b) in the case of an application with respect to a wire or electronic communication—

(i) the application is by a Federal investigative or law enforcement officer and is approved by the Attorney General, the Deputy Attorney General, the Associate Attorney General, an Assistant Attorney General, or an acting Assistant Attorney General;

(ii) the application identifies the person believed to be committing the offense and whose communications are to be intercepted and the applicant makes a showing that there is probable cause to believe that the person's actions could have the effect of thwarting interception from a specified facility;

(iii) the judge finds that such showing has been adequately made; and

(iv) the order authorizing or approving the interception is limited to interception only for such time as it is reasonable to presume that the person identified in the application is or was reasonably proximate to the instrument through which such communication will be or was transmitted.

(12) An interception of a communication under an order with respect to which the requirements of subsections (1)(b)(ii) and (3)(d) of this section do not apply by reason of subsection (11)(a) shall not begin until the place where the communication is to be intercepted is ascertained by the person implementing the interception order. A provider of wire or electronic communications service that has received an order as provided for in subsection (11)(b) may move the court to modify or quash the order on the ground that its assistance with respect to the interception cannot be performed in a timely or reasonable fashion. The court, upon notice to the government, shall decide such a motion expeditiously.

§ 2519.   Reports concerning intercepted wire, oral, or electronic communications

(1) Within thirty days after the expiration of an order (or each extension thereof) entered under section 2518, or the denial of an order approving an interception, the issuing or denying judge shall report to the Administrative Office of the United States Courts—

(a) the fact that an order or extension was applied for;

(b) the kind of order or extension applied for (including whether or not the order was an order with respect to which the requirements of sections 2518(1)(b)(ii) and 2518(3)(d) of this title did not apply by reason of section 2518(11) of this title);

(c) the fact that the order or extension was granted as applied for, was modified, or was denied;

(d) the period of interceptions authorized by the order, and the number and duration of any extensions of the order;

(e) the offense specified in the order or application, or extension of an order;

(f) the identity of the applying investigative or law enforcement officer and agency making the application and the person authorizing the application; and

(g) the nature of the facilities from which or the place where communications were to be intercepted.

(2) In January of each year the Attorney General, an Assistant Attorney General specially designated by the Attorney General, or the principal prosecuting attorney of a State, or the principal prosecuting attorney for any political subdivision of a State, shall report to the Administrative Office of the United States Courts—

(a) the information required by paragraphs (a) through (g) of subsection (1) of this section with respect to each application for an order or extension made during the preceding calendar year;

(b) a general description of the interceptions made under such order or extension, including (i) the approximate nature and frequency of incriminating communications intercepted, (ii) the approximate nature and frequency of other communications intercepted, (iii) the approximate number of persons whose communications were intercepted, (iv) the number of orders in which encryption was encountered and whether such encryption prevented law enforcement from obtaining the plain text of communications, intercepted pursuant to such order, and (v) the approximate nature, amount, and cost of the manpower and other resources used in the interceptions;

(c) the number of arrests resulting from interceptions made under such order or extension, and the offenses for which arrests were made;

(d) the number of trials resulting from such interceptions;

(e) the number of motions to suppress made with respect to such interceptions, and the number granted or denied;

(f) the number of convictions resulting from such interceptions and the offenses for which the convictions were obtained and a general assessment of the importance of the interceptions; and

(g) the information required by paragraphs (b) through (f) of this subsection with respect to orders or extensions obtained in a preceding calendar year.

(3) In April of each year the Director of the Administrative Office of the United States Courts shall transmit to the Congress a full and complete report concerning the number of applications for orders authorizing or approving the interception of wire, oral, or electronic communications pursuant to this chapter and the number of orders and extensions granted or denied pursuant to this chapter during the preceding calendar year. Such report shall include a summary and analysis of the data required to be filed with the Administrative Office by subsections (1) and (2) of this section. The Director of the Administrative Office of the United States Courts is authorized to issue binding regulations dealing with the content and form of the reports required to be filed by subsections (1) and (2) of this section.

---

186. How restrictive are the provisions authorizing wiretapping and eavesdropping for law enforcement? Section 2516, for example, restricts their use to the investigation of specific crimes. Are there any crimes that law enforcement officials are likely to want to investigate by these means that are not included?

Section 2518 provides elaborate procedures to apply for an authorization to wiretap or eavesdrop. How much do they regulate the practice? Aside from requiring probable cause, § 2518(3), do they do much more than impose a considerable burden of documentation?

Section 2518(5) provides that an authorization may cover a period up to 30 days and allows an extension for an additional 30 days. Aside from that, the principal substantive limitation is the proviso that the wiretapping or eavesdropping "shall be conducted in such a way as to minimize the interception of communications not otherwise subject to interception." The proviso is construed in Scott v. United States, 436 U.S. 128 (1978) (7–2). The Court said that the test of whether the requirement has been met is not the eavesdropping agents' "good faith" effort to minimize but an objective assessment of the agents' conduct in all the circumstances. Among the relevant circumstances, the Court said, were the percentage of nonpertinent calls (although there were situations where a high percentage of such calls might reasonably be intercepted), the nature of the crime being investigated, the type of use to which the telephone is normally put, and the ability of the intercepting agents to develop categories of calls that need not be intercepted. The Court upheld a telephone wiretap, in which all calls were intercepted. About 40% of the calls were related to the investigation for which the wiretap was sought. Many of the other calls were short and unimportant, such as wrong numbers, calls to persons who were unavailable, etc. In the circumstances, the Court concluded, the agents conducting the wiretap were unable to develop a category of innocent calls that they could avoid intercepting in their entirety.

Look again at *Katz*, p. 309 above. Consider the specific facts of that case and the circumstances in which the Court said eavesdropping would be permissible. Do the provisions of the federal statute comport with the Court's reasoning? What about the provision for 30 days plus 30 days during which electronic surveillance can be maintained?

In United States v. Koyomejian, 970 F.2d 536 (9th Cir.1992), the court said that the statute regulates aural surveillance and has no application to silent video surveillance.

187.   Section 2518(1)(b)(iv) requires the government to include in a wiretap or eavesdropping application "the identity of the person, if known, committing the offense and whose communications are to be intercepted." In United States v. Kahn, 415 U.S. 143 (1974) (6–3), the Court said that the government is not required to name anyone unless it knows both that the person is committing the offense and that his communications will be intercepted. It is not required to ascertain in advance whether a person whom it does not know to be committing the offense but whose communications will be intercepted may not be within the first category as well. The government is, however, required to name all persons whom it knows to be within both categories. The statute is not satisfied by providing only the name of the "principal target," usually the person whose telephone is monitored. United States v. Donovan, 429 U.S. 413 (1977).

Section 2518(8)(d) provides for an inventory notice to be served on persons named in the authorization order or application, which must indicate that there was an application, the period of any authorized wiretap or eavesdrop, and whether any conversations were intercepted. The judge who issued or denied the order has discretion to require service on other parties to intercepted communications "in the interest of justice." In *Donovan*, above, the Court held that the government has an obligation to furnish information about persons in the latter category sufficient to enable the judge to exercise her discretion.

Failure to meet either of the above requirements does not require suppression of evidence obtained pursuant to an otherwise valid order. *Donovan*, above (6–3).

Section 2516(1) designates specific officials in the Department of Justice who may authorize an application for a wiretap or eavesdropping order. In United States v. Giordano, 416 U.S. 505 (1974), the Court said that no other persons (in particular, the Attorney General's Executive Assistant) may authorize an application, and that evidence secured pursuant to an order issued in response to an application not so authorized must be suppressed.

The requirement of § 2518(8)(a) that recordings be immediately sealed and the provision that a failure to meet the requirement must be satisfactorily explained in order for the recording to be used or disclosed are discussed in United States v. Ojeda Rios, 495 U.S. 257 (1990) (6–3).

188.   In In re Grand Jury, 111 F.3d 1066 (3d Cir.1997), the court held, notwithstanding the general rule that proceedings before a grand jury are not subject to supervision by the courts, see United States v. Williams, 504 U.S. 36 (1992), p. 682 below, that a person whose conversation was intercepted by a private illegal wiretap has standing to quash a subpoena directing the person who placed the wiretap to produce the tape of the conversation. The court observed: "We do not believe Congress intended the grand jury and the courts to use their respective powers to compel violations of the federal anti-wiretapping statute." 111 F.3d at 1076.

189. Having probable cause to believe that persons who had rented a motel room were engaged in a narcotics operation, police officials sought to rent an adjoining room. There being none available, the motel clerk, whom they had told of their investigation, moved the suspects to another room and rented an adjoining one to the officials. Using no special devices, the officials overheard conversations, sometimes while sitting on the bed in the middle of their room and sometimes by lying prone on the floor a few inches from a crack between the door and the carpet. Are the overheard conversations admissible? See United States v. Fisch, 474 F.2d 1071 (9th Cir.1973). See also United States v. Agapito, 620 F.2d 324 (2d Cir.1980).

Can a government agent testify to what he sees and hears through an open bathroom window while standing behind a motel unit in a parking lot? See Ponce v. Craven, 409 F.2d 621 (9th Cir.1969).

See United States v. Johnson, 561 F.2d 832 (D.C.Cir.1977), in which a police officer stepped a few feet onto the grass outside a house in order to look through a basement window. The police had received a tip that narcotics activities could be seen through the window. Characterizing the intrusion as a "technical trespass," the court concluded that in the circumstances of the case, there was no violation of the Fourth Amendment. See also United States v. Wheeler, 641 F.2d 1321 (9th Cir.1981); United States v. Llanes, 398 F.2d 880 (2d Cir.1968); Texas v. Gonzales, 388 F.2d 145 (5th Cir.1968).

190.

On the night of April 6, 1967, federal investigators for the Alcohol Tax Unit of the Internal Revenue Service, acting upon information received from an unnamed informant, who they stated was a "reliable" source of information, went upon the farm of one Marzett, a co-defendant of appellant, and took up positions for observation of a house and shed from a distance. With the aid of binoculars, they observed through an open door the three defendants operating a still inside the shed, appellant in particular being recognized. They also watched the defendants load bottles of distilled spirits from the shed into a 1957 Ford automobile, and then saw the Ford leave the premises followed by a 1965 Chevrolet driven by appellant. The investigators followed the two cars for several miles, never losing sight of them, and then stopped and searched the cars and arrested the occupants. During the search, seventy-four gallons of non-taxpaid distilled spirits were found in the Ford. Thereafter, the investigators secured a warrant for search of the Marzett premises, which search took place that same night and revealed two distilleries, 1,400 gallons of mash, other miscellaneous distilling apparatus and eighteen gallons of non-taxpaid distilled spirits.

Fullbright v. United States, 392 F.2d 432, 433 (10th Cir.1968). Can the defendants' arrest and the search of the cars validly be based on the information learned by the observation of the house and shed? See also United States v. Whaley, 779 F.2d 585 (11th Cir.1986) (binoculars used to see conduct inside house that could be seen also with naked eye from location not generally accessible to public; search upheld); United States v. Taborda, 635 F.2d 131 (2d Cir.1980) (surveillance of interior of premises by telescope impermissible).

191. In California v. Ciraolo, 476 U.S. 207 (1986) (5–4), the Court held that "naked-eye" observation of a fenced-in area within the curtilage of the defendant's home, from an airplane flying at an altitude of a thousand feet, did not violate his rights under the Fourth Amendment. Police officers suspected that marijuana was being grown. They flew over the area in order to inspect it. The Court said that even though the defendant had exhibited an expectation of privacy, the expectation that he was protected from observation of this kind "in a physically nonintrusive manner" was "unreasonable and is not an expectation that society is prepared to honor." "Any member of the public flying in this airspace who glanced down could have seen everything that these officers observed." Id. at 209. It is immaterial, the Court said, that the officers flew over the area for the purpose of observing it in the course of criminal investigation. Accord Florida v. Riley, 488 U.S. 445 (1989) (5–4) (surveillance from helicopter flying at 400 feet).

See also Dow Chemical Co. v. United States, 476 U.S. 227 (1986) (5–4), p. 298 note 167 above, in which the Court held that sophisticated aerial photography of unenclosed parts of an industrial complex, which was closely guarded from ordinary observation, did not violate the Fourth Amendment. The holding was apparently based both on the nature of the premises observed, which the Court said were not clearly curtilage or open fields, and the method of observation. It intimated that more intrusive or unusual methods of observation "not generally available to the public" might have been a prohibited search. Id. at 238.

Kyllo v. United States

533 U.S. 27, 121 S.Ct. 2038, 150 L.Ed.2d 94 (2001)

■ JUSTICE SCALIA delivered the opinion of the Court.

This case presents the question whether the use of a thermal-imaging device aimed at a private home from a public street to detect relative amounts of heat within the home constitutes a "search" within the meaning of the Fourth Amendment.

I

In 1991 Agent William Elliott of the United States Department of the Interior came to suspect that marijuana was being grown in the home belonging to petitioner Danny Kyllo, part of a triplex on Rhododendron Drive in Florence, Oregon. Indoor marijuana growth typically requires high-intensity lamps. In order to determine whether an amount of heat was emanating from petitioner's home consistent with the use of such lamps, at 3:20 a.m. on January 16, 1992, Agent Elliott and Dan Haas used an Agema Thermovision 210 thermal imager to scan the triplex. Thermal imagers detect infrared radiation, which virtually all objects emit but which is not visible to the naked eye. The imager converts radiation into images based on relative warmth—black is cool, white is hot, shades of gray connote relative differences; in that respect, it operates somewhat like a video camera showing heat images. The scan of Kyllo's home took only a few minutes and was performed from the passenger seat of Agent Elliott's vehicle across the street from the front of the house and also from the street in back of the house. The scan showed that the roof over the garage and a side wall of petitioner's home were relatively hot compared to the rest of the home and substantially warmer than neighboring homes in the triplex. Agent Elliott concluded that petitioner was using halide lights to grow marijuana in his house, which indeed he was. Based on tips from informants, utility bills, and the thermal imaging, a Federal Magistrate Judge issued a warrant authorizing a search of petitioner's home, and the agents found an indoor growing operation involving more than 100 plants. Petitioner was indicted on one count of manufacturing marijuana, in violation of 21 U.S.C. § 841(a)(1). He unsuccessfully moved to suppress the evidence seized from his home and then entered a conditional guilty plea.

The Court of Appeals for the Ninth Circuit remanded the case for an evidentiary hearing regarding the intrusiveness of thermal imagine. On remand the District Court found that the Agema 210 "is a non-intrusive device which emits no rays or beams and shows a crude visual image of the heat being radiated from the outside of the house"; it "did not show any people or activity within the walls of the structure"; "[t]he device used cannot penetrate walls or windows to reveal conversations or human activities"; and "[n]o intimate details of the home were observed." Supp. App. to Pet. for Cert. 39–40. Based on these findings, the District Court upheld the validity of the warrant that relied in part upon the thermal imaging, and reaffirmed its denial of the motion to suppress. A divided Court of Appeals . . . affirmed, 190 F.3d 1041 (1999), with Judge Noonan dissenting. The court held that petitioner had shown no subjective expectation of privacy because he had made no attempt to conceal the heat escaping from his home . . . and even if he had, there was no objectively reasonable expectation of privacy because the imager "did not expose any intimate details of Kyllo's life," only "amorphous 'hot spots' on the roof and exterior wall," id. at 1047. We granted certiorari. . . .

II

The Fourth Amendment provides that "[t]he right of the people to be secure in their persons, houses, papers, and effects, against unreasonable searches and seizures, shall not be violated." "At the very core" of the Fourth Amendment "stands the right of a man to retreat into his own home and there be free from unreasonable governmental intrusion." Silverman v. United States, 365 U.S. 505, 511 (1961). With few exceptions, the question whether a warrantless search of a home is reasonable and hence constitutional must be answered no. . . .

On the other hand, the antecedent question of whether or not a Fourth Amendment "search" has occurred is not so simple under our precedent. The permissibility of ordinary visual surveillance of a home used to be clear because, well into the 20th century, our Fourth Amendment jurisprudence was tied to common-law trespass. . . . We have since decoupled violation of a person's Fourth Amendment rights from trespassory violation of his property . . . but the lawfulness of warrantless visual surveillance of a home has still been preserved. . . .

One might think that the new validating rationale would be that examining the portion of a house that is in plain public view, while it is a "search" despite the absence of trespass, is not an "unreasonable" one under the Fourth Amendment. . . . But in fact we have held that visual observation is no "search" at all—perhaps in order to preserve somewhat more intact our doctrine that warrantless searches are presumptively unconstitutional. . . . In assessing when a search is not a search, we have applied somewhat in reverse the principle first enunciated in Katz v. United States, 389 U.S. 347 (1967). *Katz* involved eavesdropping by means of an electronic listening device placed on the outside of a telephone booth—a location not within the catalog ("persons, houses, papers, and effects") that the Fourth Amendment protects against unreasonable searches. We held that the Fourth Amendment nonetheless protected Katz from the warrantless eavesdropping because he "justifiably relied" upon the privacy of the telephone booth. Id., at 353. As Justice Harlan's oft-quoted concurrence described it, a Fourth Amendment search occurs when the government violates a subjective expectation of privacy that society recognizes as reasonable. See id., at 361. We have subsequently applied this principle to hold that a Fourth Amendment search does *not* occur—even when the explicitly protected location of a *house* is concerned—unless "the individual manifested a subjective expectation of privacy in the object of the challenged search," and "society [is] willing to recognize that the expectation as reasonable." [California v.] *Ciraolo*, [476 U.S. 207 (1986)], at 211. . . .

The present case involves officers on a public street engaged in more than naked-eye surveillance of a home. We have previously reserved judgment as to how much technological enhancement of ordinary perception from such a vantage point, if any, is too much. . . .

III

It would be foolish to contend that the degree of privacy secured to citizens by the Fourth Amendment has been entirely unaffected by the advance of technology. For example, as the cases discussed above make clear, the technology enabling human flight has exposed to public view (and hence, we have said, to official observation) uncovered portions of the house and its curtilage that once were private. . . . The question we confront today is what limits there are upon this power of technology to shrink the realm of guaranteed privacy.

The *Katz* test—whether the individual has an expectation of privacy that society is prepared to recognize as reasonable—has often been criticized as circular, and hence subjective and unpredictable. . . . While it may be difficult to refine *Katz* when the search of areas such as telephone booths, automobiles, or even the curtilage and uncovered portions of residences are at issue, in the case of the search of the interior of homes— the prototypical and hence most commonly litigated area of protected privacy—there is a ready criterion, with roots deep in the common law, of the minimal expectation of privacy that *exists*, and that is acknowledged to be *reasonable*. To withdraw protection of this minimum expectation would be to permit police technology to erode the privacy guaranteed by the Fourth Amendment. We think that obtaining by sense-enhancing technology any information regarding the interior of the home that could not otherwise have been obtained without physical "intrusion into a constitutionally protected area," *Silverman* [v. United States], 365 U.S. [505 (1961)], at 512, constitutes a search—at least where (as here) the technology in question is not in general public use. This assures preservation of that degree of privacy against government that existed when the Fourth Amendment was adopted. On the basis of this criterion, the information obtained by the thermal imager in this case was the product of a search.

The Government maintains, however, that the thermal imaging must be upheld because it detected "only heat radiating from the external surface of the house," Brief for United States 26. The dissent makes this its leading point . . . contending that there is a fundamental difference between what it calls "off-the-wall" observations and "through-the-wall surveillance." But just as a thermal imager captures only heat emanating from a house, so also a powerful directional microphone picks up only sound emanating from a house—and a satellite capable of scanning from many miles away would pick up only visible light emanating from a house. We rejected such a mechanical interpretation of the Fourth Amendment in *Katz*, where the eavesdropping device picked up only sound waves that reached the exterior of the phone booth. Reversing that approach would leave the homeowner at the mercy of advancing technology—including imaging technology that could discern all human activity in the home. While the technology used in the present case was relatively crude, the rule we adopt must take account of more sophisticated systems that are already in use or in development. The dissent's reliance on the distinction between "off-the-wall" and "through-the-wall" observation is entirely incompatible with the dissent's belief, which we discuss below, that thermal-imaging observations of the intimate details of a home are impermissible. The most sophisticated thermal imaging devices continue to measure heat "off-the-wall" rather than "through-the-wall"; the dissent's disapproval of those more sophisticated thermal-imaging devices . . . is an acknowledgement that there is no substance to this distinction. As for the dissent's extraordinary assertion that anything learned through "an inference" cannot be a search . . . that would validate even the "through-the-wall" technologies that the dissent purports to disapprove. Surely the dissent does not believe that the through-the-wall radar or ultrasound technology produces an 8–by–10 Kodak glossy that needs no analysis (i.e., the making of inferences). . . .

The Government also contends that the thermal imaging was constitutional because it did not "detect private activities occurring in private areas," Brief for United States 22. It points out that in *Dow Chemical* we observed that the enhanced aerial photography did not reveal any "intimate details." [Dow Chemical Co. v. United States,] 476 U.S. [227 (1986)], at 238. *Dow Chemical*, however, involved enhanced aerial photography of an industrial complex, which does not share the Fourth Amendment sanctity of the home. . . . In the home, our cases show, *all* details are intimate details, because the entire area is held safe from prying government eyes. . . .

Limiting the prohibition of thermal imaging to "intimate details" would not only be wrong in principle; it would be impractical in application, failing to provide "a workable accommodation between the needs of law enforcement and the interest protected by the Fourth Amendment," Oliver v. United States, 466 U.S. 170, 181 (1984). To begin with, there is no necessary connection between the sophistication of the surveillance equipment and the "intimacy" of the details that it observes—which means that one cannot say (and the police cannot be assured) that the use of the relatively crude equipment at issue here will always be lawful. The Agema Thermovision 210 might disclose, for example, at what hour each night the lady of the house takes her daily sauna and bath—a detail that many would consider "intimate"; and a much more sophisticated system might detect nothing more intimate than the fact that someone left a closet light on. We could not, in other words, develop a rule approving only that through-the-wall surveillance which identifies objects no smaller than 36 by 36 inches, but would have to develop a jurisprudence specifying which home activities are "intimate" and which are not. And even when (if ever) that jurisprudence were fully developed, no police officer would be able to know *in advance* whether his through-the-wall surveillance picks up "intimate" details—and thus would be unable to know in advance whether it is constitutional.

    . . .

We have said that the Fourth Amendment draws "a firm line at the entrance to the house," *Payton* [v. New York], 455 U.S. [573 (1980)], at 590. That line, we think, must be not only firm but bright—which requires clear specification of those methods of surveillance that require a warrant. While it is certainly possible to conclude from the videotape of the thermal imaging that occurred in this case that no "significant" compromise of the homeowner's privacy has occurred, we must take the long view, from the original meaning of the Fourth Amendment forward. . . . Where, as here, the Government uses a device that is not in general public use, to explore details of the home that would previously have been unknowable without physical intrusion, the surveillance is a "search" and is presumptively unreasonable without a warrant.

. . .

■ JUSTICE STEVENS, with whom THE CHIEF JUSTICE, JUSTICE O'CONNOR, and JUSTICE KENNEDY join, dissenting.

There is, in my judgment, a distinction of constitutional magnitude between "through-the-wall surveillance" that gives the observer or listener direct access to information in a private area, on the one hand, and the thought processes used to draw inferences from information in the public domain, on the other hand. The Court has crafted a rule that purports to deal with direct observations of the inside of the home, but the case before us merely involves indirect deductions from "off-the-wall" surveillance, that is, observations of the exterior of the home. Those observations were made with a fairly primitive thermal imager that gathered data exposed on the outside of petitioner's home but did not invade any constitutionally protected interest in privacy. Moreover, I believe that the supposedly "bright-line" rule the Court has created in response to its concerns about future technological developments is unnecessary, unwise, and inconsistent with the Fourth Amendment.

I

There is no need for the Court to craft a new rule to decide this case, as it is controlled by established principles from our Fourth Amendment jurisprudence. One of those core principles, of course, is that "searches and seizures *inside a home* without a warrant are presumptively unreasonable." Payton v. New York, 445 U.S. 573, 586 (1980) (emphasis added). But it is equally well settled that searches and seizures of property in plain view are presumptively reasonable. . . . Whether that property is residential or commercial, the basic principle is the same: " 'What a person knowingly exposes to the public, even in his own home or office, is not a subject of Fourth Amendment protection.' " California v. Ciraolo, 476 U.S. 207, 213 (1986) (quoting Katz v. United States, 389 U.S. 347, 351 (1967)). . . . That is the principle implicated here.

While the Court "[t]akes the long view" and decides this case based largely on the potential of yet-to-be-developed technology that might allow "through-the-wall surveillance," ante, at 38–40 . . . this case involves nothing more than off-the-wall surveillance by law enforcement officers to gather information exposed to the general public from the outside of petitioner's home. All that the infrared camera did in this case was passively measure heat emitted from the exterior surfaces of petitioner's home; all that those measurements showed were relative differences in emission levels, vaguely indicating that some areas of the roof and outside walls were warmer than others. As still images from the infrared scans show . . . no details regarding the interior of petitioner's home were revealed. Unlike an x-ray scan, or other possible "through-the-wall" techniques, the detection of infrared radiation emanating from the home did not accomplish "an unauthorized physical penetration into the premises," Silverman v. United States, 365 U.S. 505, 509 (1961), nor did it "obtain information that it could not have obtained by observation from outside the curtilage of the house," United States v. Karo, 468 U.S. 705, 715 (1984).

Indeed, the ordinary use of the senses might enable a neighbor or passerby to notice the heat emanating from a building, particularly if it is vented, as was the case here. Additionally, any member of the public might notice that one part of a house is warmer than another part or a nearby building if, for example, rainwater evaporates or snow melts at different rates across its surfaces. Such use of the senses would not convert into an unreasonable search if, instead, an adjoining neighbor allowed an officer onto her property with a sensitive thermometer. Nor, in my view, does such observation become an unreasonable search if made from a distance with the aid of a device that merely discloses that the exterior of one house, or one area of the house, is much warmer than another. Nothing more occurred in this case.

Thus the notion that heat emissions from the outside of a dwelling is a private matter implicating the protections of the Fourth Amendment (the text of which guarantees the right of people "to be secure *in* their . . . houses" against unreasonable searches and seizures (emphasis added)) is not only unprecedented but also quite difficult to take seriously. Heat waves, like aromas that are generated in a kitchen, or in a laboratory or opium den, enter the public domain if and when they leave a building. A subjective expectation that they would remain private is not only implausible but also surely not "one that society is prepared to recognize as 'reasonable.'" *Katz*, 389 U.S., at 361 (Harlan, J., concurring).

To be sure, the homeowner has a reasonable expectation of privacy concerning what takes place within the home, and the Fourth Amendment's protection against physical invasions of the home should apply to their functional equivalent. But the equipment in this case did not penetrate the walls of petitioner's home, and while it did pick up "details of the home" that were exposed to the public, ante, at 38, it did not obtain "any information regarding the *interior* of the home," ante, at 40 (emphasis added). In the Court's own words, based on what the thermal imager "showed" regarding the outside of petitioner's home, the officers "concluded" that petitioner was engaging in illegal activity inside the home. Ante, at 30. It would be quite absurd to characterize their thought processes as "searches," regardless of whether they inferred (rightly) that petitioner was growing marijuana in his house, or (wrongly) that "the lady of the house [was taking] her daily sauna and bath." Ante, at 38. . . . For the first time in its history, the Court assumes that an inference can amount to a Fourth Amendment violation. See ante, at 36–37.

Notwithstanding the implications of today's decision, there is a strong public interest in avoiding constitutional litigation over the monitoring of emissions from homes, and over the inferences drawn from such monitoring. Just as "the police cannot reasonably be expected to avert their eyes from evidence of criminal activity that could have been observed by any member of the public," [California v.] *Greenwood*, 486 U.S. [35 (1988)], at 41, so too public official should not have to avert their senses or their equipment from detecting emissions in the public domain such as excessive heat, traces of smoke, suspicious odors, odorless gases, airborne particulates, or radioactive emissions, any of which could identify hazards to the community. In my judgment, monitoring such emissions with "sense-enhancing technology," ante, at 34, and drawing useful conclusions from such monitoring, is an entirely reasonable public service.

On the other hand, the countervailing privacy interest is at best trivial. After all, homes generally are insulated to keep heat in, rather than to prevent the detection of heat going out, and it does not seem to me that society will suffer from a rule requiring the rare homeowner who both intends to engage in uncommon activities that produce extraordinary amounts of heat, and wishes to conceal that production from outsiders, to make sure that the surrounding area is well insulated. . . . The interest in concealing the heat escaping from one's house pales in significance to "the chief evil against which the wording of the Fourth Amendment is directed," the "physical entry of the home," United States v. United States Dist. Court for Eastern Dist. of Mich., 407 U.S. 297, 313 (1972), and it is hard to believe that it is an interest the Framers sought to protect in our Constitution.

Since what was involved in this case was nothing more than drawing inferences from off-the-wall surveillance, rather than any "through-the-wall" surveillance, the officers' conduct did not amount to a search and was perfectly reasonable.

II

Instead of trying to answer the question whether the use of the thermal imager in this case was even arguably unreasonable, the court has fashioned a rule that is intended to provide essential guidance for the day when "more sophisticated systems" gain the "ability to 'see' through walls and other opaque barriers." Ante, at 35, and n.3. . . . As I have suggested, I would not erect a constitutional impediment to the use of sense-enhancing technology unless it provides its user with the functional equivalent of actual presence in the area being searched.

. . .

Although the Court is properly and commendably concerned about the threats to privacy that may flow from advances in the technology available to the law enforcement profession, it has unfortunately failed to heed the tried and true counsel of judicial restraint. Instead of concentrating on the rather mundane issue that is actually presented by the case before it, the Court has endeavored to craft an all-encompassing rule for the future. It would be far wiser to give legislators an unimpeded opportunity to grapple with these emerging issues rather than to shackle them with prematurely devised constitutional constraints.

. . .

———

192.   Is evidence obtained by a "mail cover," in which, at the request of a government agency, post office employees record and transmit to the agency information on the outside of mail to a particular individual, such as the name and address of the sender, admissible in evidence against the person "covered"? Against the senders? See United States v. Choate, 576 F.2d 165 (9th Cir.1978); Cohen v. United States, 378 F.2d 751, 759–60 (9th Cir.1967).

193.

Agents of the Federal Bureau of Investigation kept plaintiff and his home, together with his relatives, friends and associates, under constant surveillance and observation at his home twenty-four hours per day. . . .

. . .

. . . Agents of the Federal Bureau of Investigation followed the plaintiff, Sam Giancana, and members of his family as he went about his private affairs and went to the home of Mrs. Rose Flood where plaintiff and members of his family went to visit. Agents of the Federal Bureau of Investigation remained outside of the home of Rose Flood flashing the lights of their vehicles as signals and maintaining constant surveillance of the home of Rose Flood while the plaintiff Sam Giancana was in and about said residence.

. . . Agents of the Federal Bureau of Investigation followed the plaintiff Sam Giancana to the golf club where he patronizes [sic] and remained close to him and those with whom he played golf so that Agents of the Federal Bureau of Investigation numbering from two to four were directly behind plaintiff and his friends as they played golf, being immediately the next foursome following plaintiff and the group with which he was playing golf.

[T]he number of vehicles which the . . . [F.B.I.] maintained in and about the home of the plaintiff Sam Giancana at 1147 South Wenonah Street, Village of Oak Park, Illinois, numbered variously from two to as many as five each with two Agents of the Federal Bureau of Investigation for the purpose of maintaining constant twenty-four hour a day observation and surveillance of the plaintiff and his home and to follow him as he went about his private affairs.

Giancana v. Johnson, 335 F.2d 366, 370, n.1 (7th Cir.1964) (findings of the district court).

Were the constitutional rights of the plaintiff violated?

———

CHAPTER 5

EXAMINATION AND IDENTIFICATION

Rochin v. California

342 U.S. 165, 72 S.Ct. 205, 96 L.Ed. 183 (1952)

■ MR. JUSTICE FRANKFURTER delivered the opinion of the Court.

Having "some information that [the petitioner] was selling narcotics," three deputy sheriffs of the County of Los Angeles, on the morning of July 1, 1949, made for the two-story dwelling house in which Rochin lived with his mother, common-law wife, brothers and sisters. Finding the outside door open, they entered and then forced open the door to Rochin's room on the second floor. Inside they found petitioner sitting partly dressed on the side of the bed, upon which his wife was lying. On a "night stand" beside the bed the deputies spied two capsules. When asked "Whose stuff is this?" Rochin seized the capsules and put them in his mouth. A struggle ensued, in the course of which the three officers "jumped upon him" and attempted to extract the capsules. The force they applied proved unavailing against Rochin's resistance. He was handcuffed and taken to a hospital. At the direction of one of the officers a doctor forced an emetic solution through a tube into Rochin's stomach against his will. This "stomach pumping" produced vomiting. In the vomited matter were found two capsules which proved to contain morphine.

Rochin was brought to trial before a California Superior Court, sitting without a jury, on the charge of possessing "a preparation of morphine" in violation of the California Health and Safety Code, 1947, § 11500. Rochin was convicted and sentenced to sixty days' imprisonment. The chief evidence against him was the two capsules. They were admitted over petitioner's objection, although the means of obtaining them was frankly set forth in the testimony by one of the deputies substantially as here narrated.

On appeal, the District Court of Appeal affirmed the conviction. . . . The Supreme Court of California denied without opinion Rochin's petition for a hearing. . . .

This Court granted certiorari . . . because a serious question is raised as to the limitations which the Due Process Clause of the Fourteenth Amendment imposes on the conduct of criminal proceedings by the States.

. . .

[The Court's general discussion of the Due Process Clause and of due process of law is omitted.]

[W]e are compelled to conclude that the proceedings by which this conviction was obtained do more than offend some fastidious squeamishness or private sentimentalism about combatting crime too energetically. This is conduct that shocks the conscience. Illegally breaking into the privacy of the petitioner, the struggle to open his mouth and remove what was there, the forcible extraction of his stomach's contents—this course of proceeding by agents of government to obtain evidence is bound to offend even hardened sensibilities. They are methods too close to the rack and the screw to permit of constitutional differentiation.

It has long since ceased to be true that due process of law is heedless of the means by which otherwise relevant and credible evidence is obtained. This was not true even before the series of recent cases enforced the constitutional principle that the States may not base convictions upon confessions, however much verified, obtained by coercion. These decisions are not arbitrary exceptions to the comprehensive right of States to fashion their own rules of evidence for criminal trials. They are not sports in our constitutional law but applications of a general principle. They are only instances of the general requirement that States in their prosecutions respect certain decencies of civilized conduct. Due process of law, as a historic and generative principle, precludes defining, and thereby confining, these standards of conduct more precisely than to say that convictions cannot be brought about by methods that offend "a sense of justice." See Mr. Chief Justice Hughes, speaking for a unanimous Court in Brown v. Mississippi, 297 U.S. 278, 285–86. It would be a stultification of the responsibility which the course of constitutional history has cast upon this Court to hold that in order to convict a man the police cannot extract by force what is in his mind but can extract what is in his stomach.

To attempt in this case to distinguish what lawyers call "real evidence" from verbal evidence is to ignore the reasons for excluding coerced confessions. Use of involuntary verbal confessions in State criminal trials is constitutionally obnoxious not only because of their unreliability. They are inadmissible under the Due Process Clause even though statements contained in them may be independently established as true. Coerced confessions offend the community's sense of fair play and decency. So here, to sanction the brutal conduct which naturally enough was condemned by the court whose judgment is before us, would be to afford brutality the cloak of law. Nothing would be more calculated to discredit law and thereby to brutalize the temper of a society.

In deciding this case we do not heedlessly bring into question decisions in many States dealing with essentially different, even if related, problems. We therefore put to one side cases which have arisen in the State courts through use of modern methods and devices for discovering wrongdoers and bringing them to book. It does not fairly represent these decisions to suggest that they legalize force so brutal and so offensive to human dignity in securing evidence from a suspect as is revealed by this record. Indeed the California Supreme Court has not sanctioned this mode of securing a conviction. It merely exercised its discretion to decline a review of the conviction. All the California judges who have expressed themselves in this case have condemned the conduct in the strongest language.

We are not unmindful that hypothetical situations can be conjured up, shading imperceptibly from the circumstances of this case and by grada-tions producing practical differences despite seemingly logical extensions. But the Constitution is "intended to preserve practical and substantial rights, not to maintain theories." Davis v. Mills, 194 U.S. 451, 457.

On the facts of this case the conviction of the petitioner has been obtained by methods that offend the Due Process Clause. The judgment below must be

Reversed.[1]

---

194. The "shock the conscience" test of *Rochin*, above, has not generally been favored by the Court. In Irvine v. California, 347 U.S. 128 (1954) (5–4), the Court concluded over strong protest that repeated illegal, surreptitious entries into the petitioner's home and installation in the bedroom and elsewhere of eavesdropping devices did not shock the con-science. The absence of coercion was apparently the feature that distin-guished *Rochin*, see id. at 133. And in Breithaupt v. Abram, 352 U.S. 432 (1957), the Court rejected an argument that the withdrawal of a blood sample by a hypodermic needle from an unconscious man in order to perform a blood alcohol test shocked the conscience. The Court said:

> [T]here is nothing "brutal" or "offensive" in the taking of a sample of blood when done, as in this case, under the protective eye of a physician. To be sure, the driver here was unconscious when the blood was taken, but the absence of conscious consent, without more, does not necessarily render the taking a violation of a constitutional right; and certainly the test as administered here would not be considered offensive by even the most delicate. Furthermore, due process is not measured by the yardstick of personal reaction or the sphygmogram of the most sensitive person, but by that whole community sense of "decency and fairness" that has been woven by common experience into the fabric of acceptable conduct. It is on this bedrock that this Court has established the concept of due process. The blood test procedure has become routine in our everyday life. It is a ritual for those going into the military service as well as those applying for marriage licenses. Many colleges require such tests before permitting entrance and literally millions of us have voluntarily gone through the same, though a longer, routine in becoming blood donors. Likewise, we note that a majority of our States have either enacted statutes in some form authorizing tests of this nature or permit findings so obtained to be admitted in evidence. We therefore conclude that a blood test taken by a skilled technician is not such "conduct that shocks the con-

[1] Justice Black and Justice Douglas wrote concurring opinions.

science," *Rochin*, [342 U.S.] at 172, nor such a method of obtaining evidence that it offends a "sense of justice," Brown v. Mississippi, 297 U.S. 278, 285–86 (1936). This is not to say that the indiscriminate taking of blood under different conditions or by those not competent to do so may not amount to such "brutality" as would come under the *Rochin* rule. The chief law-enforcement officer of New Mexico, while at the Bar of this Court, assured us that every proper medical precaution is afforded an accused from whom blood is taken.

352 U.S. at 435–38.

In State v. Thompson, 505 N.W.2d 673, 675, 676 (Neb.1993), citing other cases, the court held that use of a choke hold ("lateral vascular neck restraint") that rendered a person unconscious for about ten seconds, in order to extract narcotic substances "between the size of a pinhead and a pea" from his mouth, was not an unreasonable search or otherwise unconstitutional. The *Rochin* "outrageous conduct" test is discussed in the context of alleged entrapment, in United States v. Tucker, 28 F.3d 1420 (6th Cir.1994), and United States v. Santana, 6 F.3d 1 (1st Cir.1993).

195. The problem of controlling illegal importation of goods, particularly narcotics, by swallowing them or concealing them in a body cavity has led the courts to allow as part of a "border search," see note 159, p. 289 above, the "stomach pump" device employed in *Rochin*, above, and body probes. E.g., United States v. Ogberaha, 771 F.2d 655 (2d Cir.1985) (reasonable suspicion is sufficient to justify search of body cavity); United States v. Aman, 624 F.2d 911 (9th Cir.1980) ("clear indication" required to justify search of body cavity). See generally United States v. Nelson, 36 F.3d 758 (8th Cir.1994) (evidence obtained by search of body cavity, not at border and in absence of exigent circumstances, suppressed).

Emphasizing the government's "plenary authority" to conduct routine searches at the border, without any requirement of probable cause or a warrant, the Supreme Court has held that "the detention of a traveler at the border, beyond the scope of a routine customs search and inspection, is justified at its inception if customs agents, considering all the facts surrounding the traveler and her trip, reasonably suspect that the traveler is smuggling contraband in her alimentary canal." United States v. Montoya de Hernandez, 473 U.S. 531, 541 (1985) (7–2). In that case, border authorities suspected that the defendant was carrying narcotics in her alimentary canal. She was detained and asked if she would undergo an x-ray at a hospital. After some discussion, she refused. She was given the option of returning to Colombia, her point of embarkation, by the first available flight, to which she agreed; but no flight was immediately available. She was then told that she would be detained unless she was x-rayed or she had moved her bowels and her stool was inspected. She was detained incommunicado and under observation until 16 hours after her plane had landed. Customs officers then sought a court order authorizing an x-ray and rectal examination, which was obtained about eight hours later. (The defendant had asserted that she was pregnant. The x-ray was made conditional on a negative result of a pregnancy test.) Balloons containing narcotics were removed from the defendant during a rectal examination; later she excreted additional balloons. An x-ray was not performed, although the pregnancy test later turned out to be negative. Conceding that the investigative detention in this case was longer than any that had previously been approved on the basis of reasonable suspicion and that the detention was "long, uncomfortable, indeed, humiliating," id. at 544, the Court concluded that, nevertheless, in view of the special responsibilities of customs officials to protect the border, it was permissible in the circumstances.

See also United States v. Couch, 688 F.2d 599 (9th Cir.1982) (x-ray of abdominal region at border upheld); Yanez v. Romero, 619 F.2d 851 (10th Cir.1980) (urine sample obtained by threat to use catheter held admissible).

Schmerber v. California

384 U.S. 757, 86 S.Ct. 1826, 16 L.Ed.2d 908 (1966)

■ MR. JUSTICE BRENNAN delivered the opinion of the Court.

Petitioner was convicted in Los Angeles Municipal Court of the criminal offense of driving an automobile while under the influence of intoxicating liquor. He had been arrested at a hospital while receiving treatment for injuries suffered in an accident involving the automobile that he had apparently been driving. At the direction of a police officer, a blood sample was then withdrawn from petitioner's body by a physician at the hospital. The chemical analysis of this sample revealed a percent by weight of alcohol in his blood at the time of the offense which indicated intoxication, and the report of this analysis was admitted in evidence at the trial. Petitioner objected to receipt of this evidence of the analysis on the ground that the blood had been withdrawn despite his refusal, on the advice of his counsel, to consent to the test. He contended that in that circumstance the withdrawal of the blood and the admission of the analysis in evidence denied him due process of law under the Fourteenth Amendment, as well as specific guarantees of the Bill of Rights secured against the States by that Amendment: his privilege against self-incrimination under the Fifth Amendment; his right to counsel under the Sixth Amendment; and his right not to be subjected to unreasonable searches and seizures in violation of the Fourth Amendment. The Appellate Department of the California Superior Court rejected these contentions and affirmed the conviction. . . .

We affirm.

I.

The Due Process Clause Claim.

Breithaupt [v. Abram, 352 U.S. 432 (1957)] was also a case in which police officers caused blood to be withdrawn from the driver of an automobile involved in an accident, and in which there was ample justification for the officer's conclusion that the driver was under the influence of alcohol. There, as here, the extraction was made by a physician in a simple, medically acceptable manner in a hospital environment. There, however, the driver was unconscious at the time the blood was withdrawn and hence had no opportunity to object to the procedure. We affirmed the conviction there resulting from the use of the test in evidence, holding that under such circumstances the withdrawal did not offend "that 'sense of justice' of which we spoke in Rochin v. California, 342 U.S. 165." 352 U.S., at 435. *Breithaupt* thus requires the rejection of petitioner's due process argument, and nothing in the circumstances of this case[2] or in supervening events persuades us that this aspect of *Breithaupt* should be overruled.

II.

The Privilege Against Self-Incrimination Claim.

Breithaupt summarily rejected an argument that the withdrawal of blood and the admission of the analysis report involved in that state case violated the Fifth Amendment privilege of any person not to "be compelled in any criminal case to be a witness against himself," citing Twining v. New Jersey, 211 U.S. 78. But that case, holding that the protections of the Fourteenth Amendment do not embrace this Fifth Amendment privilege, has been succeeded by Malloy v. Hogan, 378 U.S. 1, 8. We there held that "[t]he Fourteenth Amendment secures against state invasion the same privilege that the Fifth Amendment guarantees against federal infringement—the right of a person to remain silent unless he chooses to speak in the unfettered exercise of his own will, and to suffer no penalty . . . for such silence." We therefore must now decide whether the withdrawal of the blood and admission in evidence of the analysis involved in this case violated petitioner's privilege. We hold that the privilege protects an accused only from being compelled to testify against himself, or otherwise provide the State with evidence of a testimonial or communicative nature, and that the withdrawal of blood and use of the analysis in question in this case did not involve compulsion to these ends.

It could not be denied that in requiring petitioner to submit to the withdrawal and chemical analysis of his blood the State compelled him to submit to an attempt to discover evidence that might be used to prosecute him for a criminal offense. He submitted only after the police officer rejected his objection and directed the physician to proceed. The officer's direction to the physician to administer the test over petitioner's objection constituted compulsion for the purposes of the privilege. The critical question then, is whether petitioner was thus compelled "to be a witness against himself."

---

2. We "cannot see that it should make any difference whether one states unequivocally that he objects or resorts to physical violence in protest or is in such condition that he is unable to protest." Breithaupt v. Abram, 352 U.S., at 441 (Warren, C.J., dissenting). It would be a different case if the police initiated the violence, refused to respect a reasonable request to undergo a different form of testing, or responded to resistance with inappropriate force. Compare the discussion at Part IV, infra.

If the scope of the privilege coincided with the complex of values it helps to protect, we might be obliged to conclude that the privilege was violated. In Miranda v. Arizona, [384 U.S. 436 (1966)] at 460, the Court said of the interests protected by the privilege: "All these policies point to one overriding thought: the constitutional foundation underlying the privilege is the respect a government—state or federal—must accord to the dignity and integrity of its citizens. To maintain a 'fair state-individual balance,' to require the government 'to shoulder the entire load' . . . to respect the inviolability of the human personality, our accusatory system of criminal justice demands that the government seeking to punish an individual produce the evidence against him by its own independent labors, rather than by the cruel, simple expedient of compelling it from his own mouth." The withdrawal of blood necessarily involves puncturing the skin for extraction, and the percent by weight of alcohol in that blood, as established by chemical analysis, is evidence of criminal guilt. Compelled submission fails on one view to respect the "inviolability of the human personality." Moreover, since it enables the State to rely on evidence forced from the accused, the compulsion violates at least one meaning of the requirement that the State procure the evidence against an accused "by its own independent labors."

As the passage in *Miranda* implicitly recognizes, however, the privilege has never been given the full scope which the values it helps to protect suggest. History and a long line of authorities in lower courts have consistently limited its protection to situations in which the State seeks to submerge those values by obtaining the evidence against an accused through "the cruel, simple expedient of compelling it from his own mouth. . . . In sum, the privilege is fulfilled only when the person is guaranteed the right 'to remain silent unless he chooses to speak in the unfettered exercise of his own will.' " Ibid. The leading case in this Court is Holt v. United States, 218 U.S. 245. There the question was whether evidence was admissible that the accused, prior to trial and over his protest, put on a blouse that fitted him. It was contended that compelling the accused to submit to the demand that he model the blouse violated the privilege. Mr. Justice Holmes, speaking for the Court, rejected the argument as "based upon an extravagant extension of the Fifth Amendment," and went on to say: "[T]he prohibition of compelling a man in a criminal court to be witness against himself is a prohibition of the use of physical or moral compulsion to extort communications from him, not an exclusion of his body as evidence when it may be material. The objection in principle would forbid a jury to look at a prisoner and compare his features with a photograph in proof." 218 U.S., at 252–53.

It is clear that the protection of the privilege reaches an accused's communications, whatever form they might take, and the compulsion of responses which are also communications, for example, compliance with a subpoena to produce one's papers. . . . On the other hand, both federal and state courts have usually held that it offers no protection against compulsion to submit to fingerprinting, photographing, or measurements, to write or speak for identification, to appear in court, to stand, to assume a stance, to walk, or to make a particular gesture. The distinction which has emerged, often expressed in different ways, is that the privilege is a bar against compelling "communications" or "testimony," but that compulsion which makes a suspect or accused the source of "real or physical evidence" does not violate it.

Although we agree that this distinction is a helpful framework for analysis, we are not to be understood to agree with past applications in all instances. There will be many cases in which such a distinction is not readily drawn. Some tests seemingly directed to obtain "physical evidence," for example, lie detector tests measuring changes in body function during interrogation, may actually be directed to eliciting responses which are essentially testimonial. To compel a person to submit to testing in which an effort will be made to determine his guilt or innocence on the basis of physiological responses, whether willed or not, is to evoke the spirit and history of the Fifth Amendment. Such situations call to mind the principle that the protection of the privilege "is as broad as the mischief against which it seeks to guard," Counselman v. Hitchcock, 142 U.S. 547, 562.

In the present case, however, no such problem of application is presented. Not even a shadow of testimonial compulsion upon or enforced communication by the accused was involved either in the extraction or in the chemical analysis. Petitioner's testimonial capacities were in no way implicated; indeed, his participation, except as a donor, was irrelevant to the results of the test, which depend on chemical analysis and on that alone. Since the blood test evidence, although an incriminating product of compulsion, was neither petitioner's testimony nor evidence relating to some communicative act or writing by the petitioner, it was not inadmissible on privilege grounds.

III.

The Right to Counsel Claim.

This conclusion also answers petitioner's claim that, in compelling him to submit to the test in face of the fact that his objection was made on the advice of counsel, he was denied his Sixth Amendment right to the assistance of counsel. Since petitioner was not entitled to assert the privilege, he has no greater right because counsel erroneously advised him that he could assert it. His claim is strictly limited to the failure of the police to respect his wish, reinforced by counsel's advice, to be left inviolate. No issue of counsel's ability to assist petitioner in respect of any rights he did possess is presented. The limited claim thus made must be rejected.

IV.

The Search and Seizure Claim.

. . . The question is squarely presented . . . whether the chemical analysis introduced in evidence in this case should have been excluded as the product of an unconstitutional search and seizure.

The overriding function of the Fourth Amendment is to protect personal privacy and dignity against unwarranted intrusion by the State. . . .

The values protected by the Fourth Amendment thus substantially overlap those the Fifth Amendment helps to protect. History and precedent have required that we today reject the claim that the Self-Incrimination Clause of the Fifth Amendment requires the human body in all circumstances to be held inviolate against state expeditions seeking evidence of crime. But if compulsory administration of a blood test does not implicate the Fifth Amendment, it plainly involves the broadly conceived reach of a search and seizure under the Fourth Amendment. That Amendment expressly provides that "[t]he right of the people to be secure in their *persons*, houses, papers, and effects, against unreasonable searches and seizures, shall not be violated. . . ." (Emphasis added.) It could not reasonably be argued, and indeed respondent does not argue, that the administration of the blood test in this case was free of the constraints of the Fourth Amendment. Such testing procedures plainly constitute searches of "persons," and depend antecedently upon seizures of "persons," within the meaning of that Amendment.

Because we are dealing with intrusions into the human body rather than with state interferences with property relationships or private papers—"houses, papers, and effects"—we write on a clean slate. Limitations on the kinds of property which may be seized under warrant, as distinct from the procedures for search and the permissible scope of search, are not instructive in this context. We begin with the assumption that once the privilege against self-incrimination has been found not to bar compelled intrusions into the body for blood to be analyzed for alcohol content, the Fourth Amendment's proper function is to constrain, not against all intrusions as such, but against intrusions which are not justified in the circumstances, or which are made in an improper manner. In other words, the questions we must decide in this case are whether the police were justified in requiring petitioner to submit to the blood test, and whether the means and procedures employed in taking his blood respected relevant Fourth Amendment standards of reasonableness.

In this case, as will often be true when charges of driving under the influence of alcohol are pressed, these questions arise in the context of an arrest made by an officer without a warrant. Here, there was plainly probable cause for the officer to arrest petitioner and charge him with driving an automobile while under the influence of intoxicating liquor. The police officer who arrived at the scene shortly after the accident smelled liquor on petitioner's breath, and testified that petitioner's eyes were "bloodshot, watery, sort of a glassy appearance." The officer saw petitioner again at the hospital, within two hours of the accident. There he noticed similar symptoms of drunkenness. He thereupon informed petitioner "that he was under arrest and that he was entitled to the services of an attorney, and that he could remain silent, and that anything that he told me would be used against him in evidence."

While early cases suggest that there is an unrestricted "right on the part of the Government, always recognized under English and American law, to search the person of the accused when legally arrested to discover and seize the fruits or evidences of crime," Weeks v. United States, 232 U.S. 383, 392 . . . the mere fact of a lawful arrest does not end our inquiry. The suggestion of these cases apparently rests on two factors—first, there may be more immediate danger of concealed weapons or of destruction of evidence under the direct control of the accused . . . ; second, once a search of the arrested person for weapons is permitted, it would be both impractical and unnecessary to enforcement of the Fourth Amendment's purpose to attempt to confine the search to those objects alone. . . . Whatever the validity of these considerations in general, they have little applicability with respect to searches involving intrusions beyond the body's surface. The interests in human dignity and privacy which the Fourth Amendment protects forbid any such intrusions on the mere chance that desired evidence might be obtained. In the absence of a clear indication that in fact such evidence will be found, these fundamental human interests require law officers to suffer the risk that such evidence may disappear unless there is an immediate search.

Although the facts which established probable cause to arrest in this case also suggested the required relevance and likely success of a test of petitioner's blood for alcohol, the question remains whether the arresting officer was permitted to draw these inferences himself, or was required instead to procure a warrant before proceeding with the test. Search warrants are ordinarily required for searches of dwellings, and, absent an emergency, no less could be required where intrusions into the human body are concerned. The requirement that a warrant be obtained is a requirement that the inferences to support the search "be drawn by a neutral and detached magistrate instead of being judged by the officer engaged in the often competitive enterprise of ferreting out crime." Johnson v. United States, 333 U.S. 10, 13–14. . . . The importance of informed, detached and deliberate determinations of the issue whether or not to invade another's body in search of evidence of guilt is indisputable and great.

The officer in the present case, however, might reasonably have believed that he was confronted with an emergency, in which the delay necessary to obtain a warrant, under the circumstances, threatened "the destruction of evidence," Preston v. United States, 376 U.S. 364, 367. We are told that the percentage of alcohol in the blood begins to diminish shortly after drinking stops, as the body functions to eliminate it from the system. Particularly in a case such as this, where time had to be taken to bring the accused to a hospital and to investigate the scene of the accident, there was no time to seek out a magistrate and secure a warrant. Given these special facts, we conclude that the attempt to secure evidence of blood-alcohol content in this case was an appropriate incident to petitioner's arrest.

Similarly, we are satisfied that the test chosen to measure petitioner's blood-alcohol level was a reasonable one. Extraction of blood samples for testing is a highly effective means of determining the degree to which a person is under the influence of alcohol. . . . Such tests are a commonplace in these days of periodic physical examinations and experience with them teaches that the quantity of blood extracted is minimal, and that for most people the procedure involves virtually no risk, trauma, or pain. Petitioner is not one of the few who on grounds of fear, concern for health, or religious scruple might prefer some other means of testing, such as the "breathalyzer" test petitioner refused. . . . We need not decide whether such wishes would have to be respected.

Finally, the record shows that the test was performed in a reasonable manner. Petitioner's blood was taken by a physician in a hospital environment according to accepted medical practices. We are thus not presented with the serious questions which would arise if a search involving use of a medical technique, even of the most rudimentary sort, were made by other than medical personnel or in other than a medical environment—for example, if it were administered by police in the privacy of the stationhouse. To tolerate searches under these conditions might be to invite an unjustified element of personal risk of infection and pain.

We thus conclude that the present record shows no violation of petitioner's right under the Fourth and Fourteenth Amendments to be free of unreasonable searches and seizures. It bears repeating, however, that we reach this judgment only on the facts of the present record. The integrity of an individual's person is a cherished value of our society. That we today hold that the Constitution does not forbid the States minor intrusions into an individual's body under stringently limited conditions in no way indicates that it permits more substantial intrusions, or intrusions under other conditions.

Affirmed.[3]

———

196. In United States v. Montoya de Hernandez, 473 U.S. 531, 540 (1985) (7–2), discussed in note 195, p. 354 above, the Supreme Court observed that the reference in *Schmerber* to a "clear indication" that evidence will be found, p. 360 above, was "used to indicate the necessity for particularized suspicion that the evidence sought might be found within the body of the individual, rather than as enunciating still a third Fourth Amendment threshold between 'reasonable suspicion' and 'probable cause.'"

197. *Schmerber*, p. 356 n.2, seems to indicate that the use of "appropriate" force to make a person submit to a blood test or another such procedure is permissible, provided that the procedure itself is one that can be required. Is that proposition sound? In Hammer v. Gross, 932 F.2d 842 (9th Cir.1991), the court upheld the use of reasonable force to obtain a

---

[3] Justice Harlan wrote a brief concurring opinion, which Justice Stewart joined. Justice Black wrote a dissenting opinion, which Justice Douglas joined. Chief Justice Warren, Justice Douglas and Justice Fortas also wrote brief dissenting opinions.

blood sample from a driver suspected of drunk driving. The evidence was suppressed in State v. Ravotto, 777 A.2d 301 (N.J.2001), because unreasonable force was used.

198. The DNA Analysis Backlog Elimination Act of 2000, 42 U.S.C. § 14135a, requires persons in federal custody or on parole, probation or supervised release to provide a DNA sample, to be turned over to the FBI for analysis, the results of which are put in a data bank. All the states have enacted similar legislation mandating DNA testing and storage of the results for some similar group of persons. The data obtained by state and federal officials is kept in a unified data bank and made available to law enforcement officials. In United States v. Kincade, 345 F.3d 1095 (9th Cir.2003), vacated and rehearing granted, 354 F.3d 1000 (2004), the court held that the Fourth Amendment does not permit the involuntary extraction of blood to obtain a DNA sample, unless it is supported by individualized reasonable suspicion.

199. Relying on *Schmerber*, the Supreme Court of South Dakota held that the taking of a urine sample of an arrested person without her consent did not violate the defendant's rights under the Fourth Amendment. State v. Hanson, 588 N.W.2d 885 (S.D.1999).

In State v. Holt, 156 N.W.2d 884 (Iowa 1968), the defendant, who had been arrested for drunk driving, refused to take a blood test or a urine test at the police station. With respect to the blood test, he said that he refused to take the test because he had frequently been stuck with needles and hated them. The court held that testimony of his refusal was properly admitted in evidence against him.

In *Schmerber*, the Court declined to say whether, if a method of testing is generally proper and "for most people . . . involves virtually no risk, trauma, or pain," the wishes of "the few who on grounds of fear, concern for health, or religious scruple might prefer some other means of testing . . . have to be respected," p. 361. Should unusual squeamishness be a sufficient basis for requiring police not to employ a method of testing in a particular case?

200. In United States v. Chapel, 55 F.3d 1416 (9th Cir.1995) (en banc), noting that *Schmerber* required probable cause to arrest before a blood sample may be taken, the court held that a formal arrest before (or soon after) the blood sample is taken is not essential. In Matter of Lavigne, 641 N.E.2d 1328 (Mass.1994), the court held that a search warrant, issued after a hearing, can authorize the compelled extraction of a blood sample from a person not under arrest, to obtain evidence of a crime. So also, in Matter of Abe A., 437 N.E.2d 265 (N.Y.1982), it was held that a court may order a suspect not under arrest to furnish a blood sample, provided that there is probable cause to believe he has committed a crime, there is a "clear indication" that relevant material evidence will be obtained, and a safe, reliable method is used.

201. A Massachusetts statute prescribing an automatic 90-day suspension of the driver's license of someone who is lawfully arrested for drunken driving and refuses to take a breathalyzer test was sustained, against the claim that such suspension without a prior opportunity for a hearing is unconstitutional, in Mackey v. Montrym, 443 U.S. 1 (1979) (5–4). *Mackey* was followed in Illinois v. Batchelder, 463 U.S. 1112 (1983) (6–3).

The introduction at trial of evidence that the defendant refused to take a blood alcohol test after a police officer lawfully asked him to do so is not a violation of the privilege against self-incrimination. South Dakota v. Neville, 459 U.S. 553 (1983) (7–2).

202. Can a suspect be required to undress so that police can examine his body for scars? See McFarland v. United States, 150 F.2d 593 (D.C.Cir. 1945). Can he be required to shave before he appears in a lineup? See United States v. Crouch, 478 F.Supp. 867 (E.D.Cal.1979). See also United States v. Brown, 920 F.2d 1212 (5th Cir.1991) (defendant required to dye hair as it was alleged to be at time of crime, before appearing in lineup); United States v. Valenzuela, 722 F.2d 1431 (9th Cir.1983) (defendant required to be clean shaven at trial to facilitate identification). Are photographs of his body admissible in evidence over his objection? See People v. Smith, 298 P.2d 540 (Cal.Dist.Ct.App.1956). Are hairs clipped from the defendant's head over his protest while he is in custody admissible in evidence against him? See United States v. Anderson, 739 F.2d 1254 (7th Cir.1984) (taking of hair from scalp and beard pursuant to search warrant upheld); United States v. Weir, 657 F.2d 1005 (8th Cir.1981) (clipping strands of hair from head, beard, and moustache of arrested persons was "so minor . . . [that] fourth amendment rights were not implicated").

203. Fingerprints. As the Court indicated in *Schmerber*, above, claims that the taking of fingerprints over objection violates the privilege against self-incrimination have been rejected. E.g., United States v. Kelly, 55 F.2d 67 (2d Cir.1932). See also United States v. Richardson, 388 F.2d 842 (6th Cir.1968) (examination of hands under ultraviolet light for fluorescein power dusted on stolen goods). Nor have the courts accepted the claims, made by "respectable" defendants (for example, in antitrust cases) that the requirement of fingerprinting as to them was a punishment, e.g., United States v. Krapf, 285 F.2d 647, 650–51 (3d Cir.1960), or was an unconstitutional invasion of their privacy, United States v. Laub Baking Co., 283 F.Supp. 217 (N.D.Ohio 1968). In In re Reardon, 445 F.2d 798 (1st Cir.1971), the court ruled that if the defendant failed to comply with the district court's order to furnish a palmprint, his bail would be revoked.

204. Handwriting. In Gilbert v. California, 388 U.S. 263 (1967), the Court ruled that the taking of handwriting exemplars from a defendant following his arrest and their use against him, all without his consent, did not violate his privilege against self-incrimination. Following *Schmerber*, the Court said: "A mere handwriting exemplar, in contrast to the content of what is written, like the voice or body itself, is an identifying physical characteristic outside its protection." Id. at 266–67.[4]

4. The Court concluded also that "the taking of the exemplars was not a 'critical' stage of the criminal proceedings entitling petitioner to the assistance of counsel. . . .

Dissenting from this portion of the Court's opinion, Justice Fortas observed:

Unlike blood, handwriting cannot be extracted by a doctor from an accused's veins while the accused is subjected to physical restraint, which *Schmerber* permits. So presumably, on the basis of the Court's decision, trial courts may hold an accused in contempt and keep him in jail—indefinitely—until he gives a handwriting exemplar.

This decision goes beyond *Schmerber*. Here the accused, in the absence of any warning that he has a right to counsel, is compelled to cooperate, not merely to submit; to engage in a volitional act, not merely to suffer the inevitable consequences of arrest and state custody; to take affirmative action which may not merely identify him, but tie him directly to the crime.

Gilbert, 388 U.S. at 291–92.

In United States v. Doe, 405 F.2d 436 (2d Cir.1968), the court held that a witness who refused to comply with a court order to furnish exemplars for a grand jury could be punished by a commitment for contempt and, if he persisted in refusing and was subsequently indicted, his refusal could be considered by the jury at his trial.[5] Accord United States v. Knight, 607 F.2d 1172 (5th Cir.1979) (instructions to jury on refusal to furnish exemplar upheld); United States v. Nix, 465 F.2d 90 (5th Cir.1972). In United States v. Stembridge, 477 F.2d 874 (5th Cir.1973), the court held that the prosecutor could introduce expert testimony at the trial to explain the difference between a robbery note and the defendant's exemplars. A defendant may not, however, be required to give a handwriting sample by writing to dictation, because his spelling of the words dictated would be testimonial evidence. United States v. Campbell, 732 F.2d 1017 (1st Cir. 1984).

In United States v. Euge, 444 U.S. 707 (1980) (6–3), the Court upheld the authority of the IRS to require a person being investigated for tax liability to furnish a handwriting exemplar, under its authority to issue a summons for a person to appear and produce papers and records, etc., 26 U.S.C. § 7602.

205. Voice. In United States v. Wade, 388 U.S. 218 (1967), p. 369 below, the Court again relied on *Schmerber*, above, and held that an accused could be compelled "to speak within hearing distance of the witnesses, even to utter words purportedly uttered by the robber"; in such

---

[T]here is minimal risk that the absence of counsel might derogate from his right to a fair trial. . . . If, for some reason, an unrepresentative exemplar is taken, this can be brought out and corrected through the adversary process at trial since the accused can make an unlimited number of additional exemplars for analysis and comparison by government and defense handwriting experts."

388 U.S. at 267. See United States v. Wade, p. 369 below.

5. The witness was ordered committed for 30 days. The court of appeals indicated, contrary to Justice Fortas's speculation in *Gilbert*, that an indefinite commitment might be excessive and violate due process. 405 F.2d at 438–39.

a case, the accused is "required to use his voice as an identifying physical characteristic, not to speak his guilt." 338 U.S. at 222–23. See United States v. Leone, 823 F.2d 246 (8th Cir.1987) (defendant required to speak incriminating words recorded on tape before jury). Compare Palmer v. Peyton, 359 F.2d 199 (4th Cir.1966), in which the court held that the method used to obtain a voice identification (without a lineup) was so unreliable that its admission in evidence violated fundamental standards of due process.

Justice Fortas dissented from this portion of the Court's opinion in *Wade*:

> In my view . . . the accused may not be compelled in a lineup to speak the words uttered by the person who committed the crime. I am confident that it could not be compelled in court. It cannot be compelled in a lineup. It is more than passive, mute assistance to the eyes of the victim or of witnesses. It is the kind of volitional act—the kind of forced cooperation by the accused—which is within the historical perimeter of the privilege against compelled self-incrimination.

> Our history and tradition teach and command that an accused may stand mute. The privilege means just that; not less than that. According to the Court, an accused may be jailed—indefinitely—until he is willing to say, for an identifying audience, whatever was said in the course of the commission of the crime. Presumably this would include, "Your money or your life"—or perhaps, words of assault in a rape case. This is intolerable under our constitutional system.

> . . .

> . . . *Schmerber*, which authorized the forced extraction of blood from the veins of an unwilling human being, did not compel the person actively to cooperate—to accuse himself by a volitional act which differs only in degree from compelling him to act out the crime, which, I assume, would be rebuffed by the Court. It is the latter feature which places the compelled utterance by the accused squarely within the history and noble purpose of the Fifth Amendment's commandment.

388 U.S. at 260–61.

206. The complexity of the testimonial–nontestimonial distinction that the Court used in *Schmerber* to resolve the defendant's claim under the Fifth Amendment privilege against compulsory self-incrimination is indicated in Pennsylvania v. Muniz, 496 U.S. 582 (1990). The defendant was driving on the highway and was stopped by a patrol officer, who had reason to believe that the defendant was drunk. The officer asked him to perform three standard field sobriety tests (e.g., walk a straight line), which he performed badly. He told the officer that he did badly because he had been drinking. He was arrested and brought to a station for booking. During booking, which was videotaped, he was asked routine questions about his name, address, age, etc., and asked also whether he knew the date of his sixth birthday. He stumbled over questions about his address and age and said that he did not remember the date of his sixth birthday.

He was again asked to perform the sobriety tests, which he performed badly, attempting again to explain his bad performance. He was asked to take a breathalyzer test, which, after asking some questions and commenting about his state of drunkenness, he refused to do. No *Miranda* warnings were given until then.

The Court held that evidence about the defendant's slurring of speech and lack of muscular coordination was nontestimonial and therefore admissible. The answer to the question whether he knew the date of his sixth birthday, however, required a testimonial response; its incriminating significance lay not in its delivery but in its content. The defendant's responses to the routine booking questions and his remarks in the course of the sobriety tests and responses to the request that he take a breathalyzer test were also testimonial; but, the Court said, the former were admissible under a "routine booking exception" to the *Miranda* requirements and the latter were admissible because they were not in response to custodial interrogation. (On the *Miranda* aspects of the case, see note 240, p. 437 below.)

207. In Estelle v. Smith, 451 U.S. 454 (1981), the defendant was indicted for murder. Before trial, the court ordered a psychiatric examination to determine whether he was competent to stand trial. He was subsequently tried and convicted. At the sentencing proceeding, the psychiatrist who had examined the defendant gave testimony based on the examination, which supported the state's request for the death penalty. The defendant was sentenced to death.

The Court held that this use of the psychiatrist's testimony violated the defendant's privilege against compulsory self-incrimination and his right to counsel. As to the privilege, the Court said: "A criminal defendant, who neither initiates a psychiatric evaluation nor attempts to introduce any psychiatric evidence, may not be compelled to respond to a psychiatrist if his statements can be used against him at a capital sentencing proceeding. Because respondent did not voluntarily consent to the pretrial psychiatric examination after being informed of his right to remain silent and the possible use of his statements, the State could not rely on what he said to . . . [the psychiatrist] to establish his future dangerousness." Id. at 468. The Court noted that if the defendant had refused to answer questions, the competency examination could have proceeded on the condition that the results of the examination would be used only for that purpose. With respect to the right to counsel, the Court said that, having already been indicted, the defendant had the right to be assisted by counsel before deciding whether to submit to the competency examination.

Estelle v. Smith was distinguished in Buchanan v. Kentucky, 483 U.S. 402 (1987) (7–2), in which the defense counsel had requested the psychiatric evaluation and the prosecutor used a report of the evaluation to rebut evidence presented by the defense. See also United States v. Byers, 740 F.2d 1104, 1115 (D.C.Cir.1984), in which the court held that "when a defendant raises the defense of insanity, he may constitutionally be subjected to compulsory examination by court-appointed or government psychiatrists without the necessity of recording; and when he introduces into evidence psychiatric testimony to support his insanity defense, testimony of those examining psychiatrists may be received (on that issue) as well.'' The court rejected also a claim that the defendant's right to counsel was violated because his lawyer was not permitted to attend psychiatric staff conferences leading to an evaluation of the defendant subsequently used at his trial. The majority and dissenting opinions canvass the issues thoroughly and cite other federal cases. Estelle v. Smith is distinguished also in Penry v. Johnson, 532 U.S. 782 (2001), in which a witness referred to a psychiatric examination of the defendant prepared at the request of defense counsel in a previous unrelated case, to determine the defendant's competence to stand trial. The psychiatrist concluded that the defendant would be dangerous if released. Among the distinguishing factors, the court noted that Penry himself had made his mental condition an issue in the earlier trial and the current one, whereas in *Estelle*, the trial court had called for the examination and had chosen the examining psychiatrist; that the prosecutor elicited the testimony about the psychiatric examination during cross-examination of a defense witness, whereas in *Estelle* it had been elicited during the prosecution's affirmative case; and that in *Estelle* it was clear at the time of the psychiatric examination that future dangerousness would be an issue at trial, which was not so in this case. The Court declined to say whether these distinctions affected the merits of the defendant's Fifth Amendment claim. It said only that, for purposes of the defendant's habeas corpus petition, it was not unreasonable for the lower court to conclude that they did.

Estelle v. Smith was *not* followed in Allen v. Illinois, 478 U.S. 364 (1986) (5–4), in which, collaterally to criminal charges, the state brought proceedings to have the petitioner declared a sexually dangerous person and committed. In those proceedings, he was ordered to submit to psychiatric examinations. The testimony of the psychiatrists was introduced at the trial to determine whether the petitioner should be committed, over his objection that their information had been obtained in violation of his privilege against compulsory self-incrimination. The Court upheld the order of commitment. It said that since the state's purpose is treatment and not punishment, sexually dangerous person proceedings are noncriminal in nature and the privilege is not involved, even though the proceedings are initiated only after criminal charges are brought and in many procedural respects resemble a criminal trial.

208. The courts have generally held that the results of lie-detector tests are too unreliable to be admissible in evidence, nor is testimony that the defendant was willing or unwilling to take a test admissible. See, however, United States v. Oliver, 525 F.2d 731 (8th Cir.1975), in which the court upheld the admission of test results over the defendant's objection, because, before submitting to the test, for which the government had paid on the defendant's motion, he had agreed to admission of the results whatever they might be. The court rejected the defendant's claim that he was compelled to agree to their admission as the condition of his motion being granted. Lie-detector tests are discussed at length in Commonwealth v. Juvenile (No. 1), 313 N.E.2d 120 (Mass.1974), in which a rule like the result in *Oliver* is approved. Fifteen years later, the Massachusetts court observed that its expectation that polygraphy would gain general scientific acceptance had not materialized, and it ruled that "polygraphic evidence, with or without pretest stipulation, is inadmissible in criminal trials . . . either for substantive purposes or for corroboration or impeachment of testimony." Commonwealth v. Mendes, 547 N.E.2d 35, 41 (Mass.1989) (cases in other jurisdictions cited). See also People v. Barbara, 255 N.W.2d 171 (Mich.1977), in which the court concluded that the results of a test should continue to be inadmissible at trial but may be considered by the court in a hearing on a motion for a new trial. Lie-detector tests are discussed in United States v. Scheffer, 523 U.S. 303 (1998) (8–1), holding that a provision of the Military Rules of Evidence that makes polygraph evidence inadmissible in court-martial proceedings does not unconstitutionally restrict the right to make a defense.

———

The Court's disposition of cases involving evidence obtained by various kinds of examinations of the defendant is based on its holding and analysis of the Fifth Amendment claim in Schmerber v. California, p. 355 above (which in turn relies heavily on phrases borrowed from Miranda v. Arizona, p. 417 below). The Court's holding is that "the privilege [against self-incrimination] protects an accused only from being compelled to testify against himself, or otherwise provide the State with evidence of a testimonial or communicative nature," p. 356 above. Apparently conceding that the distinction is not always clear-cut, the Court asserted nevertheless that it provides "a helpful framework for analysis," p. 358 above.

How helpful is it? (Does the Court itself make much use of it as an analytic tool in *Schmerber*?) Why should the government, in aid of a criminal prosecution, be allowed to require that a man exhibit himself before others or speak or write, to make an impression of lines on the tips of his fingers, and to extract blood, but not be able to require that he answer questions? (How much of a factor is the comparative reliability of the evidence obtained by each technique?) In all of the situations some degree of cooperation by the defendant is needed. Equally in all of them, that the defendant is "required" to cooperate does not necessarily mean that physical force can be used to overcome his refusal to do so. (But see note 197, p. 361 above.) What interest(s) of the defendant is invaded by compelled testimony but not the other practices? (The Court acknowledges that at least the extraction of blood involves the same "complex of values" as questioning, p. 357 above.) What is the relevance in this context of the distinction between testimonial (or communicative) and nontestimonial evidence? Is it clear what the distinction is?

What is the point of the Court's observation that Schmerber's "participation, except as a donor" was irrelevant to the results of the test. Since it was Schmerber's blood that was tested, his participation as a donor was altogether crucial. Why does the Court have a difficult time with lie detector tests? How does an involuntary physiological response, see p. 358 above, which reveals guilt or innocence differ from chemical analysis of one's blood which reveals guilt or innocence?

Would there be significant value in rules that applied more literally the policy that "the government seeking to punish an individual produce the evidence against him by its own independent labors," p. 357 above, and prohibited all "use" of the defendant to procure evidence against himself after he has been taken into custody?

Lineups

United States v. Wade
388 U.S. 218, 87 S.Ct. 1926, 18 L.Ed.2d 1149 (1967)

■ MR. JUSTICE BRENNAN delivered the opinion of the Court.

The question here is whether courtroom identifications of an accused at trial are to be excluded from evidence because the accused was exhibited to the witnesses before trial at a post-indictment lineup conducted for identification purposes without notice to and in the absence of the accused's appointed counsel.

The federally insured bank in Eustace, Texas, was robbed on September 21, 1964. A man with a small strip of tape on each side of his face entered the bank, pointed a pistol at the female cashier and the vice president, the only persons in the bank at the time, and forced them to fill a pillowcase with the bank's money. The man then drove away with an accomplice who had been waiting in a stolen car outside the bank. On March 23, 1965, an indictment was returned against respondent, Wade, and two others for conspiring to rob the bank, and against Wade and the accomplice for the robbery itself. Wade was arrested on April 2, and counsel was appointed to represent him on April 26. Fifteen days later an FBI agent, without notice to Wade's lawyer, arranged to have the two bank employees observe a lineup made up of Wade and five or six other prisoners and conducted in a courtroom of the local county courthouse. Each person in the line wore strips of tape such as allegedly worn by the robber and upon direction each said something like "put the money in the bag," the words allegedly uttered by the robber. Both bank employees identified Wade in the lineup as the bank robber.

At trial, the two employees, when asked on direct examination if the robber was in the courtroom, pointed to Wade. The prior lineup identification was then elicited from both employees on cross-examination. At the close of testimony, Wade's counsel moved for a judgment of acquittal or, alternatively, to strike the bank officials' courtroom identifications on the ground that conduct of the lineup, without notice to and in the absence of his appointed counsel, violated his Fifth Amendment privilege against self-incrimination and his Sixth Amendment right to the assistance of counsel. The motion was denied, and Wade was convicted. The Court of Appeals for the Fifth Circuit reversed the conviction and ordered a new trial at which the in-court identification evidence was to be excluded, holding that, though the lineup did not violate Wade's Fifth Amendment rights, "the lineup, held as it was, in the absence of counsel, already chosen to represent appellant, was a violation of his Sixth Amendment rights ..." 358 F.2d 557, 560. . . .

I.

Neither the lineup itself nor anything shown by this record that Wade was required to do in the lineup violated his privilege against self-incrimination. We have only recently reaffirmed that the privilege "protects an accused only from being compelled to testify against himself, or otherwise provide the State with evidence of a testimonial or communicative nature...." Schmerber v. California, 384 U.S. 757, 761. . . .

. . .

[I]t deserves emphasis that this case presents no question of the admissibility in evidence of anything Wade said or did at the lineup which implicates his privilege. The Government offered no such evidence as part of its case, and what came out about the lineup proceedings on Wade's cross-examination of the bank employees involved no violation of Wade's privilege.

II.

The fact that the lineup involved no violation of Wade's privilege against self-incrimination does not, however, dispose of his contention that the courtroom identifications should have been excluded because the lineup was conducted without notice to and in the absence of his counsel. Our rejection of the right to counsel claim in Schmerber rested on our conclusion in that case that "[n]o issue of counsel's ability to assist petitioner in respect of any rights he did possess is presented." 384 U.S., at 766. In contrast, in this case it is urged that the assistance of counsel at the lineup was indispensable to protect Wade's most basic right as a criminal defendant—his right to a fair trial at which the witnesses against him might be meaningfully cross-examined.

[The Sixth Amendment] reads: "In all criminal prosecutions, the accused shall enjoy the right . . . to have the Assistance of Counsel *for his defence*." (Emphasis supplied.) The plain wording of this guarantee thus encompasses counsel's assistance whenever necessary to assure a meaningful "defence."

. . .

[I]n addition to counsel's presence at trial, the accused is guaranteed that he need not stand alone against the State at any stage of the prosecution, formal or informal, in court or out, where counsel's absence might derogate from the accused's right to a fair trial. The security of that right is as much the aim of the right to counsel as it is of the other guarantees of the Sixth Amendment—the right of the accused to a speedy and public trial by an impartial jury, his right to be informed of the nature and cause of the accusation, and his right to be confronted with the witnesses against him and to have compulsory process for obtaining witnesses in his favor. The presence of counsel at such critical confrontations, as at the trial itself, operates to assure that the accused's interests will be protected consistently with our adversary theory of criminal prosecution. . . .

In sum . . . [we are required to] scrutinize any pretrial confrontation of the accused to determine whether the presence of his counsel is necessary to preserve the defendant's basic right to a fair trial as affected by his right meaningfully to cross-examine the witnesses against him and to have effective assistance of counsel at the trial itself. It calls upon us to analyze whether potential substantial prejudice to defendant's rights inheres in the particular confrontation and the ability of counsel to help avoid that prejudice.

III.

The Government characterizes the lineup as a mere preparatory step in the gathering of the prosecution's evidence, not different—for Sixth Amendment purposes—from various other preparatory steps, such as systematized or scientific analyzing of the accused's fingerprints, blood sample, clothing, hair, and the like. We think there are differences which preclude such stages being characterized as critical stages at which the accused has the right to the presence of his counsel. Knowledge of the techniques of science and technology is sufficiently available, and the variables in techniques few enough, that the accused has the opportunity for a meaningful confrontation of the Government's case at trial through the ordinary processes of cross-examination of the Government's expert witnesses and the presentation of the evidence of his own experts. The denial of a right to have his counsel present at such analyses does not therefore violate the Sixth Amendment; they are not critical stages since there is minimal risk that his counsel's absence at such stages might derogate from his right to a fair trial.

IV.

But the confrontation compelled by the State between the accused and the victim or witnesses to a crime to elicit identification evidence is peculiarly riddled with innumerable dangers and variable factors which might seriously, even crucially, derogate from a fair trial. The vagaries of eyewitness identification are well-known; the annals of criminal law are rife with instances of mistaken identification. . . . A major factor contributing to the high incidence of miscarriage of justice from mistaken identification has been the degree of suggestion inherent in the manner in which the prosecution presents the suspect to witnesses for pretrial identification. . . . Suggestion can be created intentionally or unintentionally in many subtle ways. And the dangers for the suspect are particularly grave when the witness' opportunity for observation was insubstantial, and thus his susceptibility to suggestion the greatest.

Moreover, "[i]t is a matter of common experience that, once a witness has picked out the accused at the line-up, he is not likely to go back on his word later on, so that in practice the issue of identity may (in the absence of other relevant evidence) for all practical purposes be determined there and then, before the trial."[6]

The pretrial confrontation for purpose of identification may take the form of a lineup, also known as an "identification parade" or "showup," as in the present case, or presentation of the suspect alone to the witness. . . . It is obvious that risks of suggestion attend either form of confrontation and increase the dangers inhering in eyewitness identification. But as is the case with secret interrogations, there is serious difficulty in depicting what transpires at lineups and other forms of identification confrontations. . . . For the same reasons, the defense can seldom reconstruct the manner and mode of lineup identification for judge or jury at trial. Those participating in a lineup with the accused may often be police officers; in any event, the participants' names are rarely recorded or divulged at trial. The impediments to an objective observation are increased when the victim is the witness. Lineups are prevalent in rape and robbery prosecutions and present a particular hazard that a victim's understandable outrage may excite vengeful or spiteful motives. In any event, neither witnesses nor line-up participants are apt to be alert for conditions prejudicial to the suspect. And if they were, it would likely be of scant benefit to the suspect since neither witnesses nor lineup participants are likely to be schooled in the detection of suggestive influences. Improper influences may go undetected by a suspect, guilty or not, who experiences the emotional tension which we might expect in one being confronted with potential accusers. Even when he does observe abuse, if he has a criminal record he may be reluctant to take the stand and open up the admission of prior convictions. Moreover, any protestations by the suspect of the fairness of the lineup made at trial are likely to be in vain; the jury's choice is between the accused's unsupported version and that of the police officers present. In short, the accused's inability effectively to reconstruct at trial any unfairness that occurred at the lineup may deprive him of his only opportunity meaningfully to attack the credibility of the witness' courtroom identification.

What facts have been disclosed in specific cases about the conduct of pretrial confrontations for identification illustrate both the potential for substantial prejudice to the accused at that stage and the need for its

---

6. Williams & Hammelmann, Identification Parades, Part I, [1963] Crim. L. Rev. 479, 482.

revelation at trial. . . . [S]tate reports, in the course of describing prior identifications admitted as evidence of guilt, reveal numerous instances of suggestive procedures, for example, that all in the lineup but the suspect were known to the identifying witness, that the other participants in a lineup were grossly dissimilar in appearance to the suspect, that only the suspect was required to wear distinctive clothing which the culprit allegedly wore, that the witness is told by the police that they have caught the culprit after which the defendant is brought before the witness alone or is viewed in jail, that the suspect is pointed out before or during a lineup, and that the participants in the lineup are asked to try on an article of clothing which fits only the suspect.

The potential for improper influence is illustrated by the circumstances, insofar as they appear, surrounding the prior identifications in the three cases we decide today. In the present case, the testimony of the identifying witnesses elicited on cross-examination revealed that those witnesses were taken to the courthouse and seated in the courtroom to await assembly of the lineup. The courtroom faced on a hallway observable to the witnesses through an open door. The cashier testified that she saw Wade "standing in the hall" within sight of an FBI agent. Five or six other prisoners later appeared in the hall. The vice president testified that he saw a person in the hall in the custody of the agent who "resembled the person that we identified as the one that had entered the bank."

The lineup in *Gilbert* [v. California, 388 U.S. 263 (1967)] was conducted in an auditorium in which some 100 witnesses to several alleged state and federal robberies charged to Gilbert made wholesale identifications of Gilbert as the robber in each other's presence, a procedure said to be fraught with dangers of suggestion. And the vice of suggestion created by the identification in *Stovall* [v. Denno, 388 U.S. 293 (1967)], was the presentation to the witness of the suspect alone handcuffed to police officers. It is hard to imagine a situation more clearly conveying the suggestion to the witness that the one presented is believed guilty by the police. . . .

The few cases that have surfaced therefore reveal the existence of a process attended with hazards of serious unfairness to the criminal accused and strongly suggest the plight of the more numerous defendants who are unable to ferret out suggestive influences in the secrecy of the confrontation. We do not assume that these risks are the result of police procedures intentionally designed to prejudice an accused. Rather we assume they derive from the dangers inherent in eyewitness identification and the suggestibility inherent in the context of the pretrial identification. . . .

Insofar as the accused's conviction may rest on a courtroom identification in fact the fruit of a suspect pretrial identification which the accused is helpless to subject to effective scrutiny at trial, the accused is deprived of that right of cross-examination which is an essential safeguard to his right to confront the witnesses against him. . . . And even though cross-examination is a precious safeguard to a fair trial, it cannot be viewed as an absolute assurance of accuracy and reliability. Thus in the present context, where so many variables and pitfalls exist, the first line of defense must be the prevention of unfairness and the lessening of the hazards of eyewitness identification at the lineup itself. The trial which might determine the accused's fate may well not be that in the courtroom but that at the pretrial confrontation, with the State aligned against the accused, the witness the sole jury, and the accused unprotected against the over-reaching, intentional or unintentional, and with little or no effective appeal from the judgment there rendered by the witness—"that's the man."

Since it appears that there is grave potential for prejudice, intentional or not, in the pretrial lineup, which may not be capable of reconstruction at trial, and since presence of counsel itself can often avert prejudice and assure a meaningful confrontation at trial, there can be little doubt that for Wade the post-indictment lineup was a critical stage of the prosecution at which he was "as much entitled to such aid [of counsel] . . . as at the trial itself." Powell v. Alabama, 287 U.S. 45, 57. Thus both Wade and his counsel should have been notified of the impending lineup, and counsel's presence should have been a requisite to conduct of the lineup, absent an "intelligent waiver." . . . No substantial countervailing policy consider-ations have been advanced against the requirement of the presence of counsel. Concern is expressed that the requirement will forestall prompt identifications and result in obstruction of the confrontations. As for the first, we note that in the two cases in which the right to counsel is today held to apply, counsel had already been appointed and no argument is made in either case that notice to counsel would have prejudicially delayed the confrontations. Moreover, we leave open the question whether the presence of substitute counsel might not suffice where notification and presence of the suspect's own counsel would result in prejudicial delay. And to refuse to recognize the right to counsel for fear that counsel will obstruct the course of justice is contrary to the basic assumptions upon which this Court has operated in Sixth Amendment cases. . . . In our view counsel can hardly impede legitimate law enforcement; on the contrary, for the reasons ex-pressed, law enforcement may be assisted by preventing the infiltration of taint in the prosecution's identification evidence. That result cannot help the guilty avoid conviction but can only help assure that the right man has been brought to justice.

Legislative or other regulations, such as those of local police depart-ments, which eliminate the risks of abuse and unintentional suggestion at lineup proceedings and the impediments to meaningful confrontation at trial may also remove the basis for regarding the stage as "critical." But neither Congress nor the federal authorities have seen fit to provide a solution. What we hold today "in no way creates a constitutional strait-jacket which will handicap sound efforts at reform, nor is it intended to have this effect." Miranda v. Arizona [384 U.S. 436 (1996)], at 467.

V.

We come now to the question whether the denial of Wade's motion to strike the courtroom identification by the bank witnesses at trial because of the absence of his counsel at the lineup required . . . the grant of a new trial at which such evidence is to be excluded. We do not think this disposition can be justified without first giving the Government the opportunity to establish by clear and convincing evidence that the in-court identifications were based upon observations of the suspect other than the lineup identification. . . . Where, as here, the admissibility of evidence of the lineup identification itself is not involved, a per se rule of exclusion of courtroom identification would be unjustified. . . . A rule limited solely to the exclusion of testimony concerning identification at the lineup itself, without regard to admissibility of the courtroom identification, would render the right to counsel an empty one. The lineup is most often used, as in the present case, to crystallize the witnesses' identification of the defendant for future reference. We have already noted that the lineup identification will have that effect. The State may then rest upon the witnesses' unequivocal courtroom identification, and not mention the pre-trial identification as part of the State's case at trial. Counsel is then in the predicament in which Wade's counsel found himself—realizing that possible unfairness at the lineup may be the sole means of attack upon the unequivocal courtroom identification, and having to probe in the dark in an attempt to discover and reveal unfairness, while bolstering the government witness' courtroom identification by bringing out and dwelling upon his prior identification. Since counsel's presence at the lineup would equip him to attack not only the lineup identification but the courtroom identification as well, limiting the impact of violation of the right to counsel to exclusion of evidence only of identification at the lineup itself disregards a critical element of that right.

We think it follows that the proper test to be applied in these situations is that quoted in Wong Sun v. United States, 371 U.S. 471, 488, " '[W]hether, granting establishment of the primary illegality, the evidence to which instant objection is made has been come at by exploitation of that illegality or instead by means sufficiently distinguishable to be purged of the primary taint.' Maguire, Evidence of Guilt 221 (1959)." . . . Application of this test in the present context requires consideration of various factors; for example, the prior opportunity to observe the alleged criminal act, the existence of any discrepancy between any pre-lineup description and the defendant's actual description, any identification prior to lineup of another person, the identification by picture of the defendant prior to the lineup, failure to identify the defendant on a prior occasion, and the lapse of time between the alleged act and the lineup identification. It is also relevant to consider those facts which, despite the absence of counsel, are disclosed concerning the conduct of the lineup.

. . .

[The Court concluded that the court of appeals had not applied the proper test, stated above, for exclusion of the in-court identifications and remanded the case for further proceedings.][7]

---

[7] Justice Clark wrote a brief concurring opinion. Justice Black wrote an opinion dissenting in part and concurring in part. Justice White also wrote an opinion dissenting in

209.   In an opinion dissenting in part and concurring in part in *Wade*, above, Justice Black said: "The 'tainted fruit' determination required by the Court involves more than considerable difficulty. I think it is practically impossible. How is a witness capable of probing the recesses of his mind to draw a sharp line between a courtroom identification due exclusively to an earlier lineup and a courtroom identification due to memory not based on the lineup? What kind of 'clear and convincing evidence' can the prosecution offer to prove upon what particular events memories resulting in an in-court identification rest?" 388 U.S. at 248. Justice White, dissenting in part and concurring in part, agreed that if the state wanted to free a courtroom identification from an earlier improperly obtained identification, it had "a heavy burden . . . and probably an impossible one. To all intents and purposes, courtroom identifications are barred if pretrial identifications have occurred without counsel being present." Id. at 251.

210.   Gilbert v. California, 388 U.S. 263 (1967), was decided with *Wade*. The Court there held that "a per se exclusionary rule" was applicable to testimony of an identification at a lineup that failed to meet the standards set in *Wade*; only such a rule, the Court said, "can be an effective sanction to assure that law enforcement authorities will respect the accused's constitutional right to the presence of his counsel at the critical lineup." Id. at 273.

211.   *Wade*'s requirement of the presence of counsel applies only to the actual confrontation between a witness and the accused, and not to a conference between the witness and the prosecutor following the confrontation. United States v. Bierey, 588 F.2d 620 (8th Cir.1978) (other cases cited).

212.   The defendant was arrested for car theft. He was assigned counsel and directed to appear for arraignment two weeks later. Before the arraignment, a detective who was investigating a robbery committed a month earlier learned that the defendant fit a description of one of the robbers. The detective arranged for a victim of the robbery to be present at the arraignment, and she identified the defendant, who was subsequently convicted of the robbery. The lawyer assigned to him for the car theft case was present at the arraignment when the identification was made. Did the defendant have any Sixth Amendment right to counsel in connection with the identification? See Boyd v. Henderson, 555 F.2d 56 (2d Cir.1977).

213.   Also decided with *Wade*, Stovall v. Denno, 388 U.S. 293 (1967), established that *Wade* would not be applied retroactively. The Court observed, however, that past convictions based on an identification could be attacked on the ground that the method by which identification of the defendant was obtained "was so unnecessarily suggestive and conducive to irreparable mistaken identification that he was denied due process of law."

part and concurring in part, which Justice Harlan and Justice Stewart joined. Justice Fortas wrote an opinion concurring in part and dissenting in part, which Chief Justice Warren and Justice Douglas joined; see note 205, p. 364 above.

Id. at 302. In *Stovall*, the Court found that the defendant, who had been brought alone to a hospital where he was identified by one of his victims, had not been denied due process in "the totality of the circumstances," particularly that "an immediate hospital confrontation was imperative," *id.*

The Court applied *Stovall* in Foster v. California, 394 U.S. 440 (1969), and concluded that the facts presented "a compelling example of unfair lineup procedures," *id.* at 442. The petitioner Foster and others were charged with the armed robbery of a Western Union office.

> Except for the robbers themselves, the only witness to the crime was Joseph David, the late night manager of the Western Union office. After Foster had been arrested, David was called to the police station to view a lineup. There were three men in the lineup. One was petitioner. He is a tall man; close to six feet in height. The other two men were short—five feet, five or six inches. Petitioner wore a leather jacket which David said was similar to the one he had seen underneath the coveralls worn by the robber. After seeing this lineup, David could not positively identify petitioner as the robber. He "thought" he was the man, but he was not sure. David then asked to speak to petitioner, and petitioner was brought into an office and sat across from David at a table. Except for prosecuting officials there was no one else in the room. Even after this one-to-one confrontation David still was uncertain whether petitioner was one of the robbers: "truthfully—I was not sure," he testified at trial. A week or 10 days later, the police arranged for David to view a second lineup. There were five men in that lineup. Petitioner was the only person in the second lineup who had appeared in the first lineup. This time David was "convinced" petitioner was the man.

> At trial, David testified to his identification of petitioner in the lineups, as summarized above. He also repeated his identification of petitioner in the courtroom. The only other evidence against petitioner which concerned the particular robbery with which he was charged was the testimony of the alleged accomplice Clay.

The Court concluded that "the pretrial confrontations clearly were so arranged as to make the resulting identifications virtually inevitable." Id. at 441–43.

The Court considered the standards that apply in such cases again, in Neil v. Biggers, 409 U.S. 188 (1972). It said:

> Some general guidelines emerge . . . as to the relationship between suggestiveness and misidentification. It is, first of all, apparent that the primary evil to be avoided is "a very substantial likelihood of irreparable misidentification." Simmons v. United States, 390 U.S., at 384. While the phrase was coined as a standard for determining whether an in-court identification would be admissible in the wake of a suggestive out-of-court identification, with the deletion of "irreparable" it serves equally well as a standard for the admissibility of testimony concerning the out-of-court identification itself. It is the

likelihood of misidentification which violates a defendant's right to due process, and it is this which was the basis of the exclusion of evidence in *Foster*. Suggestive confrontations are disapproved because they increase the likelihood of misidentification, and unnecessarily suggestive ones are condemned for the further reason that the increased chance of misidentification is gratuitous. But as *Stovall* makes clear, the admission of evidence of a showup without more does not violate due process.

What is less clear from our cases is whether . . . unnecessary suggestiveness alone requires the exclusion of evidence. While we are inclined to agree with the courts below that the police did not exhaust all possibilities in seeking persons physically comparable to respondent, we do not think that the evidence must therefore be excluded. The purpose of a strict rule barring evidence of unnecessarily suggestive confrontations would be to deter the police from using a less reliable procedure where a more reliable one may be available, not because in every instance the admission of evidence of such a confrontation offends due process.

Id. at 198–99.

In Manson v. Brathwaite, 432 U.S. 98, 114 (1977) (7–2), the Court reaffirmed that "reliability is the linchpin in determining the admissibility of identification testimony" under the Due Process Clause and that pretrial identification evidence obtained by an unnecessarily suggestive procedure need not be excluded automatically, The factors to be considered in determining reliability "include the opportunity of the witness to view the criminal at the time of the crime, the witness' degree of attention, the accuracy of his prior description of the criminal, the level of certainty demonstrated at the confrontation, and the time between the crime and the confrontation," against which "is to be weighed the corrupting effect of the suggestive identification itself." Id. See, e.g., United States v. Emanuele, 51 F.3d 1123 (3d Cir.1995) (witness's viewing of defendant outside courtroom in shackles and accompanied by marshals was impermissibly suggestive; subsequent identification of defendant in court violated due process); Thigpen v. Cory, 804 F.2d 893 (6th Cir.1986) (use of identification violated due process); Solomon v. Smith, 645 F.2d 1179 (2d Cir.1981) (use of identification violated due process and right to counsel).

————

Kirby v. Illinois

406 U.S. 682, 92 S.Ct. 1877, 32 L.Ed.2d 411 (1972)

■ MR. JUSTICE STEWART announced the judgment of the Court and an opinion in which THE CHIEF JUSTICE, MR. JUSTICE BLACKMUN, and MR. JUSTICE REHNQUIST join.

. . . In the present case we are asked to extend the *Wade–Gilbert* per se exclusionary rule to identification testimony based upon a police station showup that took place *before* the defendant had been indicted or otherwise formally charged with any criminal offense.

On February 21, 1968, a man named Willie Shard reported to the Chicago police that the previous day two men had robbed him on a Chicago street of a wallet containing, among other things, traveler's checks and a Social Security card. On February 22, two police officers stopped the petitioner and a companion, Ralph Bean, on West Madison Street in Chicago.[8] When asked for identification, the petitioner produced a wallet that contained three traveler's checks and a Social Security card, all bearing the name of Willie Shard. Papers with Shard's name on them were also found in Bean's possession. When asked to explain his possession of Shard's property, the petitioner first said that the traveler's checks were "play money," and then told the officers that he had won them in a crap game. The officers then arrested the petitioner and Bean and took them to a police station.

Only after arriving at the police station, and checking the records there, did the arresting officers learn of the Shard robbery. A police car was then dispatched to Shard's place of employment, where it picked up Shard and brought him to the police station. Immediately upon entering the room in the police station where the petitioner and Bean were seated at a table, Shard positively identified them as the men who had robbed him two days earlier. No lawyer was present in the room, and neither the petitioner nor Bean had asked for legal assistance, or been advised of any right to the presence of counsel.

More than six weeks later, the petitioner and Bean were indicted for the robbery of Willie Shard. Upon arraignment, counsel was appointed to represent them, and they pleaded not guilty. A pretrial motion to suppress Shard's identification testimony was denied, and at the trial Shard testified as a witness for the prosecution. In his testimony he described his identification of the two men at the police station on February 22, and identified them again in the courtroom as the men who had robbed him on February 20. He was cross-examined at length regarding the circumstances of his identification of the two defendants. . . . The jury found both defendants guilty, and the petitioner's conviction was affirmed on appeal. . . . The Illinois appellate court held that the admission of Shard's testimony was not error, relying upon an earlier decision of the Illinois Supreme Court . . . holding that the *Wade–Gilbert* per se exclusionary rule is not applicable to pre-indictment confrontations. We granted certiorari, limited to this question. . . .

---

8. The officers stopped the petitioner and his companion because they thought the petitioner was a man named Hampton, who was "wanted" in connection with an unrelated criminal offense. The legitimacy of this stop and the subsequent arrest is not before us.

I

We note at the outset that the constitutional privilege against compulsory self-incrimination is in no way implicated here. The Court emphatically rejected the claimed applicability of that constitutional guarantee in *Wade* itself. . . .

. . .

The *Wade–Gilbert* exclusionary rule, by contrast, stems from a quite different constitutional guarantee—the guarantee of the right to counsel contained in the Sixth and Fourteenth Amendments. Unless all semblance of principled constitutional adjudication is to be abandoned, therefore, it is to the decisions construing that guarantee that we must look in determining the present controversy.

In a line of constitutional cases in this Court stemming back to the Court's landmark opinion in Powell v. Alabama, 287 U.S. 45, it has been firmly established that a person's Sixth and Fourteenth Amendment right to counsel attaches only at or after the time that adversary judicial proceedings have been initiated against him. . . .

This is not to say that a defendant in a criminal case has a constitutional right to counsel only at the trial itself. The *Powell* case makes clear that the right attaches at the time of arraignment, and the Court has recently held that it exists also at the time of a preliminary hearing. . . . But the point is that, while members of the Court have differed as to existence of the right to counsel in the contexts of some of the above cases, *all* of those cases have involved points of time at or after the initiation of adversary judicial criminal proceedings—whether by way of formal charge, preliminary hearing, indictment, information, or arraignment.

The only seeming deviation from this long line of constitutional decisions was Escobedo v. Illinois, 378 U.S. 478. But *Escobedo* is not apposite here for two distinct reasons. First, the Court in retrospect perceived that the "prime purpose" of *Escobedo* was not to vindicate the constitutional right to counsel as such, but, like *Miranda*, "to guarantee full effectuation of the privilege against self-incrimination. . . ." Johnson v. New Jersey, 384 U.S. 719, 729. Secondly, and perhaps even more important for purely practical purposes, the Court has limited the holding of *Escobedo* to its own facts . . . and those facts are not remotely akin to the facts of the case before us.

The initiation of judicial criminal proceedings is far from a mere formalism. It is the starting point of our whole system of adversary criminal justice. For it is only then that the government has committed itself to prosecute, and only then that the adverse positions of government and defendant have solidified. It is then that a defendant finds himself faced with the prosecutorial forces of organized society, and immersed in the intricacies of substantive and procedural criminal law. It is this point, therefore, that marks the commencement of the "criminal prosecutions" to which alone the explicit guarantees of the Sixth Amendment are applicable. . . .

In this case we are asked to import into a routine police investigation an absolute constitutional guarantee historically and rationally applicable only after the onset of formal prosecutorial proceedings. We decline to do so. Less than a year after *Wade* and *Gilbert* were decided, the Court explained the rule of those decisions as follows: "The rationale of those cases was that an accused is entitled to counsel at any 'critical stage of the *prosecution*,' and that a post-indictment lineup is such a 'critical stage.'" (Emphasis supplied.) Simmons v. United States, 390 U.S. 377, 382–383. We decline to depart from that rationale today by imposing a per se exclusionary rule upon testimony concerning an identification that took place long before the commencement of any prosecution whatever.

II

What has been said is not to suggest that there may not be occasions during the course of a criminal investigation when the police do abuse identification procedures. Such abuses are not beyond the reach of the Constitution. As the Court pointed out in *Wade* itself, it is always necessary to "scrutinize *any* pretrial confrontation...." 388 U.S., at 227. The Due Process Clause of the Fifth and Fourteenth Amendments forbids a lineup that is unnecessarily suggestive and conducive to irreparable mistaken identification....[9] When a person has not been formally charged with a criminal offense, *Stovall* strikes the appropriate constitutional balance between the right of a suspect to be protected from prejudicial procedures and the interest of society in the prompt and purposeful investigation of an unsolved crime.

The judgment is affirmed.[10]

-----

214. The question left open in *Kirby*, whether there had been a denial of due process in the particular circumstances, was answered in the negative, in United States ex rel. Kirby v. Sturges, 510 F.2d 397 (7th Cir.1975). The court concluded that although the identification procedure used was unnecessarily suggestive, nothing more than "sloppy" police work had been involved and that the identification was sufficiently reliable. See also United States v. Oreto, 37 F.3d 739 (1st Cir.1994) (in-court witnesses were told where defendants were sitting prior to identification; identification procedure, although improper, did not require reversal).

215. The Due Process Clause does not invariably require a hearing outside the presence of the jury on the admissibility of identification evidence that the defendant claims was obtained improperly. While such a

---

9. In view of our limited grant of certiorari, we do not consider whether there might have been a deprivation of due process in the particularized circumstances of this case. That question remains open for inquiry in a federal habeas corpus proceeding.

[10] Chief Justice Burger wrote a brief concurring opinion. Justice Powell concurred in the result. Justice Brennan wrote a dissenting opinion which Justice Douglas and Justice Marshall joined. Justice White also wrote a dissenting opinion.

hearing may often be advisable and sometimes constitutionally required, there is no rule requiring such a hearing in every case. The Due Process Clause does not require "the abandonment of the time-honored process of cross-examination as the device best suited to determine the trustworthiness of testimonial evidence." Watkins v. Sowders, 449 U.S. 341, 349 (1981) (7–2).

216. The problem of identification of the defendant in court, when there is typically no lineup and the defendant is seated next to defense counsel, is discussed in United States v. Archibald, 734 F.2d 938, modified, 756 F.2d 223 (2d Cir.1984). The court held that despite the traditional use of in-court identifications, the circumstances may be unduly suggestive and that upon a proper request by the defendant the trial court should take steps to ensure a fair identification.

217. *Wade*, p. 369 above, rather than *Kirby*, was applied to an identification of the defendant by the victim of a rape, at a preliminary hearing at which the defendant was not represented by counsel. At that point, "adversary judicial criminal proceedings" against the defendant having begun, *Wade* required the exclusion at trial of evidence of the earlier identification. Moore v. Illinois, 434 U.S. 220 (1977).

Cf. McGee v. Estelle, 625 F.2d 1206 (5th Cir.1980), holding that the adversary process is *not* begun by an appearance before a magistrate, following a warrantless arrest, for the sole purpose of advising the defendant of his rights. At the time of the appearance, prosecuting authorities were still unaware of the arrest. The court held that *Kirby*, not *Wade*, was applicable to a lineup following the appearance.

Reiterating that "the right to counsel does not attach until the initiation of adversary judicial proceedings," the Court held that prisoners were not entitled to the appointment of counsel while they were in administrative detention following a prison proceeding at which it was determined that they were involved in crimes committed in the prison. Assuming that the detention was analogous to an arrest, the Court observed that the right to counsel does not attach at the time of arrest. The right to a speedy trial and the guarantee of due process, the Court noted, concern different protections from the right to counsel. United States v. Gouveia, 467 U.S. 180 (1984) (8–1).

218.

> The present case . . . involves an immediate on-the-scene confrontation at 5 o'clock in the morning when there would necessarily be a long delay in summoning appellant's counsel, or a substitute counsel, to observe a formal lineup. Such delay may not only cause the detention of an innocent suspect; it may also diminish the reliability of any identification obtained, thus defeating a principal purpose of the counsel requirement.

> Unquestionably, confrontations in which a single suspect is viewed in the custody of the police are highly suggestive. Whatever the police

actually say to the viewer, it must be apparent to him that they think they have caught the villain. Doubtless a man seen in handcuffs or through the grill of a police wagon looks more like a crook than the same man standing at ease and at liberty. There may also be unconscious or overt pressures on the witness to cooperate with the police by confirming their suspicions. And the viewer may have been emotionally unsettled by the experience of the fresh offense.

Yet, on the other hand, recognition of a person or face would seem to be as much the product of a subjective mental image as of articulable, consciously remembered characteristics. A man may see clearly in his "mind's eye" a face or a figure which he is hard put to describe adequately in words. Though the image of an "unforgettable face" may occasionally linger without any translation into words, photographic recall is most often ephemeral. Vivid in the flash of direct observation, it fades rapidly with time. And the conscious attempt to separate the ensemble impression into particular verbalized features, in order to preserve some recollection, may well distort the original accurate image so that it is the verbalized characteristics which are remembered and not the face or the man.

Balancing all the doubts left by the mysteries of human perception and recognition, it appears that prompt confrontations in circumstances like those of this case will "if anything promote fairness, by assuring reliability...."[11]

Russell v. United States, 408 F.2d 1280, 1283–84 (D.C.Cir.1969). See Frank v. Blackburn, 605 F.2d 910 (5th Cir.1979), upholding an on-scene, one-on-one confrontation between a witness and a robber, following his arrest within a half hour of the crime.

Dissenting in *Kirby*, p. 378 above, Justice Brennan observed: "In the setting of a police station squad room where all present except petitioner and Bean were police officers, the danger was quite real that Shard's understandable resentment might lead him too readily to agree with the police that the pair under arrest, and the only persons exhibited to him, were indeed the robbers. . . . The State had no case without Shard's identification testimony, and safeguards against that consequence were therefore of critical importance. Shard's testimony itself demonstrates the necessity for such safeguards. On direct examination, Shard identified petitioner and Bean not as the alleged robbers on trial in the courtroom, but as the pair he saw at the police station." 406 U.S. at 700.

219. Photograph identifications. In Simmons v. United States, 390 U.S. 377 (1968), another aspect of which is considered in note 150 p. 278 above, one day after a bank robbery FBI agents showed photographs of two suspects to eyewitnesses. One of the suspects was identified in the photographs, which were mostly group photographs of the two suspects and others. At trial the eyewitnesses identified the defendant whose photograph they had identified earlier as one of the robbers. The Court rejected his

11. Wise v. United States, 383 F.2d at 209 [D.C.Cir.1967].

claim that the photograph identification procedure "was so unduly prejudiced as fatally to taint his conviction."

It must be recognized that improper employment of photographs by police may sometimes cause witnesses to err in identifying criminals. A witness may have obtained only a brief glimpse of a criminal, or may have seen him under poor conditions. Even if the police subsequently follow the most correct photographic identification procedures and show him the pictures of a number of individuals without indicating whom they suspect, there is some danger that the witness may make an incorrect identification. This danger will be increased if the police display to the witness only the picture of a single individual who generally resembles the person he saw, or if they show him the pictures of several persons among which the photograph of a single such individual recurs or is in some way emphasized. The chance of misidentification is also heightened if the police indicate to the witness that they have other evidence that one of the persons pictured committed the crime. Regardless of how the initial misidentification comes about, the witness thereafter is apt to retain in his memory the image of the photograph rather than of the person actually seen, reducing the trustworthiness of subsequent lineup or courtroom identification.

Despite the hazards of initial identification by photograph, this procedure has been used widely and effectively in criminal law enforcement, from the standpoint both of apprehending offenders and of sparing innocent suspects the ignominy of arrest by allowing eyewitnesses to exonerate them through scrutiny of photographs. The danger that use of the technique may result in convictions based on misidentification may be substantially lessened by a course of cross-examination at trial which exposes to the jury the method's potential for error. We are unwilling to prohibit its employment, either in the exercise of our supervisory power or, still less, as a matter of constitutional requirement. Instead, we hold that each case must be considered on its own facts, and that convictions based on eyewitness identification at trial following a pretrial identification by photograph will be set aside on that ground only if the photographic identification procedure was so impermissibly suggestive as to give rise to a very substantial likelihood of irreparable misidentification.

Id. at 383–84.

Among the factors on which the Court relied for its conclusion that the identification was not unduly prejudicial were: the need for prompt police action, the good opportunity for the witnesses to observe the defendant during the robbery, the freshness of their memory one day after the robbery, the lack of improper suggestion in the procedure (at least six photographs used, mostly group photographs, witnesses alone when shown photographs), and subsequent confirmation of the identifications. Id. at 385–86.

The defendant in *Simmons* had not been arrested when the photograph identifications were made. Relying on the historical construction of the right to counsel, the Court concluded in United States v. Ash, 413 U.S. 300 (1973) (6–3), that *Wade* did not apply to post-indictment photograph identifications. The Court said that photographic display was one of the variety of activities within the adversary system for which "the ethical responsibility of the prosecutor" was the "primary safeguard against abuses" and which were governed by the general rules and procedures of the system, including confrontation at trial. In *Ash*, almost three years after the crime and shortly before the trial was to begin, the prosecutor showed photographs including the photograph of the defendant to trial witnesses, as part of his preparation for trial. The Court did not consider whether the display violated the due process standard of *Simmons*.

The government's practice of not preserving photographic spreads shown to undercover agents for identification of suspects was sharply criticized in United States v. Sanchez, 603 F.2d 381 (2d Cir.1979).

220. Is it a denial of equal protection of the laws or otherwise constitutionally impermissible for an accused who cannot obtain his release on bail following indictment to be placed in a lineup, although other accused persons who are free on bail are not placed in a lineup? Does it matter whether the lineup concerns the crime for which the accused has been indicted or some other crime(s) of which he is suspected? See United States v. Jones, 403 F.2d 498 (7th Cir.1968); Rigney v. Hendrick, 355 F.2d 710 (3d Cir.1965). In United States v. Scarpellino, 296 F.Supp. 269, 272 (D.Minn.1969), the court observed that "one released on bail or personal recognizance can by court order, if a request from the United States Attorney is not honored, be required to return to jail or to the police department or elsewhere within reason and for a limited time to appear in a lineup." What limitations are there on such a practice? Compare Beightol v. Kunowski, 486 F.2d 293 (3d Cir.1973).

In United States v. Hammond, 419 F.2d 166 (4th Cir.1969), the district court ordered the defendant, who had been indicted for bank robbery and was detained in jail, to participate in reasonably scheduled lineups and "to wear any clothing or items, such as a false goatee; to speak any words; to walk in any manner; or to take any physical stance that may be required." The defendant refused. His conviction for criminal contempt was upheld. In Higgins v. Wainwright, 424 F.2d 177 (5th Cir.1970) (voice lineup), and United States v. Parhms, 424 F.2d 152 (9th Cir.1970), the prosecutor was allowed to bring before the jury the defendant's refusal to participate in a lineup.

How much force can be used to make an arrested person participate in a lineup? See Appeal of Maguire, 571 F.2d 675 (1st Cir.1978), upholding an order authorizing the use of "such reasonable force as is reasonably necessary" to compel a witness, then serving a long prison sentence, to appear in a lineup and submit to fingerprinting before a grand jury. See generally note 197, p. 361 above.

United States v. Dionisio

410 U.S. 1, 93 S.Ct. 764, 35 L.Ed.2d 67 (1973)

■ MR. JUSTICE STEWART delivered the opinion of the Court.

A special grand jury was convened in the Northern District of Illinois in February 1971, to investigate possible violations of federal criminal statutes relating to gambling. In the course of its investigation, the grand jury received in evidence certain voice recordings that had been obtained pursuant to court orders.

The grand jury subpoenaed approximately 20 persons, including the respondent Dionisio, seeking to obtain from them voice exemplars for comparison with the recorded conversations that had been received in evidence. Each witness was advised that he was a potential defendant in a criminal prosecution. Each was asked to examine a transcript of an intercepted conversation, and to go to a nearby office of the United States Attorney to read the transcript into a recording device. The witnesses were advised that they would be allowed to have their attorneys present when they read the transcripts. Dionisio and other witnesses refused to furnish the voice exemplars, asserting that these disclosures would violate their rights under the Fourth and Fifth Amendments.

The Government then filed separate petitions in the United States District Court to compel Dionisio and the other witnesses to furnish the voice exemplars to the grand jury. The petitions stated that the exemplars were "essential and necessary" to the grand jury investigation, and that they would "be used solely as a standard of comparison in order to determine whether or not the witness is the person whose voice was intercepted...."

Following a hearing, the District Judge rejected the witnesses' constitutional arguments and ordered them to comply with the grand jury's request. He reasoned that voice exemplars, like handwriting exemplars or fingerprints, were not testimonial or communicative evidence, and that consequently the order to produce them would not compel any witness to testify against himself. The District Judge also found that there would be no Fourth Amendment violation, because the grand jury subpoena did not itself violate the Fourth Amendment, and the order to produce the voice exemplars would involve no unreasonable search and seizure within the proscription of that Amendment. . . . When Dionisio persisted in his refusal to respond to the grand jury's directive, the District Court adjudged him in civil contempt and ordered him committed to custody until he obeyed the court order, or until the expiration of 18 months.

The Court of Appeals for the Seventh Circuit reversed. 442 F.2d 276. It agreed with the District Court in rejecting the Fifth Amendment claims, but concluded that to compel the voice recordings would violate the Fourth Amendment. In the court's view, the grand jury was "seeking to obtain the voice exemplars of the witnesses by the use of its subpoena powers because probable cause did not exist for their arrest or for some other, less unusual, method of compelling the production of the exemplars." Id., at 280. The court found that the Fourth Amendment applied to grand jury process, and that "under the fourth amendment law enforcement officials may not compel the production of physical evidence absent a showing of the reasonableness of the seizure. Davis v. Mississippi, 394 U.S. 721...." Ibid.

In *Davis* this Court held that it was error to admit the petitioner's fingerprints into evidence at his trial for rape, because they had been obtained during a police detention following a lawless wholesale roundup of the petitioner and more than 20 other youths. Equating the procedures followed by the grand jury in the present case to the fingerprint detentions in *Davis*, the Court of Appeals reasoned that "[t]he dragnet effect here, where approximately twenty persons were subpoenaed for purposes of identification, has the same invidious effect on fourth amendment rights as the practice condemned in *Davis*." Id., at 281.

[W]e granted the Government's petition for certiorari. . . .

I

The Court of Appeals correctly rejected the contention that the compelled production of the voice exemplars would violate the Fifth Amendment. It has long been held that the compelled display of identifiable physical characteristics infringes no interest protected by the privilege against compulsory self-incrimination. . . .

. . .

. . . The voice recordings were to be used solely to measure the physical properties of the witnesses' voices, not for the testimonial or communicative content of what was to be said.

II

The Court of Appeals held that the Fourth Amendment required a preliminary showing of reasonableness before a grand jury witness could be compelled to furnish a voice exemplar, and that in this case the proposed "seizures" of the voice exemplars would be unreasonable because of the large number of witnesses summoned by the grand jury and directed to produce such exemplars. We disagree.

. . .

As the Court made clear in *Schmerber* [v. California, 384 U.S. 757 (1966)], the obtaining of physical evidence from a person involves a potential Fourth Amendment violation at two different levels—the "seizure" of the "person" necessary to bring him into contact with government agents . . . and the subsequent search for and seizure of the evidence. . . . The constitutionality of the compulsory production of exemplars from a grand jury witness necessarily turns on the same dual inquiry—whether either the initial compulsion of the person to appear before the grand jury, or the subsequent directive to make a voice recording is an unreasonable "seizure" within the meaning of the Fourth Amendment.

It is clear that a subpoena to appear before a grand jury is not a "seizure" in the Fourth Amendment sense, even though that summons may be inconvenient or burdensome. Last Term we again acknowledged what has long been recognized, that "[c]itizens generally are not constitutionally immune from grand jury subpoenas. . . ." Branzburg v. Hayes, 408 U.S. 665, 682. . . .

These are recent reaffirmations of the historically grounded obligation of every person to appear and give his evidence before the grand jury. . . .

The compulsion exerted by a grand jury subpoena differs from the seizure effected by an arrest or even an investigative "stop" in more than civic obligation. For, as Judge Friendly wrote for the Court of Appeals for the Second Circuit:

> The latter is abrupt, is effected with force or the threat of it and often in demeaning circumstances, and, in the case of arrest, results in a record involving social stigma. A subpoena is served in the same manner as other legal process; it involves no stigma whatever; if the time for appearance is inconvenient, this can generally be altered; and it remains at all times under the control and supervision of a court.

United States v. Doe (Schwartz) 457 F.2d [895 (2d Cir.1972)], at 898. Thus, the Court of Appeals for the Seventh Circuit correctly recognized in a case subsequent to the one now before us, that a "grand jury subpoena to testify is not that kind of governmental intrusion on privacy against which the Fourth Amendment affords protection, once the Fifth Amendment is satisfied." Fraser v. United States, 452 F.2d 616, 620. . . .

This case is thus quite different from Davis v. Mississippi, supra. . . . For in *Davis* it was the initial seizure—the lawless dragnet detention—that violated the Fourth and Fourteenth Amendments, not the taking of the fingerprints. . . . *Davis* is plainly inapposite to a case where the initial restraint does not itself infringe the Fourth Amendment.

This is not to say that a grand jury subpoena is some talisman that dissolves all constitutional protections. . . . Grand juries are subject to judicial control and subpoenas to motions to quash. . . .

But we are here faced with no such constitutional infirmities in the subpoena to appear before the grand jury or in the order to make the voice recordings. There is, as we have said, no valid Fifth Amendment claim. There was no order to produce private books and papers, and no sweeping subpoena *duces tecum*. . . .

The Court of Appeals found critical significance in the fact that the grand jury had summoned approximately 20 witnesses to furnish voice exemplars. We think that fact is basically irrelevant to the constitutional issues here. The grand jury may have been attempting to identify a number of voices on the tapes in evidence, or it might have summoned the 20 witnesses in an effort to identify one voice. But whatever the case, "[a] grand jury's investigation is not fully carried out until every available clue has been run down and all witnesses examined in every proper way to find if a crime has been committed. . . ." United States v. Stone, 429 F.2d 138, 140. . . . The grand jury may well find it desirable to call numerous witnesses in the course of an investigation. It does not follow that each witness may resist a subpoena on the ground that too many witnesses have been called. Neither the order to Dionisio to appear, nor the order to make a voice recording, was rendered unreasonable by the fact that many others were subjected to the same compulsion.

But the conclusion that Dionisio's compulsory appearance before the grand jury was not an unreasonable "seizure" is the answer to only the first part of the Fourth Amendment inquiry here. Dionisio argues that the grand jury's subsequent directive to make the voice recording was itself an infringement of his rights under the Fourth Amendment. We cannot accept that argument.

In Katz v. United States, [389 U.S. 347 (1967)], we said that the Fourth Amendment provides no protection for what "a person knowingly exposes to the public, even in his own home or office. . . ." 389 U.S., at 351. The physical characteristics of a person's voice, its tone and manner, as opposed to the content of a specific conversation, are constantly exposed to the public. Like a man's facial characteristics, or handwriting, his voice is repeatedly produced for others to hear. No person can have a reasonable expectation that others will not know the sound of his voice, any more than he can reasonably expect that his face will be a mystery to the world. . . .

The required disclosure of a person's voice is thus immeasurably further removed from the Fourth Amendment protection than was the intrusion into the body effected by the blood extraction in *Schmerber*. . . . Similarly, a seizure of voice exemplars does not involve the "severe, though brief, intrusion upon cherished personal security," effected by the "pat-down" in *Terry* [v. Ohio, 392 U.S. 1 (1968)]—"surely . . . an annoying, frightening, and perhaps humiliating experience." Terry v. Ohio, 392 U.S., at 24–25. Rather, this is like the fingerprinting in *Davis*, where, though the initial dragnet detentions were constitutionally impermissible, we noted that the fingerprinting itself "involves none of the probing into an individual's private life and thoughts that marks an interrogation or search." Davis v. Mississippi, 394 U.S., at 727. . . .

Since neither the summons to appear before the grand jury nor its directive to make a voice recording infringed upon any interest protected by the Fourth Amendment, there was no justification for requiring the grand jury to satisfy even the minimal requirement of "reasonableness" imposed by the Court of Appeals. . . . A grand jury has broad investigative powers to determine whether a crime has been committed and who had committed it. The jurors may act on tips, rumors, evidence offered by the prosecutor, or their own personal knowledge. . . . No grand jury witness is "entitled to set limits to the investigation that the grand jury may conduct." Blair v. United States, 250 U.S., at 282. And a sufficient basis for an indictment may only emerge at the end of the investigation when all the evidence has been received. . . . Since Dionisio raised no valid Fourth Amendment claim, there is no more reason to require a preliminary showing of reasonableness here than there would be in the case of any witness who, despite the lack of any constitutional or statutory privilege, declined to answer a question or comply with a grand jury request. Neither the

Constitution nor our prior cases justify any such interference with grand jury proceedings.

The Fifth Amendment guarantees that no civilian may be brought to trial for an infamous crime "unless on a presentment or indictment of a Grand Jury." This constitutional guarantee presupposes an investigative body "acting independently of either prosecuting attorney or judge," Stirone v. United States, 361 U.S. 212, 218, whose mission is to clear the innocent, no less than to bring to trial those who may be guilty. Any holding that would saddle a grand jury with minitrials and preliminary showings would assuredly impede its investigation and frustrate the public's interest in the fair and expeditious administration of the criminal laws. . . . The grand jury may not always serve its historic role as a protective bulwark standing solidly between the ordinary citizen and an overzealous prosecutor, but if it is even to approach the proper performance of its constitutional mission, it must be free to pursue its investigations unhindered by external influence or supervision so long as it does not trench upon the legitimate rights of any witness called before it.

Since the Court of Appeals found an unreasonable search and seizure where none existed, and imposed a preliminary showing of reasonableness where none was required, its judgment is reversed and this case is remanded to that court for further proceedings consistent with this opinion. . . . [12]

---

221.   In a companion case, United States v. Mara, 410 U.S. 19 (1973) (6–3), the Court extended the same reasoning used in *Dionisio* to a subpoena to furnish handwriting exemplars to a grand jury.

222.   The appellant was a suspect in a bank robbery. The grand jury investigating the robbery subpoenaed him to appear in a lineup. When he failed to appear, he was found in contempt, and he appealed. The court of appeals, rejecting the appellant's effort to distinguish *Dionisio* and *Mara*, above, affirmed.

Appellant argues . . . that there is a crucial difference between a lineup and the identification procedures at issue in *Dionisio* and *Mara*: a lineup is inherently a less reliable identification procedure than the providing of voice and handwriting exemplars. . . . But as neither the inconvenience of responding to the grand jury's directive nor the forced display of physical characteristics such as one's voice or face make the challenged order a "seizure" within the meaning of the fourth amendment, considerations such as the reliability of the identification procedure are largely irrelevant to whether the grand jury directive to appear violates the fourth amendment. It is simply immaterial to the constitutional analysis whether a lineup is less "scientific" than finger-

---

[12] Justice Brennan wrote an opinion concurring in part and dissenting in part.   Justice Douglas and Justice Marshall wrote dissenting opinions.

printing, voice and handwriting comparison, or other identification procedures. As the Court recognized in *Dionisio*, a grand jury's investigatory powers include the right to "act on tips, rumors, evidence offered by the prosecutor, or their own personal knowledge." 410 U.S. at 15. . . . And a lineup is a well-accepted investigatory method, far preferable to individual confrontations. Indeed, it is by now well established that, whenever possible, witnesses should view suspects in lineups rather than individually to avoid the misidentification that can result from a lone confrontation. . . . To deny the grand jury the power to require a suspect's participation in a lineup is therefore to place the Government in a dilemma: if it is to let the witness view the suspect at all, it must do so under circumstances which courts have repeatedly criticized as unduly suggestive. A lineup does not pose the same potential for unfairness, particularly where the suspect's counsel is present. . . . We note that the Government wisely intends to allow appellant's counsel to be present, and hence we are not confronted with whether it is required to do so by the sixth amendment. . . . We expressly refrain from deciding that forcing a suspect to appear in a lineup without tendering the right to counsel would be constitutional.

The power to compel appearance at a lineup is, it is true, subject to possible oppressive misuse. A fingerprint or handwriting or voice exemplar need only be obtained once. There is no occasion, as with a lineup, to require the witness to return and give his evidence in other investigations. . . . One can imagine the temptation to call certain individuals with known criminal proclivities to appear repeatedly in lineups, and the absence of a standard of probable cause or reasonable suspicion adds to the potential for abuse. . . . But many investigatory powers of the grand jury are subject to abuse, and the remedy for this problem, if it should occur, is pointed out in *Dionisio*. . . . The oppressive use of orders to appear in lineups can and should be dealt with by refusal of a court to enforce the order. Here there is no suggestion of oppressive use and no need to interfere with the grand jury's power to issue the order. We conclude, therefore, that subject to the district court's continuing power and duty to prevent misuse, the grand jury is empowered to require a suspect to appear at a lineup.

In re Melvin, 550 F.2d 674, 676–77 (1st Cir.1977).

See United States v. Ferri, 778 F.2d 985 (3d Cir.1985) (grand jury subpoena to appear for ink printing of feet and shoes upheld); In re Grand Jury Proceedings (Mills), 686 F.2d 135 (3d Cir.1982) (grand jury order to furnish samples of facial and scalp hair upheld); In re Pantojas, 639 F.2d 822 (1st Cir.1980) (grand jury order to appear in lineup upheld). See also United States v. Smith, 687 F.2d 147 (6th Cir.1982) ("voluntary" production of handwriting exemplar in lieu of grand jury appearance upheld).

223. Davis v. Mississippi, 394 U.S. 721 (1969). Over a period of about ten days, the police took the defendant and at least 23 other youths to police headquarters and fingerprinted them in connection with investigation of a rape that had just occurred. The defendant did not voluntarily submit to the fingerprinting nor did the police have probable cause for his arrest at that time. Later, still without the defendant's consent and without probable cause for his arrest, the police fingerprinted him again and used the fingerprints against him at his trial for rape. Holding that none of the fingerprints had been validly obtained, the Court reversed the defendant's conviction.

The Court said:

> Detentions for the sole purpose of obtaining fingerprints are no less subject to the constraints of the Fourth Amendment. It is arguable, however, that because of the unique nature of the fingerprinting process, such detentions might, under narrowly defined circumstances, be found to comply with the Fourth Amendment even though there is no probable cause in the traditional sense. . . . Detention for fingerprinting may constitute a much less serious intrusion upon personal security than other types of police searches and detentions. Fingerprinting involves none of the probing into an individual's private life and thoughts which marks an interrogation or search. Nor can fingerprint detention be employed repeatedly to harass any individual, since the police need only one set of each person's prints. Furthermore, fingerprinting is an inherently more reliable and effective crime-solving tool than eyewitness identifications or confessions and is not subject to such abuses as the improper line-up and the "third degree." Finally, because there is no danger of destruction of fingerprints, the limited detention need not come unexpectedly or at an inconvenient time. For this same reason, the general requirement that the authorization of a judicial officer be obtained in advance of detention would seem not to admit of any exception in the fingerprinting context.

> We have no occasion in this case, however, to determine whether the requirements of the Fourth Amendment could be met by narrowly circumscribed procedures for obtaining, during the course of a criminal investigation, the fingerprints of individuals for whom there is no probable cause to arrest. For it is clear that no attempt was made here to employ procedures which might comply with the requirements of the Fourth Amendment. . . .

Id. at 727–28.

Hayes v. Florida

470 U.S. 811, 105 S.Ct. 1643, 84 L.Ed.2d 705 (1985)

■ JUSTICE WHITE delivered the opinion of the Court.

The issue before us in this case is whether the Fourth Amendment to the Constitution of the United States, applicable to the States by virtue of the Fourteenth Amendment, was properly applied by the District Court of Appeal of Florida, Second District, to allow police to transport a suspect to the station house for fingerprinting, without his consent and without probable cause or prior judicial authorization.

A series of burglary-rapes occurred in Punta Gorda, Florida, in 1980. Police found latent fingerprints on the doorknob of the bedroom of one of the victims, fingerprints they believed belonged to the assailant. The police also found a herringbone pattern tennis shoe print near the victim's front porch. Although they had little specific information to tie petitioner Hayes to the crime, after police interviewed him along with 30 to 40 other men who generally fit the description of the assailant, the investigators came to consider petitioner a principal suspect. They decided to visit petitioner's home to obtain his fingerprints or, if he was uncooperative, to arrest him. They did not seek a warrant authorizing this procedure.

Arriving at petitioner's house, the officers spoke to petitioner on his front porch. When he expressed reluctance voluntarily to accompany them to the station for fingerprinting, one of the investigators explained that they would therefore arrest him. Petitioner, in the words of the investigator, then "blurted out" that he would rather go with the officers to the station than be arrested. App. 20. While the officers were on the front porch, they also seized a pair of herringbone pattern tennis shoes in plain view.

Petitioner was then taken to the station house, where he was fingerprinted. When police determined that his prints matched those left at the scene of the crime, petitioner was placed under formal arrest. Before trial, petitioner moved to suppress the fingerprint evidence, claiming it was the fruit of an illegal detention. The trial court denied the motion and admitted the evidence without expressing a reason. Petitioner was convicted of the burglary and sexual battery committed at the scene where the latent fingerprints were found.

. . .

We agree with petitioner that Davis v. Mississippi, 394 U.S. 721 (1969), requires reversal of the judgment below. . . .

Here, as in *Davis*, there was no probable cause to arrest, no consent to the journey to the police station and no judicial authorization for such a detention for fingerprinting purposes. Unless later cases have undermined *Davis* or we now disavow that decision, the judgment below must be reversed.

None of our later cases have undercut the holding in *Davis* that transportation to and investigative detention at the station house without probable cause or judicial authorization together violate the Fourth Amendment. . . .

Nor are we inclined to forswear *Davis*. There is no doubt that at some point in the investigative process, police procedures can qualitatively and quantitatively be so intrusive with respect to a suspect's freedom of movement and privacy interests as to trigger the full protection of the Fourth and Fourteenth Amendments. . . . And our view continues to be that the line is crossed when the police, without probable cause or a warrant, forcibly remove a person from his home or other place in which he is entitled to be and transport him to the police station, where he is detained, although briefly, for investigative purposes. We adhere to the view that such seizures, at least where not under judicial supervision, are sufficiently like arrests to invoke the traditional rule that arrests may constitutionally be made only on probable cause.

None of the foregoing implies that a brief detention in the field for the purpose of fingerprinting, where there is only reasonable suspicion not amounting to probable cause, is necessarily impermissible under the Fourth Amendment. . . . There is . . . support in our cases for the view that the Fourth Amendment would permit seizures for the purpose of fingerprinting, if there is reasonable suspicion that the suspect has committed a criminal act, if there is a reasonable basis for believing that fingerprinting will establish or negate the suspect's connection with that crime, and if the procedure is carried out with dispatch. . . . Of course, neither reasonable suspicion nor probable cause would suffice to permit the officers to make a warrantless entry into a person's house for the purpose of obtaining fingerprint identification. . . .

We also do not abandon the suggestion in *Davis* . . . that under circumscribed procedures, the Fourth Amendment might permit the judiciary to authorize the seizure of a person on less than probable cause and his removal to the police station for the purpose of fingerprinting. We do not, of course, have such a case before us. We do note, however, that some States, in reliance on the suggestion in *Davis*, have enacted procedures for judicially authorized seizures for the purpose of fingerprinting. The state courts are not in accord on the validity of these efforts to insulate investigative seizures from Fourth Amendment invalidation. . . .

As we have said, absent probable cause and a warrant, Davis v. Mississippi, 394 U.S. 721 (1969), requires the reversal of the judgment of the Florida District Court of Appeal.

. . . [13]

---

224. If the police believe that they have fingerprints of an unidentified person who committed a crime, should they be allowed to summon a group of persons who are suspects to headquarters for fingerprinting (or require them to submit to fingerprinting at their homes)? What problems does that raise different from the problems raised by a requirement that all persons, say in their eighth year of school, be fingerprinted for a permanent record? If the police should have such authority, what "narrowly circumscribed procedures" should they have to follow? Could comparable procedures be developed for the application of lineups or other identification techniques to groups of suspects? Or personal searches? Or searches of

---

[13] Justice Brennan wrote an opinion concurring in the judgment, which Justice Marshall joined. Justice Blackmun concurred in the judgment.

premises in a defined area? If not, why not? If so, what procedures would you require? See generally Beightol v. Kunowski, 486 F.2d 293 (3d Cir. 1973) (police have no authority to arrest person for purpose of obtaining fingerprints and photograph).

In Thom v. New York Stock Exchange, 306 F.Supp. 1002 (S.D.N.Y. 1969), aff'd sub nom. Miller v. New York Stock Exchange, 425 F.2d 1074 (2d Cir.1970), the court upheld the constitutionality of a New York statute requiring employees of member firms of national security exchanges and others to be fingerprinted as a condition of employment. The statute was an effort to prevent thefts of securities. And in Biehunik v. Felicetta, 441 F.2d 228 (2d Cir.1971), the court of appeals held that a police commissioner could constitutionally order 62 policemen, on pain of discharge, to appear in a lineup for possible identification by civilians who claimed that they had been assaulted by policemen.

225. In State v. Hall, 461 A.2d 1155 (N.J.1983), the court upheld the authority of the state trial court of general jurisdiction to issue an order compelling a person suspected of participating in a robbery, but not arrested or charged, to appear in a lineup. The court said:

> We accordingly conclude that an evidential finding of probable cause to believe that a particular individual has committed a crime is not an absolute prerequisite for judicial authorization of an investigatory detention. We are satisfied that a court has jurisdiction to authorize an investigatory detention under the following limited circumstances. The court's authorization of an investigatory detention must, first, be based upon sufficient evidence to demonstrate that a particular crime has occurred, that the crime is unsolved and that it is under active investigation. Second, the police must demonstrate a reasonable and well-grounded basis to believe that the individual sought as the subject of the investigative detention may have committed the crime under investigation. Additionally, it must be shown that the results of the detention will significantly advance the criminal investigation and will serve to determine whether or not the suspect probably committed the crime. Further, it must also appear that these investigative results cannot otherwise practicably be obtained.

> In addition to these evidential standards that serve to limit the circumstances under which investigatory detentions may be judicially authorized without probable cause, we recognize that appropriate procedures must be fashioned to assure that the intrusiveness of the detention is properly circumscribed. Investigatory detentions can involve different kinds of evidence-gathering procedures with differing degrees of intrusiveness. The Supreme Court in *Davis* [v. Mississippi, 394 U.S. 721 (1969)] emphasized that a detention to permit fingerprinting constituted a limited intrusion into a person's liberty and privacy because fingerprinting did not "prob[e] into an individual's private life and thoughts." A detention for fingerprinting was also regarded as essentially a reliable, simple and expeditious proceeding that could be conducted fairly and without palpable abuse. *Davis* at

727. . . . Accordingly, we conclude that those identification procedures that are comparable to fingerprinting will be sustainable upon a showing of less than traditional probable cause.

In this case, we think that a lineup for the purpose of securing an identification of the criminal suspect can be conducted in conformity with such standards and likened to the fingerprinting process. The lineup involves no creative or unusual act on the part of the suspect; it involves only a display of evidence that is otherwise publicly visible. In this regard the lineup does not "prob[e] into an individual's private life and thoughts." *Davis*, supra, 394 U.S. at 727. . . . Furthermore, the lineup, when properly conducted, can protect against abuse and insure fairness. . . . When conducted properly and fairly the procedure can furnish reliable evidence and can often be an effective crime-solving tool. . . . Finally, the lineup procedure can be accomplished at a convenient time and need not entail a restraint upon the suspect for an unduly long period of time.

In order to safeguard constitutional interests and secure the overall reasonableness of such nontestimonial identification procedures, the conduct of investigatory detentions must be carefully circumscribed by other procedural protections. . . . Indeed, the Supreme Court in *Davis* observed that "abuses" can occur in an investigatory detention, mentioning specifically an "improper line-up." Davis v. Mississippi, supra, 394 U.S. at 727. . . . As a result, in order to guarantee that the detention and accompanying intrusion is not improper or abusive, it must be accomplished in a fashion designed to produce the least amount of harassment of, interference with, or prejudice to the suspect. . . . Further, in most cases, the suspect must be given sufficient notice of the proposed detention. . . . The suspect should also be given the opportunity to arrange a convenient time for the detention . . . and the opportunity to have counsel present during the detention. . . . In addition, unusual or untoward consequences to the suspect resulting from the detention should be avoided or minimized.

We think that these procedural safeguards protect citizens' constitutional rights. We are also satisfied that the evidential standard that we adopt . . . allows police to investigate serious offenses without unduly interfering with the liberty or privacy of a person who has not been charged with any crime. In our view, these procedural requirements, in conjunction with the evidential standard, represent a proper balancing of the public interest in effective law enforcement and the liberty and privacy interests of the individual under the federal and State constitutions.

. . .

Applying these judicially formulated guidelines to this case, we believe that the circumstances surrounding defendant's detention and lineup clearly and adequately satisfied his constitutional right to be free from unreasonable searches and seizures. Defendant was linked to the commission of serious offenses for which he was ultimately convicted. According to the affidavit in support of the motion to compel the lineup, defendant was identified by an informant as the robber depicted in the composite sketch that was prepared by the police with the assistance of the victims of the crime. Also, one eyewitness of the crime had already made an equivocal identification of defendant's photograph. Based on this substantial information, the prosecutor moved for a detention order. Defendant, accompanied by counsel, was permitted to contest the motion. The trial judge found that Detective Booket's affidavit established an articulable, well-founded belief that defendant was involved in the commission of the particular offenses. Thus, upon notice to the defendant and with provisions for him to be heard, the detention order was authorized by a neutral and detached judge.

Further, in this case, the degree of intrusion into the individual's interests was certainly reasonable when measured against the degree of proof presented and the government interest involved. The detention was brief. It was conducted upon ample notice and at a convenient time. Defendant was not required to perform any creative act or give evidence not otherwise readily visible. Significantly, no interrogation occurred. Unquestionably, defendant's lineup detention, safeguarded by adequate restrictions, was beyond legal reproach.

461 A.2d at 1160–63.

See In re Fingerprinting of M.B., 309 A.2d 3 (N.J.Super.Ct.1973) (order for taking of fingerprints of boys in eighth grade class, as part of homicide investigation, upheld).

CHAPTER 6

QUESTIONING

_____

Spano v. New York

360 U.S. 315, 79 S.Ct. 1202, 3 L.Ed.2d 1265 (1959)

■ MR. CHIEF JUSTICE WARREN delivered the opinion of the Court.

This is another in the long line of cases presenting the question whether a confession was properly admitted into evidence under the Fourteenth Amendment. As in all such cases, we are forced to resolve a conflict between two fundamental interests of society; its interest in prompt and efficient law enforcement, and its interest in preventing the rights of its individual members from being abridged by unconstitutional methods of law enforcement. . . .

The State's evidence reveals the following: Petitioner Vincent Joseph Spano is a derivative citizen of this country, having been born in Messina, Italy. He was 25 years old at the time of the shooting in question and had graduated from junior high school. He had a record of regular employment. The shooting took place on January 22, 1957.

On that day, petitioner was drinking in a bar. The decedent, a former professional boxer weighing almost 200 pounds who had fought in Madison Square Garden, took some of petitioner's money from the bar. Petitioner followed him out of the bar to recover it. A fight ensued, with the decedent knocking petitioner down and then kicking him in the head three or four times. Shock from the force of these blows caused petitioner to vomit. After the bartender applied some ice to his head, petitioner left the bar, walked to his apartment, secured a gun, and walked eight or nine blocks to a candy store where the decedent was frequently to be found. He entered the store in which decedent, three friends of decedent, at least two of whom were ex-convicts, and a boy who was supervising the store were present. He fired five shots, two of which entered the decedent's body, causing his death. The boy was the only eyewitness; the three friends of decedent did not see the person who fired the shot. Petitioner then disappeared for the next week or so.

On February 1, 1957, the Bronx County Grand Jury returned an indictment for first-degree murder against petitioner. Accordingly, a bench warrant was issued for his arrest, commanding that he be forthwith brought before the court to answer the indictment, or, if the court had adjourned for the term, that he be delivered into the custody of the Sheriff of Bronx County. . . .

On February 3, 1957, petitioner called one Gaspar Bruno, a close friend of 8 or 10 years' standing who had attended school with him. Bruno was a fledgling police officer, having at that time not yet finished attending police academy. According to Bruno's testimony, petitioner told him "that he took a terrific beating, that the deceased hurt him real bad and he dropped him a couple of times and he was dazed; he didn't know what he was doing and that he went and shot at him." Petitioner told Bruno that he intended to get a lawyer and give himself up. Bruno relayed this information to his superiors.

The following day, February 4, at 7:10 p.m., petitioner, accompanied by counsel, surrendered himself to the authorities in front of the Bronx County Building, where both the office of the Assistant District Attorney who ultimately prosecuted his case and the courtroom in which he was ultimately tried were located. His attorney had cautioned him to answer no questions, and left him in the custody of the officers. He was promptly taken to the office of the Assistant District Attorney and at 7:15 p.m. the questioning began, being conducted by Assistant District Attorney Goldsmith, Lt. Gannon, Detectives Farrell, Lehrer and Motta, and Sgt. Clarke. The record reveals that the questioning was both persistent and continuous. Petitioner, in accordance with his attorney's instructions, steadfastly refused to answer. Detective Motta testified: "He refused to talk to me." "He just looked up to the ceiling and refused to talk to me." Detective Farrell testified:

Q. And you started to interrogate him?

A. That is right.

. . .

Q. What did he say?

A. He said "you would have to see my attorney. I tell you nothing but my name."

. . .

Q. Did you continue to examine him?

A. Verbally, yes, sir.

He asked one officer, Detective Ciccone, if he could speak to his attorney, but that request was denied. Detective Ciccone testified that he could not find the attorney's name in the telephone book. He was given two sandwiches, coffee and cake at 11 p.m.

At 12:15 a.m. on the morning of February 5, after five hours of questioning in which it became evident that petitioner was following his attorney's instructions, on the Assistant District Attorney's orders petitioner was transferred to the 46th Squad, Ryer Avenue Police Station. The Assistant District Attorney also went to the police station and to some extent continued to participate in the interrogation. Petitioner arrived at 12:30 and questioning was resumed at 12:40. The character of the questioning is revealed by the testimony of Detective Farrell:

> Q. Who did you leave him in the room with?
>
> A. With Detective Lehrer and Sergeant Clarke came in and Mr. Goldsmith came in or Inspector Halk came in. It was back and forth. People just came in, spoke a few words to the defendant or they listened a few minutes and they left.

But petitioner persisted in his refusal to answer, and again requested permission to see his attorney, this time from Detective Lehrer. His request was again denied.

It was then that those in charge of the investigation decided that petitioner's close friend, Bruno, could be of use. He had been called out on the case around 10 or 11 p.m., although he was not connected with the 46th Squad or Precinct in any way. Although, in fact, his job was in no way threatened, Bruno was told to tell petitioner that petitioner's telephone call had gotten him "in a lot of trouble," and that he should seek to extract sympathy from petitioner for Bruno's pregnant wife and three children. Bruno developed this theme with petitioner without success, and petitioner, also without success, again sought to see his attorney, a request which Bruno relayed unavailingly to his superiors. After this first session with petitioner, Bruno was again directed by Lt. Gannon to play on petitioner's sympathies, but again no confession was forthcoming. But the Lieutenant a third time ordered Bruno falsely to importune his friend to confess, but again petitioner clung to his attorney's advice. Inevitably, in the fourth such session directed by the Lieutenant, lasting a full hour, petitioner succumbed to his friend's prevarications and agreed to make a statement. Accordingly at 3:25 a.m. the Assistant District Attorney, a stenographer, and several other law enforcement officials entered the room where petitioner was being questioned, and took his statement in question and answer form with the Assistant District Attorney asking the questions. The statement was completed at 4:05 a.m.

But this was not the end. At 4:30 a.m. three detectives took petitioner to Police Headquarters in Manhattan. On the way they attempted to find the bridge from which petitioner said he had thrown the murder weapon. They crossed the Triborough Bridge into Manhattan, arriving at Police Headquarters at 5 a.m., and left Manhattan for the Bronx at 5:40 a.m. via the Willis Avenue Bridge. When petitioner recognized neither bridge as the one from which he had thrown the weapon, they reentered Manhattan via the Third Avenue Bridge, which petitioner stated was the right one, and then returned to the Bronx well after 6 a.m. During that trip the officers also elicited a statement from petitioner that the deceased was always "on [his] back," "always pushing" him and that he was "not sorry" he had shot the deceased. All three detectives testified to that statement at the trial.

Court opened at 10 a.m. that morning, and petitioner was arraigned at 10:15.

At the trial, the confession was introduced in evidence over appropriate objections. The jury was instructed that it could rely on it only if it was found to be voluntary. The jury returned a guilty verdict and petitioner was sentenced to death. The New York Court of Appeals affirmed the conviction over three dissents . . . and we granted certiorari to resolve the serious problem presented under the Fourteenth Amendment. . . .

Petitioner's first contention is that his absolute right to counsel in a capital case . . . became operative on the return of an indictment against him, for at that time he was in every sense a defendant in a criminal case, the grand jury having found sufficient cause to believe that he had committed the crime. He argues accordingly that following indictment no confession obtained in the absence of counsel can be used without violating the Fourteenth Amendment. . . . We find it unnecessary to reach that contention, for we find use of the confession obtained here inconsistent with the Fourteenth Amendment under traditional principles.

The abhorrence of society to the use of involuntary confessions does not turn alone on their inherent untrustworthiness. It also turns on the deep-rooted feeling that the police must obey the law while enforcing the law; that in the end life and liberty can be as much endangered from illegal methods used to convict those thought to be criminals as from the actual criminals themselves. Accordingly, the actions of police in obtaining confessions have come under scrutiny in a long series of cases. Those cases suggest that in recent years law enforcement officials have become increasingly aware of the burden which they share, along with our courts, in protecting fundamental rights of our citizenry, including that portion of our citizenry suspected of crime. The facts of no case recently in this Court have quite approached the brutal beatings in Brown v. Mississippi, 297 U.S. 278 (1936) or the 36 consecutive hours of questioning present in Ashcraft v. Tennessee, 322 U.S. 143 (1944). But as law enforcement officers become more responsible, and the methods used to extract confessions more sophisticated, our duty to enforce federal constitutional protections does not cease. It only becomes more difficult because of the more delicate judgments to be made. Our judgment here is that, on all the facts, this conviction cannot stand.

Petitioner was a foreign-born young man of 25 with no past history of law violation or of subjection to official interrogation, at least insofar as the record shows. He had progressed only one-half year into high school and the record indicates that he had a history of emotional instability. He did not make a narrative statement, but was subject to the leading questions of a skillful prosecutor in a question and answer confession. He was subjected to questioning not by a few men, but by many. They included Assistant District Attorney Goldsmith, one Hyland of the District Attorney's Office, Deputy Inspector Halks, Lieutenant Gannon, Detective Ciccone, Detective Motta, Detective Lehrer, Detective Marshal, Detective Farrell, Detective Leira, Detective Murphy, Detective Murtha, Sergeant Clarke, Patrolman Bruno and Stenographer Baldwin. All played some part, and the effect of such massive official interrogation must have been felt. Petitioner was questioned for virtually eight straight hours before he confessed, with his only respite being a transfer to an arena presumably considered more appropriate by the police for the task at hand. Nor was the questioning conducted during normal business hours, but began in early evening, continued into the night, and did not bear fruition until the not-too-early morning. The drama was not played out, with the final admissions obtained, until almost sunrise. In such circumstances slowly mounting fatigue does, and is calculated to, play its part. The questioners persisted in the face of his repeated refusals to answer on the advice of his attorney, and they ignored his reasonable requests to contact the local attorney whom he had already retained and who had personally delivered him into the custody of these officers in obedience to the bench warrant.

The use of Bruno, characterized in this Court by counsel for the State as a "childhood friend" of petitioner's, is another factor which deserves mention in the totality of the situation. Bruno's was the one face visible to petitioner in which he could put some trust. There was a bond of friendship between them going back a decade into adolescence. It was with this material that the officers felt that they could overcome petitioner's will. They instructed Bruno falsely to state that petitioner's telephone call had gotten him into trouble, that his job was in jeopardy, and that loss of his job would be disastrous to his three children, his wife and his unborn child. And Bruno played this part of a worried father, harried by his superiors, in not one but four different acts, the final one lasting an hour. . . . Petitioner was apparently unaware of John Gay's famous couplet:

> An open foe may prove a curse,
> But a pretended friend is worse,

and he yielded to his false friend's entreaties.

We conclude that petitioner's will was overborne by official pressure, fatigue and sympathy falsely aroused, after considering all the facts in their post-indictment setting. Here a grand jury had already found sufficient cause to require petitioner to face trial on a charge of first-degree murder, and the police had an eyewitness to the shooting. The police were not therefore merely trying to solve a crime, or even to absolve a suspect. . . . They were rather concerned primarily with securing a statement from defendant on which they could convict him. The undeviating intent of the officers to extract a confession from petitioner is therefore patent. When such an intent is shown, this Court has held that the confession obtained must be examined with the most careful scrutiny, and has reversed a conviction on facts less compelling than these. . . . Accordingly, we hold that petitioner's conviction cannot stand under the Fourteenth Amendment.

. . .[1]

---

[1] Justice Douglas wrote a concurring opinion which Justice Black and Justice Brennan joined. Justice Stewart wrote a concurring opinion which Justice Douglas and Justice Brennan joined. Both opinions indicated that the concurring Justices believed that the right to counsel had attached after Spano was indicted.

226. Declaring that a defendant's disturbed psychiatric condition at the time a confession is made is not by itself a basis for exclusion of the confession on constitutional grounds, the Court held in Colorado v. Connelly, 479 U.S. 157, 167 (1986) (7–2), that "coercive police activity is a necessary predicate to the finding that a confession is not 'voluntary' within the meaning of the Due Process Clause of the Fourteenth Amendment."

Connelly was rejected in State v. Bowe, 881 P.2d 538 (Haw.1994). Relying on the state constitution's due process clause and privilege against self-incrimination, the court said: "[A]n individual's capacity to make a rational and free choice between confessing and remaining silent may be overborne as much by the coercive conduct of a private individual as by the coercive conduct of the police. Accordingly, we hold that admitting coerced confessions, regardless of the source of the coercion, is fundamentally unfair." Id. at 546.

In Mincey v. Arizona, 437 U.S. 385 (1978) (8–1), the Court concluded that a defendant's will was overborne by questioning while he was seriously wounded and in the intensive care unit of a hospital, and that his statements were therefore involuntary and inadmissible. See also Woods v. Clusen, 794 F.2d 293 (7th Cir.1986) (totality of circumstances, including defendant's youth and lack of previous contact with the criminal justice system, the intimidating circumstances of his arrest and questioning, and deliberate deception by the police to suggest that they already had incriminating evidence violated defendant's privilege against compulsory self-incrimination); United States v. Murphy, 763 F.2d 202 (6th Cir.1985) (confession made while defendant was being attacked by police dog was involuntary, but admission of the confession was harmless error).

In United States v. Braxton, 112 F.3d 777 (4th Cir.1997), the defendant, an adult, was interviewed at his mother's house by police officers who suspected him of illegally purchasing firearms. He was not in custody. In the course of the interview, an officer told the defendant that they "needed" to talk to him and that he could face five years in prison because he was not "coming clean"; they did not inform him of the consequences of a confession, in particular that he would subject himself to prosecution. Rejecting the defendant's contention that in the circumstances, the confession was involuntary, the court observed that "the mere existence of threats, violence, implied promises, improper influence, or other coercive police activity . . . does not automatically render a confession involuntary." Id. at 780. To hold the confession involuntary on the basis of the officers' statements, the court said, would impose on officers an obligation to give something like *Miranda* warnings even in the absence of custodial interrogation.

Whether or not a confession is voluntary is ultimately a question of law and requires an independent determination by the federal court on federal collateral attack of a state conviction. Miller v. Fenton, 474 U.S. 104 (1985) (8–1).

227. In State v. Patton, 826 A.2d 783 (N.J.Super.2003), the police arrested the defendant for murder. While he was detained at headquarters, the police fabricated an audiotape that purported to be an interview with an eyewitness to the murder, who identified the defendant. Having given the defendant *Miranda* warnings, the police played the audiotape for him, after which he confessed. At trial, the prosecutor introduced the fabricated audiotape to show that the defendant's confession was voluntary. Observing that the interview on the audiotape contained a scenario that conformed to the prosecution's theory of the case, the court declared a "bright-line" rule that "the use of police-fabricated evidence to induce a confession that is then used at trial to support the voluntariness of a confession is per se a violation of due process." Id. at 805.

———

Massiah v. United States

377 U.S. 201, 84 S.Ct. 1199, 12 L.Ed.2d 246 (1964)

■ MR. JUSTICE STEWART delivered the opinion of the Court.

The petitioner was indicted for violating the federal narcotics laws. He retained a lawyer, pleaded not guilty, and was released on bail. While he was free on bail a federal agent succeeded by surreptitious means in listening to incriminating statements made by him. Evidence of these statements was introduced against the petitioner at his trial over his objection. He was convicted, and the Court of Appeals affirmed. We granted certiorari to consider whether, under the circumstances here presented, the prosecution's use at the trial of evidence of the petitioner's own incriminating statements deprived him of any right secured to him under the Federal Constitution. . . .

The petitioner, a merchant seaman, was in 1958 a member of the crew of the S.S. *Santa Maria*. In April of that year federal customs officials in New York received information that he was going to transport a quantity of narcotics aboard that ship from South America to the United States. As a result of this and other information, the agents searched the *Santa Maria* upon its arrival in New York and found in the afterpeak of the vessel five packages containing about three and a half pounds of cocaine. They also learned of circumstances, not here relevant, tending to connect the petitioner with the cocaine. He was arrested, promptly arraigned, and subsequently indicted for possession of narcotics aboard a United States vessel. In July a superseding indictment was returned, charging the petitioner and a man named Colson with the same substantive offense, and in separate counts charging the petitioner, Colson, and others with having conspired to possess narcotics aboard a United States vessel, and to import, conceal, and facilitate the sale of narcotics. The petitioner, who had retained a lawyer, pleaded not guilty and was released on bail, along with Colson.

A few days later, and quite without the petitioner's knowledge, Colson decided to cooperate with the government agents in their continuing investigation of the narcotics activities in which the petitioner, Colson, and others had allegedly been engaged. Colson permitted an agent named Murphy to install a Schmidt radio transmitter under the front seat of Colson's automobile, by means of which Murphy, equipped with an appropriate receiving device, could overhear from some distance away conversations carried on in Colson's car.

On the evening of November 19, 1959, Colson and the petitioner held a lengthy conversation while sitting in Colson's automobile, parked on a New York street. By prearrangement with Colson, and totally unbeknown to the petitioner, the agent Murphy sat in a car parked out of sight down the street and listened over the radio to the entire conversation. The petitioner made several incriminating statements during the course of this conversation. At the petitioner's trial these incriminating statements were brought before the jury through Murphy's testimony, despite the insistent objection of defense counsel. The jury convicted the petitioner of several related narcotics offenses, and the convictions were affirmed by the Court of Appeals.

The petitioner argues that it was an error of constitutional dimensions to permit the agent Murphy at the trial to testify to the petitioner's incriminating statements which Murphy had overheard under the circumstances disclosed by this record. This argument is based upon two distinct and independent grounds. First, we are told that Murphy's use of the radio equipment violated the petitioner's rights under the Fourth Amendment, and, consequently, that all evidence which Murphy thereby obtained was . . . inadmissible against the petitioner at the trial. Secondly, it is said that the petitioner's Fifth and Sixth Amendment rights were violated by the use in evidence against him of incriminating statements which government agents had deliberately elicited from him after he had been indicted and in the absence of his retained counsel. Because of the way we dispose of the case, we do not reach the Fourth Amendment issue.

In Spano v. New York, 360 U.S. 315, the Court reversed a state criminal conviction because a confession had been wrongly admitted into evidence against the defendant at his trial. In that case the defendant had already been indicted for first-degree murder at the time he confessed. The Court held that the defendant's conviction could not stand under the Fourteenth Amendment. While the Court's opinion relied upon the totality of the circumstances under which the confession had been obtained, four concurring Justices pointed out that the Constitution required reversal of the conviction upon the sole and specific ground that the confession had been deliberately elicited by the police after the defendant had been indicted, and therefore at a time when he was clearly entitled to a lawyer's help. It was pointed out that under our system of justice the most elemental concepts of due process of law contemplate that an indictment be followed by a trial, "in an orderly courtroom, presided over by a judge, open to the public, and protected by all the procedural safeguards of the law."

360 U.S., at 327 (Stewart, J., concurring). It was said that a Constitution which guarantees a defendant the aid of counsel at such a trial could surely vouchsafe no less to an indicted defendant under interrogation by the police in a completely extrajudicial proceeding. Anything less, it was said, might deny a defendant "effective representation by counsel at the only stage when legal aid and advice would help him." 360 U.S., at 326 (Douglas, J., concurring).

. . .

This view no more than reflects a constitutional principle established as long ago as Powell v. Alabama, 287 U.S. 45, where the Court noted that ". . . during perhaps the most critical period of the proceedings . . . that is to say, from the time of their arraignment until the beginning of their trial, when consultation, thoroughgoing investigation and preparation [are] vitally important, the defendants . . . [are] as much entitled to such aid [of counsel] during that period as at the trial itself." Id., at 57. And since the *Spano* decision the same basic constitutional principle has been broadly reaffirmed by this Court. . . .

Here we deal not with a state court conviction, but with a federal case, where the specific guarantee of the Sixth Amendment directly applies. . . . We hold that the petitioner was denied the basic protections of that guarantee when there was used against him at his trial evidence of his own incriminating words, which federal agents had deliberately elicited from him after he had been indicted and in the absence of his counsel. It is true that in the *Spano* case the defendant was interrogated in a police station, while here the damaging testimony was elicited from the defendant without his knowledge while he was free on bail. But, as Judge Hays pointed out in his dissent in the Court of Appeals, "if such a rule is to have any efficacy it must apply to indirect and surreptitious interrogations as well as those conducted in the jailhouse. In this case, Massiah was more seriously imposed upon . . . because he did not even know that he was under interrogation by a government agent." 307 F.2d, at 72–73.

The Solicitor General, in his brief and oral argument, has strenuously contended that the federal law enforcement agents had the right, if not indeed the duty, to continue their investigation of the petitioner and his alleged criminal associates even though the petitioner had been indicted. He points out that the Government was continuing its investigation in order to uncover not only the source of narcotics found on the S.S. *Santa Maria*, but also their intended buyer. He says that the quantity of narcotics involved was such as to suggest that the petitioner was part of a large and well-organized ring, and indeed that the continuing investigation confirmed this suspicion, since it resulted in criminal charges against many defendants. Under these circumstances the Solicitor General concludes that the government agents were completely "justified in making use of Colson's cooperation by having Colson continue his normal associations and by surveilling them."

We may accept and, at least for present purposes, completely approve all that this argument implies, Fourth Amendment problems to one side.

We do not question that in this case, as in many cases, it was entirely proper to continue an investigation of the suspected criminal activities of the defendant and his alleged confederates, even though the defendant had already been indicted. All that we hold is that the defendant's own incriminating statements, obtained by federal agents under the circumstances here disclosed, could not constitutionally be used by the prosecution as evidence against *him* at his trial.

. . .[2]

---

228. The reach of the principle announced in *Massiah* was discussed in United States v. Henry, 447 U.S. 264 (1980) (6–3). There, the defendant had been indicted for armed robbery and was detained in jail pending trial. While in jail, he made incriminating statements to another inmate, who testified about the statements at the defendant's trial. The inmate had for some time previously been an informant for the government. Federal agents had instructed him to be alert for statements by the defendant but not to question him or initiate conversations.

The Court affirmed the ruling below that under *Massiah* the statements should not have been admitted. It said that the test is whether a government agent had "deliberately elicited" the incriminating statements within the meaning of *Massiah*. The Court said that three factors were important to its decision: (1) the inmate had been acting under instructions as a paid informant, (2) the inmate was, so far as the defendant knew, only another inmate and not a government agent, and (3) the defendant was under indictment and in custody when the conversation occurred. "By intentionally creating a situation likely to induce Henry to make incriminating statements without the assistance of counsel, the government violated Henry's Sixth Amendment right to counsel." Id. at 274.

Massiah and *Henry* were applied in Maine v. Moulton, 474 U.S. 159 (1985) (5–4). The Court said that the rule of those cases applied even though the defendant had initiated the conversations with the government informer (a codefendant). "[K]nowing exploitation by the State of an opportunity to confront the accused without counsel being present is as much a breach of the State's obligation not to circumvent the right to the assistance of counsel as is the intentional creation of such an opportunity. Accordingly, the Sixth Amendment is violated when the State obtains incriminating statements by knowingly circumventing the accused's right to have counsel present in a confrontation between the accused and a state agent." Id. at 176. The Court said also, reaffirming its conclusion in *Massiah*, that evidence obtained by circumventing the defendant's right to counsel is not admissible even though the police are also investigating other crimes for which no charges are pending. Evidence would be admissible at a

[2] Justice White wrote a dissenting opinion which Justice Clark and Justice Harlan joined.

trial for the latter crimes if the defendant were subsequently prosecuted but not at the trial for charges as to which the right to counsel was violated.

Massiah was applied in United States v. Anderson, 523 F.2d 1192 (5th Cir.1975), in which several months after the defendant, a doctor, had been indicted in connection with illegal distribution of drugs and one week before trial, a government informer visited him in his office and represented herself as a patient. The court held that her testimony about the meeting with the defendant should not have been admitted. The court said that it did not question "the propriety of continuing governmental investigation of an indicted defendant's suspected criminal activities," but that here there was no such investigation. "Rather, it appears that a special single-shot confrontation was arranged . . . to obtain from the defendant evidence of specific intent to shore up the government's case, and that it was arranged at a time, place and under circumstances that defendant's attorney would not be present." Id. at 1196.

Henry was distinguished in Kuhlmann v. Wilson, 477 U.S. 436 (1986) (6–3). An informer was placed in the defendant's cell while he was awaiting trial. The informer was there for the express purpose of listening to and reporting to the police any statements bearing on the crimes with which the defendant was charged. The particular interest of the police was to identify the defendant's confederates. Without questioning the defendant or prompting him in any way, the informant heard and reported his incriminating statements. In those circumstances, the Court said, the principle of *Massiah* and *Henry* was not violated. "[T]he primary concern of the *Massiah* line of decisions is secret interrogation by investigatory techniques that are the equivalent of direct police interrogation. . . . [A] defendant does not make out a violation of . . . [the right to counsel] simply by showing that an informant, either through prior arrangement or voluntarily, reported his incriminating statements to the police. Rather, the defendant must demonstrate that the police and their informant took some action, beyond merely listening, that was designed deliberately to elicit incriminating remarks." Id. at 459.

Henry was distinguished also in United States v. Malik, 680 F.2d 1162 (7th Cir.1982), in which an inmate deliberately elicited incriminating statements from the defendant on his own initiative, in hope of gaining some advantage with respect to his own prosecution. See also United States v. Moore, 917 F.2d 215 (6th Cir.1990), in which the defendant, while incarcerated, made incriminating statements to his girlfriend in a telephone conversation, which the police overheard and taped with her permission.

See generally Illinois v. Perkins, 496 U.S. 292 (1990), p. 469 below.

229. The *Miranda* rules provide that before a person is subjected to custodial interrogation, he must be given advice designed to protect the privilege against compulsory self-incrimination. See Miranda v. Arizona, p. 417 below. In Brewer v. Williams, 430 U.S. 387 (1977) (5–4), without deciding whether the *Miranda* rules had been violated, the court held that statements that the defendant made to a police detective had been obtained in violation of his right to counsel. The defendant had surrendered to the police on a warrant for his arrest on a charge of abduction. He was suspected of murder. He was brought before a judge who advised him of his rights and was committed to jail. At several points, he consulted with a lawyer and was advised not to make any statements. Before police transported him from the city where he was arrested to the city where the crime occurred, his lawyer stated explicitly that there was to be no questioning during the trip. During the trip, without asking questions, a detective made comments intended to elicit incriminating statements from the defendant. The Court said that the right to counsel means "at least that a person is entitled to the help of a lawyer at or after the time that judicial proceedings have been initiated against him—'whether by way of formal charge, preliminary hearing, indictment, information or arraignment'" (citing, inter alia, Kirby v. Illinois, 406 U.S. 682, 689 (1972), p. 378 above). 430 U.S. at 398. It was unquestioned that judicial proceedings had been initiated against the defendant and that the purpose of the detective in the car was "to elicit information . . . just as surely as . . . if he had formally interrogated" the defendant. The facts were, therefore, "constitutionally indistinguishable" from those of *Massiah*. Id. at 399, 400. For the subsequent history of Brewer v. Williams, see Nix v. Williams, 467 U.S. 431 (1984), p. 147 note 77 above.

In Patterson v. Illinois, 487 U.S. 285, 300 (1988) (5–4), after the defendant had been indicted, he was questioned by police officers and made incriminating statements. The questioning was preceded by *Miranda* warnings. Over the objection that *Miranda* warnings are insufficient to sustain a waiver of the right to counsel (as contrasted with the privilege against compulsory self-incrimination) the Court held that the incriminating statements were admissible. The *Miranda* warnings, properly given, advise the defendant sufficiently to make his waiver of the right to counsel "knowing and intelligent." Id. at 300.

"[W]hatever warnings suffice for *Miranda*'s purposes will also be sufficient in the context of postindictment questioning. The State's decision to take an additional step and commence formal adversarial proceedings against the accused does not substantially increase the value of counsel to the accused at questioning, or expand the limited purpose that an attorney serves when the accused is questioned by authorities. With respect to this inquiry, we do not discern a substantial difference between the usefulness of a lawyer to a suspect during custodial interrogation, and his value to an accused at post-indictment questioning." Id. at 298–99.

In Fellers v. United States, 540 U.S. ___ (2004), after the defendant had been indicted, police officers went to his home and, in a discussion with him about his involvement in the crime, elicited incriminating statements. They then took him to a jail, where he was given *Miranda* warnings. He waived his rights under *Miranda* and repeated the incriminating statements. Finding that the discussion at his house violated his Sixth Amendment rights under *Massiah*, the Court remanded the case for consideration whether the violation of the Sixth Amendment required suppression of the statements at the jail, as its fruits. See Oregon v. Elstad, p. 431 below.

On the relationship between *Massiah* and *Miranda* generally, see Rhode Island v. Innis, 446 U.S. 291, 300 n.4 (1980), p. 432 below. See also Michigan v. Jackson, 475 U.S. 625 (1986), p. 443 below.

230. Brewer v. Williams, p. 408 note 229 above, indicates that *Massiah* is not limited to the period after the defendant has been formally accused but applies after the initiation of *judicial* proceedings. See Kirby v. Illinois, p. 378 above. *Massiah* is not applicable, however, following an arrest, even though the arrest is pursuant to a complaint and warrant. United States v. Pace, 833 F.2d 1307 (9th Cir.1987); United States v. Duvall, 537 F.2d 15 (2d Cir.1976).

In United States v. Brown, 551 F.2d 639 (5th Cir.1977), rev'd on other grounds, 569 F.2d 236 (1978), the defendant was arrested by state officials on charges involving an interstate theft. Five days later, while she was waiting (in state custody) in a corridor of the county courthouse for the public defender, she was approached by two agents of the FBI. The public defender had already been appointed to represent her; she was in the courthouse for a preliminary hearing, which was scheduled to start about a half hour after the time of her meeting with the FBI agents. They gave her *Miranda* warnings and one of them questioned her. She was not indicted for a federal crime for more than six months thereafter. At her trial, she claimed that her responses to the questions should be suppressed under *Massiah*. What result?

231. In Hoffa v. United States, 385 U.S. 293, 310 (1966), the Court observed that "there is no constitutional right to be arrested." Does *Massiah* have any application before a defendant is arrested? Once the police have a clear basis for an arrest and have decided eventually to arrest a person, are they required under *Massiah* not to try to elicit incriminating statements from him in the absence of counsel? See United States ex rel. Molinas v. Mancusi, 370 F.2d 601 (2d Cir.1967); cf. Garcia v. United States, 364 F.2d 306 (10th Cir.1966); Gascar v. United States, 356 F.2d 101 (9th Cir.1965). If not, can they delay arrest in order to utilize investigative techniques that would be barred by *Massiah* after arrest (or indictment)?

232. The right to counsel is "offense-specific." McNeil v. Wisconsin, 501 U.S. 171 (1991) (6–3). It attaches only to the offense with which the defendant is charged and other offenses not formally charged that would be considered the same offense under the *Blockberger* test for double jeopardy (see note 635, p. 1216 below). Texas v. Cobb, 532 U.S. 162 (2001) (5–4). It does not apply to distinct offenses, however closely related factually. Id. In United States v. Coker, 298 F.Supp.2d 184 (D.Mass.2003), the court relied on the theory of separate sovereignties, see note 638 p. 1218 below, to conclude that the right to counsel, which had attached to the defendant with respect to state arson charges, did not bar questioning by federal agents with respect to federal crimes involving the same incident.

Suppose that after the defendant has been indicted for one crime, the police, investigating his involvement in another crime, obtain evidence against him pertaining to the crime for which he has already been indicted. Is the evidence admissible at the trial for that crime? Compare United States v. Terzado-Madruga, 897 F.2d 1099 (11th Cir.1990), and Mealer v. Jones, 741 F.2d 1451 (2d Cir.1984), with United States v. Darwin, 757 F.2d 1193 (11th Cir.1985).

Massiah does not prohibit surreptitious investigation of defendant's efforts to obstruct justice after entry of a plea of guilty and before sentence. The results of such investigation can be revealed to the judge at sentencing. United States v. Pineda, 692 F.2d 284 (2d Cir.1982).

———

Why should police efforts to obtain information from an individual be more circumscribed after the police or the prosecutor have taken official steps to institute proceedings against him? Suppose the following situation: After making a general investigation of a homicide which included questioning A and B among others, the detectives of the homicide squad conclude that A is guilty of the crime. Having probable cause to believe that he is guilty, they arrest him. They believe that B is innocent of the crime but has information which will help to convict A. A (who has been brought before a magistrate and released on bail) is ignored by the police. B is subjected to polite but insistent questioning; in entire good faith, the police urge him to tell what he knows about the crime. B gives the police information which leads to B's subsequent arrest and conviction for the crime. A is released.

Assuming that the guilt *as such* of the defendant is not the significant factor—he is after all equally guilty (or innocent) before and after he is arrested—what "happened" when A was arrested and brought before a magistrate that should deny the police access to him as a source of information? Does *Massiah* provide an answer? Is it sufficient to say that an indictment should be "followed by a trial" or that a defendant has the right to counsel after he has been indicted because that is a " 'critical period of the proceedings,' " pp. 405, 406 above?

———

Escobedo v. Illinois
378 U.S. 478, 84 S.Ct. 1758, 12 L.Ed.2d 977 (1964)

■ MR. JUSTICE GOLDBERG delivered the opinion of the Court.

The critical question in this case is whether, under the circumstances, the refusal by the police to honor petitioner's request to consult with his lawyer during the course of an interrogation constitutes a denial of "the Assistance of Counsel" in violation of the Sixth Amendment to the Constitution as "made obligatory upon the States by the Fourteenth Amendment," Gideon v. Wainwright, 372 U.S. 335, 342, and thereby renders inadmissible in a state criminal trial any incriminating statement elicited by the police during the interrogation.

On the night of January 19, 1960, petitioner's brother-in-law was fatally shot. In the early hours of the next morning, at 2:30 a.m., petitioner was arrested without a warrant and interrogated. Petitioner made no statement to the police and was released at 5 that afternoon pursuant to a state court writ of habeas corpus obtained by Mr. Warren Wolfson, a lawyer who had been retained by petitioner.

On January 30, Benedict DiGerlando, who was then in police custody and who was later indicted for the murder along with petitioner, told the police that petitioner had fired the fatal shots. Between 8 and 9 that evening, petitioner and his sister, the widow of the deceased, were arrested and taken to police headquarters. En route to the police station, the police "had handcuffed the defendant behind his back," and "one of the arresting officers told defendant that DiGerlando had named him as the one who shot" the deceased. Petitioner testified, without contradiction, that the "detectives said they had us pretty well, up pretty tight, and we might as well admit to this crime," and that he replied, "I am sorry but I would like to have advice from my lawyer." A police officer testified that although petitioner was not formally charged "he was in custody" and "couldn't walk out the door."

Shortly after petitioner reached police headquarters, his retained lawyer arrived. The lawyer described the ensuing events in the following terms:

On that day I received a phone call [from "the mother of another defendant"] and pursuant to that phone call I went to the Detective Bureau at 11th and State. The first person I talked to was the Sergeant on duty at the Bureau Desk, Sergeant Pidgeon. I asked Sergeant Pidgeon for permission to speak to my client, Danny Escobedo. . . . Sergeant Pidgeon made a call to the Bureau lockup and informed me that the boy had been taken from the lockup to the Homicide Bureau. This was between 9:30 and 10:00 in the evening. Before I went anywhere, he called the Homicide Bureau and told them there was an attorney waiting to see Escobedo. He told me I could not see him. Then I went upstairs to the Homicide Bureau. There were several Homicide Detectives around and I talked to them. I identified myself as Escobedo's attorney and asked permission to see him. They said I could not. . . . The police officer told me to see Chief Flynn who was on duty. I identified myself to Chief Flynn and asked permission to see my client. He said I could not. . . . I think it was approximately 11:00 o'clock. He said I couldn't see him because they hadn't completed questioning. . . . [F]or a second or two I spotted him in an office in the Homicide Bureau. The door was open and I could see through the office. . . . I waved to him and he waved back and then the door was closed, by one of the officers at Homicide.[3] There were four or five officers milling around the Homicide Detail that night. As to whether I talked to Captain Flynn any later that day, I waited around for another hour or two and went back again and renewed by [sic] request to see my client. He again told me I could not. . . . I filed an official complaint with Commissioner Phelan of the Chicago Police Department. I had a conversation with every police officer I could find. I was told at Homicide that I couldn't see him and I would have to get a writ of habeas corpus. I left the Homicide Bureau and from the Detective Bureau at 11th and State at approximately 1:00 A.M. [Sunday morning]. I had no opportunity to talk to my client that night. I quoted to Captain Flynn the Section of the Criminal Code which allows an attorney the right to see his client.

Petitioner testified that during the course of the interrogation he repeatedly asked to speak to his lawyer and that the police said that his lawyer "didn't want to see" him. The testimony of the police officers confirmed these accounts in substantial detail.

Notwithstanding repeated requests by each, petitioner and his retained lawyer were afforded no opportunity to consult during the course of the entire interrogation. At one point, as previously noted, petitioner and his attorney came into each other's view for a few moments but the attorney was quickly ushered away. Petitioner testified "that he heard a detective telling the attorney the latter would not be allowed to talk to [him] 'until they were done' " and that he heard the attorney being refused permission to remain in the adjoining room. A police officer testified that he had told the lawyer that he could not see petitioner until "we were through interrogating" him.

There is testimony by the police that during the interrogation, petitioner, a 22-year-old of Mexican extraction with no record of previous experience with the police, "was handcuffed" in a standing position and that he "was nervous, he had circles under his eyes and he was upset" and was "agitated" because "he had not slept well in over a week."

It is undisputed that during the course of the interrogation Officer Montejano, who "grew up" in petitioner's neighborhood, who knew his family, and who uses "Spanish language in [his] police work," conferred alone with petitioner "for about a quarter of an hour. . . ." Petitioner testified that the officer said to him "in Spanish that my sister and I could go home if I pinned it on Benedict DiGerlando," that "he would see to it that we would go home and be held only as witnesses, if anything, if we had made a statement against DiGerlando . . . that we would be able to go home that night." Petitioner testified that he made the statement in issue because of this assurance. Officer Montejano denied offering any such assurance.

---

3. Petitioner testified that this ambiguous gesture "could have meant most anything," but that he "took it upon [his] own to think that [the lawyer was telling him] not to say anything," and that the lawyer "wanted to talk" to him.

A police officer testified that during the interrogation the following occurred:

> I informed him of what DiGerlando told me and when I did, he told me that DiGerlando was [lying] and I said, "Would you care to tell DiGerlando that?" and he said, "Yes, I will." So, I brought . . . Escobedo in and he confronted DiGerlando and he told him that he was lying and said, "I didn't shoot Manuel, you did it."

In this way, petitioner, for the first time, admitted to some knowledge of the crime. After that he made additional statements further implicating himself in the murder plot. At this point an Assistant State's Attorney, Theodore J. Cooper, was summoned "to take" a statement. Mr. Cooper, an experienced lawyer who was assigned to the Homicide Division to take "statements from some defendants and some prisoners that they had in custody," "took" petitioner's statement by asking carefully framed questions apparently designed to assure the admissibility into evidence of the resulting answers. Mr. Cooper testified that he did not advise petitioner of his constitutional rights, and it is undisputed that no one during the course of the interrogation so advised him.

Petitioner moved both before and during trial to suppress the incriminating statement, but the motions were denied. Petitioner was convicted of murder. . . .

. . .

In Massiah v. United States, 377 U.S. 201, this Court observed that "a Constitution which guarantees a defendant the aid of counsel at . . . trial could surely vouchsafe no less to an indicted defendant under interrogation by the police in a completely extrajudicial proceeding. Anything less . . . might deny a defendant 'effective representation by counsel at the only stage when legal aid and advice would help him.' " Id. at 204, quoting Douglas, J., concurring in Spano v. New York, 360 U.S. 315, 326.

The interrogation here was conducted before petitioner was formally indicted. But in the context of this case, that fact should make no difference. When petitioner requested, and was denied, an opportunity to consult with his lawyer, the investigation had ceased to be a general investigation of "an unsolved crime." Spano v. New York, 360 U.S. 315, 327 (Stewart, J., concurring). Petitioner had become the accused, and the purpose of the interrogation was to "get him" to confess his guilt despite his constitutional right not to do so. At the time of his arrest and throughout the course of the interrogation, the police told petitioner that they had convincing evidence that he had fired the fatal shots. Without informing him of his absolute right to remain silent in the face of this accusation, the police urged him to make a statement. As this Court observed many years ago:

> It cannot be doubted that, placed in the position in which the accused was when the statement was made to him that the other suspected person had charged him with crime, the result was to produce upon his mind the fear that if he remained silent it would be considered an admission of guilt, and therefore render certain his being

committed for trial as the guilty person, and it cannot be conceived that the converse impression would not also have naturally arisen, that by denying there was hope of removing the suspicion from himself. Bram v. United States, 168 U.S. 532, 562. Petitioner, a layman, was undoubtedly unaware that under Illinois law an admission of "mere" complicity in the murder plot was legally as damaging as an admission of firing of the fatal shots. . . . The "guiding hand of counsel" was essential to advise petitioner of his rights in this delicate situation. Powell v. Alabama, 287 U.S. 45, 69. This was the "stage when legal aid and advice" were most critical to petitioner. Massiah v. United States, supra, at 204. It was a stage surely as critical as was the arraignment in Hamilton v. Alabama, 368 U.S. 52, and the preliminary hearing in White v. Maryland, 373 U.S. 59. What happened at this interrogation could certainly "affect the whole trial," Hamilton v. Alabama, supra, at 54, since rights "may be as irretrievably lost, if not then and there asserted, as they are when an accused represented by counsel waives a right for strategic purposes." Ibid. It would exalt form over substance to make the right to counsel, under these circumstances, depend on whether at the time of the interrogation, the authorities had secured a formal indictment. Petitioner had, for all practical purposes, already been charged with murder.

. . .

In Gideon v. Wainwright, 372 U.S. 335, we held that every person accused of a crime, whether state or federal, is entitled to a lawyer at trial. The rule sought by the State here, however, would make the trial no more than an appeal from the interrogation; and the "right to use counsel at the formal trial [would be] a very hollow thing [if], for all practical purposes, the conviction is already assured by pretrial examination." In re Groban, 352 U.S. 330, 344 (Black, J., dissenting). "One can imagine a cynical prosecutor saying: 'Let them have the most illustrious counsel, now. They can't escape the noose. There is nothing that counsel can do for them at the trial.' " Ex parte Sullivan, 107 F.Supp. 514, 517–18.

It is argued that if the right to counsel is afforded prior to indictment, the number of confessions obtained by the police will diminish significantly, because most confessions are obtained during the period between arrest and indictment, and "any lawyer worth his salt will tell the suspect in no uncertain terms to make no statement to police under any circumstances." Watts v. Indiana, 338 U.S. 49, 59 (Jackson, J., concurring in part and dissenting in part). This argument, of course, cuts two ways. The fact that many confessions are obtained during this period points up its critical nature as a "stage when legal aid and advice" are surely needed. Massiah v. United States, supra, at 204. . . . The right to counsel would indeed be hollow if it began at a period when few confessions were obtained. There is necessarily a direct relationship between the importance of a stage to the police in their quest for a confession and the criticalness of that stage to the accused in his need for legal advice. Our Constitution, unlike some others, strikes the balance in favor of the right of the accused to be advised by his lawyer of his privilege against self-incrimination. . . .

We have learned the lesson of history, ancient and modern, that a system of criminal law enforcement which comes to depend on the "confession" will, in the long run, be less reliable and more subject to abuses than a system which depends on extrinsic evidence independently secured through skillful investigation. As Dean Wigmore so wisely said:

> [A]*ny system of administration which permits the prosecution to trust habitually to compulsory self-disclosure as a source of proof must itself suffer morally thereby.* The inclination develops to rely mainly upon such evidence, and to be satisfied with an incomplete investigation of the other sources. The exercise of the power to extract answers begets a forgetfulness of the just limitations of that power. The simple and peaceful process of questioning breeds a readiness to resort to bullying and to physical force and torture. If there is a right to an answer, there soon seems to be a right to the expected answer,—that is, to a confession of guilt. Thus the legitimate use grows into the unjust abuse; ultimately, the innocent are jeopardized by the encroachments of a bad system. Such seems to have been the course of experience in those legal systems where the privilege was not recognized.

8 Wigmore, Evidence (3d ed. 1940), 309. (Emphasis in original.) This Court also has recognized that "history amply shows that confessions have often been extorted to save law enforcement officials the trouble and effort of obtaining valid and independent evidence. . . ." Haynes v. Washington, 373 U.S. 503, 519.

We have also learned the companion lesson of history that no system of criminal justice can, or should, survive if it comes to depend for its continued effectiveness on the citizens' abdication through unawareness of their constitutional rights. No system worth preserving should have to *fear* that if an accused is permitted to consult with a lawyer, he will become aware of, and exercise, these rights. If the exercise of constitutional rights will thwart the effectiveness of a system of law enforcement, then there is something very wrong with that system.

We hold, therefore, that where, as here, the investigation is no longer a general inquiry into an unsolved crime but has begun to focus on a particular suspect, the suspect has been taken into police custody, the police carry out a process of interrogations that lends itself to eliciting incriminating statements, the suspect has requested and been denied an opportunity to consult with his lawyer, and the police have not effectively warned him of his absolute constitutional right to remain silent, the accused has been denied "the Assistance of Counsel" . . . and that no statement elicited by the police during the interrogation may be used against him at a criminal trial.

　　. . .

Nothing we have said today affects the powers of the police to investigate "an unsolved crime," Spano v. New York, 360 U.S. 315, 327 (Stewart, J., concurring), by gathering information from witnesses and by other

"proper investigative efforts." Haynes v. Washington, 373 U.S. 503, 519. We hold only that when the process shifts from investigatory to accusatory—when its focus is on the accused and its purpose is to elicit a confession—our adversary system begins to operate, and, under the circumstances here, the accused must be permitted to consult with his lawyer.
. . . [4]

---

233. The Court has said that the holding of *Escobedo* is "limited . . . to its own facts," Kirby v. Illinois, 406 U.S. 682, 689 (1972), p. 378 above. See Moran v. Burbine, 475 U.S. 412 (1986) (6–3), p. 444 below.

Miranda v. Arizona

384 U.S. 436, 86 S.Ct. 1602, 16 L.Ed.2d 694 (1966)

■ MR. CHIEF JUSTICE WARREN delivered the opinion of the Court.

The cases before us raise questions which go to the roots of our concepts of American criminal jurisprudence: the restraints society must observe consistent with the Federal Constitution in prosecuting individuals for crime. More specifically, we deal with the admissibility of statements obtained from an individual who is subjected to custodial police interrogation and the necessity for procedures which assure that the individual is accorded his privilege under the Fifth Amendment to the Constitution not to be compelled to incriminate himself.

. . .

Our holding will be spelled out with some specificity in the pages which follow but briefly stated it is this: the prosecution may not use statements, whether exculpatory or inculpatory, stemming from custodial interrogation of the defendant unless it demonstrates the use of procedural safeguards effective to secure the privilege against self-incrimination. By custodial interrogation, we mean questioning initiated by law enforcement officers after a person has been taken into custody or otherwise deprived of his freedom of action in any significant way. As for the procedural safeguards to be employed, unless other fully effective means are devised to inform accused persons of their right of silence and to assure a continuous opportunity to exercise it, the following measures are required. Prior to any questioning, the person must be warned that he has a right to remain silent, that any statement he does make may be used as evidence against him, and that he has a right to the presence of an attorney, either retained or appointed. The defendant may waive effectuation of these rights, provid-

[4] Justice Harlan and Justice Stewart wrote dissenting opinions. Justice White also wrote a dissenting opinion, which Justice Clark and Justice Stewart joined.

ed the waiver is made voluntarily, knowingly and intelligently. If, however, he indicates in any manner and at any stage of the process that he wishes to consult with an attorney before speaking there can be no questioning. Likewise, if the individual is alone and indicates in any manner that he does not wish to be interrogated, the police may not question him. The mere fact that he may have answered some questions or volunteered some statements on his own does not deprive him of the right to refrain from answering any further inquiries until he has consulted with an attorney and thereafter consents to be questioned.

I.

The constitutional issue we decide in each of these cases is the admissibility of statements obtained from a defendant questioned while in custody or otherwise deprived of his freedom of action in any significant way. In each, the defendant was questioned by police officers, detectives, or a prosecuting attorney in a room in which he was cut off from the outside world. In none of these cases was the defendant given a full and effective warning of his rights at the outset of the interrogation process. In all the cases, the questioning elicited oral admissions, and in three of them, signed statements as well which were admitted at their trials. They all thus share salient features—incommunicado interrogation of individuals in a police-dominated atmosphere, resulting in self-incriminating statements without full warnings of constitutional rights.

An understanding of the nature and setting of this in-custody interrogation is essential to our decisions today. The difficulty in depicting what transpires at such interrogations stems from the fact that in this country they have largely taken place incommunicado. From extensive factual studies undertaken in the early 1930s, including the famous Wickersham Report to Congress by a Presidential Commission, it is clear that police violence and the "third degree" flourished at that time. In a series of cases decided by this Court long after these studies, the police resorted to physical brutality—beating, hanging, whipping—and to sustained and protracted questioning incommunicado in order to extort confessions. The Commission on Civil Rights in 1961 found much evidence to indicate that "some policemen still resort to physical force to obtain confessions," 1961 Comm'n on Civil Rights Rep., Justice, pt. 5, 17. The use of physical brutality and violence is not, unfortunately, relegated to the past or to any part of the country. . . .

The examples given above are undoubtedly the exception now, but they are sufficiently widespread to be the object of concern. Unless a proper limitation upon custodial interrogation is achieved—such as these decisions will advance—there can be no assurance that practices of this nature will be eradicated in the foreseeable future. . . .

Again we stress that the modern practice of in-custody interrogation is psychologically rather than physically oriented. . . . Interrogation still takes place in privacy. Privacy results in secrecy and this in turn results in a gap in our knowledge as to what in fact goes on in the interrogation rooms. A valuable source of information about present police practices, however, may be found in various police manuals and texts which document procedures employed with success in the past, and which recommend various other effective tactics. These texts are used by law enforcement agencies themselves as guides. It should be noted that these texts professedly present the most enlightened and effective means presently used to obtain statements through custodial interrogation. By considering these texts and other data, it is possible to describe procedures observed and noted around the country.

. . .

[T]he setting prescribed by the manuals and observed in practice becomes clear. In essence, it is this: To be alone with the subject is essential to prevent distraction and to deprive him of any outside support. The aura of confidence in his guilt undermines his will to resist. He merely confirms the preconceived story the police seek to have him describe. Patience and persistence, at times relentless questioning, are employed. To obtain a confession, the interrogator must "patiently maneuver himself or his quarry into a position from which the desired objective may be attained."[5] When normal procedures fail to produce the needed result, the police may resort to deceptive stratagems such as giving false legal advice. It is important to keep the subject off balance, for example, by trading on his insecurity about himself or his surroundings. The police then persuade, trick, or cajole him out of exercising his constitutional rights.

Even without employing brutality, the "third degree" or the specific stratagems described above, the very fact of custodial interrogation exacts a heavy toll on individual liberty and trades on the weakness of individuals. . . .

In the cases before us today, given this background, we concern ourselves primarily with this interrogation atmosphere and the evils it can bring. . . .

In these cases, we might not find the defendants' statements to have been involuntary in traditional terms. Our concern for adequate safeguards to protect precious Fifth Amendment rights is, of course, not lessened in the slightest. In each of the cases, the defendant was thrust into an unfamiliar atmosphere and run through menacing police interrogation procedures. . . . To be sure, the records do not evince overt physical coercion or patent psychological ploys. The fact remains that in none of these cases did the officers undertake to afford appropriate safeguards at the outset of the interrogation to insure that the statements were truly the product of free choice.

It is obvious that such an interrogation environment is created for no purpose other than to subjugate the individual to the will of his examiner. This atmosphere carries its own badge of intimidation. To be sure, this is not physical intimidation, but it is equally destructive of human dignity.

---

5. Inbau & Reid, Lie Detection and Criminal Interrogation 185 (3rd ed. 1953).

The current practice of incommunicado interrogation is at odds with one of our Nation's most cherished principles—that the individual may not be compelled to incriminate himself. Unless adequate protective devices are employed to dispel the compulsion inherent in custodial surroundings, no statement obtained from the defendant can truly be the product of his free choice.

From the foregoing, we can readily perceive an intimate connection between the privilege against self-incrimination and police custodial questioning. It is fitting to turn to history and precedent underlying the Self-Incrimination Clause to determine its applicability in this situation.

II.

We sometimes forget how long it has taken to establish the privilege against self-incrimination, the sources from which it came and the fervor with which it was defended. Its roots go back into ancient times. . . .

. . .

[W]e may view the historical development of the privilege as one which groped for the proper scope of governmental power over the citizen. As a "noble principle often transcends its origins," the privilege has come rightfully to be recognized in part as an individual's substantive right, a "right to a private enclave where he may lead a private life. That right is the hallmark of our democracy." United States v. Grunewald, 233 F.2d 556, 579, 581–82 (Frank, J., dissenting), rev'd, 353 U.S. 391 (1957). . . . [T]he privilege against self-incrimination—the essential mainstay of our adversary system—is founded on a complex of values. . . . All these policies point to one overriding thought: the constitutional foundation underlying the privilege is the respect a government—state or federal—must accord to the dignity and integrity of its citizens. To maintain a "fair state-individual balance," to require the government "to shoulder the entire load," 8 Wigmore, Evidence 317 (McNaughton rev.1961), to respect the inviolability of the human personality, our accusatory system of criminal justice demands that the government seeking to punish an individual produce the evidence against him by its own independent labors, rather than by the cruel, simple expedient of compelling it from his own mouth. . . . In sum, the privilege is fulfilled only when the person is guaranteed the right "to remain silent unless he chooses to speak in the unfettered exercise of his own will." Malloy v. Hogan, 378 U.S. 1, 8 (1964).

The question in these cases is whether the privilege is fully applicable during a period of custodial interrogation. In this Court, the privilege has consistently been accorded a liberal construction. . . . We are satisfied that all the principles embodied in the privilege apply to informal compulsion exerted by law-enforcement officers during in-custody questioning. An individual swept from familiar surroundings into police custody, surrounded by antagonistic forces, and subjected to the techniques of persuasion described above cannot be otherwise than under compulsion to speak. As a practical matter, the compulsion to speak in the isolated setting of the police station may well be greater than in courts or other official investigations, where there are often impartial observers to guard against intimidation or trickery.

. . .

Our holding [in Escobedo v. Illinois, 378 U.S. 478 (1964),] stressed the fact that the police had not advised the defendant of his constitutional privilege to remain silent at the outset of the interrogation, and we drew attention to that fact at several points in the decision. . . . This was no isolated factor, but an essential ingredient in our decision. The entire thrust of police interrogation there, as in all the cases today, was to put the defendant in such an emotional state as to impair his capacity for rational judgment. The abdication of the constitutional privilege—the choice on his part to speak to the police—was not made knowingly or competently because of the failure to apprise him of his rights; the compelling atmosphere of the in-custody interrogation, and not an independent decision on his part, caused the defendant to speak.

A different phase of the *Escobedo* decision was significant in its attention to the absence of counsel during the questioning. There, as in the cases today, we sought a protective device to dispel the compelling atmosphere of the interrogation. In *Escobedo*, however, the police did not relieve the defendant of the anxieties which they had created in the interrogation rooms. Rather, they denied his request for the assistance of counsel. . . . This heightened his dilemma, and made his later statements the product of this compulsion. . . . The denial of the defendant's request for his attorney thus undermined his ability to exercise the privilege—to remain silent if he chose or to speak without any intimidation, blatant or subtle. The presence of counsel, in all the cases before us today, would be the adequate protective device necessary to make the process of police interrogation conform to the dictates of the privilege. His presence would insure that statements made in the government-established atmosphere are not the product of compulsion.

It was in this manner that *Escobedo* explicated another facet of the pre-trial privilege, noted in many of the Court's prior decisions: the protection of rights at trial. That counsel is present when statements are taken from an individual during interrogation obviously enhances the integrity of the fact-finding processes in court. The presence of an attorney, and the warnings delivered to the individual, enable the defendant under otherwise compelling circumstances to tell his story without fear, effectively, and in a way that eliminates the evils in the interrogation process. Without the protections flowing from adequate warnings and the rights of counsel, "all the careful safeguards erected around the giving of testimony, whether by an accused or any other witness, would become empty formalities in a procedure where the most compelling possible evidence of guilt, a confession, would have already been obtained at the unsupervised pleasure of the police." Mapp v. Ohio, 367 U.S. 643, 685 (1961) (Harlan, J., dissenting). . . .

III.

Today, then, there can be no doubt that the Fifth Amendment privilege is available outside of criminal court proceedings and serves to protect persons in all settings in which their freedom of action is curtailed in any significant way from being compelled to incriminate themselves. We have concluded that without proper safeguards the process of in-custody interrogation of persons suspected or accused of crime contains inherently compelling pressures which work to undermine the individual's will to resist and to compel him to speak where he would not otherwise do so freely. In order to combat these pressures and to permit a full opportunity to exercise the privilege against self-incrimination, the accused must be adequately and effectively apprised of his rights and the exercise of those rights must be fully honored.

It is impossible for us to foresee the potential alternatives for protecting the privilege which might be devised by Congress or the States in the exercise of their creative rule-making capacities. Therefore we cannot say that the Constitution necessarily requires adherence to any particular solution for the inherent compulsions of the interrogation process as it is presently conducted. Our decision in no way creates a constitutional straightjacket which will handicap sound efforts at reform, nor is it intended to have this effect. We encourage Congress and the States to continue their laudable search for increasingly effective ways of protecting the rights of the individual while promoting efficient enforcement of our criminal laws. However, unless we are shown other procedures which are at least as effective in apprising accused persons of their right of silence and in assuring a continuous opportunity to exercise it, the following safeguards must be observed.

At the outset, if a person in custody is to be subjected to interrogation, he must first be informed in clear and unequivocal terms that he has the right to remain silent. For those unaware of the privilege, the warning is needed simply to make them aware of it—the threshold requirement for an intelligent decision as to its exercise. More important, such a warning is an absolute prerequisite in overcoming the inherent pressures of the interrogation atmosphere. It is not just the subnormal or woefully ignorant who succumb to an interrogator's imprecations, whether implied or expressly stated, that the interrogation will continue until a confession is obtained or that silence in the face of accusation is itself damning and will bode ill when presented to a jury. Further, the warning will show the individual that his interrogators are prepared to recognize his privilege should he choose to exercise it.

The Fifth Amendment privilege is so fundamental to our system of constitutional rule and the expedient of giving an adequate warning as to the availability of the privilege so simple, we will not pause to inquire in individual cases whether the defendant was aware of his rights without a warning being given. Assessments of the knowledge the defendant possessed, based on information as to his age, education, intelligence, or prior contact with authorities, can never be more than speculation; a warning is a clearcut fact. More important, whatever the background of the person interrogated, a warning at the time of the interrogation is indispensable to overcome its pressures and to insure that the individual knows he is free to exercise the privilege at that point in time.

The warning of the right to remain silent must be accompanied by the explanation that anything said can and will be used against the individual in court. This warning is needed in order to make him aware not only of the privilege, but also of the consequences of forgoing it. It is only through an awareness of these consequences that there can be any assurance of real understanding and intelligent exercise of the privilege. Moreover, this warning may serve to make the individual more acutely aware that he is faced with a phase of the adversary system—that he is not in the presence of persons acting solely in his interest.

The circumstances surrounding in-custody interrogation can operate very quickly to overbear the will of one merely made aware of his privilege by his interrogators. Therefore, the right to have counsel present at the interrogation is indispensable to the protection of the Fifth Amendment privilege under the system we delineate today. Our aim is to assure that the individual's right to choose between silence and speech remains unfettered throughout the interrogation process. A once-stated warning, delivered by those who will conduct the interrogation, cannot itself suffice to that end among those who most require knowledge of their rights. A mere warning given by the interrogators is not alone sufficient to accomplish that end. . . . Even preliminary advice given to the accused by his own attorney can be swiftly overcome by the secret interrogation process. . . . Thus, the need for counsel to protect the Fifth Amendment privilege comprehends not merely a right to consult with counsel prior to questioning, but also to have counsel present during any questioning if the defendant so desires.

The presence of counsel at the interrogation may serve several significant subsidiary functions as well. If the accused decides to talk to his interrogators, the assistance of counsel can mitigate the dangers of untrustworthiness. With a lawyer present the likelihood that the police will practice coercion is reduced, and if coercion is nevertheless exercised the lawyer can testify to it in court. The presence of a lawyer can also help to guarantee that the accused gives a fully accurate statement to the police and that the statement is rightly reported by the prosecution at trial. . . .

An individual need not make a pre-interrogation request for a lawyer. While such request affirmatively secures his right to have one, his failure to ask for a lawyer does not constitute a waiver. No effective waiver of the right to counsel during interrogation can be recognized unless specifically made after the warnings we here delineate have been given. The accused who does not know his rights and therefore does not make a request may be the person who most needs counsel. . . .

Accordingly we hold that an individual held for interrogation must be clearly informed that he has the right to consult with a lawyer and to have the lawyer with him during interrogation under the system for protecting the privilege we delineate today. As with the warnings of the right to remain silent and that anything stated can be used in evidence against him, this warning is an absolute prerequisite to interrogation. No amount of circumstantial evidence that the person may have been aware of this right will suffice to stand in its stead. Only through such a warning is there ascertainable assurance that the accused was aware of this right.

If an individual indicates that he wishes the assistance of counsel before any interrogation occurs, the authorities cannot rationally ignore or deny his request on the basis that the individual does not have or cannot afford a retained attorney. The financial ability of the individual has no relationship to the scope of the rights involved here. The privilege against self-incrimination secured by the Constitution applies to all individuals. The need for counsel in order to protect the privilege exists for the indigent as well as the affluent. In fact, were we to limit these constitutional rights to those who can retain an attorney, our decisions today would be of little significance. The cases before us as well as the vast majority of confession cases with which we have dealt in the past involve those unable to retain counsel. While authorities are not required to relieve the accused of his poverty, they have the obligation not to take advantage of indigence in the administration of justice. Denial of counsel to the indigent at the time of interrogation while allowing an attorney to those who can afford one would be no more supportable by reason or logic than the similar situation at trial and on appeal struck down in Gideon v. Wainwright, 372 U.S. 335 (1963), and Douglas v. California, 372 U.S. 353 (1963).

In order fully to apprise a person interrogated of the extent of his rights under this system then, it is necessary to warn him not only that he has the right to consult with an attorney, but also that if he is indigent a lawyer will be appointed to represent him. Without this additional warning, the admonition of the right to consult with counsel would often be understood as meaning only that he can consult with a lawyer if he has one or has the funds to obtain one. The warning of a right to counsel would be hollow if not couched in terms that would convey to the indigent—the person most often subjected to interrogation—the knowledge that he too has a right to have counsel present. As with the warnings of the right to remain silent and of the general right to counsel, only by effective and express explanation to the indigent of this right can there be assurance that he was truly in a position to exercise it.

Once warnings have been given, the subsequent procedure is clear. If the individual indicates in any manner, at any time prior to or during questioning, that he wishes to remain silent, the interrogation must cease. At this point he has shown that he intends to exercise his Fifth Amendment privilege; any statement taken after the person invokes his privilege cannot be other than the product of compulsion, subtle or otherwise. Without the right to cut off questioning the setting of in-custody interrogation operates on the individual to overcome free choice in producing a statement after the privilege has been once invoked. If the individual states that he wants an attorney, the interrogation must cease until an attorney is present. At that time, the individual must have an opportunity to confer with the attorney and to have him present during any subsequent questioning. If the individual cannot obtain an attorney and he indicates that he wants one before speaking to police, they must respect his decision to remain silent.

This does not mean, as some have suggested, that each police station must have a "station house lawyer" present at all times to advise prisoners. It does mean, however, that if police propose to interrogate a person they must make known to him that he is entitled to a lawyer and that if he cannot afford one, a lawyer will be provided for him prior to any interrogation. If authorities conclude that they will not provide counsel during a reasonable period of time in which investigation in the field is carried out, they may refrain from doing so without violating the person's Fifth Amendment privilege so long as they do not question him during that time.

If the interrogation continues without the presence of an attorney and a statement is taken, a heavy burden rests on the government to demonstrate that the defendant knowingly and intelligently waived his privilege against self-incrimination and his right to retained or appointed counsel. Escobedo v. Illinois, 378 U.S. 478, 490, n.14. This Court has always set high standards of proof for the waiver of constitutional rights . . . and we reassert these standards as applied to in-custody interrogation. Since the State is responsible for establishing the isolated circumstances under which the interrogation takes place and has the only means of making available corroborated evidence of warnings given during incommunicado interrogation, the burden is rightly on its shoulders.

An express statement that the individual is willing to make a statement and does not want an attorney followed closely by a statement could constitute a waiver. But a valid waiver will not be presumed simply from the silence of the accused after warnings are given or simply from the fact that a confession was in fact eventually obtained. . . . Moreover, where in-custody interrogation is involved, there is no room for the contention that the privilege is waived if the individual answers some questions or gives some information on his own prior to invoking his right to remain silent when interrogated.

Whatever the testimony of the authorities as to waiver of rights by an accused, the fact of lengthy interrogation or incommunicado incarceration before a statement is made is strong evidence that the accused did not validly waive his rights. In these circumstances the fact that the individual eventually made a statement is consistent with the conclusion that the compelling influence of the interrogation finally forced him to do so. It is inconsistent with any notion of a voluntary relinquishment of the privilege. Moreover, any evidence that the accused was threatened, tricked, or cajoled into a waiver will, of course, show that the defendant did not voluntarily waive his privilege. The requirement of warnings and waiver of rights is a fundamental with respect to the Fifth Amendment privilege and not simply a preliminary ritual to existing methods of interrogation.

The warnings required and the waiver necessary in accordance with our opinion today are, in the absence of a fully effective equivalent, prerequisites to the admissibility of any statement made by a defendant. No distinction can be drawn between statements which are direct confessions and statements which amount to "admissions" of part or all of an offense. The privilege against self-incrimination protects the individual from being compelled to incriminate himself in any manner; it does not distinguish degrees of incrimination. Similarly, for precisely the same reason, no distinction may be drawn between inculpatory statements and statements alleged to be merely "exculpatory." If a statement made were in fact truly exculpatory it would, of course, never be used by the prosecution. In fact, statements merely intended to be exculpatory by the defendant are often used to impeach his testimony at trial or to demonstrate untruths in the statement given under interrogation and thus to prove guilt by implication. These statements are incriminating in any meaningful sense of the word and may not be used without the full warnings and effective waiver required for any other statement. In *Escobedo* itself, the defendant fully intended his accusation of another as the slayer to be exculpatory as to himself.

The principles announced today deal with the protection which must be given to the privilege against self-incrimination when the individual is first subjected to police interrogation while in custody at the station or otherwise deprived of his freedom of action in any significant way. It is at this point that our adversary system of criminal proceedings commences, distinguishing itself at the outset from the inquisitorial system recognized in some countries. Under the system of warnings we delineate today or under any other system which may be devised and found effective, the safeguards to be erected about the privilege must come into play at this point.

Our decision is not intended to hamper the traditional function of police officers in investigating crime. . . . When an individual is in custody on probable cause, the police may, of course, seek out evidence in the field to be used at trial against him. Such investigation may include inquiry of persons not under restraint. General on-the-scene questioning as to facts surrounding a crime or other general questioning of citizens in the fact-finding process is not affected by our holding. It is an act of responsible citizenship for individuals to give whatever information they may have to aid in law enforcement. In such situations the compelling atmosphere inherent in the process of in-custody interrogation is not necessarily present.

In dealing with statements obtained through interrogation, we do not purport to find all confessions inadmissible. Confessions remain a proper element in law enforcement. Any statement given freely and voluntarily without any compelling influences is, of course, admissible in evidence. The fundamental import of the privilege while an individual is in custody is not whether he is allowed to talk to the police without the benefit of warnings and counsel, but whether he can be interrogated. There is no requirement that police stop a person who enters a police station and states that he wishes to confess to a crime, or a person who calls the police to offer a confession or any other statement he desires to make. Volunteered statements of any kind are not barred by the Fifth Amendment and their admissibility is not affected by our holding today.

To summarize, we hold that when an individual is taken into custody or otherwise deprived of his freedom by the authorities in any significant way and is subjected to questioning, the privilege against self-incrimination is jeopardized. Procedural safeguards must be employed to protect the privilege, and unless other fully effective means are adopted to notify the person of his right of silence and to assure that the exercise of the right will be scrupulously honored, the following measures are required. He must be warned prior to any questioning that he has the right to remain silent, that anything he says can be used against him in a court of law, that he has the right to the presence of an attorney, and that if he cannot afford an attorney one will be appointed for him prior to any questioning if he so desires. Opportunity to exercise these rights must be afforded to him throughout the interrogation. After such warnings have been given, and such opportunity afforded, the individual may knowingly and intelligently waive these rights and agree to answer questions or make a statement. But unless and until such warnings and waiver are demonstrated by the prosecution at trial, no evidence obtained as a result of interrogation can be used against him.

IV.

A recurrent argument made in these cases is that society's need for interrogation outweighs the privilege. This argument is not unfamiliar to this Court. . . . The whole thrust of our foregoing discussion demonstrates that the Constitution has prescribed the rights of the individual when confronted with the power of government when it provided in the Fifth Amendment that an individual cannot be compelled to be a witness against himself. That right cannot be abridged. . . .

If the individual desires to exercise his privilege, he has the right to do so. This is not for the authorities to decide. An attorney may advise his client not to talk to police until he has had an opportunity to investigate the case, or he may wish to be present with his client during any police questioning. In doing so an attorney is merely exercising the good professional judgment he has been taught. This is not cause for considering the attorney a menace to law enforcement. He is merely carrying out what he is sworn to do under his oath—to protect to the extent of his ability the rights of his client. In fulfilling this responsibility the attorney plays a vital role in the administration of criminal justice under our Constitution.

In announcing these principles, we are not unmindful of the burdens which law enforcement officials must bear, often under trying circumstances. We also fully recognize the obligation of all citizens to aid in enforcing the criminal laws. This Court, while protecting individual rights, has always given ample latitude to law enforcement agencies in the legitimate exercise of their duties. The limits we have placed on the interrogation process should not constitute an undue interference with a proper system of law enforcement. As we have noted, our decision does not in any way preclude police from carrying out their traditional investigatory functions. Although confessions may play an important role in some convictions, the cases before us present graphic examples of the overstatement of the "need" for confessions. In each case authorities conducted interrogations ranging up to five days in duration despite the presence, through standard investigating practices, of considerable evidence against each defendant. Further examples are chronicled in our prior cases. . . .

It is also urged that an unfettered right to detention for interrogation should be allowed because it will often redound to the benefit of the person questioned. When police inquiry determines that there is no reason to believe that the person has committed any crime, it is said, he will be released without need for further formal procedures. The person who has committed no offense, however, will be better able to clear himself after warnings with counsel present than without. It can be assumed that in such circumstances a lawyer would advise his client to talk freely to police in order to clear himself.

. . .

Custodial interrogation, by contrast, does not necessarily afford the innocent an opportunity to clear themselves. A serious consequence of the present practice of the interrogation alleged to be beneficial for the innocent is that many arrests "for investigation" subject large numbers of innocent persons to detention and interrogation. . . .

. . .

V.

Because of the nature of the problem and because of its recurrent significance in numerous cases, we have to this point discussed the relationship of the Fifth Amendment privilege to police interrogation without specific concentration on the facts of the cases before us. We turn now to these facts to consider the application to these cases of the constitutional principles discussed above. In each instance, we have concluded that statements were obtained from the defendant under circumstances that did not meet constitutional standards for protection of the privilege.

. . . [6]

---

[6] Justice Clark wrote an opinion dissenting in three of the cases before the Court and concurring in the result in one. Justice Harlan wrote a dissenting opinion which Justice Stewart and Justice White joined. Justice White also wrote a dissenting opinion which Justice Harlan and Justice Stewart joined.

234. In a dissenting opinion, Justice Harlan described and discussed the facts of Miranda v. Arizona:[7]

On March 3, 1963, an 18-year-old girl was kidnapped and forcibly raped near Phoenix, Arizona. Ten days later, on the morning of March 13, petitioner Miranda was arrested and taken to the police station. At this time Miranda was 23 years old, indigent, and educated to the extent of completing half the ninth grade. He had "an emotional illness" of the schizophrenic type, according to the doctor who eventually examined him; the doctor's report also stated that Miranda was "alert and oriented as to time, place, and person," intelligent within normal limits, competent to stand trial, and sane within the legal definition. At the police station, the victim picked Miranda out of a lineup, and two officers then took him into a separate room to interrogate him, starting about 11:30 a.m. Though at first denying his guilt, within a short time Miranda gave a detailed oral confession and then wrote out in his own hand and signed a brief statement admitting and describing the crime. All this was accomplished in two hours or less without any force, threats or promises and—I will assume this though the record is uncertain . . . —without any effective warnings at all.

Miranda's oral and written confessions are now held inadmissible under the Court's new rules. One is entitled to feel astonished that the Constitution can be read to produce this result. These confessions were obtained during brief, daytime questioning conducted by two officers and unmarked by any of the traditional indicia of coercion. They assured a conviction for a brutal and unsettling crime, for which the police had and quite possibly could obtain little evidence other than the victim's identifications, evidence which is frequently unreliable. There was, in sum, a legitimate purpose, no perceptible unfairness, and certainly little risk of injustice in the interrogation. Yet the resulting confessions, and the responsible course of police practice they represent, are to be sacrificed to the Court's own finespun conception of fairness which I seriously doubt is shared by many thinking citizens in this country.

384 U.S. at 518–19.

235. In 1968, Congress enacted 18 U.S.C. § 3501, which provides that in any federal prosecution, a confession is admissible "if it is voluntarily given." 18 U.S.C. § 3501(a). The test of voluntariness is the pre-*Miranda* totality-of-the-circumstances test, including but not limited to whether or not the person had been advised of his rights. Notwithstanding the statute, the courts continued to apply *Miranda*. Finally, in Dickerson v. United States, 530 U.S. 428, 444 (2000) (7–2), the Court declared that "*Miranda* announced a constitutional rule that Congress may not supersede legisla-

---

7. *Miranda* was one of four cases which the Supreme Court considered in its opinion and to which it applied the new requirements. Miranda himself was again convicted of kidnapping and rape at a subsequent trial, in which the confession which the Supreme Court had concluded was unconstitutionally obtained was not admitted. State v. Miranda, 450 P.2d 364 (Ariz.1969).

tively." Observing that the *Miranda* warnings "have become part of our national culture," id. at 430, the Court added that it would not overrule *Miranda*.

236. The *Miranda* warnings do not have to be given in the exact form stated in that opinion. California v. Prysock, 453 U.S. 355 (1981) (6–3). In particular, advising a defendant that if he is indigent, a lawyer will be appointed for him "if and when you go to court" is not defective because of the inclusion of that phrase. Duckworth v. Eagan, 492 U.S. 195 (1989) (5–4).

In United States v. Caba, 955 F.2d 182 (2d Cir.1992), the court generally disapproved the practice of having an informant or codefendant give a translation of the *Miranda* warnings to a person who does not understand English, but said that there is no per se rule to that effect.

237. At about 3:00 a.m., Hill, a 17-year-old boy, was arrested at his home and brought to the police station "for questioning" in connection with a street gang killing earlier that night. He was fully warned of his constitutional rights. In response to questioning, he denied any knowledge of the killing. Over the next three hours, on three or four separate occasions lasting about ten or 15 minutes each, the same detective questioned him again. On each occasion, he was alone with the detective in an interview room. At about 6:00 a.m., after the detective had called for a car to transport Hill to the police lockup, he called the detective back into the room and made a statement denying his guilt but implicating himself. No warnings were given after the initial warnings. "[C]onsidering the fact that the adequacy of the *Miranda* warnings is not disputed here, that the questioning was not for an inordinate period of time, that the period of interrogation had concluded as far as the police were concerned before the statement was made, that the defendant never sought to terminate the questioning, and that Hill's admission was a self protective attempt to shift the blame onto another and thereby relieve himself of all fault," the court held that the statement was admissible. People v. Hill, 233 N.E.2d 367, 372 (Ill.1968). The court declined to adopt "an automatic second-warning system," which, it said, would "add a perfunctory ritual to police procedures." Id. at 371.

In Michigan v. Mosley, 423 U.S. 96 (1975) (7–2), detectives gave the defendant the *Miranda* warnings and then questioned him about the robbery charges for which he had been arrested. When he said he did not want to answer questions, the questioning stopped. A few hours later, after repeating the warnings, other detectives questioned the defendant about a homicide for which he had not been arrested. His answers incriminated him and he was subsequently prosecuted for murder. The Court held that the resumption of questioning in those circumstances, each session being independent of the other and accompanied by warnings, did not violate *Miranda*. That case, the Court said, did not "create a per se proscription of indefinite duration upon any further questioning by any police officer on any subject, once the person in custody has indicated a desire to remain silent." So long as a person's "right to cut off questioning" is "scrupulously honored," as the court concluded it had been, a resumption of questioning is permissible. Id. at 102–103, 104.

238. An initial failure to give *Miranda* warnings does not render inadmissible statements made after the warnings are given, even though the person made incriminating admissions before they were given. Oregon v. Elstad, 470 U.S. 298 (1985) (6–3). Police arrested the defendant, who was eighteen years old, at his home. An officer questioned him briefly in the living room while another officer talked with his mother. He made brief damaging admissions. He was then taken to the police station and, about an hour later, was given *Miranda* warnings. He gave the police a full statement about the burglary for which he had been arrested.

Observing that the *Miranda* exclusionary rule may exclude a person's statements even though they are not coerced and that there has been no violation of the Fifth Amendment privilege, the Court said that the rule does not require that the statements and their fruits be regarded as "inherently tainted," Id. at 307. Provided that statements are voluntary, subsequent statements made after compliance with *Miranda* are admissible. The psychological impact of having "let the cat out of the bag" by the first statements does not, without more, render the later statements involuntary. Nor is it essential that a person have been told that his prior statements are not admissible. The Court said:

> Far from establishing a rigid rule, we direct courts to avoid one; there is no warrant for presuming coercive effect where the suspect's initial inculpatory statement, though technically in violation of *Miranda*, was voluntary. The relevant inquiry is whether, in fact, the second statement was also voluntarily made. As in any such inquiry, the finder of fact must examine the surrounding circumstances and the entire course of police conduct with respect to the suspect in evaluating the voluntariness of his statements. The fact that a suspect chooses to speak after being informed of his rights is, of course, highly probative. We find that the dictates of *Miranda* and the goals of the Fifth Amendment proscription against use of compelled testimony are fully satisfied in the circumstances of this case by barring use of the unwarned statement in the case in chief. No further purpose is served by imputing "taint" to subsequent statements obtained pursuant to a voluntary and knowing waiver. We hold today that a suspect who has once responded to unwarned yet uncoercive questioning is not thereby disabled from waiving his rights and confessing after he has been given the requisite *Miranda* warnings.

Id. at 318.

In State v. Seibert, 93 S.W.3d 700 (Mo.2002), cert. granted, 538 U.S. 1031 (2003), a police officer deliberately questioned the defendant without giving her *Miranda* warnings. After he obtained incriminating statements, he interrupted the questioning for twenty minutes and then, giving the defendant *Miranda* warnings, resumed. The officer's evident purpose was to elicit statements in the first session that the defendant would repeat after the warnings were given. The court held that the intentional violation of *Miranda* distinguished the case from *Elstad* and that in those circumstances, exclusion of the second statement was required. Contra, United States v. Orso, 234 F.3d 436 (9th Cir.2000) (en banc). See People v. Neal, 72 P.3d 280 (Cal.2003), generally in agreement with *Seibert*, in which the court concluded that in all the circumstances—the deliberate violation of *Miranda* in the first interrogation, as well as the defendant's youth, inexperience, low intelligence, and minimal education, and the deprivations and isolation of his confinement during the interrogations—the post-*Miranda* statements were involuntary.

See note 271 (Michigan v. Tucker), p. 482 below.

239. Compulsory questioning by itself does not violate the privilege against compulsory self-incrimination, if the answers are never used in any criminal proceeding. "[A] violation of the constitutional *right* against self-incrimination occurs only if one has been compelled to be a witness against himself in a criminal case." Chavez v. Martinez, 538 U.S. 760, 770 (2003) (6–3). The plaintiff, who was never charged with a crime, had brought an action against the officer who questioned him, under 42 U.S.C. § 1983.

Rhode Island v. Innis
446 U.S. 291, 100 S.Ct. 1682, 64 L.Ed.2d 297 (1980)

■ MR. JUSTICE STEWART delivered the opinion of the Court.

In Miranda v. Arizona, 384 U.S. 436, 474, the Court held that, once a defendant in custody asks to speak with a lawyer, all interrogation must cease until a lawyer is present. The issue in this case is whether the respondent was "interrogated" in violation of the standards promulgated in the *Miranda* opinion.

I

On the night of January 12, 1975, John Mulvaney, a Providence, R.I., taxicab driver, disappeared after being dispatched to pick up a customer. His body was discovered four days later buried in a shallow grave in Coventry, R.I. He had died from a shotgun blast aimed at the back of his head.

On January 17, 1975, shortly after midnight, the Providence police received a telephone call from Gerald Aubin, also a taxicab driver, who reported that he had just been robbed by a man wielding a sawed-off shotgun. Aubin further reported that he had dropped off his assailant near Rhode Island College in a section of Providence known as Mount Pleasant. While at the Providence police station waiting to give a statement, Aubin noticed a picture of his assailant on a bulletin board. Aubin so informed one of the police officers present. The officer prepared a photo array, and again Aubin identified a picture of the same person. That person was the respondent. Shortly thereafter, the Providence police began a search of the Mount Pleasant area.

At approximately 4:30 a.m. on the same date, Patrolman Lovell, while cruising the streets of Mount Pleasant in a patrol car, spotted the respondent standing in the street facing him. When Patrolman Lovell stopped his car, the respondent walked towards it. Patrolman Lovell then arrested the respondent, who was unarmed, and advised him of his so-called *Miranda* rights. While the two men waited in the patrol car for other police officers to arrive, Patrolman Lovell did not converse with the respondent other than to respond to the latter's request for a cigarette.

Within minutes, Sergeant Sears arrived at the scene of the arrest, and he also gave the respondent the *Miranda* warnings. Immediately thereafter, Captain Leyden and other police officers arrived. Captain Leyden advised the respondent of his *Miranda* rights. The respondent stated that he understood those rights and wanted to speak with a lawyer. Captain Leyden then directed that the respondent be placed in a "caged wagon," a four-door police car with a wire screen mesh between the front and rear seats, and be driven to the central police station. Three officers, Patrolmen Gleckman, Williams, and McKenna, were assigned to accompany the respondent to the central station. They placed the respondent in the vehicle and shut the doors. Captain Leyden then instructed the officers not to question the respondent or intimidate or coerce him in any way. The three officers then entered the vehicle, and it departed.

While en route to the central station, Patrolman Gleckman initiated a conversation with Patrolman McKenna concerning the missing shotgun. As Patrolman Gleckman later testified:

> A. At this point, I was talking back and forth with Patrolman McKenna stating that I frequent this area while on patrol and [that because a school for handicapped children is located nearby,] there's a lot of handicapped children running around in this area, and God forbid one of them might find a weapon with shells and they might hurt themselves.

App. 43–44. Patrolman McKenna apparently shared his fellow officer's concern:

> A. I more or less concurred with him [Gleckman] that it was a safety factor and that we should, you know, continue to search for the weapon and try to find it.

Id., at 53. While Patrolman Williams said nothing, he overheard the conversation between the two officers:

> A. He [Gleckman] said it would be too bad if the little—I believe he said a girl—would pick up the gun, maybe kill herself.

Id., at 59. The respondent then interrupted the conversation, stating that the officers should turn the car around so he could show them where the gun was located. At this point, Patrolman McKenna radioed back to Captain Leyden that they were returning to the scene of the arrest, and that the respondent would inform them of the location of the gun. At the time the respondent indicated that the officers should turn back, they had traveled no more than a mile, a trip encompassing only a few minutes.

The police vehicle then returned to the scene of the arrest where a search for the shotgun was in progress. There, Captain Leyden again advised the respondent of his *Miranda* rights. The respondent replied that he understood those rights but that he "wanted to get the gun out of the way because of the kids in the area in the school." The respondent then led the police to a nearby field, where he pointed out the shotgun under some rocks by the side of the road.

On March 20, 1975, a grand jury returned an indictment charging the respondent with the kidnapping, robbery, and murder of John Mulvaney. Before trial, the respondent moved to suppress the shotgun and the statements he had made to the police regarding it. After an evidentiary hearing at which the respondent elected not to testify, the trial judge found that the respondent had been "repeatedly and completely advised of his *Miranda* rights." He further found that it was "entirely understandable that [the officers in the police vehicle] would voice their concern [for the safety of the handicapped children] to each other." The judge then concluded that the respondent's decision to inform the police of the location of the shotgun was "a waiver, clearly, and on the basis of the evidence that I have heard, and [*sic*] intelligent waiver, of his [*Miranda*] right to remain silent." Thus, without passing on whether the police officers had in fact "interrogated" the respondent, the trial court sustained the admissibility of the shotgun and testimony related to its discovery. That evidence was later introduced at the respondent's trial, and the jury returned a verdict of guilty on all counts.

On appeal, the Rhode Island Supreme Court, in a 3–2 decision, set aside the respondent's conviction. . . . [T]he court concluded that the respondent had invoked his *Miranda* right to counsel and that, contrary to *Miranda*'s mandate that, in the absence of counsel, all custodial interrogation then cease, the police officers in the vehicle had "interrogated" the respondent without a valid waiver of his right to counsel. . . .

We granted certiorari to address for the first time the meaning of "interrogation" under Miranda v. Arizona. . . .

II

. . .

In the present case, the parties are in agreement that the respondent was fully informed of his *Miranda* rights and that he invoked his *Miranda* right to counsel when he told Captain Leyden that he wished to consult with a lawyer. It is also uncontested that the respondent was "in custody" while being transported to the police station.

The issue, therefore, is whether the respondent was "interrogated" by the police officers in violation of the respondent's undisputed right under *Miranda* to remain silent until he had consulted with a lawyer. In resolving this issue, we first define the term "interrogation" under *Miranda* before turning to a consideration of the facts of this case.

A

The starting point for defining "interrogation" in this context is, of course, the Court's *Miranda* opinion. There the Court observed that "[b]y custodial interrogation, we mean *questioning* initiated by law enforcement officers after a person has been taken into custody or otherwise deprived of his freedom of action in any significant way." Id., at 444 (emphasis added). This passage and other references throughout the opinion to "questioning" might suggest that the *Miranda* rules were to apply only to those police interrogation practices that involve express questioning of a defendant while in custody.

We do not, however, construe the *Miranda* opinion so narrowly. The concern of the Court in *Miranda* was that the "interrogation environment" created by the interplay of interrogation and custody would "subjugate the individual to the will of his examiner" and thereby undermine the privilege against compulsory self-incrimination. Id., at 457–58. The police practices that evoked this concern included several that did not involve express questioning. For example, one of the practices discussed in *Miranda* was the use of lineups in which a coached witness would pick the defendant as the perpetrator. This was designed to establish that the defendant was in fact guilty as a predicate for further interrogation. . . . A variation on this theme discussed in *Miranda* was the so-called "reverse line-up" in which a defendant would be identified by coached witnesses as the perpetrator of a fictitious crime, with the object of inducing him to confess to the actual crime of which he was suspected in order to escape the false prosecution. . . . The Court in *Miranda* also included in its survey of interrogation practices the use of psychological ploys, such as to "posi[t]" "the guilt of the subject," to "minimize the moral seriousness of the offense," and "to cast blame on the victim or on society." Id., at 450. It is clear that these techniques of persuasion, no less than express questioning, were thought, in a custodial setting, to amount to interrogation.

This is not to say, however, that all statements obtained by the police after a person has been taken into custody are to be considered the product of interrogation. . . . It is clear . . . that the special procedural safeguards outlined in *Miranda* are required not where a suspect is simply taken into custody, but rather where a suspect in custody is subjected to interrogation. "Interrogation," as conceptualized in the *Miranda* opinion, must reflect a measure of compulsion above and beyond that inherent in custody itself.[8]

---

8. There is language in the opinion of the Rhode Island Supreme Court in this case suggesting that the definition of "interrogation" under *Miranda* is informed by this Court's decision in Brewer v. Williams, 430 U.S. 387. . . . This suggestion is erroneous. Our decision in *Brewer* rested solely on the Sixth and Fourteenth Amendment right to counsel. . . . That right, as we held in Massiah v. United States, 377 U.S. 201, 206, prohibits law enforcement officers from "deliberately elicit[ing]" incriminating information from a defendant in the absence of counsel after a formal charge against the defendant

We conclude that the *Miranda* safeguards come into play whenever a person in custody is subjected to either express questioning or its functional equivalent. That is to say, the term "interrogation" under *Miranda* refers not only to express questioning, but also to any words or actions on the part of the police (other than those normally attendant to arrest and custody) that the police should know are reasonably likely to elicit an incriminating response from the suspect. The latter portion of this definition focuses primarily upon the perceptions of the suspect, rather than the intent of the police. This focus reflects the fact that the *Miranda* safeguards were designed to vest a suspect in custody with an added measure of protection against coercive police practices, without regard to objective proof of the underlying intent of the police. A practice that the police should know is reasonably likely to evoke an incriminating response from a suspect thus amounts to interrogation.[9] But, since the police surely cannot be held accountable for the unforeseeable results of their words or actions, the definition of interrogation can extend only to words or actions on the part of police officers that they *should have known* were reasonably likely to elicit an incriminating response.

B

Turning to the facts of the present case, we conclude that the respondent was not "interrogated" within the meaning of *Miranda*. It is undisputed that the first prong of the definition of "interrogation" was not satisfied, for the conversation between Patrolmen Gleckman and McKenna included no express questioning of the respondent. Rather, that conversation was, at least in form, nothing more than a dialogue between the two officers to which no response from the respondent was invited.

Moreover, it cannot be fairly concluded that the respondent was subjected to the "functional equivalent" of questioning. It cannot be said, in short, that Patrolmen Gleckman and McKenna should have known that their conversation was reasonably likely to elicit an incriminating response from the respondent. There is nothing in the record to suggest that the officers were aware that the respondent was peculiarly susceptible to an appeal to his conscience concerning the safety of handicapped children. Nor

has been filed. Custody in such a case is not controlling; indeed, the petitioner in *Massiah* was not in custody. By contrast, the right to counsel at issue in the present case is based not on the Sixth and Fourteenth Amendments, but rather on the Fifth and Fourteenth Amendments as interpreted in the *Miranda* opinion. The definitions of "interrogation" under the Fifth and Sixth Amendments, if indeed the term "interrogation" is even apt in the Sixth Amendment context, are not necessarily interchangeable, since the policies underlying the two constitutional protections are quite distinct. . . .

9. This is not to say that the intent of the police is irrelevant, for it may well have a bearing on whether the police should have known that their words or actions were reasonably likely to evoke an incriminating response. In particular, where a police practice is designed to elicit an incriminating response from the accused, it is unlikely that the practice will not also be one which the police should have known was reasonably likely to have that effect.

is there anything in the record to suggest that the police knew that the respondent was unusually disoriented or upset at the time of his arrest.

The case thus boils down to whether, in the context of a brief conversation, the officers should have known that the respondent would suddenly be moved to make a self-incriminating response. Given the fact that the entire conversation appears to have consisted of no more than a few offhand remarks, we cannot say that the officers should have known that it was reasonably likely that Innis would so respond. This is not a case where the police carried on a lengthy harangue in the presence of the suspect. Nor does the record support the respondent's contention that, under the circumstances, the officers' comments were particularly "evocative." It is our view, therefore, that the respondent was not subjected by the police to words or actions that the police should have known were reasonably likely to elicit an incriminating response from him.

The Rhode Island Supreme Court erred, in short, in equating "subtle compulsion" with interrogation. That the officers' comments struck a responsive chord is readily apparent. Thus, it may be said, as the Rhode Island Supreme Court did say, that the respondent was subjected to "subtle compulsion." But that is not the end of the inquiry. It must also be established that a suspect's incriminating response was the product of words or actions on the part of the police that they should have known were reasonably likely to elicit an incriminating response. This was not established in the present case.

For the reasons stated, the judgment of the Supreme Court of Rhode Island is vacated, and the case is remanded to that court for further proceedings not inconsistent with this opinion.

. . . [10]

---

240. *Miranda* is not applicable to "routine booking questions" or to "carefully scripted instructions" and "limited and carefully worded inquiries" related to a legitimate police procedure. Pennsylvania v. Muniz, 496 U.S. 582 (1990) (8–1).

241. After the defendant, having been arrested and advised of his rights, said that he did not want to make any statements unless his lawyer was present, police allowed his wife, at her urging, to speak with him in the presence of an officer. The officer openly taped the defendant's conversation with his wife. The Court concluded that the police action was not the "functional equivalent" of interrogation and was permissible. The Court noted that the police had not encouraged the defendant or his wife to speak to one another, but had yielded to her insistence, and that there were legitimate reasons, such as the wife's safety and security generally, to have an officer present. Arizona v. Mauro, 481 U.S. 520 (1987) (5–4).

---

[10] Justice White wrote a brief note, indicating his concurrence. Chief Justice Burger wrote an opinion concurring in the judgment. Justice Marshall wrote a dissenting opinion, which Justice Brennan joined. Justice Stevens also wrote a dissenting opinion.

Waiver

————

242. In *Miranda*, the Court said that the defendant can waive "effectuation" of his rights, "provided the waiver is made voluntarily, knowingly and intelligently," pp. 417–418 above. In a dissenting opinion, Justice White asked how a defendant could be permitted to waive his rights without first consulting an attorney, if he could not (but for the waiver) be permitted voluntarily to answer questions without the advice of counsel. 384 U.S. at 536. When is a waiver "made voluntarily, knowingly and intelligently"?

> [I]f a prisoner is told that he has a right to say nothing and that what he says may be used against him, and that he has a right to an attorney and to his presence during any interrogation, at public expense if he is indigent, the objective of *Miranda* is fully met. It is irrelevant that the prisoner, so advised, chooses to speak without counsel because he misconceives his need for aid or the utility of a lawyer. . . .
>
>   . . .
>
> There is no right to escape detection. There is no right to commit a perfect crime or to an equal opportunity to that end. The Constitution is not at all offended when a guilty man stubs his toe. On the contrary, it is decent to hope that he will. Nor is it dirty business to use evidence a defendant himself may furnish in the detectional stage. Voluntary confessions accord with high moral values, and as to the culprit who reveals his guilt unwittingly with no intent to shed his inner burden, it is no more unfair to use the evidence he thereby reveals than it is to turn against him clues at the scene of the crime which a brighter, better informed, or more gifted criminal would not have left. Thus the Fifth Amendment does not say that a man shall not be permitted to incriminate himself, or that he shall not be persuaded to do so. It says no more than that a man shall not be "compelled" to give evidence against himself.
>
> Hence while we are solicitous of the right to counsel at the trial stage to the end that a defendant shall not suffer injustice because he is not equipped to protect himself, it would be thoughtless to transfer the same right to counsel to the detectional scene. If it be granted that a man may seek legal advice as to how to avoid detection, it is not because the Constitution guarantees him that right. Surely *Miranda* does not say that a man's deed or word may not be used against him merely because he was unaware of its incriminating thrust . . . or unless he first rejected an opportunity for advice by counsel. . . . A

man could not escape his confession to a friend or relative because he thought that what he said did not constitute proof of a crime or that the friend or relative could not testify against him. It is consonant with good morals, and the Constitution, to exploit a criminal's ignorance or stupidity in the detectional process. This must be so if Government is to succeed in its primary mission to protect the first right of the individual to live free from criminal attack.

. . .

. . . Nowhere does *Miranda* suggest that the waiver of counsel at the detectional stage would not be "knowing" or "intelligent" if the suspect did not understand the law relating to the crime, the possible defenses, and the hazards of talking without the aid of counsel, or if the suspect was not able to protect his interests without such aid, or . . . if it was not "wise" of the prisoner to forego counsel or the right to silence. . . . However relevant to "waiver" of the right to counsel at trial or in connection with a plea of guilty, those factors are foreign to the investigational scene where the detection of the guilty is the legitimate aim.

Hence if a defendant was given the *Miranda* warnings, if the coercion of custodial interrogation was thus dissipated, his "waiver" was no less "voluntary" and "knowing" and "intelligent" because he misconceived the inculpatory thrust of the facts he admitted, or because he thought that what he said could not be used because it was only oral or because he had his fingers crossed, or because he could well have used a lawyer. A man need not have the understanding of a lawyer to waive one. Such matters, irrelevant when the defendant volunteers his confession to a friend or to a policeman passing on his beat, are equally irrelevant when the confession is made in custody after the coercion of custodial interrogation has been dispelled by the *Miranda* warnings. With such warnings, the essential fact remains that defendant understood he had the right to remain silent and thereby to avoid the risk of self-incrimination. That is what the Fifth Amendment privilege is about.

State v. McKnight, 243 A.2d 240 (N.J.1968).

243. 18 U.S.C. § 5033 provides that when a juvenile is taken in custody, the juvenile's parents must immediately be notified and must also be notified of his rights and the nature of the alleged offense. In United States v. Wendy G., 255 F.3d 761 (9th Cir.2001), the court held that the parents must be informed that they will have an opportunity "to advise and counsel" the juvenile before interrogation.

In Fare v. Michael C., 442 U.S. 707 (1979) (5–4), the Court held that the request of a juvenile who was in custody in connection with a murder to speak to his probation officer was not the equivalent of a request to speak to an attorney and did not, therefore, per se require that questioning stop, as would have a request to speak to an attorney, see note 246, p. 439 below. The juvenile had been given his *Miranda* warnings and had asked to see his probation officer when he was advised of his right to see an attorney. The Court declared that the question of waiver in this case should be decided on the basis of all the circumstances, and concluded that the juvenile court's finding of waiver was correct.

See United States ex rel. Riley v. Franzen, 653 F.2d 1153 (7th Cir. 1981) (*Michael C.* applied; juvenile's request to see parent invoked neither right to counsel nor right to remain silent). *Miranda* aside, state law may require police to give a juvenile an opportunity to speak to his parent or another adult before questioning him. See, e.g., Commonwealth v. Henderson, 437 A.2d 387 (Pa.1981).

244.

Three days after the commission of a homicide in the course of a robbery, the police of Newport News, Virginia, arrested Harris and took him to the police station at about 9:15 p.m. Captain Weaver of the Detective Bureau told Harris that he was charged with armed robbery and murder and correctly read him his *Miranda* rights. Harris said he understood them. Some 20 minutes later Lt. Austin repeated the *Miranda* warnings and again advised Harris of the charges against him, requesting that Harris sign a waiver-of-rights form. Harris refused to sign, but expressed his willingness to talk and reaffirmed that he understood the explanation to him of his *Miranda* rights.

Lt. Austin knew Harris' parents and telephoned the boy's mother and requested she come to the station right away. Lt. Austin also permitted Harris to telephone his girlfriend and later his sister. While all this was going on, Harris talked freely, insisting that, although present at the place of robbery and homicide, and although carrying a pistol, he did not fire it.

About an hour after beginning their conversation, Harris and Lt. Austin were joined by Harris' uncle, who had come in response to the telephone call to Harris' mother. In the uncle's presence, Harris was advised of his *Miranda* rights for the third time. He told his uncle he had not been mistreated in any way. Harris and his uncle were offered the opportunity to talk privately but declined. Harris was then asked by Lt. Austin to relate the facts of the robbery to his uncle, and Harris substantially repeated his earlier oral statement. It was this statement before his uncle that was later admitted into evidence against him.

During the course of making his confession, according to Lt. Austin's testimony, Harris explained to Austin that he was willing to talk about it but would not sign anything. The Lieutenant's testimony is susceptible to three interpretations, and for decisional purposes we read it (favorably to Harris) to mean that Harris talked freely but would not sign anything because (1) Harris thought that if he simply told about it, it would be Lt. Austin's word against his and, if he later decided to deny the conversation, the judge would believe him rather than Austin; (2) Harris thought an oral confession inadmissible in court; and (3) Harris misunderstood the elements of felony murder and thought that proof that he personally fired the gun was essential to convicting him of the graver offense.

Harris was 17 years old. His I.Q. was 67, which is within the "dull-normal" range of intelligence at about the sixth-grade level. His poorly developed language skills were at about the third-grade level. At trial the defense psychiatrist conceded, however, that Harris understood both his right to remain silent and that anything he said could and would be used against him, though, as to the latter, he might not understand "to what degree and to what extent it would be used or what charges [it would support]." The psychiatrist further testified that Harris' limited understanding of the consequences of talking would be shared by "many people even with a superior I.Q.," and that the primary source of Harris' confusion was his ignorance of the felony-murder doctrine.

Harris' confession was admitted over objection that it was not the product of a knowing and intelligent waiver of his right to keep silent within the meaning of *Miranda.*

Harris v. Riddle, 551 F.2d 936, 937 (4th Cir.1977).

Assuming that Lt. Austin perceived that Harris's willingness to answer questions was based on a misunderstanding of the law and that he would not answer questions if he understood the consequences, was Austin under any (constitutional) obligation to explain the situation?

245. In North Carolina v. Butler, 441 U.S. 369 (1979) (5–3), the Supreme Court said that *Miranda* does not require that a waiver of the right to the presence of a lawyer during custodial interrogation be made expressly orally or in writing. While the prosecution has a heavy burden of proof to establish such a waiver, "in at least some cases waiver can be clearly inferred from the actions and words of the person interrogated." Id. at 373. In Colorado v. Connelly, 479 U.S. 157 (1986) (5–4), the Court specified that the prosecution is required to prove that a defendant has waived his right to the assistance of counsel during custodial interrogation by a preponderance of the evidence. See Tague v. Louisiana, 444 U.S. 469 (1980) (7–2) (no waiver).

246. Edwards v. Arizona, 451 U.S. 477 (1981). "[W]hen an accused has invoked his right to have counsel present during custodial interrogation, a valid waiver of that right cannot be established by showing only that he responded to further police-initiated custodial interrogation even if he has been advised of his rights. . . . [A]n accused . . . having expressed his desire to deal with the police only through counsel, is not subject to further interrogation by the authorities until counsel has been made available to him, unless the accused himself initiates further communication, exchanges, or conversations with the police." Id. at 484–85.

The Court applied *Edwards* in Oregon v. Bradshaw, 462 U.S. 1039 (1983) (5–4). It was agreed by all the Justices that, under *Edwards,* questioning of a defendant who has requested counsel may not be resumed unless (1) the defendant initiates further conversation with the police, and

(2) he in fact waives his right to counsel. Beyond that, the Court indicated considerable disagreement about the stringency of the test of a waiver. See Smith v. Illinois, 469 U.S. 91 (1984) (6–3), holding that no subsequent responses of the defendant to further questions can be used to cast doubt on the original request for counsel, which bars questioning. See also Solem v. Stumes, 465 U.S. 638, 646 (1984) (6–3) (*Edwards* not applied retroactively), emphasizing the "bright line" rule laid down by *Edwards*.

The *Edwards* rule, cutting off questioning, comes into play only if a suspect "unambiguously request[s] counsel." Davis v. United States, 512 U.S. 452, 459 (1994). The Court said that it would not "extend *Edwards* and require law enforcement officers to cease questioning immediately upon the making of an ambiguous or equivocal reference to an attorney." Id. "The rationale underlying *Edwards* is that the police must respect a suspect's wishes regarding his right to have an attorney present during custodial interrogation. But when the officers conducting the questioning reasonably do not know whether or not the suspect wants a lawyer, a rule requiring the immediate cessation of questioning . . . would needlessly prevent the police from questioning a suspect in the absence of counsel even if the suspect did not wish to have a lawyer present." Id. at 460. The Court acknowledged "that requiring a clear assertion of the right to counsel might disadvantage some suspects who—because of fear, intimidation, lack of linguistic skills, or a variety of other reasons—will not clearly articulate their right to counsel although they actually want to have a lawyer present." Id. But, the Court said, "the primary protection afforded suspects subject to custodial interrogation is the *Miranda* warnings themselves." Id.

In a concurring opinion, four Justices expressed the view that the rule should be that "when a suspect under custodial interrogation makes an ambiguous statement that might reasonably be understood as expressing a wish that a lawyer be summoned (and questioning cease), interrogators' questions should be confined to verifying whether the individual meant to ask for a lawyer." Id. at 476. The majority observed that asking such clarifying questions would "often be good police practice," but made clear that it was not required. Id. at 461.

Davis was applied in Clark v. Murphy, 331 F.3d 1062 (9th Cir.2003) ("I think I would like to talk to a lawyer" not unambiguous and unequivocal). See Coleman v. Singletary, 30 F.3d 1420 (11th Cir.1994) (equivocal statement that the defendant did not want to answer further questions); Midkiff v. Commonwealth, 462 S.E.2d 112 (Va.1995) ("I'll be honest with you, I'm scared to say anything without talking to a lawyer" not "clear and unambiguous").

In Connecticut v. Barrett, 479 U.S. 523 (1987) (7–2), the defendant was given *Miranda* warnings and thereafter agreed to talk with the police but said that he would not give a written statement unless his attorney were present. At trial, the defendant testified that he understood the *Miranda* warnings. Reversing a decision of the state supreme court, the Court held that *Edwards* did not require suppression of the defendant's oral statements. Even though a request for counsel should be broadly construed, the defendant's statements to the police were not ambiguous and should be understood as he evidently intended them.

Hawaii has adopted the view of the concurring opinion in *Davis*. State v. Hoey, 881 P.2d 504 (Haw.1994) (other cases cited).

Edwards prohibits the police from reinitiating an interrogation of a suspect without counsel present, whether or not the suspect has had an opportunity to consult with counsel. "A single consultation with an attorney does not remove the suspect from persistent attempts by officials to persuade him to waive his rights, or from the coercive pressures that accompany custody and that may increase as custody is prolonged." Minnick v. Mississippi, 498 U.S. 146, 487 (1990) (6–2). *Edwards* applies, furthermore, to questioning about an unrelated crime, whether such questioning is by the same officers who elicited the request or by others. Arizona v. Roberson, 486 U.S. 675 (1988) (6–2).

In United States v. Kelsey, 951 F.2d 1196 (10th Cir.1991), after the defendant was arrested but before he was given *Miranda* warnings, he asked to speak with his lawyer. Later, he was given *Miranda* warnings and then questioned. The government contended that *Edwards* was inapplicable, because the defendant's request to speak with his lawyer preceded any questioning and the giving of the warnings. The court held that *Edwards* was applicable and that the questioning was improper.

Edwards was applied to a confession obtained by police questioning following the defendant's request for appointed counsel at an initial appearance ("arraignment") before a magistrate, in Michigan v. Jackson, 475 U.S. 625 (1986) (6–3). The Court said that application of the strict *Edwards* rule was even more appropriate for the right to counsel than for the privilege against compulsory self-incrimination and that the factual differences in the circumstances in which the request for counsel is made do not warrant a departure from the rule. Accordingly, "if police initiate interrogation after a defendant's assertion, at an arraignment or similar proceeding, of his right to counsel, any waiver of the defendant's right to counsel for that police-initiated interrogation is invalid." Id. at 636.

In McNeil v. Wisconsin, 501 U.S. 171 (1991) (6–3), the defendant was arrested on a charge of armed robbery. Formal proceedings began and his right to counsel attached. Then, police officers initiated questioning about other crimes, and the defendant waived his rights under *Miranda*. The Court held that the right to counsel that had attached for one crime did not prevent police from initiating questioning about other crimes. It said that the right to counsel as such (i.e., not in the context of custodial interrogation) being offense-specific, "[i]t cannot be invoked once for all future prosecutions, for it does not attach until a prosecution is commenced." Id. at 175.

Edwards was distinguished in Wyrick v. Fields, 459 U.S. 42 (1982) (8–1), which involved questioning following voluntary submission to a polygraph examination. After having been arrested on a charge of rape and having retained counsel, the defendant requested the polygraph examination, before which he waived the right to have counsel present. The Court said that the waiver applied to the post-examination questioning as well and that no additional *Miranda* warnings had to be given.

———

Moran v. Burbine

475 U.S. 412, 106 S.Ct. 1135, 89 L.Ed.2d 410 (1986)

■ JUSTICE O'CONNOR delivered the opinion of the Court.

After being informed of his rights pursuant to Miranda v. Arizona, 384 U.S. 436 (1966), and after executing a series of written waivers, respondent confessed to the murder of a young woman. At no point during the course of interrogation, which occurred prior to arraignment, did he request an attorney. While he was in police custody, his sister attempted to retain a lawyer to represent him. The attorney telephoned the police station and received assurances that respondent would not be questioned further until the next day. In fact, the interrogation session that yielded the inculpatory statements began later that evening. The question presented is whether either the conduct of the police or respondent's ignorance of the attorney's efforts to reach him taints the validity of the waivers and therefore requires exclusion of the confessions.

I

On the morning of March 3, 1977, Mary Jo Hickey was found unconscious in a factory parking lot in Providence, Rhode Island. Suffering from injuries to her skull apparently inflicted by a metal pipe found at the scene, she was rushed to a nearby hospital. Three weeks later she died from her wounds.

Several months after her death, the Cranston, Rhode Island police arrested respondent and two others in connection with a local burglary. Shortly before the arrest, Detective Ferranti of the Cranston police force had learned from a confidential informant that the man responsible for Ms. Hickey's death lived at a certain address and went by the name of "Butch." Upon discovering that respondent lived at that address and was known by that name, Detective Ferranti informed respondent of his *Miranda* rights. When respondent refused to execute a written waiver, Detective Ferranti spoke separately with the two other suspects arrested on the breaking and entering charge and obtained statements further implicating respondent in Ms. Hickey's murder. At approximately 6 p.m., Detective Ferranti telephoned the police in Providence to convey the information he had uncovered. An hour later, three officers from that department arrived at the Cranston headquarters for the purpose of questioning respondent about the murder.

That same evening, at about 7:45 p.m., respondent's sister telephoned the Public Defender's Office to obtain legal assistance for her brother. Her sole concern was the breaking and entering charge, as she was unaware that respondent was then under suspicion for murder. She asked for Richard Casparian who had been scheduled to meet with respondent earlier that afternoon to discuss another charge unrelated to either the break-in or the murder. As soon as the conversation ended, the attorney who took the call attempted to reach Mr. Casparian. When those efforts were unsuccessful, she telephoned Allegra Munson, another Assistant Public Defender, and told her about respondent's arrest and his sister's subsequent request that the office represent him.

At 8:15 p.m., Ms. Munson telephoned the Cranston police station and asked that her call be transferred to the detective division. In the words of the Supreme Court of Rhode Island . . . the conversation proceeded as follows:

> A male voice responded with the word "Detectives." Ms. Munson identified herself and asked if Brian Burbine was being held; the person responded affirmatively. Ms. Munson explained to the person that Burbine was represented by attorney Casparian who was not available; she further stated that she would act as Burbine's legal counsel in the event that the police intended to place him in a lineup or question him. The unidentified person told Ms. Munson that the police would not be questioning Burbine or putting him in a lineup and that they were through with him for the night. Ms. Munson was not informed that the Providence Police were at the Cranston police station or that Burbine was a suspect in Mary's murder.

State v. Burbine, 451 A.2d 22, 23–24 (1982). At all relevant times, respondent was unaware of his sister's efforts to retain counsel and of the fact and contents of Ms. Munson's telephone conversation.

Less than an hour later, the police brought respondent to an interrogation room and conducted the first of a series of interviews concerning the murder. Prior to each session, respondent was informed of his *Miranda* rights, and on three separate occasions he signed a written form acknowledging that he understood his right to the presence of an attorney and explicitly indicating that he "[did] not want an attorney called or appointed for [him]" before he gave a statement. App. to Pet. for Cert. 94, 103, 107. Uncontradicted evidence at the suppression hearing indicated that at least twice during the course of the evening, respondent was left in a room where he had access to a telephone, which he apparently declined to use. . . . Eventually, respondent signed three written statements fully admitting to the murder.

Prior to trial, respondent moved to suppress the statements. The court denied the motion, finding that respondent had received the *Miranda* warnings and had "knowingly, intelligently, and voluntarily waived his privilege against self-incrimination [and] his right to counsel." App. to Pet. for Cert. 116. Rejecting the contrary testimony of the police, the court found that Ms. Munson did telephone the detective bureau on the evening in question, but concluded that "there was no . . . conspiracy or collusion on the part of the Cranston Police Department to secrete this defendant from his attorney." Id., at 114. In any event, the court held, the constitutional right to request the presence of an attorney belongs solely to the defendant and may not be asserted by his lawyer. Because the evidence was clear that respondent never asked for the services of an attorney, the telephone call had no relevance to the validity of the waiver or the admissibility of the statements.

The jury found respondent guilty of murder in the first degree, and he appealed to the Supreme Court of Rhode Island. A divided court rejected his contention that the Fifth and Fourteenth Amendments to the Constitution required the suppression of the inculpatory statements and affirmed the conviction. . . . [T]he court noted that because two different police departments were operating in the Cranston station house on the evening in question, the record supported the trial court's finding that there was no "conspiracy or collusion" to prevent Ms. Munson from seeing respondent. 451 A.2d, at 30, n.5. In any case, the court held, the right to the presence of counsel belongs solely to the accused and may not be asserted by "benign third parties, whether or not they happen to be attorneys." Id., at 28.

After unsuccessfully petitioning the United States District Court for the District of Rhode Island for a writ of habeas corpus . . . respondent appealed to the Court of Appeals for the First Circuit. That court reversed. 753 F.2d 178 (1985). Finding it unnecessary to reach any arguments under the Sixth and Fourteenth Amendments, the court held that the police's conduct had fatally tainted respondent's "otherwise valid" waiver of his Fifth Amendment privilege against self-incrimination and right to counsel. Id., at 184. The court reasoned that by failing to inform respondent that an attorney had called and that she had been assured that no questioning would take place until the next day, the police had deprived respondent of information crucial to his ability to waive his rights knowingly and intelligently. The court also found that the record would support "no other explanation for the refusal to tell Burbine of Attorney Munson's call than . . . deliberate or reckless irresponsibility." Id., at 185. This kind of "blameworthy action by the police," the court concluded, together with respondent's ignorance of the telephone call, "vitiate[d] any claim that [the] waiver of counsel was knowing and voluntary." Id., at 185, 187.

We granted certiorari to decide whether a prearraignment confession preceded by an otherwise valid waiver must be suppressed either because the police misinformed an inquiring attorney about their plans concerning the suspect or because they failed to inform the suspect of the attorney's efforts to reach him. . . . We now reverse.

II

In Miranda v. Arizona, the Court recognized that custodial interrogations, by their very nature, generate "compelling pressures which work to undermine the individual's will to resist and to compel him to speak where he would not otherwise do so freely." 384 U.S., at 467. To combat this inherent compulsion, and thereby protect the Fifth Amendment privilege against self-incrimination, *Miranda* imposed on the police an obligation to follow certain procedures in their dealings with the accused. In particular, prior to the initiation of questioning, they must fully apprise the suspect of the State's intention to use his statements to secure a conviction, and must inform him of his rights to remain silent and to "have counsel present . . . if [he] so desires." Id., at 468–70. Beyond this duty to inform, *Miranda* requires that the police respect the accused's decision to exercise the rights outlined in the warnings. "If the individual indicates in any manner, at any time prior to or during questioning, that he wishes to remain silent, [or if he] states that he wants an attorney, the interrogation must cease." *Miranda*, 384 U.S., at 473–74. . . .

Respondent does not dispute that the Providence police followed these procedures with precision. The record amply supports the state-court findings that the police administered the required warnings, sought to assure that respondent understood his rights, and obtained an express written waiver prior to eliciting each of the three statements. Nor does respondent contest the Rhode Island courts' determination that he at no point requested the presence of a lawyer. He contends instead that the confessions must be suppressed because the police's failure to inform him of the attorney's telephone call deprived him of information essential to his ability to knowingly waive his Fifth Amendment rights. In the alternative, he suggests that to fully protect the Fifth Amendment values served by *Miranda*, we should extend that decision to condemn the conduct of the Providence police. We address each contention in turn.

A

Echoing the standard first articulated in Johnson v. Zerbst, 304 U.S. 458, 464 (1938), *Miranda* holds that "[t]he defendant may waive effectuation" of the rights conveyed in the warnings "provided the waiver is made voluntarily, knowingly and intelligently." 384 U.S., at 444, 475. The inquiry has two distinct dimensions. . . . First the relinquishment of the right must have been voluntary in the sense that it was the product of a free and deliberate choice rather than intimidation, coercion or deception. Second, the waiver must have been made with a full awareness both of the nature of the right being abandoned and the consequences of the decision to abandon it. Only if the "totality of the circumstances surrounding the interrogation" reveals both an uncoerced choice and the requisite level of comprehension may a court properly conclude that the *Miranda* rights have been waived. Fare v. Michael C., 442 U.S. 707, 725 (1979). . . .

Under this standard, we have no doubt that respondent validly waived his right to remain silent and to the presence of counsel. The voluntariness of the waiver is not at issue. As the Court of Appeals correctly acknowledged, the record is devoid of any suggestion that police resorted to physical or psychological pressure to elicit the statements. . . . Indeed it appears that it was respondent, and not the police, who spontaneously initiated the conversation that led to the first and most damaging confession. . . . Nor is there any question about respondent's comprehension of the full panoply of rights set out in the *Miranda* warnings and of the potential consequences of a decision to relinquish them. Nonetheless, the Court of Appeals believed that the "[d]eliberate or reckless" conduct of the police, in particular their failure to inform respondent of the telephone call, fatally undermined the validity of the otherwise proper waiver. We find this conclusion untenable as a matter of both logic and precedent.

Events occurring outside of the presence of the suspect and entirely unknown to him surely can have no bearing on the capacity to comprehend and knowingly relinquish a constitutional right. Under the analysis of the Court of Appeals, the same defendant, armed with the same information and confronted with precisely the same police conduct, would have knowingly waived his *Miranda* rights had a lawyer not telephoned the police station to inquire about his status. Nothing in any of our waiver decisions or in our understanding of the essential components of a valid waiver requires so incongruous a result. No doubt the additional information would have been useful to respondent; perhaps even it might have affected his decision to confess. But we have never read the Constitution to require that the police supply a suspect with a flow of information to help him calibrate his self-interest in deciding whether to speak or stand by his rights. . . . Once it is determined that a suspect's decision not to rely on his rights was uncoerced, that he at all times knew he could stand mute and request a lawyer, and that he was aware of the State's intention to use his statements to secure a conviction, the analysis is complete and the waiver is valid as a matter of law. The Court of Appeals' conclusion to the contrary was in error.

Nor do we believe that the level of the police's culpability in failing to inform respondent of the telephone call has any bearing on the validity of the waivers. In light of the state-court findings that there was no "conspiracy or collusion" on the part of the police, 451 A.2d, at 30, n.5, we have serious doubts about whether the Court of Appeals was free to conclude that their conduct constituted "deliberate or reckless irresponsibility." 753 F.2d, at 185; see 28 U.S.C. § 2254(d). But whether intentional or inadvertent, the state of mind of the police is irrelevant to the question of the intelligence and voluntariness of respondent's election to abandon his rights. Although highly inappropriate, even deliberate deception of an attorney could not possibly affect a suspect's decision to waive his *Miranda* rights unless he were at least aware of the incident. . . . Nor was the failure to inform respondent of the telephone call the kind of "trick[ery]" that can vitiate the validity of a waiver. *Miranda*, 384 U.S., at 476. Granting that the "deliberate or reckless" withholding of information is objectionable as a matter of ethics, such conduct is only relevant to the constitutional validity of a waiver if it deprives a defendant of knowledge essential to his ability to understand the nature of his rights and the consequences of abandoning them. Because respondent's voluntary decision to speak was made with full awareness and comprehension of all the information *Miranda* requires the police to convey, the waivers were valid.

B

At oral argument respondent acknowledged that a constitutional rule requiring the police to inform a suspect of an attorney's efforts to reach him would represent a significant extension of our precedents. . . . He contends, however, that the conduct of the Providence police was so inimical to the Fifth Amendment values *Miranda* seeks to protect that we should read that decision to condemn their behavior. Regardless of any issue of waiver, he urges, the Fifth Amendment requires the reversal of a conviction if the police are less than forthright in their dealings with an attorney or if they fail to tell a suspect of a lawyer's unilateral efforts to contact him. Because the proposed modification ignores the underlying purposes of the *Miranda* rules and because we think that the decision as written strikes the proper balance between society's legitimate law enforcement interests and the protection of the defendant's Fifth Amendment rights, we decline the invitation to further extend *Miranda*'s reach.

At the outset, while we share respondent's distaste for the deliberate misleading of an officer of the court, reading *Miranda* to forbid police deception of an *attorney* "would cut [the decision] completely loose from its own explicitly stated rationale." Beckwith v. United States, 425 U.S. 341, 345 (1976). As is now well established, "[t]he . . . *Miranda* warnings are 'not themselves rights protected by the Constitution but [are] instead measures to insure that the [suspect's] right against compulsory self-incrimination [is] protected.'" New York v. Quarles, 467 U.S. 649, 654 (1984), quoting Michigan v. Tucker, 417 U.S. 433, 444 (1974). Their objective is not to mold police conduct for its own sake. Nothing in the Constitution vests in us the authority to mandate a code of behavior for state officials wholly unconnected to any federal right or privilege. The purpose of the *Miranda* warnings instead is to dissipate the compulsion inherent in custodial interrogation and, in so doing, guard against abridgment of the suspect's Fifth Amendment rights. Clearly, a rule that focuses on how the police treat an attorney—conduct that has no relevance at all to the degree of compulsion experienced by the defendant during interrogation—would ignore both *Miranda*'s mission and its only source of legitimacy.

Nor are we prepared to adopt a rule requiring that the police inform a suspect of an attorney's efforts to reach him. While such a rule might add marginally to *Miranda*'s goal of dispelling the compulsion inherent in custodial interrogation, overriding practical considerations counsel against its adoption. As we have stressed on numerous occasions, "[o]ne of the principal advantages" of *Miranda* is the ease and clarity of its application. Berkemer v. McCarty, 468 U.S. 420, 430 (1984). . . . We have little doubt that the approach urged by respondent and endorsed by the Court of Appeals would have the inevitable consequence of muddying *Miranda*'s otherwise relatively clear waters. The legal questions it would spawn are legion: To what extent should the police be held accountable for knowing that the accused has counsel? Is it enough that someone in the station house knows, or must the interrogating officer himself know of counsel's efforts to contact the suspect? Do counsel's efforts to talk to the suspect concerning one criminal investigation trigger the obligation to inform the defendant before interrogation may proceed on a wholly separate matter? We are unwilling to modify *Miranda* in a manner that would so clearly undermine the decision's central "virtue of informing police and prosecutors with specificity . . . what they may do in conducting [a] custodial interrogation, and of informing courts under what circumstances statements obtained during such interrogation are not admissible." Fare v. Michael C., supra, at 718.

Moreover, problems of clarity to one side, reading *Miranda* to require the police in each instance to inform a suspect of an attorney's efforts to reach him would work a substantial and, we think, inappropriate shift in the subtle balance struck in that decision. Custodial interrogations implicate two competing concerns. On the one hand, "the need for police questioning as a tool for effective enforcement of criminal laws" cannot be doubted. Schneckloth v. Bustamonte, 412 U.S. 218, 225 (1973). Admissions of guilt are more than merely "desirable," United States v. Washington, 431 U.S. [181 (1977)], at 186; they are essential to society's compelling interest in finding, convicting and punishing those who violate the law. On the other hand, the Court has recognized that the interrogation process is "inherently coercive" and that, as a consequence, there exists a substantial risk that the police will inadvertently traverse the fine line between legitimate efforts to elicit admissions and constitutionally impermissible compulsion. New York v. Quarles, 467 U.S., at 656. *Miranda* attempted to reconcile these opposing concerns by giving the *defendant* the power to exert some control over the course of the interrogation. Declining to adopt the more extreme position that the actual presence of a lawyer was necessary to dispel the coercion inherent in custodial interrogation . . . the Court found that the suspect's Fifth Amendment rights could be adequately protected by less intrusive means. Police questioning, often an essential part of the investigatory process, could continue in its traditional form, the Court held, but only if the suspect clearly understood that, at any time, he could bring the proceeding to a halt or, short of that, call in an attorney to give advice and monitor the conduct of his interrogators.

The position urged by respondent would upset this carefully drawn approach in a manner that is both unnecessary for the protection of the Fifth Amendment privilege and injurious to legitimate law enforcement. Because, as *Miranda* holds, full comprehension of the rights to remain silent and request an attorney are sufficient to dispel whatever coercion is inherent in the interrogation process, a rule requiring the police to inform the suspect of an attorney's efforts to contact him would contribute to the protection of the Fifth Amendment privilege only incidentally, if at all. This minimal benefit, however, would come at a substantial cost to society's legitimate and substantial interest in securing admissions of guilt. Indeed, the very premise of the Court of Appeals was not that awareness of Ms. Munson's phone call would have dissipated the coercion of the interrogation room, but that it might have convinced respondent not to speak at all. . . . Because neither the letter nor purposes of *Miranda* require this additional handicap on otherwise permissible investigatory efforts, we are unwilling to expand the *Miranda* rules to require the police to keep the suspect abreast of the status of his legal representation.

We acknowledge that a number of state courts have reached a contrary conclusion. . . . We recognize also that our interpretation of the Federal Constitution, if given the dissent's expansive gloss, is at odds with the policy recommendations embodied in the American Bar Association Standards of Criminal Justice. . . . Notwithstanding the dissent's protestations, however, our interpretive duties go well beyond deferring to the numerical preponderance of lower court decisions or to the subconstitutional recommendations of even so esteemed a body as the American Bar Association. . . . Nothing we say today disables the States from adopting different requirements for the conduct of its employees and officials as a matter of state law. We hold only that the Court of Appeals erred in construing the Fifth Amendment to the Federal Constitution to require the exclusion of respondent's three confessions.

III

Respondent also contends that the Sixth Amendment requires exclusion of his three confessions. It is clear, of course, that, absent a valid waiver, the defendant has the right to the presence of an attorney during any interrogation occurring after the first formal charging proceeding, the point at which the Sixth Amendment right to counsel initially attaches. . . . And we readily agree that once the right *has* attached, it follows that the police may not interfere with the efforts of a defendant's attorney to act as a " 'medium' between [the suspect] and the State" during the interrogation. Maine v. Moulton, 474 U.S. 159, 176 (1985). . . . The difficulty for respondent is that the interrogation sessions that yielded the inculpatory statements took place *before* the initiation of "adversary judicial proceedings." United States v. Gouveia, [467 U.S. 180 (1984)], at 192. He contends, however, that this circumstance is not fatal to his Sixth Amendment claim. At least in some situations, he argues, the Sixth Amendment protects the integrity of the attorney-client relationship regardless of whether the prosecution has in fact commenced "by way of formal charge, preliminary hearing, indictment, information or arraignment." 467 U.S., at 188. Placing principal reliance on a footnote in *Miranda*, 384 U.S., at 465, n.35, and on Escobedo v. Illinois, 378 U.S. 478 (1964), he maintains that *Gouveia, Kirby* [v. Illinois, 406 U.S. 682 (1972)] and our other "critical stage" cases, concern only the narrow question of when the right *to* counsel—that is, to the appointment or presence of counsel—attaches. The right to non-interference with an attorney's dealings with a criminal suspect, he asserts, arises the moment that the relationship is formed, or, at the very least, once the defendant is placed in custodial interrogation.

We are not persuaded. At the outset, subsequent decisions foreclose any reliance on *Escobedo* and *Miranda* for the proposition that the Sixth Amendment right, in any of its manifestations, applies prior to the initiation of adversary judicial proceedings. Although *Escobedo* was originally decided as a Sixth Amendment case, "the Court in retrospect perceived that the 'prime purpose' of *Escobedo* was not to vindicate the constitutional right to counsel as such, but, like *Miranda*, 'to guarantee full effectuation of the privilege against self-incrimination. . . .' " Kirby v. Illinois, supra, at 689, quoting Johnson v. New Jersey, 384 U.S. 719, 729 (1966). Clearly then, *Escobedo* provides no support for respondent's argument. Nor, of course, does *Miranda*, the holding of which rested exclusively on the Fifth Amendment. Thus, the decision's brief observation about the reach of *Escobedo*'s Sixth Amendment analysis is not only dictum, but reflects an understanding of the case that the Court has expressly disavowed. . . .

Questions of precedent to one side, we find respondent's understanding of the Sixth Amendment both practically and theoretically unsound. As a practical matter, it makes little sense to say that the Sixth Amendment right to counsel attaches at different times depending on the fortuity of whether the suspect or his family happens to have retained counsel prior to interrogation. . . . More importantly, the suggestion that the existence of an attorney-client relationship itself triggers the protections of the Sixth Amendment misconceives the underlying purposes of the right to counsel. The Sixth Amendment's intended function is not to wrap a protective cloak around the attorney-client relationship for its own sake any more than it is to protect a suspect from the consequences of his own candor. Its purpose, rather, is to assure that in any "criminal prosecutio[n]," U.S. Const., Amdt. 6, the accused shall not be left to his own devices in facing the " 'prosecutorial forces of organized society.' " Maine v. Moulton, supra, at 170 (quoting Kirby v. Illinois, 406 U.S., at 689). By its very terms, it becomes applicable only when the government's role shifts from investigation to accusation. For it is only then that the assistance of one versed in the "intricacies . . . of law," ibid., is needed to assure that the prosecution's case encounters "the crucible of meaningful adversarial testing." United States v. Cronic, 466 U.S. 648, 656 (1984).

. . .

Respondent contends, however, that custodial interrogations require a different rule. Because confessions elicited during the course of police questioning often seal a suspect's fate, he argues, the need for an advocate—and the concomitant right to noninterference with the attorney-client relationship—is at its zenith, regardless of whether the state has initiated the first adversary judicial proceeding. We do not doubt that a lawyer's presence could be of value to the suspect; and we readily agree that if a suspect confesses, his attorney's case at trial will be that much more difficult. But these concerns are no more decisive in this context than they were for the equally damaging preindictment lineup at issue in *Kirby*. . . . For an interrogation, no more or less than for any other "critical" pretrial event, the possibility that the encounter may have important consequences at trial, standing alone, is insufficient to trigger the Sixth Amendment right to counsel. As *Gouveia* made clear, until such time as the " 'government has committed itself to prosecute, and . . . the adverse positions of government and defendant have solidified' " the Sixth Amendment right to counsel does not attach. 467 U.S., at 189 (quoting Kirby v. Illinois, 406 U.S., at 689).

Because, as respondent acknowledges, the events that led to the inculpatory statements preceded the formal initiation of adversary judicial proceedings, we reject the contention that the conduct of the police violated his rights under the Sixth Amendment.

IV

Finally, respondent contends that the conduct of the police was so offensive as to deprive him of the fundamental fairness guaranteed by the Due Process Clause of the Fourteenth Amendment. Focusing primarily on the impropriety of conveying false information to an attorney, he invites us to declare that such behavior should be condemned as violative of canons fundamental to the " 'traditions and conscience of our people.' " Rochin v. California, 342 U.S. 165, 169 (1952), quoting Snyder v. Massachusetts, 291 U.S. 97, 105 (1934). We do not question that on facts more egregious than those presented here police deception might rise to a level of a due process violation. . . . We hold only that, on these facts, the challenged conduct falls short of the kind of misbehavior that so shocks the sensibilities of civilized society as to warrant a federal intrusion into the criminal processes of the States.

We hold therefore that the Court of Appeals erred in finding that the Federal Constitution required the exclusion of the three inculpatory statements. Accordingly, we reverse and remand for proceedings consistent with this opinion.

. . . [11]

---

247. The defendant was arrested for illegal sale of firearms, while he was making a sale to an undercover agent. He was given *Miranda* warnings and signed a statement that he was willing to answer questions. He was questioned about the firearms transactions that led to his arrest. Thereafter, on the basis of information that the agents had received before the arrest, they questioned him about a homicide. The Court held that the failure to advise the defendant that he would be questioned about the homicide did not make his waiver of the right not to be questioned invalid. A valid waiver does not require that a defendant be told all information that might affect his decision to confess. Failure to tell the defendant that he would be questioned about the homicide was not "trickery" of a kind that would invalidate the waiver. Colorado v. Spring, 479 U.S. 564 (1987) (7–2).

[11] Justice Stevens wrote a dissenting opinion, which Justice Brennan and Justice Marshall joined.

248. A number of states have rejected the Court's holding in Moran v. Burbine and imposed a different rule under state law. In State v. Stoddard, 537 A.2d 446, 452 (Conn.1988), for example, the Supreme Court of Connecticut said: "In light of both the historical record and our due process tradition, we conclude that a suspect must be informed promptly of timely efforts by counsel to render pertinent legal assistance. Armed with that information, the suspect must be permitted to choose whether he wishes to speak with counsel, in which event interrogation must cease, or whether he will forego assistance of counsel, in which event counsel need not be afforded access to the suspect. The police may not preclude the suspect from exercising the choice to which he is constitutionally entitled by responding in less than forthright fashion to the efforts by counsel to contact the suspect. The police, because they are responsible for the suspect's isolation, have a duty to act reasonably, diligently and promptly to provide counsel with accurate information and to apprise the subject of the efforts by counsel." The court said that a failure to inform the arrested person does not necessarily require exclusion of his statements during detention. Rather, the trial court must consider the failure to inform in the context of all the circumstances and decide whether, had the person been informed, he would nevertheless have waived his right to the presence of counsel before making the statements. If so, exclusion is not required.

The Supreme Court of California rejected Moran v. Burbine in People v. Houston, 724 P.2d 1166 (Cal.1986), but its ruling was subsequently overturned by a state constitutional amendment providing that relevant evidence is to be excluded from criminal proceedings only if exclusion is required by the federal Constitution. See People v. Ledesma, 251 Cal.Rptr. 417 (Ct.App.1988). Other states that have rejected Moran v. Burbine include Delaware, Bryan v. State, 571 A.2d 170 (Del.1990); Florida, Haliburton v. State, 514 So.2d 1088 (Fla.1987); Illinois, People v. McCauley, 645 N.E.2d 923 (Ill.1994); People v. Chipman, 743 N.E.2d 48 (Ill.2000) (*McCauley* applicable only if attorney is present at police station); Massachusetts v. Mavredakis, 725 N.E.2d 169 (2000); Michigan, People v. Bender, 551 N.W.2d 71 (Mich.1996); and New Jersey, State v. Reed, 627 A.2d 630 (N.J.1993).

If police officers arrest a person who they believe has committed a serious crime, can they be expected to warn and advise him *effectively* about his rights? The plain import of the *Miranda* opinion is that perfunctory, ritualistic compliance with its requirements is inadequate. Can the police be expected to do more? Is it possible *effectively* to convey the information contained in the *Miranda* warnings without at least intimating that the arrested person would be well advised not to answer questions until he speaks to a lawyer? Put the matter differently: Is it likely that the arrested person will take the *Miranda* warnings very seriously if they are given by a policeman who obviously would like to ask questions and intends to do so unless the person objects? (Consider the "bright line" rule of Edwards v.

Arizona, p. 441 note 246 above, in this connection.) If not, are the *Miranda* warnings likely too often to be ineffective? Or have they some function to perform other than simply to inform arrested persons of their rights?

———

Orozco v. Texas

394 U.S. 324, 89 S.Ct. 1095, 22 L.Ed.2d 311 (1969)

■ MR. JUSTICE BLACK delivered the opinion of the Court.

The petitioner, Reyes Arias Orozco, was convicted in the Criminal District Court of Dallas County, Texas, of murder without malice and was sentenced to serve in the state prison not less than two nor more than 10 years. The Court of Criminal Appeals of Texas affirmed the conviction, rejecting petitioner's contention that a material part of the evidence against him was obtained in violation of the provision of the Fifth Amendment to the United States Constitution, made applicable to the States by the Fourteenth Amendment, that "No person . . . shall be compelled in any criminal case to be a witness against himself."

The evidence introduced at trial showed that petitioner and the deceased had quarreled outside the El Farleto Cafe in Dallas shortly before midnight. The deceased had apparently spoken to petitioner's female companion inside the restaurant. In the heat of the quarrel outside, the deceased is said to have beaten petitioner about the face and called him "Mexican Grease." A shot was fired killing the deceased. Petitioner left the scene and returned to his boarding house to sleep. At about 4 a.m. four police officers arrived at petitioner's boarding house, were admitted by an unidentified woman, and were told that petitioner was asleep in the bedroom. All four officers entered the bedroom and began to question petitioner. From the moment he gave his name, according to the testimony of one of the officers, petitioner was not free to go where he pleased but was "under arrest." The officers asked him if he had been to the El Farleto restaurant that night and when he answered "yes" he was asked if he owned a pistol. Petitioner admitted owning one. After being asked a second time where the pistol was located, he admitted that it was in the washing machine in a backroom of the boarding house. Ballistics tests indicated that the gun found in the washing machine was the gun that fired the fatal shot. At petitioner's trial, held after the effective date of this Court's decision in Miranda v. Arizona, 384 U.S. 436 (1966), the trial court allowed one of the officers, over the objection of petitioner's lawyer, to relate the statements made by petitioner concerning the gun and petitioner's presence at the scene of the shooting. The trial testimony clearly shows that the officers questioned petitioner about incriminating facts without first informing him of his right to remain silent, his right to have the advice of a lawyer before making any statement, and his right to have a lawyer appointed to assist him if he could not afford to hire one. The Texas Court of Criminal Appeals held, with one judge dissenting, that the admission of testimony concerning the statements petitioner had made without the above warnings was not precluded by *Miranda*. We disagree and hold that the use of these admissions obtained in the absence of the required warnings was a flat violation of the Self-Incrimination Clause of the Fifth Amendment as construed in *Miranda*.

The State has argued here that since petitioner was interrogated on his own bed, in familiar surroundings, our *Miranda* holding should not apply. It is true that the Court did say in *Miranda* that "compulsion to speak in the isolated setting of the police station may be greater than in courts or other official investigations where there are often impartial observers to guard against intimidation or trickery." 384 U.S. 436, 461. But the opinion iterated and reiterated the absolute necessity for officers interrogating people "in custody" to give the described warnings. . . . According to the officer's testimony, petitioner was under arrest and not free to leave when he was questioned in his bedroom in the early hours of the morning. The *Miranda* opinion declared that the warnings were required when the person being interrogated was "in custody at the station *or otherwise deprived of his freedom of action in any significant way*." 384 U.S. 436, 477. (Emphasis supplied.) The decision of this Court in *Miranda* was reached after careful consideration and was announced in lengthy opinions by both the majority and dissenting Justices. There is no need to recanvass those arguments again. We do not, as the dissent implies, expand or extend to the slightest extent our *Miranda* decision. We do adhere to our well-considered holding in that case and therefore reverse the conviction below.

. . .

■ MR. JUSTICE WHITE, with whom MR. JUSTICE STEWART joins, dissenting.

. . . The rule [that "once arrest occurs, the application of *Miranda* is automatic"] is simple but it ignores the purpose of *Miranda* to guard against what was thought to be the corrosive influence of practices which station house interrogation makes feasible. The Court wholly ignores the question whether similar hazards exist or even are possible when police arrest and interrogate on the spot, whether it be on the street corner or in the home, as in this case. No predicate is laid for believing that practices outside the station house are normally prolonged, carried out in isolation, or often productive of the physical or psychological coercion made so much of in *Miranda*. It is difficult to imagine the police duplicating in a person's home or on the street those conditions and practices which the Court found prevalent in the station house and which were thought so threatening to the right to silence. Without such a demonstration, *Miranda* hardly reaches this case or any cases similar to it.

. . .

I cannot accept the dilution of the custody requirements of *Miranda* to this level, where the hazards to the right to silence are so equivocal and unsupported by experience in a recurring number of cases. . . . Even if there were reason to encourage suspects to consult lawyers to tell them to be silent before quizzing at the station house, there is no reason why police in the field should have to preface every casual question of a suspect with the full panoply of *Miranda* warnings. The same danger of coercion is simply not present in such circumstances, and the answers to the questions may as often clear a suspect as help convict him. . . .

. . . [12]

---

249. Whether or not a person is in custody for purposes of the *Miranda* requirements depends on the objective circumstances of the interrogation. It does not depend on the subjective view of either the person interrogated or the officers who conduct the interrogation. Stansbury v. California, 511 U.S. 318 (1994) (per curiam). In *Stansbury*, the Court concluded that the California court had mistakenly given independent significance to the fact that the investigation had not yet focused on the defendant rather than considering it only insofar as it had a bearing on the objective circumstances. Following *Stansbury* and again emphasizing that whether a person is in custody depends on the objective circumstances, the Court has suggested, without quite holding, that a person's individual characteristics, including his age and experience with the law, have little, if any, relevance. Yarborough v. Alvarado, 541 U.S. ___ (2004) (5–4). The Court said that the objective test was intended to give the police clear guidance. It equivocated somewhat about whether obvious characteristics (perhaps including age) or characteristics known to the police who conduct an interrogation might properly be considered, as part of the objective circumstances.

250. Suspecting that Duffy was involved in a robbery during the course of which one of the victims had been stabbed, Nevin, a police officer, went to the house where the defendant was staying and was admitted and taken to the bedroom where the defendant was asleep. "Officer Nevin testified that upon entering the room he noticed a knife sticking out from under the mattress of Duffy's bed and, before arousing the latter, he withdrew it. He then woke Duffy and greeted him with the query, 'is this the knife you used in the fight?' According to Officer Nevin, Duffy's response was, 'no, I had it with me and I dropped it during the fight. Joe Louis picked it up. Then I got it back. I don't know who stabbed the guy.' Appellant was then arrested. . . ." Duffy v. State, 221 A.2d 653, 655 (Md.1966). Is Duffy's statement admissible in evidence against him? Does it make any difference that Duffy was not arrested until after he made the statement? Suppose Officer Nevin testified that he did not believe that he had probable cause to arrest Duffy and did not intend to arrest him until after he heard Duffy's statement.

[12] Justice Harlan wrote a brief concurring opinion. Justice Stewart wrote a brief memorandum.

251. Detectives arrested Daniel W. for car theft and were told by him that Rodney P. was his accomplice. They went to Rodney P.'s home at about 8:00 p.m. and found him standing with two friends on the side steps of the house. One of the detectives asked the two friends to leave and then questioned Rodney P. for about four minutes. Rodney P. admitted that he had taken the car. He was 16 years old. People v. Rodney P. (Anon.), 233 N.E.2d 255 (N.Y.1967). Can Rodney P.'s admission be used against him?

252.

> Shortly after . . . ["the fatal stabbing of one Marie Huggins on a public street in Valley Township, Chester County"] as a result of a phone call from headquarters, Police Officer Edward Hollingsworth, who was on patrol, proceeded to the hospital to investigate. In the hospital accident ward, he found several persons, including the defendant, Jefferson, who had a towel over her forehead and left eye. . . .

> Upon entering the hospital accident ward, Hollingsworth asked: "What happened?" Jefferson replied: "There was a fight." . . . "They jumped me and I stabbed them." Hollingsworth immediately phoned [Chief of Police] Zevtchin at his home, who responded by coming to the hospital within minutes.

> Upon his arrival Zevtchin received a short briefing from Hollingsworth in the hallway of the hospital and then entered the accident ward. He asked, "Who did the stabbing?" Jefferson raised her hand and said, "I did. I think I got the wrong one." Then in response to further questions by Zevtchin, Jefferson detailed the occurrence and its background.

Commonwealth v. Jefferson, 226 A.2d 765, 766 (Pa.1967). Is Jefferson's reply to Officer Hollingsworth admissible against her? Her reply to Officer Zevtchin's first question? Her further statements?

253. "At approximately 9:15 p.m. on the evening of March 11, 1966, nine Houston police officers, carrying a valid search warrant and firearms, entered a downtown drugstore of which Kenneth Jordan Brown was the manager. The warrant authorized a search for narcotics, and the affidavit upon which it was issued named Brown as the possessor of the suspected contraband. The doors of the store were closed, and Brown was summoned from a back room, where he had been lying down, to witness the officers as they searched the premises. After the store had been carefully searched for a period of 30 to 45 minutes, one of the officers discovered a brown paper sack under a display counter which contained two plastic bags filled with a substance later determined to be heroin. As the officer raised the sack from its place of concealment, he exhibited it to Brown and asked him 'What is this?' Brown replied: 'It's heroin. You've got me this time.'" Brown v. Beto, 468 F.2d 1284, 1285 (5th Cir.1972). Is Brown's statement admissible against him?

254. "As a result of thorough police investigation [of a holdup killing], the defendant was discovered to be staying in a certain hotel and detectives went there to apprehend him. The defendant having gone out, the detectives awaited his return; two of them were let into the room by the hotel clerk, while a third remained in the lobby. The defendant arrived at about one o'clock in the morning, carrying a package under his left arm. Spotted by the officer in the lobby, he was followed upstairs and accosted in front of the door to his room. The door opened and one of the detectives inside the room, observing the defendant 'reaching for the package' under his arm, dashed from the room and grabbed him. During the ensuing struggle, in which considerable force was required to subdue the defendant, the package was torn open to reveal a loaded gun. One of the officers yelled, 'I have the gun. I have the murder weapon.' The defendant reacted to this by blurting out, 'No, no, I was only driving the car. I didn't do it. I didn't do it. The kid did it.' " People v. Hill, 216 N.E.2d 588, 590 (N.Y.1966). Is the defendant's statement admissible against him? See also United States v. Miles, 440 F.2d 1175 (5th Cir.1971); Hill v. State, 420 S.W.2d 408 (Tex.Crim.App.1967) (*Miranda* inapplicable to "res gestae statements" by defendant arrested during commission of crime).

255.

Appellant and White lived in a second-floor room of a rooming house. At about 5:00 a.m. on Saturday, March 20, 1965, the police responded to a report initiated by Appellant that there was an unconscious man in her room. They were met by Appellant, who told them she could not rouse White. She told the police that White had arrived home from work Friday evening bleeding from a wound in his chest which he said he had received at the hands of some "jitterbugs" who had jumped, robbed, and stabbed him. The police found White dead in bed with wounds in his chest and jaw. There was a small amount of blood on the undershirt and shorts he was wearing, on the sheet and blanket, and on the floor between the bed and the wall. There was no sign of disorder in the room. The police found White's jacket, which had a hole corresponding with his chest wound, and his overcoat, which had blood on it but no hole.

The police questioned Appellant about White's habits, the route he would have taken home from work, his friends, associates, and debtors and about her own activities that evening. At 6:15 a.m. Detective Cannon sent other officers to verify the place of White's employment, which Appellant had described as a hotel near a stated intersection, and to trace his route homeward.

Cannon told Appellant he intended to take her to the Homicide Squad Office at Police Headquarters to prepare a written report of what she had told them; she was also told she would be taken home when this was finished. Detective Cannon testified that while he generally considers everyone found on the scene of a homicide as a "suspect in a way," he did not consider Appellant a suspect; in short her statements were considered plausible.

On the way to Headquarters with Appellant, the police attempted to locate White's sister and made another stop to buy a package of cigarettes which Appellant requested. They arrived at Headquarters at 6:40 a.m. and went to a private room in the rear of the Homicide Squad Office. Appellant was interviewed and her statement was typed in about two hours, 45 minutes being consumed by interruptions for Cannon to attend to other police business.

Cannon asked Appellant to read and sign the statement if she found it to be accurate. As she started to read it, she said she was "in trouble." Cannon asked what she meant by that and she responded, "Well, it just looks like I am in trouble." He offered her a phone to call a lawyer, assuring her that the lawyer "will tell you that you are a witness and what you are saying is what you know about the man's death." Shortly thereafter she signed. Cannon then offered to provide a ride home as soon as a driver was available. While they were waiting, they talked about a church where Appellant had been the previous evening and with which Cannon was acquainted. In the midst of this conversation, Appellant repeated her fear about being "in trouble," and at 9:05 a.m., she leaned forward and said "Well, I might as well tell you, I stabbed him." Cannon testified that at once he said "stop right there. I want to tell you right now you are under arrest. You are charged with homicide. You are entitled to the services of a lawyer and a bondsman. You don't have to say anything. If you do, I am going to take it down and it can possibly be used against you. If you can't get your own lawyer, the Court will appoint one."

Hicks v. United States, 382 F.2d 158, 160 (D.C.Cir.1967). Is the appellant's admission that she stabbed White admissible against her? See also United States v. Roark, 753 F.2d 991 (11th Cir.1985) (defendant initially posed as victim of crime); United States v. Cobb, 449 F.2d 1145 (D.C.Cir.1971) (same).

256. Whether a person convicted in a state court is "in custody" for the purpose of the *Miranda* requirements at the time he makes incriminating statements is a "mixed question of law and fact," which is reviewed independently by a federal court in habeas corpus proceedings, rather than a question of fact about which the state court's findings are entitled to a presumption of correctness, under 28 U.S.C. § 2254(d). Thompson v. Keohane, 516 U.S. 99 (1995) (7–2).

257. Oregon v. Mathiason, 429 U.S. 492 (1977) (6–2). Having some reason to believe that the defendant was involved in a burglary, a police officer left a note at the defendant's home, in which he asked the defendant to call the police station. The defendant was a parolee. He called and arranged to meet the officer at the station house. At the meeting, the defendant was told that he was not under arrest and was then questioned briefly about the burglary; the officer told the defendant that he believed the defendant was involved in it. Within five minutes the defendant admitted his guilt. After the questioning ended, the defendant was allowed to leave. In these circumstances, the Court said, the *Miranda* warnings were not required. "Any interview of one suspected of a crime by a police officer will have coercive aspects to it, simply by virtue of the fact that the police officer is part of a law enforcement system which may ultimately cause the suspect to be charged with a crime. But police officers are not required to administer *Miranda* warnings to everyone whom they question. Nor is the requirement of warnings to be imposed simply because the questioning takes place in the station house, or because the questioned person is one whom the police suspect. *Miranda* warnings are required only where there has been such a restriction on a person's freedom as to render him 'in custody.' It was *that* sort of coercive environment to which *Miranda* by its terms was made applicable, and to which it is limited." Id. at 495. *Mathiason* was followed in California v. Beheler, 463 U.S. 1121 (1983) (6–3). See Minnesota v. Murphy, 465 U.S. 420 (1984) (6–3), in which the defendant, as required by the terms of his probation, met with his probation officer and submitted to questioning by her. The Court concluded that *Miranda* was not applicable and that the admission of his statements did not violate his Fifth Amendment privilege.

A patient of a state psychiatric hospital was in custody for purposes of the *Miranda* requirements when he was interviewed intensively as a definite criminal suspect, in a secluded area reserved for police activities, in isolation from other patients, notwithstanding that he was told that he was free to leave the interrogation area. State v. Stott, 794 A.2d 120 (N.J.2002).

Mathiason was applied in Barfield v. Alabama, 552 F.2d 1114 (5th Cir.1977). The defendant was a suspect in a murder case. Four days after the killing, a police officer interviewed her about the murder in a conversation on the street. He asked her to come to his office for another interview on the following day, and she agreed. At the second interview, after some questions he left to get her a soda. When he returned, she was on the floor "in a fetal type position" and was talking. The officer stood at the door and listened without saying anything. She confessed to the killing. Afterwards, the officer helped her to calm herself and gave her the *Miranda* warnings. After further cooperation with the police, she was put in jail. The court observed that the defendant "was not informed that she was not under arrest, but neither was she informed that she was," and that if she was indeed told not to leave the room, as she alleged, inasmuch as she was left alone and her departure was unimpeded, the statement was "more in the nature of a precatory request than a command." Id. at 1118. See also United States v. Charles, 738 F.2d 686 (5th Cir.1984) (interview of defendants, who were police officers, in district attorney's office, not custodial interrogation).

258. Mathis v. United States, 391 U.S. 1 (1968). The defendant was a prisoner in a state penitentiary. At the prison, an agent of the Internal Revenue Service interviewed him in the course of a "routine tax investigation." The Service subsequently initiated a criminal investigation of possible tax offenses committed by the defendant and prosecuted him for tax fraud. Part of the evidence used against the defendant was obtained from him during the interview in prison. The Supreme Court reversed his conviction; it held that failure to give the *Miranda* warnings before interviewing the defendant made the evidence obtained from him inadmissible. The Court said that it was irrelevant that no prosecution was contemplated when the interview took place, because "tax investigations frequently lead to criminal prosecutions," and "there was always the possibility" that there would be a prosecution in this case. Nor was it significant that the defendant's custody was unrelated to the tax offenses; there was "nothing in the *Miranda* opinion which calls for a curtailment of the warnings to be given persons under interrogation by officers based on the reason why the person is in custody." Id. at 4–5. See United States v. Chamberlain, 163 F.3d 499 (8th Cir.1998) (interview of prisoner in prison office, in all the circumstances, was custodial interrogation).

When an agent of the Internal Revenue Service interviews a taxpayer who is *not* in custody, *Miranda* warnings are not required, even if the interview is in connection with an investigation that may lead to a criminal prosecution. Such an interview "simply does not present the elements which the *Miranda* Court found so inherently coercive as to require its holding." Beckwith v. United States, 425 U.S. 341, 347 (1976) (7–1). See United States v. Hall, 421 F.2d 540 (2d Cir.1969) (federal agents' interview with suspect in bank robbery, at his home). But see United States v. Carter, 884 F.2d 368 (8th Cir.1989) (postal investigators' questioning of bank employee in office of bank president was custodial interrogation).

In United States v. Leahey, 434 F.2d 7 (1st Cir.1970), the court held that when the IRS failed to follow its own policy (announced following the decision in *Mathis*, above) of giving such warnings when a criminal prosecution was contemplated, whether or not required by *Miranda*, information obtained from the taxpayer would be suppressed.

259.   Four members of the Court concluded that *Miranda* warnings are not required when a person testifies before a grand jury, even if he is a target of the grand jury's investigation. United States v. Mandujano, 425 U.S. 564 (1976). "[T]he *Miranda* Court simply did not perceive judicial inquiries and custodial interrogation as equivalents"; to extend its holding "to questioning before a grand jury inquiring into criminal activity under the guidance of a judge is an extravagant expansion never remotely contemplated by this Court in *Miranda*." Id. at 579, 580. Despite the lack of a majority for this view in *Mandujano*, it is understood to be the law. See United States v. Washington, 431 U.S. 181, 182 n.1 (1977) (7–2). Compare United States v. Doss, 563 F.2d 265 (6th Cir.1977) (due process violated when person already indicted is summoned before grand jury and questioned about crimes charged without disclosure of indictment).

Section 9–11.151 of the United States Attorneys' Manual, which includes policy and directives promulgated by the Department of Justice for all United States Attorneys' offices, states that "notwithstanding the lack of a clear constitutional imperative," it is the Department's policy to advise a grand jury witness of the general subject matter of the inquiry, of his right to refuse to answer a question the answer to which would tend to incriminate him, that anything he says may be used against him, and that he will be permitted to consult with counsel outside the grand jury room if he wishes. In addition, "targets" of an investigation are told that their conduct is being investigated.

260. The defendant was convicted of being an accessory to a homicide. Part of the evidence against him was a statement that he made to a detective investigating the homicide during an interview in a prosecutor's office, where the defendant was being held on another charge. The defendant made the incriminating statement after the detective told him that he was wanted only as a witness and that there was no intention to prosecute him in connection with the homicide. The detective gave this assurance in good faith; the decision to prosecute the defendant was made later. People v. Caserino, 212 N.E.2d 884 (N.Y.1965). Was the defendant's statement admissible?

261.

In the early morning hours of March 16, 1965 defendant George McKie reported to a neighborhood patrolman that he had discovered the body of Manella Morris in the second floor apartment of a two-family house located at 65 Walter Avenue, Inwood, Nassau County. The defendant had spent the night of March 15 in the first floor apartment which had been rented by his friend. He allegedly discovered the body when he went to the Morris apartment to use the toilet, since the toilet in the first floor apartment was not working.

Detective Matthew Bonora and other members of the homicide squad soon arrived at the scene of the crime and went upstairs to view the body. The face and head of the deceased were completely obscured; the head was covered with a blanket and rope was tied securely around the neck. In the course of questioning McKie outside the house, Detective Bonora asked him what he thought the police might do with respect to this serious situation. According to the detective, the defendant replied that: "We are going to have to stop whoever is going around hitting these people in the head."

At this point no one had seen the victim's head, and they all thought that death had been caused by strangulation. Detective Bonora and Dr. Lukash, the medical examiner, immediately went upstairs and cut the ropes around the neck of the deceased. Upon removing the blanket, it was revealed that it was not a strangulation but that the deceased had died from a fractured skull. The defendant naturally became the prime suspect. Concededly, defendant was taken to police headquarters and interrogated extensively about his connection with the homicide. The interrogation proved fruitless, for he neither confessed nor made a single damaging admission.

Shortly thereafter, however, as a result of evidence obtained during the over-all investigation, the defendant was arrested and charged with several unrelated misdemeanors (gambling and sale of alcoholic beverages without a license). The District Court Judge assigned Patrick Adams, Esq., to represent defendant on the misdemeanor charges. Defendant pleaded guilty to one of the charges in satisfaction of all and received a jail sentence of six months which he served.

During all this time Detective Bonora and others continued the investigation of the Morris homicide but were unable to uncover any evidence to link McKie with the crime. Following McKie's release from jail on the misdemeanor charges, Detective Bonora approached him on many occasions to question him about the homicide. This caused McKie to get in touch with Adams, the attorney who had represented him earlier. Adams told Detective Bonora not to examine or talk to McKie. . . . Adams continued to represent McKie for all purposes including the investigation of the homicide. As late as April 21, 1966, when Detective Bonora visited McKie's apartment, Adams told him over the telephone: "I told you once, I told you twice, I told you many times not to examine or not to talk to McKie."

About one month later, on May 18, 1966, Detective Bonora, Detective Oliva and Patrolman Monroe, who never ceased in their efforts to unravel the truth and build their case against their prime suspect, set out to find McKie and again question him. Detective Bonora testified that they spotted McKie on the street and followed him in their car. McKie entered a small building and the officers parked at the curb. Patrolman Monroe got out of the car and went into an apartment house near the building that McKie entered, in order to investigate a report of a prowler. When McKie came out he approached the car, leaned in the window and said to Detective Bonora, "It's not going to work, Matt. When are you guys going to stop bugging me?" At that point Patrolman Monroe came out of the building and McKie began an altercation with him shouting and yelling. As the argument became heated McKie said to Monroe, "You can be killed too," and Monroe replied, "You're not dealing with any little old lady now." Observing the intensity of this verbal duel, Bonora and Oliva got out of the car and Bonora said to McKie, "You seem to be so brave now; you weren't so brave when you killed that little old lady" to which McKie replied, "Sure I did it, but you guys can't prove it."

As a result of this statement, McKie was arrested and charged with the murder of Mrs. Morris.

People v. McKie, 250 N.E.2d 36, 36–37 (N.Y.1969).

Is McKie's statement to Bonora admissible against him?

––––––––

Dunaway v. New York

442 U.S. 200, 99 S.Ct. 2248, 60 L.Ed.2d 824 (1979)

■ Mr. Justice Brennan delivered the opinion of the Court.

We decide in this case the question reserved 10 years ago in Morales v. New York, 396 U.S. 102 (1969), namely, "the question of the legality of

custodial questioning on less than probable cause for a full-fledged arrest."
Id., at 106.

I

On March 26, 1971, the proprietor of a pizza parlor in Rochester, N.Y., was killed during an attempted robbery. On August 10, 1971, Detective Anthony Fantigrossi of the Rochester Police was told by another officer that an informant had supplied a possible lead implicating petitioner in the crime. Fantigrossi questioned the supposed source of the lead—a jail inmate awaiting trial for burglary—but learned nothing that supplied "enough information to get a warrant" for petitioner's arrest. App., at 60. Nevertheless, Fantigrossi ordered other detectives to "pick up" petitioner and "bring him in." Id., at 54. Three detectives located petitioner at a neighbor's house on the morning of August 11. Petitioner was taken into custody; although he was not told he was under arrest, he would have been physically restrained if he had attempted to leave. . . . He was driven to police headquarters in a police car and placed in an interrogation room, where he was questioned by officers after being given the warnings required by Miranda v. Arizona, 384 U.S. 436 (1966). Petitioner waived counsel and eventually made statements and drew sketches that incriminated him in the crime.

At petitioner's jury trial for attempted robbery and felony murder, his motions to suppress the statements and sketches were denied, and he was convicted. . . . [T]his Court . . . vacated the judgment, and remanded the case for further consideration in light of the Court's supervening decision in Brown v. Illinois, 422 U.S. 590 (1975). . . . The petitioner in *Brown*, like petitioner Dunaway, made inculpatory statements after receiving *Miranda* warnings during custodial interrogation following his seizure—in that case a formal arrest—on less than probable cause. Brown's motion to suppress the statements was also denied and the statements were used to convict him. Although the Illinois Supreme Court recognized that Brown's arrest was unlawful, it affirmed the admission of the statements on the ground that the giving of *Miranda* warnings served to break the causal connection between the illegal arrest and the giving of the statements. This Court reversed, holding that the Illinois courts erred in adopting a per se rule that *Miranda* warnings in and of themselves sufficed to cure the Fourth Amendment violation; rather the Court held that in order to use such statements, the prosecution must show not only that the statements meet the Fifth Amendment voluntariness standard, but also that the causal connection between the statements and the illegal arrest is broken sufficiently to purge the primary taint of the illegal arrest in light of the distinct policies and interests of the Fourth Amendment.

. . .

The County Court determined after a supplementary suppression hearing that Dunaway's motion to suppress should have been granted.

Although reaffirming that there had been "full compliance with the mandate of Miranda v. Arizona," the County Court found that "this case does not involve a situation where the defendant voluntarily appeared at police headquarters in response to a request of the police. . . ." App., at 117. . . . The County Court further held that "the factual predicate in this case did not amount to probable cause sufficient to support the arrest of defendant," that "the *Miranda* warnings by themselves did not purge the taint of the defendant's illegal seizure[,] Brown v. Illinois, supra . . . and [that] there was no claim or showing by the People of any attenuation of the defendant's illegal detention," App., at 121. Accordingly petitioner's motion to suppress was granted. . . .

A divided Appellate Division reversed. . . .

We granted certiorari . . . to clarify the Fourth Amendment's requirements as to the permissible grounds for custodial interrogation and to review the New York court's application of Brown v. Illinois. We reverse.

II

We first consider whether the Rochester police violated the Fourth and Fourteenth Amendments when, without probable cause to arrest, they took petitioner into custody, transported him to the police station, and detained him there for interrogation.

. . . There can be little doubt that petitioner was "seized" in the Fourth Amendment sense when he was taken involuntarily to the police station. And respondent State concedes that the police lacked probable cause to arrest petitioner before his incriminating statement during interrogation. Nevertheless respondent contends that the seizure of petitioner did not amount to an arrest and was therefore permissible under the Fourth Amendment because the police had a "reasonable suspicion" that petitioner possessed "intimate knowledge about a serious and unsolved crime." Brief for Respondent, at 10. We disagree.

. . .

Terry [v. Ohio, 392 U.S. 1 (1968)] for the first time recognized an exception to the requirement that Fourth Amendment seizures of persons must be based on probable cause. . . . *Terry* departed from traditional Fourth Amendment analysis in two respects. First, it defined a special category of Fourth Amendment "seizures" so substantially less intrusive than arrests that the general rule requiring probable cause to make Fourth Amendment "seizures" reasonable could be replaced by a balancing test. Second, the application of this balancing test led the Court to approve this narrowly defined less intrusive seizure on grounds less rigorous than probable cause, but only for the purpose of a pat-down for weapons.

Because *Terry* involved an exception to the general rule requiring probable cause, this Court has been careful to maintain its narrow scope.

. . .

Respondent State now urges the Court to apply a balancing test, rather than the general rule, to custodial interrogations, and to hold that "seizures" such as that in this case may be justified by mere "reasonable suspicion." *Terry* and its progeny clearly do not support such a result. The narrow intrusions involved in those cases were judged by a balancing test rather than by the general principle that Fourth Amendment seizures must be supported by the "long prevailing standards" of probable cause, Brinegar v. United States, supra, 338 U.S., at 176, only because these intrusions fell far short of the kind of intrusion associated with an arrest. . . .

In contrast to the brief and narrowly circumscribed intrusions involved in those cases, the detention of petitioner was in important respects indistinguishable from a traditional arrest. Petitioner was not questioned briefly where he was found. Instead, he was taken from a neighbor's home to a police car, transported to a police station, and placed in an interrogation room. He was never informed that he was "free to go"; indeed, he would have been physically restrained if he had refused to accompany the officers or had tried to escape their custody. The application of the Fourth Amendment's requirement of probable cause does not depend on whether an intrusion of this magnitude is termed an "arrest" under state law. The mere facts that petitioner was not told he was under arrest, was not "booked," and would not have had an arrest record if the interrogation had proved fruitless, while not insignificant for all purposes . . . obviously do not make petitioner's seizure even roughly analogous to the narrowly defined intrusions involved in *Terry* and its progeny. Indeed, any "exception" that could cover a seizure as intrusive as that in this case would threaten to swallow the general rule that Fourth Amendment seizures are "reasonable" only if based on probable cause.

The central importance of the probable cause requirement to the protection of a citizen's privacy afforded by the Fourth Amendment's guarantees cannot be compromised in this fashion. . . . The familiar threshold standard of probable cause for Fourth Amendment seizures reflects the benefit of extensive experience accommodating the factors relevant to the "reasonableness" requirement of the Fourth Amendment, and provides the relative simplicity and clarity necessary to the implementation of a workable rule. . . .

In effect, respondents urge us to adopt a multifactor balancing test of "reasonable police conduct under the circumstances" to cover all seizures that do not amount to technical arrests. But the protections intended by the Framers could all too easily disappear in the consideration and balancing of the multifarious circumstances presented by different cases, especially when that balancing may be done in the first instance by police officers engaged in the "often competitive enterprise of ferreting out crime." Johnson v. United States, 333 U.S. 10, 14 (1948). A single, familiar standard is essential to guide police officers, who have only limited time and expertise to reflect on and balance the social and individual interests involved in the specific circumstances they confront. Indeed, our recognition of these dangers, and our consequent reluctance to depart from the proven protections afforded by the general rule, is reflected in the narrow limitations emphasized in the cases employing the balancing test. For all but those narrowly defined intrusions, the requisite "balancing" has been performed in centuries of precedent and is embodied in the principle that seizures are "reasonable" only if supported by probable cause.

. . .

[D]etention for custodial interrogation—regardless of its label—intrudes so severely on interests protected by the Fourth Amendment as necessarily to trigger the traditional safeguards against illegal arrest. We accordingly hold that the Rochester police violated the Fourth and Fourteenth Amendments when, without probable cause, they seized petitioner and transported him to the police station for interrogation.

III

There remains the question whether the connection between this unconstitutional police conduct and the incriminating statements and sketches obtained during petitioner's illegal detention was nevertheless sufficiently attenuated to permit the use at trial of the statements and sketches. . . .

The New York courts have consistently held, and petitioner does not contest, that proper *Miranda* warnings were given and that his statements were "voluntary" for purposes of the Fifth Amendment. But Brown v. Illinois, supra, settled that "[t]he exclusionary rule . . . when utilized to effectuate the Fourth Amendment, serves interests and policies that are distinct from those it serves under the Fifth," 422 U.S., at 601, and held therefore that "*Miranda* warnings, and the exclusion of a confession made without them, do not alone sufficiently deter a Fourth Amendment violation." Ibid.

. . .

Consequently, although a confession after proper *Miranda* warnings may be found "voluntary" for purposes of the Fifth Amendment, this type of "voluntariness" is merely a "threshold requirement" for Fourth Amendment analysis, 422 U.S., at 604. Indeed, if the Fifth Amendment has been violated, the Fourth Amendment issue would not have to be reached.

Beyond this threshold requirement, *Brown* articulated a test designed to vindicate the "distinct policies and interests of the Fourth Amendment." Id., at 602. Following *Wong Sun*, the Court eschewed any per se or "but for" rule, and identified the relevant inquiry as "whether Brown's statements were obtained by exploitation of the illegality of his arrest," id., at 600; see Wong Sun v. United States, 372 U.S. 471, 488 (1963). *Brown*'s focus on "the causal connection between the illegality and the confession," 422 U.S., at 603, reflected the two policies behind the use of the exclusionary rule to effectuate the Fourth Amendment. When there is a close causal connection between the illegal seizure and the confession, not only is exclusion of the evidence more likely to deter similar police misconduct in the future, but use of the evidence is more likely to compromise the integrity of the courts.

Brown identified several factors to be considered "in determining whether the confession is obtained by exploitation of an illegal arrest[: t]he temporal proximity of the arrest and the confession, the presence of intervening circumstances . . . and, particularly the purpose and flagrancy of the official misconduct. . . . And the burden of showing admissibility rests, of course, on the prosecution." Id., at 603–604. Examining the case before it, the Court readily concluded that the State had failed to sustain its burden of showing the confession was admissible. In the "less than two hours" that elapsed between the arrest and the confession "there was no intervening event of significance whatsoever." Ibid. Furthermore, the arrest without probable cause had a "quality of purposefulness" in that it was an "expedition for evidence" admittedly undertaken "in the hope that something might turn up." Id., at 605.

The situation in this case is virtually a replica of the situation in *Brown*. Petitioner was also admittedly seized without probable cause in the hope that something might turn up, and confessed without any intervening event of significance. . . . No intervening events broke the connection between petitioner's illegal detention and his confession. To admit petitioner's confession in such a case would allow "law enforcement officers to violate the Fourth Amendment with impunity, safe in the knowledge that they could wash their hands in the 'procedural safeguards' of the Fifth."[13] [14]

---

262. In Kaupp v. Texas, 538 U.S. 626 (2003) (per curiam), police went to the home of the defendant, who was seventeen years old, late at night. They woke him and said, "[W]e need to go and talk." The defendant said "Okay." He was handcuffed and taken to the police station in his underwear, and, after being given *Miranda* warnings, he was questioned. The state court held that he was not arrested until after he confessed. Citing *Dunaway*, the Supreme Court summarily reversed.

Dunaway and *Brown*, p. 122 above, were applied in Taylor v. Alabama, 457 U.S. 687 (1982) (5–4).

Illinois v. Perkins
496 U.S. 292, 110 S.Ct. 2394, 110 L.Ed.2d 243 (1990)

■ JUSTICE KENNEDY delivered the opinion of the Court.

An undercover government agent was placed in the cell of respondent Perkins, who was incarcerated on charges unrelated to the subject of the

---

13. Comment, 25 Emory L.J. 227, 238 (1976).

[14] Justice White and Justice Stevens wrote concurring opinions. Justice Rehnquist wrote a dissenting opinion, which Chief Justice Burger joined.

agent's investigation. Respondent made statements that implicated him in the crime that the agent sought to solve. Respondent claims that the statements should be inadmissible because he had not been given *Miranda* warnings by the agent. We hold that the statements are admissible. *Miranda* warnings are not required when the suspect is unaware that he is speaking to a law enforcement officer and gives a voluntary statement.

I

In November 1984, Richard Stephenson was murdered in a suburb of East St. Louis, Illinois. The murder remained unsolved until March 1986, when one Donald Charlton told police that he had learned about a homicide from a fellow inmate at the Graham Correctional Facility, where Charlton had been serving a sentence for burglary. The fellow inmate was Lloyd Perkins, who is the respondent here. Charlton told police that, while at Graham, he had befriended respondent, who told him in detail about a murder that respondent had committed in East St. Louis. On hearing Charlton's account, the police recognized details of the Stephenson murder that were not well known, and so they treated Charlton's story as a credible one.

By the time the police heard Charlton's account, respondent had been released from Graham, but police traced him to a jail in Montgomery County, Illinois, where he was being held pending trial on a charge of aggravated battery, unrelated to the Stephenson murder. The police wanted to investigate further respondent's connection to the Stephenson murder, but feared that the use of an eavesdropping device would prove impracticable and unsafe. They decided instead to place an undercover agent in the cellblock with respondent and Charlton. The plan was for Charlton and undercover agent John Parisi to pose as escapees from a work release program who had been arrested in the course of a burglary. Parisi and Charlton were instructed to engage respondent in casual conversation and report anything he said about the Stephenson murder.

Parisi, using the alias "Vito Bianco," and Charlton, both clothed in jail garb, were placed in the cellblock with respondent at the Montgomery County jail. The cellblock consisted of 12 separate cells that opened onto a common room. Respondent greeted Charlton who, after a brief conversation with respondent, introduced Parisi by his alias. Parisi told respondent that he "wasn't going to do any more time," and suggested that the three of them escape. Respondent replied that the Montgomery County jail was "rinky-dink" and that they could "break out." The trio met in respondent's cell later that evening, after the other inmates were asleep, to refine their plan. Respondent said that his girlfriend could smuggle in a pistol. Charlton said: "Hey, I'm not a murderer, I'm a burglar. That's your guys' profession." After telling Charlton that he would be responsible for any murder that occurred, Parisi asked respondent if he had ever "done" anybody. Respondent said that he had and proceeded to describe at length the events of the Stephenson murder. Parisi and respondent then engaged in some casual conversation before respondent went to sleep. Parisi did not give respondent *Miranda* warnings before the conversations.

Respondent was charged with the Stephenson murder. Before trial, he moved to suppress the statements made to Parisi in the jail. The trial court granted the motion to suppress, and the State appealed. The Appellate Court of Illinois affirmed . . . holding that Miranda v. Arizona, 384 U.S. 436 (1966), prohibits all undercover contacts with incarcerated suspects that are reasonably likely to elicit an incriminating response.

We granted certiorari . . . to decide whether an undercover law enforcement officer must give *Miranda* warnings to an incarcerated suspect before asking him questions that may elicit an incriminating response. We now reverse.

II

. . .

Conversations between suspects and undercover agents do not implicate the concerns underlying *Miranda*. The essential ingredients of a "police-dominated atmosphere" and compulsion are not present when an incarcerated person speaks freely to someone whom he believes to be a fellow inmate. Coercion is determined from the perspective of the suspect. . . . When a suspect considers himself in the company of cellmates and not officers, the coercive atmosphere is lacking. . . . There is no empirical basis for the assumption that a suspect speaking to those whom he assumes are not officers will feel compelled to speak by the fear of reprisal for remaining silent or in the hope of more lenient treatment should he confess.

It is the premise of *Miranda* that the danger of coercion results from the interaction of custody and official interrogation. We reject the argument that *Miranda* warnings are required whenever a suspect is in custody in a technical sense and converses with someone who happens to be a government agent. Questioning by captors, who appear to control the suspect's fate, may create mutually reinforcing pressures that the Court has assumed will weaken the suspect's will, but where a suspect does not know that he is conversing with a government agent, these pressures do not exist. The state court here mistakenly assumed that because the suspect was in custody, no undercover questioning could take place. When the suspect has no reason to think that the listeners have official power over him, it should not be assumed that his words are motivated by the reaction he expects from his listeners. . . .

Miranda forbids coercion, not mere strategic deception by taking advantage of a suspect's misplaced trust in one he supposes to be a fellow prisoner. As we recognized in *Miranda*, "[c]onfessions remain a proper element in law enforcement. Any statement given freely and voluntarily without any compelling influences is, of course, admissible in evidence." 384 U.S., at 478. Ploys to mislead a suspect or lull him into a false sense of security that do not rise to the level of compulsion or coercion to speak are not within *Miranda*'s concerns. . . .

Miranda was not meant to protect suspects from boasting about their criminal activities in front of persons whom they believe to be their cellmates. This case is illustrative. Respondent had no reason to feel that undercover agent Parisi had any legal authority to force him to answer questions or that Parisi could affect respondent's future treatment. Respondent viewed the cellmate-agent as an equal and showed no hint of being intimidated by the atmosphere of the jail. In recounting the details of the Stephenson murder, respondent was motivated solely by the desire to impress his fellow inmates. He spoke at his own peril.

The tactic employed here to elicit a voluntary confession from a suspect does not violate the Self-Incrimination Clause. We held in Hoffa v. United States, 385 U.S. 293 (1966), that placing an undercover agent near a suspect in order to gather incriminating information was permissible under the Fifth Amendment. . . . The only difference between this case and *Hoffa* is that the suspect here was incarcerated, but detention, whether or not for the crime in question, does not warrant a presumption that the use of an undercover agent to speak with an incarcerated suspect makes any confession thus obtained involuntary.

. . .

This Court's Sixth Amendment decisions in Massiah v. United States, 377 U.S. 201 (1964) . . . [and other cases] do not avail respondent. We held in those cases that the government may not use an undercover agent to circumvent the Sixth Amendment right to counsel once a suspect has been charged with the crime. . . . In the instant case no charges had been filed on the subject of the interrogation, and our Sixth Amendment precedents are not applicable.

Respondent can seek no help from his argument that a bright-line rule for the application of *Miranda* is desirable. Law enforcement officers will have little difficulty putting into practice our holding that undercover agents need not give *Miranda* warnings to incarcerated suspects. The use of undercover agents is a recognized law enforcement technique, often employed in the prison context to detect violence against correctional officials or inmates, as well as for the purposes served here. The interests protected by *Miranda* are not implicated in these cases, and the warnings are not required to safeguard the constitutional rights of inmates who make voluntary statements to undercover agents.

We hold that an undercover law enforcement officer posing as a fellow inmate need not give *Miranda* warnings to an incarcerated suspect before asking questions that may elicit an incriminating response. The statements at issue in this case were voluntary, and there is no federal obstacle to their admissibility at trial. We now reverse and remand for proceedings not inconsistent with our opinion.

... [15]

Perkins follows the general approach to the *Miranda* requirements that was taken in Moran v. Burbine, p. 444 above: What a defendant does not know has no bearing on his state of mind and, therefore, does not implicate any issue of compulsion to speak. In both cases, the situation in which the defendant found himself, a jail cell in *Perkins* and a police station in *Burbine*, was entirely within the control of the police and not one that the defendant himself chose voluntarily. Can that fact be made the basis for an argument that *Miranda* does—or should—apply?

---

263.   Following a remand to the state trial court, Perkins claimed that he had asserted his right to counsel after his arrest on the aggravated battery charge and that the subsequent questioning by undercover agents violated his privilege against compulsory self-incrimination. People v. Perkins, 618 N.E.2d 1275 (Ill.App.1993). The court said that the government's procedure was calculated to deceive the defendant so that he was not "given an opportunity to knowingly and intelligently waive his previously asserted right to have counsel present during questioning." Id. at 1280. In those circumstances, the court concluded, Arizona v. Roberson, p. 443 above, applied.

In United States v. Ingle, 157 F.3d 1147 (8th Cir.1998), the defendant, who was being detained on an unrelated charge, agreed to be transported to a jail elsewhere, in order to talk with federal agents and appear before a grand jury in connection with the investigation of a murder which he was suspected of having committed. The public defender was appointed to represent him "in all further proceedings." After talking with counsel, he refused to talk with the investigators or to testify before a grand jury. Two inmates at the jail, one of whom wore a recording device, talked with the defendant in a jail cell. The court held that the recorded conversation was admissible in evidence. Following *Perkins*, it held that there was no *Miranda* violation. And following *Massiah* and Moran v. Burbine, there was no Sixth Amendment violation, notwithstanding the appointment of counsel, because formal proceedings had not begun.

264. Berkemer v. McCarty, 468 U.S. 420 (1984). A highway patrol officer stopped the defendant, who was driving in an erratic manner. After the defendant was out of the car, the officer decided to arrest him for drunk driving. He did not tell the defendant that he was under arrest. He asked the defendant whether he had been using intoxicants. The defendant replied that he had drunk beer and smoked marijuana shortly before. He

---

[15] Justice Brennan wrote an opinion concurring in the judgment. Justice Marshall wrote a dissenting opinion.

was then arrested and taken to the jail, where the officer asked him further questions about his having been drinking. The defendant's answers were incriminating. No *Miranda* warnings were given.

Rejecting the contention that *Miranda*'s requirements should not apply to minor offenses—misdemeanors, or traffic offenses—the Court held that "a person subjected to custodial interrogation is entitled to the benefit of the procedural safeguards enunciated in *Miranda* regardless of the nature or severity of the offense of which he is suspected or for which he was arrested." Id. at 434. The Court said that any other rule would undermine the clarity of the *Miranda* requirements, which was a "crucial advantage." Id. at 430.

Secondly, however, the Court concluded that roadside questioning of a motorist during a routine traffic stop is not "custodial interrogation" within the meaning of *Miranda*, even though the motorist is not free to leave. Such a stop, the Court observed, is usually brief, and the motorist does not feel "completely at the mercy of the police." Id. at 438. In these respects, a traffic stop resembles a *Terry* stop, to which the *Miranda* requirements do not apply, more than an arrest. If a traffic stop is prolonged and the person is treated as " 'in custody' for practical purposes," id. at 440, the *Miranda* requirements are applicable. On that basis, the Court concluded that the defendant's statements on the highway were admissible and his statements at the jail were not admissible.

See United States v. Dortch, 199 F.3d 193 (5th Cir.1999) (continued detention of defendant after justification for traffic stop was eliminated was an unreasonable seizure).

––––––––

New York v. Quarles

467 U.S. 649, 104 S.Ct. 2626, 81 L.Ed.2d 550 (1984)

■ JUSTICE REHNQUIST delivered the opinion of the Court.

Respondent Benjamin Quarles was charged in the New York trial court with criminal possession of a weapon. The trial court suppressed the gun in question, and a statement made by respondent, because the statement was obtained by police before they read respondent his "*Miranda* rights." . . . We granted certiorari . . . and we now reverse. We conclude that under the circumstances involved in this case, overriding considerations of public safety justify the officer's failure to provide *Miranda* warnings before he asked questions devoted to locating the abandoned weapon.

On September 11, 1980, at approximately 12:30 a.m., Officer Frank Kraft and Officer Sal Scarring were on road patrol in Queens, N.Y., when a young woman approached their car. She told them that she had just been raped by a black male, approximately six feet tall, who was wearing a black jacket with the name "Big Ben" printed in yellow letters on the back. She told the officers that the man had just entered an A & P supermarket located nearby and that the man was carrying a gun.

The officers drove the woman to the supermarket, and Officer Kraft entered the store while Officer Scarring radioed for assistance. Officer Kraft quickly spotted respondent, who matched the description given by the woman, approaching a check-out counter. Apparently upon seeing the officer, respondent turned and ran toward the rear of the store, and Officer Kraft pursued him with a drawn gun. When respondent turned the corner at the end of an aisle, Officer Kraft lost sight of him for several seconds, and upon regaining sight of respondent, ordered him to stop and put his hands over his head.

Although more than three other officers had arrived on the scene by that time, Officer Kraft was the first to reach respondent. He frisked him and discovered that he was wearing a shoulder holster which was then empty. After handcuffing him, Officer Kraft asked him where the gun was. Respondent nodded in the direction of some empty cartons and responded, "the gun is over there." Officer Kraft thereafter retrieved a loaded .38-caliber revolver from one of the cartons, formally placed respondent under arrest, and read him his *Miranda* rights from a printed card. Respondent indicated that he would be willing to answer questions without an attorney present. Officer Kraft then asked respondent if he owned the gun and where he had purchased it. Respondent answered that he did own it and that he had purchased it in Miami, Fla.

In the subsequent prosecution of respondent for criminal possession of a weapon, the judge excluded the statement, "the gun is over there," and the gun because the officer had not given respondent the warnings required by our decision in Miranda v. Arizona, 384 U.S. 436 (1966), before asking him where the gun was located. The judge excluded the other statements about respondent's ownership of the gun and the place of purchase, as evidence tainted by the prior *Miranda* violation. . . .

. . . For the reasons which follow, we believe that this case presents a situation where concern for public safety must be paramount to adherence to the literal language of the prophylactic rules enunciated in *Miranda*.

. . .

In this case we have before us no claim that respondent's statements were actually compelled by police conduct which overcame his will to resist. . . . Thus the only issue before us is whether Officer Kraft was justified in failing to make available to respondent the procedural safeguards associated with the privilege against compulsory self-incrimination since *Miranda*.

. . .

We hold that on these facts there is a "public safety" exception to the requirement that *Miranda* warnings be given before a suspect's answers may be admitted into evidence, and that the availability of that exception does not depend upon the motivation of the individual officers involved. In a kaleidoscopic situation such as the one confronting these officers, where spontaneity rather than adherence to a police manual is necessarily the order of the day, the application of the exception which we recognize today should not be made to depend on post hoc findings at a suppression hearing concerning the subjective motivation of the arresting officer. Undoubtedly most police officers, if placed in Officer Kraft's position, would act out of a host of different, instinctive, and largely unverifiable motives—their own safety, the safety of others, and perhaps as well the desire to obtain incriminating evidence from the suspect.

Whatever the motivation of individual officers in such a situation, we do not believe that the doctrinal underpinnings of *Miranda* require that it be applied in all its rigor to a situation in which police officers ask questions reasonably prompted by a concern for the public safety. . . .

The police in this case, in the very act of apprehending a suspect, were confronted with the immediate necessity of ascertaining the whereabouts of a gun which they had every reason to believe the suspect had just removed from his empty holster and discarded in the supermarket. So long as the gun was concealed somewhere in the supermarket, with its actual whereabouts unknown, it obviously posed more than one danger to the public safety: an accomplice might make use of it, a customer or employee might later come upon it.

In such a situation, if the police are required to recite the familiar *Miranda* warnings before asking the whereabouts of the gun, suspects in Quarles' position might well be deterred from responding. Procedural safeguards which deter a suspect from responding were deemed acceptable in *Miranda* in order to protect the Fifth Amendment privilege; when the primary social cost of those added protections is the possibility of fewer convictions, the *Miranda* majority was willing to bear that cost. Here, had *Miranda* warnings deterred Quarles from responding to Officer Kraft's question about the whereabouts of the gun, the cost would have been something more than merely the failure to obtain evidence useful in convicting Quarles. Officer Kraft needed an answer to his question not simply to make his case against Quarles but to insure that further danger to the public did not result from the concealment of the gun in a public area.

We conclude that the need for answers to questions in a situation posing a threat to the public safety outweighs the need for the prophylactic rule protecting the Fifth Amendment's privilege against self-incrimination. We decline to place officers such as Officer Kraft in the untenable position of having to consider, often in a matter of seconds, whether it best serves society for them to ask the necessary questions without the *Miranda* warnings and render whatever probative evidence they uncover inadmissible, or for them to give the warnings in order to preserve the admissibility of evidence they might uncover but possibly damage or destroy their ability to obtain that evidence and neutralize the volatile situation confronting them.

In recognizing a narrow exception to the *Miranda* rule in this case, we acknowledge that to some degree we lessen the desirable clarity of that rule. At least in part in order to preserve its clarity, we have over the years refused to sanction attempts to expand our *Miranda* holding. . . . As we have in other contexts, we recognize here the importance of a workable rule "to guide police officers, who have only limited time and expertise to reflect on and balance the social and individual interests involved in the specific circumstances they confront." Dunaway v. New York, 442 U.S. 200, 213–14 (1979). But as we have pointed out, we believe that the exception which we recognize today lessens the necessity of that on-the-scene balancing process. The exception will not be difficult for police officers to apply because in each case it will be circumscribed by the exigency which justifies it. We think police officers can and will distinguish almost instinctively between questions necessary to secure their own safety or the safety of the public and questions designed solely to elicit testimonial evidence from a suspect.

The facts of this case clearly demonstrate that distinction and an officer's ability to recognize it. Officer Kraft asked only the question necessary to locate the missing gun before advising respondent of his rights. It was only after securing the loaded revolver and giving the warnings that he continued with investigatory questions about the ownership and place of purchase of the gun. The exception which we recognize today, far from complicating the thought processes and the on-the-scene judgments of police officers, will simply free them to follow their legitimate instincts when confronting situations presenting a danger to the public safety.[16]

We hold that the Court of Appeals in this case erred in excluding the statement, "the gun is over there," and the gun because of the officer's failure to read respondent his *Miranda* rights before attempting to locate the weapon. Accordingly we hold that it also erred in excluding the subsequent statements as illegal fruits of a *Miranda* violation. We therefore reverse and remand for further proceedings not inconsistent with this opinion.

. . . [17]

---

265. In United States v. DeSantis, 870 F.2d 536 (9th Cir.1989), the court held that the *Quarles* public safety exception warranted relaxation of the *Edwards* requirement (p. 441 note 246 above) that all questioning stop once an arrested person makes a request to talk to counsel. See United

---

16. Although it involves police questions in part relating to the whereabouts of a gun, Orozco v. Texas, 394 U.S. 324 (1969), is in no sense inconsistent with our disposition of this case. . . . In *Orozco* . . . the questions about the gun were clearly investigatory; they did not in any way relate to an objectively reasonable need to protect the police or the public from any immediate danger associated with the weapon. In short there was no exi-

gency requiring immediate action by the officers beyond the normal need expeditiously to solve a serious crime. . . .

[17] Justice O'Connor wrote an opinion concurring in part in the judgment and dissenting in part. Justice Marshall wrote a dissenting opinion, which Justice Brennan and Justice Stevens joined.

States v. Mobley, 40 F.3d 688 (4th Cir.1994), in which the court agreed with *DeSantis* that *Quarles* might justify an exception to the *Edwards* requirement but concluded that the circumstances did not justify an exception in that case.

In United States v. Lackey, 334 F.3d 1224 (10th Cir.2003), the defendant was arrested on a warrant for offenses including the illegal discharge of a firearm. After he was handcuffed but before he was given *Miranda* warnings, an arresting officer asked if he had any guns or sharp objects on his person. The defendant responded that there was a gun in his car. The court held that his response was within the public safety exception to *Miranda*. Accord, United States v. Reyes, 353 F.3d 148 (2d Cir.2003).

266.   *Miranda* warnings are "not essential to the validity of a confession which has been given in a foreign country." United States v. Mundt, 508 F.2d 904, 906 (10th Cir.1974). Accord United States v. Martindale, 790 F.2d 1129 (4th Cir.1986); United States v. Chavarria, 443 F.2d 904 (9th Cir.1971).

267.   Do the *Miranda* requirements apply only to the police and other government officials engaged in criminal investigations? Or to all government officials? Does it have any application to persons who are not government officials?

"Schaumberg was a slot machine repairman employed at Harrah's. Cox, his brother-in-law, was visiting at Schaumberg's home. Shortly after 6:00 A.M. on September 21, 1964, Schaumberg was observed working on a dollar slot machine by a pit boss of Harrah's, Ovlan Fritz. After performing some mechanics within the machine, he adjusted it so that it was turned partially on the base plate and then left the area. Immediately thereafter, Cox went to the machine, moved it squarely onto the base plate, whereupon it registered a $5,000.00 jackpot. Fritz reported what he saw to two other supervisors. Together with a security guard employed by Harrah's they asked Cox to accompany them to the security office. Leaving him in the office, they proceeded to locate Schaumberg whom they found in a washroom. Schaumberg accompanied them to the manager's office. The security guard remained outside the office while two of the supervisors, Howland and Curry, questioned Schaumberg. In all, four supervisors testified Schaumberg admitted that he had rigged the slot machine because Cox needed money." Schaumberg v. State, 432 P.2d 500, 501 (Nev.1967).

The supervisors who questioned Schaumberg did not advise him of his rights. Can his admissions be used against him in a prosecution for conspiracy to cheat and defraud Harrah's? See also In the Matter of Victor F., 169 Cal.Rptr. 455 (Ct.App.1980) (school principal); People v. Raitano, 401 N.E.2d 278 (Ill.1980) (store security guard).

See generally Colorado v. Connelly, 479 U.S. 157 (1986), p. 403 note 226 above.

———

Harris v. New York
401 U.S. 222, 91 S.Ct. 643, 28 L.Ed.2d 1 (1971)

■ Mr. Chief Justice Burger delivered the opinion of the Court.

We granted the writ in this case to consider petitioner's claim that a statement made by him to police under circumstances rendering it inadmissible to establish the prosecution's case in chief under Miranda v. Arizona, 384 U.S. 436 (1966), may not be used to impeach his credibility.

The State of New York charged petitioner in a two-count indictment with twice selling heroin to an undercover police officer. At a subsequent jury trial the officer was the State's chief witness, and he testified as to details of the two sales. A second officer verified collateral details of the sales, and a third offered testimony about the chemical analysis of the heroin.

Petitioner took the stand in his own defense. He admitted knowing the undercover police officer but denied a sale on January 4, 1966. He admitted making a sale of contents of a glassine bag to the officer on January 6 but claimed it was baking powder and part of a scheme to defraud the purchaser.

On cross-examination petitioner was asked seriatim whether he had made specified statements to the police immediately following his arrest on January 7—statements that partially contradicted petitioner's direct testimony at trial. In response to the cross-examination, petitioner testified that he could not remember virtually any of the questions or answers recited by the prosecutor. At the request of petitioner's counsel the written statement from which the prosecutor had read questions and answers in his impeaching process was placed in the record for possible use on appeal; the statement was not shown to the jury.

The trial judge instructed the jury that the statements attributed to petitioner by the prosecution could be considered only in passing on petitioner's credibility and not as evidence of guilt. In closing summations both counsel argued the substance of the impeaching statements. The jury then found petitioner guilty on the second count of the indictment. . . .

At trial the prosecution made no effort in its case in chief to use the statements allegedly made by petitioner, conceding that they were inadmissible under Miranda v. Arizona. . . . The transcript of the interrogation used in the impeachment, but not given to the jury, shows that no warning of a right to appointed counsel was given before questions were put to petitioner when he was taken into custody. Petitioner makes no claim that the statements made to the police were coerced or involuntary.

Some comments in the *Miranda* opinion can indeed be read as indicating a bar to use of an uncounseled statement for any purpose, but discussion of that issue was not at all necessary to the Court's holding and cannot be regarded as controlling. *Miranda* barred the prosecution from making its case with statements of an accused made while in custody prior to having or effectively waiving counsel. It does not follow from *Miranda* that evidence inadmissible against an accused in the prosecution's case in chief is barred for all purposes, provided of course that the trustworthiness of the evidence satisfies legal standards.

In Walder v. United States, 347 U.S. 62 (1954), the Court permitted physical evidence, inadmissible in the case in chief, to be used for impeachment purposes.

> It is one thing to say that the Government cannot make an affirmative use of evidence unlawfully obtained. It is quite another to say that the defendant can turn the illegal method by which evidence in the Government's possession was obtained to his own advantage, and provide himself with a shield against contradiction of his untruths. [...]

> [T]here is hardly justification for letting the defendant affirmatively resort to perjurious testimony in reliance on the Government's disability to challenge his credibility.

347 U.S., at 65.

It is true that Walder was impeached as to collateral matters included in his direct examination, whereas petitioner here was impeached as to testimony bearing more directly on the crimes charged. We are not persuaded that there is a difference in principle that warrants a result different from that reached by the Court in *Walder*. Petitioner's testimony in his own behalf concerning the events of January 7 contrasted sharply with what he told the police shortly after his arrest. The impeachment process here undoubtedly provided valuable aid to the jury in assessing petitioner's credibility, and the benefits of this process should not be lost, in our view, because of the speculative possibility that impermissible police conduct will be encouraged thereby. Assuming that the exclusionary rule has a deterrent effect on proscribed police conduct, sufficient deterrence flows when the evidence in question is made unavailable to the prosecution in its case in chief.

Every criminal defendant is privileged to testify in his own defense, or to refuse to do so. But that privilege cannot be construed to include the right to commit perjury. Having voluntarily taken the stand, petitioner was under an obligation to speak truthfully and accurately, and the prosecution here did no more than utilize the traditional truth-testing devices of the adversary process. Had inconsistent statements been made by the accused to some third person, it could hardly be contended that the conflict could not be laid before the jury by way of cross-examination and impeachment.

The shield provided by *Miranda* cannot be perverted into a license to use perjury by way of a defense, free from the risk of confrontation with prior inconsistent utterances. We hold, therefore, that petitioner's credibility was appropriately impeached by use of his earlier conflicting statements.

Affirmed.[18]

---

[18] Justice Brennan wrote a dissenting opinion which Justice Douglas and Justice Marshall joined. Justice Black noted his dissent.

268. Doyle v. Ohio, 426 U.S. 610 (1976) (6–3). Notwithstanding *Harris*, above, the use for impeachment purposes of a defendant's *silence* following his arrest and after receiving *Miranda* warnings is a violation of due process. The defendants were prosecuted for a narcotics offense. At trial, they testified and gave an exculpatory account that they had not mentioned earlier. Over objection, the prosecutor cross-examined them about their failure to give the arresting officer their account. Reversing the convictions, the Court said: "Silence in the wake of these warnings may be nothing more than the arrestee's exercise of these *Miranda* rights. Thus, every post-arrest silence is insolubly ambiguous because of what the State is required to advise the person arrested. . . . Moreover, while it is true that the *Miranda* warnings contain no express assurance that silence will carry no penalty, such assurance is implicit to any person who receives the warnings. In such circumstances, it would be fundamentally unfair and a deprivation of due process to allow the arrested person's silence to be used to impeach an explanation subsequently offered at trial." Id. at 617–18. See United States v. Hale, 422 U.S. 171 (1975).

Doyle was applied in Wainwright v. Greenfield, 474 U.S. 284 (1986). The defendant pleaded not guilty by reason of insanity. The Court held that his silence after being given a *Miranda* warning following his arrest could not be used at trial as evidence of his sanity. Compare Greer v. Miller, 483 U.S. 756 (1987) (6–3) (prosecutor's question in violation of *Doyle*, objection to which was sustained, did not require reversal of conviction); United States v. Stubbs, 944 F.2d 828 (11th Cir.1991) (witness's brief comment about defendant's post-arrest silence not a *Doyle* violation).

In Jenkins v. Anderson, 447 U.S. 231 (1980) (7–2), the Court held that it was permissible for the prosecutor to cross-examine the defendant about his failure to give an exculpatory account of the alleged crime to the police before his arrest. The "use of prearrest silence to impeach a defendant's credibility," id. at 238, violates neither the privilege against compulsory self-incrimination nor the fundamental fairness required by the Due Process Clause. *Doyle* was distinguished on the ground that here "no governmental action induced petitioner to remain silent before arrest." Id. at 240. The Court observed that the states were free to adopt evidentiary rules admitting or excluding such evidence as they thought appropriate.

Jenkins was applied in Fletcher v. Weir, 455 U.S. 603 (1982) (7–1–1). There, the defendant was cross-examined about his failure to give an exculpatory version (self-defense) of a homicide to police officers after his arrest. There was no indication in the record that he had been given *Miranda* warnings. The Court said: "In the absence of the sort of affirmative assurances embodied in the *Miranda* warnings, we do not believe that it violates due process of law for a State to permit cross-examination as to postarrest silence when a defendant chooses to take the stand. A State is entitled, in such situations, to leave to the judge and jury under its own rules of evidence the resolution of the extent to which postarrest silence may be deemed to impeach a criminal defendant's own testimony." Id. at 607.

Doyle "does not apply to cross-examination that merely inquires into prior inconsistent statements. Such questioning makes no unfair use of silence because a defendant who voluntarily speaks after receiving *Miranda* warnings has not been induced to remain silent. As to the subject matter of his statements, the defendant has not remained silent at all." Anderson v. Charles, 447 U.S. 404, 408 (1980) (7–2).

269. *Harris* was applied in Oregon v. Hass, 420 U.S. 714 (1975) (6–2), in which a state police officer gave the defendant full *Miranda* warnings at the time of his arrest. In the patrol car, the defendant said that he would like to talk to an attorney, which the officer said he could do when they got to the police station. Before they got to the station, the defendant made incriminating statements. The officer was allowed to testify about those statements for the limited purpose of impeaching the credibility of the defendant as a witness on the stand. The Court said that it saw no valid distinction between this case and *Harris*. Here, as there, "the shield provided by *Miranda* is not to be perverted to a license to testify inconsistently, or even perjuriously, free from the risk of confrontation with prior inconsistent utterances." 420 U.S. at 722.

270. Relying on the privilege against self-incrimination in the state constitution, the Supreme Court of California rejected the holding of *Harris* in People v. Disbrow, 545 P.2d 272 (Cal.1976). Its principal objection to *Harris*, the court said, was "the considerable potential that a jury, even with the benefit of a limiting instruction, will view prior inculpatory statements as substantive evidence of guilt rather than as merely reflecting on the declarant's veracity." 545 P.2d at 279. The Supreme Court of Hawaii made a similar determination. State v. Santiago, 492 P.2d 657 (Haw.1971). *Disbrow* was presumably overturned by a state constitutional amendment, see note 248, p. 454 above.

271. Michigan v. Tucker, 417 U.S. 433 (1974) (8–1). The defendant was arrested on a charge of rape and taken to the police station. Before he was questioned, the police asked him whether he knew the crime for which he had been arrested, whether he wanted a lawyer, and whether he understood his constitutional rights. He responded that he knew why he was arrested and knew his rights, and did not want a lawyer. The police advised him that his statements could be used against him. They did not advise him, as required by *Miranda*, that he could have free legal advice if he could not afford to pay for it. During the questioning, the defendant made exculpatory statements that led the police to one Henderson. Henderson gave the police information that incriminated the defendant. The questioning of the defendant occurred before *Miranda* was decided, but his trial followed that decision. At trial, the defendant's own incriminating statements were excluded. A motion to exclude Henderson's testimony was denied, and Henderson testified against the defendant.

Declining to decide the extent to which *Miranda* requires exclusion of evidence other than responses to questions derived from violations of the *Miranda* rules, the Court held that Henderson's statements were properly admitted.

The *Miranda* rules, the Court said, established a set of "procedural safeguards" that "were not themselves rights protected by the Constitution but were instead measures to insure that the right against compulsory self-incrimination was protected." In this case, the questioning did not deprive the defendant of his constitutional right "but rather failed to make available to him the full measure of procedural safeguards associated with that right since *Miranda*." Id. at 444. The Court noted the timetable of the case in relation to *Miranda* and the fact that the police were in compliance with existing law when they questioned the defendant. It observed that exclusion of Henderson's testimony in addition to the defendant's testimony would not augment *Miranda*'s purpose to deter illegal police conduct; furthermore, failure to give the defendant the full *Miranda* warnings did not cast doubt on the reliability of Henderson's testimony.

Before the decision in Dickerson v. United States, 530 U.S. 428 (2000) (7–2), note 235 p. 429 above, courts generally concluded that *Tucker* and Oregon v. Elstad, 470 U.S. 298 (1985), note 238 p. 431 above, dictated the conclusion that physical evidence that is the fruit of a *Miranda* violation need not be excluded. E.g., United States v. Elie, 111 F.3d 1135 (4th Cir.1997). The question has been considered anew after the decision in *Dickerson*, with varying results. Several circuits have concluded that the prior rule remains valid. E.g., United States v. Villalba-Alvarado, 345 F.3d 1007 (8th Cir.2003). In United States v. Patane, 304 F.3d 1013 (10th Cir.2002), however, the court held that such evidence is not admissible. And in United States v. Faulkingham, 295 F.3d 85 (1st Cir.2002), the court held that whether physical evidence should be excluded depended on the need for deterrence of police misconduct in the circumstances of the case and that the evidence should not be excluded if the *Miranda* violation was not intentional but merely negligent. The Supreme Court has granted certiorari in *Patane*, 538 U.S. 976 (2003). A decision is expected in 2004.

In United States v. Morales, 788 F.2d 883 (2d Cir.1986), the court held that a voluntary statement that was obtained by police officers acting in good faith but in violation of the *Miranda* rules could be considered as part of the probable cause for an arrest. The defendant made the statement in response to a police officer's question while he was lawfully detained but before he was arrested. Referring to cases including *Tucker* and *Elstad*, the court said: "[W]e can find no 'valid and useful purpose' to be served by disregarding . . . [the defendant's] pre-warning statement to the officers who were acting in good faith. Where, as here, there is no indication of trickery or coercion, there is no justification for requiring a police officer to ignore incriminating admissions in arriving at a conclusion that there is probable cause for an arrest. Suppression of the uncounseled statements at the trial is sufficient to further the purposes of *Miranda*." 788 F.2d at 886.

272. Does anyone other than the person questioned have standing to object to the admission of evidence obtained in violation of the *Miranda* requirements? In People v. Varnum, 427 P.2d 772, 775 (Cal.1967), the court said no.

> Non-coercive questioning is not in itself unlawful . . . and the Fifth and Sixth Amendment rights protected by *Escobedo, Dorado*,[19] and *Miranda* are violated only when evidence obtained without the required warnings and waiver is introduced against the person whose questioning produced the evidence. The basis for the warnings required by *Miranda* is the privilege against self-incrimination . . . and that privilege is not violated when the information elicited from an unwarned suspect is not used against him. . . . Similarly the right to counsel protected by *Escobedo* and *Dorado* is not infringed when the exclusion of any evidence obtained through the violation of the rules of those cases precludes any interference with the suspect's right to effective representation. . . . Unlike unreasonable searches and seizures, which always violate the Constitution, there is nothing unlawful in questioning an unwarned suspect so long as the police refrain from physically and psychologically coercive tactics condemned by due process and do not use against the suspect any evidence obtained. Accordingly, in the absence of such coercive tactics, there is no basis for excluding physical or other non-hearsay evidence acquired as a result of questioning a suspect in disregard of his Fifth and Sixth Amendment rights when such evidence is offered at the trial of another person.

Accord People v. Denham, 241 N.E.2d 415 (Ill.1968). See also Bradford v. Michigan, 394 U.S. 1022 (1969) (testimony coerced from witness); People v. Portelli, 205 N.E.2d 857 (N.Y.1965) (same).

Further Aspects of the Privilege Against Compulsory Self-Incrimination

---

Fisher v. United States

425 U.S. 391, 96 S.Ct. 1569, 48 L.Ed.2d 39 (1976)

■ MR. JUSTICE WHITE delivered the opinion of the Court.

In these two cases we are called upon to decide whether a summons directing an attorney to produce documents delivered to him by his client in connection with the attorney-client relationship is enforceable over

---

[19] People v. Dorado, 398 P.2d 361 (Cal. 1965), in which the Supreme Court of Cali-   fornia applied the rationale of *Escobedo*.

claims that the documents were constitutionally immune from summons in the hands of the client and retained that immunity in the hands of the attorney.

I

In each case, an Internal Revenue agent visited the taxpayer or taxpayers and interviewed them in connection with an investigation of possible civil or criminal liability under the federal income tax laws. Shortly after the interviews—one day later in No. 74–611 and a week or two later in No. 74–18—the taxpayers obtained from their respective accountants certain documents relating to the preparation by the accountants of their tax returns. Shortly after obtaining the documents—later the same day in No. 74–611 and a few weeks later in No. 74–18—the taxpayers transferred the documents to their lawyer—respondent Kasmir and petitioner Fisher, respectively—each of whom was retained to assist the taxpayer in connection with the investigation. Upon learning of the whereabouts of the documents, the Internal Revenue Service served summonses on the attorneys directing them to produce documents listed therein. In No. 74–611, the documents were described as "the following records of Tannebaum Bindler & Lewis [the accounting firm]."

1. Accountant's work papers pertaining to Dr. E.J. Mason's books and records of 1969, 1970 and 1971.

2. Retained copies of E.J. Mason's income tax returns for 1969, 1970 and 1971.

3. Retained copies of reports and other correspondence between Tannebaum Bindler & Lewis and Dr. E.J. Mason during 1969, 1970 and 1971.

In No. 74–18, the documents demanded were analyses by the accountant of the taxpayers' income and expenses which had been copied by the accountant from the taxpayers' canceled checks and deposit receipts. In No. 74–611, a summons was also served on the accountant directing him to appear and testify concerning the documents to be produced by the lawyer. In each case, the lawyer declined to comply with the summons directing production of the documents, and enforcement actions were commenced by the Government under 26 U.S.C. §§ 7402(b) and 7604(a). In No. 74–611, the attorney raised in defense of the enforcement action the taxpayer's accountant-client privilege, his attorney-client privilege, and his Fourth and Fifth Amendment rights. In No. 74–18, the attorney claimed that enforcement would involve compulsory self-incrimination of the taxpayers in violation of their Fifth Amendment privilege, would involve a seizure of the papers without necessary compliance with the Fourth Amendment, and would violate the taxpayers' right to communicate in confidence with their attorney. In No. 74–18 the taxpayers intervened and made similar claims.

In each case the summons was ordered enforced by the District Court and its order was stayed pending appeal. In No. 74–18, 500 F.2d 683 (CA3 1974), petitioners' appeal raised, in terms, only their Fifth Amendment claim, but they argued in connection with that claim that enforcement of the summons would involve a violation of the taxpayers' reasonable expectation of privacy and particularly so in light of the confidential relationship of attorney to client. The Court of Appeals for the Third Circuit after reargument en banc affirmed the enforcement order, holding that the taxpayers had never acquired a possessory interest in the documents and that the papers were not immune in the hands of the attorney. In No. 74–611, a divided panel of the Court of Appeals for the Fifth Circuit reversed the enforcement order, 499 F.2d 444 (1974). The court reasoned that by virtue of the Fifth Amendment the documents would have been privileged from production pursuant to summons directed to the taxpayer had he retained possession and, in light of the confidential nature of the attorney-client relationship, the taxpayer retained, after the transfer to his attorney, "a legitimate expectation of privacy with regard to the materials he placed in his attorney's custody, that he retained constructive possession of the evidence, and thus . . . retained Fifth Amendment protection." Id., at 453. We granted certiorari to resolve the conflict created. . . . Because in our view the documents were not privileged either in the hands of the lawyers or of their clients, we affirm the judgment of the Third Circuit in No. 74–18 and reverse the judgment of the Fifth Circuit in No. 74–611.

II

All of the parties in these cases and the Court of Appeals for the Fifth Circuit have concurred in the proposition that if the Fifth Amendment would have excused a *taxpayer* from turning over the accountant's papers had he possessed them, the *attorney* to whom they are delivered for the purpose of obtaining legal advice should also be immune from subpoena. Although we agree with this proposition for the reasons set forth in Part III, infra, we are convinced that, under our decision in Couch v. United States, 409 U.S. 322 (1973), it is not the taxpayer's Fifth Amendment privilege that would excuse the *attorney* from production.

. . . The taxpayer's privilege under this Amendment is not violated by enforcement of the summonses involved in these cases because enforcement against a taxpayer's lawyer would not "compel" the taxpayer to do anything—and certainly would not compel him to be a "witness" against himself. The Court has held repeatedly that the Fifth Amendment is limited to prohibiting the use of "physical or moral compulsion" exerted on the person asserting the privilege, Perlman v. United States, 247 U.S. 7, 15 (1918). . . . In Couch v. United States, supra, we recently ruled that the Fifth Amendment rights of a taxpayer were not violated by the enforcement of a documentary summons directed to her accountant and requiring production of the taxpayer's own records in the possession of the accountant. We did so on the ground that in such a case "the ingredient of personal compulsion against an accused is lacking." 409 U.S., at 329.

Here, the taxpayers are compelled to do no more than was the taxpayer in *Couch*. The taxpayers' Fifth Amendment privilege is therefore not violated by enforcement of the summonses directed toward their attorneys.

This is true whether or not the Amendment would have barred a subpoena directing the taxpayer to produce the documents while they were in his hands.

The fact that the attorneys are agents of the taxpayers does not change this result. *Couch* held as much, since the accountant there was also the taxpayer's agent, and in this respect reflected a long-standing view. In Hale v. Henkel, 201 U.S. 43, 69–70 (1906), the Court said that the privilege "was never intended to permit [a person] to plead the fact that some third person might be incriminated by his testimony, even though he were the agent of such person. . . . [T]he Amendment is limited to a person who shall be compelled in any criminal case to be a witness against *himself.*" (Emphasis in original.) "It is extortion of information from the accused himself that offends our sense of justice." Couch v. United States, supra, at 328. Agent or no, the lawyer is not the taxpayer. The taxpayer is the "accused," and nothing is being extorted from him.

Nor is this one of those situations, which *Couch* suggested might exist, where constructive possession is so clear or relinquishment of possession so temporary and insignificant as to leave the personal compulsion upon the taxpayer substantially intact. . . .

Respondents in No. 74–611 and petitioners in No. 74–18 argue, and the Court of Appeals for the Fifth Circuit apparently agreed, that if the summons was enforced, the taxpayers' Fifth Amendment privilege would be, but should not be, lost solely because they gave their documents to their lawyers in order to obtain legal advice. But this misconceives the nature of the constitutional privilege. The Amendment protects a person from being compelled to be a witness against himself. Here, the taxpayers retained any privilege they ever had not to be compelled to testify against themselves and not to be compelled themselves to produce private papers in their possession. *This* personal privilege was in no way decreased by the transfer. It is simply that by reason of the transfer of the documents to the attorneys, those papers may be subpoenaed without compulsion on the taxpayer. The protection of the Fifth Amendment is therefore not available. "A party is privileged from producing evidence but not from its production." Johnson v. United States, [228 U.S. 457 (1913)], at 458.

The Court of Appeals for the Fifth Circuit suggested that because legally and ethically the attorney was required to respect the confidences of his client, the latter had a reasonable expectation of privacy for the records in the hands of the attorney and therefore did not forfeit his Fifth Amendment privilege with respect to the records by transferring them in order to obtain legal advice. It is true that the Court has often stated that one of the several purposes served by the constitutional privilege against compelled testimonial self-incrimination is that of protecting personal privacy. . . . But the Court has never suggested that every invasion of privacy violates the privilege. Within the limits imposed by the language of the Fifth Amendment, which we necessarily observe, the privilege truly serves privacy interests; but the Court has never on any ground, personal privacy included, applied the Fifth Amendment to prevent the otherwise proper acquisition or use of evidence which, in the Court's view, did not involve compelled testimonial self-incrimination of some sort.

The proposition that the Fifth Amendment protects private information obtained without compelling self-incriminating testimony is contrary to the clear statements of this Court that under appropriate safeguards private incriminating statements of an accused may be overheard and used in evidence, if they are not compelled at the time they were uttered . . . and that disclosure of private information may be compelled if immunity removes the risk of incrimination. If the Fifth Amendment protected generally against the obtaining of private information from a man's mouth or pen or house, its protections would presumably not be lifted by probable cause and a warrant or by immunity. The privacy invasion is not mitigated by immunity; and the Fifth Amendment's strictures, unlike the Fourth's, are not removed by showing reasonableness. The Framers addressed the subject of personal privacy directly in the Fourth Amendment. They struck a balance so that when the State's reason to believe incriminating evidence will be found becomes sufficiently great, the invasion of privacy becomes justified and a warrant to search and seize will issue. They did not seek in still another Amendment—the Fifth—to achieve a general protection of privacy but to deal with the more specific issue of compelled self-incrimination.

. . .

Insofar as private information not obtained through compelled self-incriminating testimony is legally protected, its protection stems from other sources—the Fourth Amendment's protection against seizures without warrant or probable cause and against subpoenas which suffer from "too much indefiniteness or breadth in the things required to be 'particularly described,'" Oklahoma Press Pub. Co. v. Walling, 327 U.S. 186, 208 (1946) . . . the First Amendment . . . or evidentiary privileges such as the attorney-client privilege.

III

Our above holding is that compelled production of documents from an attorney does not implicate whatever Fifth Amendment privilege the taxpayer might have enjoyed from being compelled to produce them himself. The taxpayers in these cases, however, have from the outset consistently urged that they should not be forced to expose otherwise protected documents to summons simply because they have sought legal advice and turned the papers over to their attorneys. . . . In this posture of the case, we feel obliged to inquire whether the attorney-client privilege applies to documents in the hands of an attorney which would have been privileged in the hands of the client by reason of the Fifth Amendment.

Confidential disclosures by a client to an attorney made in order to obtain legal assistance are privileged. . . . The purpose of the privilege is to encourage clients to make full disclosure to their attorneys. . . . As a practical matter, if the client knows that damaging information could more readily be obtained from the attorney following disclosure than from himself in the absence of disclosure, the client would be reluctant to confide in his lawyer and it would be difficult to obtain fully informed legal advice. However, since the privilege has the effect of withholding relevant information from the factfinder, it applies only where necessary to achieve its purpose. Accordingly it protects only those disclosures—necessary to obtain informed legal advice—which might not have been made absent the privilege. . . . This Court and the lower courts have thus uniformly held that pre-existing documents which could have been obtained by court process from the client when he was in possession may also be obtained from the attorney by similar process following transfer by the client in order to obtain more informed legal advice. . . . The purpose of the privilege requires no broader rule. Pre-existing documents obtainable from the client are not appreciably easier to obtain from the attorney after transfer to him. Thus, even absent the attorney-client privilege, clients will not be discouraged from disclosing the documents to the attorney, and their ability to obtain informed legal advice will remain unfettered. It is otherwise if the documents are not obtainable by subpoena *duces tecum* or summons while in the exclusive possession of the client, for the client will then be reluctant to transfer possession to the lawyer unless the documents are also privileged in the latter's hands. Where the transfer is made for the purpose of obtaining legal advice, the purposes of the attorney-client privilege would be defeated unless the privilege is applicable. "It follows, then, that *when the client himself would be privileged* from production of the document, either as a party at common law . . . or as exempt from self-incrimination, the attorney having possession of the document is not bound to produce." 8 Wigmore § 2307, p. 592. Lower courts have so held. . . . This proposition was accepted by the Court of Appeals for the Fifth Circuit below, is asserted by petitioners in No. 74–18 and respondents in No. 74–611, and was conceded by the Government in its brief and at oral argument. Where the transfer to the attorney is for the purpose of obtaining legal advice, we agree with it.

Since each taxpayer transferred possession of the documents in question from himself to his attorney, in order to obtain legal assistance in the tax investigations in question, the papers, if unobtainable by summons from the client, are unobtainable by summons directed to the attorney by reason of the attorney-client privilege. We accordingly proceed to the question whether the documents could have been obtained by summons addressed to the taxpayer while the documents were in his possession. The only bar to enforcement of such summons asserted by the parties or the courts below is the Fifth Amendment's privilege against self-incrimination. . . .

IV

The proposition that the Fifth Amendment prevents compelled production of documents over objection that such production might incriminate stems from Boyd v. United States, 116 U.S. 616 (1886). *Boyd* involved a civil forfeiture proceeding brought by the Government against two partners for fraudulently attempting to import 35 cases of glass without paying the prescribed duty. . . . At trial, the Government obtained a court order directing the partners to produce an invoice the partnership had received. . . . The invoice was disclosed, offered in evidence, and used, over the Fifth Amendment objection of the partners, to establish that the partners were fraudulently claiming a greater exemption from duty than they were entitled to. . . . This Court held that the invoice was inadmissible and reversed the judgment in favor of the Government. The Court ruled that the Fourth Amendment applied to court orders in the nature of subpoenas *duces tecum* in the same manner in which it applies to search warrants . . . ; and that the Government may not, consistent with the Fourth Amendment, seize a person's documents or other property as evidence unless it can claim a proprietary interest in the property superior to that of the person from whom the property is obtained. . . . The invoice in question was thus held to have been obtained in violation of the Fourth Amendment. The Court went on to hold that the accused in a criminal case or the defendant in a forfeiture action could not be forced to produce evidentiary items without violating the Fifth Amendment as well as the Fourth. More specifically, the Court declared, "a compulsory production of the private books and papers of the owner of goods sought to be forfeited . . . is compelling him to be a witness against himself, within the meaning of the Fifth Amendment to the Constitution." Id., at 634–35. Admitting the partnership invoice into evidence had violated both the Fifth and Fourth Amendments.

Among its several pronouncements, *Boyd* was understood to declare that the seizure, under warrant or otherwise, of any purely evidentiary materials violated the Fourth Amendment and that the Fifth Amendment rendered these seized materials inadmissible. Gouled v. United States, 255 U.S. 298 (1921). . . . That rule applied to documents as well as to other evidentiary items. . . . Private papers taken from the taxpayer, like other "mere evidence," could not be used against the accused over his Fourth and Fifth Amendment objections.

Several of *Boyd*'s express or implicit declarations have not stood the test of time. The application of the Fourth Amendment to subpoenas was limited by Hale v. Henkel, 201 U.S. 43 (1906), and more recent cases. . . . Purely evidentiary (but "nontestimonial") materials, as well as contraband and fruits and instrumentalities of crime, may now be searched for and seized under proper circumstances. . . . Also, any notion that "testimonial" evidence may never be seized and used in evidence is inconsistent with Katz v. United States, 389 U.S. 347 (1967) . . . approving the seizure under appropriate circumstances of conversations of a person suspected of crime. . . .

It is also clear that the Fifth Amendment does not independently proscribe the compelled production of every sort of incriminating evidence but applies only when the accused is compelled to make a *testimonial* communication that is incriminating. We have, accordingly, declined to extend the protection of the privilege to the giving of blood samples . . . to the giving of handwriting exemplars . . . voice exemplars . . . or the donning of a blouse worn by the perpetrator. . . . Furthermore, despite *Boyd*, neither a partnership nor the individual partners are shielded from compelled production of partnership records on self-incrimination grounds. . . . It would appear that under that case the precise claim sustained in *Boyd* would now be rejected for reasons not there considered.

The pronouncement in *Boyd* that a person may not be forced to produce his private papers has nonetheless often appeared as dictum in later opinions of this Court. . . . To the extent, however, that the rule against compelling production of private papers rested on the proposition that seizures of or subpoenas for "mere evidence," including documents, violated the Fourth Amendment and therefore also transgressed the Fifth . . . the foundations for the rule have been washed away. In consequence, the prohibition against forcing the production of private papers has long been a rule searching for a rationale consistent with the proscriptions of the Fifth Amendment against compelling a person to give "testimony" that incriminates him. Accordingly, we turn to the question of what, if any, incriminating testimony within the Fifth Amendment's protection, is compelled by a documentary summons.

A subpoena served on a taxpayer requiring him to produce an accountant's workpapers in his possession without doubt involves substantial compulsion. But it does not compel oral testimony; nor would it ordinarily compel the taxpayer to restate, repeat, or affirm the truth of the contents of the documents sought. Therefore, the Fifth Amendment would not be violated by the fact alone that the papers on their face might incriminate the taxpayer, for the privilege protects a person only against being incriminated by his own compelled testimonial communications. . . . The accountant's workpapers are not the taxpayer's. They were not prepared by the taxpayer, and they contain no testimonial declarations by him. Furthermore, as far as this record demonstrates, the preparation of all of the papers sought in these cases was wholly voluntary, and they cannot be said to contain compelled testimonial evidence, either of the taxpayers or of anyone else. The taxpayer cannot avoid compliance with the subpoena merely by asserting that the item of evidence which he is required to produce contains incriminating writing, whether his own or that of someone else.

The act of producing evidence in response to a subpoena nevertheless has communicative aspects of its own, wholly aside from the contents of the papers produced. Compliance with the subpoena tacitly concedes the existence of the papers demanded and their possession or control by the taxpayer. It also would indicate the taxpayer's belief that the papers are those described in the subpoena. . . . The elements of compulsion are clearly present, but the more difficult issues are whether the tacit averments of the taxpayer are both "testimonial" and "incriminating" for purposes of applying the Fifth Amendment. These questions perhaps do not lend themselves to categorical answers; their resolution may instead depend on the facts and circumstances of particular cases or classes thereof. In light of the records now before us, we are confident that however incriminating the contents of the accountant's workpapers might be, the act of producing them—the only thing which the taxpayer is compelled to do—would not itself involve testimonial self-incrimination.

It is doubtful that implicitly admitting the existence and possession of the papers rises to the level of testimony within the protection of the Fifth Amendment. The papers belong to the accountant, were prepared by him, and are the kind usually prepared by an accountant working on the tax returns of his client. Surely the Government is in no way relying on the "truthtelling" of the taxpayer to prove the existence of or his access to the documents. . . . The existence and location of the papers are a foregone conclusion and the taxpayer adds little or nothing to the sum total of the Government's information by conceding that he in fact has the papers. Under these circumstances by enforcement of the summons "no constitutional rights are touched. The question is not of testimony but of surrender." In re Harris, 221 U.S. 274, 279 (1911).

When an accused is required to submit a handwriting exemplar he admits his ability to write and impliedly asserts that the exemplar is his writing. But in common experience, the first would be a near truism and the latter self-evident. In any event, although the exemplar may be incriminating to the accused and although he is compelled to furnish it, his Fifth Amendment privilege is not violated because nothing he has said or done is deemed to be sufficiently testimonial for purposes of the privilege. This Court has also time and again allowed subpoenas against the custodian of corporate documents or those belonging to other collective entities such as unions and partnerships and those of bankrupt businesses over claims that the documents will incriminate the custodian despite the fact that producing the documents tacitly admits their existence and their location in the hands of their possessor. . . . The existence and possession or control of the subpoenaed documents being no more in issue here than in the above cases, the summons is equally enforceable.

Moreover, assuming that these aspects of producing the accountant's papers have some minimal testimonial significance, surely it is not illegal to seek accounting help in connection with one's tax returns or for the accountant to prepare workpapers and deliver them to the taxpayer. At this juncture, we are quite unprepared to hold that either the fact of existence of the papers or of their possession by the taxpayer poses any realistic threat of incrimination to the taxpayer.

As for the possibility that responding to the subpoena would authenticate the workpapers, production would express nothing more than the taxpayer's belief that the papers are those described in the subpoena. The taxpayer would be no more competent to authenticate the accountant's workpapers or reports by producing them than he would be to authenticate them if testifying orally. The taxpayer did not prepare the papers and could not vouch for their accuracy. The documents would not be admissible in evidence against the taxpayer without authenticating testimony. Without more, responding to the subpoena in the circumstances before us would not appear to represent a substantial threat of self-incrimination. . . .

Whether the Fifth Amendment would shield the taxpayer from producing his own tax records in his possession is a question not involved here; for the papers demanded here are not his "private papers," see Boyd v. United States, 116 U.S., at 634–35. We do hold that compliance with a summons directing the taxpayer to produce the accountant's documents involved in these cases would involve no incriminating testimony within the protection of the Fifth Amendment.

. . . [20]

---

273. The Court relied on its holding in *Fisher*, above, for its holding in Andresen v. Maryland, 427 U.S. 463 (1976), p. 251 note 140 above, that a defendant's privilege against self-incrimination was not violated when business records were seized during a search of his office pursuant to a warrant.

274. The Court has indicated, but not quite held, that its unanswered question in *Fisher*—whether the Fifth Amendment shields a taxpayer "from producing his own tax records in his possession," above—should be answered in the negative. In United States v. Doe, 465 U.S. 605 (1984) (6–3), a grand jury ordered a witness to produce business records of companies owned by him. The Court held that the records, which were prepared voluntarily, were not covered by the privilege, whether they were in the witness's possession or not. Although papers are not protected, their production is protected if it is an independently incriminating testimonial act.

The "act of production" privilege is discussed in United States v. Hubbell, 530 U.S. 27 (2000), in which the Court held that the defendant could not be compelled to produce a broad range of incriminating documents that the government was unable to specify with particularity. For additional cases in which an "act of production" privilege was upheld, see United States v. Grable, 98 F.3d 251 (6th Cir.1996); United States v. Fox, 721 F.2d 32 (2d Cir.1983); In re Grand Jury Proceedings United States, 626 F.2d 1051 (1st Cir.1980).

The sole shareholder of a corporation, acting in his capacity as custodian of corporate records, may not resist a subpoena to produce the records on the ground that the act of production would violate his privilege against compulsory self-incrimination. So, generally, the custodian of corporate records may not resist their production on the ground that the content of the records would incriminate him. However, since the act of production is made by the individual in his capacity as a corporate agent, no evidentiary use can be made of it as an act of the individual; it must be regarded as the act of the corporation. Braswell v. United States, 487 U.S. 99 (1988) (5–4).

[20] Justice Brennan and Justice Marshall wrote opinions concurring in the judgment.

The Fifth Amendment does not prohibit a court from issuing an order directing a defendant to sign a consent directive that would enable the government to obtain records from a foreign bank. Signing the directive does not involve a testimonial communication and can therefore be compelled. Doe v. United States, 487 U.S. 201 (1988) (8–1). The consent form that petitioner was ordered to sign pursuant to a grand jury investigation was worded to avoid any representation that the records in question existed or that any records that the bank might turn over were authentic.

The privilege against compulsory self-incrimination does not prevent the state from ordering a mother, subject to conditions imposed by the juvenile court concerning her care for her child, to produce the child, even though production of the child might be incriminating. Baltimore City Department of Social Services v. Bouknight, 493 U.S. 549 (1990) (7–2). The woman subject to the order was suspected of having abused or possibly killed her child. The Court said that the privilege did not protect her from having to produce the child in compliance with the order because "she has assumed custodial duties related to production and because production is required as part of a noncriminal regulatory regime." Id. at 555–56. The Court noted that her privilege could still be protected by appropriate limitations on the state's use of incriminating information obtained as a result of the order.

275. The defendant was classified by his draft board as a conscientious objector available for civilian work, and was mailed an order to report for work. He did not do so. When the case was considered for prosecution, counsel for the Selective Service System found that there was no indication in the file that the defendant had been mailed a notice of classification and that he had a right to appeal; without such mailing, he could not be prosecuted. The draft board wrote to the defendant, asking him to appear and to bring with him the notice of classification. He did so, and the notice showed the date on which it had been mailed. Later, the defendant was prosecuted and convicted. United States v. Casias, 306 F.Supp. 166 (D.Colo. 1969).

Was the defendant entitled to be told by the draft board why it wanted him to produce the notice of classification?

Immunity From Prosecution

Garrity v. New Jersey
385 U.S. 493, 87 S.Ct. 616, 17 L.Ed.2d 562 (1967)

■ MR. JUSTICE DOUGLAS delivered the opinion of the Court.

Appellants were police officers in certain New Jersey boroughs. The Supreme Court of New Jersey ordered that alleged irregularities in handling cases in the municipal courts of those boroughs be investigated by the Attorney General, invested him with broad powers of inquiry and investigation, and directed him to make a report to the court. The matters investigated concerned alleged fixing of traffic tickets.

Before being questioned, each appellant was warned (1) that anything he said might be used against him in any state criminal proceeding; (2) that he had the privilege to refuse to answer if the disclosure would tend to incriminate him; but (3) that if he refused to answer he would be subject to removal from office.

Appellants answered the questions. No immunity was granted, as there is no immunity statute applicable in these circumstances. Over their objections, some of the answers given were used in subsequent prosecutions for conspiracy to obstruct the administration of the traffic laws. Appellants were convicted and their convictions were sustained over their protests that their statements were coerced, by reason of the fact that, if they refused to answer, they could lose their positions with the police department. . . .

. . .

The choice given petitioners was either to forfeit their jobs or to incriminate themselves. The option to lose their means of livelihood or to pay the penalty of self-incrimination is the antithesis of free choice to speak out or to remain silent. That practice, like interrogation practices we reviewed in Miranda v. Arizona, 384 U.S. 436, 464–65, is "likely to exert such pressure upon an individual as to disable him from making a free and rational choice." We think the statements were infected by the coercion inherent in this scheme of questioning and cannot be sustained as voluntary under our prior decisions.

It is said that there was a "waiver." . . .

Where the choice is "between the rock and the whirlpool," duress is inherent in deciding to "waive" one or the other. . . .

[T]hough petitioners succumbed to compulsion, they preserved their objections, raising them at the earliest possible point. . . . The cases are therefore quite different from the situation where one who is anxious to make a clean breast of the whole affair volunteers the information.

Mr. Justice Holmes in McAuliffe v. New Bedford, 29 N.E. 517, stated a dictum on which New Jersey heavily relies:

> The petitioner may have a constitutional right to talk politics, but he has no constitutional right to be a policeman. There are few employments for hire in which the servant does not agree to suspend his constitutional right of free speech, as well as of idleness, by the implied terms of his contract. The servant cannot complain, as he takes the

employment on the terms which are offered him. On the same principle, the city may impose any reasonable condition upon holding offices within its control.

29 N.E., at 517–18.

The question in this case, however, is not cognizable in those terms. Our question is whether a State, contrary to the requirement of the Fourteenth Amendment, can use the threat of discharge to secure incriminatory evidence against an employee.

We held in Slochower v. Board of Education, 350 U.S. 551, that a public school teacher could not be discharged merely because he had invoked the Fifth Amendment privilege against self-incrimination when questioned by a congressional committee:

> The privilege against self-incrimination would be reduced to a hollow mockery if its exercise could be taken as equivalent either to a confession of guilt or a conclusive presumption of perjury. . . . The privilege serves to protect the innocent who otherwise might be ensnared by ambiguous circumstances.

Id., at 557–58.

We conclude that policemen, like teachers and lawyers, are not relegated to a watered-down version of constitutional rights.

There are rights of constitutional statute whose exercise a State may not condition by the exaction of a price. . . . We now hold the protection of the individual under the Fourteenth Amendment against coerced statements prohibits use in subsequent criminal proceedings of statements obtained under threat of removal from office, and that it extends to all, whether they are policemen or other members of our body politic.

■ MR. JUSTICE HARLAN, whom MR. JUSTICE CLARK and MR. JUSTICE STEWART join, dissenting.

. . .

I.

. . .

It would be difficult to imagine interrogations to which these criteria of duress were more completely inapplicable or in which the requirements which have subsequently been imposed by this Court on police questioning were more thoroughly satisfied. Each of the petitioners received a complete and explicit reminder of his constitutional privilege. Three of the petitioners had counsel present; at least a fourth had consulted counsel but freely determined that his presence was unnecessary. These petitioners were not in any fashion "swept from familiar surroundings into police custody, surrounded by antagonistic forces, and subjected to the techniques of persuasion. . . ." Miranda v. Arizona, 384 U.S. 436, 461. I think it manifest that, under the standards developed by this Court to assess voluntariness, there is no basis for saying that any of these statements were made involuntarily.

II.

The issue remaining is whether the statements were inadmissible because they were "involuntary as a matter of law," in that they were given after a warning that New Jersey policemen may be discharged for failure to provide information pertinent to their public responsibilities. . . . The central issues here are therefore identical to those presented in Spevack v. Klein, [385 U.S. 511 (1967)]: whether consequences may properly be permitted to result to a claimant after his invocation of the constitutional privilege, and if so, whether the consequence in question is permissible. For reasons which I have stated in Spevack v. Klein,[21] in my view nothing in the logic or purposes of the privilege demands that all consequences which may result from a witness' silence be forbidden merely because that silence is privileged. The validity of a consequence depends both upon the hazards, if any, it presents to the integrity of the privilege and upon the urgency of the public interests it is designed to protect.

It can hardly be denied that New Jersey is permitted by the Constitution to establish reasonable qualifications and standards of conduct for its public employees. Nor can it be said that it is arbitrary or unreasonable for New Jersey to insist that its employees furnish the appropriate authorities with information pertinent to their employment. . . . Finally, it is surely plain that New Jersey may in particular require its employees to assist in the prevention and detection of unlawful activities by officers of the state government. The urgency of these requirements is the more obvious here, where the conduct in question is that of officials directly entrusted with the administration of justice. . . . It must be concluded, therefore, that the sanction at issue here is reasonably calculated to serve the most basic interests of the citizens of New Jersey.

The final question is the hazard, if any, which this sanction presents to the constitutional privilege. The purposes for which, and the circumstances in which, an officer's discharge might be ordered under New Jersey law plainly may vary. It is of course possible that discharge might in a given case be predicated on an imputation of guilt drawn from the use of the privilege, as was thought by this Court to have occurred in Slochower v. Board of Education [350 U.S. 551 (1956)]. But from our vantage point, it would be quite improper to assume that New Jersey will employ these procedures for purposes other than to assess in good faith an employee's continued fitness for public employment. . . . We are not entitled to assume that discharges will be used either to vindicate impermissible inferences of guilt or to penalize privileged silence, but must instead presume that this procedure is only intended and will only be used to establish and enforce standards of conduct for public employees. As such, it does not minimize or endanger the petitioners' constitutional privilege against self-incrimination.

. . . [22]

---

[21] P. 498 below.

[22] Justice White wrote a dissenting opinion, applicable also to Spevack v. Klein, below.

Spevack v. Klein

385 U.S. 511, 87 S.Ct. 625, 17 L.Ed.2d 574 (1967)

■ MR. JUSTICE DOUGLAS announced the judgment of the Court and delivered an opinion in which THE CHIEF JUSTICE, MR. JUSTICE BLACK and MR. JUSTICE BRENNAN concur.

This is a proceeding to discipline petitioner, a member of the New York Bar, for professional misconduct. Of the various charges made, only one survived, *viz.*, the refusal of petitioner to honor a subpoena *duces tecum* served on him in that he refused to produce the demanded financial records and refused to testify at the judicial inquiry. Petitioner's sole defense was that the production of the records and his testimony would tend to incriminate him. The Appellate Division of the New York Supreme Court ordered petitioner disbarred, holding that the constitutional privilege against self-incrimination was not available to him in light of our decision in Cohen v. Hurley, 366 U.S. 117. . . . The Court of Appeals affirmed. . . .

. . .

. . . We conclude that . . . the Self-Incrimination Clause of the Fifth Amendment has been absorbed in the Fourteenth, that it extends its protection to lawyers as well as to other individuals, and that it should not be watered down by imposing the dishonor of disbarment and the deprivation of a livelihood as a price for asserting it. . . .

We said in Malloy v. Hogan [378 U.S. 1 (1964)]:

The Fourteenth Amendment secures against state invasion the same privilege that the Fifth Amendment guarantees against federal infringement—the right of a person to remain silent unless he chooses to speak in the unfettered exercise of his own will, and to suffer no penalty . . . for such silence.

378 U.S., at 8.

In this context "penalty" is not restricted to fine or imprisonment. It means, as we said in Griffin v. California, 380 U.S. 609, the imposition of any sanction which makes assertion of the Fifth Amendment privilege "costly." Id., at 614. . . .

The threat of disbarment and the loss of professional standing, professional reputation, and of livelihood are powerful forms of compulsion to make a lawyer relinquish the privilege. That threat is indeed as powerful an instrument of compulsion as "the use of legal process to force from the lips of the accused individual the evidence necessary to convict him. . . ." United States v. White, 322 U.S. 694, 698. As we recently stated in Miranda v. Arizona, 384 U.S. 436, 461, "In this Court, the privilege has consistently been accorded a liberal construction." . . . We find no room in the privilege against self-incrimination for classifications of people so as to deny it to some and extend it to others. Lawyers are not excepted from the words "No person . . . shall be compelled in any criminal case to be a witness against himself"; and we can imply no exception. Like the school teacher in

Slochower v. Board of Education, 350 U.S. 551, and the policemen in Garrity v. New Jersey,[23] ante, lawyers also enjoy first-class citizenship.

. . .

■ Mr. Justice Harlan, whom Mr. Justice Clark and Mr. Justice Stewart join, dissenting.

. . .

It cannot be claimed that the purposes served by the New York rules [requiring disclosure of the information which the petitioner refused to disclose] at issue here, compendiously aimed at "ambulance chasing" and its attendant evils, are unimportant or unrelated to the protection of legitimate state interests. . . .

. . .

Without denying the urgency or significance of the public purposes served by these rules, the plurality opinion has seemingly concluded that they may not be enforced because any consequence of a claim of the privilege against self-incrimination which renders that claim "costly" is an "instrument of compulsion" which impermissibly infringes on the protection offered by the privilege. . . . The Court has not before held that the Federal Government and the States are forbidden to permit any consequences to result from a claim of the privilege; it has instead recognized that such consequences may vary widely in kind and intensity and that these differences warrant individual examination both of the hazard, if any, offered to the essential purposes of the privilege, and of the public interests protected by the consequence. This process is far better calculated than the broad prohibition embraced by the plurality to serve both the purposes of the privilege and the other important public values which are often at stake in such cases. It would assure the integrity of the privilege, and yet guarantee the most generous opportunities for the pursuit of other public values, by selecting the rule or standard most appropriate for the hazards and characteristics of each consequence.

One such rule has already been plainly approved by this Court. It seems clear to me that this rule is applicable to the situation now before us. The Court has repeatedly recognized that it is permissible to deny a status or authority to a claimant of the privilege against self-incrimination if his claim has prevented full assessment of his qualifications for the status or authority. Under this rule, the applicant may not both decline to disclose information necessary to demonstrate his fitness, and yet demand that he receive the benefits of the status. He may not by his interjection of the privilege either diminish his obligation to establish his qualifications, or escape the consequences exacted by the State for a failure to satisfy that obligation.

. . .

23. Whether a policeman, who invokes the privilege when his conduct as a police officer is questioned in disciplinary proceedings, may be discharged for refusing to testify is a question we did not reach.

. . . The petitioner was not denied his privilege against self-incrimination, nor was he penalized for its use; he was denied his authority to practice law within the State of New York by reason of his failure to satisfy valid obligations imposed by the State as a condition of that authority. The only hazard in this process to the integrity of the privilege is the possibility that it might induce involuntary disclosures of incriminating materials; the sanction precisely calculated to eliminate that hazard is to exclude the use by prosecuting authorities of such materials and of their fruits. . . . It is true that this Court has on occasion gone a step further, and forbidden the practices likely to produce involuntary disclosures, but those cases are readily distinguishable. They have uniformly involved either situations in which the entire process was thought both to present excessive risks of coercion and to be foreign to our accusatorial system . . . or situations in which the only possible purpose of the practice was thought to be to penalize the accused for his use of the constitutional privilege. . . . Both situations are plainly remote from that in issue here. None of the reasons thought to require the prohibitions established in those cases have any relevance in the situation now before us; nothing in New York's efforts in good faith to assure the integrity of its judicial system destroys, inhibits, or even minimizes the petitioner's constitutional privilege. There is therefore no need to speculate whether lawyers, or those in any other profession or occupation, have waived in some unspecified fashion a measure of the protection afforded by the constitutional privilege; it suffices that the State is earnestly concerned with an urgent public interest, and that it has selected methods for the pursuit of that interest which do not prevent attainment of the privilege's purposes.

. . . [24]

———

276. In Gardner v. Broderick, 392 U.S. 273 (1968), the Court held that a New York City patrolman who was called before a grand jury to testify concerning the performance of his official duties could not be discharged for refusing to waive immunity from prosecution before testifying. It observed, however, that the position of the patrolman was different from that of a lawyer; "unlike the lawyer who is directly responsible to his client, the policeman is either responsible to the State or to no one." Id. at 278. Therefore, the Court said, "if appellant, a policeman, had refused to answer questions specifically, directly, and narrowly relating to the performance of his official duties, without being required to waive his immunity with respect to the use of his answers or the fruits thereof in a criminal prosecution of himself . . . the privilege against self-incrimination would not have been a bar to his dismissal." Id. Since, however, "he was discharged from office, not for failure to answer relevant questions about

[24] Justice Fortas wrote an opinion concurring in the judgment. Justice White wrote a dissenting opinion.

his official duties, but for refusal to waive a constitutional right . . . for failure to relinquish the protections of the privilege against self-incrimination," the discharge was invalid. Id.

In a companion case, Uniformed Sanitation Men Association, Inc. v. Commissioner of Sanitation of the City of New York, 392 U.S. 280 (1968), the Court reached the same conclusion respecting the dismissal of employees of the Department of Sanitation who refused on the ground of self-incrimination to testify in an investigation into their official conduct or, in some cases, to sign waivers of immunity after being called before the grand jury. Again the Court said that the men involved, "being public employees, subject themselves to dismissal if they refuse to account for their performance of their public trust, after proper proceedings, which do not involve an attempt to coerce them to relinquish their constitutional rights." Id. at 285.

Concurring in the result in both cases, Justice Harlan observed that he found in the two opinions "a procedural formula whereby, for example, public officials may now be discharged and lawyers disciplined for refusing to divulge to appropriate authority information pertinent to the faithful performance of their offices." Id. at 285.

See Lefkowitz v. Cunningham, 431 U.S. 801 (1977) (7–1) (statute removing political party officer from office and barring him from holding public or private office for five years because of assertion of privilege was invalid); Lefkowitz v. Turley, 414 U.S. 70 (1973) (disqualification of architects from public contracts following refusal to waive privilege against self-incrimination was invalid); Benjamin v. City of Montgomery, 785 F.2d 959 (11th Cir.1986) (police officers; discharge invalid); Gulden v. McCorkle, 680 F.2d 1070 (5th Cir.1982) (discharge of public employees for refusal to submit to polygraph test, without waiver of privilege, upheld); Confederation of Police v. Conlisk, 489 F.2d 891 (7th Cir.1973) (police officers; discharge invalid). See also United States v. Friedrick, 842 F.2d 382 (D.C.Cir.1988) (*Garrity* applied to FBI agent's statements in interviews with Justice Department lawyers).

277. In McKune v. Lile, 536 U.S. 24 (2002) (5–4), the defendant was imprisoned for rape. Several years before he was to be released, prison officials ordered him to participate in a Sex Abuse Treatment Program, which was designed to reduce the likelihood of recidivism. Part of the program required him to accept responsibility for the crime for which he was convicted and to give a history of his sexual activities, including criminal activities for which he had not been prosecuted. There was no immunity from use of the information in a subsequent criminal prosecution. The defendant refused to participate, on the ground that the requirements violated his privilege against compulsory self-incrimination. As a consequence of his refusal, he was moved to a less desirable prison unit and lost certain prison privileges. Noting the valid purpose of the SATP program and the limited nature of the penalties imposed, the Court held that the defendant's Fifth Amendment privilege had not been violated.

278. Immunity statutes. The use of immunity statutes to overcome the privilege against self-incrimination and obtain testimony is common. The first federal immunity statute, which gave immunity to persons testifying in a congressional inquiry, was enacted in 1857. 11 Stat. 155. The statute was modified in 1862 to prevent a witness from getting an "immunity bath" protecting him altogether from prosecution for "any fact or act touching which he shall be required to testify," 11 Stat. at 156. See 12 Stat. 333. The modified statute, however, in terms gave immunity only from the use of the witness's testimony in evidence against him. That formula, which might allow the government to use the immunized testimony as a lead to other evidence, was held insufficient to overcome the constitutional privilege against self-incrimination, in Counselman v. Hitchcock, 142 U.S. 547 (1892). After 1893, federal immunity statutes again gave full immunity from prosecution "for or on account of any transaction, matter or thing, concerning which . . . [a witness] may testify, or produce evidence." 49 U.S.C. § 46 (testimony before Interstate Commerce Commission). Federal legislation regularly authorized administrative agencies to compel testimony by giving a witness immunity. In 1968 Congress gave the Department of Justice power to compel testimony in court by granting immunity in proceedings involving any of a very broad range of federal crimes. 82 Stat. 216, since repealed, 84 Stat. 930.

Language in Counselman v. Hitchcock created doubt whether a statute that gave a witness full "use" immunity—immunity from the use of his testimony and its fruits—would be sufficient to overcome the constitutional privilege. In 1970, Congress enacted a general immunity statute covering proceedings, among others, in a court or before a grand jury. The statute grants immunity only from the use of compelled "testimony or other information" or "any information directly or indirectly derived from such testimony or other information." 18 U.S.C. § 6002. Doubt whether the statute was constitutional was resolved by Kastigar v. United States, below.

Kastigar v. United States

406 U.S. 441, 92 S.Ct. 1653, 32 L.Ed.2d 212 (1972)

■ MR. JUSTICE POWELL delivered the opinion of the Court.

This case presents the question whether the United States Government may compel testimony from an unwilling witness, who invokes the Fifth Amendment privilege against compulsory self-incrimination, by conferring on the witness immunity from use of the compelled testimony in subsequent criminal proceedings, as well as immunity from use of evidence derived from the testimony.

Petitioners were subpoenaed to appear before a United States grand jury in the Central District of California on February 4, 1971. The Government believed that petitioners were likely to assert their Fifth Amendment privilege. Prior to the scheduled appearances, the Government applied to the District Court for an order directing petitioners to answer questions and produce evidence before the grand jury under a grant of immunity conferred pursuant to 18 U.S.C. §§ 6002–6003. Petitioners opposed issuance of the order, contending primarily that the scope of the immunity provided by the statute was not coextensive with the scope of the privilege against self-incrimination, and therefore was not sufficient to supplant the privilege and compel their testimony. The District Court rejected this contention, and ordered petitioners to appear before the grand jury and answer its questions under the grant of immunity.

Petitioners appeared but refused to answer questions, asserting their privilege against compulsory self-incrimination. They were brought before the District Court, and each persisted in his refusal to answer the grand jury's questions, notwithstanding the grant of immunity. The court found both in contempt, and committed them to the custody of the Attorney General until either they answered the grand jury's questions or the term of the grand jury expired. The Court of Appeals for the Ninth Circuit affirmed. . . . This Court granted certiorari to resolve the important question whether testimony may be compelled by granting immunity from the use of compelled testimony and evidence derived therefrom ("use and derivative use" immunity), or whether it is necessary to grant immunity from prosecution for offenses to which compelled testimony relates ("transactional" immunity). . . .

I

The power of government to compel persons to testify in court or before grand juries and other governmental agencies is firmly established in Anglo–American jurisprudence. . . . The power to compel testimony, and the corresponding duty to testify, are recognized in the Sixth Amendment requirements that an accused be confronted with the witnesses against him, and have compulsory process for obtaining witnesses in his favor. . . .

But the power to compel testimony is not absolute. There are a number of exemptions from the testimonial duty, the most important of which is the Fifth Amendment privilege against compulsory self-incrimination. The privilege reflects a complex of our fundamental values and aspirations, and marks an important advance in the development of our liberty. It can be asserted in any proceeding, civil or criminal, administrative or judicial, investigatory or adjudicatory; and it protects against any disclosures that the witness reasonably believes could be used in a criminal prosecution or could lead to other evidence that might be so used. This Court has been zealous to safeguard the values that underlie the privilege.

Immunity statutes, which have historical roots deep in Anglo–American jurisprudence, are not incompatible with these values. Rather, they seek a rational accommodation between the imperatives of the privilege and the legitimate demands of government to compel citizens to testify. The existence of these statutes reflects the importance of testimony, and the fact that many offenses are of such a character that the only persons capable of giving useful testimony are those implicated in the crime. Indeed, their origins were in the context of such offenses, and their primary use has been to investigate such offenses. Congress included immunity statutes in many of the regulatory measures adopted in the first half of this century. Indeed, prior to the enactment of the statute under consideration in this case, there were in force over 50 federal immunity statutes. In addition, every State in the Union, as well as the District of Columbia and Puerto Rico, has one or more such statutes. The commentators, and this Court on several occasions, have characterized immunity statutes as essential to the effective enforcement of various criminal statutes. As Mr. Justice Frankfurter observed, speaking for the Court in Ullmann v. United States, 350 U.S. 422 (1956), such statutes have "become part of our constitutional fabric." Id., at 438.

II

Petitioners contend, first, that the Fifth Amendment's privilege against compulsory self-incrimination, which is that "[n]o person . . . shall be compelled in any criminal case to be a witness against himself," deprives Congress of power to enact laws that compel self-incrimination, even if complete immunity from prosecution is granted prior to the compulsion of the incriminatory testimony. In other words, petitioners assert that no immunity statute, however drawn, can afford a lawful basis for compelling incriminatory testimony. They ask us to reconsider and overrule Brown v. Walker, 161 U.S. 591 (1896), and Ullmann v. United States, supra, decisions that uphold the constitutionality of immunity statutes. We find no merit to this contention and reaffirm the decisions in *Brown* and *Ullmann*.

III

Petitioners' second contention is that the scope of immunity provided by the federal witness immunity statute, 18 U.S.C. § 6002, is not coextensive with the scope of the Fifth Amendment privilege against compulsory self-incrimination, and therefore is not sufficient to supplant the privilege and compel testimony over a claim of the privilege. The statute provides that when a witness is compelled by district court order to testify over a claim of the privilege:

> the witness may not refuse to comply with the order on the basis of his privilege against self-incrimination; but no testimony or other information compelled under the order (or any information directly or indirectly derived from such testimony or other information) may be used against the witness in any criminal case, except a prosecution for perjury, giving a false statement, or otherwise failing to comply with the order.

18 U.S.C. § 6002.

The constitutional inquiry, rooted in logic and history, as well as in the decisions of this Court, is whether the immunity granted under this statute is coextensive with the scope of the privilege. If so, petitioners' refusals to answer based on the privilege were unjustified, and the judgments of contempt were proper, for the grant of immunity has removed the dangers against which the privilege protects. . . . If, on the other hand, the immunity granted is not as comprehensive as the protection afforded by the privilege, petitioners were justified in refusing to answer, and the judgments of contempt must be vacated. . . .

Petitioners draw a distinction between statutes that provide transactional immunity and those that provide, as does the statute before us, immunity from use and derivative use. They contend that a statute must at a minimum grant full transactional immunity in order to be coextensive with the scope of the privilege. In support of this contention, they rely on Counselman v. Hitchcock, 142 U.S. 547 (1892), the first case in which this Court considered a constitutional challenge to an immunity statute. The statute, a re-enactment of the Immunity Act of 1868, provided that no "evidence obtained from a party or witness by means of a judicial proceeding . . . shall be given in evidence, or in any manner used against him . . . in any court of the United States. . . ." Notwithstanding a grant of immunity and order to testify under the revised 1868 Act, the witness, asserting his privilege against compulsory self-incrimination, refused to testify before a federal grand jury. He was consequently adjudged in contempt of court. On appeal, this Court construed the statute as affording a witness protection only against the use of the specific testimony compelled from him under the grant of immunity. This construction meant that the statute "could not, and would not, prevent the use of his testimony to search out other testimony to be used in evidence against him."[25] Since the revised 1868 Act, as construed by the Court, would permit the use against the immunized witness of evidence derived from his compelled testimony, it did not protect the witness to the same extent that a claim of the privilege would protect him. Accordingly, under the principle that a grant of immunity cannot supplant the privilege, and is not sufficient to compel testimony over a claim of the privilege, unless the scope of the grant of immunity is coextensive with the scope of the privilege, the witness' refusal to testify was held proper. In the course of its opinion, the Court made the following statement, on which petitioners heavily rely:

> We are clearly of opinion that no statute which leaves the party or witness subject to prosecution after he answers the criminating question put to him, can have the effect of supplanting the privilege conferred by the Constitution of the United States. [The immunity statute under consideration] does not supply a complete protection from all the perils against which the constitutional prohibition was designed to guard, and is not a full substitute for that prohibition. In view of the constitutional provision, a statutory enactment, to be valid, must afford absolute immunity against future prosecution for the offence to which the question relates.

142 U.S., at 585–86.

25. Counselman v. Hitchcock, supra, at 564.

Sixteen days after the *Counselman* decision, a new immunity bill was introduced by Senator Cullom, who urged that enforcement of the Interstate Commerce Act would be impossible in the absence of an effective immunity statute. The bill, which became the Compulsory Testimony Act of 1893, was drafted specifically to meet the broad language in *Counselman* set forth above. The new Act removed the privilege against self-incrimination in hearings before the Interstate Commerce Commission and provided that:

> no person shall be prosecuted or subjected to any penalty or forfeiture for or on account of any transaction, matter or thing, concerning which he may testify, or produce evidence, documentary or otherwise. . . .

Act of Feb. 11, 1893, 27 Stat. 444. This transactional immunity statute became the basic form for the numerous federal immunity statutes until 1970, when, after re-examining applicable constitutional principles and the adequacy of existing law, Congress enacted the statute here under consideration. The new statute, which does not "afford [the] absolute immunity against future prosecution" referred to in *Counselman*, was drafted to meet what Congress judged to be the conceptual basis of *Counselman*, as elaborated in subsequent decisions of the Court, namely, that immunity from the use of compelled testimony and evidence derived therefrom is coextensive with the scope of the privilege.

The statute's explicit proscription of the use in any criminal case of "testimony or other information compelled under the order (or any information directly or indirectly derived from such testimony or other information)" is consonant with Fifth Amendment standards. We hold that such immunity from use and derivative use is coextensive with the scope of the privilege against self-incrimination, and therefore is sufficient to compel testimony over a claim of the privilege. While a grant of immunity must afford protection commensurate with that afforded by the privilege, it need not be broader. Transactional immunity, which accords full immunity from prosecution for the offense to which the compelled testimony relates, affords the witness considerably broader protection than does the Fifth Amendment privilege. The privilege has never been construed to mean that one who invokes it cannot subsequently be prosecuted. Its sole concern is to afford protection against being "forced to give testimony leading to the infliction of 'penalties affixed to . . . criminal acts.' "[26] Immunity from the use of compelled testimony, as well as evidence derived directly and indirectly therefrom, affords this protection. It prohibits the prosecutorial authorities from using the compelled testimony in *any* respect, and it therefore insures that the testimony cannot lead to the infliction of criminal penalties on the witness.

Our holding is consistent with the conceptual basis of *Counselman*. The *Counselman* statute, as construed by the Court, was plainly deficient

---

26. Ullmann v. United States, 350 U.S., U.S. [616 (1886)], at 634. . . .
at 438–39, quoting Boyd v. United States, 116

in its failure to prohibit the use against the immunized witness of evidence derived from his compelled testimony. The Court repeatedly emphasized this deficiency. . . . The broad language in *Counselman* relied upon by petitioners was unnecessary to the Court's decision, and cannot be considered binding authority.

. . .

IV

Although an analysis of prior decisions and the purpose of the Fifth Amendment privilege indicates that use and derivative-use immunity is coextensive with the privilege, we must consider additional arguments advanced by petitioners against the sufficiency of such immunity. We start from the premise, repeatedly affirmed by this Court, that an appropriately broad immunity grant is compatible with the Constitution.

Petitioners argue that use and derivative-use immunity will not adequately protect a witness from various possible incriminating uses of the compelled testimony: for example, the prosecutor or other law enforcement officials may obtain leads, names of witnesses, or other information not otherwise available that might result in a prosecution. It will be difficult and perhaps impossible, the argument goes, to identify, by testimony or cross-examination, the subtle ways in which the compelled testimony may disadvantage a witness, especially in the jurisdiction granting the immunity.

This argument presupposes that the statute's prohibition will prove impossible to enforce. The statute provides a sweeping proscription of any use, direct or indirect, of the compelled testimony and any information derived therefrom. . . . This total prohibition on use provides a comprehensive safeguard, barring the use of compelled testimony as an "investigatory lead," and also barring the use of any evidence obtained by focusing investigation on a witness as a result of his compelled disclosures.

A person accorded this immunity under 18 U.S.C. § 6002, and subsequently prosecuted, is not dependent for the preservation of his rights upon the integrity and good faith of the prosecuting authorities. As stated in *Murphy* [v. Waterfront Commission, 378 U.S. 52 (1964)]:

> Once a defendant demonstrates that he has testified, under a state grant of immunity, to matters related to the federal prosecution, the federal authorities have the burden of showing that their evidence is not tainted by establishing that they had an independent, legitimate source for the disputed evidence.

378 U.S., at 79 n.18. This burden of proof, which we reaffirm as appropriate, is not limited to a negation of taint; rather, it imposes on the prosecution the affirmative duty to prove that the evidence it proposes to use is derived from a legitimate source wholly independent of the compelled testimony.

This is very substantial protection, commensurate with that resulting from invoking the privilege itself. The privilege assures that a citizen is not compelled to incriminate himself by his own testimony. It usually operates to allow a citizen to remain silent when asked a question requiring an incriminatory answer. This statute, which operates after a witness has given incriminatory testimony, affords the same protection by assuring that the compelled testimony can in no way lead to the infliction of criminal penalties. The statute, like the Fifth Amendment, grants neither pardon nor amnesty. Both the statute and the Fifth Amendment allow the government to prosecute using evidence from legitimate independent sources.

The statutory proscription is analogous to the Fifth Amendment requirement in cases of coerced confessions. A coerced confession, as revealing of leads as testimony given in exchange for immunity, is inadmissible in a criminal trial, but it does not bar prosecution. Moreover, a defendant against whom incriminating evidence has been obtained through a grant of immunity may be in a stronger position at trial than a defendant who asserts a Fifth Amendment coerced-confession claim. One raising a claim under this statute need only show that he testified under a grant of immunity in order to shift to the government the heavy burden of proving that all of the evidence it proposes to use was derived from legitimate independent sources. On the other hand, a defendant raising a coerced-confession claim under the Fifth Amendment must first prevail in a voluntariness hearing before his confession and evidence derived from it become inadmissible.

There can be no justification in reason or policy for holding that the Constitution requires an amnesty grant where, acting pursuant to statute and accompanying safeguards, testimony is compelled in exchange for immunity from use and derivative use when no such amnesty is required where the government, acting without colorable right, coerces a defendant into incriminating himself.

We conclude that the immunity provided by 18 U.S.C. § 6002 leaves the witness and the prosecutorial authorities in substantially the same position as if the witness had claimed the Fifth Amendment privilege. The immunity therefore is coextensive with the privilege and suffices to supplant it. The judgment of the Court of Appeals for the Ninth Circuit accordingly is

Affirmed.[27]

———

279. The meaning of "derivative use" in connection with use immunity is discussed in Pillsbury Co. v. Conboy, 459 U.S. 248 (1983) (7–2), in which the Court held that "a deponent's civil deposition testimony, closely tracking his prior immunized testimony, is not, without duly authorized assurance of immunity at the time, immunized testimony within the meaning of § 6002, and therefore may not be compelled over a valid assertion of his Fifth Amendment privilege." Id. at 263.

[27] Justice Douglas and Justice Marshall wrote dissenting opinions.

Testimony that a person gives before a grand jury pursuant to a grant of immunity cannot constitutionally be used to impeach his credibility if he is subsequently prosecuted and testifies as a witness at trial. New Jersey v. Portash, 440 U.S. 450 (1979) (7–2). Compare Harris v. New York and Oregon v. Hass, pp. 479, 482 above.

280. Cases exploring the problem of establishing an independent source of evidence against a defendant who has testified under a grant of immunity include United States v. Overmyer, 899 F.2d 457 (6th Cir.1990); United States v. Hampton, 775 F.2d 1479 (11th Cir.1985); United States v. Pantone, 634 F.2d 716 (3d Cir.1980); United States v. Romano, 583 F.2d 1 (1st Cir.1978); United States v. Nemes, 555 F.2d 51 (2d Cir.1977); and United States v. De Diego, 511 F.2d 818 (D.C.Cir.1975).

In *Nemes*, above, the court held that the government's burden of establishing an independent source could not be met simply by the prosecutor's denial that he had had access to the immunized testimony. "The inference that the prosecutor's lack of access to compelled testimony assures the existence of independent sources cannot be relied upon to afford the witness the full protection the Constitution guarantees. The prosecutor may have never seen the witness's testimony and may believe in good faith that no one associated with the federal prosecution has seen it, but such a disclaimer does not preclude the possibility that someone who has seen the compelled testimony was thereby led to evidence that was furnished to federal investigators. Only by affirmatively proving that his evidence comes from sources independent of the immunized testimony can the prosecutor assure that the witness is in the same position he would have enjoyed had his self-incrimination privilege not been displaced by use immunity." 555 F.2d at 55. See United States v. Harris, 973 F.2d 333 (4th Cir. 1992) (assistant United States attorney who heard immunized testimony later obtained indictment; indictment dismissed).

In *Hinton*, above, the court concluded that "as a matter of fundamental fairness, a Government practice of using the same grand jury that heard the immunized testimony of a witness to indict him after he testifies, charging him with criminal participation in the matters being studied by the grand jury" should not be allowed. 543 F.2d at 1010. Relying on its supervisory authority, the court prohibited the practice. Other courts of appeals have declined to adopt the per se prohibition of *Hinton* and have held only that the defendant is entitled to a hearing at which to challenge the government's claim that the indictment was based on information from independent sources. E.g., United States v. Bartel, 19 F.3d 1105 (6th Cir.1994).

The question whether a prosecutor who has had access to a witness's testimony pursuant to a grant of immunity may participate in a subsequent decision to indict the witness is explored in United States v. Byrd, 765 F.2d 1524 (11th Cir.1985). Observing that *Kastigar* does not require that the position of an immunized witness before and after testifying "remain absolutely identical in every conceivable and theoretical respect," the court concluded: "So long as none of the evidence presented to the grand jury is derived, directly or indirectly, from the immunized testimony, it can fairly be said that the defendant's immunized testimony has not been used to incriminate him." Id. at 1530.

While awaiting trial, the appellant was summoned as a witness against a codefendant being tried on the same charges. The appellant's case was scheduled for trial subsequently before the same judge and was to be tried by the same prosecutor. The appellant was granted immunity. He refused to testify on the basis that despite the grant of immunity, in the circumstances his testimony would inevitably be used against him. The court held that he could be compelled to testify, since he would have an opportunity in pretrial proceedings in his own case to object to any use of his testimony. Graves v. United States, 472 A.2d 395 (D.C.App.1984). See generally In re Sealed Case, 791 F.2d 179 (D.C.Cir.1986).

281. Observing that "in theory, strict application of use and derivative use immunity would remove the hazard of incrimination," but that "in our imperfect world . . . we doubt that workaday measures can, *in practice,* protect adequately against use and derivative use," the Supreme Court of Alaska held that the state constitutional provision against compulsory self-incrimination required transactional immunity as a condition of compelled incriminating testimony. State v. Gonzalez, 853 P.2d 526 (Alaska 1993). The court cites cases in Hawaii, Massachusetts, and Oregon reaching the same result.

282.   "Dual sovereignties." Murphy v. Waterfront Commission, 378 U.S. 52 (1964), denies to the states or to the federal government use for prosecutorial purposes of testimony obtained by the other sovereignty by a grant of immunity. *Murphy* is discussed at length and much of its reasoning is rejected in *Balsys*, note 283 below.

283. A fear of prosecution by a foreign government does not invoke the privilege against compulsory self-incrimination. United States v. Balsys, 524 U.S. 666 (1998) (7–2). Balsys had been summoned to testify before the Office of Special Investigations of the Department of Justice about activities during World War II which might make him subject to deportation. He claimed that his responses might subject him to criminal prosecution in Lithuania, Israel, and Germany. The district court found that the danger of prosecution in the first two countries was "real and substantial," id. at 671.

284. The federal statutes before 1970 gave immunity not only from prosecution but also from "penalty or forfeiture" in connection with compelled testimony. Does the Constitution require that immunity extend beyond criminal proceedings? If so, how far? What kinds of "penalty or forfeiture" are barred? See Boyd v. United States, 116 U.S. 616 (1886); Lee v. Civil Aeronautics Board, 225 F.2d 950 (D.C.Cir.1955). Does *Spevack,* p. 498 above, have a bearing on this question? If the Constitution does not require immunity beyond criminal prosecution, should it nevertheless be granted?

285. The courts have rejected a variety of grounds for refusing to testify that do not involve subsequent governmental action. In Branzburg v. Hayes, 408 U.S. 665 (1972), the Court rejected the claim that a newspaper reporter is generally privileged under the First Amendment not to reveal the names of confidential sources of news in response to questions of the grand jury. A First Amendment "scholar's privilege" was rejected in United States v. Doe, 460 F.2d 328 (1st Cir.1972). In Bursey v. United States, 466 F.2d 1059 (9th Cir.1972), however, the court upheld witnesses' refusal to answer questions on the ground that First Amendment rights were involved; the court concluded that the government had not shown a sufficiently compelling interest to overcome those rights.

In LaTona v. United States, 449 F.2d 121 (8th Cir.1971), the court refused to accept a witness's claim to be excused from testifying before the grand jury because he would be subject to "underworld reprisals" and might be killed if he testified. To the same effect, see In re Grand Jury Proceedings (Taylor v. United States), 509 F.2d 1349 (5th Cir.1975). But see United States v. Banks, 942 F.2d 1576, 1578 (11th Cir.1991), holding that a person who refuses to testify before the grand jury because of a "legitimate and well-founded fear" for his own and his family's safety cannot be convicted of corruptly endeavoring to obstruct justice.

In general, claims of a privilege not to testify against a member of one's family have been rejected. In a lengthy opinion reviewing and confirming the rule in other jurisdictions, the court held that there is no parent-child or child-parent privilege not to testify, in In re Grand Jury, 103 F.3d 1140 (3d Cir.1997).

In In re Grand Jury, 111 F.3d 1083 (3d Cir.1997), the court held that a grant of use and derivative use immunity to a witness summoned before a grand jury, by which she was promised that her testimony and any fruits thereof would not be used against her husband, who was the subject of the grand jury's investigation, and that an indictment against her husband would not be sought before the same grand jury, was sufficient to defeat her privilege against giving adverse spousal testimony.

286. A witness's assertion that the answer to a question would tend to incriminate him usually is not contested. The government may, however, challenge the assertion and oppose the witness's claim under the privilege against compulsory self-incrimination on that basis. See, e.g., United States v. Castro, 129 F.3d 226 (1st Cir.1997) (claim upheld); In re Brogna, 589 F.2d 24 (1st Cir.1978) (same).

On the issue of waiver of the privilege with respect to subsequent questions by answering previous incriminating questions, see Klein v. Harris, 667 F.2d 274, 287–89 (2d Cir.1981); United States v. Seifert, 648 F.2d 557, 561 (9th Cir.1980).

Neither a defendant's guilty plea nor her statements during the colloquy with the judge when the plea is entered constitute a waiver of her privilege against compulsory self-incrimination at sentencing. Mitchell v. United States, 526 U.S. 314 (1999).

287. If a witness refuses to testify before the grand jury, he can be committed to jail for civil contempt until he obeys the order of court directing him to testify. In a federal proceeding, the maximum period of confinement is 18 months. 28 U.S.C. § 1826. It has been held that confinement for civil contempt should not be continued once it becomes clear that the witness's detention has no coercive impact and will not induce him to testify. See Simkin v. United States, 715 F.2d 34 (2d Cir.1983). "As long as the judge is satisfied that the coercive sanction might yet produce its intended result, the confinement may continue. But if the judge is persuaded, after a conscientious consideration of the circumstances pertinent to the individual contemnor, that the contempt power has ceased to have a coercive effect, the civil contempt remedy should be ended. The contemnor will not have avoided all sanction by his irrevocable opposition to the court's order. Once it is determined that the civil contempt remedy is unavailing, the criminal contempt sanction is available." Id. at 37.

288. Reporting requirements. Federal law imposes excise and occupational taxes on the business of accepting wagers. 26 U.S.C. §§ 4401, 4411. Persons who are subject to the occupational tax are required to register with the Internal Revenue Service. 26 U.S.C. § 4412. The Service is directed to make a list of those who pay the tax available for public inspection. In Marchetti v. United States, 390 U.S. 39 (1968), noting that "wagering and its ancillary activities are very widely prohibited under both federal and state law," id. at 44, the Supreme Court concluded that the requirements of payment of the occupational tax and registration created a substantial possibility of self-incrimination and, therefore, that a person who asserted the constitutional privilege could not be criminally punished for failing to perform those acts.

In Grosso v. United States, 390 U.S. 62 (1968), the Court applied the same reasoning to the excise tax, payment of which was required to be accompanied by submission of a special tax return applicable only to those in the wagering business. On the same basis, in Haynes v. United States, 390 U.S. 85 (1968), the Court reversed a conviction for possession of a firearm that had not been registered as required by law, 26 U.S.C. §§ 5841, 5851; and in Leary v. United States, 395 U.S. 6 (1969), the Court reversed a conviction for violation of the Marijuana Tax Act, 26 U.S.C. §§ 4741, 4744.

In each of the cases, the Court declined to uphold the challenged provisions and impose a restriction on use of the information obtained thereby, because it thought that such a resolution of the competing interests was not contemplated by the statutory scheme and should be reached, if at all, by Congress rather than the Court. The Gun Control Act of 1968, 82 Stat. 1214, retained the firearm registration requirement and enacted a use restriction providing that except for a prosecution for furnishing false information, no information obtained thereby shall "be used, directly or indirectly, as evidence against that person in a criminal proceeding with respect to a violation of law occurring prior to or concurrently with the filing of the application or registration, or the compiling of the records containing the information or evidence." 26 U.S.C. § 5848(a). The amended statute was upheld in United States v. Freed, 401 U.S. 601 (1971).

In Garner v. United States, 424 U.S. 648 (1976), the Court held that since the defendant could have asserted the privilege against self-incrimination as a basis for refusing to give information on his income-tax returns, having given the information, he had no basis on which to object to the introduction of the information against him in a criminal trial. Unlike the disclosure requirements involved in *Marchetti* and *Grosso*, above, federal income tax returns are not directed peculiarly at persons engaged in illegal activities. Nor was the reasoning in Garrity v. New Jersey, 385 U.S. 493 (1967), p. 494 above, applicable, since a person who validly exercised the privilege when filing his return could not be prosecuted for failure to file a return; the possibility that the validity of a claim of the privilege would be tested in a criminal prosecution was not the kind of compulsion with which *Garrity* was concerned.

The Court held in California v. Byers, 402 U.S. 424 (1971) (5–4), that a "hit and run" statute which requires the driver of a motor vehicle involved in an accident to stop at the scene and give his name and address does not violate the privilege against self-incrimination.

———

An arrest is commonly described as taking a person into custody so that he can be held to answer a charge against him. E.g., ALI, Code of Criminal Procedure § 18 (1930). Often, however, an arrest may be more an aspect of the investigation of crime than of prosecution. While police actions are in some respects restricted after they have taken a person into custody, at least as significant are actions that may be taken as incidents of an arrest. Police have no general authority to demand information for their records from the community at large, or to fingerprint persons or examine their bodies, or to place them in lineups for observation by others. It is assumed generally that a person who has been arrested should not be held in custody until his trial but should be released as soon as possible after his arrest. In most cases the conditions of his release, if any are imposed, give little assurance of his appearance for trial; more dependable are the habits and relationships that tie him to the community and the threat of penalty if he does not appear. See Chapter Eight, below.

Each of the investigative techniques that are now incidents of arrest might be authorized without a precedent arrest. The questioning of witnesses, for example, is a major aspect of ordinary criminal investigation which does not depend on the power to arrest; rather an arrest has the effect of limiting questioning of the person arrested. With respect to both what it authorizes and what it precludes, the significance of an arrest is that it gives the arrested person the status of an "accused." Because he has been accused, a person who is arrested is required to submit to the actions described above, but, also because he has been accused, he cannot be questioned except in a carefully controlled atmosphere.

What is the quality of an accusation of crime? What, aside from its functional consequences, is its significance? Should the process of criminal investigation make so much depend on the existence of an accusation? Would it be desirable to lessen dependence on this fact, so far as constitutional doctrine permits?

In a number of contexts something of this sort has happened or has been urged. Central to the stop-and-frisk issue is the question whether police ought to have general authority to stop (and question, or frisk) persons whom they cannot validly accuse of a crime. In Davis v. Mississippi, 394 U.S. 721 (1969), p. 391 note 223 above, the Court speculated whether police might not be authorized to fingerprint persons who are not accused of a crime. It is now assumed in many jurisdictions that persons who have been arrested and released can be required to appear for inclusion in a lineup, see note 220, p. 385 above; given the factual premises of United States v. Wade, 388 U.S. 218 (1967), p. 369 above, it is plausible to suppose that police may sometimes request persons who are suspected but not accused of crime to participate in a lineup rather than be observed in less neutral circumstances.

Are official interferences in our lives, diminutions of the right to be let alone by the government, more or less to be feared if they are tied closely to the criminal process? Is the loss in human dignity greater when police engage in "aggressive patrolling" which harasses large groups in a community who are not suspected of any crime or when police stop and frisk an individual who is singled out from the community because he has behaved not criminally, but suspiciously? Does each of us lose more actually and potentially if privacy is lost to the community generally, as by a general requirement of disclosure to an official body of some hitherto private information or, if some practice like eavesdropping is authorized but limited to the investigation of (serious) crime?

———

INDEX

References are to pages.

†